TEACHING EXCEPTIONAL CHILDREN IN ALL AMERICA'S SCHOOLS

A First Course for Teachers and Principals

MAYNARD C. REYNOLDS
JACK W. BIRCH

Published by The Council for Exceptional Children

Copyright © 1977 by The Council for Exceptional Children,
1920 Association Drive, Reston, Virginia 22091

Library of Congress Catalog Number 77-082558

Design and artwork by Angeline V. Culfogienis

Photographs by Nanda Ward Haynes

Second printing 1979

Contents

Selected Key Dates and Events in the Development of Public Education in the United States, 1776-1980 ... v

About the Authors ... xi

Preface ... xiii

1. Introduction: The Currents of Change ... 1
2. Origins of Change ... 48
3. Assessment ... 104
4. Parents and Planning ... 154
5. Giftedness and Talents: High Rate of Cognitive Development ... 192
6. Mental Retardation: Low Rate of Cognitive Development ... 261
7. Learning Disabilities and Behavior Disorders ... 331
8. Physical and Health Impairments ... 393
9. Emerging Trends and New Partners ... 439
10. Speech Problems ... 482
11. Hearing Impairment ... 513
12. Visual Impairments ... 603
13. Emerging Programs ... 639
14. Facing the Future: Emerging Trends and Issues ... 670

References ... 703

Appendix A Organizations and Agencies Concerned with Exceptional Persons ... 723

Appendix B Teacher Training Materials ... 727

Name Index ... 763

Subject Index ... 775

Selected Key Dates and Events in the Development of Public Education in the United States, 1776-1980

1776   The 13 states unanimously declared their independence and their joint commitment to "life, liberty and the pursuit of happiness."

1779   Thomas Jefferson's School Bill for Virginia; First state school system proposal.

1791   Passage of Tenth Amendment to the United States Constitution reserves education to the states.

1817   First educational program for exceptional children and youth formally established in the United States—American Asylum for the Education and Instruction of the Deaf (now American School for the Deaf), Hartford, Connecticut.

1818   First grants of money paid by the federal government to states.

1821   English high school for boys organized in Boston.

1823   United States' first normal school for teachers privately established in Vermont.

1826   First nursery school of the nation opened in New Harmony, Indiana.

Bowdoin College first in United States to award a degree to a Black person, John Russwurm.

1829   Massachusetts passes first state high school law.

First residential school for blind pupils in the United States incorporated in Watertown, Massachusetts; initially called the New England Asylum for the Blind, now the Perkins School for the Blind.

1839   State supported normal school for teacher training started at Lexington, Massachusetts.

1840   Rhode Island passed first state compulsory education law.

1845   First statewide associations of teachers founded in New York and Rhode Island.

1848   Eduard Seguin came from France to describe his educational procedures there with mentally retarded pupils and to urge the establishment of schools for mentally retarded children and youth in the United States.

Dorothea Dix confronted the Congress with the inhumanity of many programs for the "mentally ill."

1852	Massachusetts passed the second compulsory school attendance law.
1855	The United States' first kindergarten established at Watertown, Wisconsin.
1857	National Education Association formed, initially called the National Teachers' Association.
1859	Nation's first residential school for persons with mental retardation started in South Boston under the name Massachusetts School for Idiotic and Feeble-Minded Youth. Samuel Gridley Howe, then head of the Perkins School for the Blind, was most influential in enlisting legislative and public support for this new facility.
1867	Congress created a National Department of Education, later to become the United States Office of Education, now under the Secretary of Health, Education and Welfare.
1869	First day classes for any exceptional children were begun for deaf pupils in Boston, Massachusetts.
1873	Nation's first permanent public kindergarten initiated by the St. Louis, Missouri, public schools.
1878	Day classes for mentally retarded pupils proposed by August Schenck of Detroit in a speech before the American Teachers Association.
1891	Teacher training launched at Gallaudet College in the area of deaf education.
1893	Committee of Ten report promulgated, the initial report of a series on curriculum from the National Education Association.
1895	United States educators with management responsibilities formed the American Association of School Administrators.
1896	First public school day classes for mentally retarded pupils initiated in Providence, Rhode Island.
1898	National Congress of Mothers organized; now called National Congress of Parents and Teachers.
1899	First public school day classes for crippled children and youth started in Chicago, Illinois.
1900	First public school day classes for blind pupils begun in Chicago, Illinois.
	Two states, Wisconsin and Michigan, authorized subsidies to expand classes for deaf pupils in local public schools, the first such state financial support for excess educational cost for any exceptional children and youth.
1904	Vineland Training School started summer training sessions for teachers of the retarded.
1905	E. L. Thorndike conceptualized and planned a scale to measure educational achievement.
1906	Approximate time medical inspections were introduced in the schools for the detection and prevention of contagious infectious diseases.

1908	Establishment of first public school day classes for children with lowered vitality.
1908	Speech correction initiated in New York public school.
1909	First White House Conference on Children and Youth.
	National Education Association cites the Goddard translation and revision of the Binet-Simon Scale of Intelligence as a useful test with exceptional children and specifically with mentally retarded children.
1910	Nation's first public junior high schools opened in Berkeley, California and Columbus, Ohio.
1911	Countrywide survey by United States Bureau of Education found 6% of cities reporting special classes for gifted pupils.
1913	Roxbury, Massachusetts started first classes for partially seeing pupils.
1915	*Laggards in Our Schools* by Leonard P. Ayres was published; it became one of the first special education texts.
1916	Organization of American Federation of Teachers as an affiliate of the American Federation of Labor.
	Lewis Terman produced the Stanford-Binet Scale of Intelligence tests with an elaborate standardization and the inclusion of the intelligence quotient concept proposed by Stern in 1912.
1917	Federal support for vocational education furnished through Smith-Hughes Act.
1918	All states had legally effective compulsory education.
	The Seven Cardinal Principles of Secondary Education was published.
1920	First presidential proclamation of American Education Week.
	Federal Civilian Rehabilitation Act signed by President Woodrow Wilson.
1922	Founding year of The Council for Exceptional Children.
1923	World Confederation of Organizations of the Teaching Profession organized in San Francisco, California; original name was World Federation of Education Associations.
1926	First prototype of teaching machine and programed instruction invented by Sidney Pressey at Ohio State University.
1930	In a national conference on child health and protection called by President Hoover one committee was assigned to study the needs of exceptional children.
1931	A section on exceptional children was formed in the United States Office of Education and a professional educator was named a Senior Specialist to head the unit.

1941	The National Society for the Study of Education devoted a yearbook to the education of exceptional children.
1944	Initial GI Bill for veterans' education passed by Congress.
1950	National Association for Retarded Citizens formed; other parent groups with focus on specific exceptional conditions also began to press for special education and other necessary services.
	Thirty-four states had laws subsidizing public school classes for all recognized groups of exceptional children.
1952	Federal Communications Commission reserved more than 200 channels for noncommercial television, providing functional base for educational television.
1957	Cooperative Educational Research Program launched by the US Office of Education, with problems of the mentally retarded a priority concern.
1958	National Defense Education Act approved by Congress to improve instruction in sciences, mathematics, and languages.
	Congress passed Public Law 85-926 to provide one million dollars to be allocated to colleges and to universities to train professional educators for special education of mentally retarded pupils.
1960	First book published on programed instruction.
1961	Congress added funds to support preparation of teachers of deaf children and youth.
1963	Congress legislated funds to support training of educators for all recognized groups of handicapped children and youth and to subsidize research regarding their education.
1965	Elementary and Secondary Education Act provided major breakthrough in federal support of the schools, particularly for programs serving disadvantaged children and youth.
	National Teacher Corps approved by Congress. Head Start made a year-round program. Elementary and Secondary Education Act authorized educational benefits directed mostly toward low income families.
1966	Regional educational research and development centers and laboratories established through the United States Office of Education.
	Federal effort on behalf of handicapped pupils given added status, elevated to Bureau for the Education of the Handicapped in the Office of Education.
1967	Education Professions Development Act adopted by Congress.
1971	Special study of educational needs of gifted and talented pupils initiated by United States Commissioner of Education.
1972	Conclusions from legal actions in Pennsylvania and in the District of Columbia initiated a national move to open and improve education for all exceptional pupils within the context of regular education to the fullest extent possible and with guarantees of due process.

1973 Rehabilitation Act amendments guarantee rights of the handicapped in employment and in educational institutions that receive federal monies.

1974 US Supreme Court upheld right of non-English speaking students to bilingual compensatory education in English (*Lou v. Nichols*).

1975 Education of All Handicapped Children Act (Public Law 94-142) passed by the Congress and signed by President Gerald Ford.

1976 All states have laws subsidizing public school programs for exceptional children and youth.

The National Education Association and the American Federation of Teachers pass resolutions in support of teaching exceptional children in regular classes (mainstreaming) with appropriate support personnel and facilities.

Four states require by law all regular class teachers to have preparation to include exceptional pupils in their classes.

1978 Public Law 94-142 (The Education of All Handicapped Children Act) becomes effective, assuring all handicapped children a full public education and a variety of accompanying rights.

1980 Full educational opportunities for all exceptional children by this date set as goal by the United States Commissioner of Education.

About the Authors

Maynard C. Reynolds is Professor and Chairman of the Department of Psychoeducational Studies and Director of the Leadership Training Institute at the University of Minnesota, Minneapolis. He has been involved, as a professor and contributor, in the field of special education for nearly thirty years. Dr. Reynolds has served on such national and state committees as: Chairman of the Minnesota State Advisory Commission on Handicapped Children (1957-1961); Member of the Advisory Committee, Division of Training Programs, Bureau of Education for the Handicapped, US Office of Education; and Chairman of the Committee to Advise on a Possible Merger of State Braille Sight Saving School and the State School for the Deaf (1974-1975). Dr. Reynolds also served as President of The Council for Exceptional Children from 1965 to 1966. He holds membership in many professional and academic associations. He has contributed to numerous journals and has authored or edited many major publications in the field of special education. Dr. Reynolds received CEC's highest award, The J. E. Wallace Wallin Award for Service to Handicapped Children in 1971 and The Mildred Thomsom Award from Region VIII of the American Association on Mental Deficiency in 1975.

Jack W. Birch is Professor of Special Education and Professor of Educational and Developmental Psychology in the School of Education at the University of Pittsburgh. He began his career as a teacher of special children in 1937 and has since worked as a teacher of exceptional children and a school psychologist. He was Director of Special Education and of the Psychoeducational Clinic in the Pittsburgh Public Schools from 1948 to 1958. Dr. Birch is a Fellow of the American Psychological Association and the American Association on Mental Deficiency, and a Diplomate of the American Psychological Association. Dr. Birch was also President of The Council for Exceptional Children in 1960-1961. He is responsible for over 100 publications dealing with the education and rehabilitation of exceptional children and adults. Some special honors include an Award of Merit (1955) by a Pittsburgh parents' association in recognition of outstanding service to the mentally retarded and a similar award in 1976 from the National Accreditation Council for Agencies Serving the Blind and Visually Handicapped.

Preface

Special educators and all other public and private educators are moving rapidly into a new set of relationships. Many terms could be used to describe the change process, but we prefer *renegotiation*. For us, the term holds implications of dealings between equals, of adaptations that are undertaken consciously and voluntarily in order to achieve a new "fit," and of the careful reassessment of what each has to offer the other. The stimulus for this renegotiation springs from parent advocacy, from forward thinking educators, and from the adjudications and legislation that have reaffirmed the right to education for exceptional children in least restrictive environments according to individualized plans. Thus, for many handicapped and gifted children, special education and services are being brought into the regular class and special and regular education teachers find themselves working together to meet the judicial and legislative mandates.

Until now, textbooks concerned with education of exceptional students have started from the premise that most trainees were going to be specialists working alone with children who had particular handicaps or were gifted. Different skills are needed, however, when most of the children are to be served in the regular class and when the person providing an important share of the day to day instruction and services is a regular educator.

Mainstreaming does not make the special educator redundant. Indeed, mainstreaming forces recognition that the special educator has a broadened role, one calling for preparation to be a valuable resource for all teachers in a school and for all children with any kind of handicap or learning problem. Thus, this book is oriented toward special education in the mainstream, that is, toward special education as a resource for all teachers in all of the schools.

The mainstream approach offered in this book includes a cluster of characteristics that are unique for education trainees:

- The key role of the regular-special educator team is emphasized. The book is addressed primarily to teachers and principals, both those in preservice training and those in continuing and in-service education.

- The book applies with equal force to all educators. It is planned for use as a text in the preparation of all preschool, elementary, secondary, and special subject teachers, and for those readying themselves to be administrators or to be specialists with exceptional children.
- A deliberate advocacy role is encouraged for all educators, pressing toward improved education for all children, including exceptional children.
- The book emphasizes the "why" and "how" of educational matters, in addition to the "what." The content is devoted to both the practical and theoretical. Utility is the chief criterion for determining the extent of background material that is included.
- Special education is presented as "a part of" rather than "apart from" all the rest of education. Emphasis is on initial and progressive inclusion of exceptional children with all other children during schooling.
- The presentation is structured to make it adaptable for teacher preparation institutions that are trying to develop rapidly their capacity to offer mainstream instruction to many teachers. A special appendix contains a list and description of training resources for teacher training.

The authors have had unusual opportunities during the past decade to work with literally hundreds of special and regular teachers and principals in school systems and departments of special education in colleges and universities where change processes have been under way. We are grateful for the opportunities afforded through Don Davies, Bill Smith, Malcolm Davis, and Edward Moore who, as federal officers, were associated with the experimental programs sponsored under the Education Professions Develpoment Act, the National Center for the Improvement of Educational Systems, and the Teacher Corps. More recently, we have been associated with similar projects sponsored by the Bureau of Education for the Handicapped, led by Thomas Behrens, Edwin Martin, and others. Work in the context of these federally supported projects has given us much opportunity to visit and learn about the renegotiations that are most significant for special education in the context of regular education.

To some readers, this book may seem like a radical departure from the existing literature in special education, and so it may be. But we believe that it is among the first of a stream of books that will reflect the changing structures now evident in the ways schools are going about providing education for students with unusual needs.

The preparation of this book has involved many people. On the Minnesota side much appreciation goes to colleagues, including Karen Lundholm, Sylvia Rosen, Evelyn Deno, S. Pike Hall, Reece Peterson, Robert Prouty, Sue Bye, and Ann Nevin. Special thanks go to Bonnie Warhol for careful management of all typing and references. On the Pittsburgh side Jane Birch, William Craig, Hannah and Jack Matthews, Mary Moore, June Mullins, Ralph Peabody, James Salem, Godfrey Stevens, and Naomi Zigmond gave various combinations of professional and personal support and encouragement to the endeavor that were thoroughly appreciated.

Maynard C. Reynolds
Jack W. Birch

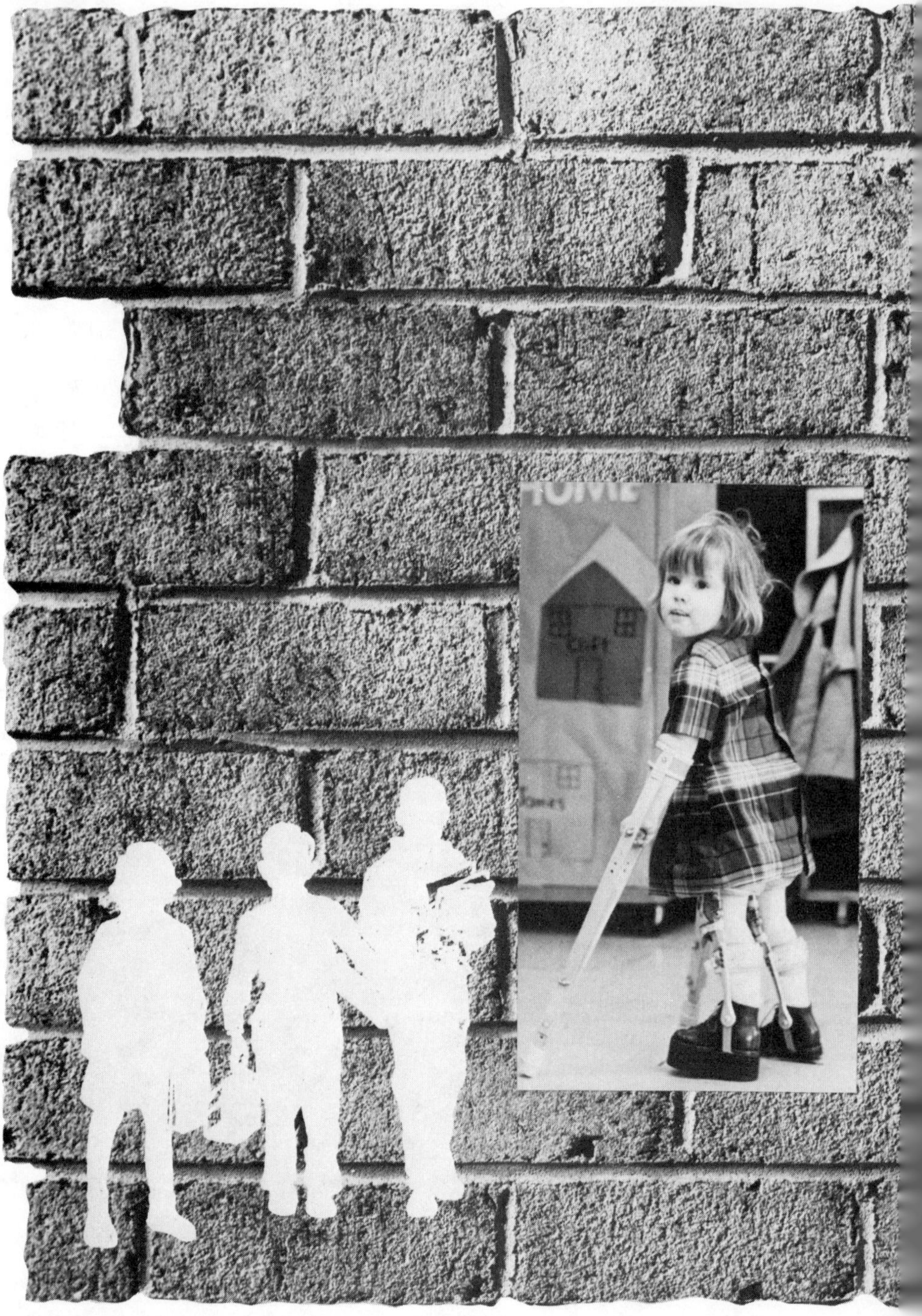

1. Introduction: The Currents of Change

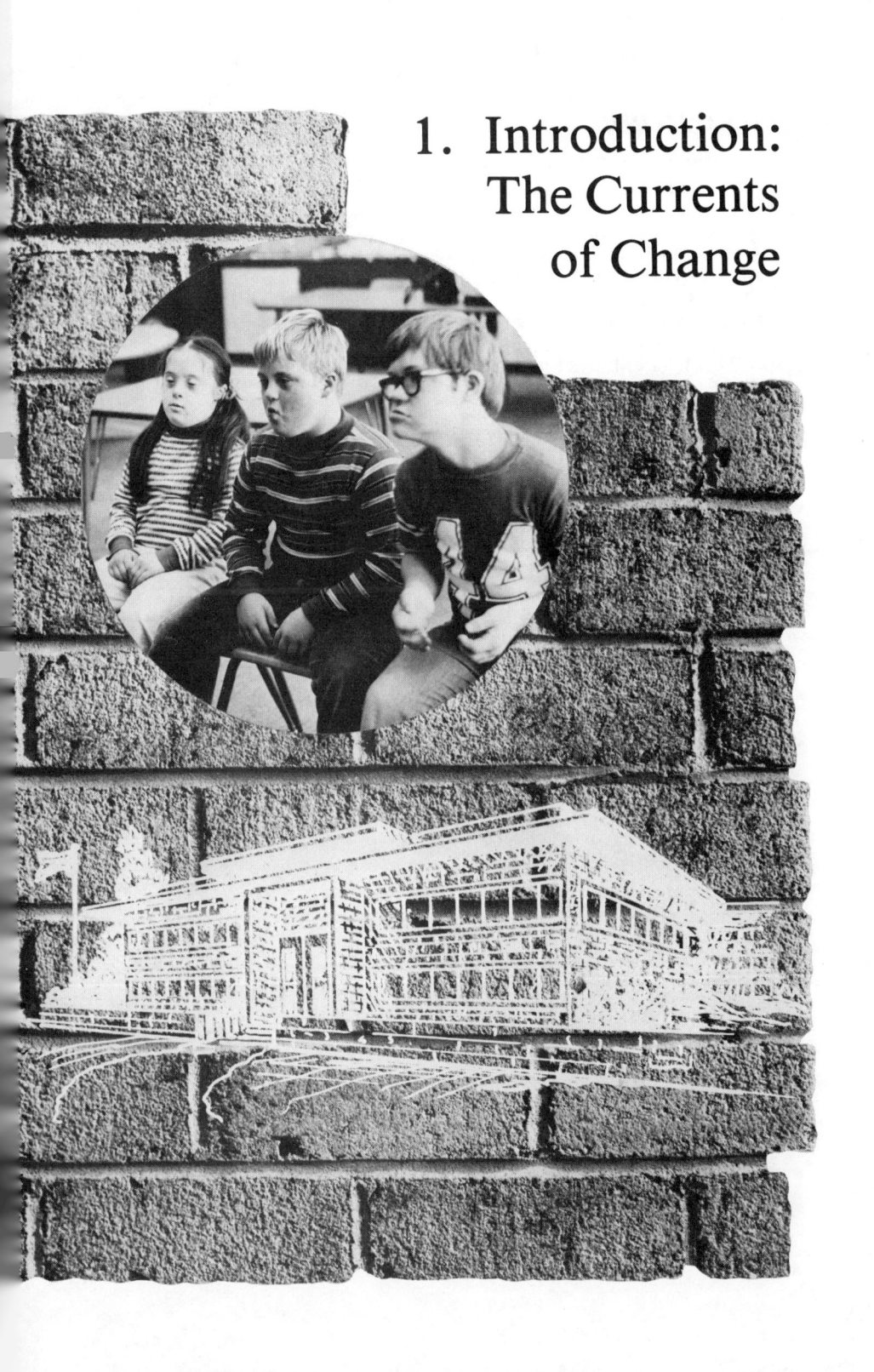

CHAPTER OUTLINE

CHANGES IN SPECIAL EDUCATION
EMERGING PRACTICES IN SCHOOLS
   An Elementary School
   A Secondary School
   A Minischool within a Comprehensive High School
   An Area Vocational Technical Institute
   The Dissolution of a Special School
   Exceptional Children
   Gifted and Talented Children
PREVAILING VERSUS PREFERRED PRACTICES
HISTORICAL PERSPECTIVE
   19th Century: Residential Schools
   Early 20th Century: Community Prototypes
   1945 to 1970: Explosion of Simple Models
   The 1970's: Negotiating for More Inclusive Arrangements
FORCES AND TRENDS OF THE 1970's
   Aggressive Categorical Parent Groups
   Minority Groups
   Federal Legislation
CHANGING PATTERNS OF ADMINISTRATIVE ARRANGEMENTS
   The Original Cascade Model
   New Perspective on the Cascade Model
MAINSTREAMING IN THE BROADER COMMUNITY
   How Many Exceptional Students?
   The Legal Base
CONCLUSIONS
SUGGESTIONS FOR STUDENTS AND INSTRUCTOR
TOPICAL BIBLIOGRAPHIES

CHANGES IN SPECIAL EDUCATION

Many changes are occurring in education for handicapped and gifted students that affect the roles of all teachers and principals. Consider the following events and developments:

1. *The wave of judicial pronouncements concerning the right to education, right to appropriate education in the least restricted environment, and right to participation in placement decisions.* Following a federal court case conducted in 1971 *(PARC v. Pennsylvania)* the state of Pennsylvania found itself obligated to undertake a search for all retarded children in the state and to initiate immediately programs that would provide each individual with an appropriate education.
2. *The virtual "shutdown" on school exclusions, expulsions, and suspensions.* In a landmark decision in 1975 *(Goss v. Lopez)* the Supreme Court moved a long way in protecting student rights against school demissions of any kind and making it clear that school principals and teachers may face legal action if students are suspended or expelled from school for any but the most compelling reasons and, even then, by careful procedures.
3. *The return of many persons from residential institutions to the community, resulting in the obligation of local schools to serve many seriously handicapped students.* In many states the population of state operated schools and hospitals has been reduced by more than half in less than a decade; the impact of this shift is apparent in every aspect of local school operations—in the buses, in the classrooms, and on the school board agenda.
4. *The launching by local schools of programs for persons formerly believed to be uneducable.* Most school systems have for some years conducted programs for handicapped students, but now the press is on to extend schooling to those the schools have previously excluded.
5. *The rapid erosion of the traditional boundaries between regular and special education.* The refer-test-classify procedures by which many children were sent to isolated classes and centers have been cast in doubt and now one sees more handicapped students in regular classes.
6. *The emergence of new support or indirect roles for special education teachers that involve teaming with regular educators.* As fewer children with special needs are referred out of regular school programs, the specialists are found more often in the "regular" school setting, teaming up with regular teachers to assess, plan for, and teach exceptional children.
7. *The requirements that parents be notified before any special "diagnosis" or assessment of their children is undertaken in educational*

planning. What has always been considered good practice in many school districts is now being established formally as a right of parents under federal and state statutes.
8. *The serious objections by many parents and minority groups to the prevailing systems for testing, classification, and placement of children in special classes in the schools.* In California, educators have had to give up the use of individual intelligence tests because of court cases in which advocates of minority group children argued persuasively that such tests have been used unfairly to classify and stigmatize some children.

These developments have a common theme: the greater inclusion of exceptional children in the mainstream of community and school life. They signify the reversal of the negative, rejection oriented cascade that permitted the removal of some children from the mainstream of education and isolated them in "special" settings. They also signify the demise of what has been called the "two box" theory of education, that is, that there are two kinds of children—exceptional and normal—and two kinds of school systems: one "special" for the exceptional children and one "regular" for the normal children. In sum, the developments encourage a unified school system in which exceptional children are part of the educational mainstream to the maximum extent feasible.

The education of exceptional children in the mainstream, or mainstreaming, requires more than merely placing handicapped children in regular classrooms, however. Refusing to refer children to special education or simply dumping children back into community schools or into regular classes is a cruelty to everyone involved: pupils, teachers, and parents. Many children would be placed in environments where they are poorly understood and served.

The locus of action in mainstreaming is the regular class and school; the major effort required there is to develop and support the classroom settings and programs so that they can serve effectively the children who have special educational needs. One of the basic components of mainstreaming is the provision of individualized school programs for all children, including those who are exceptional, so that fewer displacements from the mainstream to special, isolated settings are necessary.

Broadly speaking, mainstreaming is based on an inclusive attitude or general predisposition toward the education of children; that is, to provide education for as many children as possible in the regular class environment. But the regular teacher, alone or with help, will not always be the optimal instructor for all pupils; hence a full continuum of instructional arrangements to meet the needs of individual children is integral to mainstreaming, but each displacement from a regular teacher to a specialist in another setting, even in the same school, must be justified and negotiated with the student and parents.

In 1976, The Council for Exceptional Children, then a national organization with a membership of 60,000 special educators, described the school environment in which exceptional children should be educated in an official definition of mainstreaming:

> Mainstreaming is a belief which involves an educational placement procedure and process for exceptional children, based on the conviction that each such child should be educated in the least restrictive environment in which his educational and related needs can be satisfactorily provided. This concept recognizes that exceptional children have a wide range of special educational needs, varying greatly in intensity and duration; that there is a recognized continuum of educational settings which may, at a given time, be appropriate for an individual child's needs; that to the maximum extent appropriate, exceptional children should be educated with nonexceptional children; and that special classes, separate schooling, or other removal of an exceptional child from education with nonexceptional children should occur only when the intensity of the child's special education and related needs is such that they cannot be satisfied in an environment including nonexceptional children, even with the provision of supplementary aids and services. ("Official Actions...," 1976, p. 43)

This statement envisages a transformation in both special and regular education. For decades, the rhetoric of progressive education centered on individualized schooling for every child. Special education now is adding its energies and skills to the achievement of that lofty goal.

It is sometimes useful to distinguish between several kinds of mainstreaming—academic, social, and physical. It is not uncommon, for example, for a child to be *physically* located in a mainstream school situation but to be isolated there socially and academically. Similarly, sometimes a child is well integrated into a mainstream *academic* program, but is excluded *socially*—perhaps because of physical stigmata or for other reasons that have not been dealt with adequately in the school. It is assumed here that several kinds of mainstreaming are preferred over isolation whenever they are compatible with the student's developmental needs.

EMERGING PRACTICES IN SCHOOLS

To bring into somewhat closer focus the kinds of innovative things that are going on in schools today, a number of vignettes are presented here. These illustrations are not intended to be viewed as the "only ways" of serving children with special needs. Indeed, there are many administrative structures for appropriate individualized education. But these brief vignettes show something about how the capacity to deal with the exceptional needs of pupils can be built into the regular school environment.

An Elementary School

A former special class teacher who had prepared for intensive diagnostic and prescriptive teaching teamed up with the school librarian, who was steeped in instructional materials, to build an active center for helping children who were not progressing well in their regular classrooms. A regular teacher who became concerned about a pupil joined with the former special education teacher and the librarian to study the child (always involving the parents) and to see what they could arrange. Two well trained paraprofessionals gave them the time to meet and later helped with much of the specific teaching.

This team was able to deal on the spot with most of the children who were of special concern due to learning or behavior problems. Occasionally, a psychologist and a social worker were invited in from the central office to help extend the study and planning. (Actually, the psychologist was frequently in the school building helping to install, through training efforts, a new instructional management system.)

The school district conducts several special classes and manages several special centers in cooperation with other community agencies to serve children who have highly specialized and distinctive needs which, beyond question, require a special teacher in a separated environment, at least for a period of time. But, in the main, elementary schools do not contain special classes. The school library has several very special centers adjacent to the resource room out of which the special education teacher works, but that is all.

A Secondary School

A special resource center is conducted in an inner city junior high school. An eighth grade boy who is having great difficulty in his academic classes because of a severe reading problem is a typical client of the center. His school attendance has been going down steadily and he feels bitter and alienated from his teachers; he feels that they know and care little about him. His parents are mostly inattentive and unconcerned except when he misbehaves, which happens with increasing frequency.

The boy comes to the center and is met there by two fellow students. They give him several simple tests and inventories, and they are very sensitive to his feelings about his limited reading ability. The assessment takes about a half hour. The students have learned how to conduct them through other students and the teacher in charge of the center. An agreement with the boy about his difficulties in two classes is reached. The outcome is a proposed contract that the students will help the boy to work out with his two teachers. In return for the boy's regular attendance and strong, regular efforts in the classes, the students will seek out reading materials that he can handle, and the teachers will free him for some time each day so he can come to the center for intensive reading instruction.

Through a succession of cases like this boy's, virtually every teacher in the building is in and out of the center; they meet students there who, with the help of other students, are petitioning for adjustments in their school programs. The center itself is rich in materials. It is led by a sensitive, specially trained teacher who often consults with classroom teachers about accommodations in programs for students who have special needs.

Several things about this situation should be noted: the involvement of regular teachers in making accommodations in the program; the indirect or supportive role of the specialized teacher; and the responsibility students themselves take to create a school environment that is livable and helpful. Imagine how many special classes might be needed in such a building if self containment was chosen as the way to go.

A Minischool within a Comprehensive High School

A faculty group in one of the Roseville, Minnesota, public high schools became concerned about the significant numbers of students who were "not making it"—they were underachieving, without goals, hostile toward adults, uninvolved in school activities, in difficulty with the law, frequently absent from school, and generally headed for trouble. About one in ten students was identified as "not making it" and not more than a third of them were getting any special help or support.

A planning activity was launched by teachers in cooperation with parents, police, welfare, and corrections professionals that led to a specific plan for a minischool within the regular high school. A team of regular teachers, special education teachers, and vocational educators was formed to work on alternatives in curriculum that needed to be installed in the school; basic skills in English, modified social studies, mathematics, occupational relations, and work experience. Students were enrolled in the minischool program; in addition, all FOCUS students also enrolled one hour per day in "Family"—a group process oriented activity for small groups consisting of a staff person and 8 to 10 students.

The program has been described as emphasizing caring, positive expectations, and definite structure. Students in the FOCUS program have very significant roles in governance of the whole operation. FOCUS students take responsibility for bringing non-FOCUS students to the program so that it is seen as a well integrated alternative program in the building and they (the FOCUS students) are responsible for keeping their parents informed and bringing them to school for conferences. Through FOCUS it is felt that "mainstream" programs of the building, of area vocational programs and community resources are being used more effectively than ever. (For more details see Larsen, 1977).

An Area Vocational Technical Institute

The area vocational technical institute serves a large region that includes several high schools. The institute has taken seriously the federal mandate to serve handicapped and disadvantaged students, teenagers, and young adults. About 350 of the 2,500 full time students qualify as handicapped, as defined by special educators, and more could qualify as disadvantaged. The institute has set up a strong vocational evaluation unit in which students can explore their abilities and interests and then try out various occupational roles through work sample situations. Several vocational evaluators had special training to work with the handicapped students, but all the students, including the handicapped, come into the same evaluation unit. Some may get more attention than others but, if they do, it is in the context of their specific strengths, limits, needs, and interests. The staff is proud of its program for handicapped people, although they do not think of them as handicapped. There is no list of handicapped students nor do handicapped students go to special places; the total program has been constructed to accommodate students with very special needs. The mainstream in that school has changed.

The school also conducts an intensive support system for students who need extra academic help in order to survive in the various vocational training programs. The students who come to the learning center need to be there. If one had to classify them, there would be, to be sure, "LD's," "EM's," and others,* but there is no such labeling in the school. Incidentally, attendance and retention rates are especially good at this institute and behavior problems are at a minimum.

If one were to follow students who have special needs in this school, one would see "interpreters for the deaf" working with teachers in the various shops, labs, and classrooms—supporting students who need special accommodations. Similar supports have spread through the building, but only in such obvious measure and periods of time as essential. Students move on their own as soon as feasible.

---

*Special educators have made common use of a variety of abbreviations for various "categories" of exceptional children—for example, LD = learning disabled, EMR = educable mentally retarded, SLBP = special learning and behavior problem and TMR = trainable mentally retarded. The authors prefer to use such terms sparingly and to make other approaches to issues concerning the classification of children. However, it is necessary for regular teachers to be familiar with the most common of these abbreviations.

The Dissolution of a Special School

This vignette concerns the dissolution of a small special school for deaf and hard of hearing children in a community that, for years, had conducted a segregated program. At the request of parents the school was disbanded and the whole operation was moved into a regular school building where the children could be integrated with normal hearing children for at least part of their schooling.

In the regular school, 2 third grade teachers had classes of 30 children each. The special teacher of the deaf joined them with 5 hearing impaired children and all were placed in one unit. The ratio became 1 teacher to about 22 pupils. The hearing impaired children were integrated for most of the time.

The special teacher helps with the hearing children (a rich background in languages is highly useful) in addition to seeing that the hearing impaired children get the specialized help they need. The program has been implemented in a highly successful way. Indeed, the early success of this program made it possible to move toward a much broader program of integration for handicapped children in the school. "Normal" students soon were helping with accommodations for those with motor handicaps and many of them began learning the rudiments of manual communication systems used with deaf pupils.

Exceptional Children

Until recently the *prevailing* definition of *exceptional children* listed, in one way or another, those who are gifted, retarded, blind, partially seeing, deaf, hard of hearing, crippled, neurologically impaired, disturbed, maladjusted, speech and language impaired, special or general learning disabled, developmentally disabled, and others, plus combinations of these. But it is recognized now that it is the *educational work to be done with the pupil* that has to be the teacher's and principal's concern, more than the medical or legal name of the child's condition. Thus, a preferred definition of exceptional children, for us, includes all those pupils who need some form of special education—part time or full time, for short or long periods—at some stage in their sequence of schooling.

In the recent past special education was thought of as instructional activity carried on outside the regular class by an expert with a particular type of pupil. The view coming into prominence today sees special education as the individualized application of techniques, procedures, instructional materials, and equipment designed to accommodate to unusual forms or rates of cognitive, affective and motor status or development, to sensory deprivation, to lack of earlier schooling, to ineffective earlier instruction, or to any other personal or environmental conditions that stand in the way of a broad and thorough education. Most, if not all, of its techniques, procedures, materials, and equipment are readily adaptable for use by regular class teachers. Hence, an exceptional child's individualized educational program is usually a combination of regular and special education. Most of the time, too, it can be conducted as an integral part of regular class activities under the regular teacher's direction, with support from specialists, aides, and pupils.

Special education thus considered does attend to the particular educational needs of all the groups who have ordinarily been named as its targets. The terminology we use to denote exceptional children in the chapters which follow attempts to bridge historical and contemporary usage while providing guides to the immediate future. That is necessary in this time of transition. Also, where there are educationally significant nuances of meaning connected with expressions they are indicated in the context.

Gifted and Talented Children

Relatively little has been said so far about gifted and talented children, those with high cognitive abilities and talents who are able to learn very rapidly, even complex subject matters, at early ages. These students need to be well understood and served lest they suffer special kinds of delay and denial in education. Much of the federal legislation and court action about special education has been restricted to handicapped children and has not included the gifted and talented. A few states have organized strong efforts on behalf of gifted students, however. For example, in North Carolina and Pennsylvania provisions for specialized support of programs for the handicapped were extended fully to the gifted. Many local school districts include special efforts on behalf of the gifted regardless of governmental actions or inactions in the field.

In recent years, fortunately, a concerted interest in these students is evident at both state and federal levels. The US Office of Education has launched small programs of support for training and research in the education of the gifted and talented, and responsibilities for leadership in the area are beginning to be clarified in federal offices. Many states are proceeding with plans to develop programs for gifted and talented children. Attention of special educators should flow fully to all students who have special needs—gifted as well as handicapped; and, equally, regular teachers should be concerned about the full range of talents and needs represented by students.*

PREVAILING VERSUS PREFERRED PRACTICES

All human services—social welfare, law, medicine, and education— alter their practices when new values and information impinge on them.

---

*Whenever the term "exceptional" is used it refers to handicapped, gifted, and talented.

Improvements in practice rarely "take over" suddenly. Instead, they replace existing procedures at a slow and often uneven pace. But some changes come more easily and rapidly than others. The rate of change depends on such factors as cost, complexity, clarity of evidence supporting the changes, and the social values and pressures that are present.

Sometimes the urgency for progressive change is recognized in almost all of the quarters in which power resides; social, judicial, legislative, financial, professional, and popular support converge with sufficient force to quickly close the gap between what is and what should be. As the rate of change accelerates, all participants are thrust quickly into what had seemed a distant tomorrow. Such a change is occurring for teachers and most other educators with respect to the education of all exceptional children and youth.

In the context of the change, it is more necessary than ever that teachers in training and experienced teachers look in a new way at special education and the exceptional pupils who have been in its sole charge for many years. A variety of changes in functions and roles may be anticipated. Regular class teachers at all school levels and in all curricular areas will become much more knowledgeable about and competent at teaching exceptional pupils of all kinds. They will not replace *specialist* teachers of exceptional pupils; rather, the two will work closely together and with parents to identify, plan for, guide, instruct, and evaluate the progress of exceptional pupils. Regular teachers can be expected to take on more instruction of exceptional children in their classes as more schools build up strong support systems, including consultation, teaching assistance, and adequate materials. To the greatest extent practicable, all children will be in the regular class environment. The proper arrangement of this transition is the challenge.

Because of this altered perspective, it is essential that all teachers be familiar with current practices in the education of exceptional pupils and with the desired trends for the future, that is with *prevailing practices* and *preferred practices*.

The movement from prevailing toward preferred practices is of great import to teachers. *Prevailing practices* are those in widespread use; *preferred practices* are those that are in limited use but should be adopted, we believe, by more personnel. Preferred practices are advances that have been shown to be appropriate, effective, and feasible. One example is the trend to start exceptional children in kindergarten or first grade along with their other peers. Another example is the tendency to recognize teachers, regular and special, as the coequal coordinators of program placement and instructional planning for exceptional children.

Not all emerging practices are preferred. The line that is drawn between prevailing and preferred practices blurs in actuality because school systems are constantly in a state of becoming. Ultimately, it is the teacher and parents who determine, by what they accept as best for the education of children and youth, which professional practices will prevail.

In this book, most chapters contain a section in which prevailing and preferred practices are contrasted. The device is used to summarize quickly the practices most likely to be encountered in school programs for exceptional children, and then to present immediately an image of how the programs ought to be conducted. The first set of prevailing and preferred practices, covering certain general considerations that are presented in this first chapter, is presented here.

Prevailing Practices	Preferred Practices
1. Special education is conducted mainly in separate, specialized settings, such as special classes, resource rooms, or special schools.	1. Special education is conducted as an integral part of the unified school system; as much of it as possible is made portable and provided in regular classes and schools. Specialized settings are used only for essential purposes and limited periods of time.
2. Special education is managed mainly by highly centralized and specialized officers of the school system, all distinctly set apart from the general educational leadership system.	2. The administrative management of special education, as well as instructional programs, is highly decentralized; a maximum effort is made to accommodate exceptional children in their neighborhood schools.
3. Educational programs tend to start at 5 or 6 years of age for most exceptional children, with some special programs, such as those for deaf children, starting earlier.	3. Special education begins at birth or as soon thereafter as it is needed.
4. Handicapped students tend to be excluded from many programs at secondary and higher levels of education, and especially from vocational education.	4. Exceptional students are given full opportunities for education in secondary and vocational schools, colleges, and expanding lifelong learning programs.

Prevailing Practices	Preferred Practices
5. Placements in special settings are made on the basis of the child's classification into a "category" of handicapping condition or giftedness.	5. Children are separated from regular classes only when necessary for specific forms of instruction; many children, consequently, even those with severe handicaps, remain in regular school settings all or most of the time.
6. Special educators, school psychologists, speech clinicians, school social workers, and other specialized staff members provide services directly to children and families in clinical settings.	6. Special educators, school psychologists, speech clinicians, school social workers, and other specialized staff emphasize training as a function, and they work to "give away" as many of their competencies as possible to teachers and other staff members.
7. As spaces for instruction, schools consist mainly of series of "boxes" that have little provision for variety, easy access, and flexibility.	7. Schools, as physical settings for education, provide barrier free, safe, interesting, flexible spaces for all children, including those who are handicapped.
8. Special education financial aids to local school districts are allotted mainly to programs that isolate exceptional children in separate school settings.	8. Special education financial aids are used to support all forms of special instruction, including those conducted in regular classroom settings.
9. Instructional materials for regular school programs are very limited and separated from those that are available to special education instructors.	9. Adequate instructional supplies and materials are provided to all teachers, thus improving their accommodative power in dealing with individual differences among learners.
10. Teachers "refer" special "problem children" to specialists.	10. Teachers call in specialists to help with problem children right in the classroom.

Prevailing Practices	Preferred Practices
11. Parents are informed—usually—about the specialized programs that are provided for their children.	11. Parents participate fully with teachers and other staff members in all decisions regarding specialized programs for their children.
12. Reading instruction is conducted at multiple levels in most elementary school classrooms, but other aspects of the curriculum are standardized for all children.	12. Modern management systems for instruction and curriculum differentiation permit a wide variety of programing to accord with individual readiness and needs in all subjects.
13. Some children start every school year in the regular classes of their schools while others always start to attend and have their basic enrollment only in special education programs.	13. Every child, including the handicapped, starts his first year of schooling and every successive year in a regular school program.

HISTORICAL PERSPECTIVE

Before we try to gain additional perspectives on the theme of accommodating exceptional children in regular school programs, it may be helpful to take a brief excursion into the history of special education and to look, particularly, for those trends and forces that created our current conditions and that may continue to define and energize future activities.

The history of education for exceptional children is a simple story of massive neglect, denial, and rejection. For every Helen Keller and the other notable few who received intensive special help, tens of thousands of other exceptional children, both gifted and handicapped, were doomed to constricted lives; it was believed that they could not be taught, were not worth teaching, or could proceed on their own. In a sense, the development of special education can be recounted as an assault on this discriminatory attitude. It began in the early 19th century with a handful of dedicated pioneers such as Gaspard Itard (1774-1838) and his student Edouard Seguin (1812-1880), who began the study and training of mentally deficient children; Samuel G. Howe (1801-1876), who started the first school for the blind in the United States and proved by his work with blind and deaf Laura Bridgeman that the blind could be educated; Thomas H. Gallaudet (1787-1851), who organized the first school for the deaf in this country; and Louis Braille (1809-1852), the inventor of the system of writing that bears his name. In the early years of the 20th century Sidney L. Pressey, Lewis Terman, and Leta Hollingworth publicized the educational potentialities of gifted students, and their neglect. Tracking (separate sections for the most able students) began in 1886 in Elizabeth, New Jersey, and in St. Louis, Missouri, in 1871. Separate special classes for the gifted, sometimes called opportunity rooms, are recorded at Los Angeles State Normal School in 1924 and in Cleveland in 1922 (Newland, 1976).

Formal arrangements for the education of exceptional children in the United States can be divided into four periods, as shown in Table 1-1. Brief reviews of each of the first three periods are followed by a somewhat more extended treatment of the new trends that appeared rather suddenly in the 1970's and promise to persist for some period of time.

19th Century: Residential Schools

The first organized arrangements in the United States for the education of blind, deaf, and retarded children were copied from the residential schools and asylums of Europe; they became the models and set the dominant early pattern for special education in the United States. They tended to be narrowly categorical in orientation. Since colleges and universities were not yet involved in relevant professional training programs, the residential schools prepared teachers for the specialized work in on the job training. The roles of teachers, therefore, were defined categorically as of the blind, the deaf, or the retarded.

Most states established residential schools, sometimes after private institutions had demonstrated that the target population was educable. Nevertheless, all exceptional children could not be accommodated in the institutions. Facilities were limited in the state operated schools and the private ones were too expensive for many families. Some parents considered separation from their children more onerous than depriving them of educational opportunities. And children with severe and multiple handicaps were often not eligible for admission to any school.

Residential schools, both public and private, are still in existence but more and more they are being used only for selected individuals who present severe and multiple educational problems that may be best served there, or students from extremely isolated communities where the specialized resources necessary to instruct them have not yet been developed.

Early 20th Century: Community Prototypes

Community based programs specifically designed for the education of exceptional children began to appear at the turn of the century as special classes and public day schools. In their earliest forms, these programs

TABLE 1-1
Education of Exceptional Children
in the United States

Rough time periods	Events	Modal programs format
Late 19th century	1. European models for education are transported to the United States by immigrants and visitors. 2. Most states begin to accept a *public* responsibility for the education of the handicapped—earliest progress is made in areas of blindness and deafness, and later in mental retardation.	Residential school
Early 20th century (ca 1900-1945)	1. Many cities begin local special classes. 2. Residential institutions begin to train specialized teachers for local school special programs.	Prototype community based programs—the special class and special school
ca 1945-1970	1. Parents of exceptional children organize for political action. 2. Many colleges and universities launch preparation programs for specialized teachers. 3. State and federal legislative action moves strongly to support special education.	Explosion of the simple special class model
Beginning ca 1970	1. Parent groups move increasingly to the courts to stimulate more services for handicapped and gifted children. 2. The civil rights movement spreads from race and sex to the handicapped. 3. Minority groups object to high rates of negative classification of children. 4. Regular teacher education begins to include components on exceptional children. 5. Comprehensive federal legislation incorporates concepts of rights to education and least restrictive alternative (Public Law 94-142).	Negotiations for more inclusive arrangements; the period of least restrictive alternative, mainstreaming, or progressive inclusion

were dependent on residential schools for leadership, curricula, and teacher preparation. Gallaudet College, for example, which was then serving deaf children, started a teacher training program in the 1890's (Craig, 1942), and in 1904 the Vineland Training School in New Jersey began summer training sessions for teachers of retarded children (Hill, 1945).

At their best, these early programs reflected a bare tolerance of exceptional children in community schools except for the gifted who, often undetected, were "getting by." The community school movement developed slowly. For the first half of this century, most children who were noticeably difficult to teach were in schools for minimum periods only. Children who progressed slowly in academic subjects frequently were forced to repeat grades until they became embarrassingly oversized in comparison with their classmates. When special classes or "opportunity" rooms were instituted for such children, the labels that often were attached to the children took on derogatory connotations.

Until comparatively recently, of course, public schools had never seriously tried to serve all children, and especially not those who were difficult to teach. Indeed, during the first decades of this century, most children attended school only long enough to acquire the rudiments of a basic education. Consequently, school systems were not prepared physically, philosophically, or financially to operate far reaching programs for exceptional children. Special education is costly by definition because of its emphasis on individual problems and needs. When school budgets were limited, as during the Depression of the 1930's, in particular, special class programs were not expanded.

The rather pervasive neglect of atypical children that was evident well into the 20th century was not a deliberate and callous deprivation, perhaps, but an outgrowth of certain ideas that were pervasive at the time. Sloan (1963), for example, attributed the educational lethargy of the early 1900's to the widespread public misinformation on genetics and criminal tendencies and to the accepted attitude that mental retardation was generally a hopeless condition. It was also widely believed that mental precocity was closely akin to mental illness and that unusual brightness was most often a temporary flash in the pan in children. "Early ripe, early rot" was accepted as an axiom.

In *Buck v. Bell* (1927), Supreme Court Justice Oliver Wendell Holmes supported a sterilization policy for retarded citizens. He wrote, "It is better for all the world, if instead of waiting to execute degenerate offspring for crime or to let them starve from their imbecility, society can prevent those who are manifestly unfit from continuing their kind" (p. 207).

In the 1930's, research findings about the "rigidity" of the mentally retarded (Zigler, 1969) tended to become diffused in the public consciousness and to make the provision of special educational opportunities for them seem hopeless. Thus delay and denial were the educational lot of most children with any kind of handicap throughout at least the first half of the 20th century.

Nevertheless, during 1920's and 1930's, bits of progress were evident. For example, formal programs to train specialized teachers for the exceptional were instituted in a few universities, first at Wayne State University and the Teachers College of Columbia University, and then at Eastern Michigan University at Ypsilanti and the University of Wisconsin at Milwaukee. The roles for which teachers were prepared were mainly modeled on those developed in the residential schools. On the basis of existing practices, it was assumed that exceptional children should receive the services of special teachers in special environments. Very little attention was given to orientating regular teachers to the needs of these students.

1945 to 1970: Explosion of Simple Models

As if to make up through one large effort the neglect of centuries, a remarkable surge of activities on behalf of all exceptional children began shortly after World War II. Our largest states launched programs to serve exceptional pupils in the public schools on a broad scale, and numerous colleges and universities organized programs to train teachers in special education to serve the children.

The change that occurred over the quarter of a century is best reflected in statistics. In 1948, 442,000 children were enrolled in special education programs; in 1963, 1,666,000 were enrolled (Mackie, 1965); and according to estimates of the Bureau of Education for the Handicapped, during the 1971-72 school year, 2,857,551 handicapped children were receiving special education services. These data reflect more than a sixfold increase, and they do not include what was happening with gifted pupils.

The increase in training programs for special education teachers was almost as great. About 77 colleges and universities were providing training sequences for special education teachers in one or more categories in 1948; by 1954, the number was 122 (Mackie & Dunn, 1954), and by 1973, it was over 400. In 1976, it was estimated that the number of colleges and universities involved in this field exceeded 600. The rapid increases in college programs in the 1950's and 1960's reflected the new involvement of the federal government in the financial support of special education training efforts. In addition to special teachers, school systems were employing growing numbers of administrators and supervisors for the rapidly proliferating programs in special education that were spreading across more and more categories. Beginning about 1965 many of those new positions were in connection with programs for gifted pupils.

Although it is impossible to determine all the influences that brought about the rapid development of public school programs for exceptional children between 1960 and 1970, three can be recognized. They were new on the educational scene.

First, parents of exceptional children formed a number of organizations, such as the National Association for Retarded Citizens (known earlier as the National Association for Retarded Children), which was chartered in 1950. It became socially and politically active, and influenced state legislatures and the Congress. In response, the federal government established a national program in the field of special education. In 1957, supports were provided for research and leadership training in the area of mental retardation; in 1963; the supports were extended by Congreess to cover virtually all exceptionalities except the gifted; and in 1966, a new Bureau of Education for the Handicapped (BEH) was established to administer the burgeoning new programs. In fiscal year 1976 BEH distributed more than $200 million to state departments of education, colleges, and local school systems for a broad spectrum of programs. Under legislation passed in 1975 (Public Law 94-142, The Education for All Handicapped Children Act) there is considerable promise that appropriations will escalate rapidly over a five year period beginning in 1977. The beginning structure is in place for a similar movement on behalf of gifted students. Money will not solve problems, but it is one essential.

Second, many state legislatures, in response to pressure from parents' groups, passed new legislation that mandated instruction in the schools for many categories of exceptional children. The legislatures provided "excess cost" aids in one form or another to local school districts that launched special education programs. Excess cost aids are special categories of state or federal funding of special education programs designed to assure that local districts do not experience any "excess cost" when they provide specialized programs for students who have special needs. Presumably, it is possible for local districts to design programs for handicapped children without experiencing strains on their budgets and without being biased for or against a "special" program just because of its cost. Because of the financial assistance provided by state legislatures and later by the federal agencies, many school districts found that the operation of special education programs not only permitted the provision of services for exceptional children but also helped to improve the services for the school population as a whole.

Third, as the nation became aware of and made necessary provisions for the rehabilitation of World War II and Korean War veterans who had been seriously injured, facilities in veterans' hospitals were enlarged and new research programs to further aid the veterans were established in various institutions and agencies. In colleges and universities, departments of clinical psychology, speech pathology, and physical medicine were expanded through federal rehabilitation funds, and the influences of their investigations on behalf of veterans spread to the research and training being carried on for exceptional children. For example, because blinded veterans rejected isolation and dependency as their fate, programs for mobility and occupational training were begun for them at veterans' hospitals. Leaders of these programs soon became involved in preparing teachers of blind children in mobility and orientation techniques. Many more school systems discovered that blind children could function in integrated day school programs that were based on a resource teacher model, that is, programs in which the children spent only part of the day away from the regular class. These programs forced serious examination of the past practices of automatically referring blind children to special schools or classes.

It should be noted that the sheer quantitative leap in programing for exceptional children between 1945 and 1970 is not attributable to any great technological or ideological advances. There were some innovations, such as the development of low vision and individual electronic hearing aids, and of techniques for the rapid production of enlarged print books (for children with partial sight), but they are of limited account in the context of the massive change. On the whole, the period can be said to have been one of rapid development based on the simple models of the past. The teachers who were prepared in the 1950's and 1960's were, in most cases, prepared for "special classes and schools" of the familiar model of earlier decades. This is not to imply that the 25 years were totally barren of new ideas; in fact, some of the trends that are discussed in the next section were generated during these important years.

As part of the studies stimulated by the late President John F. Kennedy in the mid 1960's, a great many US special educators were enabled to investigate developments in special education in other parts of the world. Visitors to the Scandinavian countries encountered what is known as the process of *normalization,* that is, the principle of educating handicapped persons in and for the "normal" environment of the nonhandicapped, to the maximum feasible extent. This process requires major development of community based support systems for the handicapped.

The boundary lines of the categories of exceptional children began to be seriously examined. Strong pressures were developed to extend special education services to children who were obviously very much in need of specialized forms of education but were as yet unserved. The cases that were argued most strenuously in the 1950's concerned whether schools should serve the "trainable" as well as the "educable" retarded and whether gifted and talented pupils really need special education. See the famous debate between I. Ignacy Goldberg and William M. Cruickshank (Goldberg & Cruickshank, 1958)...Recent judicial and legislative mandates relating to the schools' responsibility to all handicapped children have made this debate of historical interest only.

Special education categories were increased to include children who do not fall into any of the traditional special education classifications. In the late 1960's, the largest increases in special education enrollment were in "learning disabilities," which many observers do not consider a category in the traditional sense but, rather, a diverse set of residuals from other categories. The inclusion of the category in special education's province was welcomed by many persons, nevertheless, because it represented a move away from the overly simple medical and psychometric models of categorization, which have increasingly come under attack, and permitted the extension of service to neglected children, even if the definitional problems provided a major professional embarrassment.

Overall, one characteristic of the postwar period may be of the greatest importance for the future: For the first time diverse programs of special education were consolidated in single schools making it possible to look at and to work across all categories and to consider how they might be related to each other. That consolidation began to be reflected in the research and training programs of many colleges and universities. However, many difficulties about the "category" problem remain to be solved.

During the busy period of the 1960's, the long standing patterns of special education began to draw their share of skepticism and even hostility. Although blessed with rapidly increasing amounts of money, school districts did not generate serious evaluation of their programs. When evaluation studies were undertaken, as in the 1960 series of mental retardation special class "efficacy" studies, the evaluation methodology was usually at least as doubtful as the practices purported to be evaluated. The orientation has often been narrowly psychometric in such studies, with too little attention to matters of values and morals.

Some very influential special educators, such as Dunn (1968), and some people outside of the professional ranks were skeptical. For example, the following comments were offered to a group of special education administrators in 1970 by US Congressman Albert Quie:

> One of the great problems of being in political office these days is that there is very little that is sacred. One was generally always safe being for motherhood, the flag, apple pie, and handicapped children. But today with the women's liberation movement and the pill, motherhood is being challenged, the flag seems to be continually getting into trouble, apple pie is being tested by the Food and Drug Administration, and I am afraid

that handicapped children might not be too far behind. If the public is going to significantly invest in the education of the exceptional child... [it is necessary] to establish clear objectives for the programs, to explain to the public what its dollars will buy, and to demonstrate that the objectives have been achieved. (Quie, 1970)

The 1970's: Negotiating for More Inclusive Arrangements

Fundamental changes are in process in the 1970's based on a broad new agenda for educators. A renegotiation of boundaries between regular and special education and between community based and residential institutions is under way. Perhaps the period can be summarized under the rubric "least restrictive alternative" or "mainstreaming," or in its broadest sense, "progressive inclusion" or "integration."

Before proceeding into the current scene, a summary is in order. The whole history of education for exceptional children can be told in terms of one steady trend that can be described as progressive inclusion. Exceptional children have come, in a period of less than two centuries, from total neglect, first into isolated residential schools, for just a few—then into isolated community settings, mostly in the form of special classes for a limited population—and now into more integrated arrangements for many children. In the 1970's, we are in the midst of what undoubtedly will be recorded by future historians as a remarkable reversal of the negative cascade that sent these children off to isolated classes and centers. The agendas of local school boards in communities all across the country now reflect the influx of children with complex and severe educational problems, pupils who had been sent off to hospitals and residential centers earlier; and virtually every school principal in every school district is facing difficult questions about the accommodation of more exceptional children in regular classrooms.

The movement of special education toward mainstream education is found in other countries, too. Witness this statement about Sweden:

Stress has been laid during the last decade on efforts to integrate handicapped pupils as far as possible into ordinary education.

At one time the characteristics of special education could be summed up as individualized teaching methods, specially constructed programs, step-by-step learning, a psychological approach to the child's problems and difficulties, mental hygiene as an aspect of the methods and treatment adopted by teachers, and so on. On the whole, the emphasis was not only on the pedagogic aims of education, as evaluated in terms of knowledge, skill, achievement, but also on the social and emotional development of the child. All these criteria, however, have now been incorporated in modern education and it is therefore no longer reasonable to regard special education as fundamentally different from general education. Throughout the world the general school systems seem to have changed their characteristics. In Sweden, the modern school aims at a method of work whereby each student can obtain exactly what he requires in respect of teaching, upbringing and care. The aim is to offer each individual student a course of study that suits his particular aptitudes and needs and gives him an opportunity to perform according to his ability.

The aim...is also valid for special teaching. It implies the creation of better opportunities in the school system as a whole for children and young people with some sort of special difficulty or handicap. Special education in Sweden nowadays can thus be described as an essential part of general education, as one of the elements designed to make it possible for all pupils, including the handicapped, to benefit by access to learning or training. At the same time, special education requires a greater degree of specialist contributions, coordinated with the pedagogic work in "ordinary" education. Medical, technical, social and psychological experts are needed as are specially trained teachers and specially devised teaching aids combined with ordinary materials. Hence, it is still correct to talk of special education as a reality in the sense that it involves concentrated educational efforts for the individual handicapped pupil. (Lundstrom, 1974, pp. 119-120).

This historical perspective suggests that the current mainstreaming trend is not a minor pendulum swing or a temporary enthusiasm. There has been a steady, progressive, inclusive trend in special education from the beginning, from unconcern to distal (far away) to proximal (near) arrangements. It would be naive to assume a straight line, uncomplicated, and continuing trend but there appear to be fundamental forces at work supporting the general trend toward more inclusive arrangments for the education of children with special needs. Administrative arrangements are seen increasingly as dependent variables that can be modified to meet individual human needs, rather than as certitudes for the disposition of children diagnosed or "carved by nature" to fit particular slots. These topics are given detailed treatment in the rest of this chapter.

FORCES AND TRENDS OF THE 1970's

As used here, the term *forces* signifies those influences that relate to special education but are larger than special education in scope and effect. They are, essentially a clustering of ideological and social phenomena that energize and define movements in special education. Because they are of critical importance at this time, they should be understood in relation to possible future educational developments.

Aggressive Categorical Parent Groups

For a quarter of a century the schools and other institutions serving exceptional children have been stimulated by organized groups of parents of exceptional children to increase and improve the services they provide. Professionals have sometimes felt threatened by parent groups but they have found constructive ways of interacting with parents to create a broadly coordinated voice in such activities as achieving legislative consideration at state and federal levels. Occasionally the professionals have tried but never really successfully, to absorb the associations. Parent groups are the watchdogs of the institutions that serve their children, and they are quick to make themselves heard at all levels—school, community, state, and nation—whenever programs appear to be inadequate.

At first, parent associations and most individual parents tended to be strictly local in their orientation. Letha Paterson, an early leader in the parents' movement in Minnesota, used to say that all parents of the handicapped go through three stages: (a) they ask, "Why did this happen to me?" and make themselves the object of concern; (b) then they ask, "How can I better help my child?" and (c) finally, they begin to ask "How can I help other children and families who have similar problems?" When large numbers of parents reach this third stage, broad patterns of support for services, teacher training, and research begin to be forged.

The more recently formed groups of parents concerned with improved education for gifted children follow a similar pattern only their first question is, "Why does the school neglect my child's gifts instead of fostering them?" Where children were both handicapped and gifted, as is the case with many, their efforts have needed to go in several directions, including colleges and other postsecondary schools.

The associations of parents of the exceptional that emerged after World War II quickly turned to the use of political power. Beginning in about 1970, however, they looked to the courts as a means of promoting public action. This fact may be more important than any other in accounting for the changes in special education that occurred in the early 1970's and are likely to continue, at least into the near future. Court actions are here subsumed under the rubric of parent groups because, clearly, the parent groups are the basic planning and motivating forces behind them. When the leverage provided by the courts recedes, other stratagems unquestionably will be employed to secure changes in policies and programs. Indeed, a demonstration was given in 1975; much of the important new federal legislation (Public Law 94-142) was achieved through the pressures of representatives of parent groups.

In the context of recent court decisions, right to education, right to treatment, due process, and least restrictive alternative have emerged as concepts that may change the face of special education and, indeed, of all of education. A landmark in this extension of educational rights to handicapped children was the case *PARC v. Pennsylvania* (1971). Although the *PARC* (Pennsylvania Association for Retarded Children) and certain subsequent cases were not taken through the full legal course, either because they were settled by consent agreements or have not been appealed to the US Supreme Court for constitutional determination, they have been extraordinarily persuasive in establishing the principle that every child, no matter how variant from others, has the right to education. In other words, public schools have the obligation to provide appropriate education for literally all children, either in their own facilities or by arrangement with other agencies (Lippman & Goldberg, 1973).

These cases also established a broad concept of education. The appropriate function of public education was decided judicially to include equipping children with "life skills," a principle that goes far beyond the goal of transmitting academic or strictly intellectual skills. The court made clear that it considered the enhancement of individual development to be the critical objective of education rather than the consideration of the returns society might expect from providing the individual with education.

The *PARC* case also established the right of parents to participate in major decisions affecting their children. The State Secretary of Education in Pennsylvania was directed to train hearing officers to conduct proceedings for parents and school representatives whenever there were disagreements on such matters as school placement.

The court also expressed the preference for placing exceptional children in regular classes for their education, with displacements to special classes and special schools requiring extraordinary justification. This least restrictive alternative, which has been supported in other recent cases, portends major changes in the kinds of evidence required for and the basic logic of placement processes. When there is no clear evidence that an alternative setting is advantageous, the child is required to be served in the regular classroom. The need for support systems to work with regular teachers to meet these new imperatives is obvious.

The concept of *least restrictive alternative,* is quite new in education and will deserve close scrutiny. A discussion advanced by leaders of The Council for Exceptional Children proceeds as follows:

> Effectively complying with due process requirements contributes to the designing of educational programs to meet the individual needs of each child. Determination of both the child's needs and the appropriate program is the purpose of due process. The process, however, is also designed to insure that handicapped children receive their education in the least restrictive setting. Such a concept assumes that there are a variety of alternative settings in which the child can be placed. These settings range from the usual or regular classroom with nonhandicapped peers to more restrictive settings such as special classes on a full or part time basis, special schools, or residential institutions which are the most restrictive.
>
> The concept is frequently referred to as mainstreaming. From a legal view, the concept means that any removal of an individual from a normal situation into one which is restrictive as a matter of public policy, is a limitation of that individual's liberty. Thus, placement in a special class as

opposed to a regular class deprives the individual of some liberty, and is restrictive...

In light of the judicial mandates and those which are based in statutes, adherence to due process in placement decisions means that for each child regardless of the severity of his handicap, the schools must propose a placement in the most normal setting possible. Further, within the due process context, the schools must be prepared to accept the responsibility for demonstrating the appropriateness of their recommendation not only as the best setting for the educational service but also as the least restrictive. This same obligation occurs each time a change is proposed in the child's educational program. Further, it has been recommended that a hearing officer's decision to approve a proposed education plan "shall indicate why less restrictive placement alternatives could not adequately and appropriately serve the child's educational needs." (Abeson, Bolick, & Hass, 1975, p. 29). (Abeson, in Jones & Wilderson, 1976, pp. 23-24)

Another approach to the concept is provided in the draft regulations of the US Office of Civil Rights in implementation of amendments to the Rehabilitation Act of 1973; in the following, the term *recipients* refers to any educational agency that receives federal funds in any form.

84.35 Most normal setting feasible.

A recipient shall provide educational services to each qualified handicapped person who resides in the recipient's jurisdiction, regardless of the nature or severity of the person's handicap, in the most normal setting feasible and may not remove a handicapped person from, or place such person in a setting other than, the regular educational environment except when the nature or severity of the person's handicap is such that education in regular classes with the use of supplementary aids and services is demonstrated by the recipient not to be in the best interest of such person. (*Federal Register,* Vol. 41, No. 96, 1976)

While the above sources refer specifically to handicapped pupils, the same concept applies to gifted pupils. In Pennsylvania the least restrictive alternative principle is mandated in state law as applied to gifted children, effective in September 1977. Under mandate of the same law, due process and hearings on program admissions and program appropriateness are the rights of parents, pupils, and school districts.

Another set of cases, developed mainly in the context of institutional placements, established the individual's *right to treatment,* which was defined to include education. The *Wyatt v. Aderholt* (1971) case has been of crucial interest because it helped to establish the principle that lack of funds is not an acceptable justification for the failure to provide treatment. Public agencies are required either to raise sufficient funds or to reallocate existing resources to fulfill their treatment responsibilities to patients.

A cautionary note concerning right to education concepts arises from a 1976 three judge federal court case in Ohio (*Cuyahoga County Association for Retarded Children and Adults v. Essex,* 1976). The court concluded that:

> In dealing with a system of mandatory free public education a state which determines that only those children who can derive actual benefit from a broadly based public education system are to be included therein cannot be said to be acting arbitrarily.

In effect the court ruled that a discretionary system "structured so that the greatest emphasis is placed upon aiding individuals with, relatively speaking, greater intellectual capacity," was not constitutionally defective.* It may be significant that the court added a final footnote noting that Public Law 94-142, the Education for All Handicapped Children Act of 1975, might alter the issues of the case in consideration and require extension of education to all children as a matter of right.

Minority Groups

The parent groups organized around exceptional children have, except for those concentrating of the gifted, drawn their memberships and active participants from among parents of severely handicapped children. A high proportion of the membership is White, middle class, and relatively affluent. The programs instigated by the organizations, however, are by no means directed at only middle class, severely handicapped children. Indeed, a major impact of the groups' activities during the period of rapid expansion of special education (1945 to 1970) was felt in urban ghetto schools.

The proliferation of funds for special education led to the widespread organization of EMR (educable mentally retarded), ED (emotionally disturbed), and SM (socially maladjusted) programs for children who were hard to teach. These categories carry far more stigma than classification such as blind, crippled, or deaf. In urban and rural ghetto schools, minority group children were placed in the ED, SM, and EMR programs at a considerably higher rate than children in other schools. By the same token, programs for gifted pupils included few minority pupils. Thus, from the viewpoint of many minority group parents, the effects of special education were negative; indeed, many felt that this was an expression of racist attitudes and not what parents really wanted.

The President's Committee on Mental Retardation (1968) found that children from impoverished and minority group homes are 15 times more likely to be diagnosed as retarded than are children from higher income

---
*See *Mental Disability Law Reporter*, 1976.

families, and that three-fourths of the nation's "mentally retarded" are found in the isolated and impoverished urban and rural slums. Awareness of the spreading presence of special classes in ghetto schools aroused resentment and resistance among parents. As a result, administrators of school systems in our largest cities were placed under a virtual mandate to reverse the expansion of special education programs and to eliminate the testing, categorizing, and labeling practices that are associated with placement in the programs. In his review of Michael Young's book, *Rise of Meritocracy*, David Riesman (1967) lauded this "resistance of parents to having their children fall like brass in Plato's social system" (p. 905).

In professional associations, such as The Council for Exceptional Children, minority group members have also voiced their concern for the institutionalized racism and prejudice that is represented in the excessive placement of minority group children in programs that remove them from the mainstream of education, and they are working within their associations to change the policies and operations of schools. In fact, there is a rising and broad demand among special educators for the elimination of any activity that degrades and stigmatizes children.

The minority groups and professionals who challenge the excesses of special placements and the simple categorizing and labeling of children have taken a position that is, in fact, discordant with the exceptionality categories and a political problem of some proportion has resulted. While associations of parents of exceptional children sometimes seek to expand the traditional forms of special education for their children, minority group members tend to take strongly questioning attitudes toward much of the activity conducted in the name of special education. The categorical systems of special education sometimes appear to be a disguise for racial segregation. Their doubts and questions have proved to be particularly pressing in some of the largest cities in the nation where civil rights officers of the Department of Health, Education, and Welfare have ordered the desegregation of schools, often with special directives relating to special education classes. A major problem to which teachers will need to address themselves in the immediate future is the determination of means by which the energies of both groups of parents—those organized by exceptionality and those who are members of ethnic minorities—can be joined to support developments that serve all children with appropriate and good effects. There is, obviously, a common interest in providing intensive, appropriate education to children who have special needs, but it is complicated by the current political stirrings of both groups. A recent volume edited by Jones (1976) deals specifically with prospects and problems of the confluence of mainstreaming trends regarding race and exceptionality; in summary, the

Jones treatment offers a cautious hope for mainstreaming in its broadened meaning if conducted and evaluated with sensitivity.

Federal Legislation

Since the late 1950's, the role of the federal government in leading and supporting special education programs has grown steadily. At first, support went mainly to research and leadership training, but in more recent years funds have begun to flow directly to state and local school systems to finance the delivery of services to children. Currently the concepts enunciated by the courts are being reflected in the enabling legislation at both state and federal levels.

Many of the judicial principles—right to education, least restrictive alternative, individualized programing, and due process—have been embodied in Public Law 94-142, the Education for All Handicapped Children Act of 1975. This Act proposes a substantial escalation of federal funding for special education programs beginning in 1977; but to qualify for the funding, states must comply with a broad new set of standards on assessment and planning for individual children, and the involvement of parents in planning and other procedures.

The Act is a detailed and comprehensive blueprint for federal participation in special education programs of all kinds at state and local levels. Because of its pervasive and detailed nature, it is regarded by some education administrators as extraordinarily intrusive in state and local school operations, especially since education in America is legally a state, not a national responsibility. Also, it is noted that Congress contributes no more than 10% of the cost of education in the United States. However, if the legislation is administered with flexibility and the dollar appropriations are substantial, it can be a powerful tool for achieving special education goals in the coming years. Public Law 94-142 provides some procedural safeguards and promises some resources, but of course much more is required to assure appropriate education.

A related piece of legislation is the Rehabilitation Act, which was enacted by the US Congress and signed by the President in 1973. This Act adds the category of handicapped to race and sex in the statement of social principle or policy that guarantees individual rights. It explicitly excludes the use of handicapping conditions as a basis for negative decisions in schooling, employment, and the broader affairs of society. Section 504 of that Act reads, in part, as follows:

> No otherwise qualified handicapped individual in the United States...shall solely by reason of his handicap be excluded from participation in, be denied the benefits of, or be subjected to discrimination under any program or activity receiving Federal financial assistance. (Rehabilitation Act of 1973, 29 U.S.C. 794)

The pattern of federal involvement in education for the exceptional, through both legislative and judicial actions, adds strength to the long-standing dominant trend in the field of special education. That trend can be described as progressively inclusive in the sense, first, of extending rights and opportunities to more and more persons and, second, of making a place for these children in the mainstream settings of our society whenever possible.

CHANGING PATTERNS OF ADMINISTRATIVE ARRANGEMENTS

The administrative arrangements for special education in most schools of the nation well into the 1960's and even into the 1970's, in many places, can be described in terms of the "two box" theory. From this point of view, in local school buildings there are two kinds of classrooms (regular and special), two general classes of children (regular class children and exceptional children), and two sets of teachers (regular educacation and special education). In effect, two separate school systems are operated, each with its own supervisory staff and funding system.

Under the two box theory, a child who shows difficulty in a regular class is referred by the teacher to a psychologist and/or other specialist for study. If the child meets the standards for some category of special education (such standards often are defined by state regulations that specify the conditions for special categorical funding), placement is made in a special class or special school. Too often, psychological testing is the sole basis on which a final placement decision is made.

It is not unusual for a large elementary school operating under the two box theory to have perhaps 24 regular "boxes" or classrooms and 4 or 5 special "boxes" for educable mentally retarded children, learning disabled children, remedial reading cases, and Title I children (programs for children who need supplementary help in schools with a significant proportion of students from low income families). Speech and hearing clinicians and other itinerant specialist teachers may be in and out of the building for part time services to some students.

The teachers serving the special education classrooms in such schools generally receive their training in the special education departments of colleges and universities across the country, and they hold specialized certificates from state departments of education for their particular categories of competency. On the average, going into the 1970's, states offered seven or eight different kinds of special education teacher certification. Among the more common areas of specialization are: educable mentally retarded, trainable mentally retarded, speech and hearing, learning disabilities, hearing impairments, visual impairments, crippled and other health impaired, and emotionally disturbed. Of course, there are many variants among the categories. Depending on the state, it would be possible for a teacher to be certified to teach in such additional categories as hard of hearing, partially sighted, brain damaged, perceptually impaired, gifted, and many others.

To complete the brief story of two box organization, one must add that most of the development of this kind of organization occurred at the elementary school level. At secondary and postsecondary levels, students most often are left to sink or swim without special supports; and the story at these higher levels is told more in terms of sink than swim. In particular, students in more advanced levels of schooling have been denied opportunities, have become frustrated and have withdrawn, and, in many instances, have been excluded.

The Original Cascade Model

In the 1960's, a somewhat more complex administrative model for the organization of special education programs emerged. It is sometimes described as a cascade or continuum of administrative arrangements, not just two kinds of boxes (see Figure 1-1). However, it was still oriented mainly to the *places* or *administrative structures* of special education. Some distinct features are included in the model:

1. It proposed that support be given to regular classrooms as one means of meeting the special needs of the children who are maintained there.
2. It proposed that children *not* be classified and given special placements on a permanent basis but, rather, that they be moved to special stations only for as long as necessary and that they be returned to regular classrooms as soon as feasible. Thus, no indelible labels were involved. The total number of children served over time in special settings greatly exceeds the numbers served at any given time.
3. It proposed that the boundary lines between special education and regular education be renegotiated and opened so that students might pass back and forth easily, as dictated by their educational needs.
4. It proposed that regular and special education staff members become more interactive or collaborative in their daily work, such as sharing responsibilities for students, rather than to remain isolated in their separate centers and classrooms.
5. It proposed that extraordinary justification be required whenever a child was removed from the regular school environment, especially when removal was from both home and school environments for placement in a residential center.

A new teacher entering such a school system is likely to encounter a broad continuum or cascade of instructional arrangements; and college students who are preparing for work in special education under cascade

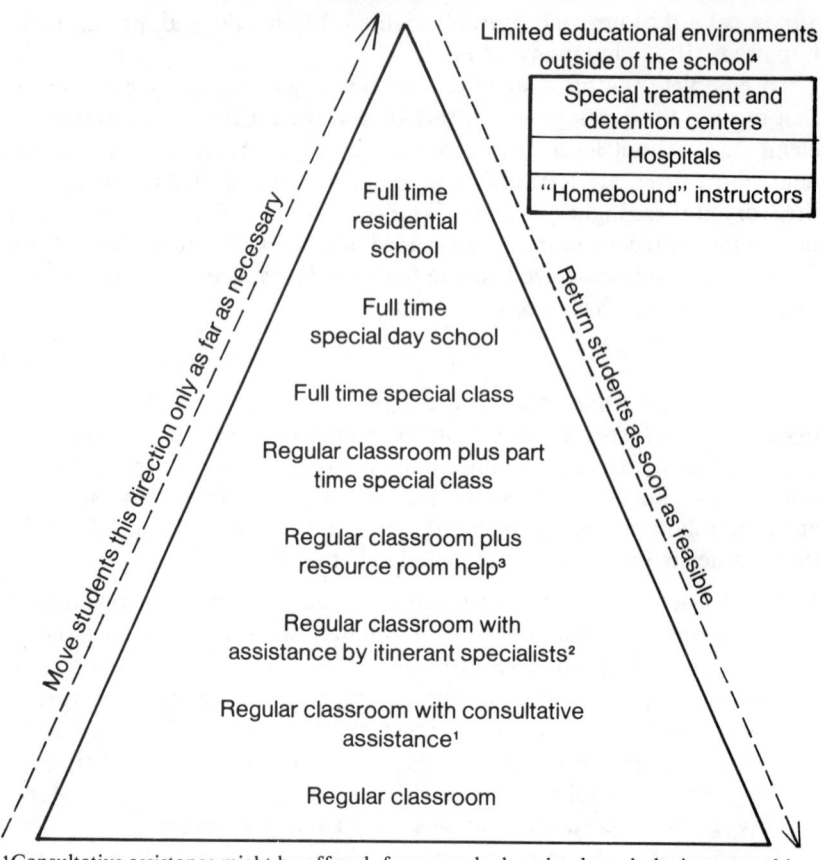

FIGURE 1-1
The Original Special Education Cascade

Limited educational environments outside of the school[4]

| Special treatment and detention centers |
| Hospitals |
| "Homebound" instructors |

- Full time residential school
- Full time special day school
- Full time special class
- Regular classroom plus part time special class
- Regular classroom plus resource room help[3]
- Regular classroom with assistance by itinerant specialists[2]
- Regular classroom with consultative assistance[1]
- Regular classroom

Move students this direction only as far as necessary

Return students as soon as feasible

[1] Consultative assistance might be offered, for example, by school psychologists, consulting teachers, resource room teachers, supervisors or others. The term *consultative* denotes only *indirect* services and no *direct* service or instruction to the child by the consultant.

[2] Itinerant specialists commonly include speech and hearing clinicians and mobility instructors for the blind, for example. They offer some *direct* instruction to the students involved.

[3] A resource room is a special station (classroom) in a school building that is manned by a resource teacher who usually offers some direct instruction to selected students but also usually offers consulting services to regular teachers. Sometimes resource teachers are categorical (such as resource teacher for the blind) but increasingly resource teachers are employed for a more generic, noncategorical role.

[4] This special set of environments is included here in set-aside fashion because usually students are placed in these settings for reasons other than educational. For example, they go to detention centers on order of courts for reason of conviction for some criminal offense; or they go to hospitals or are held at home because of health problems. Special educators often work in these *limited* environments and some degree of specialization in education is required. But, in the main, there is strong preference, from an educational point of view, for return of the students to regular school environments as soon as feasible.

model conditions are likely to find the job market expanding for some of the stations of the cascade (i.e., resource teachers) and diminishing for narrowly categorical, two box classrooms.

Nevertheless, the original cascade model can be subjected to a variety of criticisms. One particularly telling observation is that it is still too much "place" oriented. Although it proposed that administrative arrangements and places be conceptualized as providing variable and flexible services to students and that pupil placements within the cascade be monitored and revised as necessary, it is nevertheless true that the model put the clearest focus on administrative structures and places. The only reason for providing the diversity in administrative arrangements, presumably, is to enable the development and scheduling of instructional programs. Why not, then, develop the models and the dialogue in a way that emphasizes the instructional diversity?

This criticism of the original cascade becomes even more valid as changes occur at different administrative levels in the capacity to offer specialized instruction. What if, for example, deaf pupils could be given the specialized instruction they need in the regular school environment? Or, what if detailed diagnostic procedures could be coordinated through teaming arrangements within the regular school setting, thus reducing sharply the use of referral and special placement procedures for children who are not progressing in academics or who show behavior problems? In fact, precisely these kinds of developments are taking place now; we are learning to provide specialized instruction outside of specialized places.

Current changes can be represented schematically, as shown in Figure 1-2. Diagnostic and specialized instructional procedures are coming down to the regular class base of the cascade. There is a growing recognition that not all specialized instruction needs a special place and, in fact, that it is likely to be disadvantageous to confine children in special places or limited environments for long periods of time.

Specialists tend to design environments that only specialists can manage. Thus, specialized teachers of hearing impaired children, for example, often design educational programs that include extraordinary controls of the acoustic environment, intricate arrangements of amplification equipment, and very heavy focus on the language development problems of the hearing impaired children. Similarly, psychologists sometimes assume that teachers ought to work on a one to one basis with every child in a way that permits constant individual monitoring and only dyadic interactions. It is important for regular teachers to take a stand when such misapprehensions are aired. They should insist, of course, that children receive the intensive special help they need, but that the educational settings—both physical and social—be diverse and bear

FIGURE 1-2
Changes Occurring in the Cascade (Fewer Specialized Places; More Diverse "Regular" Places)

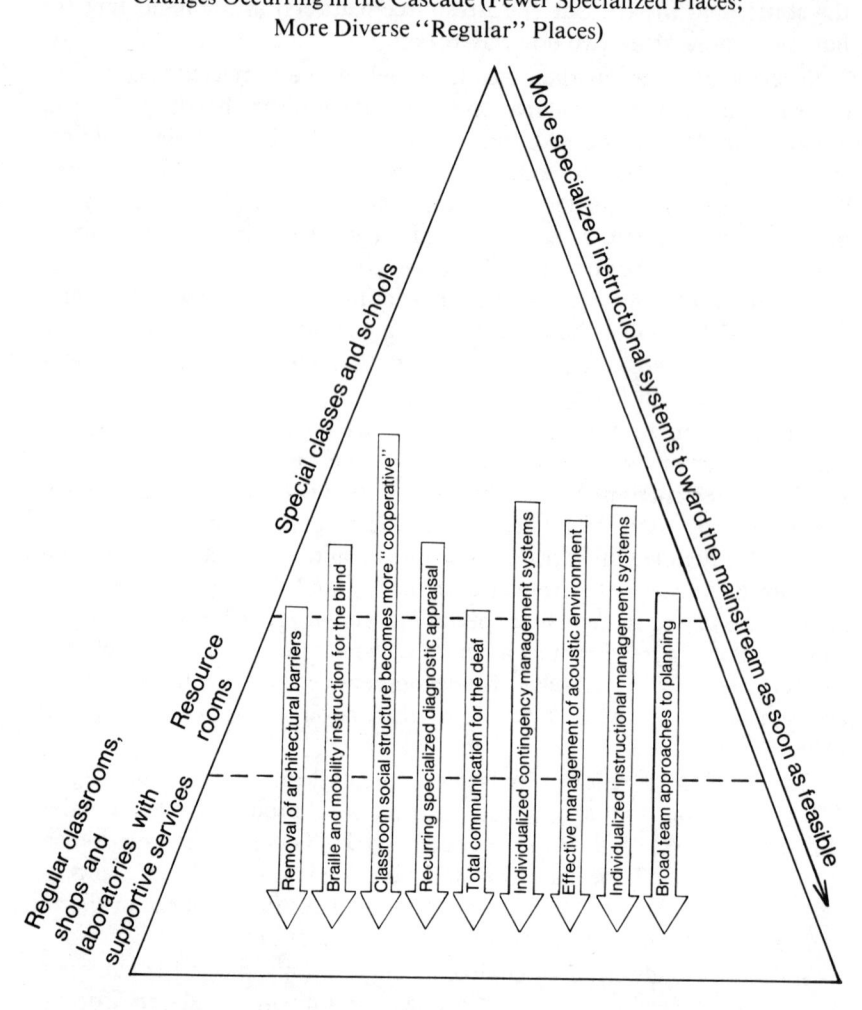

Triangle diagram showing, from apex to base: Special classes and schools; Resource rooms; Regular classrooms, shops and laboratories with supportive services. Right side label: "Move specialized instructional systems toward the mainstream as soon as feasible." Downward arrows within the triangle are labeled: Removal of architectural barriers; Braille and mobility instruction for the blind; Classroom social structure becomes more "cooperative"; Recurring specialized diagnostic appraisal; Total communication for the deaf; Individualized contingency management systems; Effective management of acoustic environment; Individualized instructional management systems; Broad team approaches to planning.

some concordance with the real or ordinary situations of community life.

While specialized places may offer opportunities for intensive and specific instruction, they tend to be *limiting* in several other respects.

1. Specialized places offer limited curricula. It is unlikely, for example, that specialized classes and schools created for a category of children will be able to develop broad programs in vocational or even academic areas. The rich offerings of regular schools need to be opened as widely as possible to all children. Thus, there is strong need and pressure to create more diversity and support systems in regular school

programs at all levels—preschool, elementary and secondary, vocational, and institutions of higher education—so that a full range of curriculum possibilities is available to all students with special needs.
2. Special places tend to enroll students within a limited category. For example, a setting may serve only students who are gifted, blind, deaf, disturbed, or pregnant, and so on. This limitation restricts models of behavior, opportunities for friendships, and the awareness and appreciation of diversity, both for the students in the category and others.
3. Systems for the narrow categorical placement of students in specialized environments lead to oversimplified public dialogue and social policy development. Categories of children tend to become hardened and the categorical group characterization becomes stereotyping, which leads, in general, to poor quality planning and programing. There is little chance for the appreciation of diversity to develop among students unless they experience diversity. If school environments tend to allocate children by category narrowly and rigidly, then distrust, misunderstanding, and fear of the children can be expected as outcomes because no basis for mutual understanding and appreciation has been provided.
4. Sometimes, of course, special places totally fail to offer the intensive or specialized education they are intended to offer, and the results are only watered down curriculum and lowered expectations.

New Perspective on the Cascade Model

A new perspective on the cascade is proposed as a way of conceptualizing preferred practices for the future (see Figure 1-3). It proposes that regular classes be made more educationally diverse, which would diminish the need to develop and use separate specialized educational environments. Regular schools and classes should have diversified staffing and should offer many forms of individualized instructional programs so that a great variety of students could be accommodated there with good results. By such a policy, regular school spaces would be treated acoustically and employ amplification devices, for example, so that pupils with limited hearing could be instructed in the regular spaces and still use their hearing maximally. Such spaces would have a variety of learning centers, equipment, facilities, and materials to serve students with special needs and preferences. Regular teachers would be challenged to become broadly resourceful in managing the diverse environment and serving the broad range of needs of a diverse student population. Special educators and other professionals with highly specialized knowledge and skills would be employed in collaborative teaching and supportive roles with regular teachers.

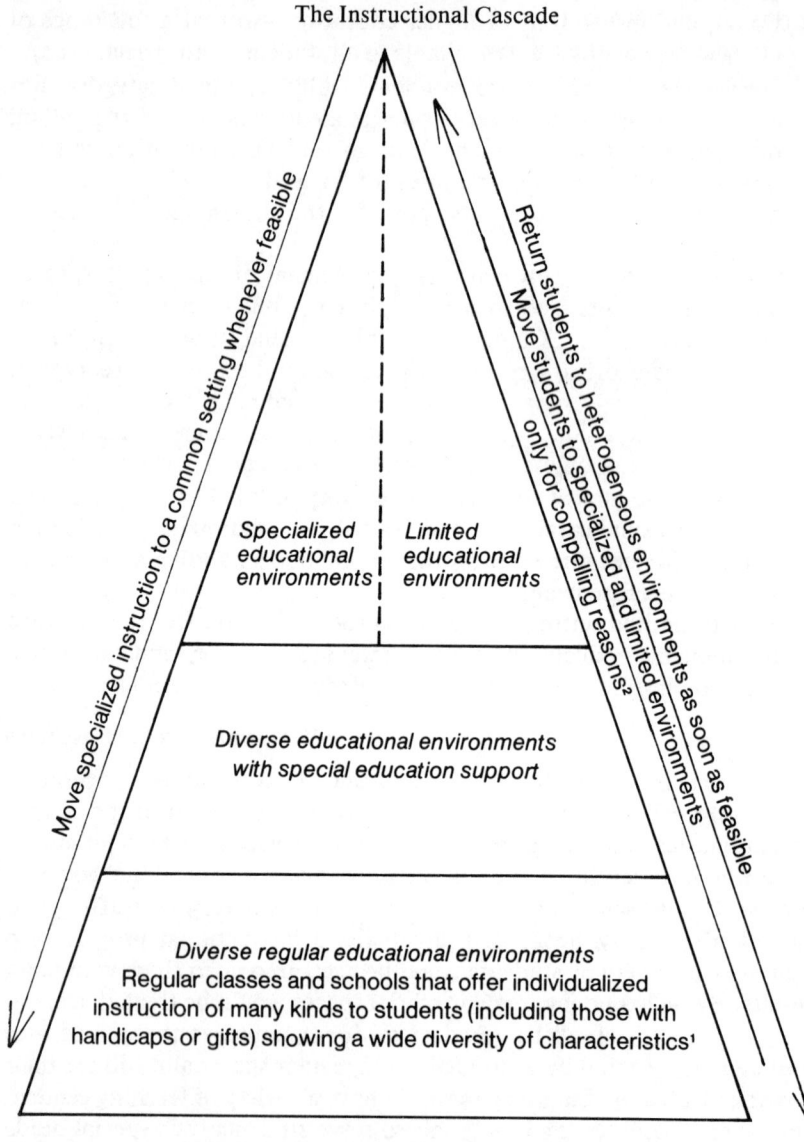

FIGURE 1-3
The Instructional Cascade

Move specialized instruction to a common setting whenever feasible

Return students to heterogeneous environments as soon as feasible

Move students to specialized and limited environments only for compelling reasons[2]

Specialized educational environments | Limited educational environments

Diverse educational environments with special education support

Diverse regular educational environments
Regular classes and schools that offer individualized instruction of many kinds to students (including those with handicaps or gifts) showing a wide diversity of characteristics[1]

[1] It is assumed that no educational "place" is impervious to change and development and that through good efforts many of the varieties of specialized and intensive forms of education can be moved into a developing mainstream.

[2] Here, as in the case of the original cascade, it is assumed that students should be removed from the mainstream only for limited periods and compelling reasons, that when in specialized and limited environments their progress should be monitored carefully and regularly, and that they should be returned to the mainstream as soon as feasible.

The instructional cascade puts first priority on moving the various forms of specialized instruction into regular school structures. There would remain (see the top part of the schema in Figure 1-3) some separate specialized and limited educational environments. Examples of the separate specialized environments that might be included are:

1. Broad psychiatric treatment/ educational settings used for periods of especially intensive help to selected students.
2. Special settings for intensive treatment/education dealing with severe motor problems.
3. Settings in which profoundly and severely multiply handicapped children are offered a totally specialized curriculum.
4. Settings that are constructed for maximal efficiency in acoustic management and amplification for the intensive education of hearing impaired students.
5. Special classes for the intensive education of children who are simply floundering in or are unresponsive to regular school environments.

In the instructional cascade both specialized and limited programs have been included (see the upper portions of the schema). Children are moved to specialized environments only for educational purposes. In the case of limited settings placements often are made for reasons other than optimizing education. In the schema representing the original cascade, a small offset section describes these programs. Included are detention centers, hospitals or other medical settings, and homes. Children are placed in or confined to such settings, not for educational reasons, but because they are ill, have broken the law, or have severe mobility limitations. Occasionally, children are still confined, or set aside, in limited settings because of presumed moral failures (e.g, pregnant girls or drug addicted youth).

Special educators often administer programs in such limited settings, but the settings are not necessarily specialized in the sense that is proposed in the instructional cascade. Many children in those special locations really need only regular education; they are there for other reasons. In general, educators assume that the placement of students in limited environments—limited both socially and physically—ought to be held to an absolute minimum. Of course, no matter how long the children must be confined to such places, their education still needs careful attention. In Figure 1-3 limited settings are included within the general cascade arrangement, suggesting that educators ought to be involved in placements in detention centers and similar settings to ensure appropriateness of education and to achieve careful coordination with other school programs. There is much need for developmental work to improve educational offerings in the home, at the bedside, and in detention centers. A child who lacks opportunities and support for development is denied a sense of the future; children in these limited settings too often have little reason to feel confident, optimistic, and hopeful as they look to the future.

In Odessa, Texas, a collaborative effort was initiated by probation officers, a county judge, and school administrators to create facilities and programs by which youth who had broken the law and were "incarcerated" in the local jail could receive appropriate education. A plan was devised to bus students from the jail to a community setting in which a comprehensive educational program was available. Through broad cooperation between county and school officials a major vocational training unit was added to the school. More than a third of the students in the facility were reported—in 1976—to be those who had been in difficulty with the law, but who nevertheless were in a broad-based school program. (See Dial, 1977).

The general attitude or view taken here is that all students should begin their formal education in regular classes, with the special help they need first brought to them there, and should be moved to specialized and limited settings only after thorough and comprehensive trial in regular classes and only for compelling reasons. If placement in specialized settings is necessary, the children should be returned to the mainstream as soon as feasible.

It is doubtful if present day assessment procedures are, on their own, able to indicate with sufficient certainty that children will need to be educated outside the mainstream. Actual experience, first, in an integrated setting is necessary before that determination can be made. Strong efforts should be made to build appropriate instructional capacity into the mainstream for every child possible, thus limiting extrusions to other settings and hurrying the return of those children who are removed from the mainstream for any period of time.

A particular difficulty exists, of course, when an educational environment is both specialized and limited. For example, if a residential school enrolls only deaf children and offers instruction by specialized methods in only limited specialized domains, it is a doubly homogeneous environment and is poorly equipped to prepare students for open community life. Similarly, a juvenile delinquent who lives only with other delinquents and receives an educational program that is very limited in range, is also in a highly homogeneous and, in this case, a potentially damaging environment.

It is strongly desirable for children who live overnight in institutions to be moved into broad, community based, daytime educational programs so that they can experience as fully as possible the richer diversity of students and programs available in the community. See, for example, in Chapters 6 and 11, the ingeneous solutions to these two problems implemented by the Lexington School for the Deaf and Western State School and Hospital in Pennsylvania. Similarly, if students need, for a period of time, highly specialized educational environments that are not available within reasonable transport from their homes, perhaps small group homes for them should be developed in the communities that offer a wide range of educational environments and instruction.

The courts and Public Law 94-142 posit the general principle that children should be educated in the *least restrictive environment*. The education must also be *appropriate*. The regular class in the neighborhood school is presumed generally to be able to supply both, if properly planned, staffed, and equipped. The least restrictive environment that is appropriate for a particular pupil's education may, for a time, require part time instruction in a resource room or even full time instruction in a special class. Plans for every individual must meet both tests, that is, be appropriate and in the least restrictive alternative.

The instructional cascade proposal entails several broad policies that are listed here; they are discussed in greater detail in later chapters of this book. The instructional cascade proposes:

1. A decentralization policy—to develop the capacity to conduct specialized forms of education in many settings, rather than in a few.
2. A "give away" policy for educational specialists, that is, the willingness to teach aspects of their specialties to less specialized professionals and sometimes to aides and to parents.
3. A joining of responsibilities for assessment, planning, and instruction in a single setting, as opposed to a policy of referral to special centers for child study and prescription.
4. Descriptions of students that are made mainly in terms directly relevant to instruction, rather than in terms of abstract categories, such as *retarded* or *disturbed*.

MAINSTREAMING IN THE BROADER COMMUNITY

The changes occurring in educational programs for exceptional children are part of a more comprehensive set of changes. They are broader than special education. The court orders and emerging legislation articulate new imperatives for general superintendents and boards of education, not just special education departments. What they direct is not just a minor in-housing reordering of special education programs but a general reordering of total school systems—the ways children are assessed, assigned, and served. The same kinds of changes can be seen in other forms of service as well.

In mental health, for example, many of the clinicians (psychiatrists, clinical psychologists, and social workers) have abandoned their special enclaves and function within the context of the community. Instead of working directly and solely to "fix" or "cure" the individual who comes to them with problems, their energies have turned to providing environmental supports for that person. Employers, wives, children, neighbors, storekeepers, and clergy are enlisted to build support systems to maintain the individual in familiar surroundings.

The diagnostic studies required in this broad context extend beyond the individual's immediate condition to his total life situation. The treatment that is prescribed is also directed to the total situation, that is, directed to all relevant elements of the person's life setting. In the process of such work, the professionals work within a framework of community relationships that they turn to preventive and therapeutic purposes. And so it is in the schools.

Restrictive boundaries are eroding outside the realm of professional services as well. In one large city, for example, handicapped persons have banded together to press for better services by the city bus system. Persons with motor handicaps often are not able to board the buses in the quick style required, and those in wheelchairs may be totally immobilized by the public transportation system. They want lifting devices to help take wheelchairs on board the buses. The bus company has offered to send special minisize "handicabs" for them, but the handicapped persons have insisted on being mainstreamed, that is, being able to use the bus system. And so it is in the schools.

At the 1976 Convention of the American Association for the Advancement of Science (AAAS), another example of broad changes was evident. Even before the convention was committed to the city of Boston, clearances were obtained to assure all handicapped scientists who attended the convention that they would have full access to all sessions and that all hotels and other meeting places would have external and internal ramps to permit scientists in wheel chairs to move readily to all sessions, restaurants, restrooms, and hotel rooms. It meant also that the special symphony concert for convention registrants was held in a hall with appropriate ramps. Deaf scientists attending convention sessions were provided with interpreter services in the preferred communication mode; and, whenever feasible, blind scientists received advanced manuscripts of presentations that used visual aids. During the convention, 400 handicapped scientists met to help map strategies to permit all scientific meetings to be mainstreamed, that is, to determine how special services can be provided, not in set-aside stations, but in the mainstream of conventions. The AAAS has published a guide for use by other associations in arranging barrier free meetings (Redden, 1976). Handicapped persons want full entry, opportunities, and participation in all mainstream activities.

A further example of what is happening in communities is the widow to widow program. In the grief in the wake of the death of a husband, many widows are turning to networks of other widows for help; there they find immediate understanding relationships and support that are far different from the services available from the clinical psychologist or psychiatrist. Indeed, such professionals increasingly find themselves involved in creating and supporting networks for mutual help among widows. Thus the specialist is less involved in direct services to a particular clientele and more involved in changing and developing community structures to serve persons with special needs. In such a process, the psychiatrist and psychologist find themselves engaged in the indirect processes of helping broad groups of helpers to help, rather than in helping directly a limited number of clients at very high cost. They "give away" some of their special insights and skills and take on an indirect support role rather than a direct service role. And, again, so it is for many specialists in the schools. In many communities mental healthmental retardation councils or planning bodies have been formed to help construct the broad, integrated programs required in a "full service" era.

One of the reasons for these changes is the sheer impossibility of providing specialized help in one to one treatment situations for all individuals who have specialized needs. There is little chance of providing all the manpower that would be needed to deal individually with all learning and adjustment problems if services are provided only by specialists working in specialized environments; and it is doubtful that the nation could afford such services even if the specialized manpower problems were soluble. But beyond economics and manpower problems, it seems clear that developments in mainstream settings that lead to the appreciation of diversity and its accommodation in treatment are vastly to be preferred, on qualitative grounds, to referral to segregated settings.

How Many Exceptional Students?

How many students are exceptional? How much program are we buying in the name of special education? Visits to different school systems would probably lead to a variety of answers. In one major city, for example, estimates of special education services result in five different answers to the first question.

1. 5%—About 5% of the students have received one or more types of special services regularly for the entire school year. Included in this group are profoundly and multiply handicapped students, young students who receive daily instruction in braille or other highly specialized subjects, and some particularly vulnerable or fragile students who have needed rather protracted help in a specialized environment.

2. 10%—About 10% of the students receive specialized assistance on any one school day. This estimate includes the 5% who receive services in year long programs. The other 5% is made up of students who receive only short term or occasional help from specialists such as speech therapists, resource teachers, or others.
3. 20%—About 20% of the students receive some kind of special service over the period of a school year under the same conditions as the 10%. The 20% figure simply includes all of the students who receive service over a year. Obviously, the identificiation of exceptional students is not a one time operation. To provide 10% of the students with some form of special services on the average school day, the schools actually serve some 20% of the total student population in a given year.
4. 40%—If students were followed from kindergarten through grade 6, how many would be found to need at least brief periods of speech therapy or crisis intervention for an emotional problem, or display distinct learning or behavior problems, or need to repeat a full grade? In one of the few studies available to answer this question (Rubin & Balow, 1971) it appears that about 40% of elementary school children may need a special service at some time.
5. 80%—Professors Rubin and Balow (1971) have now extended their longitudinal study into secondary school years, reporting informally that the percentage of children needing specialized assistance at some time in their public school experience continues to rise beyond the 40% level.

Returning to the question of how many exceptional children there are, we can see that the answer is complex. In general, special educators consider themselves responsible for about 10% to 12% of all children. Many states have been quite willing to fund special education programs at that level. Sometimes, that percentage is broken down into categories, with speech correction and educable mental retardation, for example, each credited with 2 out of every 10 exceptional children; but for modern, dynamic educational planning it is no longer very helpful to think in terms of a static set of children at the 10% to 12% level that can be distributed among subsets by traditional categorical labels. The Rubin and Balow (1971) studies make that plain. The facts and the bases of the rationale for specialized programs requires more openess to a changing and larger set of students.

The Legal Base

Traditionally, the operations of schools have been determined by local and state initiative. The fundamental obligation to offer educational opportunities to children rests at the state level. Most state constitutions contain language requiring the operation of a "general and uniform" school system; the language varies but the intention does not. For some years, school buses have been rolling over the most isolated mountain roads and across swollen streams to find every "normal" child and to see that pupils get to school.

In spite of long standing laws requiring local school districts to provide education for all children and to compel all children of certain ages to attend the schools provided, in the past various categories of children have been excused or excluded from the schools and many school authorities have felt quite free to expel for any reason individual students who were troublesome or difficult. Few people noted that the so called compulsory school attendance laws were generally not being administered with vigor and, outside of the immediate families, the demissions of individual children also went largely unnoticed. The situation was such that in most communities no one really knew how many children were out of school. In large cities, where mobility of families is high, the situation was even more difficult to assess.

Radical changes in demissions have been occurring, however, in part because of the activities of students themselves. They have become too aware of their rights to be denied valuable educational opportunities by arbitrary procedures. Lawyers, often supported by organized groups of parents and service organizations, have been eager to press cases for individual students; and professionals who, from various points of view, see the rights of individual students as fundamental to a democratic society and surpassing in importance all rights and conveniences of institutions, have added their weight. In addition, legislators have removed categorical bases for the demission of children from schools, such as the repeal of laws allowing the exclusion of the trainable retarded, thus forcing the schools to deliberate each proposed admission or demission on an individual basis.

Recently, state legislatures and the US Congress, most notably with Public Law 94-142, have taken the situation to the ultimate position. It has been made abundantly clear that every child has a constitutional and lawful right to education and that it is the obligation of the local district to provide the education, preferably within its own school system or, if not, then by special arrangements with other districts or agencies. The fundamental expression of this right is found at the constitutional level in the equal protection clause of the 14th Amendment.

Educators are enjoined not only to enroll literally all children who are presented to the schools but to actively seek out all children, through census and special finding procedures for those with special needs and to insure their enrollment in appropriate school programs. Categorical exclusions from school are illegal. The difficult problems of individual pupils must be dealt with in accordance with principles of due process, not in class or categorical procedures; if demission from the school is directed, special arrangements for out-of-school education must be provided. The effect of these policies and legal requirements is to harden the compulsory attendance laws, to safeguard at the highest levels the right of each student to appropriate education, and to add force for the reorganization of the schools so that individual needs become a paramount concern.

CONCLUSIONS

New imperatives, judicial and moral, make more inclusive arrangements for schooling a necessity. What one might speak of as the era of mainstreaming, least restrictive alternative, progressive inclusion, or integration is a further advancement of a long trend in American education. The movement can be seen as advance beyond the two box theory of treatment in which a person is either normal and law abiding and needs no special treatment, or is sick, poor, disturbed, asocial, or old and therefore institutionalized for treatment and care.

What is required is that the regular school environments be transformed to provide for a greater diversity of students and instructional offerings. Following such developments it will become increasingly unnecessary to displace some students to specialized and limited environments. Such specialized and restrictive environments have enormous limitations both in their immediate services and in their longer range implications for the students involved. It is anticipated, of course, that not all students will be well served in mainstream settings; thus it is expected that some specialized school programs will continue to be conducted in special classes and other special settings. But the processes that are used to place students in the special settings will need to be justified with great care. This total process of development and placement is what is meant by mainstreaming.

Obviously, the mainstream trend makes new demands on both regular class and special education teachers. The remainder of this book explicates some of these demands and the opportunities they present. Some educators may wish that special education would continue its separate status, take its exceptional pupils off to separate enclaves, and use all the special funds for the purpose, and thus leave the regular schools without this additional challenge and burden. But it is not to be so. The agenda before all educators is to create a single, unified school system that serves *all* children in the most inclusive possible ways; and that is a challenging and worthy undertaking.

SUGGESTIONS FOR STUDENTS AND INSTRUCTOR

1. Secure for review copies of state laws, policies, and regulations concerning the operations of special education programs in your state, looking particularly for implications for regular classes.

2. Invite representatives of local or state associations of parents of exceptional children to meet with you to discuss current policies, practices, and problems in implementing special education programs in your community or state. Or, attend meetings of such associations to observe their concerns and programs.
3. Seek films or slide tape modules that treat public policy topics. Information about such items is readily available through The Council for Exceptional Children, Area Learning Resource Centers, state department of education, and many universities.
4. Secure and study copies of recently published proceedings of hearings of the Congress (US House of Representatives or the Senate) on legislation relating to the handicapped and gifted. Major publications of this kind are available almost every year and may be obtained by writing to one of your congressional representatives.
5. Administer and review results on scales for measurement of attitudes toward handicapped persons and about various arrangements for the education of exceptional children. For example, try the Rucker-Gable Educational Programming Scale (1974).
6. Visit local schools and interview teachers about local arrangements for education of exceptional children, checking particularly on trends that reflect the emerging policies as discussed in this chapter. How much change in special education practices in your schools is taking place at this time?
7. Compile a directory of personnel and agencies within your schools and in the broader community that could be used to arrange for careful studies and consultation concerning exceptional pupils.
8. Prepare a list of topics you think need to be studied by regular teachers if they are to participate effectively in mainstreaming programs. Have a group of teachers respond to the list, indicating the degree of interest and commitment they have in regard to the several topics.
9. Secure the report from the Invisible College entitled *All Together Now* (Jordan, 1976) from The Council for Exceptional Children and review readings and tapes on various facets of mainstreaming. Also see Appendix B for descriptive information on other "packaged" materials for training.

Instructors may suggest that students use the topical bibliographies that follow this section, and that follow subsequent chapters, to do investigations in depth for papers and class discussions.

TOPICAL BIBLIOGRAPHIES
History and General

Beery, K. *Models for mainstreaming*. San Rafael CA: Dimension, 1972.

Dunn, L. M. Special education for the mildly retarded—Is it justifiable? *Exceptional Children,* 1968, *35,* 5-22.

Elam, S. (Ed.). Special issue on special education. *Phi Delta Kappan,* 1974, *55*, 513-560.

Hobbs, N. *The futures of children.* San Francisco: Jossey-Bass, 1975.

Jordan, J. B. (Ed.) *Exceptional child education at the bicentennial: A parade of progress.* Reston VA: The Council for Exceptional Children, 1977.

Meyen, E. L., Vergason, G. A., & Whelan, R. J. (Eds.). *Strategies for teaching exceptional children.* Denver: Love, 1972.

Nazzaro, J. N. *Exceptional timetables: Historical events affecting the handicapped and gifted.* Reston VA: The Council for Exceptional Children, 1977.

Reger, R. What does "mainstreaming" mean? *Journal of Learning Disabilities,* 1974, *7,* 513-515.

Reynolds, M. C. (Ed.). *Futures of education for exceptional students: Emerging structures.* Reston VA: The Council for Exceptional Children, 1978.

Reynolds, M. C. (Ed.). *Mainstreaming: Origins and implications.* Reston VA: The Council for Exceptional Children, 1976.

Sloan, W. Four score and seven. *American Journal of Mental Deficiency,* 1963, *68*(1).

Warfield, G. *Mainstream currents: Reprints from* Exceptional Children, 1968-74. Reston VA: The Council for Exceptional Children, 1975.

Wolfensberger, W. *The principle of normalization in human services.* Toronto: National Institute of Mental Retardation, 1972.

Training

Grosenick, J. K., & Reynolds, M. C. *Teacher education: Renegotiating roles for mainstreaming.* Reston VA: The Council for Exceptional Children, 1978.

Jenkins, J. R., & Mayhall, W. F. Development and evaluation of a resource teacher program. *Exceptional Children,* 1976, *43,* 21-29.

Jordan, J. B. (Ed.). *Teacher, please don't close the door—the exceptional child in the mainstream.* Reston VA: The Council for Exceptional Children, 1976.

Lilly, M. S. A training based model for special education. *Exceptional Children,* 1971, *37,* 745-749.

Thiagarajan, S., Semmel, M., & Semmel, D. *Instructional development for training teachers of exceptional children: A sourcebook.* Reston VA: The Council for Exceptional Children, 1974.

Administrative Arrangements

Deno, E. *Instructional alternatives for exceptional children.* Reston VA: The Council for Exceptional Children, 1973.

Hammill, D. D. The resource-room model in special education. *Journal of Special Education,* 1972, *6*(4), 349-354.

Jordan, J. B. (Ed.). *Teacher please don't close the door—The exceptional child in the mainstream.* Reston VA: The Council for Exceptional Children, 1976.

Lanza, L.G., & Vassar, W. G. Designing and implementing a program for the gifted and talented. *National Elementary Principal,* 1972, *51*(5), 22-24.

The Legal Base

Ballard, J. *Public Law 94-142 and Section 504—Understanding what they are and are not.* Reston VA: The Council for Exceptional Children, 1978.

Higgins, S. T. *Special education administrative policies manual.* Reston VA: The Council for Exceptional Children, 1977.

Weintraub, F. J., & Abeson, A. New education policies for the handicapped, the quiet revolution. *Phi Delta Kappan,* April, 1974, 526-529.

Weintraub, F. J., Abeson, A., Ballard, J., & LaVor M. L. (Eds.). *Public policy and the education of exceptional children.* Reston VA: The Council for Exceptional Children, 1976.

Wilken, W.H., & Porter, D.O. *State aid for special education: Who benefits?* Washington DC: National Foundation for the Improvement of Education, 1977.

Mainstreaming in the Broader Community

Begab, M. J., & Richardson, S. A. *The mentally retarded and society.* Baltimore: University Park Press, 1975.

Braddock, D. *Opening closed doors: The deinstitutionalization of disabled individuals.* Reston VA: The Council for Exceptional Children, 1977.

Caplan, R. B. *Helping the helpers to help.* New York: The Seabury Press, 1972.

Rhodes, W. C., & Gibbins, S. *Environmental forces impinging upon normal and disturbed children in a regular classroom.* Final Report. Ann Arbor: Michigan University, Institute for the Study of Mental Retardation, 1971.

Rosenblum, G. (Ed.). *Issues in community and preventive mental health.* New York: Behavioral Publications, 1971.

Wolfensberger, W. *The principle of normalization in human services.* Toronto: National Institute on Mental Retardation, 1972.

Zigler, E., & Balla, D.A. Impact of institutional experience on the behavior and development of retarded persons. *American Journal of Mental Deficiency,* 1977, 82(1), 1-11.

Media

Ballard, J., Nazzaro, J. N., & Weintraub, F. J. *P.L. 94-142, The Education for All Handicapped Children Act of 1975* (multimedia). Reston VA: The Council for Exceptional Children, 1976.

Nazzaro, J. N. *All together now* (cassette album). Reston VA: The Council for Exceptional Children, 1974.

Nazzaro, J. N. *Exceptional times: An historical perspective of special education* (16mm film). Reston VA: The Council for Exceptional Children, 1977.

2. Origins of Change

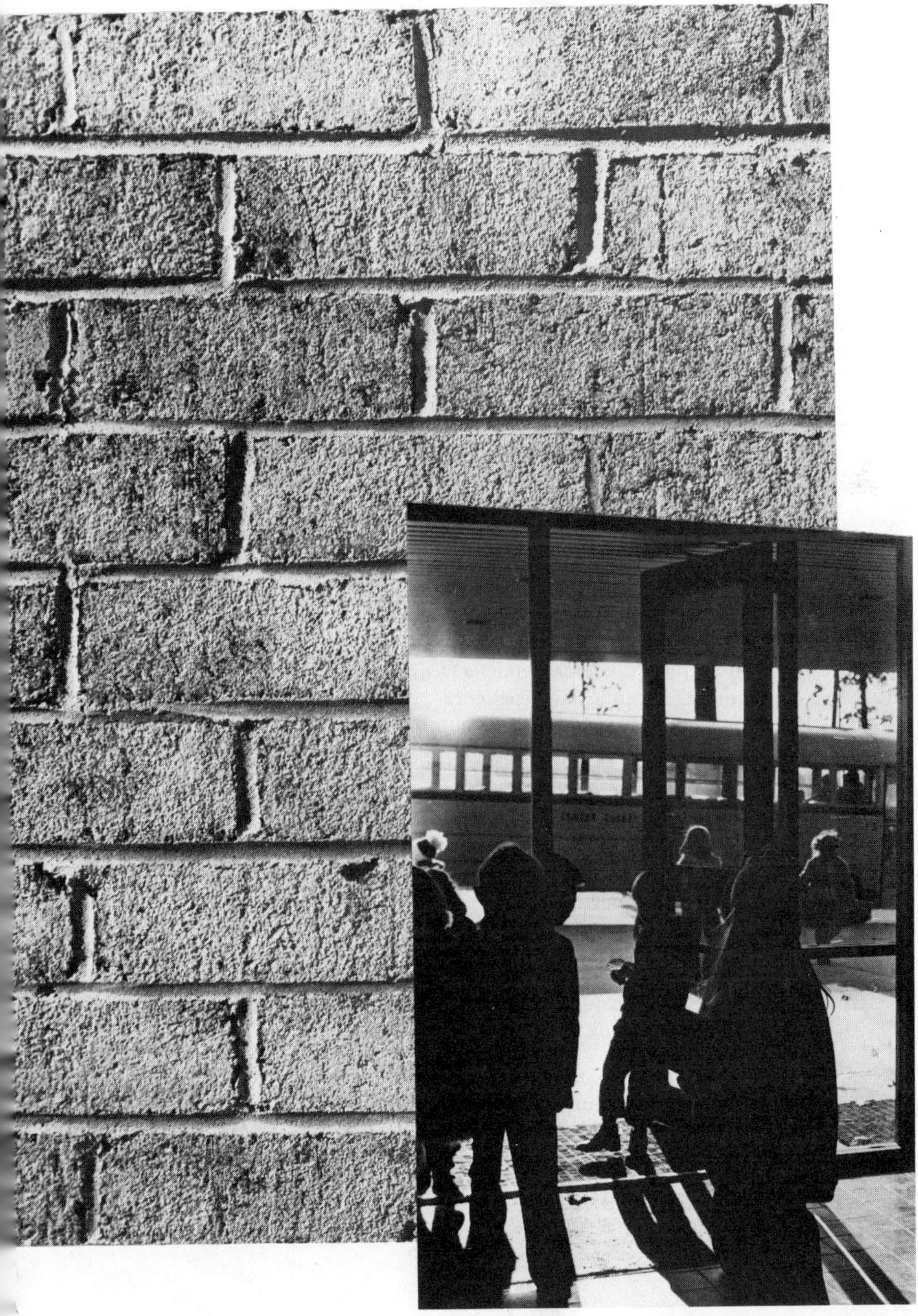

CHAPTER OUTLINE

INTERNAL AND EXTERNAL FORCES ON PROFESSIONALS
SOME CONCEPTUAL SHIFTS
   A Value Change: Primacy of the Individual
      The Private Role of Education
      The "Payoff" of Individualization
      The Central Principle of Enhancing Individual Lives
   Consulting Processes: From Dyadic to Triadic Relationships
   Changing Systems of Measurement
      Norm Oriented Versus Domain Oriented Measurements
      A Decision Oriented Framework
         Predictive Instruments
         The Aptitude-Treatment-Interaction Assumption
         Experimentation with Different Learning Approaches
         Domain Referenced Testing
      Grading in the Schools
   The Concept of Expectancy in Children
   The Classification and Grouping of Children
      Purposes of Classification
      A Formula for Classification
      The Concept of the Person-Environment Match
PREVAILING VERSUS PREFERRED PRACTICES
THE EMPIRICAL BASE FOR MAINSTREAMING
   Classes as Social Settings
      Cooperative Class Procedures
      Increasing Attentiveness—Reducing Disturbing Behavior
   Mainstreaming Research and Experience
      Feasibility and Value of Mainstreaming
   Suspected Intellectual, Perceptual, Physical, Emotional, and Academic Handicaps
      Blind Children
      Autistic Children
      Children with Hearing Impairments
      Children with Severe Learning Disabilities and Behavior Disorders
      Physically Handicapped Children
      Gifted Children
      Trainable Mentally Retarded Children
      Educable Mentally Retarded Children
   Needs of Regular Educators
   Impact of Mainstreaming on Regular Class Pupils
   Costs of Mainstreaming
   History of Regular Educator Roles in Mainstreaming
   Acceptance of Mainstreaming
   Cautions about Mainstreaming
   Summary
SUGGESTIONS FOR STUDENTS AND INSTRUCTOR
TOPICAL BIBLIOGRAPHIES

INTERNAL AND EXTERNAL FORCES ON PROFESSIONALS

Change is a characteristic of every profession. Often the forces for change are internal, that is, originating in the profession's drive for excellence, and they are relatively slow acting. The rate of change is accelerated, however, when external forces, such as discoveries in related fields or sharp shifts in national policies or social values, act on the profession in conjunction with the internal forces. Thus, in virtually every profession, practitioners are under the constant imperative to keep themselves abreast of new developments, and the more rapid the rate of change, the more urgent that imperative is, otherwise their clients are deprived of rightful opportunities for increased health, justice, technology, happiness, or education. All professions, consequently, support viable structures through which their practitioners can learn of the new developments that are changing their fields and of the applications of these developments.

In this chapter, some of the discoveries and innovative processes that have provided substance for the rapidly moving mainstreaming process are identified and explicated. The discussion is focused on, first, a clarification of the set of events leading to mainstreaming that otherwise may appear to be largely unconnected and irrational, and second, providing the rationale and motives for the attitudes and behaviors that are frequently associated with mainstreaming. Although some of the topics examined can be traced to events or ideas that originated many decades ago, others are the consequence of a major turning point in the social philosophy of education, which means that a new set of concepts has surfaced to become the framework for new kinds of educational planning.

The topics range over a broad territory, from value changes to highly technical developments. They could well engage the concerns of educators at any level of schooling but, as is proposed here, they are especially appropriate for study by teachers and principals. Specifically, this chapter discusses (a) some of the major conceptual shifts that seem to be inherent in the mainstreaming movement and (b) the general state of the empirical base—experience and research—that underlies the movement.

SOME CONCEPTUAL SHIFTS

A Value Change: Primacy of the Individual

Until recently, the schools in the nation did not seriously try to provide education for all children. Despite the long history of the constitutional "equal protection" clause and of compulsory school attendance laws in virtually all states, until recently significant numbers of children either were never admitted to the schools or they were demitted (excused, excluded, suspended, or expelled) from the schools at an earlier age than most other children. In the congressional testimony on the Education for All Handicapped Children Act of 1975, it was estimated that one million exceptional children in the United States were receiving no education whatsoever.

In almost every school system, while the large proportion of children have been selected for education within the mainstream, others have been isolated in special stations, not always on the basis that the special stations provided better services for the children, and hundreds and even thousands of others have been removed totally from local schools, families, and community life for placement in residential centers of various kinds. Obviously, some children have needed the specialized attention that is available in the special settings to which they have been assigned; but for many other children the demissions from the mainstream of society were determined by the convenience or comfort of the mainstream institutions and the failure to broaden the mainstream and make it more inclusive.

Now we are in a zero demission era; schools are required to make plans and implement them for the education of every child. None can be excluded totally from educational opportunity, and any decision to displace a child from the mainstream for educational purposes must be justified in terms of enhancing the child's opportunities and life.

The Private Role of Education

Public education in the United States has both private and public roles. Currently, the emphasis is shifting to the private role.

> The private role of education is to provide a chance for individual fulfillment, principally intellectual but also artistic, social, cultural, vocational and societal, to give an individual an opportunity to find the education he needs to achieve his own ends. The public role of education is to serve the society that supports it by acting as a medium for social cohesion and social advancement, maintaining and passing on the national culture, refreshing and adding to our body of knowledge, sorting out talent, and providing an education that will match a great variety of talent and career opportunity. (Eurich, Bronk, Millet, Perkins, & Wexler, 1973, p. 160)

This shift reflects the belief that education directed to literally all children and emphasizing their private *ends* will lead to sufficient socialization and commitments to the public good to sustain our society and, indeed, to further nurture its growth of freedom and prosperity.

Educators are being mandated not only to enroll all children who are presented to the schools and to place them in appropriate programs, but also to actively seek out all children for enrollment, including those with special needs. Implicit in this movement is the concept that the rights of the individual supercede institutional and even societal requirements.

The ability or potential of the individual to contribute to society or its institutions is no longer a proper test in considering a child's enrollment in school. It is sufficient if all that can be anticipated for handicapped people is the enhancement of their own lives.

The emergence of individual priority over institutional convenience and the evaluation of programs in terms of individual rather than social returns lead to important changes in educational practices: in educational measurement and monitoring the emphasis is shifting to the individual; journals accept research studies based on a single subject; new management systems, such as individually guided education (IGE), stress individual development; curricula stress individual adaptations, as in individual prescribed instruction (IPI); and innumerable systems for individualizing instruction through computerized assistance have been developed. The applied behavior analysts now working in the schools follow the principles developed by Skinner, Bijou, Lindsley, Haring, and others, to give preeminence to data on and instruction for the individual. These workers have taught us to conduct single child "experiments" wherein we systematically change the conditions of stimulation and/or the consequences of behavior so that we can choose a pattern of instruction that "matches" with the individual's needs. Individualization* of education is widely accepted, as evidenced by the responses of education leaders in a recent opinion survey (Spears, 1973). Unquestionably, the present focus on the individual student reflects changes in values as well as practices.

The "Payoff" of Individualization

To further explicate the concept of the individual as the primary object of education it is sometimes useful to contrast three levels of payoff: societal, institutional, and individual. In some situations, societal goals are held to be paramount and institutions and individuals are manipulated as necessary to achieve them. Such situations might be characterized as highly "sovietized." Democratic societies permit the domination of societal payoff at times of extreme national crises, such as during war, but ordinarily, most people focus on individual lives and the fostering of free institutions. In other words, most people would state the ultimate goals of a democratic society in terms of individual lives and free institutions, leaving it to faith that the aggregate results produce good society.

In the past decades, however, decisions about the exceptional have not always been made in terms of individual payoff; rather, they have

---

*The term *individualization* is used to denote education that is carefully matched to the individual's developmental status and needs; it may include group as well as individual (solitary) activities.

been made and justified in terms of payoff to institutions or society as a whole. As late as the 1950's it was argued that some exceptional children, those considered very limited in potential, need not be served by the schools when their returns to society are minimal. In one famous debate it was argued that

> Public education is...based on the belief that as a result of learning, the individual will be able to assume a self-directed role in society, and that he will probably assume responsibility for others—his wife and children or parents. (Goldberg & Cruickshank, 1958, p. 622)

In pleas for more funds and expanded programs for some exceptional children, it was often claimed that when those persons were educated and trained so that they could become self supporting, their removal from welfare rolls and payments of income taxes repaid society for the investment. It has also been argued that education and employment of limited potential workers is "good business"—or provides dollar payoff for institutions. These "rate of return" arguments and claims may be true in most cases but they no longer are acceptable as the starting point in planning for even the least educable students.

The Central Principle of Enhancing Individual Lives

The truly noteworthy fact here is that payoff to society or particular institutions has not been the focus of recent policy statements in our society, as expressed through the Congress and the courts. Nor do the institutional values dominate the scene in due process hearings for exceptional students. Rather, it is the principle of enhancing the life of the individual that has taken the central, commanding position. For example, even if it takes more public funds to teach severely crippled children to feed themselves than it takes to give them a liquid nutritional gruel to drink three times daily, the policy now is that educators shall get on with the teaching-learning tasks involved in self feeding. The aim is to insure that every individual shall have, to the extent that is feasible and equitable, opportunities to set purposes and order in their own lives, pursue their goals on the basis of well developed skills, and enjoy a fair share of life's pleasures in a pattern of their own choosing.

The strong shift to the primacy of the individual is observable in broader aspects of our society as well. Much of the accountability movement in all institutions is expressed in terms of individuals; that is, the tests of institutional functioning most often come in the form of individual grievances that sometimes result in formal actions wherein an individual makes a claim against the institution. Witness the cases of grievance on the basis of racial or sex biases in employment, complaints for the lack of effective treatment in hospitals, or complaints of unsafe working conditions or toxic chemicals in industrial plants.

Happily, there need be no neglect of the larger needs of the community when attention is given primarily to the individual. Careful attention to the development of everyone in the population means that the aggregate of human development in the community is advanced and the supply of resources for institutional development is optimized.

The strong commitment to a primary emphasis on the individual, it can be argued, serves as a balance for the requirement that children attend school for a number of years, usually to age 16. If children were confined to schools that did not attend to their needs in an individualized way, where they might be attitudinally rejected yet not be permitted to leave, there would be personal disaster. In the early years of schooling, when curricular attention goes mainly to what Stoddard has termed the "cultural imperatives"—the basics of language, mathematics, social skills, health, and safety—we owe to each child a school program and setting, both physical and social, that expresses appreciation of that individual. When students pass on to the postcompulsory point of education (beyond age 16) perhaps a different emphasis—one that deals realistically with the students' opportunities or selectability in various institutions (for advanced schooling or for employment)—can be justified.

Consulting Processes: From Dyadic to Triadic Relationships

As more exceptional children are enrolled in regular classes, specialists and special educators are moving to construct support systems for such pupils. Regular teachers find themselves joined with resource teachers, psychologists, speech clinicians, teacher aides, or other adult workers in attempting to serve each student. Thus schooling increasingly involves significant adult-adult-child relationships. Instead of the relatively simple dyadic relationship of teacher and pupil, we face the triad of consultant, client, and target. The consultant may be a special teacher, a school psychologist, a school social worker, a special supervisor, an audiologist, or any one of many other specialists.

The consultant is in the indirect role, the teacher in the direct instructional role. Often, special teachers provide direct instruction as well—on special topics, such as braille, auditory training, or Gillingham reading methods—but our concern here is their functions in the indirect or consulting role. Regular teachers are now learning how to use consultants of many kinds.

Consulting, in the present context, is a temporary relationship undertaken voluntarily to help improve instruction for one or more pupils. The teacher is the client and the pupil is the ultimate target (Figure 2-1). The consulting relationship proceeds on the assumption that everyone involved is well motivated and equally dedicated to effective instruction. Often, too, they are professional peers.

FIGURE 2-1
The Consultation Triad

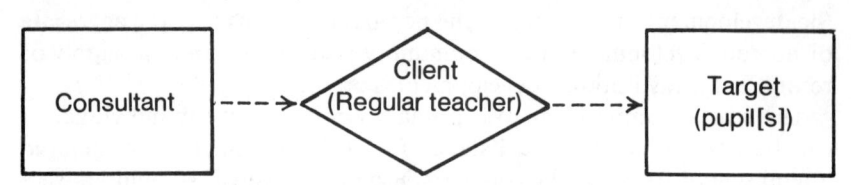

Consultant ---→ Client (Regular teacher) ---→ Target (pupil[s])

The following list suggests a few guidelines for regular teachers to keep in mind when they work with consultants. These suggestions have been derived from broad theoretical work and experience in consultation functions, but they seem applicable to the rapidly expanding role of the regular teacher as user of consultation (Parker, 1975).

1. Remember that the teacher "owns" the problem and is in charge of the education of the pupil or the class procedures that are under consideration.
2. The teacher should be sure that there is early agreement with the consultant on the nature of the "problem" and on how decisions about plans for solution will be made. An oral or written contract should be drawn up early in the relationship on goals, methods, and responsibilities.
3. Be sure that it is clear that the teacher is the client and that all communication flows to him/her. The consultant is there to help structure the client/teacher's work not somebody else's. This relationship does not preclude some direct assessment of children and observations in the classroom by the consultant if agreed on as part of the contract.
4. Status problems should be avoided. Consultants and clients are coequals.
5. The teacher should avoid entering personal subjective materials (letting attention shift to personal needs and problems); instead, the content of the relationship should remain centered on the child and the instructional situation.
6. The teacher should seek alternative suggestions from the consultant rather than a single or set plan.
7. Teachers should try to use each consultation as a learning experience in increasing effective communication and listening, building trust among professionals, and maximizing instructional effectiveness.
8. Each consultation experience should be evaluated objectively and the teacher's conclusions should be shared with the consultant.

Changing Systems of Measurement

The shift of concern to the individual entails new measurement and decision systems in the schools. Historically, educational measurement systems have been oriented to interpreting the performance of the individual against age-grade norms or through social comparison processes. Measurement theory emphasized the construction of tests and test items that produced interpersonal variance, large differences among those tested; and the results usually were expressed as percentiles to tell what proportion of children were surpassed by a particular child, or as "standard" scores to give the individual's standing on a distribution of scores in the social comparative context. In addition, testing systems were strongly oriented to simple predictions and selection-rejection decisions. These kinds of measurement have come to be recognized as very amenable to discriminatory and unfair uses.

In her presidential address to the American Psychologist Association, Tyler (1973) examined what she called a "frontal onslaught" on the whole structure of testing in our society. She described one of the important conceptual shifts as follows:

> Instead of assuming that someone is going to use the test...to select the persons most likely to succeed in a particular situation..., it is possible to begin with an assumption that the purpose of the test is to analyze what each person who takes it has to offer, so that a suitable place can be found for him. Another way of putting it is to say that tests are being designed for the benefit of test takers rather than for the benefit of employers or admission offices. (p.1023)

Glaser (1973) made a complementary point in a statement on the changing nature of testing.

> [Testing]...will become an integral part of the educational process itself. For instructional purposes, tests will be interpreted in terms of performance criteria so that student and teacher are informed about the student's progress relative to standards of competence, and, in this way, provide information for deciding on an appropriate course for instruction. (p. 564)

The current trend, one to which special education is making a strong contribution in the restructuring of education, is toward measurement systems that:

- Are domain and/or criterion referenced.
- Are directly related to instructional purposes.
- Can be interpreted without social comparisons or "norms."
- Lend themselves to systematic and individualized management systems for instruction.
- Recapture for the individual the concept of aptitude in relation to how the individual learns most efficiently, rather than how much of a personal trait is salable to an institution.

Norm Oriented Versus Domain Oriented Measurements

The preceding discussion moved quickly through several concepts about testing that need more detailed consideration. Most school measurement in the past was norm referenced testing. Such tests are interpreted through social comparisons. A group is specified and tested so that one can say, for example, that an individual's score is at the 55th percentile (it exceeds the scores of 55% of the group), above the mean, or at a point "two standard deviations" above or below the mean. The results are not always directly interpretable in terms of the domain or whatever it is that is being tested. In fact, the test may have been constructed with items that yield discrimination (increase variance) data among individuals but neglect careful adherence to a domain. Many so-called intelligence tests, for example, can be described as "hodge podge" as far as domain is concerned; the orientation in their construction has more often been to maximizing of variance, prediction, and selection than to clarity of domain.

In domain or criterion oriented testing, on the other hand, emphasis is placed on clearly delineating whatever it is one intends to measure. For example, given the 26 letters in the alphabet and the "sounds" they represent in English phonetics, it is possible to test children for knowledge of the sounds as a "domain" and to interpret the results without reference to any norm group; then it would be meaningful to say that a child knows the sounds of 70%, 90%, or 60% of the letters of the alphabet. Or, we could test a skeet shooter and say that his "average" is 70% hits on target under certain conditions. Measurement of change or improvement in the domain is quite straightforward. A different quality of information is provided when one speaks directly and quantitatively about a person's achievement in a domain than when one compares the individual with a "norm" group. The teacher who is clear about the goals of instruction and who carefully specifies the detailed tasks and sequences of instruction probably finds the domain orientation in testing and measurement an essential tool.

A Decision Oriented Framework

Much of the earlier testing was oriented also to a kind of simple prediction about the achievements of children. It has been said that the investment in the prediction of academic achievement has been greater than that in any other field, except, possibly, in the prediction of horse races and the stock market. The purpose of schooling, however, differentiating it from racing or the stock market, is not so much to *make predictions* (about the lives of children) as it is to *make a difference* (in the development of children). Norm referenced tests are probably the preferred device for making predictions and selection-rejection decisions. But schools are no longer permitted to make basic selection-rejection decisions. Schools are to be all inclusive no matter how exceptional the needs of children may be, and each student is to be offered a uniquely appropriate education. For purposes of instructional decision making, domain oriented approaches are usually to be preferred.

In an earlier section of this chapter a distinction was made among three levels of payoff: societal, institutional, and individual. It can be said that most testing in the schools has been oriented to institutional payoff which depends on simple predictions and selection-rejection decisions. What is needed is more testing oriented to individual payoff and to assisting the teacher in making instructional decisions.

Predictive instruments. Educators have tended to use devices, such as IQ tests, that predict academic achievement in the schools with some success, to separate out children for special settings—some children going to classes for the retarded, others for the gifted, and so on. The problem is that the IQ does not indicate whether any child will do better in a segregated setting; it only indicates that the low scoring child is unlikely to do well and that the high scoring child is likely to do well in the existing, regular school program. A high IQ predicts success in many institutions or programs but it does not include information that helps the gifted individual to choose among them, and a low IQ predicts relatively poor success in many settings but does not help the individual to choose among them. Knowledge of IQ's helps only to identify children who may be selected or rejected for some institutional goal but it does not help much in improving instruction for the individual. The widespread use of norm referenced tests and correlational predictive procedures in test validation is a sign of the strong orientation to selection-rejection decisions and to institutional goals that have permeated the schools. In this context some observers have said that the schools have followed an industrial rather than a school model.

For the purposes of enhancing individual payoff, it is not enough to use predictive instruments and to make rejection decisions when the predictions are unfavorable. If educators are truly concerned about each child and if they commit themselves to making no rejection (demission) decisions, a wholly different quality of information about children and their life situations is required.

As shown in Table 2-1, one can make selection-rejection decisions that maximize institutional payoff whenever one has a predictive device and a situation that permits selecting only some individuals. Traditionally, psychological testing in the schools has been undertaken within this kind of framework. The tests most commonly used have been validated on the basis of simple predictions, and test items have often been selected on the basis of their discriminatory power rather than their adequate representation of some meaningful domain. The manuals for such tests typically have provided norms based on age or grade.

Norm referenced testing has a variety of valuable uses, such as giving an individual useful self knowledge. Festinger (1954) argued persuasively

TABLE 2-1
A Decision Payoff Matrix

Who gets the payoff?	Data required	Type of decision
Institutions	Simple predictions—depending mostly on norm referenced tests or observations on variables that magnify individual differences and correlate with outcomes that have institutional utility	Selection-rejection
Individuals	1. Aptitude-treatment-interactions (ATI) and/or 2. "Rate" of performance or learning in different systems and/or 3. Domain or criterion referenced test results in competency areas	Instructional placement—the matching of instruction with individual readiness for instruction

that one of the methods used by individuals to build self concepts is making active comparisons with other people. For example, it is probably not sufficient for all purposes for individuals to have only domain oriented assessments or even absolute data on their own performances, as in speed of running the 100 yard dash; it adds something to the knowledge of the performance to be able to compare theirs with others; to see themselves, in other words, in the context of "norm groups."

Furthermore, it is useful for an individual to have both norm referenced data and predictive indexes of the very best kinds when making decisions on future educational programs, vocational roles, or institutional affiliations. And, of course, norm referenced tests can be used quite legitimately to make institutional decisions, as when a professional school chooses the most promising candidates from a large pool for an expensive training program.

Thus, although there are legitimate and important uses for norm referenced tests and institutionally oriented decisions, additional approaches to measurement and decision making are essential in the contexts of today's schools. The dominant use of norm referenced evaluation procedures in early schooling, in which all children are required to participate, is part of a system that has made it difficult for some children to feel fully valued and accepted in the schools and community.

The aptitude treatment interaction assumption. When the aim is to maximize individual payoff (Table 2-1), the problem of testing becomes one of choosing or helping in the design of appropriate educational environments and procedures to maximize performance for each child.

Placement decisions would be simple, indeed, if one assumed that all children can and should be educated through exactly similar procedures. However, teachers make what might be called the aptitude-treatment-interaction (ATI) assumption, that is, the assumption that children differ markedly in important aptitudes or other attributes which, in turn, indicate the use of different instructional programs to optimize education for each individual. The clearest cases are the totally blind or profoundly deaf children who, obviously, cannot learn all subjects by the methods and materials that are commonly used with other pupils. Other and more subtle differences among children should be equally important for instructional planning.

The ATI idea had its origin in education in the work of Cronbach and Gleser (1965). In technical terms, it requires demonstration that an aptitude or attribute is acted on positively by a treatment; for example, if there are two possible instructional procedures, the variable that produces a disordinal* interaction with the treatments provides the basis for decisions to optimize the opportunities for individuals. In the measurement context, it is notable that the differential slant of two or more regression lines is the critical data rather than the simple high regression coefficients or high prediction.

Teachers are constantly making informal ATI decisions, that is, in deciding on methods or approaches to education that will be most useful to individual children. For example, a teacher may decide that a particular child will learn best when given short, closely monitored assignments, while another child may organize his own work over long time segments. The teacher's day is filled with microdecisions of these kinds, always matching instruction to the particular needs or most promising approaches for a child.

Informal ATI type decisions are common also in many of the day by day placement decisions made by school workers. A school principal, for example, may wisely place a pupil in the classroom of teacher A rather than with teacher B. In this case the teachers are the "treatments" and it could be judged that one treatment (teacher) was better matched than the other with the aptitudes (attributes) of the child. Or, a placement team might propose to place a particular handicapped child in a given school situation because it has an especially good language program. In such situations one sees careful consideration going to both the child and the potential treatments and the decisions involve the ATI logic, if only informally.

---

*The disordinal interaction requires demonstration that one treatment is best for some subjects and another treatment, for others. For a discussion of disordinal and ordinal interactions, in the context of ATI decision theory, see Bracht & Glass (1968).

Experimentation with different learning approaches. Something functionally similar to an ATI decision can be achieved quite differently by trying out or experimenting with several different methods or environments with a child and assessing carefully which approach works best. Teachers follow these procedures whenever, for example, they try teaching a specific skill within the framework of a game or drill procedure, or when they compare rates of a child's performance in a highly structured versus an open framework. The applied behavior analysts use these procedures when they establish, through experimental means, what will serve as a "reinforcer" for a particular child.

Domain referenced testing. A final approach indicated in Table 2-1 is domain and/or criterion referenced testing procedures. In carefully sequenced and individualized instruction it is important to use tests that represent various domains of knowledge or skill and about which one can make meaningful decisions without norm references. When a child has completed all of the essential prerequisites, as checked on domain referenced tests, the child can then proceed to the next level of work.

Grading in the Schools

The preceding discussions of measurement and decision processes finally reach their most meaningful form for students themselves in the grading system used in the schools they attend. The exceptional student may wind up in a difficult situation. Suppose that a student who has shown longstanding difficulties in reading and general verbal comprehension is enrolled in a regular social studies or English class at the high school level; further, let it be supposed that all students take essentially identical programs and are examined by the same tests. Predictably, our hypothesized student would fall at or near the bottom of the class on nearly every daily, weekly, or monthly quiz, and summary report card grades would be consistent *D*'s or *F*'s. In one sense, the grades would be accurate, but in another sense the grades reflect a situation that is hardly healthy for the student and perhaps not for the rest of the class as well. The grading system may be particularly troublesome if it is highly competitive, as in "grading on the curve." Any time that grades are so distributed that only preset portions are "good" and "bad," then a kind of hydraulic or competitive effect is observed. One child's "good" grade subtracts from another's ability to achieve a good grade. Gifted children, under this system, may receive top grades while being undereducated, also. But in a domain oriented or mastery orientation system, no such competitive processes are involved because, potentially, all students can master any particular domain. In many schools and communities, however, grading tends to be competitive and problematic.

Grading is one of the particulars that needs to be dealt with as we try to provide a greater diversity of programs for a greater diversity of students in mainstream school settings. In day by day school operations our aim should be (a) to develop individual plans that specify goals and objectives for each student, (b) to provide information to students and parents on progress in fulfilling those individual plans, (c) to use grading methods that report details of the progress of each student and thus become part of the reinforcement system in the instructional process. It is of the utmost importance in day by day schooling that grading become a positive, information sharing process rather than a competitive, social comparison process in which some students are constantly devalued.

In summary, it can be said of grading that what students and their parents require is honest and useful information. In day by day, week by week operations, the grading information of greatest value is on progress in meeting the objectives set for that student's unique program.

Is long division mastered or not? The specific rules of punctuation? The use of the cross-cut saw? Can the student demonstrate a reasonably comprehensive and balanced understanding of the Civil War or of the processes of cellular division? The ability to sustain individual work? The attitudes and skills of cooperative work? The answers to these and similar questions are obtainable through carefully developed domain oriented assessments. In the daily school situation the individual student does not require percentiles, stanines, normal curves, or any of the appurtenances of norm oriented, competitive measurements.

Occasionally, norm oriented, longer range assessments of rate of development and predictions of likely development and selectability are important. Again, one must provide the best possible information to all students, with attention focused on helping the individual to make decisions about the future. Comparisons with others may be useful in this context.

The Concept of Expectancy in Children

As noted, educators have had great interest in predicting child achievement. Such predictions often have been translated into statements about the *capacities* of and *expectations* for children. The linkage of the concepts of simple prediction and capacity was taken for granted.

An early side effect of the academic prediction movement, which mostly used general intelligence test results as the predictors, was the development of individualized grading systems. It became a matter of misguided fairness that some children should be "expected" to achieve more and some less, and that school report cards should reflect each child's achievement in relation to his individual capacity. Let it be said immediately that being accurate about what to "expect" of every child is a sure impossibility.

A refinement of this procedure was the special attention given to those children whose capacity was high but achievements were low—the so-called underachievers or learning disabled. Somehow, children achieving below capacity were made a special clinical group. It might equally have been argued that all children were doing exactly what should be expected of them if only we knew enough to make accurate predictions or to judge their capacities and life situations appropriately. In any case, the discrepancy cases might have been called the "overpredicted," putting the onus on the testers, rather than the "underachievers," which put the onus on the child. Discrepancies between mental age and achievement age or between IQ and AQ (Achievement Quotient, computed by taking the ratio of achievement "age" over mental "age") are not necessarily indicators of special aptitude for better work; yet millions of dollars were invested to support the assumption. Formulae that adjust expectations for the regression of achievement on IQ and for years in school still contain the basic logical problems.

Strangely, these discrepancy variables, which reflect differences between so-called capacity and achievement, never have been carefully studied although they have been enormously popular in drawing distinctions between remedial or learning disability cases and retardation. The assumption was that children with high capacity but low achievement belonged to a different category than those showing uniformly low, flat profiles, and there was a pervasive pessimism about the educability of children with low capacity estimates (the retarded) because so little was expected of them. It is no wonder parents of some "retarded" children became negative in attitudes toward schools.

A subtle form of discrepancy analysis, using profile interpretations, involved the assumption that the general level of a profile yields some kind of capacity or expectancy level and that departures from the flat median line represent needs and potentialities for remediation. By some mystical process, the average of several scores becomes the "expected" level on each variable, and presumably flat profiles are preferred over irregular ones. This form of discrepancy analysis will stand up to rigorous examination no better than simpler approaches using general intelligence as the standard. Profiles across a whole battery of tests that show some high and some quite low scores are assumed to be anomalous in some intrapersonal way and thus are an appropriate basis for remedial action. The low scores presumably represent "defects" destined for special treatment; yet it is entirely possible that very rapid learners show similar profiles.

A particular problem with many profile procedures is that reliability is low on some scales, and the proper use of regressed profile scores can sometimes turn a profile on its head. For example, let it be supposed that a child has been given a variety of tests that purport to show how that individual learns under various conditions. The obtained scores may show a very high result on "visual learning" and a somewhat lower score on "auditory learning." Each of the scores is an estimate of the true ability of the individual along these two dimensions and each of the measurements has many limitations. Each of the scales has limited reliability which is to say that the score obtained in any one testing may vary considerably from the "true" score. When an extremely high or low score is obtained and reliability is low it is advisable to use regressed estimates of the attribute; that is, to assume the individual's true score is not so extreme as the obtained score. If the reliabilities of the scales are different, regressed scores may actually show a different profile than the obtained scores; yet few diagnosticians use the proper procedures.

Few testers or teachers have built up the skills and habits necessary to the use of such regressed scores in the practical interpretation of profiles. Instead most school workers make the simplest and most direct interpretations of profiles using simply the obtained scores. Unhappily, such procedures often lead to complicated misjudgments of children's capacities and needs (Cronbach, Gleser, Nanda, & Rajaratnam, 1972).

Lately, a variety of influences has broken the rigid molds of past notions about capacity for learning or what it is reasonable to "expect" of learners. Scholars, reexamining studies on the nature-nurture controversy, have helped to create a much more open idea of nurturance of intelligence (Hunt, 1961), and studies in international education have helped to clarify the great influence of social forces in the achievements of individual human beings (Halsey, 1961). Minority groups have militantly demanded a more guarded use of general intelligence tests as a basis for creating expectancies and classification systems.

B. F. Skinner has argued that we have permitted the adjective, as in *intelligent* behavior, to become the noun *intelligence,* and then we make futile speculations about its determinants. Bijou and others, who have urged the educational community to adopt the viewpoint of the applied behavior analyst, have argued that "a retarded individual is one who has a limited repertory of behavior evolving from interactions with his environmental contacts which constitute his history" (Bijou, 1963). In this framework a concept of general capacity seems to be superfluous. Lindsley (1964) took what might be the ultimate position when he wrote,

> Children are not retarded, only their behavior in average environments is sometimes retarded. In fact, it is modern sciences' ability to design suitable environments for these children that is retarded. (p. 62)

The behaviorists, such as Bijou and Lindsley, believe, as do religious missionaries, that behavior can be changed if the response is defined carefully and the environment is controlled to influence the probabilities of response; they make little reference to concepts of fixed capacity.

The sources of new viewpoints on human capacity are many, but suffice it to say that our views are much less fixed now than they were earlier. What might be expected of a person is seen, in important part, to be a function of culture and a particular environmental history. It is increasingly appreciated also that "intelligent" behavior has many non-cognitive determinants. Classifications of individuals according to simple intelligence test results or other capacity estimates are not secure; and classifications according to discrepancy systems involving differences between capacity and achievements are tenuous, indeed. In this context, consequently, specific doubts and embarrassments inevitably arise over such classifications as "retarded," "underachiever," "remedial case," and "learning disabled." These classifications have little valid use in making instructional decisions. (As may be noted in other parts of this text, the authors prefer to make direct observations of rates of cognitive development and of academic development.)

The implications of changing views on human capacities include making early childhood education a primary target for action, particularly in disadvantaged communities. The pervasive attitude in this book is that where the rates of child development are low, perhaps more can be done through systematic enrichment of the environment to produce fuller and more rapid development. The assumption is not that the children's "capacities" are necessarily low; indeed, it is hard to know how to advance a decent hypothesis about the capacities of individuals, but we can proceed with attempts to improve learning environments and learning rates everywhere.

In summary, one can say simply that there is no such thing as *the capacity* of a child for learning. One might say that children have many different capacities for learning or that it is reasonable to expect different rates of learning from them depending on how they are taught and what their other life experiences are. Children in ancient Rome learned Latin by age 2. So it is with complex, culturally related learning: What can be expected of children must take account of the characteristics of both the children and their environments. The orientation required is ecological.

Children and youth all over the nation are being taught and are learning at levels far above the levels "expected" of them. Nowhere is this more obvious than in the burgeoning new centers for severely handicapped persons. There is reason to wipe out much of what has been said about children's "capacities" and to accept, instead, a greater responsibility for arranging environments that make a positive difference in what one can expect of and achieve with them.

The Classification and Grouping of Children

A visit to almost any school will reveal remarkably complex patterns in the movement and classification of children. In elementary schools, children are grouped mainly by age and grade. Later, students move to junior and senior high schools where groups are organized by subject matter as well as by age and grade.

Much of the general grouping in schools is controlled by central administrators and school boards who declare which buildings shall be elementary schools and which shall be junior high schools and so on. But a great deal of classification and grouping goes on within each classroom or instructional setting. The band director decides who shall play first trumpet and who shall play second trumpet, and the pupils space and engage themselves accordingly. Or, the teacher sets up three or four reading groups, and because some pupils are ready for more advanced work, they are grouped separately.

The major variable used in schools for purposes of general classification and grouping is chronological age. In most school districts, kindergarten is entered in September of the calendar year in which a child reaches age 5 and then the pupils progress year by year in age-grade groups. Some districts permit or encourage early entrance for children who show very high achievements and readiness for school. But this brief account is not the whole story.

A broad set of complications in the classification of children has come from special education. Special education often sifts children into a variety of "categories": mental retardation, learning disabilities, speech handicaps, emotional disturbance, hearing impairment, vision impairment, and crippling and other health impairments. Classroom groups, teacher certification, legislative funding systems, and parent groups have tended to follow the same categorical delineations. Patterns differ somewhat from one state to another so that, for example, Texas provides for a classification of brain injured children while most other states do not. Regular teachers have learned to refer children according to existing systems of categories, and school psychologists and other personnel workers have performed their functions at the gateways.

A number of problems emerge in connection with the categorizing of children and programs, especially when labels with negative implications are attached to individuals who are categorized, as in mentally *retarded,* emotionally *disturbed,* or learning *disabled.* Hobbs (1975) saw such classifications and labels as potentially harmful.

> Classification, or inappropriate classification. . .can blight the life of a child, reducing opportunity, diminishing his competence and self-esteem, alienating him from others, nurturing a meanness of spirit, and making

him less a person than he could become. Nothing less than the futures of children is at stake. (p. 1)

It is assumed here that some forms of classification are necessary; not all children can be educated effectively in the same environment. Human dialogue and the practical organization of work require some classification and grouping. But whatever system is used it nevertheless must give primary attention to the individuality of children.

Purposes of Classification

As a start in considering what might be an appropriate approach to classification, it may be useful to consider the purposes of classification. Educators who work with physicians or psychologists frequently find themselves trapped in classification schemes that may better serve purposes other than those of education. Zubin (1967), a clinical psychologist, cited three purposes for the diagnosis and classification of what he called behavior disorders: (a) to search for etiology, (b) to make a prognosis, and (c) to select a therapy. Physicians and clinical psychologists tend to be oriented to these purposes. How they observe the individual, what they choose for attention, and which groupings or classifications they select vary with their purposes. In anticipation of the discussion that follows, it can be stated immediately that only a third of these purposes has any relevance for educators; yet our information systems tend to become distracted and cluttered by the other two purposes Zubin listed.

Certainly it is clear that classification merely according to Zubin's first purpose, etiology, is not a useful approach in education. Knowing the cause of poor sight gives one little help in deciding how the child with poor sight should be taught. Similarly, it usually does not matter in educational planning whether the child's attentional problems stem from brain injury or other causes. Etiological variables may be useful in education but only in the context of the educational decisions to be made; the causes of behavior are relevant to education only in relation to the difference they make in how teachers proceed with instruction and examples of this are hard to find.

Similarly, prognosis has limited usefulness for instruction. Educators are employed to influence children's learning, not simply to predict it. Educational decisions require attention to variables or characteristics that interact with instruction, that is, that help educators to make a difference rather than a simple prediction. This requirement is far beyond the content of psychological reports written in simple terms of capacity, expectation, or underachievement, all of which are prognostic in orientation.

Zubin's third purpose, the selection of treatment, does have relevance in the present context because the important purpose of educational classification is to design or select treatment or instruction. Two general classes of treatment should be distinguished, however. The first is oriented to negative criteria, in which case we use terms like *prevention, cure,* or *amelioration;* and the second, to positive criteria, in which case we use terms like *development, competency,* or *achievement.* In the second case, the concept of prevention is not meaningful in any full sense.

Educational treatments are almost always positive, that is, oriented to competency or achievement. They are concerned with teaching and learning, not with the recovery from defects or the simple prevention of problems. The educator "prevents" reading failure not by building antibodies but by teaching reading or its prerequisites with greater resourcefulness and better effect to more children. To be educationally relevant and to engage the teacher, the treatment must involve learning and development.

The view proposed here is consonant with Zubin's third purpose but only in the context of a developmental rather than a deficit oriented view of treatment. Unfortunately, there is still much talk among educators about dysfunctions, deficits, impairments, and disabilities, as if these deviations were the starting points in education and recovery from or remediation of them were the goal. Obviously, one prevents problems and creates a kind of invulnerability to insult whenever important competencies are engendered, but let it be remembered that human development, the competencies and the breadth it gives to life, is the goal.

A Formula for Classification

Cromwell (1976) suggested a formulation of the classification problem based on four classes of information, as follows:

A—Antecedent (historical, etiological) events.
B—Current observations which might include test results plus other forms of data.
C—Treatments (or instructional interventions).
D—Outcomes.

The various relations among the ABCD's can be used to create a knowledge base. An example of an AD relation would be information showing that low birth weight babies (A) tend to become below average academic achievers (D) in the elementary school. An example of a BD relation would be that children with highly punitive parents (B) tend to show high "acting out" behavior (D). Finding that the use of social reinforcement, such as praise or recognition (C), produces good results (D) for a particular student illustrates a CD relationship. An observation that students who show a relatively low "conceptual level" in a field of study (B) do best (D) when instruction is highly structured by the teacher (C) illustrates a BCD relationship.

Psychometrically oriented psychologists tend to be oriented to BD relationships, that is, to giving tests and making general predictions. Physicians tend to be very much interested in the causes of current conditions—which is to say they tend to attend to A's and B's—and to their prognostic significance or to medical treatments. The problem is that those who consult with the teacher must always deal with the C's, the interventions—and, in particular, the interventions the teacher can undertake.

The critical element for educators in this formula is C—the treatment or instructional interventions. AD, BD, and ABD relations are strictly prognostic and are of little interest to the educator, although they may be to others. The critical question is whether one can make a difference in outcome (D) through an intervention (C). Thus, from an educator's viewpoint, the critical relations are ACD, BDC, ABCD, and CD—all involving intervention. The educator becomes a significant factor in the life of the child precisely when the outcome (D) is conditional not just on the characteristics of the child (A + B) but also on the characteristics of the school environment (C). In the aptitude-treatment-interaction paradigm the A's and B's become the aptitudes and the C's, the treatments; the problem is to allocate children to treatment (or to design a treatment) that will optimize the outcome (D) (see Figure 2-2).

FIGURE 2-2
Intervention-Outcome Interactions

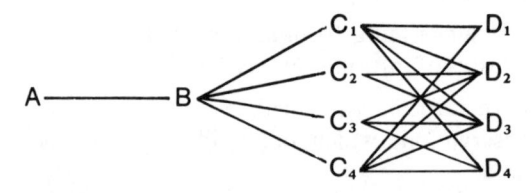

$$A \longrightarrow B \begin{array}{c} C_1 \\ C_2 \\ C_3 \\ C_4 \end{array} \begin{array}{c} D_1 \\ D_2 \\ D_3 \\ D_4 \end{array}$$

The Concept of the Person-Environment Match

To put the problem in the language that is now emerging in education, the problem is to provide a "match" of the child's characteristics and the features of the instructional program in such a way as to yield best outcomes for the child.

An obvious implication of these considerations is that children need to be studied in their school and life settings. Planning for them, the making of an appropriate "match," requires study of both child and situation. Special education teachers, psychologists, and other specialists who join with regular teachers to make educational plans for a pupil must be ecologically oriented in that they always look at the child in relation to a setting—school, home, and playground, for example—and in terms of how the setting, environment, or treatment might be changed. The problems of children are not understood if one looks only at children and labels them as defective, or looks only at teachers and blames their inadequacies for children's failures. Pupils, teachers, and their interactions in a complex setting, as well as family life, must be understood if the most promising plans for children are to be devised.

The test of a classification scheme, for educators, is its educational outcome. Does a scheme permit the allocation of each child to a school situation that is most productive for that child? Obviously, the simple traditional classifications and grouping systems of special education do not supply positive answers. Simple psychometric formulations followed by classification, labels, and special placements are often a serious disservice to children.

There are many myths among regular educators about the categories of the handicaps and the mystique of special education. The assumption seems to be that the special categories of teachers know special things to do to "fix" the problems of children in certain categories. In fact, special educators often have highly refined skills for the systematic and intensive instruction of children, but the skills do not have to be exercised in private and they are less specific to the traditional "categories" than is commonly assumed. They can be joined with the skills of regular teachers to create diverse environments that will appropriately accommodate all, or nearly all, children.

Hunt's (1975) concept of person-environment "match," a practical extension of the ATI (aptitude-treatment-interaction) model, brings together several of the concepts discussed in the preceding section and provides a useful example for special education. Several characteristics of the model have received particular emphasis. First a match must be considered in a developmental context; that is, a student's characteristics may change and, in fact, should be expected to change, in the school situation. For example, a child might be classified for instruction on the basis of low conceptual level, low creativity, or poor response to social reinforcers. All of these characteristics can change and, indeed, can be made the object of training. Thus, no one match can be expected to hold for a long period. Reclassification is required periodically. Second, it is important to consider the effects of a person on the environment as well as of the environment on the person. It is possible that a given child produces some negative reaction from a particular teacher which makes it difficult for that teacher to be effective with that child. So, mutual interactions must be considered in making educational plans.

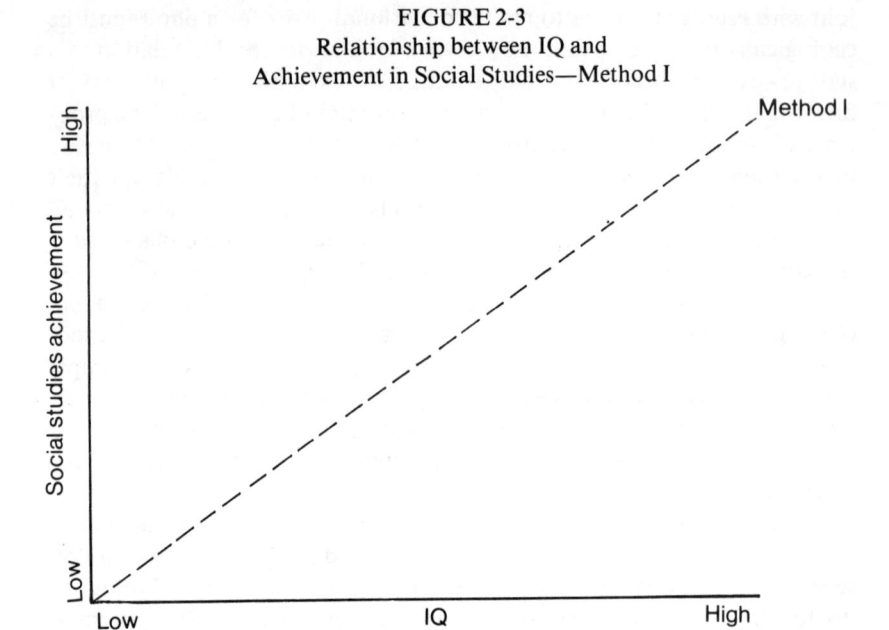

FIGURE 2-3
Relationship between IQ and
Achievement in Social Studies—Method I

To explicate the concept of the "match," consider the following hypothetical case. (Research findings are generally consistent with the case as it is outlined here.) Suppose that in a classroom group taught by the teacher's usual methods there is a substantial relation between the general intelligence of pupils (IQ) and achievement in social studies. This relation is represented in Figure 2-3.

IQ's are distributed across the base line from low to high, and achievement in social studies along the vertical axis, again, from low to high. The broken line represents the relation between IQ and achievement under instructional Method I, a relatively low structured method in which students have many choices of activities and materials. The teacher offers a rich variety of learning opportunities with little systematic structure. Under these conditions, students low in IQ tend to achieve only at low levels; and students with high IQ's achieve much higher in social studies (Figure 2-3). For the best prediction on how any student will achieve, the teacher locates the relevant IQ at the base line, goes straight up to the broken line, and then crosses horizontally to the left to the achievement line.

Suppose, however, that another approach to social studies instruction—Method II—can be created in the school. In this case, instruction is highly structured; the teacher defines a definite sequence of carefully graduated steps in the learning process. Each student proceeds smoothly through materials in which new concepts are carefully developed and their expanding relations are shown. The relations between IQ and achievement might be quite different in this case (see Figure 2-4). The regression line or line of best fit (the dotted line) shows some positive relation between IQ and achievement but the degree of the relation is much less sharp. In practical terms, it appears that low IQ pupils show less of a disadvantage under Method II; but high IQ pupils appear to do less well. The structure seems to help those with low IQ's but impedes those with high IQ's.

Now let us superimpose Figures 2-3 and 2-4 so that we can look simultaneously at the relations between IQ and social studies achievement under both teaching methods (Figure 2-5). The two regression lines intersect or cross—they are disordinal—indicating that we may have evidence of one way of matching different students to different methods of instruction. Here we demonstrate that low IQ children profit best by the highly structured method of instruction, but that the highly structured method is limiting for high IQ students. The latter will do better if they are left relatively free to do their own structuring (Method I). The point in the IQ distribution where the regression lines intersect indicates how the group should be divided for instruction by the two methods.

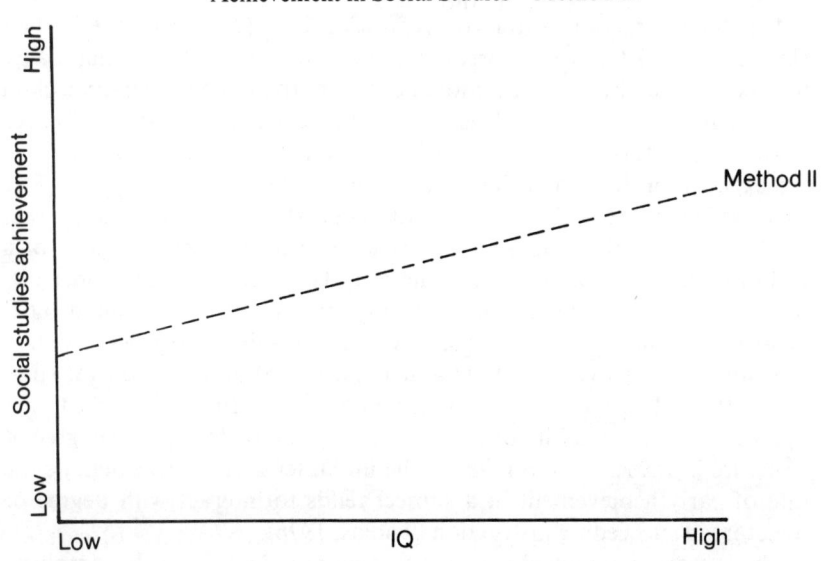

FIGURE 2-4
Relationship between IQ and
Achievement in Social Studies—Method II

FIGURE 2-5
Relationship between IQ and Achievement in Social Studies—
A Comparison of Method I and Method II

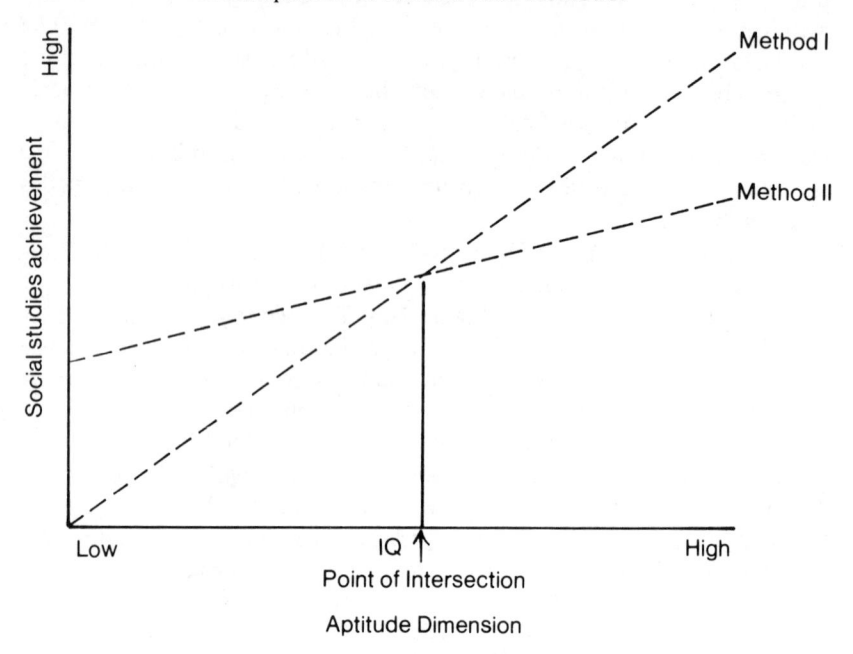

Point of Intersection

Aptitude Dimension

It is the interaction of the two regression lines (the difference in their slants) or the differences in prediction under the two methods that makes it possible to make the instructional decision: to match or classify a child for instructional purposes. It is also noteworthy that the expectation for a child depends on the method of instruction that is used. In Figure 2-5, the expectation for a high IQ child, for example, would be higher under Method I than Method II. It was in this context that we stated earlier that there is no such thing as *the* capacity of or *a* singular expectation for a child in school learning; rather, one expects different results under different conditions. The capacity of children cannot be estimated independently of their life situation and even then is subject to gross errors.

Studies by Cartwright (1971) and Hunt (1975) and the general summary of ATI studies by Cronbach and Snow (1977) suggested that general intellectual ability or conceptual level interacts with the degree of structure in instruction. Similarly, the initial level of achievement or the rate of early achievement in a subject tends to interact with degree of structure in succeeding instruction (Tobias, 1976).

Much more is involved in the matching paradigm than the simplistic example given here. The figures illustrate mainly the statistical side of the problem to show how measurement and observation can be juxtaposed with different instructional approaches to arrive at decisions for matching individuals with the most promising approaches. But let us consider the matching procedures more generally and in practical terms.

Suppose that a teacher has called for consultation about a child's learning problem with a special education teacher and a psychologist. If they wanted to use the matching system, how would they proceed? First, they would study the school's current alternatives for instruction and possibilities for further alteration. That is, they would consider the characteristics of the various curricula, materials, available alternative teachers, and administrative arrangements to see what different "treatments" might be possible. In their study of the child, they would attempt to specify current needs and characteristics that seem particularly relevant to decisions on the arrangement of programs. These would be achievement in skills and content subjects, interests, motivations, work habits, ambitions, and so on. They would also study the family and ask the parents for their insights.

Only after all of these studies would they begin to make decisions about programing for the child. They would constantly consider both the child's characteristics and the likely interaction of the characteristics with treatment alternatives. They likely would find it unnecessary to classify and label the child in any one of the gross categorizations, such as "gifted," "mentally retarded," "learning disabled," or "emotionally disturbed." Instead, they would proceed from their data directly to an educational plan. Their plan would be stated in immediate, developmental terms designed to enhance the child's learning and development. Unfortunately, the classification systems still used in many schools to serve exceptional students are gross, unsystematic, and limited in usefulness at best, and degrading and misleading at worst.

The traditional categories for exceptional children do not "carve nature at its joints." They are not usually real, necessary, meaningful, or useful; in fact, they often serve only to devalue the child and cloud the issue. Although the categories were designed to represent a practical, human construction of problems, the problem can be addressed more effectively in other ways. We suggest an approach that is based on the analysis of both the student and the student's life setting, the latter to include the instructional processes that are used or are potentially usable in the classroom. The aim should be to achieve such a *match* of child and environment as will be maximally productive for the development of the child. The system for classification should,

> deemphasize the familiar but gross categories of exceptionality. It should specify instead the services required to assist the child or his family and school in the interest of the child's fullest development. (Hobbs, 1975, p. 234)

PREVAILING VERSUS PREFERRED PRACTICES

So far, in this chapter, brief consideration has been given to a number of conceptual shifts that are occurring in educational provisions for exceptional students. Following is a brief summary of the prevailing and preferred practices as related to concept shifts.

Prevailing Practices	Preferred Practices
1. Education is a privilege.	1. Education is a right.
2. Children who are difficult to teach are demitted.	2. Zero-demission is the accepted policy.
3. Payoff is oriented to the institution.	3. Payoff is oriented primarily to the individual.
4. Norm oriented testing dominates.	4. Domain oriented testing grows in importance.
5. Grading is competitive in classes.	5. Grading (noncompetitive) relates to individual goals.
6. Testing is prediction oriented.	6. Testing is decision oriented.
7. Aptitude is a salable trait.	7. Aptitude is the way the individual learns best.
8. Aptitudes and treatments are dealt with separately.	8. Aptitudes are conceptualized in terms of interactions with treatments.
9. Learning difficulties are attributed to the child.	9. Learning difficulties are seen as arising from both child and the environment in interaction.
10. Assessment is focused only on the child.	10. Assessment is focused on both the child and the child's life/school setting.
11. Children are described in general terms of "expectancy."	11. The singular concept of "expectancy" is abandoned.
12. Exceptional children are placed in negatively labeled categories.	12. Exceptional children are dealt with in terms of functionally relevant characteristics and matched to the most promising instructional procedure.

THE EMPIRICAL BASE FOR MAINSTREAMING

A wide range of research and experience is relevant to the main topic of this book, educational mainstreaming: for example, research on architecture and environmental management, such as lighting and acoustic control; the full history of the civil rights movement; sociological and psychiatric research on labeling practices and effects; data reflecting the effectiveness and general evaluation of institutions for the handicapped; and the history of and research on homogeneous grouping practices in the schools. None of the above topics is reviewed systematically here, however, because of space limitations. Topical bibliographies at the close of the chapter will help interested students pursue them.

Probably of more immediate relevance for review are two other topics: (a) a sample of studies that deal quite specifically with classrooms as social and physical environments for the accommodation of exceptional pupils and (b) a longer review of research and experience addressed specifically to mainstreaming issues.

Classes as Social Settings

Briefly reviewed in this section are two lines of investigation that focus on behavior within the class. Each has a strong theoretical basis that has been translated into practical application. Each significantly increases the capacity of teachers and children to deal with exceptional pupils in the mainstream.

Cooperative Class Procedures

Traditionally, teachers have been trained to focus attention on the academic learning of children and to give relatively little systematic attention to the social processes in their classes. Educational policy making bodies have shown a similar pattern of emphasis on limited cognitive objectives and neglect of other potential goals. For example, almost everyone agrees that social studies—the knowledge of history and of major governmental and cultural institutions and systems—is an important school subject; yet few persons pay explicit and systematic attention to teaching children the skills and attitudes of cooperative behavior on which the survival of our social system may depend.

The class itself is a complex social system that can be organized to enhance or impede the development of social goals. The way classes are conducted markedly influences their capacity to accommodate children who have special needs. Johnson and Johnson (1975), contrasting instructional operations that they characterized as (a) cooperative, (b) competitive, or (c) individualized, showed by both research and practical procedures that cooperative classes are supportive social environments for exceptional students.

Cooperative classes are structured to encourage and reinforce sharing, mutual support, coordination, free communication, and trust among pupils; students are taught effective skills of listening and communication; evaluations are domain rather than social comparison or norm oriented. As teachers make explicit these process outcomes and work toward them, the results, as shown by research findings, tend to be positive in both the cognitive and affective domains for exceptional students and other students as well. "In a cooperative structure...differences (among pupils) are positively valued as greater resources to help the group accomplish a variety of goals" (Johnson & Johnson, 1975, p. 95).

Research suggests that there really is no such thing as an impervious regular class; each class and every teacher has the capacity for many forms of structure and for seeking many different goals. It is possible to structure classes to emphasize cooperative goals, to encourage positive interpersonal behavior, and to reduce disabling anxieties, thus creating a positive environment in which mainstreaming becomes a reality for many children who, otherwise, would be rejected and isolated.

Increasing Attentiveness—Reducing Disturbing Behavior

Another line of research that has fundamental implications for mainstreaming focuses on the attentional and disturbing behaviors of students. Probably no other topics are more frequently cited as the causes of negative attitudes toward some pupils and of referrals of pupils out of regular classrooms.

Using broad observational procedures in classroom situations, Kounin (1970) advanced a number of hypotheses about the poor attention and disturbing behavior of individuals and groups of children in classes. One simple hypothesis was that if, when asking questions in group situations, teachers first asked the question, paused briefly, and then called on a pupil by name (proceeding randomly over time to include all pupils), better attentional behavior resulted than if the pupil were named first and the question followed. Other hypotheses dealt with group alerting techniques and transitions (changing from one activity to another) that seemed to be critical in control of classroom behavior.

Borg (undated) developed the Kounin theoretical and observational work into a brief teacher training system covering about a dozen similar procedures for improving the attention and reducing the disturbing behavior of pupils; the system has been tried and shows strong and positive results in the behavior of children where teachers have been trained. This suggests that the mainstream itself—the teacher managed class setting—can be changed through teacher controlled processes to increase student attention and cooperation, to reduce disturbing behavior, and to make the setting more accommodating to mainstreamed students.

As part of the mainstreaming movement, it is of high importance that the research and developmental work of people like the Johnsons and Borg be supported, that results be carefully evaluated, and that when results are positive they be disseminated widely to teachers. It is abundantly clear that many behavior problems can be dealt with in regular school situations if sufficient insight and the necessary tools are available.

Mainstreaming Research and Experience

In the following section of this chapter attention is given to research and other forms of empirical evidence relating specifically to mainstreaming issues. In many school districts the least restrictive environment doctrine began its stirrings with considerable force but little rationale. School leaders and teachers have badly needed a summary of the empirical base for the movement; indeed, special education leaders suggested that research in the area is one of their highest priorities (Loe & Becker, 1975). We proceed by posing some of the key questions in the field, each question followed by a summary of the empirical data we found available.

Feasibility and Value of Mainstreaming

What published evidence supports the feasibility and value of mainstreaming, full or part time, for exceptional children?

The doctrine of least restrictive alternative is best implemented by starting all pupils in kindergarten or first grade together and then making special educational adjustments to individual differences as soon as the need is noted. The need may be known and adjustments planned before the first day of school in the case of children who are known to be physically impaired, deaf, blind, or severely limited in cognitive development. Other children who are disposed toward school-learning problems may not be noted until the regular kindergarten or first grade teacher attempts to instruct them. Children with speech and language limitations, who are hard of hearing or partially seeing, might make up this group.

The evidence supporting mainstreaming from the first day of the first year of school is positive and strong, and it comes from many sources. For youngsters who have been identified as needing special education before the usual school age reports of effective integration date as far back as 1962. The practice was operating systemwide in Tacoma, Washington, even earlier (Bertness, 1976). Descriptions of programs that brought identified exceptional children into kingergarten or first grade along with their neighborhood peers are found in some of the following summaries of research. In other research, the identification and integration of the exceptional pupils occurred later.

Suspected intellectual, perceptual, physical, emotional, and academic handicaps. The large scale investigation of Cantrell and Cantrell (1976) supports the practice of integration from the start of schooling. The

Cantrells studied the achievement of 723 pupils in the first grades of 20 school districts under conditions in which support teachers were available to help first grade teachers "to solve children's problems prior to referral for formalized services which would demand labeling and possible exclusion from the opportunities normally available to non-problem children" (p. 382).

Two specific hypotheses were tested: (a) that in first grade classes for which expert consultation was available, the children would have significantly higher achievement scores than children in classes lacking such consultation, and (b) fewer children would be referred for psychological and special services by teachers with access to expert consultation than by teachers who did not have such consultation. Both hypotheses were supported strongly by the results of the study. The authors found:

> Regular classroom teachers who have access to resource personnel. . .can effect significant achievement gains for students at all levels of IQ functioning [the IQ range was 50 to 139]. . .no one IQ level of experimental school students achieved more at the expense of any other IQ level. High IQ students within experimental schools continued to achieve commensurate with expectations for their own developmental rates even though consultation centered primarily on the problems of lower functioning students. (Cantrell & Cantrell, 1976, p. 385)

Further, the Cantrells found that the referral rates for psychological services were lower the following year in those schools that provided immediate aid to teachers for pupils with difficulties. This finding suggested that the availability of immediate support services is viewed by teachers as sufficient, in the majority of cases, for dealing with the problems. The actual number of psychological referrals from the first grades dropped to less than one-fourth of what they had been before trained teacher support services were made available. The implication is that a diminution in labeling may occur under the support teacher plan because the referrals that were made used such categorical terms as *suspected intellectual handicap, suspected perceptual handicap, underachievement, physical handicap,* and *suspected emotional handicap.*

Cantrell and Cantrell's (1976) report signifies that, if a cadre of teachers are given training in special education consultation procedures and they are encouraged to work as supportive partners with teachers in regular first grades, a marked reduction may be seen in the number of children who are referred out to special classes.

Koppitz (1976) reported a summary of certain results of a 5 year followup study of 177 children, ages 6 to 12, who had been admitted to a public school program for children with learning disabilities. (The first report of the study was made in 1971.) The average age at admission was almost 9 years; mean IQ was 92, with a range from 70+ to 143. The children's learning and behavioral disorders were varied, as were their social backgrounds and the diagnoses with which they had been labeled. The pupils showed combinations of emotional, behavioral, and learning difficulties, and most displayed signs of minimal brain dysfunction.

The study is detailed and includes a number of conclusions. The one that is most relevant here follows:

> Most of the youngsters who were able to return successfully to regular classes after only one or two years in the special classes (roughly one-fourth of the 177) probably would not have had to come to the learning-disability program at all, if they had received the extra help and attention they required in the primary grades. (Koppitz, 1976, p. 47)

The Koppitz report iterates Cantrell and Cantrell's findings.

Blind Children. Campbell (1955) characterized mainstreaming as an "exciting" development for blind children.

> An exciting new world is opening up to a few of the thousands of blind children in the United States who are fortunate enough to live in or near one of the few communities where they are offered educational and social opportunities in the schools with sighted children. (p. 73)

Campbell was alluding to what was dubbed the "unsegregated" educational design, which was begun in 1951 in California by the Temple City Unified School District and the Pasadena Pacific Oaks Friends Nursery School. Preschool blind children started to attend the latter along with seeing children. The regular teaching there, and subsequently in Temple City's Longden Avenue School, was supplemented as needed by special educators.

The nursery school philosophy emphasized the acceptance of individual differences:

> It is a practice which we examine regularly in the light of our experience and new knowledge. . . .When we accept that "normal" is a range the "special" needs become more a matter of degree than of different nature. (Campbell, 1955, p. 75)

Campbell's (1955) descriptive analysis and evaluation of mainstreaming blind children indicates that inclusion was practiced to the satisfaction of parents, educators, and the community approximately a quarter of a century ago. The program elements, as described by Campbell, from starting all children to school together, through using special educators to team with regular class teachers, to relating to other community resources along the way and linking with specialized vocational guidance, are essentially the same as those recommended for high quality program designs today.

Autistic children. Integration of preschool age autistic children in regular nursery class programs was undertaken in Toronto, Canada, in 1956.

The inclusion procedure had progressed to third grade for some of the autistic children at the time the report of the results was published (Lovatt, 1962). The children were described initially as follows:

> Unresponsive even to their own parents, they seemed to live in a dream world of their own, unrelated to reality. They appeared mentally retarded, and most of them lacked speech. They were unable to play. Our child guidance clinics were reluctant to serve such children since experience had shown that play therapy sessions, even when tried over a long period of time with such children, had produced little constructive results. (p. 103)

A teacher-therapist began working with the autistic children in the project on a one to one basis in a separate play area. As rapport was established, the teacher-therapist moved the autistic children into contact with children and staff in the regular nursery. Over a period of time, sometimes many months, the one to one relationship with the teacher-therapist became less necessary. Some autistic children needing less and less individual staff support progressed at age 5 or 6 to regular kindergarten.

At the close of the period reported in this study, four of the first pupils were progressing satisfactorily in second and third grades. Other autistic children, who had started later, were in regular class at lower grade levels.

Children with hearing impairments. Beginning in 1972, 5 year old hearing and deaf children attended kindergarten together at the Lexington School in New York City. By 1975-1976 the arrangement had been extended to include such merged classes through third grade. Connor (1976) reported that parents of hearing pupils were favorably impressed by the individualized instruction, enthusiastic and innovative teachers, progressive curriculum approach, and excellent academic development.

> The achievement test results for the hearing children confirm the parents' evaluation, with six-year-old hearing children reading at the second-grade level and with math achievement even higher. . . .[The faculty] urged the Lexington administration to enroll as many normally hearing pupils as possible. . .so that the speech, language and reading achievement of the deaf students can be upgraded. The faculty value the hearing children and their parents as models to improve their own classroom efforts. (p. 79)

Partial mainstreaming in a Vermont elementary school for a 9 year old girl with a severe hearing impairment was described in detail by the teachers who were involved (Coleman, Eggleston, Collins, Holloway, & Reider, 1975). The child had attended a special school for three years prior to entering the regular elementary school. One objective was to maintain or improve her already established rate of learning in language, speech, reading, and other subjects in the new school setting. During the first year, the child was removed from the regular class 90 minutes per day for tutoring. All language instructional objectives were attained and reading achievement increased two full grade levels by the end of the first term. Social gains were also satisfactory.

The tutor, who was experienced in teaching hearing impaired pupils, not only had instructed the girl individually and apart from the class for 90 minutes per day but also had assisted the youngster as needed during the rest of the school day which she spent with peers in large and small group activities. The program illustrates partial mainstreaming with 100% special education instruction.

The heavy investment of professional support service was necessary the first year. For the second year, it was planned that the tutoring would be gradually withdrawn.

Many residential schools have tested the feasibility and values of integrating deaf and hearing students. By 1975, 30 residential schools had established plans for such experiences. Craig and Salem (1975) reviewed 12 publications that dealt with integration, reported on their own mail survey of 75 residential schools, and presented narrative reports on several schools that they visited. They concluded that partial mainstreaming should be considered a valuable extension of existing residential school instructional patterns.

Children with severe learning disabilities and behavior disorders. Newman (1959) studied six boys, aged 8 to 10 years, who showed "severe disturbances of learning and school adjustment" and were characterized as "hyperaggressive boys with behavior disorders." They were within the normal intelligence range. In 1954, at the beginning of the study, and throughout its three year term, the boys were inpatients on a closed ward at the Clinical Center of the National Institutes of Health and attended school there.

Analysis of critical incidents in the boys' behaviors guided the medical treatment and educational procedures that were applied to bring their behavior within acceptable bounds and to turn it in productive directions.

> Differences between acceptable and tolerated activities in the classroom had to be clearly communicated, and a great deal of time and effort had to be spent on transmitting the message that what is tolerated at one period would not be tolerated at a later date. For example, the reading of comics in school was tolerated in school originally in order to communicate the message that the child was wanted in school and could stay there so long as he was not too disturbing to others. Later, comics were tabooed in school since at this time the message to be communicated was that there were some things appropriate to school and others inappropriate for the best use of schooltime. (Newman, 1959, p. 633)

From the beginning, the overall approach combined individual psychotherapy and a planned school program, the latter conducted by two special teachers. By 1959, two years after the three year intensive project was terminated, the boys were attending regular schools full time. "They received only marginal individual tutoring from the teaching staff (of the Institute) on the request of their present schools" (Newman, 1959, p. 641).

In the 1969-1970 school year in a suburb of Buffalo, New York, there was initiated an integrated design for the education of children with learning problems within the regular class setting (Reger & Koppmann, 1971). The new design, which established child evaluation centers in the local schools, was devised as an alternative to special classes for students with serious learning difficulties. The centers were staffed by the local elementary or secondary school's professional teachers only—no psychologists, social workers, or medical personnel were brought in. Parents were involved in every step of each child's assessment and in the preparation of educational plans. No data were kept confidential. Any regular class pupils with whom teachers wanted help were eligible for review. Although not every child who benefited from the center would have been placed in a special class, many would have been.

The center operates as a resource for the pupil and the pupil's teacher. It is staffed full time by a special educator and, from time to time, by other teachers. Scheduling to the resource room, just like admission to the program itself, is a local school function of the teachers who are involved, the parents, and the principal.

Data gathered in the first two years of operation showed that the demand for this program design more than doubled—from 11 to 23 units. Cost per pupil serviced was found to be $300.00, in contrast to the $2,000 to $3,000 cost per pupil for services in special classes. A major advantage is the regular class teachers' belief that they are being helped by the program in their professional work with their pupils (Reger & Koppmann, 1971).

The carefully planned inclusion of a group of learning disabled children into a regular secondary school was described by Vogel (1976). The nine youngsters had occupied a self contained sixth grade classroom the year before. Their inclusion in the departmentalized seventh grade of a large junior high school was monitored over a one year period. Conclusions were drawn about the adequacy of the procedures used and recommendations were offered for the future.

Positive consequences were reported for academic, social, and attitudinal growth. The strengths and limitations of the operation were analyzed and listed. Effects on other children and the core teachers were appraised. The general conclusion was that "the integration of severe LD children in a combined homogenous and heterogenous organized structure appeared to have many educational, attitudinal and social rewards" (Vogel, 1976, p. 54). Moreover, all of the teachers reported that their own day to day instruction had improved because they took part in the program of partial mainstreaming.

Physically handicapped children. The enrollment and maintenance of children with physical handicaps in schools with all other children has been the subject of a number of widely different anecdotal or case reports. There is extreme heterogeneity among the pupils classed as "physically handicapped, home bound, and hospitalized" or "crippled and chronically ill." The variety of impairments of muscles and bones, neurological conditions, mobility restrictions, and ill health in the group makes it difficult to generalize about them.

Despite the evident differences among these pupils and their mainstream experiences, one theme is common: Inclusion usually can be arranged, to the satisfaction of parents and teachers and to the benefit of the child, if appropriate procedures are devised and followed. Often, the procedures call for a combination of creative planning and the willingness to deal in a matter of fact way with the realities of life for a handicapped person.

A particularly illuminating investigation of inclusion was reported from England by Anderson (1973). Study involved 99 moderately and severely disabled children who were educated in "ordinary" primary schools. The first words of the first chapter of Anderson's book are: "No handicapped child should be sent to a special school who can be satisfactorily educated in an ordinary school." The study followed children with cerebral palsy, spina bifida, thalidomide deformities, hemophilia, and a variety of other disorders into the "ordinary" schools not just to test how well they were doing, but to seek guidance on how better program planning might proceed. The report of the study is at book length and includes much detail on school, family, and community aspects of programing for the physically handicapped in regular schools.

The general findings of the study can perhaps be summarized through a series of brief quotations from Anderson's "concluding comments."

> There can be little doubt that the majority of the parents. . .preferred ordinary school placement. (p. 289)

> The amount and quality of social integration between handicapped and non-handicapped children both inside and outside of school was very encouraging. (p. 290)

> Findings suggest that most children without neurological disorders are able to cope, emotionally, with the environment of an ordinary primary school. (p. 293)

It is not the physical handicap *per se* but the existence of learning disorders which is important. (p. 297)

Given special provisions of the kind I have described, it is possible to offer even severely handicapped children a satisfactory education in an ordinary school. Given imagination, backed up by expertise and by financial resources, it is possible to provide for children with additional specific learning difficulties without segregating them. (p. 303)

Gifted children. In 1952, Hildreth (1952) listed the arguments that had been offered in favor of teaching the gifted in separate classes in elementary schools.

When gifted children remain in regular school classes they tend to be idle and are neglected.

The gifted child's classmates in a regular class adopt unfavorable attitudes toward him.

A curriculum specially designed for the gifted can be developed for these children grouped in separate classes.

Acceleration in learning can be provided without the disadvantage of skipping grades.

The gifted child meets a greater challenge to his abilities in separate classes.

Separate classes at elementary school level prepare the pupils for special class work at higher school levels.

A congenial school life can be provided for the gifted in separate classes.

The teachers of separate classes for the gifted are specially trained and chosen for that work. (pp. 253-256)

Hildreth concluded her remarks on these alleged advantages with the following statement:

If the whole level of childhood education could be improved by putting instruction more largely on an individual basis and providing greater enrichment in all classrooms, there would be less argument for separate classes even in populous city areas. (p. 256)

Even while Hildreth was preparing the quoted list, an investigation (Dunlap, 1955) was under way in University City, Missouri, which shed light on the question of whether separate schools or even entirely separate classes were really necessary to secure for gifted pupils the educational opportunities they need. The investigation focused on elementary age gifted boys and girls of similar intelligence—approximately 130 IQ and above—as determined by the Stanford-Binet administered individually by psychologists.

The thrust of the study was to evaluate the effectiveness of a program design by which gifted children were maintained in regular classes between 90% and 95% of the time and given specialized instruction in groups of 8 to 10 in their own school buildings by teachers of the gifted for two 45 minute periods per week. The special instruction was individualized; it consisted mainly of material not usually covered in the regular curriculum or, if in the prescribed program, not attended to intensively. The specialized teachers of the gifted worked closely with the regular class teachers to exchange information and make sure of opportunities to coordinate the regular classes and the enrichment sessions.

The followup assessments made in the seventh grade compared the students from the enrichment program with each other, with the total seventh grade, and with seventh grade honor roll pupils at the close of the first nine week marking period. In addition, there were reported reactions to the program and its values from teachers, principals, parents, and the pupils themselves. The results gave clear support to the program in which gifted pupils were separated from their regular classes for only 90 minutes a week.

Advanced high school students have sometimes been encouraged to attend full time separate schools or separate classes. From the outset, however, there has been evidence that superior and gifted students can be accommodated quite satisfactorily in their own secondary schools with individualized program designs. An investigation of such a design in required courses such as social studies and English was reported as early as 1956 by Mallis.

Mallis (1956) grouped the students in his high school English classes and arranged a seminar format for those identified as high in achievement and ability. Independent study was a major part of the format. The seminar students spent the major portion of their scheduled class time using the library and community resources in pursuit of selected individual projects. Presentations on the study topics were made by the students to their classes for the marking period exams.

Mallis concluded that "the seminar approach to gifted students is the most feasible method of spurring such youngsters to developing their greatest potential on their own" (p. 178).

The Dunlap and Mallis reports of mainstream efforts for gifted students were included in a book of readings by French (1959). They indicate that positive findings on the mainstreaming of elementary and secondary school gifted children were being reported 20 and more years ago.

Other aspects of mainstreaming—those relating to the attitudes and preferences of gifted pupils—can be examined by checking the reports of students who attended separate special classes. The classic study on this topic was made by Barbe (1955). He analyzed the questionnaires returned by 456 graduates of the Cleveland, Ohio, Major Work Program. Responses were about equally divided between men and women.

Barbe tabulated the former pupils' opinions of the special classes they had attended. In percentages, the reactions were as follows:

Approved with enthusiasm	47.2%
Approved with hesitancy	37.0%
Undecided	6.4%
Disapproved	5.5%
Strongly opposed	2.4%
No reply	1.5%

Somewhat less than half of the respondents approved special classes with enthusiasm. However, when the least liked aspects of the separate special classes were tallied, the two most frequently cited by both sexes were found to be "attitudes of other students and teachers" and "lack of social contact with other pupils." Approximately 40% of the respondents made one of these two statements or an equivalent.

The same viewpoints were prominent in answers to a question about changes that ought to be made in the program. The change most frequently suggested was that there be more mixing, particularly socially, with other students. About 1 out of 10 of the respondents suggested the change.

It seems fair to conclude that a substantial proportion of the graduates of those nationally recognized special classes for gifted elementary and secondary school pupils missed the advantages of day to day interactions with their nongifted peers and other teachers.

The preceding reports were selected from a larger literature because they are among the better designed and reported studies, are not affectively charged statements of faith, are relevant to the topic under discussion, and illustrate that the empirical support for the inclusion concept goes back far more than a quarter of a century.

Trainable mentally retarded children. The feasibility and value of constructive educational interactions in regular public schools among trainable mentally retarded pupils and other pupils has been recognized for many years by teachers who are experienced in conducting classes for such retarded children in elementary or secondary schools. Verification of the feasibility and value is found in Ziegler and Hambleton (1976).

Twice during one year the investigators compared the behaviors outside of classroom situations of two groups of trainable mentally retarded children: (a) a group that had been moved from a school for the retarded to a regular public school where they were able to interact daily with the regular school population in nonacademic settings and (b) a matched group of trainable mentally retarded children in a school for the retarded. An interaction analysis was performed using the variables of retarded and nonretarded children, sex, and a variety of positive and negative forms of interactive behavior. The observations, totaling 35 hours, were made on the playground interaction site.

Nonretarded children did not single out and make retarded children their victims.

> Interactions involving only retarded children...at both schools were... predominantly positive in character, but included more provoked aggression and much less teaching, intervening and comforting/helping than interactions involving non-retarded and retarded children. It is important to note that retarded children *help, intervene* and *comfort,* although apparently less frequently and less effectively than non-retarded children in comparable situations.
>
> ...Independent measures were used to assess how well known the retarded students were as individuals to the non-retarded children. A surprisingly large number of regular students knew the special class children, not only as a group, but individually and by name. (p. 460)

Ziegler and Hambleton concluded,

> The placement of the special classes in a regular school was extremely effective in promoting interaction between the retarded and non-retarded students, and thus in providing a more normal environment for the retarded children. (p. 460)

Educable mentally retarded children. Haring and Krug (1974) affirmed that return to regular classes was feasible for 54% of the educable mentally retarded pupils attending special classes in a school in a disadvantaged area of a large city. They emphasized the need for proper preparation of the pupils for the move. Followup studies and conferences with regular class teachers a year after the transfer showed that the pupils had maintained academic and social development at rates equivalent to those they showed when they were in special classes full time. The regular teachers said that three-fourths of the pupils transferred to their classes did not need special help. The other one-fourth needed some assistance from a special teacher who came into the room from time to time to team with the regular teacher. According to the regular teachers, special class placement was not advisable for 54% of the educable mentally retarded children.

In Texas, Carter (1975) compared the reading achievement of 20 educable mentally retarded pupils who had been in Plan B (special classes) for at least two years with the same number of educable mentally retarded pupils who had been in Plan A (mainstream) programs for the same time. No significant difference was found in the reading attainments of the two groups. Carter also tested 20 educable mentally retarded pupils who were in regular classes and who had not been programed into either Plan A or Plan B. Their reading achievements were not significantly different from those of the pupils in the other two groups.

The findings are open to a number of different interpretations. One of the most parsimonious, however, is that educable mentally retarded pupils in a mainstream program (Plan A) are at no disadvantage in reading achievement as compared with similar pupils in other instructional settings or models. When the investigator examined the correlations between measures of mental ability and reading achievement, he found that the correlation was higher for the retarded pupils in the mainstream arrangement.

A series of studies in Texas, known collectively as Project PRIME, sponsored by the Bureau of Education for the Handicapped, is beginning to be reported—all bearing on the issues raised as Texas schools move from Plan B (traditional) to Plan A (mainstream) orientation in the organization of special education programs. In one study it was shown that of educable mentally retarded students ($N = 576$) returned from special classes to situations involving both regular teachers and supportive special teachers, only one-third of the pupils received reading instruction together with regular children. The fact that two-thirds of these educable mentally retarded students received reading instruction outside of the regular classroom was interpreted as casting "some doubt about the ability of regular classes to accommodate EMR children for academic instruction" (Gottlieb, Agard, Kauffman, & Semmel, 1976, p. 211).

Another important series of studies has emerged from California where a massive "decertification" of educable mentally retarded pupils occurred between 1969 and 1972 following certain court decisions (*Diana v. State Board of Education,* 1970 and *Larry P. v. Riles,* 1972). In the period from October 1969 to June 1973 the numbers of children certified as educable mentally retarded and assigned to classes for the retarded was reduced from 55,519 to 35,110.

A study conducted in 12 school districts to determine the "success" of decertified educable mentally retarded pupils upon return to regular classes has been reported by Yoshida, MacMillan, and Meyers (1976). The findings are reported as mixed: the rate of "poor adjustment" for those decertified was found to be "very low," average academic achievement for the group was below the average of their regular classmates but showed "considerable overlap" with many regular class pupils—about one-third of those decertified were "at least average or better than their regular classmates in achievement"; fewer than half of the teachers who received "transition aid" thought it was helpful. Transition aids took various forms, including paraprofessional aides and resource teachers. Apparently much is yet to be learned about how to make such supports satisfactory to regular teachers in a period of very rapid change.

Keogh (1976) reported a broad post hoc look at transition programs in some 250 of the California school districts. With regard to transition programs themselves, Keogh and her associates recommended, as a first priority concern in mainstreaming efforts, the preparation of regular school personnel to deal with exceptional students—to include teachers and the full range of other professionals and paraprofessionals employed in schools. They also concluded that a variety of program options or models are required in supporting mainstream education and that there is urgent necessity for good record keeping and research as schools move into mainstream programs.

A well designed study by Budoff and Gottlieb (1976) took advantage of the closing of three inner city schools and the assignment of pupils to a new school to contrast the outcomes of special classes and almost full mainstreaming for 34 educable mentally retarded pupils aged approximately 8 to 14 years; 15 were girls and 16 were boys, and almost 10% were Black.

All of the pupils had been in self contained special classes for at least one year prior to the move; in the new school, 14 were assigned to a special class and 17 were assigned to regular classes where the teachers and pupils received support from a well staffed and well equipped learning center in the building. To equalize the staff-pupil ratio, the teacher of the self contained class received help from another fully qualified special education teacher and a practice teacher. Thus the student-staff ratio was approximately 7 to 1 in each classroom condition. The final comparison data were collected after a full school year in the new settings.

Assessment of the pupils included a number of measures of achievement, motivation, cognitive style, and teachers' observations of behavior. At the end of the school year, the investigators found that the mainstreamed students "felt more positively about their prospects in school, expressed an increased sense of control vis-à-vis their environment, tended to view their own capability as students more positively, and behaved more reflectively than when they were still in special class and in contrast to the students who remained in the special class" (p. 9). No differences were found between the groups in measures of achievement over the school year.

The sample size was not large in this investigation. The one year period represented only a small portion of formal schooling. Thus the findings should be viewed as limited in general applicability and not fully conclusive. Yet the tight design, the careful controls, and the variety of measures yielding consistent results make the study an important indicator.

The investigations summarized in this section are part of the published evidence substantiating that most exceptional children and youth of all sorts can be successful in education's mainstream. Perhaps attention should be drawn, also, to the fact that the degree of exceptionality is relatively immaterial. Rather, factors such as planning, staff preparation, and well designed instruction are the keys to positive results.

Needs of Regular Educators

What is necessary for regular educators to successfully manage mainstreaming in its various forms and degrees? This question has been the object of five investigations that are summarized in this section.

The first investigation, Zawadzki (1974), used an adaptation of the Flanagan critical incident technique and queried a sample of 158 regular class teachers, kindergarten through senior high school, from low, medium, and high income school districts in the Pittsburgh, Pennsylvania, region. Zawadzki asked the teachers (a) what might deter them from effective teaching if educable mentally retarded pupils were assigned to their classes and (b) what would be needed to allow them to be effective under those circumstances.

The deterrents listed by the teachers fell into the following 15 categories:

1. Inappropriate classroom behavior on the part of the retarded pupils.
2. Concerns about the curriculum and how to adjust it.
3. Negative behavior of regular pupils toward the retarded pupils.
4. Problems of organizing for instruction.
5. Lack of teacher preparation and/or experience.
6. Emotional problems of the retarded child.
7. Negative attitudes of teachers and/or parents toward retarded pupils in regular classes.
8. Lack of supportive services.
9. Problems of physical defects.
10. Concerns about safety.
11. Inadequate assessment of achievement.
12. Special health factor problems.
13. Unfair grading policy of the school.
14. Family problems of retarded children.
15. Concerns about teacher liability.

In every instance teachers had ready practical suggestions of ways to resolve these problems and remove the deterrents.

Three major findings of the study were that (a) regular class teachers did not summarily reject the idea of including mentally retarded pupils; (b) the teachers identified 15 considerations that they believed would make it difficult to assimilate retarded pupils; and (c) the teachers listed the forms of assistance they felt would be necessary to remove the deterrents and allow the teachers to be successful in instructing educable mentally retarded youngsters along with all others.

Boote (1975) inquired about teacher and principal reactions to in-service education for elementary school teachers that was intended to assist the regular class teachers in dealing with pupils referred to as emotionally disturbed, learning disabled, educable mentally retarded, visually handicapped, and hearing handicapped. Many such pupils were already assigned primarily to the regular classes taught by those teachers.

Questionnaire responses were received from 136 teachers, grades 1 through 6, and 50 elementary school principals in suburban public schools in the Philadelphia, Pennsylvania, area. The results were clearcut on a number of points.

1. Teachers and principals both expressed a need for in-service education aimed at increasing their skills to integrate exceptional children.
2. Teachers, particularly, would like to see such dramatic changes in the in-service programs they receive as (a) fewer lectures and more workshop and participatory demonstrations, linked to graduate credit; (b) more opportunities to attend professional meetings; and (c) more emphasis on teaching exceptional children and resources available for them and less emphasis on behavior management.
3. There were significant differences between teachers and principals on the items in 2, with the principals interested in most of the same things but not to the same degree.

Boote's work, like Zawadzki's (1974), shows that teachers can and will identify those professional understandings and skills they feel they need in order to establish and maintain high quality education for all pupils in a setting where regular and exceptional pupils are merged.

Do administrators, like teachers, recognize the need for preparation? Swatzenbarg (1975) pointed out that one outcome of the mainstream effort has been the shifting of the responsibility for the education of the handicapped child from special education personnel back to regular classroom teachers under the authority of individual school principals. In the fall of 1975, Swatzenbarg investigated the status of superintendents and principals in Utah, Idaho, and Nevada on background in special education, training in supervision of teachers of handicapped children, and the training needed by elementary and secondary principals for their changed roles. Sixteen superintendents and 62 principals responded.

The superintendents of districts, almost all of which had special classes for exceptional children, said that the principals needed two categories of training: "Motivation of teachers and evaluation of instructional outcomes" (p. 4). Of the principals, 82% did not have specific training in the supervision of special education and 85% said such training would help them. The principals said that college credit, release time from the job, and money, in that order, would serve as incentives for them to obtain the added preparation they knew they needed.

Redden (1976) went even further in making systematic inquiries of teachers regarding the requirements to integrate exceptional children effectively. She asked teachers of grades 1 through 8 from 24 schools in different Kentucky communities to indicate what they regarded as examples of their own effective and ineffective mainstreaming practices. All of the 184 teachers who responded were actively mainstreaming one or more pupils designated as "learning disabled; retarded; emotionally disturbed; or visually, auditorily, and/or orthopedically impaired" (p. 121). Mainstreaming was defined "as the practice of including mildly handicapped students in regular classrooms with supplemental instructional support being provided by both material and human resources" (p. 125).

The Flanagan critical incident technique was used to collect data from the teachers. The yield was 515 reports of effective and 313 reports of ineffective teacher behavior incidents.

Redden's material, compressed into six functions, each with three to six competencies under it, is clear testimony that elementary teachers with positive experience in mainstreaming can specify the necessary elements of professional preparation for the job. The six general functions were: developing orientation strategies for mainstream entry, assessing needs and setting goals, planning teaching strategies and use of resources, implementing teaching strategies and utilizing resources, facilitating learning, and evaluating learning.

Although the research was conducted in different parts of the United States and somewhat different approaches were employed, the works of Zawadzki, Boote, and Redden lead to similar conclusions. Almost all of Zawadski's and Boote's findings fit well into Redden's summary listing. It is possible to identify and specify the professional behaviors that can make mainstreaming feasible. Moreover, many teachers are already employing these behaviors effectively.

Two other recently published investigations bear on the same question: What is necessary for regular educators to be successful in managing mainstreaming? First was an analysis of six school districts varying in size and pupil makeup that had established programs for mainstreaming educable mentally retarded children (Birch, 1974).

The investigation focused on school districts that had histories of systemwide mainstreaming policies and practices (some as long as 17 years) and whose mainstream operations were viewed as successful by parents, communities, teachers, and school administrations. Visits were made to the schools; teachers, administrators, pupils, and parents were interviewed; classes were observed; and documents were reviewed. The how and why of the workings of each district were detailed. That information was then synthesized into the principles credited with making mainstreaming successful.

Ten key factors were judged to be essential to sound systemwide mainstreaming of educable mentally retarded pupils.

1. Regular class and special education teacher concerns need consideration.
2. The potential problems of regular class teachers identified by Zawadzki (1974) need to be discussed openly and arrangements made to deal with them.
3. Positive teacher attitudes most conducive to success are:
    a. Belief in the right to education for all children.
    b. Readiness of special education and regular class teachers to cooperate with each other.
    c. Willingness to share competencies as a team on behalf of pupils.
    d. Openness to include parents as well as other professional colleagues in planning for and working with children.
    e. Flexibility with respect to class size and teaching assignments.
    f. Recognition that social and personal development can be taught and that they are equally as important as academic achievement.
4. In-service education is a requirement.
5. Pupil placement practices call for sensitive administration.
6. Identified pupils should be kept in regular grades.
7. Educational assessment and diagnostic teaching should be emphasized.
8. Local school autonomy of operation helps.
9. Line administrative support should be assured.
10. Informed parents can be very helpful.

The accuracy of the case report of each school system was verified by a responsible school official. Also, a list of 76 additional locations where mainstreaming could be observed was included.

A second study by Birch (1975) used essentially the same investigative procedure to look for the components of successful mainstreaming with deaf and hard of hearing pupils. The 14 examples described were representative of operative programs in various parts of the country and different types of schools, from preschool through college, and at different developmental stages.

The same 10 factors that were key considerations in mainstreaming mentally retarded pupils were found to be important in the case of hearing impaired pupils. But others were found, too.

Teachers noted five factors as most important in removing their fears and preparing them for successful beginnings with deaf and hard of hearing pupils in their regular classes:

1. Assignment of hearing impaired pupils to regular classes only with teachers' prior knowledge and consent; regular class teachers take part in making the decisions and they have options.
2. In-service instruction is made readily available for all faculty and staff *before* mainstreaming is started.
3. The hearing impaired pupils who attend regular classes have academic skills and achievements in keeping with those found in the rest of the class.
4. The regular teachers and pupils receive sufficient orientation so that communication with hearing impaired pupils does not constitute a major problem.
5. Assistance, both continuing and crisis, is always on hand. The special education teacher and other helping personnel, as needed, team with the regular teacher on a schedule they establish to their mutual satisfaction. Also, the regular teacher knows that the special teacher and the principal will give immediate response to an SOS.

When the successfully operating mainstream programs for hearing impaired pupils were studied, five common principles emerged:

1. A particular teaching strategy (preteach, teach, postteach) was applied.
2. Teaching was aimed toward hearing world participation.
3. A planned, organized, systematic approach was used.
4. Commitment and direction were unified and consistent.
5. Special education was brought into the regular class.

The investigations by Zawadzki, Boote, Redden, and Birch, taken together, show that teachers and their colleagues in education are successfully mainstreaming a variety of exceptional children at all school levels and in all parts of the nation. The findings of the studies provide empirical foundations on which to build preservice and in-service professional preparation for teachers. The results of the studies can be used as checklists to assess the strengths and/or weaknesses of programs now in operation. The studies supply guidelines for administrators who are interested in program planning and development. It becomes plain, too, that relatively few professional competencies apply to only one exceptional condition; the majority are common not only to exceptional children but to individualized instruction for all children.

State education agencies and their advisory groups can find in these studies significant items that call for consideration when teacher certification standards are being drafted and regulations on the special education of exceptional children, promulgated. Organizations of educators can use the findings to plan collectively negotiated employment agreements. Boards of education and school administrators can determine from the studies policies and practices statements that are best for them. Perhaps most important, individual teachers can use the reports to inform themselves on successful mainstreaming and what it implies for now and the future of their everyday professional activity.

Impact of Mainstreaming on Regular Class Pupils

What is the impact of mainstreaming on regular class pupils? Is their education interfered with? How do they react to classmates who are "different"?

No research bearing directly on the three questions has been found. On the other hand, there is growing evidence that many school aged children, particularly young children, are limited in their understanding of the range and nature of human differences by the cultural isolation in which they are reared.

It is difficult for even the best intentioned parents and teachers to help children acquire openness, individual acceptance, and mutual respect that are free of ethnic, racial, religious, and other forms of stereotyping. Miel and Kiester (1967) described how a relatively homogeneous community can raise children in an atmosphere in which many of the basic differences among people are fenced out. The authors did not focus on exceptional conditions calling for special education, nevertheless five of their findings have high potential relevance to the question of children's reactions to exceptional conditions among their peers.

1. Children are often insulated from chance introductions to lives different from their own; extraordinary effort is required to assure an encounter between a child of the suburbs and people from different backgrounds.
2. Under such conditions, children in the early elementary years learn to be hypocritical of differences. Though prejudiced, they are drilled to consider the expression of such feelings "not nice."
3. Whatever the nature of the prejudices of the intact group, they take root early and are already deeply ingrained in 6 and 7 year olds.
4. Although parents in society's enclaves hold prejudices, they express desires for the schools to give greater emphasis to certain kinds of human difference to hold in check the childhood seeding and growth of similar prejudices.
5. There is a tendency to ignore differences (i.e., economic inequality) right in the neighborhood and to take up the study of the poor of other nations, instead. Academic consideration rather than direct involvement is encouraged.

The work of investigators such as Miel and Kiester, although aimed more at religious, racial, ethnic, and socioeconomic differences, has evident implications for educators and their responsibilities with exceptional pupils. There is already a substantial amount of anecdotal material that suggests that very young children readily learn to accept wide differences under the guidance of adults who are positive models of the desired behavior. Followup of such leads through research would be of value.

Costs of Mainstreaming

Is mainstreaming more or less costly than other ways of delivering special education?

Information about how much different forms of education cost is very useful. It is even more important to know how much progress pupils make in relation to financial outlay. To illustrate, let us say that Type A education costs $1,000 per year per pupil and the pupils average 0.8 years' gain in achievement per year. Type B education costs $1,100 per year per pupil and the average annual gain is 1.0 years in achievement. Which type is more cost-effective? Type A delivers 0.8 years of achievement; Type B, 0.91 years of achievement, for every $1,000 spent. Thus, what at first appears to be more expensive is really more economical.

Noffsinger (1974, 1975) and his associates undertook a most careful comparison of four styles of education for educable mentally retarded pupils. Descriptions of the service delivery models and the 1973-1974 per pupil costs of each follow:

Self-Contained (Cost per pupil—$1,354.00)—This is the most traditional type of model for programing EMR children. Basically, it concerns itself with anywhere from 12 to 28 or 30 children in a self-contained situation with a single EMR teacher. The children may have educational programing, such as Physical Education or Math or any other content area outside of their self-contained class, but at all times they are with all EMR children. They may go to a special music class but that music class is all EMR children. They may have a special vocational education program, but during that program they are with EMR children.

Selected Academic Placement (Cost per pupil—$1,253.00)—This is a variation of the self-contained model. The student is assigned to a special education teacher, attends the special education self-contained class most of the school day, but is integrated into academic and non-academic subjects with regular education students. That integration may be for half an hour or it may be for a substantial portion of the day, such as 2 or 3 hours.

Learning Center (Cost per pupil—$1,409.00)—The basic characteristic of this model is that EMR students are assigned to regular education classes. They come from those regular classes to a special learning center where a special teacher provides educational assistance basically in core area subjects, such as reading, math, writing, and other basic academic areas. The key difference between this and the self-contained model is that the students are assigned to regular education and are identified on a regular education teacher's roll of students.

Mainstream (Cost per pupil—$1,529.00)— This unit requires the EMR students to be in the regular education program all day. The special teacher tutors and assists with the curriculum and instruction of the EMR students. (pp.1-2)

The small number of school settings involved in the study, and the great variation in sample sizes (self contained, 21; selected academic placement, 11; learning center 22; mainstream, 4) made conclusions risky. Another complicating factor is that major cities, suburbs, small cities, and rural areas were unevenly represented in the samples. Finally, some of the programs were relatively new; others were well established. These same conditions clouded the findings on pupil achievement and other measures. There do not yet appear to be solid enough findings to regard any of the four special education delivery systems as significantly different in cost or cost-effectiveness.

It should be emphasized that decisions on the style of program to offer may be made not only on the basis of cost. The principle of least restrictive alternative takes priority over budgetary considerations.

History of Regular Educator Roles in Mainstreaming

Historically, have regular educators fostered the inclusion of exceptional children in the mainstream?

Mainstream education is more than a program, a school placement, or the admission of exceptional and other children to the same classrooms. Mainstreaming is all of these descriptions but it is also a point of view. That point of view involves the individualization of instruction for all pupils.

Some of the earliest explicit statements about the benefits of inclusion appear in a paper by Anderson (1955), an elementary education leader. He advocated an ungraded organizational pattern in the first three school years after kindergarten because of its cognitive and affective benefits. In reporting his experiences over six or more years in Milwaukee, Wisconsin, and Park Forest, Illinois, Anderson called attention to how well the ungraded arrangement accommodated pupils who made unusually slow or unusually fast progress. For youngsters with apparent social, emotional, or intellectual limitations or assets, the ungraded organization allowed for deceleration or acceleration of schooling commensurate with individual requirements without conspicuous failures or skips and without "grade labels." With regard to slower or faster movement through the normally three year ungraded sequence, he reported that only about 5 or 6% were taking four years to complete the program, that the children involved were relatively unaware of their "failure," and that parents were quite able to accept the arrangement.

Thus, at mid century in the United States, evidence was beginning to be accumulated that (a) individualization of instruction could be practiced in the everyday setting of the public schools, (b) labeling was recognized as a potentially opprobrious quality, and (c) the effective integration of certain exceptional children could be demonstrated.

Acceptance of Mainstreaming

Is inclusion of exceptional pupils full time or part time in regular classes here to stay? What is the evidence regarding its degree of acceptance?

Probably the clearest research response to the two questions is found in a state by state nationwide survey by Delp and Boote (1975). They found that every state was making serious efforts for mainstreaming and that this was reflected in a high number of school districts. Those researchers concluded that "regular education and special education *must* begin immediately to ask not *whether* but *how* mainstreaming can best be implemented in each school district and each school building" (p. 19).

Cautions about Mainstreaming

Sound mainstream programing calls for careful planning and execution. One of the most frequent warning notes is that regular teachers need to be prepared (MacMillan, Jones, & Meyers, 1976; Keogh, 1976). Unfortunately, it is quite likely that when guidelines drawn from direct, successful experience are not heeded, less than satisfactory results will follow.

Care is necessary, also, in regard to determining what research has direct bearing on mainstreaming. There is a considerable body of published material on exceptional children who are enrolled with other children in regular classes; but the material is of limited relevance to mainstreaming if the children studied are not in deliberately planned and executed programs that are staffed by regular and special teachers who are prepared for integrating their instruction.

Even the irrelevant research has some value, however, because it shows (a) how teachers and pupils react when the range of individual differences in their life space is beyond their capability to cope with the situation, (b) how negative attitudes toward individuals and school work can be generated, and (c) how the study of situations in which professional educators with no preparation for work with pupils with special needs can clarify what needs to be done to provide better school conditions for all of the pupils and their teachers. Reference to such studies, as well as to others, are given in the references.

Summary

This section has been limited to the review of investigations that address mainstreaming as it was defined earlier: the enrollment of exceptional children in regular classes, with all other children, to the maximum degree possible, and there bringing to them the special educational services they need while maintaining high quality education for all the other children. More work relating to such inclusion is certainly needed, both to guide educators and to evaluate their mainstreaming efforts. Case studies, objective program development descriptions, comparisons between groups of pupils and groups of procedures, surveys of practices, assessments of instructional materials—these and many other forms of investigation can be pertinent. It is more and more important, too, that teachers themselves call attention to subjects for research and also take active part in the design and day to day conduct of studies that will affect their professional lives. Finally, however, one cannot examine the published research and experience regarding legitimate mainstreaming, part or full time, without being impressed by two points: (a) mainstreaming works, and (b) its positive results are found only where there are close cooperative relationships between regular teachers and special educators.

The substantial body of research and experience reviewed in this chapter all bear quite directly on issues relating to mainstreaming. The set of conceptual shifts in basic values and educational procedures underlying mainstreaming also has been reviewed. The aggregate of knowledge is impressive; but it must be said that we still have before us the major jobs of careful evaluation of mainstream progress. So far, much of the shift toward mainstreaming has been based mainly on value shifts and disaffection with the segregating tendencies of special education. The clearest case of the latter can be found in the public outcry in recent years against residential institutions for retarded persons. Much remains to be done in constructing a full and adequate empirical base for mainstreaming and its various alternatives.

SUGGESTIONS FOR STUDENTS AND INSTRUCTOR

1. Secure materials from one or more of the major training systems for regular teachers (see Appendix B) and try modules on topics covered in this chapter, such as consultation, testing, or classification.
2. Read materials on criterion referenced and domain referenced testing, then experiment with the construction of domain assessment devices.
3. Review case records of recent litigation pertaining to exceptional students (such cases are probably available in almost every state) to see whether primacy of attention is given to *individual* or *societal* needs.

4. Secure the Johnson and Johnson (1975) text and rate several classrooms (perhaps your own) on social climate and effectiveness in teaching social skills.
5. Study systems of classification of exceptional pupils used in your community and state. Examine them against criteria suggested in Hobb's *The Futures of Children* (1975).
6. Examine the ATI concept as advanced by Cronbach and study its relationship to statistical procedures for examining interaction effects.
7. Examine grading and reporting systems used in local schools with a view toward assessing them against criteria implied in this chapter. Are the objects specific? Mainly domain oriented? Mainly norm oriented or social comparative? Are arrangements made for long range predictive assessments? How can they be improved?
8. Secure the Borg training materials on classroom management and try modules on question asking, group alerting or other topics (Borg, undated).

TOPICAL BIBLIOGRAPHIES
Changing Measurement and Grading Procedures

Hively, W., & Reynolds, M. (Eds.). *Domain-referenced testing in special education.* Reston VA: The Council for Exceptional Children, 1975.

Mischel, W. On the future of personality measurement. *American Psychologist,* 1977, *32*(4), 246-254.

Salvia, J., & Ysseldyke, J. *Assessment in special and remedial education.* Boston: Houghton Mifflin, 1977.

Simon, S. B., & Bellanca, J. A. (Eds.). *Degrading the grading myths: A primer of alternatives.* Washington DC: Association for Supervision and Curriculum Development, 1976.

Weinberg, R. A., & Wood, F. H. (Eds.). *Observation of pupils and teachers in mainstream and special education settings: Alternative strategies.* Reston VA: The Council for Exceptional Children, 1975.

Consultation

Bradshaw, J.A., Langton, P.G., & Patterson, V.W. *Contiguity and continuity in general and special education.* Boulder CO: Western Interstate Commission for Higher Education, January 1972.

Gredler, G.R. (Ed.). *Ethical and legal factors in the practice of school psychology.* Harrisburg: Pennsylvania Department of Education, 1972.

Parker, C.A. (Ed.). *Psychological consultation: Helping teachers meet special needs.* Reston VA: The Council for Exceptional Children, 1975.

Reynolds, M.C. *Psychology and the process of schooling in the next decade: Alternative conceptions.* Minneapolis: Department of Audio-Visual Extension, University of Minnesota, 1971.

Value Changes and Classification Issues

Cromwell, R. L. Ethics, umbrage and the ABCDs. In M. Reynolds (Ed.), *Mainstreaming: Origins and implications.* Reston VA: The Council for Exceptional Children, 1976, pp. 42-47.

Hobbs, N. *The futures of children.* San Francisco: Jossey-Bass, 1975.

Kenowitz, L.A. & Edgar, E. Intra-community action networks: The ICAN system. *Mental Retardation,* 1977, *15*(3), 13-16.

Reynolds, M. C. *Futures of education: Emerging structures.* Reston VA: The Council for Exceptional Children, 1978.

The Civil Rights Movement

Baldwin, A. Y., Gear, G. H., & Lucito, L. J. (Eds.). *Educational planning for the gifted: Overcoming cultural, geographic, and socioeconomic barriers.* Reston VA: The Council for Exceptional Children, 1978.

Billingsley, A., & Giovanni, J. M. *Children of the storm: Black children and American child welfare.* New York: Harcourt, Brace, Jovanovich, 1972.

Castaneda, A., James, R. L., & Robbins, W. *The educational needs of minority groups.* Lincoln NE: Professional Education Publications, 1974.

Johnson, J. J. Special education and the inner city: A challenge for the future or another means of cooling the mark out? *Journal of Special Education,* 1969, *3,* 241-251.

Jones, R. L. (Ed.). *Mainstreaming and the minority child.* Reston VA: The Council for Exceptional Children, 1976.

Research

Barry, N. J., & Overmann, P. B. Comparison of the effectiveness of adult and peer models with EMR children. *American Journal of Mental Deficiency,* 1977, *82*(1), 33-34.

Gallagher, J. J. (Ed.). *Application of child development research to exceptional children: A noncategorical approach to research on exceptional children.* Reston VA: The Council for Exceptional Children, 1975.

Goldstein, H., Moss, J., & Jordan, L. *The efficacy of special class training on the development of mentally retarded children.* (Cooperative Research Project No. 619, July 1, 1959 to November 30, 1964.) Champaign IL: Institute for Research on Exceptional Children, University of Illinois, 1964.

Grosenick, J. K. Assessing the re-integration of exceptional children into regular classes. *TEACHING Exceptional Children,* 1970, *2*(3), 113-119.

Johnson, G. O. Special education for the mentally handicapped—A paradox. *Exceptional Children, 29,* 1962, 63-69.

Kaufman, M. J., Semmel, M. I., & Agard, J. A. Project PRIME—An overview. *Education and Training of the Mentally Retarded,* 1974, *9*(2), 107-112.

Media

Gilhool, T. K. *The right to education* (tape cassette). Reston VA: The Council for Exceptional Children, 1973.

Schneider, S., Lantzer, J. N., Makuch, G. J., & Larsen, L. A. *Improving services: Court action and child advocacy* (tape cassette). Reston VA: The Council for Exceptional Children, 1973.

3. Assessment

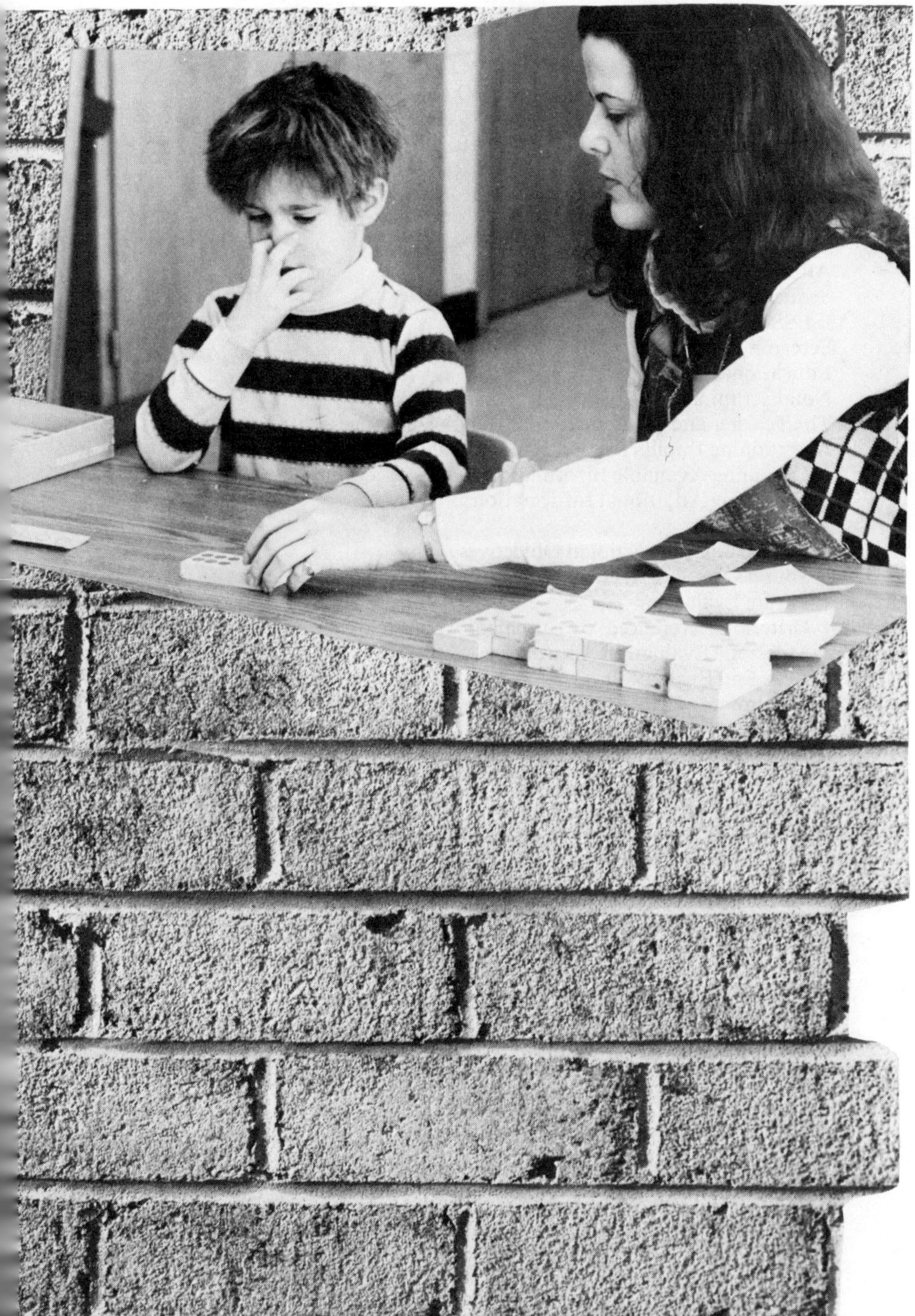

CHAPTER OUTLINE

ACHIEVING A MATCH OF STUDENT AND PROGRAM
THE NATURE OF INDIVIDUALIZED INSTRUCTION
CULTURAL IMPERATIVES VERSUS CULTURAL ELECTIVES
COMPULSORY VERSUS POSTCOMPULSORY EDUCATION
WAYS OF INDIVIDUALIZING INSTRUCTION
    Variation of Specific Objectives
    Variations in Rate and Duration
    Variation of Intensity
    Alternative Instructional Methods
    Sequential Selection
ASSESSMENT OF INDIVIDUALS
    Screening
    Educational Diagnosis
    Nondiscriminatory Assessment
    The Teacher and the Educational Diagnostic Process
    Ascertaining Pupil's Present Educational Levels
        Obtaining Available Information
        Collecting Additional Information
    Annual Goals
        Short Term Instructional Objectives
        Sources for Short Term Instructional Objectives
    Program Evaluation
        Criterion Referenced Measurement Approach
        Milestone Evaluation Approach
        Year End Evaluation
        Determining Effectiveness of Instruction
ASSESSMENT OF PROGRAMS
    Space and Facility Accommodations to Physical Impairment
    Teaching-Learning Settings
    Materials
    Classroom Management (Organization for Instruction)
    Social Environment
    Recognizing and Appreciating Cultural and Socioeconomic Differences
    Control of and Responsibility for Environment
    Content (Curriculum)
    Degree of Structure
    Instructional Methods
    Rate of Learning
    Evaluation
PREVAILING VERSUS PREFERRED PRACTICES
SUGGESTIONS FOR STUDENTS AND INSTRUCTOR
TOPICAL BIBLIOGRAPHIES

ACHIEVING A MATCH OF STUDENT AND PROGRAM

The focus of this chapter is assessment—the assessment of both students and programs—and planning to achieve a desirable match of the two, that is, of student and program. Essentially, we will be looking at differences or variability among students and asking, What differences among students should one attend to in order to plan effective individualized educational programs? And, correspondingly, in what ways can programs be varied or differentiated so that each student is well served? In our thinking about both students and programs, the focus should be on factors that *interact,* that is, factors that really make a difference and, thus, should be the determinants of decisions about instruction.

THE NATURE OF INDIVIDUALIZED INSTRUCTION

Individualized or personalized instruction places the emphasis of the instructional process on each individual pupil's skills, interests, abilities, learning styles, motivation, goals, rate of learning, self discipline, problem solving ability, and prognosis for moving ahead in various skill and content aspects of curriculum. To put instruction on that basis is a tall order, to be sure. Yet pupils can differ on all of those dimensions and more.

In this style of instruction the teacher assumes the assessment functions of an educational diagnostician and also becomes the planner or prescriber of learning objectives and the means for reaching them. The teacher also operates as a learning facilitator, consultant, and guide for the student to learning resources and progress evaluation procedures.

Emphasis on the individual's needs and assets includes placing more responsibility for learning on the student and making better use of the professional knowledge and skill of the teacher as a creative monitor and expediter. In a sense, the teacher sizes up the problem, helps to select plays, and runs interference, but the pupil carries the ball.

Examine this illustration. During Thanksgiving the class had been discussing and gathering information on the original Thanksgiving celebrated by the Pilgrims and Indians. Four students in the group approached the teacher with the idea that they would like to write a play dealing with that historic occasion. The teacher acted as a consultant to the children as they researched the necessary material and then wrote the play and made the settings and costumes. Finally, they performed the play for their own classmates and before other groups in the school.

During this same time span another student became avidly interested in the background of the actual tribe or tribes of Indians with whom the Pilgrims had been in contact. The project called for a time set aside to research the specific topic of interest in the school library, coordinated with a period when the librarian could help. Another child, one with a temporary but currently consuming interest in geology, could not be accommodated adequately by the materials and equipment in the class science center, and the teacher could not work with that pupil as much as they both wanted. The teacher arranged times, usually two times a week, when that student could join in on a geology science activity going on in another class in the school. The teacher also made up individual work packets the youngster could work on independently or with occasional consultation in class or in the library when other work was done.

Can you analyze the illustration to find examples of the teacher functions that are part of individualized or personalized instruction? Can you imagine some things that might have gone on before the activities described, or after, that would also illustrate those teacher functions? Finally, can you tell whether any of these were exceptional pupils? What makes you think your conclusions are correct?

Ideally, the instruction in the individualized program "matches" the child. Each child is taught using the approach that suits him and he learns at his own pace. There is variety in the materials and motivational techniques that are used to promote interest for individual students. This does not mean there is never group instruction. Students are grouped according to common need. Sometimes a whole class is instructed at once in a given skill.

Consider one more illustration. In one ninth grade social studies class there are two pupils who cannot read the textbook. The teacher's assessment of their reading skills is consistent with that of their previous teacher—they can read at about fourth grade level and are slowly improving. But the improvement does not promise to progress fast enough to help the two students digest the ninth grade social studies text material this term. Also, they have histories of occasional disruptive behavior. One of the students had had an altercation with a teacher which, in that teacher's view, bordered on assault.

The social studies teacher, with the help of a special education teacher, designed a plan. The goal was to help these pupils attain the informational and conceptual objectives of the social studies course. It was clear from the outset, though, that the textbook as such would be of little use in that direction.

Four major strategies were featured in the plan. One was the use of tape recorders. The two teachers arranged for the text of the social studies book, plus some related references, to be transcribed onto tape cassettes. The two target pupils had the use of the taped material to listen to while other students read the assignments.

The second strategy was to organize in-class pupil lead discussion groups for a part of most class periods. The two who were limited readers were seeded into groups where their oral language skills were on a par with the other group members, but the two were not put in the same group. When they rotated into turns as discussion leaders, they were able to conduct the discussions satisfactorily. One of the jobs of the discussion leader was to prepare a summary of the discussion to read to the rest of the class later. These two pupils were allowed to use tape recorders to take notes during classes and in discussion groups. They then made oral summaries that they taped and played back to the class instead of reading written summaries as other discussion leaders did.

The third strategy was to do all testing orally with the two limited readers. They took the same tests as other pupils, but they listened to the questions instead of reading them and they spoke their answers instead of writing them. They were, of course, held to the same standards on each quiz or major test as the other pupils. The testing was often done by an aide, a volunteer, or another class member after the regular test had been taken.

The social studies teacher found other pupils very cooperative, especially when they learned they could have the same options that the two primary target pupils had, if they wished. Many became quite adept at using tapes as study aids. Also, the teacher found that there was a wealth of audiovisual material that was located and made available for the whole class to use, through the help of the special education teacher.

The fourth strategy was to help the two pupils to continue to improve in reading skill, but not to have to face daily the huge (to them) gap between how well they could read and how much the text demanded. The two teachers, working together, obtained books of high interest and low vocabulary load, books about the persons and places in the ninth grade social studies curriculum, and used them to stimulate the further development of reading skills.

When you analyze these illustrations do you find additional examples of teacher functions that are essential components of individualized or personalized instruction? What preceded them, do you imagine? What followed: How might the rest of the regular class pupils participate in helping in instruction? Would it be worthwhile for them, too? Can you point out why the nature of the exceptional child's educational status and skills is more relevant than any medical, psychological, or legal label that might be put on the child?

CULTURAL IMPERATIVES VERSUS CULTURAL ELECTIVES

In considering educational plans it may be useful to make a distinction between the subject matters and skills that are required of all students (the cultural imperatives) and those that are deemed to be not so uniformly essential (the cultural electives). (The terms *cultural imperatives* and *cultural electives* were first used, as far as the authors are aware, by George Stoddard in *The Dual Progress Plan,* 1961.)

In a complex culture such as ours, there may well be, and we think there are, some areas of learning that are virtually as essential for thriving to human beings as adequate calcium intake is for physical health. These *imperatives* are the basics of education, the tools of the culture, without which a person is confined to fundamental ignorance and limited choice. However much the particular list of imperatives we draw up may be argued about, the consensus is still likely to be substantial at any particular time and place. For the United States in the late 20th century, the imperatives by consensus, we think, would include the following:

1. Language—speaking, listening, comprehending, reading, and writing.
2. Mathematics—at least the rudimentary forms of quantitative thinking and behavior that are required in the marketplace and for daily life.
3. Health and safety—the knowledge to provide the basics of self care, health, and protection in an open community environment, if possible.
4. Social skills—at least for the rudimentary and acceptable patterns of behavior in group life (nondestructive, at least mildly responsive, cooperative, etc.) and in citizenship.
5. Career education—beginning preparation at least for employment or an economically useful life and other life roles.

Much education in the imperatives is provided during early childhood in the home. As children enter the schools, a coalition of home and school is formed to further educe development in these essential areas. There are no demissions from this development except, possibly, in the most extreme cases. Some children have difficulty in these essential areas; by not progressing well in the initial stages of learning and instruction they become the cause of concern. The children must be located through screening procedures, followed, and studied so that special help or extra help can be arranged for them. But the help must be *persistent* because it is in areas that are so essential to basic human awareness, growth, and survival.

The *electives* are different. Our society does not require that all students take up the flute, the higher branches of mathematics, poetry, or even the use of the cross cut saw. We are remarkably tolerant of people's lifelong ineptitude in many kinds of skills. However, the schools can and should help students to catch a vision of, and explore the broad range of, electives in our society for their own development; but students can opt in or out of the areas of electives as they choose through a greater variety of programs.

The principal reason for distinguishing between imperatives and electives is to note the different logic involved in approaches to individualizing instruction. In the case of imperatives, no basic, in or out, options are allowed; in the case of electives, options are provided. We need now to consider another distinction, one that relates to assessment procedures and instructional decisions.

COMPULSORY VERSUS POSTCOMPULSORY EDUCATION

This second distinction, in considering educational planning, is between periods of compulsory and postcompulsory education. (For a discussion of the distinction between the compulsory and postcompulsory periods as concepts in educational planning, see the report of the *Conference on Future Structures of Post-Secondary Education,* 1974.) In most states children are required to attend school between ages of about 6 and 16; in that age period there are no options either for students or for schools on matters of attendance. Children must attend—literally all children, no matter how exceptional or different they may be; and correspondingly, the schools must provide appropriate programs for all students. On this latter point, there are no excuses—for lack of money, teachers, or facilities. Parents, of course, have the option of using private schools, parochial schools, or free public schools. The first two may set their own admission and demission criteria. The public schools, though, in effect have a *contract* with each student of school age to offer an appropriate program, and for breach of contract—failure to provide a suitable program—school board members and other school officials face liability issues. In the period of compulsory education there are no basic selection or rejection decisions about enrollment of students in public schools; there are only instructional decisions.

As a kind of trade-off with children for confining them to schools for a substantial period of time it seems reasonable that the schools should do at least six things:

1. Show genuine appreciation for each child.
2. Make decisions about the child's program in a strictly child advocate or individual payoff mode.
3. Provide sufficient variability in instructional programs so that each child's developmental needs can be accommodated.
4. Remove the child from the mainstream only under the most compelling of circumstances.
5. Emphasize basic tools such as reading ability, but without confinement as to what is to be read—thus expanding rather than limiting each child's opportunities for awareness and growth in unique ways.
6. Comply with rights granted to the child under law or the Constitution.

At more advanced stages of education, the "rules of the game" change considerably. At postcompulsory level (beyond age 16 in most states) students may withdraw from school either for limited periods of time or permanently. And, although students have *rights* to education that extend into the postcompulsory age level—usually to age 21—they do not have a right to enter all educational institutions or any program of their own choice. Their right to education guarantees that students have a right to a place and an appropriate program in the public school environment at least through high school graduation or to age 21 (which ever comes first) but they increasingly face the realities of the sorting processes as advanced training programs and employers come to the forefront.

Programs at the postcompulsory age levels tend to become much more specialized and to be more in the nature of "electives"; they tend to act strongly as "sorters" for various institutions of society so that, for example, students get into and stay in welding classes, medical schools, teacher training and business schools only to the extent that they make good progress and appear likely to be certified or selectable in some way into employment following prescribed periods of schooling. Here we are dealing not mainly in the imperatives of the culture, but in electives; and schools increasingly reserve their right to make selection and rejection decisions. Responsibilities at advanced levels of training often run to standards of the trades and professions and their utility in the public service; thus, student desires and needs are not the only consideration in decision processes.

There are many problems yet to be solved on behalf of the handicapped at the postcompulsory levels: making sure that they do have appropriate opportunities for education during the full period of their *rights,* making sure that they are not rejected from opportunities for education in vocational and professional schools on the basis of faulty information or clear failure to provide training program and job modifications that are feasible, making sure that handicapped students have the fullest opportunities compatible with their interests and abilities for advanced liberal education and for lifelong learning. Our society provides a richer fare in education for the gifted, but careful attention is necessary if each student of high ability, including those who are poor or disadvantaged in some other way, is to have a full opportunity for postcompulsory education.

WAYS OF INDIVIDUALIZING INSTRUCTION

Considered together, the concepts of cultural imperatives and cultural electives and of compulsory and postcompulsory education can help to define ways of individualizing programs as summarized in Figure 3-1.

Assessment / 113

FIGURE 3-1
The Individualization of Education in Relation to Cultural Imperatives
and Electives and Compulsory and Postcompulsory Schooling

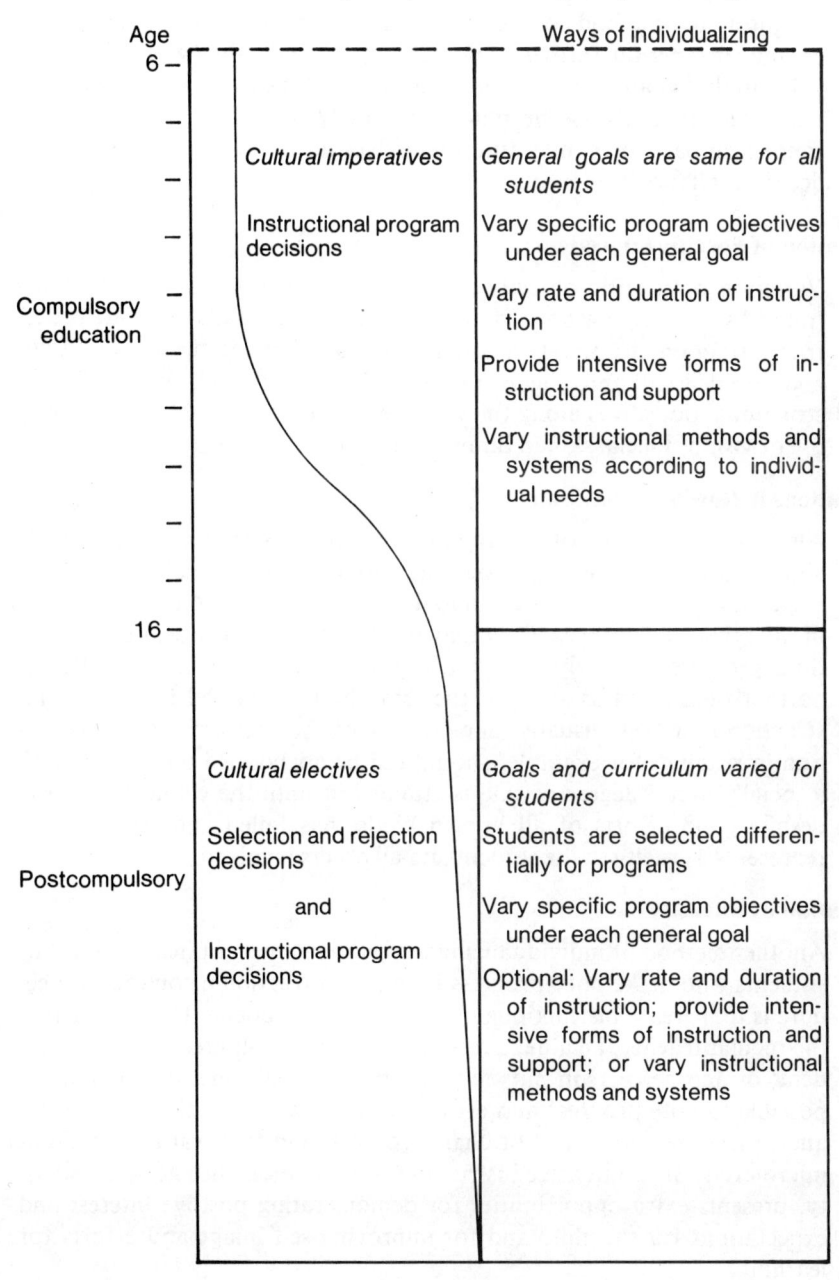

Age		Ways of individualizing
6 —		
Compulsory education	*Cultural imperatives*	General goals are same for all students
	Instructional program decisions	Vary specific program objectives under each general goal
		Vary rate and duration of instruction
		Provide intensive forms of instruction and support
		Vary instructional methods and systems according to individual needs
16 —		
Postcompulsory	*Cultural electives*	Goals and curriculum varied for students
	Selection and rejection decisions	Students are selected differentially for programs
	and	Vary specific program objectives under each general goal
	Instructional program decisions	Optional: Vary rate and duration of instruction; provide intensive forms of instruction and support; or vary instructional methods and systems

For the cultural imperatives there is no difference among students in general goal setting, but there are other ways of individualizing as noted in Figure 3-1. That is, they all get instruction in language, but rates, duration, and methods or systems of instruction may vary. In the post-compulsory period further opportunities for individualization are provided in that goals may be varied, but this is at the expense that selection and rejection decisions become increasingly allowable and the handicapped, in particular, may find themselves on the rejection side of such decisions all too frequently.

Variation of Specific Objectives

Variation of specific objectives under each general goal may be illustrated by contrasting how the goal of acquiring habits basic to pedestrian safety on city streets is attained for blind children, deaf children, and crippled children. Each can attain the goal, though the specific instructional objectives along the way (i.e., cane travel and listening, total use of vision, special skill in timing and use of ramps) differ for each.

Variations in Rate and Duration

Also among methods of individualizing programs are variations in rate and duration of training programs. Some children make very poor responses and progress in the initial stages of instruction in reading or in the other imperatives. They may need to have a great deal of instruction, progressing slowly, with much practice in one or more of the important fields; and as a result, the total duration period for formal instruction may be unusually long. As one of the "imperatives," instruction in reading, for example, should not be abandoned unless and until a socially useful degree of skill is attained or until the whole enterprise, despite good efforts of all known kinds, has failed and continuation represents a cruelty to the student and all others involved.

Variation of Intensity

Another method of individualizing is to vary intensity of instruction. For students who make poor progress in initial instruction a common procedure is to increase instructional attention to the student. This means that the regular teacher, an aide, a resource teacher, a volunteer, a fellow student, or another person puts in extra instructional time, thus making it possible to note progress and errors, to organize instructional materials and procedures, to record or chart progress, and to reward the child at microlevels. Such intensive instruction, if carried on with good sensitivity, presents extra opportunities for demonstrating positive interest and expectations for the child and for improving self image and efforts for learning.

Increasing intensity of instruction is not necessarily a highly specialized activity, so that with good supervision it can sometimes be conducted by peers or other nonprofessional persons, such as aides or volunteers. Regular teachers, if class enrollments are limited, have opportunities to intensify instruction when needed. For the most part, intensity adjustments involve rate and structure variations—instruction proceeds slowly, with much practice and with all steps smoothly organized in careful sequence.

Some forms of high intensity instruction require specialized preparation and are conducted only by well prepared personnel. The precision teaching procedures that involve pinpointing of objectives and highly precise management of instruction on both the stimulus and consequence sides illustrate such a procedure. This may involve the daily logarithmic charting of the performance of students on instructional tasks at microlevels and extremely careful sequencing of precisely defined tasks. Full implementation requires highly disciplined and intensive instructional management.

Alternative Instructional Methods

Another way of varying instruction is in differential use of alternative instructional methods or systems. Perhaps the most distinct of all alternatives here is in the choice of braille or sight reading systems for students who have visual impairments. A similar set of alternatives exists for students with severe hearing impairments: between oral-lipreading, manual, and total approaches to communication. These decisions are often difficult and depend on the characteristics of both students and teachers, as well as on other school personnel they encounter.

There are other variations in instructional methods that have importance; for example, among major systems for the teaching of reading such as totally nonoral methods, highly phonetic systems, or multisensory systems. Teaching by such methods requires careful preparation by the teacher and consistent adherence to procedures for the full implementation of the system. The assumption in the differential use of such methods is that students vary in approach that will be most useful to them, and thus, a "matching" problem exists. It is in the offering of highly specialized methods or systems of instruction that the field of special education finds its clearest definition.

Sequential Selection

Finally, a method of individualizing is to select sequentially students permitted into instructional situations. For example, only successful first year German language students might be permitted into the second year program; or, only students who show very high achievement in all academic subjects, but especially in science, might be admitted to the premedical program; or, only very good basketball players make the varsity team. Assessments leading to sequential selection decisions tend to increase, as noted previously, in the postcompulsory period of education. The result tends to be the emergence of sets of rather distinct educational programs or tracks that serve only selected students.

ASSESSMENT OF INDIVIDUALS

Screening

The study of students for purposes of individualizing programs often proceeds sequentially through two steps: screening and educational diagnosis. The first step, screening, serves merely to locate or surface students who may need special attention. Educational diagnosis then proceeds to more detailed levels to help make decisions on what instructional modifications might be essential. Sometimes the distinction between screening and educational diagnosis is blurred or unnecessary and the teacher moves directly to analysis that has instructional significance. Whenever possible, of course, it is desirable to proceed directly to careful diagnosis of every student. The extra step of screening serves mainly as a means of conserving time and money.

Methods of Screening

Screening is provided in many ways: physicians may note certain *stigmatic* or *pathognomic* signs at birth or at very early periods in life; for example, conditions such as slant eyes, deeply fissured tongue, and stubby fingers are often associated with Down's syndrome or mongolism, which is a highly reliable predictor of significantly low rates of cognitive development. Physicians may also be able to detect a severe hearing or visual impairment through special exams and then alert school officials to special needs. Parents or others who observe children may screen them informally by noting unusual rates of development, unusual behavior or episodic functioning problems. This process may be systematized somewhat by giving parents and others cues on the kinds of observations to make. The North East Ohio Regional Resource Center (NEO/RRC) for example, in making a search for handicapped children as required by federal law (Public Law 93-380), asked parents to complete a form that included the following section:

What is your child's age?_____

For his age, do you feel he often has too many difficulties in any of the following areas? If so, please put an "X" in front of those areas he has difficulty in.

___Walking	___Accepting responsibility
___Talking	___Controlling temper
___Seeing	___Dressing
___Hearing	___Following directions
___Eating	___Handling small objects
___Toileting	___Learning new things
___Sleeping	___Emotions
___Fighting	___Reading, writing, or arithmetic
___Playing with other children	
___Talking with adults	___Sexual behavior
___Playing by themselves	___Thinking clearly

Screening may also be conducted by scanning records of health serving agencies, conducting "awareness" campaigns through newspapers or other media, through special preschool, school related, and in-school screening activities. Vision and hearing screening systems are commonly conducted in cooperation with or within schools, using rough instruments to detect hearing or vision problems.

Screening systems are often quite subjective or use "broad band techniques"; that is they involve rather superficial scanning across broad domains. They result in nothing very reliable or precise; their principal concern is simply to locate or surface children who may be in need of special attention. Those identified by screening procedures need to go on into further study to determine if there is any basis for making a special schooling arrangement.

Screening Efficiency

Two kinds of errors can occur in screening—false positives and false negatives. A *false positive* is an incorrect identification of a problem or some other characteristic requiring special study; a *false negative* is a failure to detect a real problem. In general, at screening levels there is more concern for avoiding false negatives than false positives; you do not want to miss the child who has a significant problem or need. On the other hand, the screening procedures can be highly inefficient and simply refer too many children as having problems. In the ultimate case, of course, one could avoid all false negatives by asserting that everyone has all possible problems and thus perform detailed diagnostic studies on everyone.

Sometimes concepts of *effectiveness* and *efficiency* are used in connection with screening procedures. A procedure may be said to be effective according to the percentage of people who should be located who are actually identified by the procedure. Thus, a test that is intended to locate children with serious articulation problems and locates 100% of such children may be said to be 100% effective. It would be easy to be highly effective, of course, simply by referring at very high rates. The concept of efficiency takes account of this problem. A screening procedure is defined as efficient according to the percentage of those referred who are correctly referred (Pegnato & Birch, 1959).

Negative Labels

A particular difficulty occurs when children are given negative labels on the basis of crude screening procedures. Usually this does not create a problem in areas of screening for vision, hearing, or other physical impairments. However, there are frequent difficulties when labels such as "mentally retarded," "emotionally disturbed," or "learning disabled" are used.

There has been an unfortunate tendency in recent years to use doubtful, technically inadequate, techniques at early childhood levels to identify and label children. This has been encouraged by federal funding systems for special services that require eligibility to be established by categorical assignments of specific children, some of which tend to be stigmatic. For example, a massive psychological screening program, known as the Early and Periodic Screening Diagnosis and Treatment (EPSDT), was authorized by Congress in 1967. Applied at the level of very young children, the procedures sometimes result in doubtful labels such as "mentally retarded," "brain damaged," "learning disabled," or "hyperkinetic."

Teachers should reject the notion that children are assigned to such categories as mentally retarded or emotionally disturbed on the basis of screening procedures. Not only are such categorizations and labels stigmatic, they are almost totally lacking in relevance to the individualizing of educational programs. Mental ability, as measured by IQ tests, shows little relationship to progress in the short term learning of specific tasks in the school setting; and even if IQ did issue prediction it is not certain that it would interact with alternative procedures and thus be a proper basis for an educational decision.

We propose that screening procedures other than those that are health related (vision, hearing, and other health conditions) can usually be omitted in favor of moving directly to the areas of achievement or learning with which the school is concerned. Thus, it is proposed that the schools go immediately to the assessment of progress in language, mathematics, social skills, and other essential areas—in which interpretations can be made directly, rather than through concepts of mental retardation, emotional disturbance, or the like. Similarly, we would urge that diagnosis proceed mainly in directly interpretable instructionally relevant terms. Perhaps even more important is that educational diagnosis be extended to the child's total life situation as well as to the child.

Educational Diagnosis

After screening, attention turns to detailed educational diagnosis. It is important to recognize several aspects of this transition. First, the variables that were useful in screening may not and often are not relevant to educational diagnosis. The clearest cases may be in total deafness or total blindness. Identification or screening may be based on these sensory deficiencies; but educational diagnosis, in the sense that we now must proceed with studies to lay out an educational plan, obviously must look to other variables. If the child has no hearing, education must proceed through other channels and it is to the latter that attention must go. A child who shows a very slow rate of cognitive development, for example, might profit more from a program that emphasizes social skills and strong motivation for achievement than from a program that proceeds from an analysis of cognitive development itself. Thus, screening and educational diagnosis are often quite distinct problems, often developed on different variables.

It has been suggested that screening deals with mere *surfacing* variables, while a different set of *decision* variables are those that assist in planning the educational program. Surfacing and decision variables are often different variables; they are the same only in those instances where the screening or surfacing variables interact with treatment (Reynolds & Balow, 1972).

A second observation is that good instructional procedures are not always available to treat (or educate) children who may be screened as having educational problems. Until Louis Braille created the reading system that bears his name, the possibilities of teaching totally blind persons to read was virtually nil. Today there are great difficulties in teaching all that we would like to some of the most severely multiply handicapped children. Unfortunately educators—as with other professionals—must be prepared to accept some casualties. In the long range, treatments may be created to deal with problems that now seem insoluble, but for now there are limitations and realities to be confronted.

A third consideration, as noted earlier in Chapter 2, is that educational diagnosis and classification depend on the purposes for which the analysis is undertaken. Here the concern is with education and we suggest that the principal concern is to allocate the child to the most promising educational intervention. In Cromwell's (1976) terms our aim is to examine the A's and B's to result in assignment to a C to optimize D, where:

A's are historical data—what may be relevant about the child's past.

B's are concurrent data—what we can learn now about the child's present characteristics through tests or other sources.

C's are alternative educational programs.

D's are outcomes.

Or to use Hunt's (1975) terminology, the problem is to secure a "match" between the child's characteristics and the environment (educational program).

A fourth consideration in educational diagnosis is to be able to differentiate the tasks to be learned and something about their sequence in whatever learning domains might be considered, for the most obvious and essential aspect of diagnosis in education is to assess the child's existing knowledges and skills and to use this information in proposing next steps in the learning process. For example, Schwartz and Oseroff (1975) proposed a set of prereading skills, which in one small beginning section, are as follows:

  1.0 Pre-reading
    1.1 Auditory Discrimination
    1.2 Auditory Memory
    1.3 Auditory Comprehension (p. 171)

Each of these is further analyzed into measurable and teachable components. For example:

  1.1 Auditory Discrimination
    1.1.1 Sound discrimination (simply noting when gross differences occur)
    1.1.2 Rhyming
    1.1.3 Single consonant discrimination
    1.1.4 Initial consonant discrimination etc. (pp. 177-183)

The analysis proceeds systematically through what amounts to a reasonable set and sequence of learning tasks that, with teaching and learning, can result in achievement of the larger goal of independent general reading ability, at least for most subjects who have intact sensory systems. The detailed analysis and specification of tasks and their transformation into domain or criterion referenced assessment systems is often critical for students whose progress in less well oriented instructional systems is poor. Such students tend to require high structure.

Diagnosis involves much more, of course, in many cases and may include the most detailed and penetrating analysis of student characteristics and those of the family and community in attempting to specify a good "match" with instructional approaches.

Nondiscriminatory Assessment

A great deal of attention has been given in recent years to matters of unfair discrimination in assessment. Much of the concern has arisen from minority groups (and others who have realized what has happened to minority children) who feel that their children have often been misjudged, slandered, and misplaced in school programs as a result of biased testing procedures. The famous case of Larry P. in a California law suit (*Larry P. v. Riles,* 1972) resulted in an injunction against the use of intelligence tests in the case of minority group children. The case involved a finding that several Black children had been inappropriately classified as mentally retarded on the basis of intelligence test results. Following this case, a sharp general reduction occurred in the use of individual intelligence tests and in the numbers of children classified as "educable mentally retarded" in California. In a period of about six years following the *Larry P.* decision in California, enrollments in educable mentally retarded classes in that state were reduced virtually by half.

Because relatively high proportions of minority group children tend to be classified as exceptional—in one category or another—the claims of assessment bias against minority group children has immediate, if indirect, importance for special education.

Similar problems exist directly for students with sensory or other impairments. Quite obviously if educational and psychological testing procedures assume that all children can hear, see, speak, and move in adequate fashion, the assumption is incorrect and children who have impairments of these kinds will fall systematically behind other children, perhaps in misleading ways that have unfortunate outcomes. Similarly, if tests assume that all children tested in a given way have identical or equivalent experiential backgrounds, that assumption will be incorrect and may result in unfair or discriminatory judgments or decisions about some students, such as eliminating them from consideration for programs that focus on giftedness and creativity.

Sometimes particular groups of children will show up systematically in excessive numbers at screening levels and be labeled negatively without justification. Suppose a test is given, for example, that systematically results in low scores for handicapped students—as shown on the base line of Figure 3-2. Further let it be supposed that the correlation between the test and the criterion achievement test is the same for both the handicapped and nonhandicapped. This is shown by the similar slant of the regression lines in Figure 3-2. Let it be assumed, further, that the handicapped can actually achieve (or perform on the job) just as well as the nonhandicapped—again as shown in Figure 3-2; see the similar distributions on the vertical axis. In such a case it would be fair to say that the handicapped have been unfairly judged by the screening system; and if this were a selection decision, the handicapped might easily be rejected systematically and unfairly rather than selected at equal rates with the nonhandicapped as should have been the case. One way of adjusting for

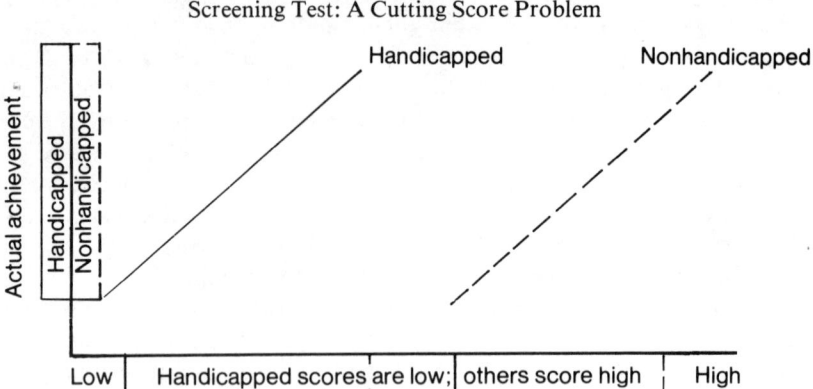

FIGURE 3-2
Screening Test: A Cutting Score Problem

[Figure 3-2: Graph with "Actual achievement" on y-axis and Low to High on x-axis. Two regression lines labeled "Handicapped" and "Nonhandicapped". Brackets on y-axis show "Handicapped" and "Nonhandicapped" ranges. X-axis shows "Handicapped scores are low; others score high".]

this situation would be to use different "cutting scores" for the two groups.

An interesting example of how a group of Black children might have been misjudged by traditional testing procedures has been provided by Baldwin (1977). In 1966, a group of 66 Black children who were then completing the fourth grade were selected for a "gifted" class even though their mean IQ on the Otis Intelligence Test was only 112. At that time (end of fourth grade) they were at grade level (average 4.93) in paragraph meaning on the Stanford Achievement Test. After one year their group mean on paragraph meaning was 7.85. Very rapid gains were shown on other measures as well. All 21 of the children who were followed in long term entered college and some were making distinguished records. Baldwin said, "The point about using standardized tests. . . is not that *they will not predict* achievement. . . . Rather, the tests can seriously underestimate potential or intellectual ability to process information" (p. 621). In other words, if only one regression equation were used for all of these students, it is quite likely that these Black children would have been seriously underestimated. Within their own group, the correlation of IQ and achievement was substantial (the prediction was at about usual level) but what might have been badly misjudged was the general level at which the children could and did achieve.

If the handicapped score lower than the nonhandicapped and there is a relative systematic difference in their output, as in Figure 3-3, then it is still possible that discriminatory factors are at work, but if so they are not so apparent. If, after a search, no discriminatory factors are found, lacking other forms of bias, we may simply face the facts in this case.

A different and more subtle form of inappropriate discriminatory assessment occurs when a testing procedure is used that systematically produces regression lines against a criterion of different slant for dif-

FIGURE 3-3
Screening Problem: The Handicapped May Be Handicapped Indeed

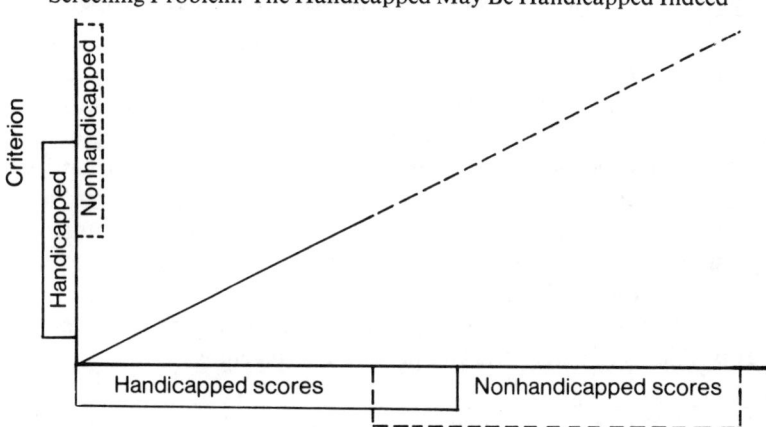

[Figure 3-3: A graph with "Criterion" on the y-axis showing ranges for Handicapped and Nonhandicapped, and x-axis showing Handicapped scores and Nonhandicapped scores, with a regression line.]

ferent groups and when this is not taken into account. For example, it might be the case that a certain test—say in language ability—predicts quite well for normal hearing students in a course related to printing (see Figure 3-4). On the contrary, the test may predict much less well for hearing impaired students (note the flatter degree of slope of the regression line for the hearing impaired). Such a finding would indicate that low scoring hearing students might be poor risks for printing school; but such would not be true for the hearing handicapped. In such instances, we would systematically disadvantage hearing handicapped students if we used only one regression equation for all applicants—the one that for most students shows the highest prediction.

FIGURE 3-4
Screening: The Problem of Differential Regression

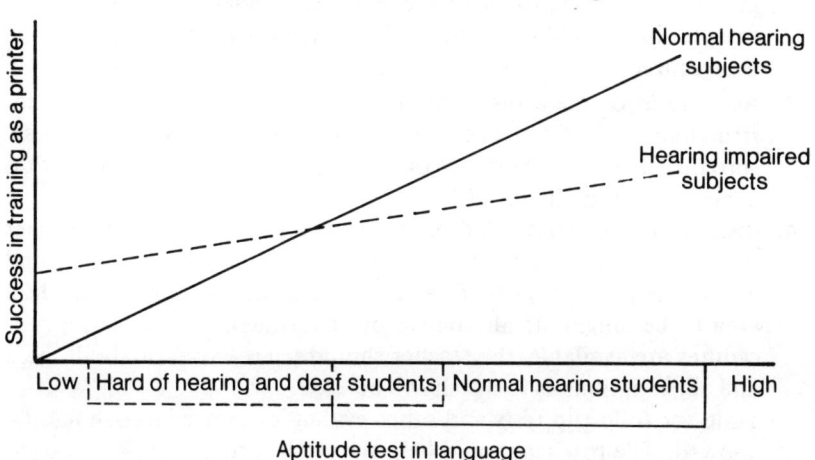

[Figure 3-4: A graph with "Success in training as a printer" on the y-axis and "Aptitude test in language" on the x-axis, showing two regression lines: a steeper solid line for Normal hearing subjects and a flatter dashed line for Hearing impaired subjects. The x-axis shows ranges from Low to High, with Hard of hearing and deaf students on the lower end and Normal hearing students on the upper end.]

Thus, the problems of discriminatory assessment are complex indeed. Perhaps the major solution to the problem is to make as few indirect assessments and predictions as possible and to proceed more directly to assessments in the domain of instruction. Give the deaf a chance in printer's training and assess directly; diagnose reading problems directly in the reading domain rather than to go to indirect predictions and equations about expectations and the like. Enormous financial and social costs could be eliminated, we believe, by emphasizing direct, domain oriented assessments. Teachers themselves might well do most of the assessing and put the results to use immediately in their day to day instruction of the pupils involved. At the same time that would allow the teachers to call on assessment specialists for assistance with more complex problems of diagnostic and prescriptive teaching.

The Teacher and the Educational Diagnostic Process

Suppose that a student's school progress or adjustment is out of place so far as the regular teacher, the parents, the student, or all of these are concerned and that they want to proceed systematically to diagnose the matter and to prescribe an educational program that matches the student's requirements. Following is a series of steps that the teacher might use.

1. The teacher should explain to the student what is about to occur and what will be expected; the student can be negotiated with as needed to reach mutually acceptable understanding of how learning problems and possibilities will be studied together.
2. The student's background knowledge and skill in the curriculum area of concern should be assessed, as well as his basic reading and quantitative skills if these are relevant. Often the assessment will be informal; the teacher simply checks the student quickly in work samples or domains in a reasonable sequence as the subject or skill is organized.
3. As a result of the assessment, the teacher can prepare specific instructional objectives. The student should be negotiated with to assure that there is concurrence on the objectives. (Parents should also concur if they are involved.)
4. Instructional materials and procedures can be selected. The teacher should be sure they fit the students' basic skill levels (reading and math), general background, and particular needs in the curriculum area to be taught. If alternative but equivalent materials and procedures are available, the teacher should tell the student about them and allow options as to which will be used.
5. Time for followup tests and other evaluation procedures should be allowed. The teacher should help the student to participate in deci-

sions about the timing and the nature of tests and other evaluations.
6. Tests and evaluations should be prepared. The teacher should be sure they are criterion referenced, clear as to domain, and as objective as feasible.
7. The instruction should be carried out. As much as possible the teacher should employ supplemental pupil self instruction, guidance by aides, and peer teaching. The teacher should always be available for consultation with the pupil.
8. The teacher should be flexible enough to change the objectives if the original assessment is found to be inaccurate in some areas.
9. The teacher should apply tests and evaluations, using self testing by the pupil as much as possible.
10. Depending on the evaluation results, the teacher should follow one of the following procedures:
    a. If criterion is not reached, the instruction should be repeated, using alternate materials and methods, if feasible.
    b. If criterion is reached, the teacher should reward the pupil. A predetermined reward should be used to assure it fits pupil's concept of a reward. The cycle can now be reentered at Step 1 and new instructional objectives for next phase of continuum of educational process can be set.
    c. If serious problems appear and the teacher feels that the diagnosis of the problem is unsuccessful or that the instruction is not working, then a special education teacher, or other consultant can be called in to help in the analysis of the problem, in arranging the instruction, and possibly for help in conducting instruction.

Regular teachers should expect to come to option 10c rather frequently and should not hesitate to use the knowledge and skills of other persons in helping professions. That includes especially the special education teacher, but may include others such as social workers, physicians, nurses, speech clinicians, audiologists, optometrists, and psychologists.

When starting the sequence of steps the teacher needs to remember that the chief purpose is to design an individualized education program, one that states the specific education and the related services to be provided to the child. The core of that statement is the list of special education activities or modified regular education activities needed. The "services" refer to transportation, medical diagnosis, and the like that may be found to be necessary accompaniments if the particular special or modified regular educational procedures are to be effective for a given pupil. In some states speech and language remediation or adaptive physical education or other developmental, corrective, and supportive activities may be defined as *related services* and in other states as special or modified regular education. In planning for a pupil it is valuable to know how such matters are defined in the state of the pupil's residence.

Ascertaining Pupil's Present Educational Levels

This section includes information and suggestions to the teacher who is in the process of working through the 10 steps in the diagnostic procedure outlined previously.

Determining present levels of educational performance is a necessary first step in educational prescriptive planning. Setting appropriate goals for a student depends on first determining what the child knows and needs to learn. Establishing the present level of a pupil's educational performance calls for collecting, surveying, and using all available information. Assembling that information is a two step process. The teacher first surveys available data and then adds to it by means of formal and informal assessment.

Obtaining Available Information

The teacher should start with pupil information that is currently on file in the school and confer with persons who have had contact with the student. Student files often include psychological reports; medical reports; developmental, social, and educational histories; speech and language evaluations; and reports of educational specialists (including those of reading specialists, the referring teacher, or prior teachers in special education). Persons with knowledge that may be of assistance include previous teachers, referring teachers, educational specialists, parents or guardians, guidance counselors, principals, psychologists, home and school visitors or social workers, and school nurses.

File information can highlight academic strengths and weaknesses and suggest directions for instructional planning. Personally communicated information from resource personnel often supplements file data and helps to clarify the student's past educational performance.

Already available information should be scanned particularly for evidences of hearing and vision tests. Sometimes sensitive young people know they need hearing aids or glasses but do not wear them for personal reasons. Some puzzling educational and social behavior is illuminated if the teacher learns that the pupil in question is either ignoring or attempting to disguise a vision or hearing problem.

Collecting Additional Information

After the survey of available information, the teacher may have a fairly good impression of how the child is functioning in instructional areas. However, for a clearer picture of the child's educational performance, supplementation through standardized formal and informal assessment procedures is usually needed.

Standardized formal assessment. Standardized tests require uniform procedures in administration and scoring. These tests are usually norm referenced, giving a means for comparing a child's performance to a population sample. The score may be expressed as a grade or age equivalent. The manuals for administering and scoring the tests should be studied to make sure the tests and their results are interpreted properly.

General achievement tests usually sample a number of instructional areas and give an idea of the student's academic strengths and weaknesses. This information can be used to determine those areas requiring further assessment. General achievement tests provide gross estimates of achievement.

Formal diagnostic tests in reading or arithmetic, for instance, enable one to determine pupils' specific instructional levels in particular areas. With some evaluation instruments, one can also analyze pupil performance to determine what content has been learned and to designate the next appropriate instructional step.

Informal assessment. A child's skills are assessed through informal tests to discover what he or she can or cannot do, rather than in terms of achievement relative to some norm, as in formal assessment. These tests are usually given individually.

Criterion referenced tests typically assess one particular skill or content area. Criteria are established to help in determining specific strengths and weaknesses. The results show what skills or content the child has mastered and indicate the next appropriate instructional point more precisely than either general achievement tests or even most formal diagnostic tests.

Informal diagnostic tests include inventories and checklists used to analyze a child's performance on a task and to identify error patterns. They may also indicate specific instructional levels. These tests have been found especially useful in helping to match student needs with appropriate materials and teaching methods.

Diagnostic teaching is more and more frequently used by superior teachers in program planning to confirm, negate, or supplement information from tests. After analyzing student performance, and after trying out various teaching methodologies, the teacher may be able to identify the most effective teaching strategies to use with that student. Diagnostic teaching can provide information about the student's rate of learning as well as the student's most favored style of learning.

Systematic observation while the pupil works can provide detailed information on efficient or inefficient behaviors. Thus, one can learn not only what a pupil can do but also how he or she approaches a task.

Commercially prepared prescription kits are offered by some publishers to supplement their instructional packages. They contain tests designed to assess a pupil's ability to perform the skills included in the packages.

The teacher's task, in estimating present educational levels, is to determine what skills and content the student has mastered. The approach ought to be practical and content oriented. Only limited attention need be given to cognitive processing or other esoteric concepts. Remember that the assessment derived information must be detailed enough to allow for the projection of realistic goals in each instructional area.

Annual Goals

Annual (or sometimes shorter range) goals are statements of the learning changes expected to result from the child's educational program. These goals are the targets of individual learning. They project the growth that it is hoped will take place during an academic year (or a major part of one). They should be general. Yet, they ought to be specific enough to focus the pupil's program on certain skills and content. The legal requirements about preparing both goals and the subordinate specific instructional objectives related to the goals are discussed later. Here we are interested in the continuing linkage of assessment and teaching.

The writing of annual goals is most realistic when it is closely linked to the process of assessment used in determining the child's present educational levels. It is an effort to look at the pupil's present functioning in appropriate instructional areas and to determine what content and which skills should be emphasized in the future.

Using the information revealed by assessment about present educational levels, teachers can determine and state long term pupil goals in each instructional area. They may use curricular sequences, developmental theory, and educated and reasonable logic, but they should approach the question systematically.

In determining the scope of an annual goal, the program planner must carefully consider many factors, including the child's health, the child's special abilities, the child's past rate of learning, behavioral factors such as attentional skills, and motivation (or the likelihood that the child will cooperate in the long term learning endeavor). Failure to consider these factors and others such as learning style may defeat the intent of goal development.

The teacher and others should consider the following guidelines in writing goals:

1. Projections should fall within the range of reasonable anticipation for attainment for the exceptional child. They should not be so difficult that they lead to frustration.
2. Projections should have sufficient scope to hold open the possibility that the child will make unexpected gains or enhance expected ones.

A goal is an expression of anticipated growth in a pupil's skill and knowledge resulting from participation in an educational program over time. Annual goals serve as the framework for the teacher's instruction and other daily activities with the child.

Short Term Instructional Objectives

Short term instructional objectives ought to derive from the goals. They include smaller, more manageable learning tasks, each of which a child must master on the way to a more general and complex goal. As such, they enable the teacher and others to record progress by noting when the pupil completes each objective. That charting of progress is intimately related, also, to assessment. In fact, it is an essential part of what is meant by continuous assessment; it keeps both teacher and pupil informed about the pupil's present functioning level.

Unlike goals, which represent global changes in a child's knowledge, skills, and learning, short term instructional objectives represent specific units of learning. Goals may take as long as a year or more to achieve. Short term instructional objectives should be mastered in relatively less time. Progress is influenced by the learning characteristics of the child and the specificity with which objectives are stated. Generally a short term instructional objective might be mastered in a time range from one or two instructional sessions to several months. Teachers might designate few or many short term instructional objectives for each goal, depending on the student's needs. Objectives may also be stated in the form of a series of steps, or subobjectives, each leading to the next.

Sources for Short Term Instructional Objectives

Teachers and others may draw on a variety of sources, including published curricula, collections of objectives published for a specific instructional area, and teacher written objectives. Objectives must also include a method of pupil progress evaluation, based on observable objective criteria and subject to a schedule for determining the effectiveness of the instruction. Thus we see again that assessment and instruction interlock in practice, as teachers look for the optimum match between pupil characteristics and tasks to be learned.

Published sequences of objectives that are part of a commercially or locally developed curriculum are sometimes referred to as "curriculum imbedded" or "curriculum based." These are usually specifically related to the content of the curriculum for which they were designed. (Many curriculum based sequences of objectives do, however, have application beyond the particular curriculum for which they were developed.) Collections of objectives are commonly found in reading and mathematics curriculums. Curriculum based objectives are also often packaged with assessment instruments for determining entry into the curriculum sequence and with criteria measures for assessing progress on the program's objectives.

Published collections of objectives can be found for many instructional areas. They vary in content emphasis, comprehensiveness, and provision for measurable criteria, but they all serve the same general function. That is, they are a source of instructional objectives in specific content areas. Materials that prepare teachers to utilize specific objectives are also available. For example, see the comprehensive set of materials for teacher training in setting objectives, criterion referenced testing, and individualizing instruction prepared by Popham, Baker, and several collaborators (UIMCET ASSOCIATES, Inc., P.O. Box 24714, Los Angeles, Calif., 90024).

Teacher written objectives reflect the skills and imagination of the teacher. Specific guidelines for the preparation of teacher written objectives (and objective referenced measures) are available from a variety of sources. Bibliographies of curriculum bound objectives and of instructional objectives collections are included in the bibliography at the end of the book. Some sources offer specific measurement criteria and measuring instruments for the objectives they list or guidelines for the preparation of measurement instruments, again showing their interactions with assessment.

The instructional situation should dictate the use of a particular source. For example, the presence of relative homogeneity in pupils' achievement and an emphasis on group instruction in some special classes may encourage a curriculum based approach to the selection of objectives.

Conversely, the tutorial, part time format and wide diversity in student achievement in resource rooms, in itinerant teacher programs, and in most classes mandates the use of a variety of objectives. Teacher written objectives are sometimes sufficient, but they are generally more useful as supplements to already available sources.

Optimum use of teacher written objectives requires a teacher trained in the preparation, sequencing, and evaluation of objectives for instructional purposes. Today's shortage of resources, time, and clerical support for teachers may make the use of curriculum based objectives a must, until that kind of teacher training is more widespread and until more paraprofessional help is provided in schools.

Program Evaluation

Appropriate objective criteria and evaluation procedures will help determine whether the short term instructional objectives are being achieved. This determination should be made on a periodic basis.

Observable, *objective criteria* are necessary to determine whether a pupil has mastered the short term instructional objectives. The criteria for demonstrating mastery of the task can be an integral part of the statement of the objective. Many published collections of instructional objectives include criteria for mastery of the objectives.

Criteria can be expressed in the frequency, percentage, or consistency of behavior specified by the instructional objectives. The criterion for successful mastery of an objective may be 80% success for three consecutive instructional periods, for instance. In certain curricular areas, the statement of criteria may represent little more than a single demonstration of performance, like swimming a given distance unaided.

Evaluation procedures for assessing mastery of instructional objectives vary in their provisions for participants in the process, in the degree of standardization of the process, and in the frequency of evaluations.

The following approaches to evaluation are widely used: the criterion referenced measurement approach, the milestone evaluation approach, and the year end evaluation approach. (For a more detailed discussion see Burger, Ciani, Miller, Grigsby, Brown, Duffy, Yoh, Biacci, Wingate, & Duffy, 1977.) Described here are simplified examples of these approaches for evaluating student progress.

Criterion Referenced Measurement Approach

The criterion referenced measurement approach includes a scheme for evaluating each objective both before and after instruction. It employs the same operations as those used in criterion referenced assessment to determine present educational levels, thus illustrating another tie between assessment and instruction. The pretest informs the teacher whether the pupil needs instruction on the objective. The posttest on the objective lets the teacher know the extent to which the content has been learned and avoids the possibility of progressing to new, often more complex learning before the more basic objective has been mastered. The test-teach-test design is continued, objective by objective. The evaluation of student progress is an integral and continuous part of the instructional process.

Criterion referenced measurement is known by many names (e.g., mastery learning, diagnostic-prescriptive teaching, precision teaching, and individually prescribed instruction). It appears in many varieties and forms, but it is always dependent on the systematic use of objective referenced measures, or tests, to assess mastery of instructional objectives on specified criteria. The criterion referenced measurement approach is found in commercial instructional management systems and in teacher generated objective sequences. (A detailed illustration of constructing such a measure for speech articulation can be found in Hively & Reynolds, 1975, pp. 2-4.)

Commercial instructional management systems. Publishers have increasingly adopted the principles of criterion referenced measurement in their design and organization of curriculum, especially in reading and mathematics. Curricula reflecting this approach provide sequences of behavioral objectives and sets of objective referenced measures to assess mastery of each objective. A set of forms or charts is usually included for recording and tracking student progress.

Teacher application of criterion referenced measurement principles. After sufficient training teachers can apply the principles of criterion referenced measurement without using a commercially packaged instructional management system. The teacher may use collections of instructional objectives and objective referenced measures without turning to those commercially available. Or if the teacher uses published materials, teacher written objectives and measures can be added.

Milestone Evaluation Approach

The mastery of instructional objectives can be evaluated at established review periods throughout the year. The timing of review periods can be determined by such projected events, or milestones, as completion of a previously specified number of instructional sessions or completion of instruction on a unit or sequence of instructional objectives. Milestones can also represent the dates on which reviews of a student's instructional program are to take place. These dates or milestones would be part of an annual schedule for evaluating student progress.

Year End Evaluation

A meeting could be scheduled at the end of the school year for the purpose of evaluating student achievement of instructional objectives. If a year end meeting is the only planned evaluation, it represents a minimal level that ignores what is known about the pupil benefits that can be generated by more frequent evaluations.

If it is not the sole but is the major evaluation format, the year end evaluation procedure should include some structured procedure for determining mastery of the instructional objectives specified for the child. The evaluation of mastery of each short term objective will be a next to impossible task if it is held off entirely until the end of an instructional year. One solution is to evaluate blocks of objectives as they collect within each annual goal, and finally, as they reflect the attainment of the annual goal itself.

Determining Effectiveness of Instruction

Dates and methods for determining the effectiveness of instruction will depend on the objective evaluation approach selected by the teacher. In a criterion referenced system, evaluation may occur on a daily to monthly basis. Milestones, especially those related to report periods, tend to be on a regularly scheduled basis. Annual evaluation, of course, will occur once a year. Preferably, a schedule for evaluation of objective mastery should be flexible so it can be responsive to what is uncovered about the child's progress and about changes in the child's learning behavior and style during continuing assessment. For that reason, primarily, we recommend the use of a criterion referenced system wherever feasible.

ASSESSMENT OF PROGRAMS

In the preceding section, attention is focused on the individual student. At this point, attention shifts to programs in the regular classroom setting and, specifically, to the programs that can be conducted there. Classrooms can vary as much as students.

The organization followed here is simply to provide a series of 12 ways in which programs can vary. In each case, a crude rating scale is included. It is intended mainly to serve as a device for communicating about the individualizing of programs, but it can also serve as a self situation assessment device and includes space for "checking" or rating (see left side of each scale). Teachers could rate their teaching situation on each of the five point scales and secure a kind of profile. Individuals might also use the scales to consider the particular dimensions on which changes or improvements are desired. Near each of the separate rating scales is a brief statement of background, rationale, and resources related to the topic. Taken at their highest levels, the scales propose a standard that would be very hard to meet. It should be understood that the scales are intended more for rhetorical and planning purposes than for evaluation; no one should feel guilty for not rating at "4" or "5" on an item.

Space and Facility Accommodations to Physical Impairment

Perhaps the most obvious barriers to education for the handicapped in regular classes and schools are the physical obstructions and abrupt elevation changes that the physically handicapped often cannot negotiate. It should be noted that these also effectively exclude handicapped parents from access to their nonhandicapped children's schools and bar handicapped teachers, administrators, and teacher educators from employment. Fortunately, more schools are now being constructed with ramps in addition to stairs, with elevators for movement up and down floors, with guard and safety rails on stairways and at other danger points, with wide doors and toilet stalls for students' wheelchairs, and with other architectural features for accommodating handicapped persons.

Less obvious architectural features also need attention: acoustical treatment of all instructional spaces; good lighting; back up safety equipment, for example, in areas requiring artificial light; modified chairs and furniture; modified water fountains; telephones; and laboratory tables and other equipment.

A truly adequate space and facilities arrangement will include more storage space and more flexible space than is typically provided in schools, so that a large supply of materials can be stored and used and so that varieties of social groupings are possible on a regular basis.

Birch and Johnstone (1975) combined educator-architect backgrounds to show how to move older buildings and newly projected schools into today's frame of reference. Their book illuminates both the architectural and instructional requirements of schools that can make them truly inclusive and offers practical solutions to these problems for teachers, administrators, and boards of education.

The improvement of space and facilities is partly a matter of demand and competent use by teachers and, equally important, a matter of

Rating Sheet 1
Space and Facility Accommodations to Physical Impairments

	1. (a) The classroom is essentially untreated for sound; (b) access to the class involves difficult elevation and entry problems for students in wheelchairs; (c) there are no amplification devices; (d) there are no partitioned areas for small group work; (e) movement to washrooms, lunch rooms, and other essential areas is difficult for the orthopedically or visually impaired students; (f) space is very limited—thus inflexible; and (g) storage space is almost totally lacking in classroom.
	2. At least four of the seven limitations (*a* through *g* above) are characteristic of the classroom spaces.
	3. General architectural accommodations (elevation changes) have been managed, but internal spaces are essentially untreated and inflexible.
	4. Basic architectural accommodations are adequate. Classroom and other spaces are generally adequate in size and sound treatment is adequate; but storage, furniture, and flexibility of space are significant problems.
	5. The classroom is carpeted and/or otherwise treated effectively for sound control; access and entry present no problems for any student; storage, flexible partitioning possibilities, sound amplification, varied furniture, and like matters are provided adequately.

budget and community support. But there is no denying that they are part of the essential conditions for the effective individualization of programs for all students. On Rating Sheet 1, one might guess that most classrooms would be rated at one of the three lowest levels.

Teaching-Learning Settings

It is difficult to imagine that rectangular rooms with wall to wall chairs in neat rows and columns and all students facing the teacher's desk can provide for the recognition of individual differences without extraordinary exertion on the part of a bionic teacher. Activities must be varied through time and for different students, and settings must be specific to activity. Thus, it seems reasonable to assume that whatever space and equipment are available will be used creatively to differentiate settings and activities.

Variation in settings should correlate with variation in provisions for learning styles, rates, and media. Uniformity of simple desk and chair arrangements usually denotes total teacher control of a narrow range of activities and a lack of movement and choice by students.

Obviously, changes in settings do not guarantee more individualized programs or better accommodation of exceptional students; but limitations in space and facilities are a frequent source of frustration when attempts are made to diversify programs to accommodate exceptional students (Aiello, 1976).

Rating Sheet 2
Teaching-Learning Settings

	1. Desks of uniform design are placed in neat rows and columns, all facing a teacher's desk.
	2. Desks of uniform design are placed in neat rows and columns, all facing in the same direction; at least one "special interest center" is added.
	3. Students sit in desks or at tables that are not in row by column arrangements and that interact with variously spaced interest centers.
	4. Instructional space is complex, involving a variety of learning centers and a variety of ways students can place themselves.
	5. Instructional space is divided into a variety of areas or learning centers that include room for both materials and students. Areas outside of the classroom, both within the school and in the larger community, are used with significant frequency and in organized ways.

Materials

The academic classroom that has a limited set of textbooks or other materials that are limited in their range of difficulty is patently unable to meet the individual needs of students in most groups. In a 1970 survey of 11th grade students, one-third of the students were found to have difficulty in reading the materials provided (Flanagan, 1973). "I read material over and over again without really understanding what I read" (p. 551). In the same survey, Flanagan found that 66% of 11th grade students had reading comprehension abilities requisite for understanding "half the points" included in typical paragraphs from the writings of Robert Louis Stevenson; 37% could understand at the level of "half the points" of the writings of Rudyard Kipling; and only 10% could understand the writings of Jane Austen. In elementary schools, it has been common for differentiations to be made in levels of materials that are used for formal instruction in reading, but not in most other subjects.

Rating Sheet 3
Materials

	1. The instructional materials include essentially only one or at most three textbooks of standard grade level difficulty that are used with near uniformity by all students.
	2. Instructional materials include several levels (different reading levels) of basic textbooks covering content of the class. Additional materials from the library are on hand regularly for use by students.
	3. All the items in 2 are available, plus occasionally the teacher uses films, filmstrips, audio tapes, overhead projections, and similar audiovisual aids.
	4. All of the items in 2 and 3 exist plus permanent provision of a variety of materials in established interest centers for use in the teaching-learning of the class.
	5. Instructional materials include several levels of reading materials, plus collections of audiovisual materials, instructional games, and competency examinations. Students are able to "store" in the classroom their individual sets of materials and records. Students are competent in use of all equipment. Special instructional materials centers and consultants are available to assist teachers.

Here is an obvious area for improvement in both the supply and competent use of materials. Fortunately, quite good attention has been given by special educators to the supply of instructional materials. Over the past decade, many school districts have been enabled, through federal grants, to build up substantial instructional materials centers so that teachers can obtain examination copies of a wide range of materials and consult with experts on their use. The National Center on Educational Media and Materials for the Handicapped (NCEMMH), funded by the US Office of Education, and the several regional repositories help to provide this important service.

In times of receding "real dollar" school budgets there are tough battles to be fought even to maintain materials budgets, let alone to improve them. Regular teachers need and deserve support in these matters. It is hoped that special educators will use resources that are becoming available through the programs funded under Public Law 94-142 and other avenues to help provide instructional resources for mainstreamed exceptional students and their teachers. Many of these materials are useful and attractive to regular class pupils; regular class teachers should find their work made more satisfying when they have opportunities to employ these materials in their daily work.

Classroom Management (Organization for Instruction)

The incidence of problem behavior in school is by no means totally a function of the inherent or even transitory characteristics of children. Management that provides inadequate or inconsistent cues, fails to alert groups when effective group alerts are intended, leaves children in confusion for long periods of time, completes activities before clarifying next expectations, leaves materials in poor order, leaves consequences of behavior promised but neglected—all of these and other management characteristics produce disorder and what finally might be labeled misbehavior. What requires diagnosis, then, when behavior disturbances appear, are child, group, and classroom situations; and required treatment may go equally to teacher, child, and/or situation.

These matters frequently point to the needs for improved teacher preparation as well as consultation. Fortunately, a supply of materials and systems for dealing with class management problems is becoming available. For example, the Borg training materials (Borg, undated), developed as an effort to translate the observational work of Kounin (1970), is a most promising approach to classroom management that seems to reduce the incidence of "disturbing" behaviors in regular classes. Training on such topics can well be a joint enterprise at the interface of regular and special teacher educators. Each group brings many skills to share with the other in this important matter.

Rating Sheet 4
Classroom Management

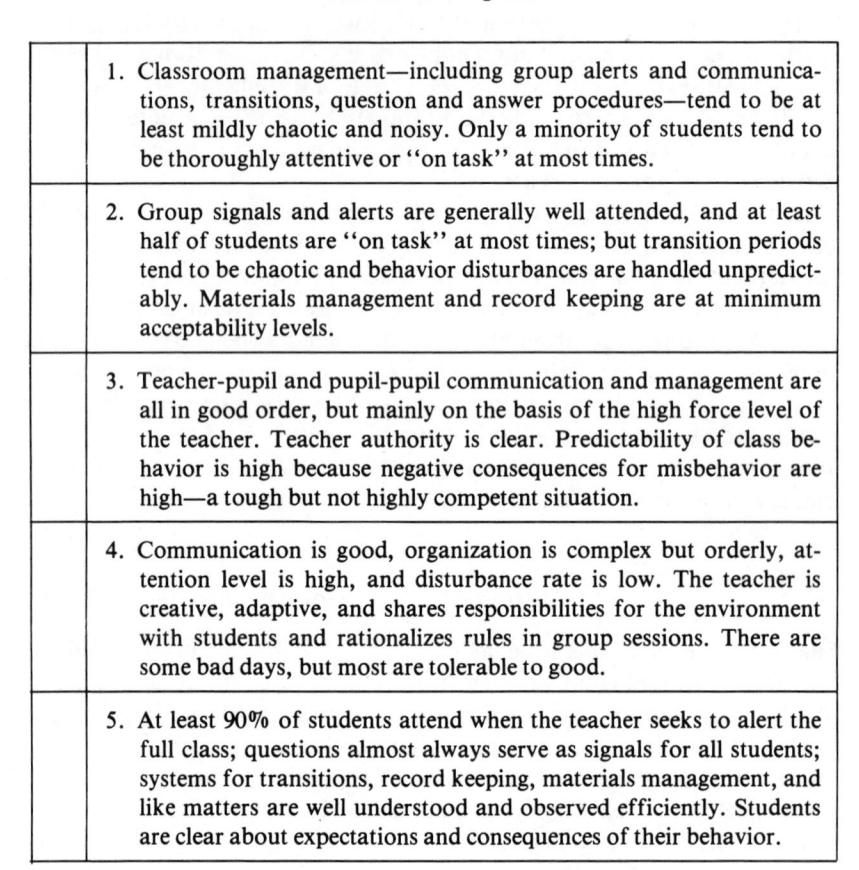

	1. Classroom management—including group alerts and communications, transitions, question and answer procedures—tend to be at least mildly chaotic and noisy. Only a minority of students tend to be thoroughly attentive or "on task" at most times.
	2. Group signals and alerts are generally well attended, and at least half of students are "on task" at most times; but transition periods tend to be chaotic and behavior disturbances are handled unpredictably. Materials management and record keeping are at minimum acceptability levels.
	3. Teacher-pupil and pupil-pupil communication and management are all in good order, but mainly on the basis of the high force level of the teacher. Teacher authority is clear. Predictability of class behavior is high because negative consequences for misbehavior are high—a tough but not highly competent situation.
	4. Communication is good, organization is complex but orderly, attention level is high, and disturbance rate is low. The teacher is creative, adaptive, and shares responsibilities for the environment with students and rationalizes rules in group sessions. There are some bad days, but most are tolerable to good.
	5. At least 90% of students attend when the teacher seeks to alert the full class; questions almost always serve as signals for all students; systems for transitions, record keeping, materials management, and like matters are well understood and observed efficiently. Students are clear about expectations and consequences of their behavior.

Social Environment

As attempts are made to accommodate exceptional children in regular classrooms, it is particularly important to encourage social structures and behaviors that create friendly and helpful interactions among pupils. There are classes in which students are not intended to come into focus on one another in any way, as if the complex of the class is just a set of dyadic relationships of teacher and child, 30 times over, and there are classroom situations in which student-helping-student is considered to be illegitimate if not cheating. The atmosphere can be very competitive among students, with no encouragement, instruction, or recognition for cooperative group activities. If more cooperation is desired it may be assumed that social behavior is not learned and that somehow the cooperativeness is supposed to appear spontaneously.

The following scale, however, indicates that the social environment can be positive. It is not that children should never behave individually or competitively; social comparisons and competition are, perhaps, inevitable. But there are good reasons to teach for more caring and skillful group behavior among students. Children who are the most different have the most to gain in cooperative groups and the most to lose when the social environment encourages competition or isolation. This is no "zero sum" situation. All children gain when they have learned to cooperate, when they have transcended their differences and undertaken joint efforts of significance. The Johnson and Johnson (1975) materials provide an example of how regular and special educators can join their efforts in this important domain.

Rating Sheet 5
Social Environment

	1. Students are expected to work essentially alone as far as instructional tasks are concerned. Student-student relationships tend to be nonsharing, even competitive. The teacher rewards individual performance and seems nondeliberate about group processes.
	2. Students work mainly in isolation, but occasionally in small groups. The teacher praises and supports friendly interactions, but no systematic provision for education in group processes is provided. Evaluation tends to be individually oriented and to encourage competition.
	3. Students work in small groups frequently and must share materials. All records are individual. Students are expected to learn to work with each other, but goals are nonspecific.
	4. Students are clustered so that they can interact freely. Some group projects are assigned with considerable frequency. Group projects are evaluated informally, but grade records emphasize individual achievements. Social skills are valued.
	5. The development of positive social skills and attitudes is one avowed objective of the teacher. Students are expected to interact and share with each other and to help one another. Sometimes they work on group projects, dividing up work. The teacher assists in group process and rewards effective group work. Students have every reason to be mutually helpful. Definite efforts are made to provide socially integrative experiences for exceptional students.

Recognizing and Appreciating Cultural and Socioeconomic Differences

The changes occurring in special education are closely interlinked with changes taking place in education that respects and cherishes the cultural ties of children from minority groups. The racial desegregation of schools is an aspect of that outreach for true cultural pluralism as well as an attempt to provide equal opportunities in education. There is some overlap, too, with programs, to enhance education and life opportunities for the poor. All of these represent special kinds of mainstreaming efforts. Jones and Wilderson (1976) commented as follows on the related trends in racial and special education mainstreaming:

> Inappropriate tests, poorly trained teachers, or irrelevant curriculum and a failure to understand the intersection of cultural differences and learning problems could be as much to blame for the *learning problems* as the characteristics and *deficits* of the children themselves, who typically were labeled emotionally disturbed, learning disabled, or educable mentally retarded, and educated in self-contained special classes. (pp. 1-2)

Dabney (1976) put the problem as follows:

> Many children who have previously been segregated in special education classrooms are not mentally retarded, nor are they suffering from neurological or other physiological pathology. Their behaviors are generally perceived as demonstrating deficits or shortcomings which derive from physical, emotional, family or community pathologies. Seldom are the behaviors perceived as having arisen as the child struggled to demonstrate capability for autonomy and control. The burden of this struggle falls more heavily upon poor children than upon children of the middle classes and more heavily upon nonwhite than upon white children. For these children the school serves as an instrument of *negative credentialism*. . . certifying the children of the poor as socially inferior. (pp. 109-110)

Such statements of the problems of some students who come from minority cultural backgrounds require the schools to respond with individualized programs.

Speaking from the perspective of American Indians, Pepper (1976) suggested that such differences in values as the following between American Indian children and those of the dominant society need to be understood as a basis for adapting instruction to individuals. (A larger set of contrasts is listed by Pepper, 1976, pp. 133-158).

American Indians	*Dominant society*
Wisdom of age and experience is respected. Elders are revered by their people.	Older people are made to feel incompetent and rejected.
Children participate in adult activities.	Adults participate in children's activities.

Family life includes the extended family.	Family life includes the nuclear family.
People express their ideas and feelings through their actions.	People express themselves and attempt to impress others through speech.
Indians have a shorter childhood and the male is held to be a responsible person at age 16.	There is an extended childhood and the male is held to be a responsible person at the age of 21.

Rating Sheet 6
Recognizing and Appreciating Cultural and Socioeconomic Differences

	1. Instruction proceeds with little or no explicit recognition of cultural differences. The majority values and styles dominate the scene.
	2. Special arrangements for remedial work are made for students who may have second language problems or who have different developmental patterns and learning styles associated with race or ethnicity. Teachers may have had required human relations training.
	3. Special projects oriented to needs of minority students are arranged to supplement the regular school programs such as special preschool language classes, bilingual youth advocates, or special units on American Indian education or Black studies.
	4. Efforts are made to go beyond special projects and to redesign the basic curriculum to include valid elements from all relevant cultures—so that all children can feel that both their past and their future are given studied and valued consideration.
	5. Content, materials, and methods of instruction are made meaningful to minority group children, as well as to all others; the commitment to cultural pluralism is real, especially as reflected in curriculum. Both students and parents from minority communities feel engaged and well understood in the school situation; they feel as equals among equals. Aesthetic experiences of the school include samples from all cultures represented by the school.

Control of and Responsibility for Environment

Students greatly need a sense of growing autonomy to develop feelings of potence or power, the feeling that they own at least a part of their own development and life. Difficulties arise when school programs are poorly attuned to a student's needs or concepts of self and, in addition, deny to the student all effective means of controlling the situation. The child who has problems but lacks opportunities even to talk about them or to impact on possible solutions is potentially in a disastrous situation.

In the rating scale on control and responsibility for environment, it is proposed that students be given expanded opportunities to control the school environment and, correspondingly, to take responsibility for the control. It assumes that most of the errors made in this area in the past have been on the conservative side, that is, on the side of underestimating the readiness of students to take responsibilities for creating good school environments, including shared responsibility in teaching, curriculum development and planning, instructional management, setting behavior standards and sanctions, creating activity options, solving specific problems, dealing with instances of particular misbehavior, and the like.

Rating Sheet 7
Control of and Responsibility for Environment

	1. Each individual class and the school is a rule governed operation; with rules based almost totally on the teacher's "police" power and competencies.
	2. Students share occasionally in discussion of how the school environment shall be managed. A degree of "consent of the governed" is achieved.
	3. Formal arrangements are made for the regular involvement of students in governance—as in student government, student management of classroom materials, weekly class meetings, or the like.
	4. Individual students and groups of students are given special training and responsibility for management of much of the school environment and processes. Included are technical matters such as running audiovisual machines, administering competency exams, orienting new students, and showing the school to visitors. In addition, training may be included in counseling skills (listening, reinforcing, etc.) and other aspects of interpersonal and group behavior.
	5. Students share significantly in the governance (policy making and administration) of their classes and school. Their obligations run to other students as well as to school officials; they are expected to help make the learning environment productive. They receive instruction, where necessary, to help them take responsibilities. The teacher shares in all of this as well, but gives particular attention to instruction for constructive initiatives and "autonomy" by students.

It is not proposed here that students should be involved all of the time and in every detail in the management of schools, any more than everyone is given a whistle to blow at a football game. There are occasions for setting general policies and creating structures for their implementation that may well engage the whole community, but there are also situations in which only the teacher "blows the whistle." Sometimes, though, students can help even with the "whistle blowing" and grow in the process.

At the highest point in the rating scale, emphasis is given not only to the sharing of control and responsibility for the school environment with students but to the preparation or training of them for their roles in this regard. (See McLaughlin, 1976, for a review of literature on the related topics of self control.)

Content (Curriculum)

Children learn on the basis of experience. If the substance or content of learning is totally imposed by the teacher or by "the book," the children must be expected to feel particularly impotent in the design of and responsibility for their own education. There is little market or reward for men and women in a free society who have learned a persistent impotence.

At the earliest stages of learning—the basics or "cultural imperatives" —children are given little choice. We do not ask infants in the crib what language they wish to learn; we proceed to interact with them and to teach them basic skills so that they can gradually build a basis for seeking out their own learning and life goals. It seems reasonable that autonomy, feelings of self as potent molder and selector of experience, should be constructed gradually. Thus, it is imperative that students be given increasing opportunities, encouragement, and reinforcement for initiative in setting some of the content or substance of their studies by themselves.

As student influence on content is expanded, clear differentiation appears according to individual interests and preferences, which is of immediate significance for the individualizing of programs. But the differentiation also impacts on attitudes and learning and individual responsibility and accountability for the learning enterprise.

Degree of Structure

Except for beginning instruction at an appropriate developmental level, no other factor is quite as basic to the individualization of instruction, possibly, as the management of structure. Children who show relatively poor progress in the initial phases of acquiring basic skills seem to profit

Rating Sheet 8
Content (Curriculum)

	1. Content is defined totally by the textbook or teachers' guide, including the sequence of topics of activities. The content and sequence are uniform for all students.
	2. The teacher basically follows a textbook or teachers' guide in setting content and sequence of topics, but introduces significant modifications or "special" topics, designed to accommodate the general interests of the group and the teacher's judgment of priorities. The program is almost totally uniform for all students.
	3. The teacher basically follows a textbook or curriculum guide but uses more than one level or set of textbooks in heterogeneous classes.
	4. Content for particular students is specified by the teacher; several levels of textbooks are used along with varieties of other instructional materials. Task sequences are carefully defined. Students are assessed individually and entered into instructions at appropriate levels.
	5. Student interests guide selection of a significant portion of the content. The program for each student is sequenced according to evaluation of previous performance and achievement. Attempts are made to integrate specific tasks across broader domains of the curriculum.

most when intensive, carefully structured instruction is offered. Their programs proceed only from strength to strength, from achievement to achievement, and task to task in smooth steps (Tobias, 1976).

There is some indication, also, that children whose rate of general cognitive development is slow may profit most when instruction is "smooth," that is, organized in small, carefully sequenced steps (Cronbach & Snow, 1977). All that we know of task anaylsis and sequencing comes to play in such instruction.

On the other hand, in some instances structure is overly tight and the students feel confined and bored; they may prefer to create a structure of their own, to discover missing conceptual linkages by themselves. There is some evidence that high conceptual level students—bright students—will tend to achieve better in low structured situations (Hunt, 1975).

Structure can be varied and used creatively by teachers. Rating Sheet 9 suggests a continuum from the total lack of a system for dealing with structure up to one in which the teacher has high control to go either way on structure, according to the individual needs of students. It is assumed that the optimal situation is one with a capacity to use varying degrees of structure according to the needs of individual students. To provide the highest degree of structure and most intensely monitored instruction, the regular class teacher may often need help.

A *low degree of structure* is evident when students have choices on the sequence of the topics they take up. Thus, linkages among concepts and broader patterns of meaning must be discovered by the students themselves. In low structure situations, it is assumed that much incidental learning will occur, that students will be able to take initiative, even in ambiguous situations—indeed, that they will be excited by the extra adventure involved in being "on their own."

A *high degree of structure* is evident when the teacher has analyzed the content and has organized it into small, smooth steps. Concepts are linked and ordered by careful design as part of the instructional plan.

Rating Sheet 9
Degree of Structure

	1. Structure is attended to only casually. No systematic effort is made to control the degree of structure.
	2. Structure is imposed on some topics—those considered most essential; all students tend to receive similar treatment.
	3. All students receive a carefully structured approach in introducing concepts or new content. Students who complete work rapidly are free to proceed in their own way in their "extra" time.
	4. Instruction is varied in degree of structure, so that all students have a variety of experiences. Degree of structure tends to be a function of teacher interest and not fully a function of student need, but all students experience variety.
	5. Degree of structure is varied systematically so that students who need high structure get it and those who achieve better by creating their own structure are encouraged to do so. The teacher has structure clearly worked out for his/her teaching area and uses it creatively.

Instructional Methods

Apart from braille, total communication for the deaf, and a limited number of other instructional systems that are uniquely applicable to exceptional students, a variety of methods of instruction can be used with any student or in almost any class. The assumption here is that students differ from one another and from time to time in the methods that are optimal for them; thus, an important aspect of instruction is to provide alternative methods and to introduce the alternatives efficiently.

Probably the most common of all methods is simple, direct instruction—a teacher lecturing or "telling," with or without occasional audiovisual adornments. Other methods put the structuring and discovery burden mainly on the student, not simply to shift the burden, but in the belief that individual discovery incites interest, meaning, and more permanent learning. Precision teaching and other methods derived from the applied behavior analysts have had expanding influence in special education. Precision teaching, possibly, represents the extreme case of high structure, microteaching; it involves the detailed pinpointing of objectives, careful arrangement of the instructional environment, and management of the consequences of each response by the child. In developmental teaching, the psychological development of students is made the explicit object of education, as in moral development (Kohlberg, 1969). Varieties of such teaching methods are described by Joyce and Weil (1972).

We assume that the teacher who is able to use various methods of instruction is in a better position to "match" with a student's needs than the teacher who confines instruction to a single approach. But the teachers need not expect to offer all approaches at all times, nor even to know them all well; they can expect their partners in special education or fellow teachers to help them to acquire options to meet particular needs.

Following is a list of some of the methods that can be used with almost any student or class:

1. *Direct instruction*—gives lecture with or without correlated visual aids and/or demonstration.
2. *Inquiry-discovery methods*—provides opportunities for students to inquire and reach generalizations independently; may or may not involve interactions among students.
3. *Group investigations*—involves the democratic process.
4. *Precision teaching*—uses methods of the applied behavior analysts.
5. *Instructional games*—embeds concepts to be taught in game situations.
6. *Creativity*—emphasizes divergent problem solving and other forms of productive rather than reproductive thinking.
7. *Psychoeducational diagnostic-prescriptive procedures.*
8. *Peer or cross age tutoring.*
9. *Developmental teaching* as in direct psychological education for moral development.

Rating Sheet 10
Instructional Methods

	1. In a typical month, the teacher uses systematically no more than two of the methods listed.
	2. In a typical month, the teacher uses systematically no more than three of the listed methods.
	3. In a typical month, the teacher uses systematically at least five of the listed methods.
	4. In a typical month, the teacher uses systematically at least five of the above methods and is studying or consulting with other school staff members about additional approaches for some students.
	5. The teacher is able to use at least six of the above methods and has collaborative arrangements with special education teachers, school consultants, psychologists, or others to help implement additional methods as needed.

Rate of Learning

Rate of learning, perhaps, is the most obvious difference among students. However, since they vary in their rate of behaving or performing, this rate must be considered also. The child who reads slowly cannot be judged fairly on any other trait that involves rapid reading. Consider the case of the sixth grader who knew all about "first aid" as it was studied in her class. The child had been very interested in the unit and carried her enthusiasm home where her mother joined in careful reviews on every detail of the subject. But on exam day, the child came home in tears for failing "first aid"—the test involved rapid reading. Assessments of rate mean nothing unless they are regarded with care in class management.

Or, consider the case of the second grade teacher whose "low group" in reading is being pressured to finish the beginning grade level reader and accompanying workbook. There is such anxiety about getting on to the next level of the reader that several children are being pushed beyond their ability levels and their incorrect response rates are rising regularly. It is as if getting on to the next level is more important than anything— even the learning of reading.

Children also vary within themselves in the rates at which they learn various skills or content; and general ability tests are not good predictors in specific areas. For example, some children may learn rapidly and easily in mathematics but be terribly slow in the music class. Each domain must be checked carefully and individually.

Classroom management skills meet a thorough test in this dimension. All students in a class do not complete learning tasks in standard time blocks nor do they all behave or perform equally in equal time periods after completing a learning task. Teachers who fail to take these observations into account are themselves a part of the problem. In this domain, the application of broad systems for the management of instruction, such as the individually guided education system developed at the University of Wisconsin, are helpful if not essential (Klausmeier, Quilling, Sorenson, Way, & Glasrud, 1971).

Rating Sheet 11
Rate of Learning

	1. All students are given fixed, uniform assignments to complete in uniform periods of time.
	2. All students are given uniform minimum assignments for standard periods of time. Students who complete work rapidly are usually free to work on *unrelated* activities. Students who do not complete work successfully continue with classmates in spite of poor background. Some extra help to "laggards" may be given.
	3. All students are given uniform minimum assignments for standard periods of time. Students who complete tasks rapidly and well are allowed informally to proceed to more advanced *related* topics. Students who fail to complete tasks satisfactorily are given extra tasks and/or assigned to others for extra help, such as aides or resource teachers.
	4. Students are given mastery examinations at *set times* such as at the beginning or end of each semester. After each evaluation, subgroups proceed at different rates and in different levels of the curriculum.
	5. Students proceed with instruction at rates indicated by mastery examinations. Such exams may be taken at any appropriate time, followed by pretests for succeeding tasks or topics. Entry to new areas may proceed at any time.

Evaluation

The continuum proposed in the rating scale on evaluation runs the gamut from strictly norm referenced testing procedures to more varied systems that include observations, informal assessments, and domain oriented testing. Excesses of norm oriented testing are at the base of many difficulties in individualizing school programs; the use of alternatives, therefore, is essential.

What is required is that we become much more clear about the objectives of instruction and develop assessment procedures that are clearly related to the domains of each major objective. If we are clear about a domain and represent it well in test items, it is not so essential to use the paraphernalia of norm referenced testing to say meaningful things about

Rating Sheet 12
Evaluation

	1. Evaluation is almost totally test oriented and always involves comparisons with other class members. Results are recorded as percentiles, percentages, standard scores, or some such metric, usually with no breakdown for diagnostic purposes. Scores are not interpreted in "mastery" terms. Atmosphere stresses grades and competition.
	2. Evaluation is test oriented and norm oriented, but with careful attention to domain. Some modest degree of use is made of results in assigning "makeup" work or in other limited adjustments of the program.
	3. Evaluation is mainly domain oriented and reasonably clear for domain. All exams are "handed back," but attention is mainly on "grading," rather than on the planning of instruction. Procedures tend to be somewhat inconsistent.
	4. Most assessments are mastery oriented and clear about domain and are used effectively and regularly in planning instruction. Feedback to students on all tests is complete and clear. However, term grades tend to be assigned quite strictly on a norm or social comparison basis. Students are encouraged to evaluate their own work independently.
	5. Assessments are partly test oriented, but include informal observations and assessments as well. All evaluation is clear as to domain and is mastery oriented. Assessments are quite frequent and integral parts of instruction. Occasionally norm oriented tests are used to give students a basis for comparison of their rates of development with that of others. All students have a solid chance for sensing progress. The teacher is aware that not all learning can be assessed by another person and that people must evaluate their own growth and what conditions for growth are optimal—as part of the total evaluation program.

outcomes. It will be possible—with domain clarity—to say something about what a child can do and cannot do in individual terms. And that kind of assessment can help in setting the starting points and the sequence of instruction. This area provides a good example of how special and regular teacher educators, together, may need to seek changes in the "foundations" courses offered for teachers—in this case negotiating for more orientation to criterion and domain oriented assessment and for more attention to observational as well as traditional assessment procedures (Hively & Reynolds, 1975).

With the preceding sections on student and program analysis in mind, we can now proceed to consider the problem of creating individual plans that match student needs with appropriate programs. Because of the importance of one other set of observations, those of the parents of each child, the topic of the "match" or of working out individualized educational programs is treated in the next chapter in which we also discuss generally procedures for collaborative planning with parents.

PREVAILING VERSUS PREFERRED PRACTICES

This chapter has provided a brief overview of processes for the study of exceptional children and of school programs for the purposes of achieving a good "match" of the two. It has assumed that the processes should be conducted on a widely decentralized basis—out in the schools where the teachers and students are located and where programs will be delivered. Following the procedure developed in earlier chapters, there is presented here a brief summary of some of the main points of the discussion.

Prevailing Practices	Preferred Practices
1. Individualization in programing for elementary pupils limited mainly to reading.	1. Individualization of programing for elementary pupils is provided in all subjects.
2. Handicapped students tend to withdraw or to be rejected from schooling beyond compulsory age levels.	2. Provisions are made for appropriate education of the handicapped at postcompulsory levels—including high schools, vocational schools, institutions of higher education, and lifelong learning centers.
3. Children tend to be screened and labeled into various categories of exceptionality.	3. Screening is conducted as a basis for further study of some persons, but without labels—especially labels of behavioral character.

Prevailing Practices	**Preferred Practices**
4. Educational diagnosis is mainly classification in terms of exceptionality categories.	4. Educational diagnosis is strictly oriented to the planning of instruction.
5. Assessment tools and techniques are mainly unmodified for use with the handicapped or those with minority cultural backgrounds.	5. Assessment procedures and interpretations are carefully attuned to the particular needs of each person—so as to be nondiscriminatory in any unfair way and to be maximally useful in planning instruction.
6. Educational diagnosis refers only to the child.	6. Educational diagnosis refers to both the child and the program.
7. Specialized assessments are conducted mainly by psychologists, special educators, or other "specialists."	7. Most assessments, even those of "specialized" character, are conducted by regular teachers, using whatever consultation and assistance by specialists may be needed.

SUGGESTIONS FOR STUDENTS AND INSTRUCTOR

1. Secure and review copies of the regulations of your state department of education for implementation of special education legislation, noting particularly sections on due process safeguards and hearings, parent notifications, individual educational plans, and nondiscriminatory assessment.
2. Examine tests in various subject areas of the school, such as reading and math, and compile suggestions of procedures for conducting informal assessments of pupil skills.
3. Visit with a school or public health nurse to obtain information on procedures used in your community for "screening" preschool children for health and school related problems.
4. Using the 12 scales included in this chapter for rating regular classes, visit several classes (perhaps your own) and rate them. Consider one or two dimensions of the ratings that interest you most and develop a special project in that area.
5. Study Hunt's (1975) concept of "matching" in detail and then observe the processes of child study and program analysis in your community in light of the concept.
6. Examine your school or community for its racial and ethnic diversity and propose a particular set of concepts, skills, or experiences that

might be helpful in individualizing programs to take account of this diversity.

TOPICAL BIBLIOGRAPHIES
Psychoeducational Aspects of Diagnosis

Gagne, R. M. (Ed.). *Learning and individual differences.* Columbus OH: Charles E. Merrill, 1967.

Hively, W., & Reynolds, M. C. (Eds.). *Domain-referenced testing in special education.* Reston VA: The Council for Exceptional Children, 1975.

Maloney, M.P. & Ward, M.P. *Psychological assessment: A conceptual approach.* New York: Oxford University Press, 1976.

Salvia, J., & Ysseldyke, J. *Assessment in special and remedial education.* Boston: Houghton Mifflin, 1977.

Nondiscriminatory Assessment

Bogatz, B. *With bias toward none.* Proceedings of a national planning conference on nondiscriminatory assessment for handicapped children. Lexington KY: University of Kentucky, Coordinating Office for Regional Resource Centers.

Journal of Educational Measurement on bias in selection, entire issue, 1976, *13*(1).

Novick, M. R., & Ellis, D. D. Equal opportunity in educational and employment selection. *American Psychologist,* 1977, *32*(5), 306-320.

Southwest Regional Resource Center. *Unbiased assessment.* Salt Lake City: Department of Special Education, University of Utah, 1977.

Space, Facilities, and Educational Settings

Aiello, B. (Ed.). *Places and spaces: Facility planning for handicapped children.* Reston VA: The Council for Exceptional Children, 1976.

Birch, J. W., & Johnstone, B. K. *Designing schools and schooling for the handicapped.* Springfield, IL: Charles C Thomas, 1975.

Redden, M. R., Fortunato-Schwandt, W., & Brown, J. W. *Barrier-free meetings: A guide for professional associations.* Washington DC: American Association for the Advancement of Science (Publication No. 76), 1976.

Social Environment

Barbe, W.B. A study of the background of the gifted. *Journal of Educational Psychology,* 1956, *47*(5), 302-309.

Hamblin, R. L., Buckholdt, D., Ferritor, D., Kozloff, M., & Blackwell, L. *The humanization processes.* New York: Wiley, 1971.

Johnson, D. W., & Johnson, R. T. *Learning together and alone.* Englewood Cliffs NJ: Prentice-Hall, 1975.

Leifer, A., & Lesser, G. *The development of career awareness in young children.* Washington DC: National Institute of Education, 1977.

Recognizing and Appreciating Cultural Differences

Bransford, L.A., Baca, L., & Lane, K. *Cultural diversity and the exceptional child.* Reston VA: The Council for Exceptional Children, 1973.

Jones, R. L. (Ed.). *Mainstreaming and the minority child.* Reston VA: The Council for Exceptional Children, 1976.

Moore, J. J. *Comprehensive implementation processes for special education services in the Bureau of Indian Affairs with Public Law 94-142 compliances: Conference proceedings.* Salt Lake City: Southwest Regional Resource Center, Department of Special Education, University of Utah, 1977.

Torrance, E. P. *Discovery and nurturance of giftedness in the culturally different.* Reston VA: The Council for Exceptional Children, 1977.

Teaching Methods

Jenkins, J. R., Mayhall, W. F., Peschka, C. M., & Jenkins, L. M. Comparing small group and tutorial instruction in resource rooms. *Exceptional Children,* 1974, *40,* 245-250.

Joyce, B., & Weil, M. *Models of teaching.* Englewood Cliffs NJ: Prentice-Hall, 1972.

Merkin, P., & Deno, S. *Data based program modification.* Reston, VA: The Council for Exceptional Children, 1977.

Ysseldyke, J. E., & Salvia, J. Diagnostic-prescriptive teaching: Two models. *Exceptional Children,* 1976, *41,* 181-186.

Screening and Early Identification

Bower, M. J. *Early identification of emotionally handicapped children in the school.* Springfield IL: Charles C. Thomas, 1974.

Martinson, R. A. *The identification of the gifted and talented.* Reston, VA: The Council for Exceptional Children, 1975.

Renzulli, J.S., Hartman, R.K., & Callahan, C.M. Scale for rating the behavioral characteristics of superior students. In W.B. Barbe & J. S. Renzulli (Eds.). *Psychology and education of the gifted* (2nd ed.). New York: Irvington, 1975.

Yahraes, H., & Prestwich, S. *Detection and prevention of learning disorders.* DHEW Publication No. (ADM) 77-337. Washington, DC: Superintendent of Documents, US Government Printing Office (Stock No. 017-024-00524-0), 1976.

Workshop

Nazzaro, J. N. *How can tests be unfair? A workshop on nondiscriminatory testing.* Reston VA: The Council for Exceptional Children, 1975.

4. Parents and Planning

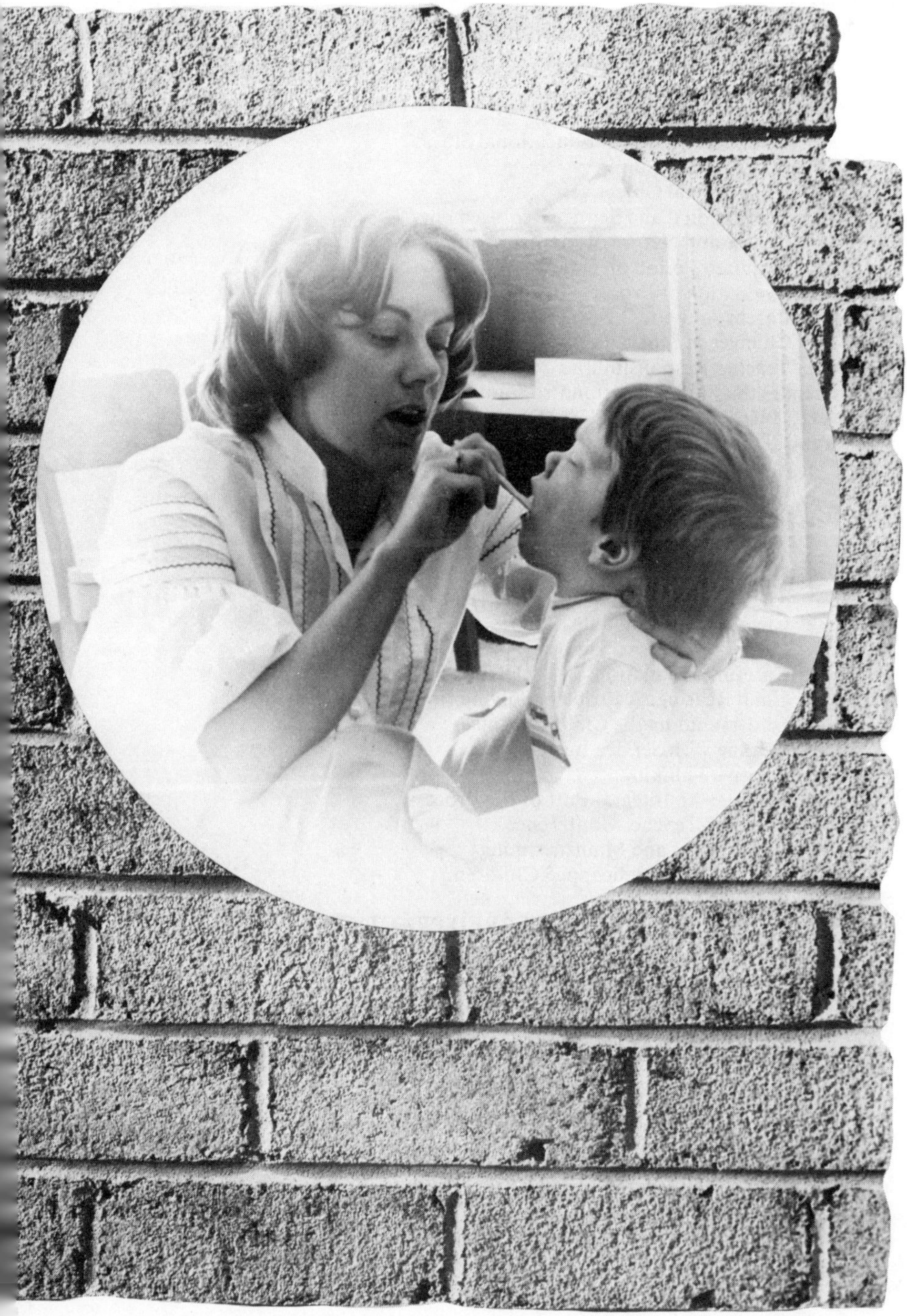

CHAPTER OUTLINE

THE INDIVIDUALIZED EDUCATION PROGRAM
  Basic Questions about an IEP
  The Content of an IEP
    The Pupil's Current Educational Status
    Goals for the Pupil
    Instructional Objectives
    Instructional and Service Requirements
    Degree and Nature of Mainstreaming
    Required Period of Time
    Evaluation of Progress toward Goals
    Parent Activities
    Changes in School Environment or Programs
    Teacher Responsibilities
  Individualized Education Program Forms
DUE PROCESS SAFEGUARDS
TEACHER-PARENT INTERACTION
  New Roles for Teachers and Parents
  What Parents Hope for from Teachers
    Assessment of Needs
    A Realistic Management Plan
    Knowledge of Community Resources
    The Parent as a Member of the Team
    Clear, Understandable Reports
    Parental Access to Reports
    Careful Explanations of a "Diagnosis"
    Child Rearing: A Problem Solving Process
    Understanding the Child's Assets
    Dealing with Service Insufficiencies
    Positive Thinking
    Parents: An Integral Part of the Process
  The Parent-Teacher Conference
  Parent Groups and Mainstreaming
  Parents of Nonhandicapped Children
  Conclusion
PREVAILING VERSUS PREFERRED PRACTICES
SUGGESTIONS FOR STUDENTS AND INSTRUCTOR
TOPICAL BIBLIOGRAPHIES

THE INDIVIDUALIZED EDUCATION PROGRAM

In this chapter we consider how student and program assessments can be matched to provide individualized programs for each exceptional student. Because this important planning process should involve deeply the parents of each child, this chapter brings together the discussion of these two elements—planning and parents.

Federal legislation has made explicit the expectation that parents should be involved in shaping educational plans for exceptional children by requiring a written individualized education program (IEP), prepared cooperatively by parents and school officials for all children affected by federal funding systems. While not intending to say that planning for individual students should be undertaken only because of federal laws and regulations, the discussion that follows uses much of the language and format of the federal regulations for IEP's.

Each state education agency that wishes to receive funds under Public Law 94-142* is required to promulgate procedures to guarantee that local education agencies prepare written individualized education programs for each handicapped student. The local education agency is expected to develop the programs and to individualize education for the pupils within the first 30 days of the 1978-79 school term. If an individualized program already exists, it is to be reviewed and updated within that time period. Thereafter, programs are to be reviewed and revised at least annually.

An individualized education program (IEP) is defined as a written statement about the objectives, content, implementation, and evaluation of a child's educational program. IEP's are necessary for children in public schools who need special education and related services and for children who receive special education in private schools with public education agency approval. The IEP is not a legally binding document but is a jointly arrived at formulation of what educational objectives are proposed for the child, how they are to be attained, and how the results will be evaluated.

Basic Questions about an IEP

The IEP can be the most significant document in the exceptional child's educational career. For the regular class teacher, the responses to the following questions may help to put the individual educational program

---

*The proposed rules related to this Act, which appear on pages 56966-56998 of the *Federal Register* dated Thursday, December 30, 1976, were drawn upon and amplified in this section. Another source that can be helpful in understanding and designing IEP's is *A Primer on Individualized Education Programs for Handicapped Children* published in 1977 by the Foundation for Exceptional Children (Torres, Ed.).

into perspective. Fortunately, several states were using essentially the same process before the enactment of Public Law 94-142, so their experiences were helpful, too, in drafting the questions and answers.

First, *for whom is an IEP made?* Plans are to be written for all "handicapped" pupils who need to receive special education. The age range in Public Law 94-142 extends from 3 to 17, inclusive, as of September 1, 1978, and from age 3 to age 21 as of September 1, 1980. Thus, by the latter date those pupils who need special education because of speech, vision, hearing, physical and health impairments, or because of learning disabilities/behavior disorders, mental retardation (slow cognitive development), and combinations of these conditions are required to be assured a free and appropriate public education from age 3 to 21 planned for according to an IEP. In some states the IEP process applies to special education for gifted and talented pupils, too.

Second, *who makes and agrees to the IEP?* Preparation of an IEP calls for a meeting of and agreement by (a) the teacher or teachers (regular and special) who have responsibility for instructing the child, (b) one or both of the child's parents, and (c) an employed professional representative of the local school district other than one of the child's teachers. This is usually an administrator or supervisor. The child, too, should be encouraged to take part in the meeting, if it appears that meaningful participation would result.

Other persons or records and reports from other persons are properly part of the meeting if needed. One person (often the school principal) convenes and coordinates the initial session, seeing that all persons and materials needed are present and that records are kept. More than one session is sometimes necessary before a mutually satisfactory understanding is reached.

Parental participation may require interpreters because of deafness or language differences, telephone conferences with parents who are immobile, and other adaptations. It is the responsibility of the local education agency to take whatever action is necessary to assure that the parent is truly involved and has a strong influence in the proceedings.

Third, *who takes the initiative to develop the first draft of an IEP?* Any of the participants may do so. Sometimes more than one draft is brought to the planning sessions. In some cases, such as that of a junior high school girl who is gifted and has a physical impairment, the IEP may be largely developed by the pupil herself and ratified by the other members of the planning team after a few helpful additions. In the case of a new kindergarten entrant who is blind and of average cognitive development rate, the first approximation of an IEP would more likely be drafted by the regular kindergarten teacher and a teacher especially competent in the education of visually impaired pupils, after learning from the parents and records about the child's prekindergarten education. They would probably put their ideas on paper after two or three weeks of assessment through observation and diagnostic teaching in the regular kindergarten.

Fourth, *what should an IEP include?* An IEP should be useful to each member of the team and other school and community personnel, not merely paperwork done for the sake of compliance with a law. The IEP preparation is an opportunity to objectify the overarching strategy for a child's instruction. It should be constructed by teachers and others for the purpose of general guidance.

By referring frequently to the IEP, teachers should be better able to design their day to day teaching tactics. When the teacher prepares lesson plans, instructional prescriptions, or pupil-teacher contracts, it shourd be possible to see their implementing relationships to the broader IEP.

The advent of the IEP furnishes a point of focus for the first time for all the specialists who contribute in various ways to the education of exceptional children. The school psychologist can now frame reports in terms of what is most relevant for the IEP. So can the physician, the school social worker, the counselor, the educational diagnostician, and others. This is not to say that the IEP should review psychological, medical, social, or other background data. Rather, there should be education related recommendations in the reports from those professional areas. They should be shorn of psychological, medical, social work, or other technical data, diagnoses, and terminology, and stated in language for possible inclusion directly in the IEP.

The Content of an IEP

An IEP should include, as minimum essentials, the following content: a picture of the pupil's current educational status, a look ahead at goals that may be a year away, a sequence of short term instructional objectives leading to each goal, a list of the instructional and service requirements to allow the program to operate, an indication of how much and what aspects of the program will be in the mainstream, the program's beginning and ending dates, the criteria and schedule for evaluation of its effectiveness, and a statement of the role of parents in relation to the plan and the specification of changes to be made in the school situation—in staffing, training, or other aspects.

The Pupil's Current Educational Status

Accurate information is needed on the pupil's present educational achievements in the cultural imperatives (basic skills), and other curricular areas appropriate to the level and placement in school. These should be stated in terms of actual present levels of in-school performance as observed informally by teachers and others as well as in terms of standardized test results. Care should be taken that actual achievements are not masked by discriminatory assessment procedures, as when a partially seeing child might take an achievement test whose type size or time limits constitute a barrier to demonstrating what the child really knows.

Goals for the Pupil

A one year projection of educational goals is needed for the pupil. These need to be stated as objectively as possible. They must start with present performance. For each component of curriculum there should be behavioral statements of anticipated outcomes. For reading, the goal might be an increase of rate and comprehension to a specified criterion level. For physical education, which must be included in each child's program, it might be a specific level on a physical fitness scale plus acquisition of a particular set of skills in tumbling and games. For music it might be a level of vocal or instrumental performance. For social studies, it might be evidence of the acquisition of certain knowledge and the ability to understand and apply certain concepts, such as representative government or legislative-judicial-administrative checks and balances. These are illustrative. The main idea is that the one year forecast of goals must be *feasible* and *appropriate* for the specific child under consideration, in the eyes of those who agree to the IEP.

Instructional Objectives

Step by step instructional objectives are necessary, too, as the means of reaching longer range goals. These are the formative elements of the IEP. They have a role both in implementation and in evaluation. If a goal for a pupil is to attain ability to eat unattended in the school cafeteria one shorter range objective might be to learn to carry a full tray from the line to a table without incident. Another might be to become skilled at cutting meat with knife and fork. Other steps would follow that would be determined by what the child already can do, where the gaps are, and in what sequence the remaining tasks might best be taught. Instructional objectives to be included in the IEP should be major milestones. Depending on the curricular area, there may be 3 or 4 to 8 or 10 during the course of the year. These should be stated in behavioral terms, should be sequenced under the proper goals, and "best estimates" of expected times of accomplishment for each milestone should be included.

Instructional and Service Requirements

Instructional and service requirements ought to be detailed in the program. Otherwise the regular class teacher or the others involved may not receive the help needed to carry out their work. This section of the written statement might have four parts:

1. *What professional and instructional support staff will be required, for what duties and for how much time?* Regular class teachers usually need some of the time of specialist teachers to work with them in the regular class. Also, they often need instructional aides (readers, interpreters) and volunteers. Consultation time with supervisors, psychologists, and others should be anticipated, too. These and any other personnel needs should be listed, with responsibilities and time estimates.
2. *What instructional facilities, materials, and media will be required, and when?* A gifted physically impaired junior high pupil may require special access to high school or college libraries and laboratories to assure an "appropriate" education. Typewriter, tape recorder, Optacon, and tactual shapes and forms are some of what may have to be supplied at home and in the kindergarten for the blind beginner referred to earlier. The regular and special teachers, working from the statements of goals and objectives, can assemble this list and give approximate times as to when they will be needed.
3. *Educational ancillary services must be thought of in advance and specified.* These might be transportation to and from school, assistance in moving about the school, food services, and other similar matters.
4. *Special education related nonschool services important for the child ought to be noted also, and arrangements proposed for them in ways that will not interfere with education.* Parents may need help in scheduling physical and occupational therapy or other health related treatments during time other than school time.

Degree and Nature of Mainstreaming

The degree and nature of mainstreaming must be spelled out in terms of where the child's education is to take place and how much of it is to be special. Some pupils may be able to participate most of the school day as members of the regular class with little or no special education being supplied, as long as it is available when needed. An example might be a child whose only exceptional characteristic is an articulation disorder such as a /th/ substitution for the /s/ sound. On the other hand, 4 or 5 young deaf children, even though they attend school all day every day in a class with 15 hearing pupils, may be receiving special education 100% of the time, for the teacher of the whole class may be a regular class teacher who is also a qualified teacher of the deaf.

Thus it is important to point out in the IEP the extent to which, and the conditions under which, the pupil will be able to participate in regular education programs. That may alter during the year in a preplanned way too; a major objective may be to move the student into a less restrictive environment with support.

Required Period of Time

The required period of time to be covered by the IEP is one year. However, there are many short term but very significant special education interventions. That is particularly true with pupils with behavior disorders or those with illnesses that keep them out of school for periods from two weeks to three or four months. The plan's beginning date and expected ending date should be specified. A new IEP conference should be scheduled at the call of any member of the team.

Evaluation of Progress toward Goals

Evaluation of progress toward the IEP's goals needs to be described in the document. The plan's evaluation should be formative. The group who planned the program ought to ask, periodically, about each short term instructional objective: "Are we getting there? Are we on time?" Affirmative answers justify a positive evaluation and the continuation of the program. Other answers should suggest alterations in relevant parts of the IEP in the areas that are not proceeding as expected. An IEP is agreed on originally with the understanding that it is the soundest approach the joint planners can develop. If it proves to be imperfect, it should be amended by the same process that brought it into being in the first place. It must be evaluated in terms of whether it accomplished what it set out to do.

Parent Activities

A statement of activities that will be undertaken by parents or others outside of the school situation as part of the collaborative effort on behalf of the child is advisable.* For example, children who have great difficulties with academic work sometimes are tutored by a father or mother to the point of excess, in view of what the school may be undertaking, and sometimes the efforts of parents and teachers are inconsistent and counterproductive. It is important that in forming IEP's there be careful analysis and planning with reference to family, home, and community experiences so that they will be supportive of the total program for a child.

---

*Items in this section and the next one are not strictly required by existing regulations under Public Law 94-142. They are included because they appear to the authors to be logical and essential parts of an IEP.

Changes in School Environment or Programs

Specifications of changes in the school environment or programs that may be necessary to serve a child should be enumerated. It may be the case, for example, that the schools do not employ or deploy a sufficient number of specialists to conduct programs needed by a particular child; or it might be the case that the in-service education program of the school district has failed to include the preparation of school personnel to perform functions essential to serve certain exceptional students. Both the assessment and planning processes need to attend to these situational requirements, and the IEP should specify whatever changes are required.

Above all, IEP designers are not to be limited in what they propose by inadequacies of personnel or other resources in the school district. The IEP should call for the specific education and services the child needs, without regard to whether they are currently available.

Teacher Responsibilities

In addition to the four questions posed and just responded to, a fifth is also timely: What is the teacher's responsibility for the attainment of the goals of the IEP? How is accountability allocated?

The question is sometimes put in terms of whether the teacher should be expected to produce specified outcomes in achievement with the pupil or whether one should look instead at the consistency and quality of the teacher's professional performance as the index of accountability. Certainly the two should interact. Satisfactory attainment by the pupil should result from good quality teaching and consistently sound teaching should produce suitable achievement.

But the teacher has control, actually, only over the teaching itself. Many factors beyond the teacher's control can intrude between the teaching and its impact on the child's achievement. Also, matters over which the teacher has only limited influence may have caused the wrong teaching approach to be taken in the first place. There might be a clumsy fit between what the pupil needed and the instruction planned, so it would be ineffective instruction no matter how expertly applied.

Therefore, when the implementation of the IEP is evaluated, we believe the adequacy of the teacher's performance should be judged by the consistency and quality of the program's execution rather than by the pupil's achievements. That is in keeping with the principle of *consensus doctorum*, namely that agreement among professionally qualified individuals defines a reasonable standard of practice in a field. At the same time, we believe that it should be a "hard" test. Acceptable professional performance should include being alert to when teaching or other services are unproductive and being energetic about bringing the planning conference back together to reconsider the educational strategy and tactics it adopted in the IEP initially.

Individualized Education Program Forms

There will no doubt be differences from state to state and within states on forms used for IEP's. The following sample forms, completed to show how they might be used in actual case work, were developed by the staff of the Wasioja Area Special Education Cooperative in Minnesota. They include forms for use in requesting an individual educational assessment, reporting assessment findings, and recording an individual educational program. The final criterion for a good set of forms should be, of course, whether they really help educators, parents, and other key persons put together a program truly helpful to the child.

REQUEST FOR INDIVIDUAL EDUCATIONAL ASSESSMENT/RE-ASSESSMENT FORM

Student's Name: *Sebastian Whynott*   Age: *10-7*   Grade: *5*

School Building: *Sleepy Hollow Elementary*

Date of Conference: *3/15/75*   Teacher/Referrer: *Mrs. Portia Streight*

Parent/s Name: *Olga & Ole Whynott*   Address: *114½ Plumb Ave.*   Phone: *CU2-0000*

Rationale For Assessment: *Sebbie has significant difficulty with academics and cannot attend to a task for any length of time. He cannot read any of the classroom material. What can be expected of him and should he be in a special program?*

Pre-assessment/Re-assessment Staffing Team Members (parents, etc.): *Mr. & Mrs. Ole Whynott (parents), Mr. Dilly Dillingham (principal), Mrs. Portia Streight (5th grade teacher), Miss Aggie Knolage (SLBP teacher).*

Objectives To Be Addressed (code to assessment team members):

1. *To determine his capability to learn and the most appropriate styles and modalities to be used in learning processes for him.*
2. *To determine his levels of reading in all components: comprehension, attack skills, etc.*
3. *To determine his levels of academic success in areas other than reading: math, science, spelling, etc.*
4. *To determine his levels of functioning in all areas of perceptual development.*

Assessment Team Members (code responsibility/objectives, when, where to be accomplished: *Miss Wilma Reedit, Remedial Reading Teacher (2,3)— Dr. Yen, Optometrist (4)*
Mr. Herkimer Humperdinck, Psychologist (1,4)
Mrs. Portia Streight, 5th Grade Teacher (1,2,3)
Mrs. Aggie Knolage, SLBP Teacher (1,2,3,4)
☐ Additional Data on Attached Sheet.

Assessment Summarization/Verification Date: *3/30/75*

I (we) consent to the individual educational assessment described above, in order to determine the educational needs of my (our) child.

SIGNATURE *Mr. and Mrs. Ole Whynott* _____ DATE *3/15/75*
(Parent/s-student)

I (we) do not consent to the individual educational assessment described above, in order to determine the educational needs of my (our) child.

SIGNATURE_____DATE_____
(Parent/s-student)

If the Parent/s-Student Reject the Assessment, State the Reasons and an Acceptable Alternative:

The following RIGHTS and procedures MUST be reviewed prior to the conducting of the individual educational assessment:

Parent's-Student's rights to review and receive copies of all assessment records, information, and results.

Parent's-Students' rights to obtain an independent educational assessment at their own expense.

That Parents-Student may request assistance in locating the names, addresses, etc., and fee structures of resources that they may go to for an independent educational assessment.

That the student's educational status will not change unless the parent/s have signed the individual educational plan.

That a "conciliation conference" may be requested if the parent/s - student refuse to permit the assessment.

That an "impartial hearing" may be requested if mutual agreement is not reached after the conciliation conference.

Any Objection Should Be Sent To: _____
(Administrator)

Any Objection Must Be Received By: _____
(date)

Address Objection Is To Be Sent To: _____
_____

Date Received: _____

Report Completed By: *Miss Aggie Knolage, Case Facilitator*

Copy of Report To Parent/Student: *3/15/75* Parent/Student: ____*O. W.*____
(date Received)   (initialed)

Case Management Log Updated: *3/15/75* Update By: *Miss Aggie Knolage*
(name)

INDIVIDUAL EDUCATION ASSESSMENT REPORT

Student's Name: *Sebastian Whynott*

Assessment By: *Miss Aggie Knolage*　　　　*SLBP Teacher*
　　　　　　　　　(name)　　　　　　　　　　(position)

School: *Sleepy Hollow Elementary*　　Phone: *CU4-0002*

Date/s Assessment Conducted: *3/16, 18, 20/75*

Specific Objectives Addressed By Specialist:
All (1 thru 4): 1-capability to learn and styles/modalities of learning; 2-reading levels; 3-other academic success; 4-perceptual development.

RESULTS:

a. Indicate Assessment Setting and Materials Used:
Setting: Sleepy Hollow Elem. School—SLBP room and classroom. Instruments used: Informal observations and tests in classroom and resource room; Detroit Test of Learning Aptitude; Peabody Individual Achievement Test; Key Math Diagnostic Arithmetic Test; Durrell Analysis of Reading Difficulty.

b. Specific Results (indicate by number from "Specific Objectives To Be Addressed")

1. *Sebbie will need considerable help throughout all learning, emphasis on a tactile kinesthetic approach should be utilized both in the regular classroom and the resource room. Based on informal assessment Sebbie appears to be a very bright child that certainly has the capability to learn.*

2. *Based on the PIAT, the Durrell, and informal assessment, Sebbie is functioning approximately one year below grade placement. Major areas of difficulty were in listening comprehension, work recognition and analysis, hearing sounds in words, and phonic spelling of words.*

3. *Based on the PIAT, Key Math, and informal assessment, Sebbie is functioning approximately one year below grade placement in spelling, and approximately five months below in math. No attempt was made to measure others areas of academic achievement.*

4. *Based on the Detroit and informal assessment, Sebbie is noted to be having significant difficulty in areas of auditory discrimination and closure.*

c. Additional Comments and/or Recommendations For Additional Assessment(s)/Specialist(s) (specify objectives to be addressed).
Sebbie is very interested in athletics and finds a great deal of success in it, even though he is small. He should be encouraged to participate in any extra-curricular activities of the nature as well as at recess.

Additional assessment may be needed as to physiological and neurological factors.

d. Statement of Constraints On Performance Or On Special Learning Conditions.
Sebbie has difficulty listening and needs to have concrete visual clues presented to him at the same time. He needs concrete, specific directions and repetition of instructions within short time frames. Sebbie works best through direct involvement with tactile/kinesthetic approach.

e. Recommended Application Of Results In Performance Statements.
Sebbie should receive approximately one-third of his educational program from the resource programs. Provisions need to be made between the regular classroom and the resource rooms so that when Sebbie needs a break from the classroom he can go to the resource rooms to do his work. (This should not become a daily ongoing activity.) Sebbie should receive a special reading program provided by the remedial reading teacher dealing with specific skills in phonics and other word attack skills; listening skills, etc. He should be provided services by the SLBP program dealing with math, auditory skills, and attention. Within the classroom expectations should be matched with supplementary services provided by the resource programs. Emphasis should be placed on a tactile/kinesthetic approach to learning. Verbal instructions should be short, to the point and reinforced with visual clues. Parents should be incorporated into the educational plan to help reinforce newly learned skills. This should not be a laborious task.

☐ Additional Data On Attached Sheet.

Signature: _Miss Aggie Knolage_ DATE: _3/22/75_
(specialist)   (completed)

Copy of Report To Parent/Student: _3/30/75_   Parent/Student _O.W._
(date received)   (initialed)

Case Management Log Updated: _3/30/75_   Update By: _Aggie Knolage_
(date)   (name)

INDIVIDUAL EDUCATIONAL ASSESSMENT/VERIFICATION STAFFING SUMMARY REPORT

Student's Name: *Sebastian Whynott*

Assessment Team Members (name, position, phone, address):
Miss Wilma Reedit—Remedial Reading Teacher, CU4-0002, Sleepy Hollow Elem.
Miss Aggie Knolage— SLBP Teacher, CU4-0002, Sleepy Hollow Elem.
Mr. Herkimer Humperdinck—Psychologist, CU2-4000, Sleepy Hollow Admin. Office
Mrs. Portia Streight—5th Grade Teacher, CU4-0002, Sleepy Hollow Elem.
Dr. Yen—Optometrist—CU2-4002, Medical Center of Sleepy Hollow

Date Of Meeting: *3/30/75*

Results—Specific Objectives (INDIVIDUAL ASSESSMENT REPORTS **MUST BE ATTACHED**)

1. *Sebbie is above average in intellectual functioning and will be functioning academically at grade level within two years as measured by group standardized achievement tests. Learning modalities that are not of a tactile/kinesthetic nature are extremely difficult for him. Visual clues should be used to reinforce any verbal directions.*

2. *Sebbie will make a minimum of at least three months growth by the end of the school year (June 10) in reading. Growth shall be measured based on pre-post*

assessment conducted by the remedial reading teacher. A special summer program in reading shall be developed and implemented for him, at the end of which he will have made an additional three months gain based on pre-post assessment conducted by the remedial reading teacher. At the conclusion of the summer program he will no longer be in need of special instruction in phonics and other word attack skills, as measured by sampling his oral reading and other appropriate assessment.

3. By the end of the year Sebbie will be completing his spelling tests each week, correctly spelling at least 14 of 20 words. Special help will be provided by his 5th grade teacher and reinforced by exercises at home with his parents. Through an individualized math program, Sebbie will be able to demonstrate three months growth in math by the end of the school year, which will be measured by the SLBP teacher with the Key Math Test. The parents will be given supplementary math materials to work with Sebbie during the summer to insure maintenance of the skills that he has gained prior to summer break. (Practice time will not interfere with his summer recreational activities.)

4. Sebbie will be able to demonstrate four months growth on the ITPA in auditory skill development by the end of the school year, after receiving individualized instruction from the SLBP teacher.

5. By the end of the school year, Sebbie will not be leaving his seat without prior permission. After that time he will be held accountable to a plan that has been agreed to by himself and his teacher/s.

☐ Additional Summarization Data On Attached Sheet:

Report Completed By: *Miss Aggie Knolage, Case Facilitator*

Copy Of Report To Parent/Student: *3/30/75* Parent/Student: ___*O-W*.___
                                (date received)   (initialed)

Case Management Log Updated: *3/30/75*   Updated By: *Miss Aggie Knolage*
                (date received)   (name)

Additional Comments: *The parents are very concerned that no matter what plan is developed that it be carried out and not forgotten about. They have requested that the providers of the program meet with them on at least a monthly basis to review progress and to re-address what they can do to help. Concentration of academics shall be on reading, math, and spelling.*

INDIVIDUAL EDUCATION PLAN

Student's Name: *Sebastian Whynott*   Date Completed: *3/30/75*

Assessment Team Members (name, position, phone, address):
Miss Wilma Reedit—Remedial Reading Teacher, CU4-0002, Sleepy Hollow Elem.
Miss Aggie Knolage—SLBP Teacher, CU4-0002, Sleepy Hollow Elem.
Mr. Herkimer Humperdinck—Psychologist, CU2-4000, Sleepy Hollow Admin.
  Office
Mrs. Portia Streight—5th Grade Teacher, CU4-0002, Sleepy Hollow Elem.
Dr. Yen—Optometrist, CU2-4002, Medical Center of Sleepy Hollow

Description Of Needs: *Sebbie has a prolonged history of poor academic achievement: difficulty with auditory discrimination and closure, reading and spelling levels, year below grade placement, doesn't complete assignments, and can't seem to sit still in classroom.*

Learning Style/Modality: *Sebbie learns best with concrete materials and a tactile/kinesthetic approach. Verbal instructions should be in short time frames and reinforced with visual clues; it may be necessary to repeat several times.*

Measurable Physical Constraints: *Auditory discrimination and closure appears to be the basis of the majority of Sebbie's problems.*

Statement Of Specific Type Of Service Needed: *Sebbie will need special supplementary instruction in reading which shall be supplied by the remedial reading teacher (a summer program shall be supplied). He will receive special help from his regular teacher in the area of spelling and completion of appropriate assignments. The SLBP teacher will supply special help to Sebbie in the areas of math and auditory discrimination and closure. A joint program will be worked out by his classroom teacher, the remedial reading teacher and the SLBP teacher dealing with his staying in his seat, etc.*

Annual Goals: *Sebbie will be able to demonstrate the following gains within 12 months.*
1. *No problem with being out of his seat without prior permission.*
2. *In reading a 12 month gain in functional level.*
3. *In math to be functioning within 2 months of grade level.*
4. *In spelling to be within 4 months of grade level.*
5. *In auditory development to be within 4 months of his age level.*

Short Term Objectives With Criteria For Attainment (1st 3 months):
1. *By June 10, Sebbie will not leave his seat more than twice per day without prior permission of the teacher. The teacher will keep appropriate charts of his behavior.*
2. *By June 10, after receiving remedial reading instruction, Sebbie will demonstrate at least a 3 month growth in reading level based on pre-post assessment as measured by the remedial reading teacher.*
3. *By June 10, Sebbie will be able to demonstrate at least a 3 month growth in math skills as measured by pre-post assessment on the Key Math Test. The SLBP teacher will be responsible for carrying out the supplementary services in math.*
4. *By June 10, Sebbie will consistently complete his spelling tests and spell correctly at least 14 of 20 words on each weekly test. His regular classroom teacher shall be responsible for supplying supplementary instruction in the area of spelling.*
5. *By June 10, Sebbie will demonstrate a minimum of 4 months growth based on pre-post assessment on the ITPA, after having received special help from the SLBP teacher.*

Long Term Objectives With Criteria For Attainment (beyond 3 months for school year): *Objectives 1, 4, and 5 will be further addressed in the new educational plan that will be developed in Sept.*

2. *By Sept. 1, after receiving special reading instruction throughout the summer, Sebbie will demonstrate a 6 month gain (from this date 3/30/75) in reading as measured by pre-post assessment administered by the remedial reading teacher.*

3. By Sept. 1, Sebbie will demonstrate that he has maintained the 3 months growth that he had achieved by June 1, through a maintenance program carried out by his parents during the summer. This level of achievement shall be demonstrated by pre-post assessment on the Key Math Test.

Special Instructional Materials/Supplies/Equipment:
None—

Other Specific Modifications: *Approximately one-third of his individual educational plan shall be carried out in the resource rooms. A special program in reading will be carried out during the summer. The parents will be given special materials to use during the summer to insure that Sebbie maintains his math skills.*

Specify Means Of Coordination With Other Programs (regular classroom, etc.):
SLBP remedial reading and regular classroom teachers will meet at least weekly to review progress on the instructional objectives and to further coordinate activities. Each specialist will spend at least 20 minutes per week in the regular classroom providing assistance in Sebbie's program. Monthly meetings will be held with the parents.

Personnel Responsible For Providing Service—Include Telephone Numbers, Addresses, etc. (regular classroom teacher, etc.):
Miss Aggie Knolage—SLBP Teacher, CU4-0002, Sleepy Hollow Elem.
Miss Wilma Reedit—Remedial Reading Teacher, CU4-0002, Sleepy Hollow Elem.
Mrs. Portia Streight—5th Grade Teacher, CU4-0002, Sleepy Hollow Elem.

Location Of Program To Carry Out Plan: *Sleepy Hollow Elem. School—regular classroom and resource rooms.*

Describe Transportation Plan If Needed: *None*

Program Will Begin: *4/1/75*   Number Of Days Per Week/Month/Year: *5 days/week; 20 days/month; for the remainder of the year—48 days.*
Daily Duration Of Plan: *2 hrs. 20 minutes per day*

Method And Frequency Of Initial And Periodic Reviews (dates, etc.):
Assessment Team Members—Initial Review—6/9/75
Ongoing monitoring of program with parents and teachers—at least monthly.

Description of Integrated Educational Activities (must be included when the student's primary placement is in special education):
Not pertinent

I (we) consent to the individual educational plan described above.

SIGNATURE: *Mr. and Mrs. Ole Wynott* DATE: *3/30/75*
                (parent/s-student)

I (we) do not consent to the Individual educational plan described above.

SIGNATURE: _____ DATE:_____
                parent/s-student

If The Parent/s-Student Reject The Individual Educational Plan, State the Reason And An Acceptable Alternative:

Report Completed By: *Aggie Knolage, Case Facilitator*

Copy Of Report To Parent/Student: *3/30/75*   Parent/Student: *O-W.*
                                            (date received)   (initialed)

Case Management Log Updated: *3/30/75*   Updated By: *Aggie Knolage*
                                       (date)   (name)

DUE PROCESS SAFEGUARDS

In the process of screening children for special needs, performing educational diagnoses, or writing out educational programs it is possible that serious disagreements may develop or events may occur about which the child, the parents, the regular teacher, or others feel their interests or rights have been violated. Increasingly in our society, formal arrangements are being provided by which individuals who feel aggrieved by any procedure or decision may have a review of the situation; at the same time, safeguards are being constructed into regular procedures in order to assure "fairness" in all procedures and to avoid unnecessary formal confrontations.

Under Public Law 94-142, "due process safeguards" are required to be made available as of October 1977 to parents and children in any matter concerning a child's identification, evaluation, or placement in an educational program. In any state receiving federal funds under this law this means that:

1. Prior notice is given to parents before any special educational diagnoses are performed.
2. Prior notice is given to parents before any change in the program (such as placement in a special class or the involvement of a resource teacher in the child's instruction) is made for a child.
3. Parents have full access to school records relevant to their child's school situation.
4. A "surrogate parent" may be designed to use procedures on behalf of children who are wards of the state or whose parents are unknown or unavailable.

If disagreements develop about any matter concerning the evaluation of or programing for a handicapped child, local school districts are obligated to provide impartial due process hearings. In any such hearings, the parent has a right to:

1. Be accompanied by a lawyer or other counselor.
2. Present evidence.
3. Confront, compel, and cross examine witnesses.
4. Obtain a transcript of the hearing or a written decision by the hearing officer.

If dissatisfied with the decision of a hearing officer, the parents have a right to appeal to their state educational agency and, if still dissatisfied, to federal or state court.

A common area of disagreement that seems to reach formal due process hearings with some frequency is a claim by some parents that their handicapped children are not well served by the public school and should be referred to private schools, with costs underwritten on public school funds.

It is to be noted that there are two parties to each hearing and appeal and that school teachers and officials have every right to seek formal hearings when they feel the plan that is emerging for any child is inappropriate. Indeed, it is a professional obligation of teachers to undertake formal action on behalf of a child or themselves when they believe a serious disservice is involved. Teachers and other school officials have rights to seek counsel, to present evidence, and to act in other such matters just as do parents and others. It is hoped that procedures will be regularized in school districts and/or through professional associations to provide counsel to school staff members who undertake due process hearings and appeals.

TEACHER-PARENT INTERACTION

Until recently few teachers received professional preparation and supervised practice in relating to parents. Also, until recently, most parents knew little more about elementary and secondary schools than what they remembered from being pupils themselves. Parent-Teacher Association participation helped to some degree but, chiefly, in out of class relationships.

For some time, and in recent years particularly, parents and other citizens have had increased reasons for taking a more direct part in the daily activities of the schools:

1. Parents of handicapped children are expected to be active participants in developing individualized education programs for their children.

2. Schools have become employers of more parents, particularly in paraprofessional and other positions, which brings them in daily contact with teachers and pupils.
3. Schools have been made the focus of the volunteer activities of many community organizations, ranging from those with broad interests, like the good citizenship stimulation of veterans' organizations to the specific program directed work of parent groups, such as the National Association for Retarded Citizens and the United Cerebral Palsy Association.
4. Social changes, nationally and locally, are being deliberately engineered through the public schools. They include, for example, attempts to upgrade the readiness of certain pupils for entry to school (e.g., Head Start) and racial integration, with its attendant potential for conflict.

New Roles for Teachers and Parents

Teachers are called on to take several different roles in relation to parents. They include the following:

1. Supervise parents who are employed or volunteer to assist teachers.
2. Evaluate the educational progress of pupils and report and interpret the evaluation to parents.
3. Participate with parents in planning and decision making regarding school policies and practices.
4. Consult with parents about the problems of and with their children.
5. In effect, *be* the child's parent when it is necessary and proper. The teacher role under the doctrine of *in loco parentis* has been eroding in recent years in a legal sense but remains strong in less formal ways.
6. Explain the work of the schools to parents in general as well as to other citizens in the school area whose taxes support the school.
7. Take part with parents in organizing and conducting general community improvement and maintenance activities.

Each role carries strains for teachers, even after the best of professional preparation. Many roles are relatively new for teachers who were not prepared for them in the past by either specific professional instruction or forewarning. Moreover, not all teachers believe that all the roles are appropriate, and they feel that teachers should not accept the responsibility for them. In addition, the way each of the seven categories of teacher-parent interaction takes place, if it does, is conditioned by whether the parent has one or more exceptional children and whether the local school has adequate staff, facilities, materials, and other resources for both regular and special education. Some parents are deeply distrustful of schools because their children have not been accepted or learned acceptably; and in such cases, the interactions with parents can be difficult. Further complicating the whole matter is the general tendency for the parent-teacher relationship to be with only one parent—the mother.

The rest of this section deals more fully with each of the seven roles briefly noted. A general point must be made first, however. One of the best ways to begin to establish competence and self confidence in these roles is to observe other teachers who carry them out well. Ask about competent teachers who may be currently engaged in such activities. Make arrangements to accompany them as learners into a number of situations. Afterward, ask questions and discuss what you did not understand. Then volunteer to take on some similar responsibilities, with a competent colleague to supervise you. Technically called *modeling*, the procedure means learning by fashioning one's own behavior after that of someone who is a good example.

What Parents Hope for from Teachers

Parents have tried to make their aspirations known. In 1975, The Council for Exceptional Children devoted a journal issue to "The Parent-Professional Partnership" (*Exceptional Children,* 1975, Vol. 41, No. 8). It included several informative parent statements. Following is some advice from one parent that certainly provides important leads (Gorham, 1975). Interspersed with the quoted comments are suggestions for implementing Gorham's requests. The suggestions are applicable to everyone who works with children, and particularly teachers as they assume more and more the centrally responsible position in the assessment, planning, and instruction for pupils.

Assessment of Needs

Gorham's first request concerns assessing the child's educational and related needs:

> Let the parent be involved every step of the way. The dialogue established may be the most important thing you accomplish. If the parent's presence is an obstacle to testing because the child will not "cooperate" in his presence, the setup should include a complete review of the testing procedure with the parent. (Remote video viewing or one-way windows are great if you are richly endowed.) (p. 523)

Note the assumption that the teacher has something to say about whether the parent is involved and, also, about the testing and where and how it is done. Parents need to know that a professionally prepared teacher is in charge of the education of their child, just as they would want a professional physician to be responsible for the health of their child. In this instance, the parent is reacting to a frequent assumption by educational diagnosticians, school psychologists, counselors, and, sometimes, teachers—namely, that the child is less likely to be cooperative in working with another adult if one or both of the parents is also present. Naturally, the professional person assessing or teaching the child wants the child to be able to perform well without distractions.

The parent, however, can misread a teacher's desire to work alone with the child as trying to hide something. Then, too, some children are comfortable working with an adult when one or both parents are present, perhaps even more comfortable and able to work more effectively. The teacher may need to interpret this situation to parents and other professional workers, and, after open discussions, arrange the best possible situation for all concerned.

It is emphasized that the teacher is the best person for such a mediating and arranging role for three reasons: First, the parents will want to have direct and final recourse to the teacher, and they should see the teacher as having central control over what happens with their child in school. Second, the teacher usually knows the child and parents best and knows the other professionals in the situation best; thus the teacher is in the logical position to assert generalship. Third, the teacher is the person who will have to live with and use the results of consultations about and assessments of the child and who, finally, will be accountable for the child's educational progress. For that reason, too, the teacher needs to have a key role in all matters relating to the child's schooling, including planning for parental involvement in decisions and planning for the child's instruction.

A Realistic Management Plan

The second of Gorham's suggestions is that teachers

> make a realistic management plan part of the assessment outcome. Give the parents suggestions for how to live with the problem on a day to day basis, considering the needs of the child, the capacities of the family, and the resources of the community. Let the parents know that you will suggest modifications in any aspect of the management plan that does not work. (p. 523)

There is increasing evidence that a child's educational progress is accelerated when teachers and parents work in close partnership—a rediscovery of "homework," though at a much more advanced stage. Homework in its early form was practice, study, and writing assignments for the children in a class, with parental supervision limited to making sure that the children spent time on the assignment. Now it is more than that: It is individualized and it calls for active parental involvement as well as supervision. Often, it calls for increased parental monitoring of their own behavior, too, to increase their contribution to the child's educational stability, improved concentration, or acceptable social behavior.

Three things stand out regarding this point: (a) A management plan must be realistic, both in the sense that it deals with the problems uncovered in the assessment and that it appears to be workable—it is not an unobtainable ideal; (b) the parents must be involved in making the plan, implementing it, determining if the plan is working, and helping to make needed modifications in the plan; and (c) communication about the plan of management must be a two way street in that the teacher keeps the parents informed about its progress and vice versa. Be ready to accept changes suggested by the parents and by the pupil as well. Any proposed teacher changes in the management plan should be pretested with parents and pupil before initiation, if feasible.

Clearly, not all parents will be equally responsive to joint planning and followup work with teachers. It is essential, though, that the teacher make serious efforts to establish a positive cooperative relationship in each case. Records should be kept by the teachers of such endeavors, and overtures to parents should be made from time to time, even though the parents may not have responded positively in the past. It may be found that sometimes they are simply shy or uncertain of how to relate comfortably to a teacher; sometimes, the situation that made their cooperation difficult in the past will have changed for the better.

Knowledge of Community Resources

Because community resources are valuable both to teachers and parents, Gorham advised the teacher to

> inform yourself about community resources. Give the parents advice on how to go about getting what they need. Steer them to the local parents organization. (p. 523)

Today, almost every exceptional condition is represented by an association in which parents, professional persons, and other public spirited citizens participates. Some organizations include several exceptionalities (i.e., speech, hearing, and crippling conditions) and sometimes more than one organization deals with the same condition (i.e., deafness, blindness, cerebral palsy, emotional disturbances). Therefore, it is not a simple matter for parents (or teachers, for that matter) to wend their way through these various groups to maximize their usefulness for a particular child. A beginning step for the interested teacher is to obtain whatever social agency directories there may be for the locality. Usually such directories will be available through supervisors of special education programs or other staff members, such as a school social worker or psychologist. The directories are typically inexpensive; they usually contain the names, addresses, staff and officer names, and summaries of the functions of governmental and volunteer agencies serving the region.

Direct familiarization with the local groups is best for both teachers and parents. That means talking on the telephone with or visiting the executive of an agency, attending relevant meetings, and observing the facilities and activities. A teacher looking for resources for a gifted child in one city, for example, called an organization that conducted Saturday morning painting instruction for elementary school pupils who were recommended because of apparent potential talent. The contact led to another similar program, not listed in the directory, for budding writers. The latter proved to be the one that met a major need of the child and his family and could be related to the youngster's daily work in school.

It is highly important, when parents are advised to call on another agency, that the information provided be accurate, that the agency is actually in the position to take on another client or member, and that the parents will not be required to start from "scratch" in providing information. Preferably, the teacher (or other school representative), with the parents' permission, will have exchanged information with the agency before the parents make their first contact.

The Parent as a Member of the Team

Gorham also advised that wherever possible, the teacher

> make the parent a team member in the actual diagnosis, treatment or educational procedures. It will give you a chance to observe how the parent and child interact. (Gorham, 1975, p. 523)

Both parent and teacher should have the opportunity to observe each other interact with the child. Each may find the other's child management skills refreshing and well worth emulating; and each may gain insights.

There are other reasons, too, why the teacher gains from making the parents partners in these professional activities. The assessment, planning, and daily instruction of the child are fundamental educational functions. The more the parents are privy to them and in a position to react directly to the teacher and other professionals, the smoother and more consistent is the delivery of instruction to the child. The parents' participation furnishes an added feedback loop for the teacher to use as well as a source for added ideas.

Making the parents part of the team also gives them opportunities to learn how the teacher works and to adapt what they observe in what they do with their children at home.

Helping parents to be more effective coworkers with teachers is so important that it deserves more attention then any of the other points we make about the teacher-parent interactions in this chapter. Veteran teachers sometimes say they were taught to discourage parents from helping their children out at home with school work. That advice grew out of concern that over eager mothers and fathers might push too hard or teach in ways that conflicted with the school approach. Today, however, there is good reason to believe that most parents, with hints from teachers, can take an active and effective part in the encouragement and guidance of their children's instruction.

In the very early childhood years, before formal schooling begins, coping skills essential for education, as well as cognitive growth, can be fostered or inhibited in children by what parents do and how they do it. Thus, if parents ask how to help get a very young child ready for school, they can be assured that there are many positive moves they can make in that direction. The principles that ought to guide parent efforts from the earliest years are as follows:

- Talk to the child; converse about what you are doing, giving enough direct attention through occasional eye to eye contact and actual touch to be sure the child is aware of being the target of the conversation.
- Encourage responses from the child, especially those that indicate growth in understanding of new words and ideas. Help expand the child's vocabulary.
- Allow the child as much freedom of movement in the house as safety will allow. Encourage exploration.
- Respond when the child seeks your attention or help, even if it is sometimes inconvenient. Encourage the child to initiate interaction and allow some of the direction of the interactions to come from the child.

Teachers can tell parents about these principles and illustrate them for preschoolers, beginning at birth. At the end of the chapter, there is a topical bibliography that can be used to help parents discover more details about what they can do in those early years.

As to teaching school age pupils at home, parents should be encouraged to try. If they can be relaxed and if they can work with the child on interesting tasks for sensible periods of time, parents can be very effective in complementing the teacher. When parents show they would like to try, it is good to set up some homework with which they can help. Keep in mind that short time periods, specific directions, and interesting tasks will tend to produce success; and that can lead to more success.

Parental participation in homework is a good idea if it is not pressed too far. Children should do at least half of their homework on their own. That does not rule out occasional consultation from a parent, though, even on that half. It is natural to need help from time to time and knowing how to get it and use it is a valuable life skill.

Assistance by parents in teaching language arts and numbers skills can be especially valuable as a starting place. These are matters in which tasks can be detailed and in which the role of the parent can be clearly specified.

High school age pupils can be helped by the cooperative relationships they establish with parents in the earlier grades about homework, if the interaction continues through secondary school. Teenagers sometimes feel estranged from their parents and have difficulty talking about themselves to adults. A recent national poll (Gallup, 1977) asked teenagers what they considered the key problems facing young people today. One out of five (20%) said a high priority problem was getting along and communicating with parents. School work and related activities can serve as a common ground on which to build easy communication and habits of joint problem solving between high school students and their parents, if it starts early and continues in a mutually rewarding climate.

When planning with parents for their children's work at home, use this as a check list to assure that you have talked about the essentials:

- Is there a good place for homework to be done?
- Do the child and the parents have clear ideas of what is to be done?
- Is the work relevant, interest holding, and well within the child's capacity to do?
- Can the parent or child get an SOS to the teacher, if necessary?

Not all parents are aware of the values of youth clubs, hobbies, walking tours, and museums and galleries for informal education. Neither do they always think of the home use of calculators, typewriters, chalk boards, colored pencils, bulletin boards, newspapers, and diaries as rewarding motivational devices to catch and hold the interest of the children. Many parents, though, are quick to grasp these ideas when the teacher suggests them. Moreover, many parents, in turn, originate and offer creative suggestions to teachers, once the communication lines open between them as educational team members.

Clear, Understandable Reports

Gorham suggested that teachers

> write your reports in clear and understandable language. Professional terminology is a useful shortcut for your own notes, and you can always use it in communication with others of your discipline. But in situations involving the parent it becomes an obstacle to understanding. Keep in mind that it is the parent who must live with the child, help him along,

shop for services to meet his needs, support his ego, and give him guidance. You cannot be there to do it for him, so the parent *must* be as well informed as you can make him. Information that he does not understand is not useful to him. The goal is a parent who understands his child well enough to help him handle his problems. (Gorham, 1975, p. 523)

Parental Access to Reports

Gorham recommended that from the outset, teachers let parents know that they are welcome to see and to have copies of the work their child does, the teacher's written comments on the work, and copies of any reports prepared or received about the child. The teacher should tell the diagnostician, counselor, school psychologist, and anyone else who gives reports on the child that he or she expects to receive them in that spirit of helpful openness. There will be occasions, perhaps, when that point of view will have attendant difficulties and they will have to be worked out with the other professionals involved; but contemporary codes of confidentiality, laws, and court decisions are on the side of the position just stated.

Select reports that should be part of a family's records, in your judgment.

> Give copies of the reports to parents. They will need them to digest and understand the information in them, to share the information with other people close to the child, and to avoid the weeks or months of record gathering which every application to a new program in the future will otherwise entail. (Gorham, 1975, p. 523)

With families becoming more and more mobile, school records are very important, especially for exceptional children who may be moved from one part to another of the country's "nonsystem" of special education (Birch & Johnstone, 1975).

Careful Explanations of a "Diagnosis"

Gorham urged teachers to

> be sure the parent understands that there is no such thing as a one shot, final, and unchanging diagnosis. Make sure he understands that whatever label you give his child (if a label must be given) is merely a device for communicating and one which may have all kinds of repercussions, many of them undesirable. Make sure he understands that it says very little about the child at present and even less about the child of the future. Caution him about using that label to "explain" his child's condition to other people. (Gorham, 1975, pp. 523-524)

Sometimes, parents become impatient with what seems protracted assessments of their children and the inability of educatonal personnel to make up their minds. Yet, parents are quick to understand the caution of repeated careful assessments if the procedures and their purposes are carefully explained. In the same way, if a handicap label must be applied to a child, the application is more readily accepted by the parents if the reasons are expressed in plain and meaningful language. Children and their peers also show understanding of an exceptional child's condition if it is explained to them in terms they can understand.

Child Rearing: A Problem Solving Process

Another of Gorham's suggestions is that teachers

> help the parent to think of life with this child in the same terms as life with his other children. It is an ongoing, problem solving process. Assure him that he is capable of that problem solving and that you will be there to help him with it. (Gorham, 1975, p. 524)

Child rearing is basically a joyous process for most parents; yet it also contains problems—even burdens—whether the children are exceptional or not. Parents range widely in their ability to cope with the problems. Teachers, of course, cannot usurp parental functions, but they can provide judicious words of encouragement or warning, according to the situation, if they do not intrude. Teachers can bring different parents together to learn and acquire strength from each other. Moreover, teachers can help parents when indicated by calling attention to available community resources.

Understanding the Child's Assets

Teachers should also

> be sure that the parent understands his child's abilities and assets as well as his disabilities and deficiencies. What the child *can* do is far more important than what he cannot do, and the parent's goal thereafter is to look for, anticipate, expect and welcome new abilities and to welcome them with joy when they appear. Urge him to be honest with his child. Tell him that the most important job he has is to respect his child, as well as love him, and to help him "feel good" about himself. (Gorham, 1975, p. 524)

The way the teacher behaves about the child is perhaps the most important and effective way to "tell" parents about their child. This is also true of the way other people of consequence act.

Children are especially sensitive to the attitudes of teachers toward handicaps. For example, a boy with very complex multiple handicaps was nominated by the pupils in his mainstream class to serve on a schoolwide committee on student behavior standards; and a trio of deaf girls won first prize in the junior high talent show by their beauty and grace in "singing" a popular song. Teachers can help to create opportunities, but it is up to the children and their parents to seize and capitalize on them.

Dealing with Service Insufficiencies

Few complete and comprehensive "systems" of special education can be found anywhere. Nor are there comprehensive "systems" of social welfare, health care, recreation, public transportation, or other essential community operations that accommodate readily to exceptional persons. In one city, a young man in a wheelchair could not enter the public library building because of steep steps and doors that were too narrow. In the same library, a 10 year old mentally gifted girl was emphatically denied admission to or borrowing privileges from any but the children's collection, so she was barred just as effectively. In a nearby community, a hard working young pediatrician tried in vain to get the local hospital to tool up to provide genetic counseling although he had evidence that several families whose children he treated both needed and desired it. There remain the three great enemies: ignorance, tradition, and prejudice.

> Warn the parent about service insufficiencies. Equip him with advice on how to make his way through the system of "helping" services. Warn him that they are not always helpful. Tell him his child has a *right* to services. Tell him to insist on being a part of all decisions about his child. (Gorham, 1975, p. 524)

Parents are often quite willing to serve as the shock troops in assaults on community and regional service failings, whether in the schools or other parts of the public sector. Linked together in organizations or on their own, parents are listened to by legislators, board members, and administrators. Teachers often can help today's children and future generations by alerting parents and groups to educational and related needs and to the procedures to follow that lead to attaining satisfaction.

Positive Thinking

Finally, Gorham suggested that teachers

> explain to him [the parent] that some people with whom he talks (teachers, doctors, professionals of any kind, or other parents) may emphasize the negative. Help train the parent not only to think positively but to teach the other people in his child's life to do so. (Gorham, 1975, p. 524)

It is not suggested that reality be discounted, or that everyone act like a Pollyanna. One can make the effort to deal realistically with negative facts while building toward a constructive, positive outcome.

Parents: An Integral Part of the Process

The preceding discussion and suggestions cover the most significant elements of the teachers' work with parents. Obviously, the suggestions do not apply to all parents or all situations, but each can be adapted to the particular case and leavened with the teacher's personal qualities. There are, no doubt, some instances in which it is not possible to establish meaningful interactions with parents. In other cases, the parents may be so competent that the teacher learns from them. Nevertheless, communicating with and guiding parents is now an integral part of the teacher's responsibility. Other school staff members (counselors, social workers, principals, psychologists, supervisors) may assume some of the responsibility, but in the final analysis it is the teacher-parent interaction that is essential.

The Parent-Teacher Conference

The meeting of parents with the teacher of their child often has profound significance for all parties, especially when the child's educational progress is problematic. The parents are likely to be deeply emotional about any "problem" they perceive; they may feel guilt, hostility, and inadequacy, and it may take time to reach a good working relationship with the teacher. Equally, the teacher may be apprehensive about a meeting with parents. Following are a few guidelines for the regular teacher who increasingly will be the key figure in conferencing with parents of exceptional children.

First, if possible, the teacher should meet with both parents for all conferences. Teachers and other professionals who have experience in conferencing with the parents of exceptional children will almost uniformly warn against the assumption that talking with one parent results in good communication to a second parent. Suppose a teacher has had a seemingly very successful conference with the mother of a child who is not responding effectively to instruction. It might appear that the facts of the situation and an appropriate program have beeen agreed on. The teacher then assumes that the father is "filled in" by the mother and that all is agreeable. This is not always the case.

Conferring with but one parent when there are two is an incomplete and sometimes dangerous procedure. It fails to consider the information that the absent parent could provide; it fails to include one of the significant parties in the planning and commitments involved; and it risks creating or enlarging differences between parents in perceptions of the child and of their roles in helping processes. On the other hand, when both parents are involved they can be assisted in understanding how important their mutual support to each other and to the child may be in creating a healthy environment for growth.

Second, the teacher should assume good intentions by parents. Even when it appears to teachers that care and attention to a child at home are minimal or that there have been specific neglects, it is *always* the appropriate assumption about parents when conferring with them about school problems and plans that they intend to be helpful and to wish good things for their children. The word *intend* has been used in this context because it expresses both will and caring; the root word *tend* is ambiguous and yet marvelously appropriate for expressing the positive attributes both of motivation and of genuine care and concern. Similarly, teachers deserve to be regarded as advocates for all children, but there is no chance for such regard and trust unless it is mutual.

Third, the teacher should listen to the parents. Professional people at conference time tend to err consistently on the side of assuming that they have most to communicate and should set the agenda. Too little time, usually, is left for listening to the parents. It is amazing what we do not know about children if we see them only in school, and it is genuinely important to listen and then listen some more to parents. They know a great deal about their children. Usually it is a different kind of information because it grows out of the special sensitivities of home and family and out of the unpredictables of the child's life instead of the regularities of school life; but it is extremely important information.

Fourth, the teacher should consider all alternatives with the parents. Sometimes professionals, in the process of assessing children and their school situations, will proceed to the point of making tentative plans and decisions, then ask essentially only for confirmation by the parents. For example, it might be decided that a child should go to a resource room for a period each day for help in reading; that a child will receive extra help in speech; or that a child is "not making it" in the local school and should be transferred to the behavioral learning center downtown—expecting that the parent conference will come to early focus on the preferred new arrangement. The point of view urged here is that it is no mere courtesy to back up a bit and involve the parents in discussion of all alternatives for planning. Rather, the observations of the parents and their views of the alternatives are essential elements in planning. If they lack information about some of the alternatives, then they should be given opportunities to learn about them—through visits; further conversation with people involved, professionals, other parents, or both; or readings—and the parents' choice of alternatives should be confirmed if at all possible, at least for a period of continuing study and planning.

Fifth, the teacher must expect criticism. Parents whose children are not responding well to school programs or whose programs are unusual and perhaps not well understood frequently are deeply apprehensive or frustrated. Sometimes they may have been more aware of the child's special and continuing needs for a longer period of time and in more detail than the current teachers of the child, and they may be tired of and disappointed about schooling in general. Teachers represent schools and sometimes become targets for the aggressions of frustrated parents.

Sometimes it works in reverse as well; that is, teachers may generalize their disappointments in parents of their community and aggress toward particular parents. It helps to anticipate the likelihood that, as a teacher, one will, more often than is comfortable, become the object of hostility and criticism. Usually, it need not be interpreted as a direct, personal attack, and often the negatives will erode and a turn will be made to a very good relationship if broad perspective is maintained and responses are made only to realities and constructive aspects of the situation.

Sixth, the teachers should not expect too much from one conference. Because conferences are often deeply emotional experiences it is unrealistic to expect a great deal of progress in any one discussion. Facing up to the learning problem of a child and talking through the anxieties and concerns about it can be a disabling experience for parents, an experience not always conducive to good listening or rational decision making. As situations become difficult, it is often wise to take a break for some time and to pick them up at a future conference. And when starting the succeeding conference it is probably a good idea to summarize what was discussed and agreed on at the earlier session(s). Memories of difficult conferences are often unsure, so that careful note taking, summarizing, and review are important.

Parent Groups and Mainstreaming

In implementing the "least restrictive alternative" or mainstreaming principle, we can expect the basic school enrollment of more children with gifts, talents, and handicaps to be in regular classes. However, many members of local associations of parents of exceptional children have had experience mainly with special classes and special schools. Thus, it should be anticipated that not all parent groups are well informed about, or fully supportive of, mainstreaming programs. Indeed, it is most likely that parent groups usually will be most supportive of the kinds of programs in which members' children are enrolled.

Parent associations are usually alert to mainstreaming trends and issues and they are active in formulating attitudes about such trends. Following is an abbreviated version of a report drafted by a committee of one local association (Minneapolis) for retarded citizens. It reflects the kinds of questions that are being raised by parent groups and the developments the local group would like to see in their community.

1. Question: *What does the word "integration" mean when it's applied to the education of students who are mentally retarded?*

    Answer: Integration of handicapped students usually refers to the placement of these students into the most "normal" educational settings that are possible in light of their particular abilities and disabilities. Integration could entail limited placement in regular classrooms combined with support services, or assignment to special classrooms or special wings of a school building. In the latter two cases, contact between handicapped and non-handicapped students could still occur during nonacademic activities like music, art and gymnasium classes and during lunch hours and recesses. The concept of integration calls for the maximum contact that is possible and still appropriate to the nature of the individual child's particular abilities.

Integration as well as "mainstreaming," as educators repeatedly point out, are *not* the "wholesale return of all handicapped students in special classes to regular classes." The concepts of integration and mainstreaming are flexible and are adjusted in each individual case to fit the needs and capacities of a particular child.

2. Question: *Can integration really benefit an exceptional child or would he or she be better off in an isolated situation with other handicapped children?*

Answer: It has been shown that handicapped children under appropriate circumstances can derive great benefits from integration into regular schools. Ten children who are trainable mentally retarded were brought together with non-handicapped children for music, phys-ed, and recesses during the 1972-73 school year in the Southview elementary school and made substantive advances in language skills and social awareness. It was found that the mentally retarded students began to model their behavior after the non-handicapped students. They became more concerned with their appearance and refined their adaptive skills.

Similar benefits have resulted in integrated programs for students who are trainable mentally retarded in various other states including Washington and Arkansas. School buildings in Tacoma, Washington, have been restructured to accommodate students of all abilities and disabilities. The Arkansas State Board of Education has directed that by the 1979-1980 school year all handicapped children in Arkansas should be educated in "regular classes, where possible" and in "special classes located in regular schools, where necessary."

3. Question: *Can an exceptional child receive services in a regular school that compare to those that are presently available in special schools?*

Answer: There can be no doubt that special schools...because of their size and the homogeneity of their population, are able to provide a vast array of services and a staff that is qualified in various special fields. The problem of providing such staff and services in a decentralized setting has been resolved in certain cases by the use of itinerant teachers: speech therapists, occupational therapists, physical therapists and others who travel between schools and spend a certain number of hours at each.

It is often the parents' option whether to place their child in an integrated setting with itinerant teachers, or whether to place him or her in a special station. While self-care skills might be developed to a greater extent in a more concentrated special station, the experimental programs in other counties have indicated that social skills are more likely to develop in a more "normalized" setting.

4. Question: *Will integration subject handicapped children to nonacceptance and teasing by other children?*

Answer: Teasing is a risk that almost all children incur in school, though non-acceptance or even ridicule are more likely and often more severe for handicapped children. To avoid such problems, the Southview elementary school, prior to integration of trainable mentally retarded children in Fall, 1972, prepared their non-handicapped students by teaching them about various types of disabilities. A "buddy system" was developed under which four non-handicapped children were chosen to work with each of the mentally retarded students, teaching them about games and at the same time instructing them in appropriate behavior. In larger settings and in the playground, it was the responsibility of the non-handicapped children to watch over the exceptional children and help them through difficulties. The buddy system proved extremely successful, and the handicapped children met with acceptance from most of the other students. When parents of the mentally retarded children took their kids shopping, they found that other students greeted and talked with their children, rather than staring as they had once been prone to do. Of course there can be no guarantee that all handicapped children will meet with this degree of acceptance. But if teachers adequately prepare their non-handicapped students beforehand, it is more likely that both handicapped and non-handicapped children will derive advantages from an integrated setting.

5. Question: *Will teachers be ready to accept handicapped children into their classrooms?*

Answer: This is a key question because so much of the success of an integration program will depend on the teachers' acceptance of handicapped children. Parents and educators seem to agree that the teachers' opinions and responses will be greatly affected by an inservice training received preparatory to integration of handicapped children. In the Southview elementary school teachers were shown films and were told about mental retardation and about the particular children who were going to enter the school.

The...Legislature endorsed this concept of inservice training and appropriated [funds] for pilot programs in inservice training for regular teachers in techniques of teaching retarded and mildly learning disabled children. An advisory council will be formed to recommend uses of these funds.

6. Question: *Is it financially possible to provide adequate staff and services for small numbers of handicapped children or is it only possible to have large facilities?*

Answer: It probably will be possible to provide programs in decentralized settings that are as adequately staffed as those in large facilities. Since state financial support for local school districts is based on essential school personnel, it should be as feasible to have a certain number of staff in one setting as it is in another. The Legislature has demonstrated its support for the hiring of special education personnel by increasing the state reimbursement to local school districts [for] special education personnel.

7. Question: *Will a teacher in a regular classroom be able to devote sufficient time to both her/his handicapped and non-handicapped students?*

Answer: It probably will be difficult for a person who is teaching music or art, for example, to both handicapped and non-handicapped students to devote sufficient time to all of the students. For this very reason, it will be essential in all integrated school programs to have adequate support staff. This supportive staff would take some of the pressure off the main teacher and provide supplementary assistance and attention to individual students. (Minneapolis Association for Retarded Citizens, 1976, pp. 3-5)

Parents of Nonhandicapped Children

The profound changes occurring in education for exceptional students call for broad understanding by all parents. Perhaps the least involved and most underinformed parents are those whose children are nonhandicapped. Such parents, however, increasingly are hearing reports of handicapped students in their "regular" classes, and more often, if they attend meetings of the PTA, they are hearing expressions of concern by parents of handicapped children.

Teachers and other school staff members must increasingly expect the need to interpret to parents of the nonhandicapped the changes occurring in programs for exceptional children. Most important of all, perhaps, is factual information on what is happening and why and help in understanding how the emerging programs provide new opportunities for all children to learn to appreciate human differences and to grow in understanding of how we can be mutually helpful to one another—with no exceptions.

Conclusion

Two current themes are increasing in strength, each reciprocally challenging to the other. Professionals who work with exceptional children must involve parents in the planning and provision of programs for their children; parents must learn to exercise their right to understand their child's diagnosis and the reasons for special treatment or educational placement. (Warfield, 1975, p. 559)

Warfield's comment puts the point of this chapter succinctly; we add only the important point about keeping all parents—including those who have nonhandicapped children—informed and involved in school affairs. These directions are new. There are clear responsibilities stated more boldly than ever before both for parents and professionals. And there is an urgency in the air that makes her use of the word *must* entirely appropriate.

PREVAILING VERSUS PREFERRED PRACTICES

As a brief summary there follows a set of contrasts between prevailing and preferred practices in areas of educational planning and involvement of parents.

Prevailing Practices

1. Planning for individual pupils is informal and nondocumented in terms of specific objectives and processes.

2. Educational plans are made strictly by professionals.

3. Responsibilities for implementing educational plans are relatively unspecified.

4. Disagreements about educational plans or placements are essentially decided locally by professionals—with no formal "hearings."

5. Children are examined by psychologists and other specialists by referral from teachers and principals.

6. School records are not reviewable by parents of children.

7. Most parent conferences with exceptional children are arranged by special education teachers and supervisors, social workers, or psychologists.

Preferred Practices

1. Individualized educational programs are drawn up recurrently and specifically for each child, listing specific objectives and procedures.

2. Educational plans are negotiated by professionals with students and parents.

3. Responsibilities for delivery on individualized educational programs are clearly specified.

4. All parties to educational plans for a child have a right to impartial hearings and appeals, if necessary, in case of disagreements.

5. Children and their school situations are assessed only on concurrence of school officials and parents.

6. School records of children are fully open to review by parents.

7. Most parent conferences with exceptional children are arranged to include regular teachers as primary participants.

SUGGESTIONS FOR STUDENTS AND INSTRUCTOR

1. Secure and review a copy of *A Primer on Individualized Education Programs for Handicapped Children,* published by the Foundation for Exceptional Children (Torres, 1977).
2. After reviewing materials of a "case" study, conduct simulated meetings to (a) develop an individualized education program, (b) a due process hearing, and (c) a regular teacher-parent conference.
3. Secure and review copies of materials used by local schools and your state department of education to inform parents of handicapped children concerning their rights to participate in the planning and monitoring on school programs for their children.
4. Interview parents of handicapped children who have been particularly active in implementing the emerging new policies concerning parental involvement in school planning.
5. Attend parent group meetings in your community, especially meetings that focus on the problems of school planning.
6. Secure, review, and criticize written individualized education programs prepared in your community. It should be possible to arrange with local special education administrators to see several programs that have had names removed and have been made anonymous.
7. Interview regular teachers who have been engaged in both preparation and implementation aspects of individualized education programs and get their views of what works, what is troublesome, and what could be improved.

TOPICAL BIBLIOGRAPHIES

The Psychoeducational Match

Cronbach, L. J., & Gleser, G. C. *Psychological tests and personnel decisions* (2nd ed.). Urbana IL: University of Illinois Press, 1965.

Cronbach, L. J., & Snow, R. E. *Aptitudes and instructional methods.* New York: Irvington, 1977.

Hunt, D. E., & Sullivan, E. V. *Between psychology and education.* Hinsdale IL: Dryden, 1974.

Hunt, D. E. Person-environment interaction: A challenge found wanting before it was tried. *Review of Educational Research,* Spring 1975, *45*(2), 209-230.

Merkin, P., & Deno, S. *Data based program modification.* Reston VA: The Council for Exceptional Children, 1977.

Nathanson, D.E. Designing instructional media for severely retarded adolescents: A theoretical approach to treatment interaction research. *American Journal of Mental Deficiency,* 1977, *82*(1), 26-32.

Individualized Educational Programs

Abeson, A., Bolick, N., & Hass, J. *A primer on due process.* Reston VA: The Council for Exceptional Children, 1975.

Jordan, J. B. (Ed.). Progress by partners in step. Special Issue on IEP. *TEACHING Exceptional Children,* 1978, *10*(3).

Sullivan, H. J. *Consideration in selecting and using instructional objectives.* Los Angeles: Instructional Objectives Exchange, Box 24095, Dept. B.

Torres, S. (Ed.). *A primer on individualized education programs for handicapped children.* Reston, VA: Foundation for Exceptional Children, 1977.

Weiner, B. B. (Ed.). *Periscope: Views of the individualized education program.* Reston, VA: The Council for Exceptional Children, 1978.

Parent Counseling

Egg, M. *The different child grows up.* New York: Day, 1969.

Kaufman, F. *Your gifted child and you.* Reston, VA: The Council for Exceptional Children, 1976.

Kroth, R. L. *Communicating with parents of exceptional children.* Denver: Love, 1975.

Kroth, R. L., & Scholl, G. T. *Getting schools involved with parents.* Reston, VA: The Council for Exceptional Children, 1978.

Kvaraceus, W. L., & Hayes, N. E. *If your child is handicapped.* Boston: Sargent Publications, 1969.

Schaefer, E. S. Parents as educators. In W. W. Hartup (Ed.), *The young child: Reviews of research* (Vol. 2). Washington DC: National Association for the Education of Young Children, 1972.

Southwest Educational Development Laboratory. *Working with parents of handicapped children.* Reston VA: The Council for Exceptional Children, 1976.

Media and Workshops

Cawley, J. D., Korba, W. L., & Pappanikou, A. J. *Special education placement: Issues and alternatives—A decision making module* (16mm film and manual). Reston VA: The Council for Exceptional Children, 1976.

Foundation for Exceptional Children. *Individualized education programs for handicapped children* (multimedia). Reston VA: Author, 1977.

Nazzaro, J. N. *Preparing for the IEP meeting: A workshop for parents.* Reston VA: The Council for Exceptional Children, 1979.

5. Giftedness and Talents
High Rate of Cognitive Development

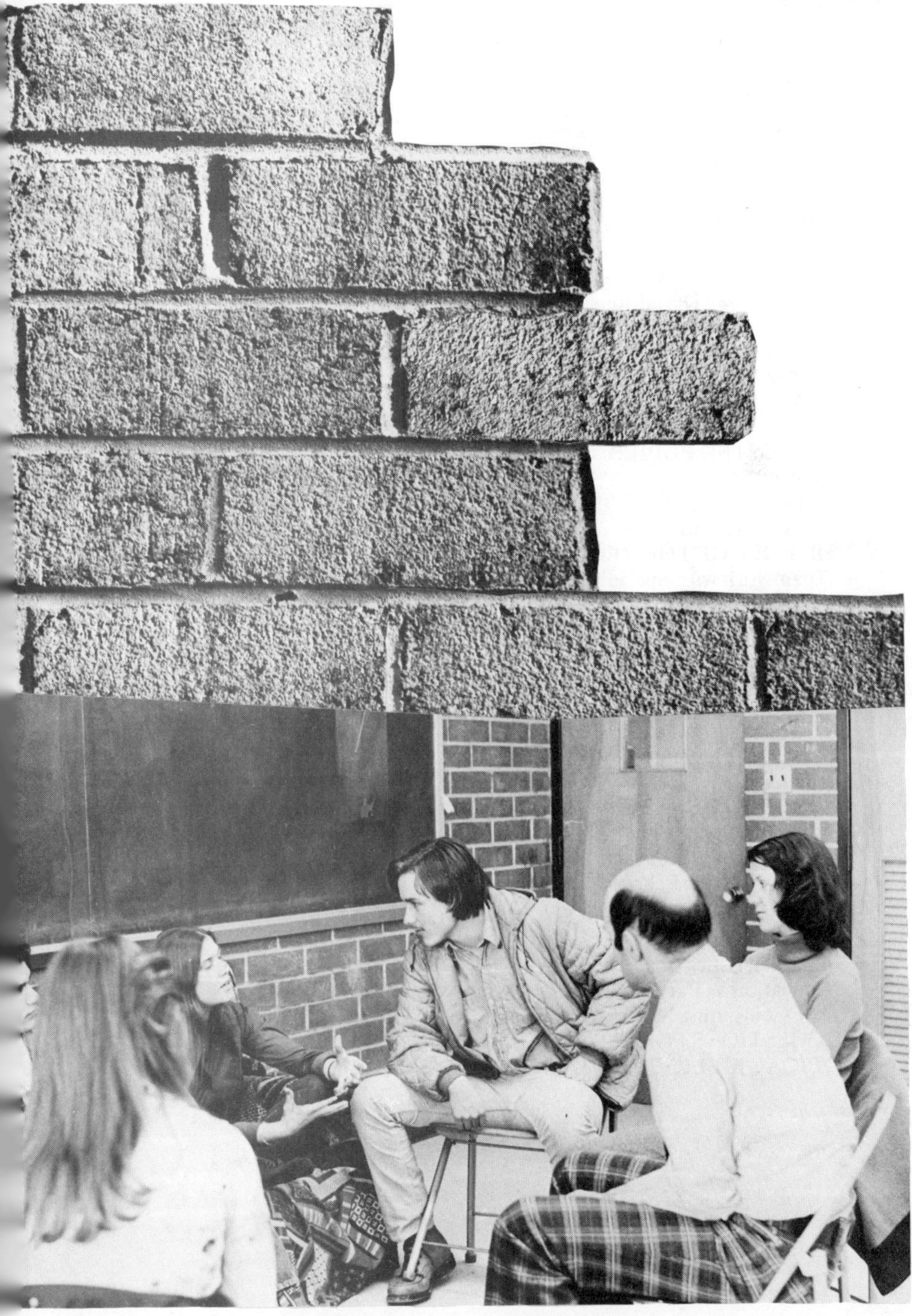

CHAPTER OUTLINE

THE CHALLENGE TO EDUCATORS
  Legal Considerations
  Medical Considerations
  Social Welfare Considerations
  Educational Considerations
  Emerging Changes in Terminology
  The Person Who Is Called Gifted or Talented
DEFINITION OF GIFTEDNESS AND TALENT
  Historical Perspectives
  Recent Approaches to Definitions
  Present-Day Definitions and their Applications
    Definitions
    Applications
    The Matrix Planning Chart
PREVAILING VERSUS PREFERRED PRACTICES
THE BEGINNING OF SPECIAL EDUCATION FOR GIFTED AND TALENTED PUPILS
  Recent Past
  Present Status
  Current Trends
THE ROLE OF THE REGULAR CLASS TEACHER
  Teamwork with Specialists
  Special Education in the Regular Grades
  Individualization of Instruction
    Curriculum Individualization
    Methods of Teaching
    Instructional Materials
    Organization for Instruction
    School Physical Plant
    Summary
EXAMPLES OF SPECIAL SCHOOL PROGRAMS
  Westside Community Schools, Omaha, Nebraska
  Three County Programs in Florida
  Executive High School Internships
COMPREHENSIVE PROGRAMING FOR PEOPLE WHO ARE GIFTED AND TALENTED
  Characteristics of a Comprehensive Education Program
  Education as Part of a Broader Group of Services
  The Continuing Need for Teachers
SUGGESTIONS FOR STUDENTS AND INSTRUCTOR
TOPICAL BIBLIOGRAPHIES

THE CHALLENGE TO EDUCATORS

What are today's gifted and talented children like? They certainly are different from one another and they certainly are not typical students. Yet they maintain more commonality with all the rest of their own generation, their parents and their teachers than might be expected by those who do not know them intimately.

This biographical sketch of a spectacularly gifted and talented student allows us to glimpse the many facets of one such person.

Harry Galanty

Harry Galanty is one of three children who grew up in the small brick house on 1474 Wessington Drive in Atlanta, Georgia.

He is a graduate of Grady High School, an integrated inner-city school, which was once known as Boys High and which once served the prominent young men from Atlanta's best families. Today, Harry is a freshman at Harvard on one of the College's 50 National Scholarships.

Twin sisters of Harry's, Carole and Diane, are sophomores at Georgia State University. Carole is concentrating on public relations and communications; Diane is not as definite in her goal.

Harry's father is a postal clerk, holding a job he has had all the years Harry and his sisters were growing up on Wessington Drive.

When Harry was nine and his sisters were 12, their mother died.

At 18, Harry—tall, thin (perhaps from missing too many meals while absorbed in a project), and wearing horn-rimmed glasses—looks the epitome of the student-scholar.

As Harry was growing up, no one at home urged him to learn or shaped and shared his academic life and goals.

"A student such as Harry Galanty refutes the belief that all academically gifted students come from verbal, high socioeconomic, academic-achieving backgrounds," says Margaret Bynum, education adviser for the Georgia Department of Education's Program for the Gifted.

"I didn't need home to learn," says Harry, "and I didn't need school to learn. I teach myself and I can do that anywhere. What I needed at school were the library for its books, the laboratories for my experiments, and the students and teachers for my social interaction."

By all measures, indices, and scales, Harry Galanty is a gifted student—a genius or near genius.

"We define students as gifted if their cognitive powers when developed allow for innovation, evaluation, problem solving, leadership, and/or coping effectively in the complex realm in which they live," says Margaret Bynum. "We expect about 3 percent of our students to fall into this category, with all of them scoring at least 1.3 standard deviations above the mean on a standardized test. On that basis, Georgia has an estimated 30,000 gifted students and the country has about 4 million."

"My greatest problem in the past was being considered one thing or another, a mathematician or a scientist or a genius," says Harry. "I hate the idea of being condemned to being one thing. I am seeking a balance now. In ninth and tenth grades, I was seeking to be a classical scientist; in eleventh grade, a mathematician; in twelfth grade, a poet; and now and in the years ahead, my goal is to be a simple human being.

"A simple human being has a balanced life, appreciates what others are doing, and accepts himself. No one is gifted at birth in becoming a simple human being. No one is born naturally happy with life. That is a real mountain to scale."

Two of his high school friends traced Harry's progression from excelling in only one area to seeking a balance in skills in all areas.

"I've known Harry since he was a ninth grader and I was a tenth grader," says Duke University sophomore, Neil Williams. "We were working on our science projects together and had a common interest. But he branched out into other things like computers and poetry and intricate math projects.

"No doubt Harry would have been an excellent student wherever he went to school, but Grady High has been a good place for him because he has been free to do research and to study on his own. He would have been like a robot in a school if he had been forced into a highly structured situation."

Randy Picklesimer, a freshman at Georgia Tech, has known Harry since they shared a ninth grade German class together. "I used to want to discuss far-out ideas, and no one would discuss them with me but Harry," says Randy.

"Harry used to feel that he was alone in his feelings. But now he is interested in literature, and it has given him a feeling that he is not alone, that he doesn't struggle by himself. After reading Ibsen, Strindberg, and T. S. Eliot, he is aware that others feel what he feels. He loves poetry. He is becoming aware of the universal nature of feelings."

Lewis Terman, pioneer in studies on identifying, testing, and educating the gifted, suggested several conditions for their education: Gifted students should work at their own pace, be accelerated beyond their age group, work independently much of the time, develop persistence and creativity, meet and work with other gifted students, and have ample access to guidance in reaching major decisions.

Grady High School's approach to scheduling Harry's work has included all of Terman's conditions.

During his academic career at Grady, Harry amassed some impressive honors and awards. His tenth grade science project, "Planetary Tidal Waves and Their Relation to Solar Flares," a computer-calculated project, was Grand Winner in the Atlanta Science Fair and First Place Winner in Geophysics at the International Science and English Fair in San Diego.

"In my 35 years of teaching," says Grady mathematics teacher Martha Barnes, "I have never taught a student more able or more personable than Harry. He not only won first place in geophysics at the Fair, but he was, in my opinion, the best-liked student there."

During the summer between tenth and eleventh grades, Harry went to Ohio State University, where he was honored as one of the top 25 mathematics students in the nation by the Mathematics Association of America.

"The 'Olympiad' at Ohio State brought together the brightest of the bright," says Mrs. Barnes. "Students took a special test to earn this honor, and Harry made it on his own. All he ever needed a teacher for was enrichment. He taught himself trigonometry, analytical geometry, integral and differential calculus, and computer science. He never scored less than 800 on the advanced math section of the College Board exam, and although he never had a formal course in physics, Harry scored 780 on the College Board exam in physics in tenth grade and 800 on that exam in eleventh grade."

"Analyzing the L Game" was Harry's eleventh grade science project, again an Atlanta First Place Winner and a First Place Award Winner at the International Science Fair held at Notre Dame.

Between eleventh and twelfth grades, Harry took part in the Georgia Governor's Honors Program, one of 400 advanced students in the state to attend. His area of excellence was mathematics. [See "Georgia's GHP" in the May 1973 issue of *Today's Education* for more about this program.]

Senior year brought additional awards and honors. Harry was elected co-president of the student body; achieved the top National Merit Score in Georgia; was STAR Student in the Atlanta School System; and was offered four full scholarships, accepting the one at Harvard.

Other significant achievements of Harry's high school career included attending the National Junior Achievement Conference at Indiana University for two years. One year Harry won Third Place for being an Outstanding Businessman. He also won a First Place Award for Public Speaking.

Deeply involved over the past two years with inventing his own words and concept families, a skill frequently associated with the academically gifted, Harry finds this new area of study his greatest challenge and the arena in which he may make his greatest contribution. Feeling like Leonardo da Vinci in that he senses himself to be the first to come to this questioning of the meaning and applicability of words, Harry has come up with a new philosophy and a new word system to describe it.

"*Essentialism,* my new philosophy which complements existentialism, comes down from the inner essence in response to the part of you that's always there; it has three principles—freedom, respect, and love," says Harry.

Involved in poetry as a means of expressing his philosophy and as a means of showcasing his new words, Harry is now writing "the poem of my youth" to personify his philosophy of essentialism.

Titled *Water, Earth, and Sky,* the poem uses 10 of Harry's new words, and he is interested to see if they will catch on. "The poem will make a big break with poetry," he says. "It will refer to itself, not other existing creations. It has its own mythology and will have very specific scientific passages."

> Appraising his own abilities, Harry sees himself as a *monoversalist*, one who has dreams in life and pursues those dreams, a person who takes the problems of life and works on them. Omniology will be the means Harry will use in his monoversalist approach to life. *Omniology,* the study of everything, is another of Harry's word inventions.
>
> "In terms of true learning, I plan to learn all my life," says Harry. "I know I could easily become a scientist and not much more. Maybe even a good one.
>
> "But I have a different picture of myself in the future. One of my next dreams is to travel from place to place. I feel homeless in myself. I feel everywhere is my home. I am trying to find a new path."
>
> Not all the gifted in our nation who attempt to travel a new path will travel it with quite the depth, brilliance, and range of Harry Galanty. Yet their success, as his, depends on how much freedom they are given to find themselves and their way and how much confidence they can maintain along the way to become, as is Harry's goal, a simple human being. (Murphy, 1976, pp. 29-30)

It should not be assumed that all gifted and talented children will find their own way and take good care of themselves. Certainly some have survived inadequate schooling with their natural capabilities largely intact and have, as adults, made enormous contributions to civilization's development and welfare. But even in those cases we do not know how much more the individual's gifts and talents might have flourished under better education. Moreover, we do know that a very significant proportion, perhaps three-fourths, of potentially gifted and talented persons do not attain the educational levels of which they are capable (Jackson & Boston, 1976).

Recently a US Commissioner of Education said:

> Studies show that gifted children in our schools today are locked in by structural and administrative restrictions that inhibit their development. They are denied open access to advanced materials, a cruel kind of censorship of the mind. They are unsatisfied in their mature concern about ethical and moral questions as well as in their intellectual pursuits. (Marland, 1972, p. 19)

The following example illustrates this problem: A 9 year old gifted pupil, already deeply interested in the comparative study of religions and their different guiding principles, did not have access to the high school library. It was miles away, and was not open evenings or weekends, and there were no provisions for elementary school children or their teachers to borrow from it. The youngster went to the public library in the company of a teenage sister, only to be told that the kinds of books wanted were classified "adult" and could not be withdrawn by a child. To use Marland's words, that pupil was "locked in by structural and administrative restrictions in the local school system and community and denied open access to advanced materials." The pupil could not satisfy a legitimate, "mature concern about ethical and moral questions," an integral part of any intellectual study of religions.

Torrance (1973) told of an artistically talented Black child whose graphic accomplishments, under the warm encouragement of an elementary school teacher, far outstripped academic achievement. The youngster's extraordinarily well done and botanically precise drawing of a flower was denied entry in a science contest. The reason: one of the school administrators did not believe that a pupil of limited academic attainments could produce such a picture without help.

As will be seen later in this chapter, there is no lack of information about sound ways to assure optimum educational opportunities for gifted and talented children and youth. The central problem for teachers and other educators is to dispel misunderstandings about gifted and talented individuals and to move what is known about the best ways to educate them from the relative obscurity of textbooks and journals into action in the daily life of America's schools. That is the challenge.

Why should teachers give attention to the challenge to provide high quality education for all gifted and talented young people? What makes it a matter that should claim any priority? To understand the responses to these queries it is first advisable to look at certain legal and medical factors. Also, there are reasons that have special meaning for society and for education, as an institution and as a profession. Finally, and most important, there are reasons that focus on the individual gifted or talented person.

Legal Considerations

Historically, the relationship of gifted and talented people to the law and the courts has been essentially the same as that of most other people. There were and are no factors intrinsic to them that would call for care, protection or any other form of monitoring by the courts. In fact, people who show a higher than usual rate of cognitive growth tend to be relatively free of legal involvements in any negative sense (Terman & Oden, 1947).

That status began to change, however, with the unprecedented consent agreement reached in response to the Pennsylvania Association for Retarded Citizens (PARC) suit in 1971. It mandated that, at public expense, all mentally retarded children between ages 6 and 21 be searched for and supplied with education suited to their needs. Following that mandate were requests that the same treatment be accorded other exceptional children, including the gifted and talented.

The right to education, with due process to be invoked to ensure it, began to spread across the nation. There is no doubt that the subsequent ramifications of the PARC suit against the Pennsylvania Department of Education and its secretary stimulated the development of a legal base for special education of gifted and talented individuals in at least two ways. It gave additional support in those states that already had specific provisions for this group in their school laws and it stimulated future oriented legislation and state board of education action in those states that had not moved earlier.

As an example, in 1956 Pennsylvania enacted a permissive provision that encouraged school systems to give special education to gifted and talented pupils. There was financial support from the state for those that did. But, as Schible (1975) suggested, under the new requirement for compliance by the Pennsylvania State Board of Education,

> . . .there will now be no excuse for school units to make such statements as "no such youngsters exist" or "we're already taking care of them within basic education." . . . Fortunately, as authorities have known for some time, much of value for high potential youngsters can take place within regular classrooms but, until the State Board Action there had often been no strong motivation for teachers to plan such provisions. (p. 22)

Federal legislation and planning, too, had begun to consider gifted and talented pupils in the broader context of special education program support (See Marland, 1971). Examples include the Elementary and Secondary Act Amendments of 1969 and Public Law 93-380 Section 404. Together with state laws and both state and federal court decisions and decrees, there is a growing legal substructure on which programs can build. Teachers in different states can determine just where their states are with respect to legal considerations and plan their own professional decisions and directions accordingly.

Medical Considerations

Until recently the chief medical interest in gifted and talented persons focused on their mental health. In the 17th century, Dryden wrote: "Great wits are sure to madness near allied, and thin partitions do their bounds divide." He bespoke the view of his day and that view can be traced to early Greek misconceptions of genius. Erroneously farfetched notions grew, linking mental illness with precocity and creativity until the end of the 19th century. The attitude is perhaps best summed up in this statement published in 1893 by a leading physician, Cesare Lombroso:

> The frequency of genius among lunatics and of madmen among men of genius explains the fact that the destiny of Nations has often been in the hands of the insane. . . . It seems as though nature had intended to. . .preserve us from being dazzled by the brilliancy of those men of genius who might well have been compared, not to the planets which keep their appointed orbits, but to falling stars, lost and dispersed over the crust of the earth. (p. 361)

Gallagher (1975) offered Lombroso's inaccurate conclusion as an example of why even the most penetrating and intensive clinical case observations need to be evaluated against a broad background of objective research. Had Lombroso looked more carefully at the published work of a contemporary, Francis Galton (1869), it might have tempered his confidence in what he felt was true. Galton's was the first recorded effort to study objectively the backgrounds and characteristics of a representative group of eminent persons. While such persons were not without defects, Galton's work found them to display a strength and integrity of character that outweighed any personality aberrations. Moreover, Lombroso might have found some fellow psychiatrists in truly violent disagreement with him. Karl Kraus, a contemporary of Freud, said:

> Nerve doctors who ruin genius for us by calling it pathological should have their skulls bashed in by the genius' collected work. . . . One should grind one's heel into the faces of all rationalistic helpers of "normal humanity" who give reassurance to people unable to appreciate works of wit and fantasy. (quoted in Janik & Toulmin, 1973)

The need for such passionate utterances diminished as the work of Terman and his associates became better known from its beginning in 1921 to date. It is clear now that gifted and talented people enjoy, on the average, not only better mental health, but also better physical health than the bulk of their contemporaries. That favored status was summarized in 1951 by Terman and Oden: "There is no law of compensation whereby the intellectual superiority of the gifted tends to be offset by inferiorities along non-intellectual lines" (p. 24).

Yet there are gifted and talented children and youth who require additional forms of special education because of additional exceptional conditions. These multiexceptional individuals are only now beginning to receive the added attention they need on a general scale. The story of Joe Hall, one such youngster, follows. It is presented at this point in the context of special education for children who show markedly accelerated cognitive capabilities. Later in this book it can be referred to again, when the special education of pupils with physical handicaps is the topic under consideration.

Prodigy From Plumtree
by Allen Rankin

When Jim and Judy Hall took their firstborn child, Joe, home to the peaceful Blue Ridge hamlet of Plumtree, N.C., ten years ago, they expected to settle down quietly. But the physiological mysteries that produce

---

Reprinted with permission from the August 1976 *Reader's Digest*. Copyright 1976 by Reader's Digest Association, Inc.

genius—indeed the miracle of life itself—swiftly changed all that. At 14 months, Joe sprang his first major surprise. Exploring the floor, he found and popped into his mouth a felt-point pen. To show him that pens were not to be eaten but written with, his mother wrote the letters a b c on a tablet. Joe took the pen and copied the letters in a remarkably good and steady hand. Judy Hall, not sure she had really seen what she thought she had, then wrote the whole alphabet. Her infant son, not to be outdone, copied that, too—every letter of it!

Soon Joe was writing the entire alphabet from memory. Well before he was two, he drew a very good picture of a cat and under it wrote c a t. "Look at that!" exclaimed an aunt, pointing out the feat to a visiting schoolteacher. "Yes, I see it," said the teacher. "But," she added, "of course he can't do that." This was to be a typical reaction to Joseph Hall performances. People refused to believe what they were seeing or hearing.

Toward the end of his third year, Joe was reading everything he could lay hands on, including a highschool science textbook. And he was asking a hundred questions a minute about his favorite subjects, space and electronics.

Pride and Alarm. Before long, he had discovered the piano, and was playing chords and harmonious passages. His father, who is band director for county high schools, put off giving him his first piano lesson until the morning of his fifth birthday. A few months later, the little prodigy had mastered the simpler works of Bach, Beethoven and Mozart, and was composing some rather elaborate music of his own!

By now Jim and Judy Hall's pride was tinged with genuine alarm. How could they cope with a child who was physically and emotionally five years old but already had the original and probing mind of an adult scientist-artist?

A psychologist friend told them that Joe might well become another Mozart or Einstein if he could get the *right* training in his formative period. But who knew what that was?

An educator suggested that they move to a big city that would have special programs for gifted children, concluding: "There's nothing in a little place like Plumtree for a boy like Joe."

The Halls disagreed. "There's nothing here for Joe," Judy argued, "except maybe his best chance to have a normal childhood. He'll have a long time to be smart, but not much longer to be a little boy."

Then, suddenly, it seemed that Joe's time might be shorter than anyone had thought. He had begun suffering from acute weakness and faintness. The diagnosis was leukemia.

Stunned, the Halls tried to keep the facts about the disease away from Joe, but he read up on leukemia and later even discussed the technical aspects of his treatment with Dr. Richard Patterson, head of the children's cancer program at the Bowman Gray School of Medicine in Winston-Salem.

One night, the five-year-old said to his mother, "I suppose my statistical chances don't look too promising, do they?" That night, and for many nights thereafter, he asked Judy to sit at his bedside and keep him company until he fell asleep.

Now the situation had changed. The Halls agreed that Joe must live and learn as much and as fast as possible. Like other parents of superkids, they soon found, however, that there is still comparatively little financial and psychological help for exceptionally gifted children.

Fearing that Joe, who longed to go to school, might not live to arrive there at age six, Judy wangled permission for him to "audit" the first grade at five. But Joe, by this time an eager student of astronomy, was bored nearly to tears.

Off the Scale. Judy managed to get him transferred to another school and skipped to the second grade. Joe loved his new teacher, Lola Young, who let him lecture the class on the wonders of planets and stars. And when the results of a standard intelligence test leaked out, the citizens of Plumtree, some of whom were hostile toward the "Know-It-All Kid," realized what a prodigy was in their midst. Most experts consider an I.Q. score of 175 or 180 an indication of top-level intelligence. Joe's score soared up the test scale, and he was assigned an I.Q. of 200!

"This means that in intellect this mountain child is probably far rarer than a one-in-a-million phenomenon," later commented Richard Stahl, director of the program for gifted and talented children at Appalachian State University.

Meanwhile, Jim and Judy Hall, who had long wondered why a boy like Joe had happened to *them,* were learning some interesting—if not too helpful—facts about giftedness:

• A gifted person might be described as an individual whose genes and control chemicals happen to arrange themselves in lucky patterns during his conception, and thus combine the highest abilities of parents and/or ancestors, enabling him to excel in the proper environment.

• Potential geniuses are often firstborn children (as was Joe) or are the offspring of at least one "older" parent (Jim had been 35 when Joe was conceived).

• Super-giftedness crops up in families of every walk, race or social stratum.

• When a child's brilliance soars to an I.Q. of 180, or more, he is likely to suffer from being "too different" and to be unable to fulfill his bright promise—*unless* he gets an accelerated education, is exposed to special enrichment programs at the normal grade level or is put in touch with minds as brilliant as his own.

Shadow of Leukemia. Joe's parents did all they could to make their gravely ill prodigy's days interesting. Further straining a budget weakened by medical bills, they bought him *some* of the books he begged for, the best chemistry set they could find and a splendid new grand piano. To make ends meet, Jim raised most of the vegetables and beef the family ate, and Judy canned hundreds of jars of produce.

Between spells of illness, Joe, at six, became a frequent pianist with the high-school bands his father directed. He won a county-wide talent contest with an impressive original composition titled "Five Thousand Miles of the Universe."

A reporter asked him, "What are you going to be when you grow up?"

"I don't know," the little boy replied, then added quietly, "I'm not sure I'm going to be anything."

Joe's sixth summer was bad. Sick much of the time, he was restless as a caged animal. He had exhausted the resources of the local library and was making constant demands for more reading matter than the family could possibly afford. Desperate, Judy hoisted an SOS to the Army, the Navy, the Air Force, NASA, the Atomic Energy Commission and The Reader's Digest. "Do you have any technical material you can send Joe?" she wrote. "Anything at all!"

A week later, an Army staff car pulled up at the Halls' door and three officers got out, staggering under the weight of 400 pounds of technical manuals on subjects from the space program to guerrilla warfare.

Joe was ecstatic and, for a while, so was his mother. "I thought that 400 pounds of stuff would entertain him all summer," she says. Joe went through it in three weeks. Reprints of scientific articles from The Digest and brochures from NASA and the AEC were also quickly exhausted.

In March 1975, Wernher von Braun, the rocket wizard, sent a copy of his book *History of Rocketry and Space Travel*. Delighted, Joe raced through the volume—and spied an error. "If that Saturn V had been powered by J-2 engines," he wrote von Braun, "it would never have gotten off the ground." The great scientist sent back thanks. "You detected a mistake that had crept through all the painstaking proofreading."

That summer, the Halls received a visit from another superbright young man—29-year-old Pat Gunkel, a researcher with New York's brainy Hudson Institute. "Talk?" recalls Judy Hall happily. "You should have heard those two talk! About galaxies and time and relativity and eternity. It was as though neither of them had ever had anyone to talk to before!"

A Place for Joe. About that time, his mother heard of a new School for Gifted Children sponsored by Appalachian State University, at Boone, just 39 miles from Plumtree. Offering college-like courses on six consecutive Saturdays, this enrichment program, limited as it is, fills such a local need that 580 of the smartest kids in nine surrounding counties, ranging from preschool to ninth grade, were enrolled. But Joe's mind, says director Richard Stahl, "was simply too far ahead of most of the others at the school. Exploding with a thousand things, he was an disruptive as a bomb in the classes he chose."

Looking for a place where Joe might fit in, Stahl took him to a regular college-sophomore class in astronomy. This didn't work out much better. "Wow!" said one college student. "He doesn't belong in sophomore astronomy. Put him in graduate school."

In the end, Joe, today age ten, returned to Plumtree. I met him there recently—a slightly built, plucky little boy whose wise blue eyes twinkle mischievously behind horn-rimmed glasses.

He confided his belief that flying saucers are real and are "manned" by robots. His gadget-cluttered room serves as headquarters for the

Joseph Hall UFO Research and Investigation Committee. The one-boy "committee" sends out a neatly mimeographed technical questionnaire to people all over the world who have reported sighting a UFO. He has received scores of completed forms from sighters—plus some 2000 letters from other precocious children or their parents.

Joe still has problems aplenty. Though he has skipped two years of school, he must endure a sixth-grade classroom that probably lags 10 or 12 years behind his learning capacity. That is, it lags in subjects he *likes*; in those he scorns as "unimportant," he's no better than his slowest classmates.

Still, despite this, Joe is as normal as any potential genius could possibly be. He loves to romp and whoop in the woods, to play baseball, to bedevil his three younger brothers and to be teased by them. He is explosively enthusiastic about his parents, his friends and his dog, Poochie. In other words, he is having a happy childhood and, as his mother notes, "Nobody can take that away from him."

Furthermore, Jim and Judy believe that if Joe had not had the extra drive, grit and zest for life that are the legacy of most superior children, he would not have won the fight, so far, against leukemia. Dr. Patterson adds, "Of the several hundred kids I've treated, Joe is one of eight or ten who have been in remission for five years or longer."

In comparison to this, any musings about whether he will become a great concert artist or an astronomer fade into insignificance. "Whatever the future brings," says Judy Hall quietly, "Jim and I have had Joe with us long enough to be forever grateful for that miracle, and for all the special wonder, joys and challenges he has already brought us." (pp. 54-58)

Teachers who instruct gifted and talented pupils need to be familiar, too, with special education for pupils with learning disabilities and behavior disorders, speech impairments, visual or hearing impairments, or other physical or health impairments. It will be necessary for teachers to accommodate the many gifted and talented pupils whose educational needs are complicated by the medical and psychological consequences of one or more of those conditions, too.

It has been pointed out by Mauser (1975) that gifted persons with other special educational needs sometimes find themselves to be paradoxes in society. On the one hand, they are underestimated because: "The extreme intellectual and special talents that they possess are often misled by society's sharp focuses on physical and social variation" (Mauser, p. 30). On the other hand, even when their intellectual prowess is recognized, architectural barriers and human prejudice sometimes combine to keep them out of training or jobs at which they would be very successful, if allowed.

The contemporary biographical sketch of Joe Hall, of Plumtree, North Carolina, calls sharply to our attention the comingling of difficulties and joys that can be found in a combination of physical illness and gifts and talents in the same little boy.

Social Welfare Considerations

All about us is evidence that America and the world needs its best minds and talents. The relatively high quality of life enjoyed by all regions of the nation has, as some of its essential ingredients, the planning, guidance, inventions, and creations in the arts and sciences, the sense of humor, and the sound moral-ethical positions characteristic of the country's wisest and most creative citizens. In industry, agriculture, government, and all the other sectors of the economy major problems need the continuing attention of our most capable and best educated specialists. The same is true for the more personal side of our lives, in friendships and marriage, and in such institutions as church and school.

The emergence of new knowledge and technology at a pace that outstrips our ability to assimilate and use it effectively, the shift taking place in our society from a work dominated to a leisure dominated national style of life—these are but examples of large emerging social changes that spawn multitudes of problems. Such problems, of course, affect everyone, and everyone can contribute in some way to their solution. It is the gifted and talented, however, who are best able to produce the grand designs needed to attack such large scale issues in ways that promise success.

In order to direct some of the creative, problem solving energies of these potential leaders toward society's needs they must be educated toward responsible attitudes toward their families, their communities, and their nation. They must be taught so they will grow in both social productivity and compassion toward others. Thus it is in society's interest that potentially gifted and talented children and youth be well educated both in content and in character, and that none of their capabilities be stunted, lost, or wasted because of weaknesses or omissions in their schooling.

Educational Considerations

Teachers, as members of the largest of society's "helping professions," are particularly aware of large tasks that confront them and of the relatively limited resources society allocates in support of the educational enterprise. It should be encouraging, then, to find that in 1976 a policy on the education of the nation's gifted and talented youth was stated by the US Office of Education, as follows:

> The United States Office of Education recognizes the need to assist States and school districts in providing quality education to meet the individual needs of all students. Commensurate with the overall purposes and objectives of education today, the U.S. Office of Education advocates educa-

tional services for those students who have demonstrated outstanding potential in a variety of fields.

In 1971, the United States Commissioner of Education in a special report to the Congress of the United States cites as a pressing educational problem the lack of differentiated educational services for the nation's gifted and talented youth. This is particularly prevalent in the educational services available to minorities and other disadvantaged populations. In response to this need, in 1972 the United States Office of Education established an Office of Gifted and Talented.

The primary responsibility for instructional programs and related activities in education rests with the states and localities.

It is our belief that increased attention on the part of all concerned: states and local education agencies, community and professional organizations, educational institutions, decision makers at all levels, representatives of specialized fields of endeavor, such as the arts, will help to effect a significant advance in delivery of educational services to the gifted and talented.

In view of these considerations, our policy is as follows:

1. The United States Office of Education recognizes the education of the gifted and talented as being an integral part of our educational system and supports the endeavors of all those who are involved in providing increased educational opportunities for these students.
2. The United States Office of Education is particularly interested in encouraging an investment by the private sector in a cooperative venture with the public sector for the purpose of providing needed specialized services to improve the quality and relevance of instruction for the gifted and talented student.
3. The United States Office of Education encourages states and school districts, wherever possible, within the administration of their programs, to consider actions which target upon the special needs of the gifted and talented population.
4. The United States Office of Education and its regional offices of education, in order to implement this policy, will provide technical and supportive services to state agencies, state and local institutions and all individuals interested in gifted and talented education.

This policy represents the position of the Department of Health, Education and Welfare, the United States Office of Education. (Trotter & Bell, 1976, p. 4).

Particularly noteworthy for all teachers are these points that can be derived from the policy statement.

1. The term *gifted and talented* is given official sanction to describe the special needs group under consideration.
2. The gifted and talented are students who have demonstrated outstanding potential in a variety of fields.
3. Differentiation of educational services is the process of choice to supply the help needed by the gifted and talented.

4. Minorities and other disadvantaged populations are specifically included as population sectors whose gifted and talented youth are to be served.
5. Cooperation and contributory investment are sought from all the nation's nongovernment sources.
6. Primary responsibility for implementing action is clearly with the states and local school systems, with the national role being technical assistance and support.

These points should help teachers clarify their own positions, both as individuals and as members of professional organizations. Also, the items might well give clues as to the major arterial pressure points in the body politic, national and state, when teachers, as individual citizens or as groups, wish to influence the directions their own profession and the larger society will be taking. Particularly relevant here are the comments by Marland and Torrance on pages 198 and 199, respectively.

The broad outline of educational considerations given so far will be further elaborated and detailed in later parts of this chapter. It will be seen that some of the things left unsaid in the Trotter-Bell Policy Statement are as important as those said.

Emerging Changes in Terminology

Teachers and other educators who start to explore the professional and academic literature on this topic encounter a profusion of terms. Expressions like *bright, high-IQ, superior, most able, genius, near-genius, highly intelligent, brilliant, mentally advanced, high achiever, major work, advanced placement, accelerate, creative, cognitive, divergent, eminent,* and others vie with each other for attention.

In an effort to maximize both readability and rationality we decided to let *gifted and talented* be our workhorse term. It has the virtue of broad contemporary usage in technical and professional publications. Also, it seems to us that it can be justified on theoretical grounds.

The popular understanding of *gifted* and *talented* seems to put the former more on the academic-intellective side and the latter more on the performing arts-creative side. It is actually the intent that both of those views be encompassed in the expression *gifted and talented* as we use it. There will be times when some of the other terms in the first paragraph of this section will need to be used because they are quotes from other writers. Also, we occasionally try to enliven a sentence by substituting a synonym where it appears likely not to be misleading. Generally, however, *gifted and talented* is our choice, and it will be defined operationally where it seems necessary in the context.

As to a rationale for the expression, it rests on our position that, for educators, cognition is the chief and central process that is implicated in differentiating gifted and talented persons from others (just as we considered cognition to play the same role in persons who are called mentally retarded). Influencing the rate of cognitive development, to be precise, is what we view as the essential concern of the educator.

Of all the components of cognition, the chief one that characterizes the gifted and talented is the heightened ability to manipulate symbols and particularly to manipulate *systems* made up of symbols. The most prevalent of such symbol systems are:

- *Oral words organized into a system called a language.* (The symbols are sounds to which meanings are attached.)
- *Written or printed words that represent the oral words.* (The symbols are groups of visible marks to which meanings are attached.)
- *Numbers, signs, and mathematical terms.* (Like written or printed words, the symbols are visible marks with standard meanings. They can also be pronounced and understood in oral form. The symbols taken altogether constitute a specialized and systematic form of language that can be understood in common by persons who use different oral language systems.)
- *Musical notations, signs, and terms.* (The symbolic structure and form has, in principle, the same characteristics as that of mathematics.)

These four symbol systems, namely oral language, printed language, mathematics, and music, are used by humans roughly in that order of frequency. Also, each one may be translated into each of the others.

Additional important visual symbol systems that may be less generally known are employed in sculpture, painting, the dance, the theater in general, and mime in particular. These symbol systems, somewhat like everyday human body language, may be more idiosyncratic and less tightly structured that the first four noted above.

The common quality called ability to manipulate symbolic systems, exemplified above, helps one to link the seemingly separate notions of giftedness and talent. The manipulations, also, are initially mental in all cases before they are transformed into oral words, writing, body movement, or some combination of the three. Thus, the painter, the writer, the mathematician, the dancer, the inventor, the poet, or the composer "thinks it through" or "thinks it out" as an essential early step leading to production.

Intelligence is, of course, more than simply the mental manipulation of symbols and symbol systems to some end. Intelligent behavior by an individual has to be understood as an expression of some level of cognitive development under conditions of awareness of intent and direction, of logical deduction and consistency, and it must be worthwhile in the view of the group affected (Wechsler, 1975). We take the position, though, (perhaps with Wechsler) that what we consider to be giftedness and talent is also a high degree of what intelligence tests *hope* to measure: "the capacity of an individual to understand the world about him and his resourcefulness to cope with its challenges" (Wechsler, 1975, p. 139).

Our concern, moreover, is not the assessment of capacity as an end in itself. Rather, it is *to help the teacher know where to begin work on the enhancement of cognitive development,* which is the major motive for any assessment. And that enhancement process, in our view, has common elements that cut across all gifts and talents. Gallagher (1975) said, "The ability to manipulate internally learned symbol systems is perhaps the *sine qua non* of giftedness" (pp. 10-11). We take that to apply across the board to what are, in ordinary usage, called giftedness and talent.

The Person Who Is Called Gifted or Talented

Even more important than society's claims under American democracy are the rights and welfare of the individual. Gifted and talented children and youth are sufficiently different from most in creative and intellectual potentialities that self fulfillment for them often requires adaptations and adjustments in the usual educational fare if they are to attain full personal development. Their interests, skill development, and knowledge stretch beyond typical curricula. Individual self actualization, healthy self concept, realistic self understanding, opportunity to develop at one's potentiality—these are the kinds of overriding educational rights implied for all children in federal and state constitutions and statutes. To make them explicit for gifted and talented pupils, however, is an important obligation that has yet to be responded to fully in most parts of the United States. Until that is done, not only is society the loser, but also the gifted and talented of the nation are being denied full citizenship. Happily, there is much progress being made toward remedying past neglect of the education of gifted and talented children and youth.

DEFINITION OF GIFTEDNESS AND TALENT

Some manifestations of giftedness have been acclaimed for centuries. They include leadership in government, exploration, navigation and prowess in arms, feats of athletics, literary achievement, acting, musical composition and performance, scientific discovery, invention, and other worthy kinds of behavior. Persons displaying these characteristics to an outstanding degree are listed among the world's most honored citizens, now or in the past. In view of that, Paul Witty (1953), one of this country's most significant educators concerned with gifted children and youth, offered in 1953 this definition of a gifted child: "any . . .whose performance, in a potentially valuable line of human activity, is consistently remarkable" (p. 256). Other definitions, to be discussed later, take different forms. But before turning to more recent (though not necessarily better) definitions, it might be valuable to take note of some historical background and some fallacious beliefs that have clouded the concepts of giftedness and talent.

Historical Perspective

One of the most persistent untruths about eminent women and men is that they were indifferent scholars as children. Perhaps some were, but the general rule holds that the potential for adult greatness shows itself in the early years. If one were to look for evidence of that among outstanding painters, it could be found in the Picasso Museum in Barcelona, Spain. An unusually complete record of the painter's work as a child and as a teenager vividly shows the extraordinary mastery of techiques plus early evidence of the creative imagination that the whole world came to admire during his mature years.

The story that Winston Churchill was a poor student as a boy may have long comforted some British schoolboys, but it was thoroughly debunked in 1975. Churchill attended Stoke Brunswick, a junior school, from 1884 to 1888. John Bartlett, the headmaster, found old reports and letters that showed the young Winston to have been quite bright. Bartlett is quoted as saying:

> It gave Sir Winston some amusement to pretend in his later life that he had always been bottom of his class, but it was certainly not true. Our contemporary records show he worked hard and that he had very real ability. In his last year he was top in every subject except geography, in which he came in second. (*International Herald Tribune,* Dec. 1, 1975, p. 14)

Wherever objective data have been available for impartial examination, the popular but unwarranted notion that outstanding leaders were poor achievers as youngsters has been refuted. Teachers, particularly, can find such erroneous beliefs cropping up frequently during interviews with parents and other persons in the community who are not familiar with the consistent superior achievement shown by highly able students when they are under good educational direction.

Another false conception holds that most children and youth who display superior achievement are "flash in the pan" performers. The most telling evidence on this point is the mass of data reported by Terman and Oden (1959). Terman and his associates located 1,000 elementary school children with individual Stanford-Binet intelligence quotients of 140 or higher. They were first contacted in the 1920's in California. Followup studies continue to this day, with few having been lost. Now mature adults, these "early bright" individuals have enviable records of accomplishment in subsequent education, in the arts and sciences, in business, in the professions, and in the quality of their personal and family lives. The flash of creative intelligence, ingenuity, and social consciousness, once lighted, tends to burn with a steady flame.

The single talent concept is another common fallacy. It is applied to suggest that a great mathematician, for example, can be expected to be childishly simple about the challenges of everyday life. Or it might be said of great artists that they are wanting in practical abilities. There are gifted individuals, it is true, who become known for their tremendous capabilities at particular pursuits. The vast majority of them, however, are well rounded people, though their public images are sometimes lopsided because it is their major interests that are most often presented to the world.

Leonardo da Vinci is one well known exception to the single talent concept, since his breadth of interest and activity was recorded and widely acknowledged. Varied capabilities in the same gifted and talented person are the rule, not the unusual case.

Another artist, an example of a multitalented person, Diego Rodriguez DeSilva y Velazquez (1599-1660), was studying painting by the time he was 10 years old and began a formal apprenticeship at age 12. By the age of 18 he was beginning to establish himself as a known painter in Seville. By age 24 he was a widely heralded artist, and he remained creative and productive until his death at age 61. A little noted fact that is important here is that Velazquez was also one of the most able and effective administrators in the Spanish Court, being Grand Chamberlain of the Palace of Philip IV, with major management responsibilities that cut across all state matters and even foreign affairs.

The richness of Thomas Jefferson's gifts and talents are familiar to many Americans. Architect, writer, politician, government administrator, philosopher—this array of achievements speaks again to the breadth that can be expected from such exceptional persons.

The eminent Swiss psychologist, Jean Piaget, was interested in natural history before psychology. In 1907 at the age of 10 he had an article published in a journal of natural history. It dealt with an unusual Albino sparrow. A few years later his writings about mollusks excited the attention of the director of the Geneva Museum of Natural History. There was a vacancy on the museum's staff. Inquiries were initiated to determine if this very able young scientific writer might be interested in the post of curator of the mollusk collection. Imagine the museum director's surprise when it was discovered that the curatorship was being considered for a schoolboy then 14 years of age.

Fortunately for psychology, a few years later Piaget became an assistant to Theodore Simon in the Binet Laboratory in Paris. His interests moved toward psychology, particularly learning and language development, and their relationships to biology. His developmental concepts of intelligence have made him one of today's giants in the science of psychology.

Another mistaken idea that has been hard to lay to rest is that gifted and talented persons, if not actually mentally ill, do tend to be odd. Certainly mental illness does occur among all parts of society, and there are eccentrics in every sector of life. But both longitudinal studies and cross sectional studies (Terman & Oden, 1947, 1959) demonstrate that gifted and talented persons are generally more stable in their emotional lives than the population as a whole.

Why are such false notions so widely held and so difficult to refute with success? Only speculation can be offered in answer to that question. Perhaps the general population is uncomfortable at the thought of a group of persons who are *generally* superior in physique, mentality, and emotional and social stability and adaptability. It might be easier to live with the concept that a high capability is usually balanced by a deficiency in another capability.

Teachers need to know about these fallacious beliefs and how to combat them. In many situations those ideas and others like them may need to be answered by facts in order to allow educational programs for gifted children and youth to develop. Lack of accurate knowledge about what education is most useful for gifted pupils is probably the most common deterrant to instructional program development for them. And that lack of knowledge on the part of the general public, gifted persons themselves, board of education members, and some educators, too, can be further clouded by prejudices of the kinds described.

Recent Approaches to Definitions

With the bewildering array of accomplishments the term *gifted and talented* brings to mind, it is no wonder that a satisfactory definition has been slow to emerge. Attempts to find commonly acceptable meanings for the terms have been complicated, too, by misconceptions such as those described before.

From our point of view, as we have said earlier, gifts and talents are primarily manifestations of a high rate and quality of cognitive development that has been cultivated richly and systematically. That conception puts the fostering of gifts and talents equally in the domain of the teacher, since the advancement of cognitive growth is major and central among teachers' responsibilities.

As a start toward understanding existing definitions as they have been proposed by respected authorities, three points about terminology are of fundamental importance to teachers and other educators. First, as they are used in education, the expressions *gifted* and *talented* are future oriented. Teachers may work with pupils who are capable of high achievement in school, encouraging the pupils to maintain or improve that achievement. But usually not until those pupils are in their late teens or early twenties will there be much solid evidence that they show gifts and talents that meet contemporary adult world standards. There are a few exceptions to that rule, particularly in the dance, swimming, acrobatics, and figure skating, where extraordinary motor skill, stamina, purposefulness, and grace sometimes combine with fine teaching to allow earlier world acclaimed performance. Apart from such exceptions, however, teachers in programs for gifted and talented pupils are working with youngsters who they believe *act like they will become* the leaders of their and later generations. Thus, teachers are judging that selected pupils have the *potential* for gifted or talented performance as adults. The special education given to those pupils is designed to enhance that potential—in short, to help the *predicted* future of each such pupil become a reality. The futuristic orientation noted here helps to account for the futuristic tone found in many definitions of giftedness and of talent.

Second, giftedness or talent is a social judgment, reflecting what a particular society or culture values most highly at a particular time. The person who produces what society values most highly, is almost without doubt going to be considered eminent in comparison with others. Those among the eminent whose productions are also most influential in solving society's problems and in setting new directions for cultural and scientific and social movement will tend to be later identified as geniuses. Thus, giftedness and talent are evidenced in what an individual does and in what reactions that product causes in others. A well reasoned, modern view of the meaning of *genius* is

> anyone who. . .produces, over a long period of time, a large body of work that has a significant influence on many persons for many years; requiring these people, as well as the individual in question, to come to terms with a different set of attitudes, ideas, viewpoints, or techniques before all can have "peace of mind," that is, a sense of resolution and closure.
>
> The work associated with this person must be presented to others, for their use and evaluation; it is a public work and takes other talented men and women years to understand, to implement, and equally important, to surpass. It is others' *necessary* effort that makes up the basic thrust of this person's impact. Others often spend their own careers working out the implications of this work, for in the end they must come to terms with it. It is this aspect that is so important, whether it is wanted by others or predictable.
>
> Acknowledgement usually occurs through the work being referred to often and being explicitly incorporated in others' work. The individual most responsible for the work receives institutional awards, for example, the Nobel Prize, and lastly, . . . becomes the object of archival interest, first within a profession and . . . eventually among a wider, interested lay public (evidenced in popular and "serious" biographies).
>
> The key ingredient to genius is productivity—large in volume, extraordinary in longevity, more or less unpredictable in content. The impact of the work is dislocation or sudden reorganization constituting a major shift,

that is, productions of "originality" rather than of reasonable extension. (Albert, 1975, pp. 140-151)

The third point is that there are differences in the degree to which gifted and talented persons turn out to be productive and influential. (That may have been inferred already from the preceding paragraphs.) There have been serious efforts to link the aptitudes and achievements shown by preschool and school age children with their later productivity. Individually administered intelligence tests, particularly the Stanford-Binet Intelligence Test and the Wechsler Intelligence Scale for Children (WISC), prove to be the most helpful instruments for that purpose. There is more than enough evidence that these tests, used by trained examiners, can locate the great majority of potentially gifted and talented children in the general population of children as early as 3 years of age, and with even greater precision by ages 5 to 7. With somewhat less accuracy, the differences among the children in later school achievement are positively related to the scores attained on the tests. When relatively wide differences are compared (i.e., children with 120 IQ, with 140 IQ, and with 180 IQ), significant differences in school and postschool achievements are reliably predictable, too. Thus, there is an empirical base for the inclusion of references to individual intelligence test findings that are found in some definitions of giftedness and talent.

Eight definitions published since 1950 will be discussed in what follows. They illustrate the several approaches teachers can expect to encounter as they gather background to help them understand and plan educational programs for gifted and talented pupils.

Psychometric definitions make specific reference to tests or to cutoff points in terms of percentages or intelligence quotients, though they may also refer to other attributes without indicating how they are to be quantified or what the criteria are for establishing their presence.

The American Personnel and Guidance Association, in 1961, gave this definition:

> The academically talented student is one who receives scores of about 115 or over on a Stanford-Binet Intelligence Test or falls above a similar point in one of the Wechsler Intelligence Scales. (cited in Love, 1972, p. 35)

Fliegler and Bish, in 1959, proposed this:

> The term gifted encompasses those children who possess a superior intellectual potential and functional ability to achieve academically in the top 15-20% of the school population; and/or talent of high order in such special areas as mathematics, science, expressive arts, creative writing, music and social leadership; and a unique creative ability to deal with their environment. (Quoted in Newland, 1976, p. 9)

These two definitions, both basically quantitative, show the range of definiteness-indefiniteness with which the quantitative approach can be expressed. Each extreme carries problems with it when practical applications are considered.

Definitions derived from psychological characteristics tend to specify particular traits or behavior patterns presumed to separate gifted and talented pupils from other pupils.

The Educational Policies Commission promulgated this trait based definition in 1950: "The gifted is one who has a high order of ability to handle ideas, to produce creatively, and to demonstrate social leadership" (quoted in Love, 1972, p. 36).

A definition by Lucito (1963) said that the gifted are:

> Students whose potential intellectual powers are at such a high ideational level in both productive and evaluative thinking that it can be. . .assumed they could be future problem solvers, innovators, and evaluators of the culture if adequate educational experiences are provided. (Quoted in Wisland, 1973, p. 308)

In 1964, Durr said,

> The gifted student is likely to have: above average language development; persistence in attacking difficult mental tasks; the ability to generalize and see relationships; unusual curiosity; a wide variety of deep interests. (Quoted in Love, 1972, p. 35)

Definitions such as these refer to individual characteristics that are open to many different interpretations. Teachers and others, including psychologists, recognize in almost all children almost every one of the qualities named in the definitions, at least to some degree and in some form.

Definitions conditioned by social need are exemplified by that of Witty, quoted earlier, and Newland's (1976) statement. Newland started from

> the assumption that if x percent of the present (U.S.) working population were involved in high-level roles, the schools were obligated to regard at least that percentage of the general school population as needing to be prepared to fulfill those kinds of roles. (pp. 12-14)

Newland's definition also differentiates between (a) those children termed gifted, with the greatest potential for conceptualizing, giving them the assignment of filling society's highest levels of responsibility, and (b) those children dubbed talented, whose greatest strengths are in other intellective activities more related to physique, emotions, and leadership. The proportion of all children designated for special education by Newland's formulation is a quantitative response to social need, estimated in 1976 as the most apt 8%. That calls for an intelligence quotient cutoff of 120 to 125. While the definition includes a psychometric quantification for purposes of implementation, Newland's approach, like that of Witty, is grounded in social need.

Educationally oriented definitions include an acknowledgment of high learning potential, but they focus on the distinctive qualities of schooling that are important to gifted and talented pupils. Fair put it this way:

> The talented child is a pupil with an especially high potential in one or more specific areas, whose potential cannot be adequately developed without special provision with the curricular, extra-curricular, and counseling programs. (Quoted in Love, 1972, p. 38)

Gallagher (1975) offered a very specific definition that is pointedly focused on education:

> Gifted and talented children are those identified by professionally qualified persons who by virtue of oustanding abilities are capable of high performance. These are children who require differentiated educational programs and services beyond those normally provided by the regular school program in order to realize their contribution to self and society.
>
> Children capable of high performance include those with demonstrated achievement and/or potential ability in any of the following areas:
>
> 1. General intellectual ability
> 2. Specific academic aptitude
> 3. Creative or productive thinking
> 4. Leadership ability
> 5. Visual and performing arts
> 6. Psychomotor ability (p. 10)

Gallagher's definition considers high ability, social contribution, and personal development, while holding differentiated educational programs and services in the center of attention.

A final example of an educationally oriented definition is found in recent federal legislation. Section 404 of Public Law 93-380 provides a program of grants and contracts to support the education of gifted and talented children. On May 6, 1976, the rules and regulations for these grants and contracts were published in the *Federal Register*. For purposes of this Act,

> "Gifted and Talented" means children and, where applicable, youth who are identified at the preschool, elementary, or secondary level as (1) possessing demonstrated or potential abilities that give evidence of high performance capability in areas such as intellectual, creative, specific academic, or leadership ability; and (2) needing differentiated education or services (beyond those being provided by the regular school system to the average student) in order to realize these potentialities. (Sec. 160b.2[c])

Identification must be accomplished by the use of multiple methods. "No child shall be denied entry into a program or project on the basis of only one method of identification" (Sec. 160b.3[b] [iii]). The rules and regulations cover a variety of programs including information services; planning, development, operation, and improvement of programs; training of state and local educators; leadership personnel training; and model projects.

Present-Day Definitions and Their Applications

Definitions

The various approaches discussed here have all made important contributions. That is illustrated by their continued appearance in the definitions now in use in school systems.

Contemporary definitions, though, include some factors not mentioned earlier and they go into more detail about other factors. For instance, cultural differences, language differences, socioeconomic differences, family differences, physical differences, and other differences are acknowledged in the newer definitions. So, for instance, are distinctions among measures of creativity. For example, when Gourley (1976) analyzed 113 programs across the nation, he found 178 identification instruments and procedures in use. He found "the term 'gifted' to mean 'outstanding or exceptional ability' in the areas of intelligence, creativity, leadership, psychomotor performance and the fine and performing arts" (pp. 31-32).

Another feature of present-day definitions is the move away from the effort to make them universal—one definition applicable in all the nation's schools. Instead, it is being urged that each school system develop its own operational definition, so long as it is within the range of relatively broad state guidelines. There are, for example, substantial differences from state to state in the proportion of the school population recommended for inclusion in specified programs: California, 2%; Connecticut, 5%; Georgia, 3%; North Carolina, 10%.

Minority groups represent another important variable that impinges on definition, identification, and program planning. Valuable insight regarding this variable is emerging from such studies as that of Reyna and Bernal (1976) in which they "approached the study of giftedness as perceived by the Mexican Americans themselves" (p. 9). They wanted to "discover the group's values, definition of talent, and productive goals" (p. 9). Admittedly an exploratory study, it nonetheless gave useful preliminary data which suggests that localized operational definitions have a significant part to play in mediating between state guidelines and the day to day activities of the schools themselves.

Most important, the beginning of program planning itself is encouraged concomitant with or even prior to the establishment of local definitions, so the two can interact. The hoped for result is to achieve a fit between the kinds of special education programs a school can mount and the nature of the gifted and talented children to be served by the programs.

In-service training of teachers and of other educators ought not to be separated from the determination of the character of the specialized programs to be offered or from the determination of which pupils would take part. Thus we see the current trend to link all components of program development rather than to try to deal separately with the definition problem, as has been the case up to now. This fits well within the Aptitude/Treatment Interaction formulation we consider fruitful for instruction.

Teachers who take part in planning for and who instruct gifted and talented pupils in their classes will be influenced most in their day to day work by the definitions promulgated through their state and local education agencies. It will be increasingly important, too, that teachers themselves take active roles in writing those definitions. That is why the history and background is important for teachers. That is also why a concrete example is given below of a definition cast in operational form—a model definition from which teachers and other educators may draw support and ideas as they contribute to the overall design and implementation of programs in their state, regional, and local school systems. This definition is drawn from the North Carolina regulations.

> A child who is gifted and talented is one who falls within the upper ten percent in the total school district on intelligence tests, achievement tests, and/or scales that rate behavior characteristics. This child has academic talent and generally performs above average in his classwork and/or may demonstrate a special talent in areas such as creativity, communication, leadership, decision making, forecasting and planning, as indicated by the use of behavioral scales and checklists. Consideration must be given to the ethnic composition of the pupil population. (North Carolina State Department of Public Instruction, 1976, p. 16)

Before moving on to see how that kind of definition can be put to use, it should be noted that it is quite specific with respect to pupil characteristics, the use of tests, and attention to ethnic differences. Moreover, the 10% figure is an outer limit, not a set requirement. Local schools, therefore, may have programs involving less than one-tenth of the total pupil enrollment. As the implementation of the definition is illustrated next, it will be seen that the local schools, and the teachers and others who plan and take part in the local identification process, have great flexibility as to how they proceed, so long as they attend to the general guidelines.

Applications

In searching for pupils who are potentially gifted and talented it is our recommendation that every reasonable means be employed. It is true that some ways have been shown to be more efficient and more effective than others (Pegnato & Birch, 1959). When experts were asked, they recommended the following tools, in this order of preference:

1. Individual intelligence test scores
2. Earlier achievements, including academic record
3. Teacher nomination based on observations
4. Standardized achievement test scores
5. Scores on creativity tests
6. Scores on group intelligence tests.

All of these six procedures received a favorable vote from at least 65% of the experts. The two leaders received a 90% and a 78% endorsement, respectively.

A key point to hold in mind is that there is a constant danger of letting the *tools* one uses to locate the children become synonymous with the *definition* of gifted and talented. That can be avoided only if teachers and others hold fast to the position that *they study and interpret what data the tools provide* rather than take the data at face value and use them in connection with hard and fast cutoff points. The final word as to whether a pupil is to be provided with a special education program should be made by the responsible teachers and other professional educators. The decision should be based on their objective and subjective appraisal of the pupil, the nature of the special educational program or activity contemplated, the atmosphere in which the pupil lives and goes to school, and the interactions among them. Parents should be included in discussions and should be advised of the educators' recommendations. That calls for professional judgment that makes use of test results and other data, rather than allowing the decision to be made by the data's relation to such arbitrary, preset points as specific scores or grade averages.

The Matrix Planning Chart

The following discussion of the matrix planning chart was adapted with permission from a bulletin by Tongue and Sperling (1976). It was produced under the auspices of 3 State Educational Agencies—Kentucky, Louisiana, and North Carolina. Those 3 states were operating in the context of a consortium of 10 states, the others being Alabama, Florida, Georgia, Mississippi, South Carolina, South Dakota, and Wyoming. Thus there is a broad base to the definition and identification process described below. It was possible for the member states to bring together nationally recognized leaders for advice and consultation. While all consultants and participants took part directly or indirectly, Tongue and Sperling give principle credit to Dr. Francis Williams of Salem, Oregon, for formalizing the "matrix" concept employed.

Organization of the matrix planning chart. Along the horizontal axis of the matrix planning chart for identification procedures (Figure 5-1) the matrix is divided into three broad categories: test data, performance data, and developmental data. These categories have been subdivided into specific procedures. Along the vertical axis are listed five categories:

1. *Academic/intellectual*—High academic aptitude and/or achievement in one or more fields of study.
2. *Artistic/expressive*—Visual and/or performing arts.
3. *Leadership/psychosocial*—High level of leadership, social and communications skills, and superior moral judgment.
4. *Divergent production/processes*—Advanced insight, outstanding imagination, innovative or creative reasoning ability, problem solving ability, and original and productive thinking.
5. *Kinesthetic*—Manipulative skills (sculpture, mechanics), expressive and artistic body movement.

Use of the matrix planning chart. The identification process should include procedures from each of the three horizontal categories. Program goals will determine which vertical categories are used.

If intelligence tests are to be used, individual measures such as the Stanford-Binet or the Wechsler Intelligence Scale for Children, which sample many aspects of cognitive development, are the best. Martinson (1974) said, "The Stanford-Binet is the best identification currently available" (p. 1). Thorndike (1975) said that the Stanford-Binet is the most stable over the years, having been revised in 1937 and 1960 and renormed in 1972.

With children who do not handle language well or who are from other than the dominant culture, educators must look to behavior correlates (attention span, perseverance, curiosity, energy, etc.) and behavioral scales and checklists. Some of the other forms of tests named in the matrix are applicable here.

Many bright pupils are diligent workers and high achievers. They obviously enjoy the challenge of learning; they are eager to attack new tasks; and they are fairly sure of themselves. These qualities call many gifted and talented children and youth to the favorable attention of teachers. Perhaps two-thirds to three-fourths of these youngsters can be identified in the first pass of teacher nominations, based on observations in elementary and secondary schools.

Teacher nomination, though, useful as it is, needs to be buttressed by other procedures because of three soft spots. Teacher nomination, by itself, tends to overrefer; it misses a significant number of pupils who should be referred, and it does not indicate very well *how* gifted and talented identified pupils might be.

The overreferral comes about when individual, well motivated, hard working children of average or a slightly better cognitive development

222 / Teaching Exceptional Children in All America's Schools

FIGURE 5-1
Matrix Planning Chart for Identification Procedures

Key
X — The prevalent culture gifted student
O — The culturally different gifted student

	Test data							Performance data					Developmental data
	Intelligence	Achievement	Creativity, divergent thinking	Aptitude	Divergent feeling	Biographical inventory	Culture free	Grades	Demonstration of skills	Teacher and/or other school personnel	Peer	Parent	Self	Case studies, anecdotes, biographical data and interviews
										Nominations, checklists, scales				
Academic/intellectual	X	X	XO	XO		X	X		XO	X	XO	XO	XO	XO
Artistic/expressive			XO	O	X	XO			XO	XO	XO	XO	XO	XO
Leadership/psychosocial				X		XO			XO	XO	XO		XO	XO
Divergent production/process			XO	O	X				XO	XO	XO	XO	XO	XO
Kinesthetic				X					XO	XO	XO	XO	XO	XO

are included in the teacher nominations because of their diligence, good achievement, and constructively striving behavior. Such students deserve commendation, but they do not usually require additional individualized special educational programing.

Teacher nomination misses one-fourth to one-third of the potentially most able, according to individual intelligence tests. That significant group is made up of pupils whose school performance is less than remarkable because they are unchallenged, unconcerned, and uncertain of themselves. They are unnoticed and undertaught. It is easy to see why teachers might not nominate them in searches for gifted and talented students; their limited school productivity would disguise their real capabilities.

Then there are also real, educationally important differences among mentally advanced pupils in their rates of cognitive growth. Two gifted and talented pupils, each performing in school in an equally outstanding fashion, may be extremely different in the degree to which their potentialities are being developed. One may be matched to an appropriate set of learning activities. The other may be partially matched, floating along easily, learning to be comfortable while remaining relatively unproductive. If the procedures used to locate gifted and talented pupils provide data on their individual differences in speed of cognitive growth, the pace of instruction can be individually adjusted more readily.

Checklists to focus teacher attention on particularly significant behaviors of gifted children are increasingly used. Teacher nominations should be made well into the year when teachers are familiar enough with the children to assess them accurately.

Parent nominations are particularly relevant at the early childhood level. Although parents of young children tend to overnominate, their perceptions of their children's behaviors and characteristics are valuable additions to those of teachers.

Identification and assessment, of course, should be done in the context of the standard procedures adopted by the state in whose jurisdiction the education of the child is being provided. These procedures protect the child's rights, help to assure that professional educational practices are respected, guide the procedures in an orderly way and safeguard due process for the parents or others concerned.

PREVAILING VERSUS PREFERRED PRACTICES

The practices usually found in schools are contrasted here with the preferred practices found operating successfully in schools which, though perhaps few in number, are the ones whose programs are showing the way to others.

Prevailing Practices	Preferred Practices
1. Identification is sporadic, usually delayed until grade 3, 4, or later. Identification is based on group intelligence test scores, grade averages, standardized achievement test scores, teacher recommendations, or a combination of those.	1. Systematic identification and assessment of preschool age children is available for possible early admission to kindergarten or first grade. Deliberate efforts are made to locate children of high promise from kindergarten on, with special attention to searching in minority group and disadvantaged populations. Use of individual intelligence tests, creativity tests, social development level tests, behavioral checklists, parental nominations, and teacher nominations, characterize the identification process.
2. Prior to educational program decisions about children there is little systematic educational assessment and planning.	2. Individualized educational needs assessments are made for each identified child (often largely done as part of the identification process) prior to educational program decisions. The needs assessment findings guide the program decisions which, themselves, are individualized.
3. Program coordination, either in the local school or throughout the whole school system, is absent or haphazard.	3. A school system staff person is responsible for the overall program coordination for gifted and talented pupils.
4. Special attention to a gifted or talented pupil comes only when a regular class teacher takes an interest.	4. Individualized programing is available from preschool years through secondary schools, including liaison with higher education institutions. Continuous progress is monitored by regular class and specialist teachers from kindergarten through 12th grade.

Prevailing Practices	Preferred Practices
5. Parents may know that their children are in special programs, but they are not consulted about the placement or the program.	5. There is full involvement of parents and the child in decision making about the educational planning and the evaluating of individualized programs.
6. Age-grade acceleration is arranged for a few pupils through early admission to school, double promotion, or early college placement.	6. Each identified pupil's progress is reviewed at least annually to consider possible age-grade acceleration and program redesign.
7. When program adaptations are arranged it is with minimal participation by specialists in education of the gifted.	7. The regular class teacher uses fellow teachers who have specialized in the education of the gifted when arranging program adaptations for pupils.
8. Special art, music, creative writing, or other classes for elementary or secondary age students are occasionally offered, either during school hours or on Saturdays.	8. There is flexible, personalized scheduling across and up and down regular classes and grade levels to accommodate special abilities and interests and to take advantage of the many special competencies possessed by particular regular class teachers. There is open access, under reasonable supervision, to libraries and laboratories so pupils can pursue individual projects.
9. A few larger cities maintain special secondary schools, some for high achievers in general and some designated for the sciences or the performing arts, for instance.	9. Emphasis is kept on bringing special educational facilities and activities to gifted and talented children in the context of the regular class rather than moving the child to a special school or class.
10. Advanced placement college courses are available in less than one out of six high schools.	10. Advanced placement is available and pupils are encouraged, with professional guidance, to explore the various options it affords.

Prevailing Practices	Preferred Practices
11. There are few teachers who have specialized in the education of gifted and talented pupils.	11. There is a staff of teachers who have specialized in the education of gifted and talented pupils, approximately 1 to each 500 pupils in the total enrollment, in elementary and secondary schools to consult and to team teach with regular class teachers. Each specialist teacher has two aides who can be assigned to work with teachers or pupils or do other work as the regular class and specialist teacher determine.
12. There is little or no preservice or in-service preparation for regular class teachers to work with gifted or talented pupils.	12. Periodic in-service minicourses are offered for regular class teachers to maintain and update understandings and skills about individualizing programs for these and other children and youth. In these minicourses, teachers often teach each other and their successful completion is counted toward professional and salary advancement.

THE BEGINNING OF SPECIAL EDUCATION FOR GIFTED AND TALENTED PUPILS

If a thorough history is ever prepared on this topic it may unearth some amazing information. As it is, we must settle for biographical anecdotes about the early training of great personages of the past and incidental material culled from histories prepared for other purposes (Cox, 1926; Goertzel & Goertzel, 1962; Sumption & Luecking, 1960).

Plato recommended that Greeks of outstanding ability be educated from childhood for responsible governmental positions. To detect future leaders, he suggested that promising juveniles be observed while being made to perform actions in which they were most likely to be deceived, and those who remembered and were not deceived were to be selected and those who failed in the trial were to be rejected.

The Emperor Charlemagne, according to legend, urged the education at state expense of promising children among the common people.

Comenius, in his 17th century writings, frequently referred to students of extraordinary aptitude for learning. He advocated financial aid for bright students from poor homes.

The rapid rise of the Ottoman Empire in the 1500's has been credited in large part to Suleiman the Magnificent's three step special education process. He sent teams to find the fairest, strongest, and brightest youth in the empire, regardless of their social class and whether they were Christian, Moslem, or adherents to other faiths. It was made worth their while to accept tutelage under his protection in the Moslem religion, in the learned disciplines of that day, and in martial arts. A robe of honor was given to each boy for exceptional work in attaining strength and knowledge. Finally, the successful graduates were offered posts of honor and responsibility in the armed forces, in the arts and sciences, and in government.

The Chinese emperors sponsored instruction and a system of civil service examinations. These brought into government employ not only able clerks, managers, and generals, but also poets, artists, and other creative persons.

The tales of other civilizations may well contain similar themes. The full story of the development of leadership in the Aztec and Inca civilizations, for instance, has yet to be told. Equally unstated are the approaches to giftedness and talent on the part of the nations of the African continent, the American Indians, and the Japanese.

Recent Past

In 1955 Pressey put in capsule form the tenets of an educational program aimed at fostering the capabilities of gifted and talented youth. He titled the topic "Toward More and Better American Geniuses" and he said:

> A practicing genius is produced by giving a precocious able youngster early encouragement, intensive instruction, continuing opportunity as he advances, a congruent stimulating social life, and cumulative success experiences. (p. 14)

Pressey went on to say about curriculum adaptations that "in proportion as they are very able and especially as they have special talents, special adaptations of the usual curriculums are likely to be desirable" (p. 16). With respect to acceleration, he added:

> Admission to the first grade on the basis of readiness for school rather than chronological age, replacement of the first three grades by a "primary pool" out of which children would move early or late depending on when they finish primary work, rapid-progress sections doing three years work in two in junior and senior high school, and credit by examination in

college—should permit each youngster to move through educational programs at his own pace, without being conspicuous if his rate is not that of the average. (pp. 123-129)

The recipe offered by Pressey—early identification, encouragement, special instruction, sequential successes, curriculum adaptation, and personally paced progress—was grounded solidly in the research of the day. A few school systems, too, were heeding the research, at least parts of it. But it would have been rare to find any school systems, public or private, that had installed all of the components of a comprehensive design for its most able pupils.

At about the same time, Terman (1954) commented on the lag between what was known and what was put into practice in the schools.

> I have always stressed the importance of *early* discovery of exceptional abilities....The striking thing is...how early in life the period of maximum creativity is reached. In nearly all fields of science, the best work is done between ages 25 and 35, and rarely later than 40. The peak productivity for work of lesser merit is usually reached 5 to 10 years later; this is true in some twenty fields of science, in philosophy, in most kinds of musical composition, in art, and in literature of many varieties. The lesson for us is that the youth of high-achievement potential should be well trained for his life work before too many of his creative years have been passed.
>
> This raises the issue of educational acceleration for the gifted. It seems that the schools are more opposed to acceleration now than they were thirty years ago. The lockstep seems to have become more and more the fashion, notwithstanding the fact that everyone who has investigated the subject is against it. (p. 222)

There were scattered efforts in the United States before and during the 1950's to promote school adaptations in line with the Pressey and Terman formulations for gifted and talented pupils. Some of them took root and flourished.

The special arrangements varied. Examples include special secondary schools such as those in New York City and Cincinnati, more or less separate clusters of special classes such as those known as Major Work Classes in Cleveland, and the classes in University City, Missouri, and early admission to kindergarten and first grade like those pioneered in Brookline, Massachusetts, and in several counties and towns in Nebraska.

These and other real life settings helped materially in keeping alive the interest in special education for the nation's most able pupils. They furnished operational evidence that many of the needed adaptations could work. However, the impact of that evidence was blunted against the stonewall tactics of those who did not welcome the idea of special education for gifted and talented children and youth.

Martinson (1973) identified reasons why so many educators rejected efforts to extend special education to this group.

Two major ones were (1) concern about the establishment of a meritocracy and (2) the fear of snobbery within an elite group. Others include (3) fear of pressures on children and (4) the deprivation of gifted and average children of contact with one another. (p. 221)

Further, Martinson pointed out that the notion on the part of some educational leaders that special groupings are undemocratic prompted articles in professional journals promoting that view. Economy moves, too, found existing special classes easy targets in time of competing pressures.

Despite difficulties, however, more programs slowly appeared. States employed coordinators at the state education department level to give overall encouragement and leadership. The Association for the Gifted (TAG), a division of The Council for Exceptional Children, promoted national and regional meetings, often cooperating with other interested groups, both national and state. The Ford Foundation, the Carnegie Corporation, and other foundations gave modest but meaningful support to the preparation of program development leaders. The Russian launching of Sputnik sparked US Congressional interest in improvements in American secondary school education, especially in mathematics and the sciences. That Congressional interest materialized as the National Defense Education Act, a platform from which added support for programs of education for the gifted and talented took sustenance.

So, despite a lukewarm to cool level of interest from most educators, education designed for the nation's gifted held onto most of its limited beachheads and made some small gains during the recent past. It was not until the present, though, that a substantial spurt of activity on the topic began.

Present Status

This is a time of burgeoning interest and of major organizational moves. Late 1975 saw the second White House Conference on the Education of the Gifted and Talented and a national symposium at Johns Hopkins University on progress since the publication of the first volume of Terman's *Genetic Studies of Genius* in 1925.

In 1976 TAG had over 1,500 members. A national conference was held in the same year on the gifted handicapped in cooperation with the American Association for the Advancement of Sciences. Regional TAG conferences on the gifted and talented were convened in Atlanta in 1975 and in Toledo in 1976. A US Office of Education Leadership Training Institute for the Talented and Gifted held summer institutes and offered technical assistance for regional, state, and local program development. A national TAG committee on the culturally diverse gifted was active. In 1976, 39 states had organized parent and advocate groups on behalf of gifted and talented children. One state had as many as 38 local community groups affiliated with the state organization.

The California Association for the Gifted Annual Conference in 1976 registered 2,300 persons. Most states have directors or coordinators of education for the gifted and talented and many have several associated staff members. There is a strong wave of interest in requiring advanced training for teachers who specialize with the gifted and in recognizing that advanced training through certification.

Local school systems are beginning, most for the first time, to think in long range terms about program designs for their gifted and talented pupils. (This is a good time to look back at pp. 224-226, where currently prevailing practices are outlined.) It is still true that most schools in America have not yet applied the recipe suggested in Pressey in 1955 (pp. 227-228), or any other plan that promises to produce comprehensive educational opportunities for this group. Yet, interest in making overall plans is stirring.

One of the fully researched and readily available adaptations of conventional schooling for gifted and talented pupils is acceleration (Keating, 1976; Reynolds, Birch, & Tuseth, 1962). Age-grade acceleration, in which a pupil moves ahead to join pupils somewhat older, has been studied extensively. If the move is made by early admission to kindergarten or first grade or if it is made later, the results are positive, so long as the process is worked out thoroughly beforehand and carefully monitored. The same is true for curriculum acceleration, in which skills or content for which the pupil is ready are taught at an earlier age than usual. Each of these forms of acceleration, used separately or together, can be very effective, and each has been thoroughly tested in research and in practice.

Age-grade and curriculum acceleration by themselves do not make a comprehensive model of special education for gifted and talented pupils. In view of the present relatively undeveloped status of model development, however, acceleration is a process that can be put to wider use, while other adaptations are tested, improved, and added, to produce the more comprehensive models needed. Also, acceleration is well suited to the point of view that gifted and talented pupils should be educated in the mainstream, since that is where acceleration best takes place.

There is something about accelerating bright children that disturbs many people. For one thing, they are often reluctant to believe that it is a healthy thing to do—either for the pupils being accelerated or the rest of society. A great deal of careful, followup study has shown that acceleration has a number of positive results and no negative effects have been found. It would be well in that connection to listen to what mentally advanced pupils who experience acceleration have to say about it.

Early Entry in College Hailed As Blessing by U.S. Prodigies*
by Gene I. Maeroff

BALTIMORE, Nov. 9—"I like going to college," said Eric, a chunky 13-year-old who two years ago was a sixth grader in a New York public school. "In elementary school, the teachers didn't know how to handle a kid like me. I was looked on as a bother by many of them."

Eric, who declined to give his last name or identify his New York college, "because I'm bothered enough by people who think I'm an oddity," joined 15 other youngsters on a panel of mathematical prodigies held last week at Johns Hopkins University.

It was part of an annual symposium on early childhood education and a highly unusual event because such youngsters ordinarily shy away from publicity and academic officials strive to protect their youngsters' privacy.

Thus, for many of the 300 researchers, teachers and others in the audience, it was a rare opportunity to get a personal perspective on the joys and frustrations of giftedness.

Tell of Exasperation

Seated behind a row of tables stretching the width of the auditorium stage, the youngsters told of the exasperation at being trapped in an elementary school or junior high ill-equipped to cope with genius and described their relief at finding a high school or college program in which to accelerate their studies.

"In the first grade," said Eric, who has now covered the equivalent of five semesters of college mathematics, "my teacher saw I was uninterested in the mathematics we were doing so she gave me second and third-grade workbooks but I was still uninterested."

"If I hadn't entered college after the sixth grade," he continued, "I might have become frustrated in all my subjects. Teachers would rather have normal students they know how to take care of."

Terri Hill, who has chosen to remain enrolled in her high school in Columbia, Md., while doing extra, college-level work in mathematics, said that she thought part of the problem for the teachers was the fear of being proved wrong by gifted students.

Fear Factor Cited

"A student wants to get something from a teacher," said the slim, soft-spoken 16-year-old, who throws the discus on the girl's track team. "A teacher can't sit back and be afraid of being corrected by a student if the student is right."

"I didn't feel at all out of place in skipping four grades and going to college," said Joseph Bates, 20, a doctoral candidate in computer science at Cornell University. "I made friends easily. I didn't date much but I wasn't ready for it. Now, I have more time for dating."

---

*Copyright© 1975 by the New York Times Company. Reprinted by permission.

Gifted students are impelled toward college level work, in part, by their impatience with some of the public school tasks they consider mundane and boring.

"I know when I comprehend a book and I don't want to write book reports," complained Mark Greenberg, a 12-year-old 10th grader, a shade less than 5 feet tall, who is taking a third-year calculus course by mail from the University of Wisconsin. "I know when I've read a book and I don't care if the teacher knows."

The matter of acceleration comes into focus early, if one looks at what some very able children achieve in elementary school. Martinson's (1972) report allows us to highlight the difficulties teachers face if they attempt to stick to typical age-grade linked curricula, even if they also apply "horizontal enrichment." In recounting the educational characteristics of 1,000 gifted pupils she noted that:

> In the kindergarten group, the average performance of gifted students was comparable to that of second grade students....
>
> The average for fourth and fifth grade gifted children was beyond that of seventh grade students.
>
> The average for gifted eighth grade students was equal or beyond the typical performance of 12th grade students. (p. 81)

The following statement by Marland (1976) neatly summarizes the status of the Advanced Placement Program, a major national form of acceleration.

Advanced Placement
by Sidney P. Marland, Jr., President
College Entrance Examination Board,
New York City

Some 20 years ago, my predecessors at the College Board established the Advanced Placement Program (AP), which allows able high school students to study college-level courses while still in school and offers them possible advanced placement in colleges on the basis of their AP examinations.

AP provides schools with curriculum descriptions, in a variety of disciplines—American history, art, biology, chemistry, classics, English, European history, French, German, Latin, mathematics, music, physics, and Spanish. Talented and conscientious school and college teachers from each field prepare these course descriptions, descriptions that can readily be adapted to local initiatives. The course outlines and tests are revised biennially to keep current with college offerings.

The three-hour AP examinations are given each year in May. Then between May and July, AP readers assemble to grade the written portions of the examinations and to compute the final scores. Scores are given on a five-point scale—a five indicating the highest recommendation for credit and a one indicating not recommended for credit.

Candidates' grade reports, examination booklets, and other materials in support of their application for advanced placement or credit are sent to the college they will enter. It is up to the college to decide whether it will give credit for the AP work.

For several reasons, secondary schools should seriously consider introducing the program if they have not already done so.

First, the lockstep traditional system of education is being abandoned in many schools to suit the styles and needs of individual students. AP has been in the forefront of this trend, giving able students an opportunity to stretch their minds. Every indication persuades us that more and more of our ablest students now seek this kind of intellectual challenge.

Second, the solemn progression from grade 12 to 13, long a glacial monument to the great silence between schools and colleges, is beginning to thaw as schools define multiple paths to the high school diploma and as colleges exercise flexibility in their admissions policies. Yet the abyss between school and college faculties in the curriculum area remains deep.

AP does not provide a full solution, but each year it does offer a systematic and influential meeting ground for school and college teachers, when the AP readers from both secondary schools and colleges gather to review and grade the examinations and share a full week of hard work, illuminating exchanges, and camaraderie.

Third, college credit earned by examination in myriad forms and styles is increasingly in the air. While college faculties express concern that some of these programs may result in a cheapening of academic degrees, they do not seem to view AP in this context. Perhaps this is because college faculties have always played a major role in developing the AP program.

Fourth, in the years ahead, the decline in the school-age population, already evident in the elementary grades, will move into high school and into college, where there may well be sharp declines in enrollments. This will no doubt stimulate competition among colleges for able students who have not yet received their high school diploma. Some collegiate institutions already enroll eleventh graders. More programs of this type will come.

But secondary schools can stand their ground and preserve their eleventh and twelfth grade programs in this sharpening competition if they can do the job for able students in these grades as effectively as the colleges can. AP is one proven way to do this.

Many schools around the country have demonstrated that AP can be installed for a modest or even negligible incremental cost.

To institute the program, a school needs a capable staff. But most schools already have talented teachers on their staffs who are capable of teaching AP or who could become so by taking additional university courses.

A school also needs to have college-level materials available, and many schools have these on hand or can obtain them from nearby libraries. Some AP courses require appropriate laboratories and equipment, but a great many high schools now have equipment that is as good as or better than what students find available for freshman courses in many of the colleges.

Beginning an AP program in a school, even for only one or two subjects, can create a dynamic concern for academic excellence that permeates the entire school and exerts a positive influence on other classes and courses as well as on members of the faculty.

Experienced AP users have found the program to be an effective instrument for serving gifted but socially disadvantaged students. I found this particularly true in my years with the Pittsburgh schools, and I suspect the same would be true in other inner-city schools where pride in the program often helps urban school leaders change negative stereotypes held by some parents and segments of the public. (pp. 43-44)

Acceleration discussions always bring up questions about social adjustment and about social maturity. Some additional insight on that matter is provided by Gallagher (1975). He reported a study of his own that examined the social standing among schoolmates of children with high intelligence test scores. He stated, "There is little or no question about the general social status of high-IQ elementary school children. It is high" (p. 39).

Then Gallagher (1975) went on to summarize other findings related to the social positions of such children, as follows:

1. The social status of gifted children seems to show a relative decrease at the secondary level.
2. Gifted children are able to identify correctly the social status of others and themselves better than the average.
3. Gifted children tend to choose each other for friends when they are removed from the classroom for a period of time each day.
4. Gifted children lose some general social acceptance when removed from the classroom for a special workshop.
5. Acceleration at the elementary level does not seriously affect their social adjustment.
6. Gifted children seem to serve as an ego-ideal to the average child, who chooses him [sic] even though he sees differences between himself and the gifted youngster. (pp. 39-40)

These generalizations about gifted children's social status can be useful when the teacher is planning individualized programs and working with parents and others in counseling and consultation. For instance, items 2, 4, and 6 can be interpreted to give support to mainstream program designs rather than to separate schools or classes. Also, item 5 primarily and all the others in supplementary ways, can argue for moving confidently in age-grade acceleration in the elementary years.

Caution is advisable, of course, against overgeneralizations of any kind. These statements about social status hold quite well for gifted and talented children who are already superior performers in school and who are solidly adjusted in the dominant culture's milieu. They may work well for other highly able children and youth, too, but that is not so certain. Special education programs that are most likely to bear full fruit are those that not only capitalize on such generalizations as those listed by Gallagher but also build on the individual characteristics of the gifted and talented pupil and match with the local school and community environment and its resources.

A search is on for comprehensive models. Most school districts that have programs of any kind for gifted and talented pupils can supply only pieces of models rather than complete ones. Relatively few have attained the comprehensiveness of the four models illustrated later in this chapter, and even those are still increasing their range and coverage.

Thus, the present status is characterized by two features. One is active and rapid growth of the governmental, parental, and professional support structures that must form the essential framework of any educational program if it is to have stability. That building goes on at national, state, and local levels simultaneously. The second feature is educational program development in local schools, with almost everyone looking elsewhere for operating examples of programs they might adapt or emulate.

Current Trends

Vigorous activism by parents brought about legislation and court determinations that propelled special education sharply ahead, at the same time setting it on a course into the mainstream of the nation's education. Though initiated for children and youth with mental retardation, the impact now has generalized to all the exceptional, including the gifted and talented.

Examples of the consequences of parent initiated legislative and judicial actions are found in these eight statements of current trends in a growing number of states.

1. Special education is mandated (required by state law) for all school age gifted and talented children and youth.
2. It is the responsibility of each local school district, primarily, to see that the special education is forthcoming.
3. The state provides earmarked funds, over and above usual state educational support to local districts, to help pay for the required special education.
4. Teachers who have specialized in the education of gifted and talented pupils must be made available.
5. A professional certification is set forth for specialists in teaching the gifted and talented.

6. Special education for these pupils is to be conducted in the regular context, with regular and specialist teachers working as a team and offering consultation to each other.
7. Personalized education plans must be put in writing for each gifted and talented pupil and reviewed periodically.
8. Parents must be asked for permission to assess their children, must have access to all records about their children and must be asked to consent to the inauguration of or change in any special education program for their children.

The legal decisions that raised new expectations regarding the right to education, due process, and least restrictive alternative first for pupils with mental retardation, then extended to other exceptional pupils, have begun to affect school arrangements for gifted and talented pupils. Pennsylvania, for example, has mandated, starting in 1977, special education that satisfies those conditions for all gifted and talented children and youth.

In actual practice, that spells changes. Ways will have to be devised to assure that gifted and talented youngsters will obtain, in the regular class setting, those individualized educational benefits now provided mainly in fully or partially segregated groupings.

The excellent qualities of earlier programs are being built upon as states and local school systems move toward compliance with the now clearly articulated national and state policies. At the same time the several concerns identified by Martinson (1973) as deterrants are being reduced or eliminated as a consequence of those policies.

THE ROLE OF THE REGULAR CLASS TEACHER

It is not new for regular class teachers to have all day long responsibilities for gifted and talented pupils, whether in the primary, middle or secondary years. What is new is that:

1. Particular attention is now called to these pupils,
2. Individualized educational plans are required for them,
3. There are specialized staff plus particularized instructional procedures to buttress the regular class teacher's work.
4. Parental involvement is increased.

These can all contribute to a positive thrust if regular class teachers also receive preparatory training and are allowed sufficient time to capitalize on their added resources.

Teamwork with Specialists

In the past, regular class teachers had responsibility only for their own interactions with their pupils. That responsibility now extends to the coordination of the activities of a resource teacher and other pupils with the gifted and talented pupils in the class.

The regular class teacher's role includes the joint preparation of individualized educational plans with the specialist teacher. The children for whom the plans are prepared, and their parents, will often be party to the planning. Because the regular class teacher will be the leader of that team effort, added management skills are called for, too.

It may be helpful to envision the regular class teacher and all the pupils, including the gifted and talented ones, in the center of focus, with various services and consultants surrounding them. These services (i.e., library, guidance counseling, instructional materials center) and consultants (specialist teacher, teacher aide, volunteers) come into the regular class if requested by the regular class teacher. They are intended primarily for gifted pupils, but they may very well splash over in beneficial ways, either planned or incidentally, for other pupils. The regular class teacher exercises professional generalship on behalf of the whole class while making sure that each gifted and talented pupil is accommodated by whatever forms of acceleration and enrichment are most suitable.

Special Education in the Regular Grades

Gifted and talented pupils, for the most part, learn the standard curricular skills and content quickly and easily. They often move far beyond the conventional curricular offerings into advanced areas. Therefore, they need teaching that does not tether them to a limited range. They need teaching that is not preoccupied with piling up information, even advanced information. The regular class, for them, needs to be a forum for research, inquiry, and projects alive with real products and applications. That is true from kindergarten through high school and postsecondary education.

These pupils are quick to evaluate feelings and hard evidence and to make well reasoned choices. With encouragement, they learn readily to produce imaginative, unusual, yet soundly grounded ideas, and to employ them in problem solution. They are persistently curious. They need teacher encouragement to maintain confidence in their own good ideas when those ideas differ from the norm or the vogue, and the confidence to live with the consequences of their independence.

Such characteristics, when they appear in regular classes, challenge the breadth and depth of professionalism in any teacher. It is no small quality to be able to direct work in widely divergent areas, to help pupils test their work's relevance, and to support and supply guidance for further inquiry, either personally or by putting them in effective contact with others in the school or community who can help.

Aware that gifted and talented pupils are not a species apart, regular class teachers see them on a continuum with all other pupils. The chief dimension of the continuum in an abstract sense is cognitive development, to be sure. Yet realistically, gifted and talented pupils have their ups and downs on all sorts of educationally significant qualities. They intermingle with all others in more ways than they differ. This can be well illustrated through examining the "Talent Totem Poles" in Figure 5-2. Taylor (1968) indicated that there are many qualities that need attention as personalized education is planned for children and youth.

FIGURE 5-2
Taylor's Talent Totem Poles

Source: C. W. Taylor, Be talent developers as well as knowledge dispensers. *Today's Education,* 1968, *57,* 67-69. Reprinted with permission.

A central tone of the mainstream theme is that adults are more likely to work effectively together if they have practice in doing so as children and youth. Thus a premium is placed on the regular class teacher's skill in helping pupils of all ages to work together, to achieve satisfying socialization without sacrificing their independence and creativity. To do that it is necessary to establish an environment in which some students can pursue highly advanced topics, often beyond the reach not only of most other pupils but also outside the competence of the teachers, too. For the gifted and talented pupils, then, their teacher may more often need to be a guide, introducer, and facilitator rather then an expert in skills and content.

Regular class teachers who work in well staffed and well equipped mainstream settings with gifted and talented pupils find it exciting and rewarding. They find that they not only help the most able children, but they also are encouraged to enrich their own professional competencies and their capabilities of stimulating the other pupils under their tutelage.

Individualization of Instruction

Gifted and talented pupils should work their way through the typical curriculum, plus. They should do so at a faster rate than others and their comprehension at any given stage should be deeper and more substantial. That applies whether the pupils come from minority cultures or from the dominant societal group.

Within the regular curriculum, plus, each highly able student's work should be individualized. A key characteristic of individualization is flexibility. Certainly there should be a fairly consistent format for each personalized plan of education. (See Chapter 4). But there should also be much openness and maneuvering room.

Curriculum Individualization

So far as curriculum content is concerned, there are four principles that apply from kindergarten through the rest of the school years for gifted and talented children and youth.

First, the teacher should be sure that all the gifted and talented pupils acquire the basic skills and content of the standard curriculum, and that they do so thoroughly. This does not mean laboriously going over what the pupils already know. Rather, it means checking carefully to see that there are no real gaps, no serious slippage resulting from the speed and informality with which much of the learning has taken place. Instruction should then be carried out to fill in the holes. Speed and informality should be fostered and rewarded.

Second, the students should be encouraged to go ahead in the standard curriculum (reading, motor development, writing, sciences, mathematics, oral languages, music, art, literature) as rapidly as fits each pupil's individual pace. There should be advanced books, materials, and instruction readily available in a systematic and orderly way, and the child's efforts in curriculum acceleration should be reinforced.

Third, the scope of the standard curricular offerings should be extended by crossing over the typical streams. For example, typing, shorthand, bookkeeping, and various technical and specialized vocational shops and laboratories can be added at times when gifted and talented students can schedule them, or can be used to replace courses passed by examination.

Fourth, the teacher should help each child to follow any personal inclinations to reach outside the standard curriculum. The teacher could use informal independent study or the more formal advanced placement program. In these cases, however, the parents *must* be involved in planning, and the teacher *must* have their full cooperation. Thus, if a 10, 12, or 16 year old wishes to pursue such added content areas as astronomy, animal husbandry, ethics, epistemology, morality, Moslem cultures, paper making, or population control, it is more than ordinarily important and highly desirable that there be full understanding and cooperation between home and school. Such prearrangement can be helpful in giving the parents a part in what is going on as well as ensuring that their own values on the relevance and the propriety of particular studies are respected.

These four principles deal with curricular subject matter or content. Curricula also include processes. The latter consist mostly of ways of behaving about learning, whatever the content or subject might be. There are six curriculum process principles, which, while significant for all pupils, have particular bearing on the education of gifted and talented children and youth. According to these principles, the teacher should:

1. Teach pupils to be efficient and effective at independent study, instilling and polishing the skills called for in self directed learning and in analyzing and solving problems on one's own.
2. Help pupils to invoke and apply complex cognitive processes such as creative thinking, critiques, and pro and con analyses.
3. Encourage pupils to press discussions of questions or issues all the way to the culminating activity of decision making and to the clear communication to others of plans, status reports, or solutions based on the decisions.
4. Establish the human interaction skills necessary to work smoothly with groups of all ages and of all levels of cognitive development.
5. Aid pupils in acquiring respect for all other humans, whatever their gifts or talents and understanding themselves in relation to all others.
6. Build in pupils positive expectations about careers and about lives as adults that optimize their talents and gifts.

Curriculum individualization should be viewed as a significant part of the *treatment* in the aptitude treatment interaction model of instruction. In that perspective, individualization of curriculum should be personalized to match the unique *aptitude* factors of each pupil. (The reader might now review the concept and reason through its possible application here.)

Methods of Teaching

Some principles of teaching gifted and talented pupils cut across all subjects, skills, and all age levels. They derive from the learning characteristics that are common to such pupils.

Pupil Learning Characteristics	**Derived Teaching Principles**
1. Learning can move at a faster rate than in other pupils.	1. Accelerate the pace at which all elements of the curriculum move.
2. Learning can attain more complex levels than in other pupils.	2. Deliberately introduce and teach important abstract concepts and ideas in the skills and disciplines earlier than usual.
3. Self directed learning can begin and can be habituated earlier.	3. Expand opportunities for independent study, discovery, and synthesis, rather than let the gifted pupil be a passive receiver of teacher presented material.

These derived principles sound three more themes that reverberate through all high quality instruction of gifted and talented youth. Note how they interlock with the preceding statements on curriculum individualization. A rich variety of examples can be found in Gallagher (1975) for all subjects and ages. The reader may wish to elaborate on these or add others, especially, examples that might also work with (a) children whose school performance is consistently poorer than their out-of-school attainments and inventive and leadership qualities suggest it should be (underachievers) and (b) children whose family and cultural backgrounds are markedly different and whose potential gifts and talents may not immediately be evident in the dominant culture (i.e., minority group children from culturally different backgrounds). The teacher who invents the means to implement any of these three principles in ways that appeal simultaneously to underachievers, to minority and culturally different pupils, and to the more easily identified gifted and talented achievers from the dominant culture has found treasures of teaching techniques that deserve to be shared with others.

Instructional Materials

In one sense there is an almost unending store of instructional materials for gifted and talented pupils. These materials are the contents of the nation's libraries, museums, and galleries; all the textbooks and references ever written, whether elementary, secondary, or collegiate; all our natural resources; all our businesses, churches, national parks, universities, laboratories, and factories; and all our citizens. Certainly all of these, and more, may be thought of as instructional materials there for the taking. They are especially appropriate for pupils who are insatiably curious and who are particularly capable at independent learning.

Yet, not all gifted and talented children and youth are self starters. Also, teacher, parents, and these children do not really have quick and easy access to the treasure trove of existing material. That is particularly true of the handicapped gifted. Moreover, there are cultural, ethnic, and racial minority groups that can rightly claim that they have been shortchanged in the collections and institutions of the majority. So a number of steps are necessary before the stockpile of existing instructional materials can be used effectively.

First, winnowing is needed. Not all resources are of good quality and there are duplications. Second, access needs to be arranged. Remember, for instance, the child (p. 182) who could not obtain library books. Third, organization and curriculum planning are necessary. Most resources are either not catalogued at all or are catalogued for social-commercial use (yellow pages and files) or for reference use (library and encyclopedia), rather than for teacher directed sequential instruction or independent study.

Simultaneously, a number of specialists are producing instructional materials designed for use with gifted and talented pupils. Ideas about some of these can be found in Torrance and Myers (1970). A publication by Kaplan (1974) contains relevant practical information. A groundbreaking example of promising ready to use instructional material is Renzulli's series, which began in 1975, for gifted and talented pupils. Additional sources of information about instructional materials will be found in Appendix B.

Organization for Instruction

As noted earlier, this topic refers to how a teacher or group of teachers deploy themselves, their pupils, and their instructional resources for maximum effect. Organization for instruction, in other words, includes decision making by teachers and other educators with reference to the tactics of instruction, once the grand strategy has been determined.

Enrolling gifted and talented pupils in regular classes, while bringing excellent individualized special education to them there, has been emerging as the preferred practice, so far as grand strategy is concerned. Thus, organization for instruction is planned, preferably, in the context of full mainstreaming or partial mainstreaming. Pupil separation from the regular class group is kept to a minimum. Kaplan's (1974) conception of three broad program prototypes (grouping students, accelerating students, and guiding or counseling students) is a useful way to think, within the mainstream concept, about overall organization for instruction for gifted and talented pupils.

Fortunately, special education programs that have grown up in America seldom separate pupils all day every day. Partial mainstreaming has been much more common.

The direction now is to be sure that the amount of separation is kept to a defensible minimum and that its justification is in terms of bona fide instructional need rather than administrative or fiscal convenience. For example, it is conceded that gifted and talented pupils need opportunities to socialize, plan, work, and discuss with others like themselves. School clubs, seminars, summer institutes, and the like, designed for and attended by gifted and talented pupils, may be necessary upon occasion to satisfy that need if it is not adequately satisfied in the usual course of regular class activities. But transporting gifted and talented pupils to a specialized school or to special classes is not acceptable. If the gifted are aggregated and separated to make for ease of staffing or other administrative conveniences, it would be questionable on instructional grounds when the grand strategy calls for inclusion rather than segregation.

Listed in Figure 5-3 are a number of expressions that denote ways of organizing for instruction. Some are suggested by Kaplan's (1974) lists. We have arranged them to indicate the probable degree to which they would or would not require segregation.

FIGURE 5-3
Ways of Organizing for Instruction

Full Mainstreaming ← → **Complete Segregation**

- Special summer programs
- Special schools
- Clustered special classes in regular schools
- Limited enrollment seminars and courses
- Resource rooms and clinical centers
- Limited participation field trips and events on school time
- Cluster groups within the regular class
- Limited participation before and after school groups
- Tutoring carried on in regular class
- Independent and individualized study in the context of the regular class

All of these approaches may need to be used under some circumstances as bases for organization for instruction. The procedures of choice are those that are most compatible with the greatest amount of mainstream school life for the gifted and talented pupils.

School Physical Plant

Gifted and talented children and youth are found among almost all other exceptional groups. Some of the most able students are affected, as suggested earlier, by architectural barriers, safety considerations, and inadequacies of light and sound factors in school building design. For more information on the implications of these factors and others and for their remedies see Birch and Johnstone (1975).

If one attempts to apply individualized instruction, team teaching, and cluster grouping of gifted pupils within the regular class it can be done in traditional classrooms and in open space. However, it will be more easily done where open space is the rule, because of the increased flexibility.

Finally, the kindergarten through 12th grade single campus building site arrangement provides a more satisfactory setting for the education of gifted children and youth than does an arrangement of widely dispersed buildings. It is even more helpful if there are weatherproof passages from building to building on the campus. The chief advantage is that elementary and middle school gifted and talented pupils can readily be offered the use of the studio, library, laboratory, personnel, and other resources of the grades above their own. Additionally, gifted and talented pupils of differing grades but of similar interests and abilities can readily meet and, if they wish, discuss and work together.

Summary

It continues to be a challenge to educators to bring together the five components—curriculum, teaching methods, materials, organization for instruction, and school physical plant—into a coordinated package that will let them bring out the best in pupils. It is no accident that we have grouped those components under the heading "Individualization of Instruction". Unless they are linked to that objective and designed to help the teacher accomplish it, the result will be slippage and loss of traction. On the other hand, the teacher's job can be made immeasurably more effective and satisfying if each of the five is shaped to fit well into the other. Teachers need to play a leadership role in forming the components to achieve that fit.

EXAMPLES OF SPECIAL SCHOOL PROGRAMS

There is an active search by local school systems for models they might use for their own guidance. It makes sense to learn from experiences elsewhere. That is one reason illustrative programs are included. We recommend, though, that teachers and other educators build from the ground up in their own localities, using state guidelines plus principles and suggestions extracted from the following examples.

The programs described here were chosen because they are comprehensive (a) in range, extending from elementary through secondary school, and (b) in the spread of kinds of gifted and talented pupils eligible. They illustrate a variety of ways to meet special pupil needs; they include an array of degrees of mainstreaming; they depend heavily on the teachers themselves for program leadership; and they emphasize rich parental and community involvement. It would be possible to find additional examples of exemplary local school district programs in California, Illinois, North Carolina, and a number of other states.

Westside Community Schools, Omaha, Nebraska

This report was taken from an article by Morton (1975).

"We do not want our gifted children exploited—nor isolated from their regular classmates. We DO want enrichment and imaginative development. The answer does NOT lie in providing a greater quantity of the same type of work assigned to others. We want them to be challenged to explore and develop their abilities and potentials." These were the comments of parents whose gifted and talented children are enrolled in the Westside Community Schools, District 66, in Omaha.

"There are many types of giftedness, not all of them of the intellectual academic type. We know that current I.Q. tests measure only 1/12 of the multiple talents now classified. We need inspiration and new ideas in working with talented and gifted students. Such students need not be isolated, but they would benefit from occasional closer association with peers of equal intelligence, and with similar interests." These were the comments of administrators and teachers.

The task before the Westside Community Schools was great. Concetrated work with community, parents, board members, administrators, teachers and students had resulted in outlining eighteen goals of the system of nearly 10,000 pupils. Twelve elementary feeder schools of three junior highs were divided into consortia, with each consortium developing and concentrating on disciplines to be shared throughout the district in meeting specific aspects of major goals—cognitive, affective, and psycho-motor, K through 12.

The concept is commitment to individualization. Special services have long been available to slow learners, educably trainable, handicapped, visually impaired, and those with speech deficiencies. Separate inter-disciplinary teams work with physical development, and with behavioral, language, and academic development. Resource teams made up of pediatricians, psychiatrists, audiologists and others, work with referred students. Reading and media specialists, traveling teachers and advisors work through the system.

A Talented and Gifted (TAG) parent organization had been formed and had asked for visible results. Creative teachers had been placed in each of the consortium schools to work with TAG students. A modest budget was set aside for TAG student resources. Two TAG consultants were hired to function in the three consortia.

Previously the intellectually gifted had been identified by licensed psychologists. Now a new philosophy was called for—one which did not isolate or exploit those identified. It became desirable to include many types of talented students not yet identified. The TAG consultants, in conjunction with superintendent, director of Special Education, other administrators, principals, teachers, parents, media specialists and students developed a unique philosophy. It was in keeping with previous ground work within the school community, yet had a different emphasis. From this base, proposals were developed as a beginning for our K through 12 program.

A district-wide identification of talented students, as well as those intellectually gifted in grades K through 6 was begun.

An orientation session of this philosophy was given separately to principals. Faculty meetings were then held with teachers. They were asked to administer group activity tests as suggested by Kuck, De Haan and Havinghurst for talented and academically gifted, and to indicate those scoring highest on a referral blank. The top 10 to 15 percent of the high scores in intellectual academic achievement, creative writing, art, music, physical education, dancing, dramatics, or social leadership were then referred to a licensed psychologist for further testing.

Consultants met with each principal following the identification phase, and outlined a program to meet the needs indicated. Teachers then select a particular area of talent, and students with related abilities meet with this teacher during one or more periods each week. In most of the twelve elementary schools, mini-courses are designed to develop latent talents. TAG consultants were asked to examine the curriculum itself to determine where creative instruction could be introduced. Resources and ideas are constantly being added and improved. Teachers are sent ideas of creativity each week by the TAG Consultants voluntarily, and special requests are handled as expediently as is possible. Teachers met with each principal following the identification phase, and outlined a program to meet the needs indicated.

Teachers were given a TAG communique form showing periods when each was free to discuss details of this developing program. Each teacher contributed her own ideas and shared creative suggestions to the TAG consultants. Subsequent workshops help teachers to develop and implement these ideas for use with TAG students. These workshops are filled to capacity. In this way positive attitudes toward the program are rapidly developing.

Once the program was off and running, it became evident that something more tangible and immediately visible must be developed. It was found that positive reinforcement of action taken was essential. For this we turned to two of our most valuable community resources—the Swanson Public Library, and the downtown Joslyn Art Museum. TAG consultants met with museum director and staff members and asked them to initiate a comprehensive exploration and educational program for TAG students—one that other students with similar interests might participate in. Eagerly accepting this challenge, their eventual plan combined resource people with talks, slides, illustrations of crafts and exhibits in the following areas: Pioneer Life; Light in Art from Rembrandt to the Laser Beam; the Medieval Way of Life; Magic Carpets—Oriental Rugs from the 19th and early 20th Centuries; Egypt of the Pharoahs, and Discovery of Line. Careful advance preparation is made, with follow-up discussion to answer questions raised at the programs. When possible, TAG students share their experiences and knowledge, and enthusiasm with other members of their classes.

At the Swanson Library resources were provided which were not available in our own schools. From a lengthy list, the following areas of research were selected: astronomy; Indian culture; vanishing wildlife, archaeology, agronomy, origin of crafts, electronics, careers, psychology, geology and mineralogy; history of sports and Olympics; nuclear physics, economics, and underwater exploration.

An Arbor Heights Junior High mini-computer course was designed for students of accelerated math at the elementary level. A creative stitchery sewing class has engaged the interest of creative students. Dramatics is under the supervision of a man long experienced in Children's Theatre. His expertise is also available to elementary students and he is scheduled to conduct inservice for teachers. Mini-courses have been added in cardboard carpentry, vocational trades, photography, creative writing, typing skills, and crafts as needs have been perceived. The local educational TV station is following the activities of primary students who have displayed leadership potential. Their study of local government of a period of several weeks will result in the formulating of their own curriculum guide.

An elementary group representing eight talents has been developed as a television company, and works weekly with the high school TV production group. They are currently working on a Bicentennial theme.

Transportation requirements for these classes are met through consulting the district bus manager. He was able to schedule the necessary 216 trips to the Library and Museum this past school year. Volunteer parents accompany the buses, and many provide supplemental transportation in private cars.

A consistent effort has been made to provide TAG students with as many opportunities as possible, utilizing available facilities without additional cost. Over nine thousand opportunities have been provided for our elementary students this year. Our main concentration has been at the elementary level, and plans are being made to expand programs already prevalent at the secondary level. The A in TAG stands for *and* interested. No child is excluded if he has a specific interest in any of the programs offered.

Parents, teachers, and principals have given us positive support. Teachers say: "We're implementing the ideas; keep them coming." Principals respond: "We're pleased to be given a new direction, the help for our teachers, and the stimulation for students." Parents say, "We think it's great!"

I often think of the kindergarten boy who came along on a trip to the

Swanson Library. He was concerned because he could not write a report of what he had learned for his friends. He was assured that it was enough to remember to talk about what he had seen. Later we learned that he not only drew chalk pictures of the earth and planets for his kindergarten room, but also gave the first grade class a half hour lecture with chalkboard illustrations!

It's rewarding to hear enthusiastic discussions of programs at the Joslyn Museum. "We got to touch all those old articles from the pioneers," was the awed remark of primary youngsters. In one classroom a pioneer breakfast with pioneer food and costumes was a follow-up of this interest area.

A nine week study of a cultural exchange of foreign students from the University of Nebraska at Omaha has been set up. Ninety-six students from thirty or more foreign countries visit throughout the district's twelve elementary schools, talking and exchanging their cultures with the talented, gifted *and interested* students of District 66, Omaha, Nebraska.

A TAG advisory board, with a parent representing each of the sixteen schools, meets with the consultants.

The advisory board, and a committee of principals and teachers met in May with the TAG Consultants, to go over the hundreds of students', teachers', parents', and administrators' evaluations. Together they helped to set up the general course of action and suggested new interest areas, and resources to utilize in the following year's program.

As the over-all TAG program continues, we find that we have only begun to tap our community resources. More parents in professions and skilled trades and crafts are volunteering their time to assist; and our appreciation of the community resource people and their generous help is growing steadily. All students benefit from this closer relationship. (pp. 25-26)

Three County Programs in Florida

These reports from Dade, Pinellas, and Polk counties in Florida are reproduced from the 1975 articles by Garcia, Peterson, and Estroff, respectively.

Dade County Public Schools

Update—

Well into our sixteenth year now with gifted education in Dade County, our programs are getting bigger, more varied, and above all better!

In 1958, Mrs. Harriet Ehrhard, Dade County Science Consultant, approached several laboratory scientists in the community about taking gifted senior high school science students to work side-by-side with them in their labs. They were enthusiastic; she identified two students and the Community Laboratory Research Program was under way. The program grew and eventually Jim Miley was hired to coordinate that program. For some years Jim was the Teacher on Special Assignment for the Gifted in Dade County. In cooperation with Mrs. Ehrhard, Jim developed the Motivation in Depth summer science program.

When the Florida legislature earmarked 25 teaching units for the gifted in 1968, Jim was ready with a program proposal. We secured 4 units and our first elementary learning center was formed.

Our growth in the past 4 years has been nothing short of phenomenal. There are presently 10 gifted/talented programs in Dade County Schools serving children ages 5-18 in grades K-12. Approximately 3,300 students are involved in these programs. The state prevalence figure for the gifted is 2% indicating that we are at present serving about 70% of eligible students.

The "It Figures" mathematics program and advanced placement courses are taught by regular classroom teachers. Motivation in Depth summer science program is taught by senior high school teachers who are contracted for each summer. The Deep Accelerated Mathematics Program utilizes the teaching services of Florida International University teachers. Students in the Oceanographic Laboratory Program for Inner City Youth are placed with scientists at N.O.A.A.

Five of the gifted/talented programs utilize the services of 47 special education teachers. All of these teachers are certified for regular education which is the appropriate certification for teaching the gifted/talented according to state regulations. Thirty-five teachers are full time and twelve are full time itinerants. Students are served from 5 to 25 hours per week depending upon the program. Conceivably a student may participate in several programs a total of 13 years. The Dade County Procedures and the State Guidelines determine the requirements for student participation. Basically students in programs for the academically gifted must have an IQ score of 130+ and be achieving two years above grade level. Students in the Talent program must score in the superior range on a test of creativity and demonstrate performance or product before a screening committee.

Subject content for the elementary academic centers and the secondary resource program includes all disciplines with strong emphasis on thinking processes. The expressive arts program emphasizes the visual and performing arts. Learnings in the Community Laboratory Research Program and the Student Leadership Development Program are determined by the student's placement in the community.

The gifted/talented program is generally still expanding and will continue to do so until the maximum number of eligible students are being served. The strengths lie in the program formats, the teacher competencies, and strong school and community support. Needs for the program would include more adequate facilities for elementary centers, a means of creating a better understanding of the program among personnel in general education, and a training program for teachers prior to their working with gifted students.

Present plans include additional elementary academic centers in the South and Southwest Areas during this school year. Further expansion would involve an expressive arts center in South, Southwest, South Central and Northeast Areas, a secondary resource program in Southwest, implementing the Leadership program throughout the county, exploring alternative programs for senior high school students, and investigating ways and means of providing for the learning disabled and emotionally disturbed gifted students.

Gifted/Talented Programs

1. *Community Laboratory Research Program*—Students in the eleventh and twelfth grades do scientific research in laboratories in the community during the school year, taking regular courses in their schools in the morning. They work 7-20 hours per week and receive one unit of high school science credit each year.
2. *Student Leadership Development Program*—High School juniors and seniors take a twoquinmester leave from their schools to work full time as community leaders in government, business, civic associations, etc. Students receive 2½ credits for their experience.
3. *Oceanographic Laboratory Program for Inner-City Youth*—Talented high school juniors and seniors from disadvantaged areas work during the summer with research scientists in oceanographic laboratories. Students receive a small remuneration for their work.
4. *Deep Accelerated Mathematics Program*—Students in grades 9-12 attend classes on Saturdays at Florida International University in college algebra, trigonometry, calculus, computer math, and advanced math. Students may earn 20-26 semester hours of college credit.
5. *Advanced Placement Program*—Eleventh and twelfth grade students take advanced courses in the various academic disciplines designed to qualify them for the College Entrance Board Examinations.
6. *Motivation in Depth Science Program*—Students spend the three summers after grades 8, 9, and 10 taking advanced biology, physics, and laboratory orientation and instrumentation.
7. *Resource Program for Gifted Secondary Students*—Students in grades 7-9 are scheduled one hour each day for independent study under the direction of two itinerant teachers. Research skills, in-depth academic projects, enrichment, and community involvement are stressed.
8. *"It Figures" Mathematics Program*—Sixth grade students participate in an accelerated math program utilizing lessons on television followed up in the classroom with validated work sheets.
9. *Learning Centers for Gifted Elementary Students*—Academically gifted children in grades K-6 attend centers two full days a week. Teams of 3-5 teachers develop a challenging, sophisticated program with strong emphasis on community resources.
10. *Centers for the Expressive Arts*—Talented elementary and junior high school students spend one full day each week in a center with three fine arts specialists. (Garcia, 1975, pp. 7-8)

Pinellas County Public Schools

The Gifted Program in Pinellas County has doubled its staff this year to 22 teachers and serves the gifted population in 53 schools. The program reaches from grade 1 through junior high.

Pinellas County uses a variety of methods to provide programs for the schools. We have set up two centers which have large physical facilities and enables us to bus in children from 24 elementary schools. They are there one day a week and have the opportunity to use the services of many resource people in the area besides the 5 teachers of gifted assigned to the centers. They have drama, music, folk craft and many other cultural components in addition to the academically-oriented subject matter.

In addition to the two centers, eight of our teachers are itinerant with either 2 or 3 schools to serve. They remain at each school the entire day, which allows them plenty of contact time for the faculty, a criticism we heard often in the past when each teacher literally sped from one school to another each day! Having the youngster the entire day once a week has some drawbacks, but in light of how much it has done to improve communication it is well worth it.

The remaining 9 teachers are appointed to one school because of exceptionally high gifted populations. This includes our junior highs which offer our gifted program in two ways. One method is as an elective to identified students and they see the teacher one period each day. Another way has been in conjunction with a Language Arts Program, with the understanding that we may not *always* be adhering strictly to a Language Arts format! In these programs, we may have a bigger block of time, but only twice a week.

Since Florida is blessed with so many people *and places* that are truly fascinating to these youngsters, we spend a lot of time on the road, fossil hunting, museum searching, bird-watching, ecology protecting, etc. Our local Science Center has written special components for our students which we can take advantage of in the areas of Photography, Computers, Energy, Chemistry and Ecology. We are always indebted to our children's parents who through even the worst part of the gas shortage never let the youngsters down, but drove them on various field trips.

The Executive Intern Program is also a part of our gifted umbrella. This is an opportunity for High School Juniors and Seniors to work with local officials in business and government. They participate full time as special assistants for a semester with full academic credit. This first semester has been so successful that there is every indication the program will be expanded next year.

We are in our fourth year now and are having growing pains, of course. Part of the problem lies in our fast growth and lack of facilities. These are being worked out with the help of an administration who firmly believe in each child's right to develop his or her potential to the greatest degree. (Peterson, 1975, p. 8.)

Polk County Public Schools

Polk County's program for the gifted and/or talented, now in its fifth year of state funding, is basically an itinerant program at the elementary level. At the present time we have 17 "gifted specialists" who serve as itinerant teachers working with approximately 100 children each in several schools, meeting with them in small groups twice or three times a week for 1 or 2 hour periods. In our largest urban areas with the greatest concentration of identified children, our teachers have split the schools, some serving grades K-3, others 4-6. Scheduling children out of their regular classes to meet with the specialist takes careful planning and, often-times, space in which to meet becomes an acute problem. Somehow we seem able to adapt to hallways, broom closets, stages, cafeterias, library corners, etc.

Our basic programming concerns itself with process rather than product. We are more preoccupied with implementing teaching strategies to encourage divergent-productive thinking in our gifted students than we are in a "project" as such though, certainly, there are products which emerge. Taking the children's interests where they are and the expertise of their teachers, curriculum that evolves can be as varied as "improvization for the theatre", to devising a social studies game celebrating the Bicentennial, to competitive Equations Game to movie-script writing, computer programming, Junior Great Books, values clarification, fetal pig dissection, etc.

Our 7th, 8th and 9th graders are involved on an after-school basis at our excellent Community College. I have established a cooperative agreement with the faculty to teach our eligible youngsters who enthusiastically participate from all over the county. This has been a highly successful project and until we have enough personnel to serve these students directly at their schools, this does seem to fill a significant need. We also have a cooperative teacher-training arrangement with a local private 4 year college in which we teach several education classes a series on Gifted Child Education and they, in turn, prior to actual internships in the schools, teach our Junior High students in an after-school series.

For the past four summers we have had two three-week sessions, full time, for gifted/talented 4th, 5th, 6th graders serving approximately 140 youngsters at each session. One fortunate summer, our junior and senior high students participated in a Cultural Arts endowed program in art and theatre at Florida Southern College. An original musical, "PIPER" was produced and declared a huge success.

In the past we have had some excellent county-wide one day seminars: Paleontology, Why Man Creates, City Planning, Cardboard Carpentry, Ringling Art Museum Workshop, etc. These were truly great but our school administration is not too happy with the 'movement of the troops' and we have had to curtail these somewhat. Unfortunate, I feel.

There are advantages and disadvantages to any type of administrative arrangement to meet the special needs of our gifted and talented. The resource room or center provides better teaching facilities especially if team teaching occurs, but the carry over into the classroom and contact with the regular classroom teacher is at a minimum. Self-contained classes can best function in large urban areas or middle-school situations. Labeling as "gifted" sometimes poses a problem and we find ourselves referring to our "Enhanced Learning" situation. Our Parent Group, PAGE, is just now beginning to grow.

There are additional possibilities for junior and senior high students such as the Executive Intern Program and the Advanced Placement Program. (Estroff, 1975, pp. 10-11)

Executive High School Internships

This nationwide program (Executive High School Internships of America, New York City, New York) forges impressive ties with the schools and society's other organizations. It has particular implications for vocational education in secondary schools, as described in the following report quoted from an article by the program's national director, S.P. Hirsch (1976).

Executive High School Internships
A Boon for the Gifted and Talented

Almost 2,500 gifted and talented juniors and seniors from 26 school districts in 17 states are learning about organizational leadership from the top—as Executive High School Interns to business executives and managers, government commissioners and administrators, newspaper editors, television producers and directors, hospital administrators, judges and attorneys, and directors of social service agencies and civic associations.

For a full semester, on sabbatical from regular classes, they are immersed in the world of organizations and administration, learning how decisions are made and earning a full range of academic credit in the process.

A Utopian Experience

"It's like utopia," says Vicki Cook (Hillsborough County, Florida), who has spent her Executive Internship semester with the president of Ensslin Advertising in Tampa. The week finds her variously meeting with clients, presenting storyboards, editing TV commercials (including those in which she has appeared), and spending time in areas such as accounting and production.

Another Hillsborough intern, Karl Miller, is equally delighted with the experience. "Since I've joined the program, I feel like one of the best informed citizens in Hillsborough," he reports.

Karl's placement with the executive director of the Hillsborough County Planning Commission involves law and city planning, areas he hopes to combine in a future career. His internship responsibilities include attending public hearings of the commission and updating research and analytical information on economic development in the county.

Both placements were arranged by coordinator JoAnn Hunter of the Hillsborough County Public Schools, which initiated the first Florida model in 1973. Ms. Hunter has been largely responsible for spreading word about the program to her colleagues in Gifted and Talented Education throughout Florida. One offshoot of the Hillsborough model is in the Orange County Public Schools, where coordinator Doris Prather has just completed her second year. Ms. Prather learned that Joe Finger, an Oak Ridge High School senior who ranks second in his class, was interested in a career in broadcasting so she found him the perfect spot, with WKIS Radio in Orlando, where he has written commercials and news stories and even broadcast sports reports. "The program has given me an opportunity to gain some exposure to the business world," he adds.

"I have a natural interest in making money," grins Kevin Hanks (Pinellas County, Florida) in explaining his selection of an Executive Internship with the president of Raymond, James & Associates, where he has developed expertise in the stock market and in the management of a brokerage house with 12 offices throughout Florida.

His placement has brought Kevin into contact with other brokers, analysts, and "a multimillionaire oilman." A research report on nonferrous metals which he prepared was used in an analyst's speech.

Kevin, who is pursuing an accounting course through independent study, reports that he has offered his father some advice on investments. "I gave him a tip that wasn't so hot," he adds with a shrug.

The Pinellas County Public Schools coordinators are Jan Rouse and Stan LeBoss who, like their other Florida counterparts, are operating models of the program funded as gifted and talented education through a special state formula.

The strong interest in law found among many high school students is reflected in a Palm Beach placement with the counsel to the Florida State Commission. There, Executive Intern Patrick Healy can be found researching pretrial information on securities frauds and "an occasional murder."

One of the highlights of his semester was accompanying his sponsor to the state capitol, Tallahassee, where he met with the lieutenant governor and other officials. "Law used to be a remote interest, but now I'm very caught up in it," reports the Palm Beach intern. Winner of several scholastic awards and selected by the American Legion to attend Boys State, he has addressed both the Lions Club and a school board meeting about the programs.

Problem Solving Curriculum

Besides the excitement of their placements, which extend from Monday through Thursday during the entire business day, the interns also attend Friday seminars on management, administration, and decision making. Adapted from the Harvard Business School case study approach, the curriculum emphasizes a problem solving focus in which interns learn to function, management consultant fashion, as analysts of organizational problems.

After the first few weeks of reading prepared cases, the interns take over and begin to develop their own. "I was hesitant at first about presenting a case study to the Palm Beach group," recalls Patrick Healy. "However, the other interns quickly got caught up in it."

Role of the Coordinator

The Palm Beach County Public Schools coordinator Harriet "Penny" Hogan considers her job ideal. Ms. Hogan and other coordinators throughout the country are responsible for identifying potential sponsors, developing the role of the high school student, briefing the teachers and additional school personnel, and recruiting students in the high schools. Coordinators speak to student groups; perform the necessary administrative tasks of distributing applications and program materials; and personally follow up with students who have displayed an initial interest in the internship program.

In addition, the coordinators orchestrate sponsor and student interviews, decide which students will be seen by what sponsors, and arrange final placements based on mutual preferences.

Students keep extensive records of their experiences through daily logs, which are reviewed by the coordinators.

A National Base

Like the other program managers, Coordinator Hogan was initially prepared for her assignment through a week-long National Coordinators Training Academy sponsored by the parent organization, Executive High School Internships of America. Located in New York City, the national office provides training and ongoing technical assistance to participating districts, along with program materials, coordinators' bulletins, newsletters, and intern insurance. An annual National Staff Training Institute brings together all the Executive Internships coordinators from around the country, and the National Conference of Executive High School Interns attracts student delegates from each of the districts to Washington, D.C., for a week.

The national office works with school systems that agree to fund a full time coordinator position for the program; release students full time for participation, without having to attend classes or keep up with schoolwork; provide optional independent study opportunities, and award a full semester of academic credit for participation.

Founded in 1971 as a joint undertaking of the New York City Human Resources Administration and Board of Education, the program has been expanded around the country through the national office, which opened in 1973. Its support has come from major foundations, including Ford and Rockefeller, the National Institute of Education (NIE), participating school systems, and corporations such as Exxon Company, USA. NIE is underwriting a two year evaluation of the program through the Center for Vocational Education at Ohio State University. (pp. 22-23).

COMPREHENSIVE PROGRAMING FOR PEOPLE WHO ARE GIFTED AND TALENTED

Almost everyone recognizes that gifted and talented children constitute one of the nation's most important natural resources. Yet only recently has serious consideration been paid to conserving and nurturing the resource. Where that does occur, attention comes to focus on educators, because the informed public recognizes the major role teachers have to play if these pupils are to attain what they should.

Characteristics of a Comprehensive Education Program

A fully developed educational scheme for gifted and talented pupils should have these attributes:

1. The education of the selected pupils should be conducted in the same schools and, for the most part, in the same class groups where all other pupils are.
2. All education for these pupils (and others) should be personalized.
3. All teachers, whether of kindergarten, music, secondary mathematics, or physical education, should have at least the basic competencies in understanding and teaching gifted and talented pupils.
4. There should be an operating system that locates all pupils who need special education because of their unusually rapid rate of cognitive development.
5. A firm linkage should be evident between the selection of pupils and the specialized teaching they are to receive. A psychoeducational match based on treatment/aptitude interaction is essential between what assessment shows that a pupil needs and the particular instruction to be supplied to that pupil.
6. There should be a staff of teacher specialists in the education of gifted and talented pupils, with supporting aides.
7. The teacher specialists should work in parallel with regular class teachers to assess needs, plan, carry out instruction, and evaluate outcomes.
8. The school's program should begin, if parents wish, in the earliest years with help in the child's home in guiding the child's development. As soon after birth as parents feel that precocity begins to evidence itself, they should be able to call on the schools for discussion and advice.
9. All components of the program should be under the surveillance of regular class teachers, special educators, parents, and the pupils themselves. That should be done with ready availability of other educational personnel like counselors, psychologists, supervisors, and administrators. In particular, the preferred practices listed earlier should be present.
10. Opportunities for pupils with high rates of cognitive development to study and to socialize with others like themselves, (older, younger, and of the same age) should be readily available within the wider setting of the mainstream of school and community.

Teachers, according to future projections, will have more and more opportunities to show professional leadership and to exert influential guidance concerning program development in the schools. It is to be expected that the 10 points listed here will be shaped and sharpened further by their contributions.

Education as Part of a Broader Group of Services

Gifted and talented pupils soon find that others are interested in them. The business and industry sector reaches out to them through supporting science fairs, junior achievement programs, and major sports drafts. Patriotic and fraternal organizations sponsor essay contests. Private secondary schools offer scholarships and higher education institutions do likewise on a much larger scale. Gifted and talented pupils who have handicaps readily capture the attention of both volunteer and tax supported rehabilitation agencies.

Teachers and other educators who are aware of these and other in-school and extraschool factors can be very helpful to gifted and talented pupils and their families. Pupils and their families turn to their present and former teachers for advice. Thus it is important that teachers be well informed about where to refer parents and pupils for expert guidance. Moreover, some such pupils from minority or disadvantaged backgrounds do not learn about opportunities unless their teachers inform them and, where necessary, intercede on their behalf. In this connection, it can be advantageous if teachers are knowledgeable about organizations of parents and others that take advocacy positions respecting the gifted and talented.

The probability seems good that more systematic and widespread community based services of all kinds, in addition to school services, will focus on highly able children and youth. Teachers will certainly have opportunities to relate to the services suggested above. More than that, teachers with special competencies may well find such agencies interested in them as prospective part or full time staff members.

The Continuing Need for Teachers

Most school systems in America are in the earliest stages of program development for gifted and talented students. Every school system in the country has such students and is, or likely soon will be, under some pressure to move forward on the matter.

Teachers are a fundamental necessity for program development, in every department and at every level of the school system. Specialist teachers will need to be prepared and employed. Also, regular class teachers who have not prepared as specialists but who have acquired basic special education competencies are in thin supply. These factors argue in favor of the viewpoint that a shortage exists. There will be a substantial need for professional educational personnel in the forseeable future.

SUGGESTIONS FOR STUDENTS AND INSTRUCTOR

1. Visit school programs where gifted and talented pupils are being taught. These should cover preschool through secondary schools and a range of settings from a full and partial mainstreaming to complete segregation.
2. Ask students to query successful teachers about their most useful teaching techniques. Help them prepare a bulletin describing the techniques, with credit for authors and contributors.
3. Have students discuss and decide what characteristics they would look for if they wished to locate elementary or secondary age children who have high promise of attaining moral and ethical leadership as adults. Would they be different if one were looking for prospective scientific leaders?
4. How do you think *gifted and talented* would have been defined in King Arthur's Court? How is it defined today in China? How might it be defined here in the year 2000?
5. Sit in with teachers who are planning individualized instruction plans for gifted and talented pupils. What competencies appear most important in that task?
6. Arrange for students to attend and report on a meeting of the local group that advocates programs for gifted and talented persons. Students might wish to divide activities according to their interests and report to each other on what they observe and learn.
7. Obtain copies of several different sets of state regulations governing education of the gifted and analyze them. What are the educational justifications for each regulation? How could the regulations be improved?

TOPICAL BIBLIOGRAPHIES

Assessment of Gifted and Talented Pupils

Baldwin, A. Y., Gear, G.H., & Lucito, L. J. (Eds.). *Educational planning for the gifted: Overcoming cultural, geographic, and socioeconomic barriers.* Reston VA: The Council for Exceptional Children, 1978.

Kaufmann, F. *Your gifted child and you.* Reston VA: The Council for Exceptional Children, 1976.

Martinson, R. A. *The identification of the gifted and talented.* Reston VA: The Council for Exceptional Children, 1975.

Pegnato, C. W., & Birch, J. W. Locating gifted children in junior high school: A comparison of methods. *Exceptional Children,* 1959, *25*, 300-304.

Renzulli, J. S. The identification and development of talent potential among the disadvantaged. *Contemporary Education,* 1971, *42,* 122-125.

Renzulli, J. S. *New directions in creativity.* New York: Harper & Row, 1975.

Renzulli, J. S. & Smith, L. A. Two approaches to identification of gifted students. *Exceptional Children,* 1977, *43,* 512-518.

Tongue, C., & Sperling, C. *Gifted and talented: An identification model.* Raleigh NC: Division for Exceptional Children, State Department of Public Instruction, 1976.

Torrance, E. P. *Discovery and nurturance of giftedness in the culturally different.* Reston, VA: The Council for Exceptional Children, 1977.

Biographies of Gifted and Talented Persons

Beth, W. R. *The infirmities of genius.* New York: Philosophical Library, 1952.

Goertzel, V., & Goertzel, M. *Cradles of eminence.* Boston: Little Brown, 1962.

Hollingworth, L. S. *Children above 180 I.Q.* Yonkers NY: World Book, 1942.

Terman, L. M., & Oden, M. *The gifted child grows up: Genetic studies of genius* (Vol. 4). Stanford CA: Stanford University Press, 1947.

Creativity in Children and Youth

Getzels, J. W. *Creativity and intelligence.* London, New York: Wiley, 1962.

McClelland, D.C., Baldwin, A.L., Bronfenbrenner, U., & Strodtbeck, F.L. *Talent and society.* Princeton NJ: Van Nostrand, 1958.

Renzulli, J. S. Talent potential in minority group students. *Exceptional Children,* 1973, *39,* 437-444.

Early Childhood of Gifted and Talented Persons

Cox, C. *Genetic studies of genius* (Vol. 2). *The early mental traits of three hundred geniuses.* Stanford CA: Stanford University Press, 1969.

Goertzel, V., & Goertzel, M. *Cradles of eminence.* Boston: Little Brown, 1962.

Hollingworth, L. S. *Children above 180 I.Q.* Yonkers NY: World Book, 1942.

Terman, L.M. The discovery and encouragement of exceptional talent. *American Psychologist,* 1954, *8*(6), 221-230.

History of Genius

Albert, R. S. Toward a behavioral definition of genius. *American Psychologist,* February 1975, 140-151.

Galton, F. *Hereditary genius.* New York: Macmillan, 1869.

Pressey, S. L. Concerning the nature and nurture of genius. *Scientific Monthly,* September 1955, 123-129. (Reprinted in J. L. French, *Educating the gifted.* Columbus OH: Holt, 1959.)

Sumption, M. C., & Luecking, E. M. *Education of the gifted.* New York: Ronald, 1960.

Witty, P. The gifted child. *Exceptional Children,* 1953, *19,* 255-259.

Special Classes, Schools, and Programs for Gifted and Talented Pupils

Barbe, W. B. Evaluation of special classes for gifted children. *Exceptional Children,* 1955, *22,* 60-62

Barbe, W. B., & Renzulli, J. S. (Eds.). *Psychology and education of the gifted* (2nd ed.). New York: Irvington, 1975.

Dunlap, J. M. Gifted children in an enriched program. *Exceptional Children,* 1955, *21*, 135-137.

Hall, T. *Gifted children: The Cleveland story.* Cleveland: World Publishing, 1956.

Henson, F. D. *Mainstreaming the gifted.* Austin TX: Learning Concepts, 1976.

Hildreth, G. H. *Educating gifted children at Hunter College Elementary School.* New York: Harper, 1952.

Kaplan, S. N. *Providing programs for the gifted and talented.* Reston VA: The Council for Exceptional Children, 1975.

Mallis, J. A. Seminar for superior students. *Clearing House,* November 1956, 175-178.

Marland, S. P. Advanced placement. *Today's Education,* January-February 1976, 43-44.

Reynolds, M., Birch, J., & Tuseth, A. Review of research on early admission. In M. C. Reynolds (Ed.). *Early school admission for mentally advanced children.* Reston VA: The Council for Exceptional Children, 1962.

Scheifele, M. *The gifted child in the regular classroom: Practical suggestions for teaching* (No. 12). Teachers College, Columbia University. New York: American Book-Stratford Press, 1953.

The nation's commitment to the education of gifted and talented children and youth—Summary of findings from a 1977 survey of states and territories. Reston VA: The Council for Exceptional Children. 1978

Special Methods for Teaching Gifted and Talented Pupils

Boston, B. O. *Gifted and talented: Developing elementary and secondary programs.* Reston VA: The Council for Exceptional Children, 1975.

Gallagher, J. J. *Teaching the gifted child.* Boston: Allyn & Bacon, 1975.

Kaplan, S. N. *Providing programs for the gifted and talented: A handbook.* Reston VA: The Council for Exceptional Children, 1975.

Keating, D. K. (Ed.). *Intellectual talent: Research and development.* Baltimore: Johns Hopkins University Press, 1976.

Maker, C. J. *Training teachers for the gifted and talented: A comparison of models.* Reston VA: The Council for Exceptional Children, 1975.

Maker, C. J. *Providing programs for the gifted handicapped.* Reston VA: The Council for Exceptional Children, 1977.

Newland, T. E. *The gifted in socio-educational perspectives.* Englewood Cliffs NJ: Prentice-Hall, 1976.

Phillips, M. Confluent education, the hidden curriculum, and the gifted child. *Phi Delta Kappan,* 1976, *58*(3), 238-241.

Pressey, S. L. *Educational acceleration: Appraisals and basic problems.* Columbus: Ohio State University, 1949.

Renzulli, J. S. *New directions in creativity.* New York: Harper & Row, 1975.

Sisk, D. Teaching the gifted and talented teacher: A training model. *Gifted Child Quarterly,* 1975, *19*(9), 81-88.

6. Mental Retardation
Low Rate of Cognitive Development

CHAPTER OUTLINE

THE CHALLENGE TO EDUCATORS
- Legal Considerations
- Medical Considerations
- Social Welfare Considerations
- Educational Considerations
- Emerging Changes in Terminology

THE PERSON CALLED MENTALLY RETARDED

MODERN CONCEPT AND SIGNIFICANCE OF MENTAL RETARDATION
- Definition of Mental Retardation
- Meaning of the Criterion Variables
- Degrees of Mental Retardation
- Impermanence of Mental Retardation
- Causes of Slow Cognitive Development
- Prevention of Mental Retardation

PREVAILING VERSUS PREFERRED PRACTICES

THE BEGINNING OF SPECIAL EDUCATION FOR MENTALLY RETARDED PUPILS
- Present Status of Special Education
- Current Trends in Special Education

THE ROLE OF THE REGULAR CLASS TEACHER
- Teamwork with Specialists
- Individualization of Instruction
  - Curriculum Individualization
  - Methods of Teaching
  - Instructional Materials
  - Organization for Instruction
  - School Physical Plant
  - Summary

A PUBLIC SCHOOL PROGRAM IN TACOMA, WASHINGTON
- Decentralization and Progressive Inclusion
- Parent Involvement
- Preparation of Teachers
- Teacher Response
- Results

TEACHING MENTALLY RETARDED PUPILS IN RESIDENTIAL SETTINGS
- Western State School and Hospital, Pennsylvania
- Group Community Residences

SELF CONTAINED SPECIAL CLASSES AND DAY SCHOOLS
- Background
- Current Practices

COMPREHENSIVE PROGRAMMING FOR PERSONS WITH ATTENUATED RATES OF COGNITIVE GROWTH

EDUCATION AS PART OF A BROADER GROUP OF SERVICES

THE CONTINUING NEED FOR TEACHERS

SUGGESTIONS FOR STUDENTS AND INSTRUCTOR

TOPICAL BIBLIOGRAPHIES

THE CHALLENGE TO EDUCATORS

The original concept of mental retardation is rapidly diminishing in importance in education. The terminology historically associated with mental retardation is fading from use. Despite those tendencies, though, the impact of mental retardation is still strongly felt in important ways both in education and in other sectors of society. It will certainly continue to have a significant influence in the health and welfare professions, in law, and in the daily lives of a great many families and individuals.

The first reasons for defining mental retardation were legal and medical. During the 19th century courts began to take official note that mentally retarded persons required special consideration. At about the same time physicians began serious efforts to analyze and treat the condition. Each of these background elements is discussed in this chapter. The challenge the condition now presents to educators is a significant one, including a reformulation of the concept of mental retardation itself.

Legal Considerations

It was apparent early that certain persons required guidance and protection because they showed poor insight and they did not profit readily from experience. They were easy prey to the unscrupulous. If left to their own devices they failed to attend to their own health, dress, and safety from the elements. They made unreliable parents and workers. If they inherited money or property, they did not manage it well. The courts termed this cluster of characteristics mental retardation (or deficiency), a condition associated with inability to look after one's day to day affairs and to plan one's future with ordinary prudence and sound judgment. The courts appointed guardians for persons of means who were judged to be mentally retarded. Those who had no assets or families to care for them were placed in asylums or allowed to roam as beggars.

The 20th century, particularly its second half, witnessed heightened concern for the legal status of all retarded persons. With the recognition that special education could improve judgment, planning, and daily living skills, the legal approach to mental retardation changed appreciably. Instead of being considered a static condition requiring guidance, supervision, and sometimes custody, a dynamic view of mental retardation began to emerge. Through instruction the condition could be ameliorated. The right to this needed special education, therefore, became an issue, as did all other personal and civil rights of retarded persons.

The right to equality of educational opportunity and to equality in other civil matters now has been established for mentally retarded citizens through a series of decisions and consent agreements. These rights are now being implemented. As this is being written the US Supreme Court has agreed to hear arguments on the proposal that mentally retarded children be represented by counsel and have the guarantee of a hearing if their parents wish to have them placed in institutions. This promises to be one more step on the road to assured civil rights for all retarded persons.

The slow rate of cognitive development called mental retardation is well recognized in law. A body of legislation and jurisprudence is growing around it. These legal considerations affect everyone. Most of all they tend to project persons with mental retardation into full and first class citizenship.

Medical Considerations

The initial interest of physicians in mentally retarded persons centered on their physical status and general health. Before 1850 students of human physiology had observed that mentally retarded persons were not all alike. The more extreme, rare, and highly visible forms first excited physicians' attention. A complex list of medical terms came into being to describe various forms of mental retardation. Since physicians were particularly interested in causes, some of the newly coined medical terms combined descriptions and implications of cause. An example is *hydrocephaly,* which is evidenced by enlargement of the cranium due to pressure from cerebrospinal fluid whose drainage passage into the rest of the body is blocked. The pressure also limits development of the cerebral cortex, which presumably results in some degree of mental retardation. Others were simply descriptive of how the retarded person looked. *Mongolism,* for example, is a name for a genetically linked condition that limits to varying degrees the maturation of a number of body systems, including the central nervous system. Physically, the individual tends to have an external eye structure resembling that of Orientals, hence the name. The condition is now called Down's syndrome after the physician credited with first describing it.

The custom of the health professions was to indicate the gravity of any condition in a systematic way. Degrees of retardation were described as borderline, moron, imbecile, or idiot. Later, more general terms were used: mild, moderate, severe, and profound.

Medical efforts to understand, prevent, correct, or ameliorate mental retardation have met with increasing success. Some of the causes are now under almost complete control. An example is *cretinism,* which is the term for mental underdevelopment arising from thyroid insufficiency in early childhood.

Some problems can be anticipated before birth by *amniocentesis.* That is a procedure by which a sample of the fluid that surrounds the unborn child is drawn off and analyzed. Clues from the analysis can lead to preventive measures in some instances. Other retardation producing anomalies yield to surgery, as when improved drainage of cerebrospinal fluid reduces the impact of hydrocephaly.

At the same time, medical advances increase the number and kinds of mentally retarded persons each year. Some occur as the result of side effects of new medications, like the thalidomide babies of the late 1950's and early 1960's (Dacarie, 1969). Others result when improved care in general decreases infant morbidity.

Despite important medical advances in managing mental retardation, there remains much more to be done. Hospital and university affiliated units and health professions research units aimed at preventing and correcting mental retardation, and supported with taxes and through private funds, press back the boundaries of the unknown a little more each year. Because of the variety and multiplicity of causes, however, it is doubtful that one can expect a major breakthrough that would eliminate the condition, as in the case of poliomyelitis a few years ago. In the meantime, mental retardation continues to be defined for the purposes of health workers in terms of its causes and in terms of the degree to which it is present.

Social Welfare Considerations

Social welfare agencies have responsibilities toward mentally retarded persons, too. Whether tax supported or volunteer, those agencies supply much of the supervision, daily living guidance, sheltered employment, and recreation services for retarded individuals who need them. For example, since 1965 the nation has seen a sharp increase in the return of young mentally retarded adults to large and small communities from segregated residential institutions. Group living arrangements, where 8 to 16 retarded persons enjoy a homelike, family style setting under general supervision by a live-in married couple, are growing in popularity as an alternative to institutional life. Social welfare personnel, many of them social workers, rehabilitation counselors, or psychologists, locate, plan for, and manage groups of such halfway houses. Support comes from civil authorities through county or regional mental health/mental retardation agencies and local affiliates of organizations like the National Association for Retarded Citizens.

Probably no group has a more wide ranging set of responsibilities in dealing with the daily life problems of mentally retarded persons than the social welfare professionals. Their functions stretch from safety, housing, and police on the one hand to employment services and recreation on the other. In that array of interactions the agencies and their staff members operate from a base that requires that slow cognitive development be acknowledged and defined so their clients can be assured of the services to which they have a right. Thus, they tend to use legal definitions of mental retardation.

Educational Considerations

There is less and less need in education for use of the term *mental retardation* as such. Certainly teachers need to know what is meant by mental retardation in the legal, medical, and social welfare senses. Teachers interact increasingly with other professionals from those areas, so it is necessary to understand key concepts in each other's technical language. Moreover, teachers need to understand enough of the legal, medical, and social welfare background and current status of persons with slow cognitive development to be well informed professionals themselves. They may sometimes need to discuss matters in those individual areas with the persons themselves and their parents or guardians. But, for the purposes of education—for the instructional planning, the teaching, and the evaluation of pupil progress that teachers do every day—the legal, medical, and social welfare concepts and terminology of mental retardation no longer have much relevance. In fact, in the view of some educational leaders, their use in education may actually be counter-productive.

It is obviously necessary to use the term *mental retardation* and other technical expressions associated with it in this chapter and elsewhere in this book. A transition to more appropriate language is under way, but it is still far from complete. The fact that terminological changes are taking place in education, too, does not mean that other relevant groups such as legislatures, lawyers, the judiciary, the health professions, and the public welfare professions will move away from the conventional terminology at the same time or pace. Such moves occur, usually, over fairly long periods of time.

More important than the change in terminology is the change in the way the condition is conceptualized. Educators are concerned primarily with fostering development. Their function is first to determine each pupil's present level of cognitive, affective, and motor achievement and second to help each individual pupil enhance and build on those foundations toward higher attainments. Moreover, each pupil's goals need to be individually formulated and the measure or progress must be personally unique, rather than a comparison with an external average or norm. It is this conceptualization, *individualized education,* that is now actually embracing such unusual developmental conditions as mental retardation and rendering untenable the early thinking about it as a status outside the range of regular education.

Emerging Changes in Terminology

Changes in how society has viewed persons with what some call mental retardation can be inferred from the alterations in the name of the major United States professional and scientific organization devoted to the study of slow cognitive development. Past names of the association and the dates of adoption are as follows:

1876—Association of Medical Superintendents of American Institutions for Idiotic and Feeble-Minded Persons
1906—American Association for the Study of the Feeble-Minded
1938—American Association on Mental Deficiency
1976—(Proposed Change) American Association for Mental Development (Sloan & Stevens, 1976)

As S.A. Warren, president of the Association, said about arguments in favor of the proposed change (1976):

The proposed name indicates our interest in persons with special needs who may not fit clearly under a strict interpretation of the diagnostic classification.

Use of the term "mental development" may add to the present de-emphasis on labels and may include some persons (e.g., Borderline, some EMR) who seem to be excluded by the recent Manual's definition.

The proposed name seems a more moderate description, stressing positive aspects, emphasizing something to be achieved, offering what some see as more acceptable language, and fostering a concept of development rather than disability and deficit.

The proposed name seems consistent with the current emphasis on generic services, including mainstreaming.

The proposed name seems to reflect a more accurate description of the population served than "mentally deficient," a term that in some contexts connotes the more seriously, neurologically impaired and thus may seem not to apply to the majority of retarded population.

The new name stresses a process which may lead to improvement, growth, and development, instead of reliance on a static diagnosis and the condition as we find it.

Warren's reasons reflect national trends of great moment to teachers. They accurately represent the cresting of a wave that is moving this and other countries toward more humane behavior with those who have traditionally been called mentally retarded and with other handicapped persons, too. It is a move toward full and equal citizenship and opportunity to participate in all sectors of society.

THE PERSON CALLED MENTALLY RETARDED

Persons with slow cognitive development are just plain people, like everyone else. There are no general personality or character factors that distinguish them from others. They are neither happier nor sadder. They are neither more nor less friendly, kind, or honest. The vast majority are as handsome or plain as their brothers and sisters and neighbors who are not dubbed mentally retarded. Except for a few, mainly among those who are severely or profoundly slow, they will not be identified by physical appearance. They may be spirited or solemn, their eyes may dance with mischief or be direct and serious. They can run and jump and sing songs. They can play jacks, hopscotch, basketball, and ride horses. They can be warm and loving, angry, disappointed, thrilled, or grieved. They are, like all of us, part of the infinitely variable human race.

Then why has it seemed necessary to provide special education for children and youth said to show mental retardation? Any why has so much of that special education separated these pupils from the rest of their age mates? Moreover, why have laws been enacted on behalf of persons with mental retardation particularly and why have groups of their parents and friends needed to organize into local, state, and national associations to safeguard their rights and further their interests?

The answer is complex, but its central core is that life in our society makes heavy demands on each person's cognitive power and on that power's reflection in social adaptive qualities. That is precisely where mental retardation strikes most devastatingly at human functioning.

It is society's efforts, through schooling, to improve social adaptability and cognitive functioning that have prompted each state to provide special education, special legal provisions, and special organizations to work for the improved development of those who have been called mentally retarded. Teachers in public and private schools find themselves in the very heart of that effort.

These two real life stories, the first about Danny and the second about David, were published in 1976. They are included here to help give a first person feel for the kind of individuals teachers who work with retarded pupils really get to know and understand.

Being Retarded Does Not Bother Danny Wheeler*

It is not easy to ask a retarded person how he feels about being retarded but it is reassuring to hear one of them say, "Oh, it doesn't bother me."

Whether that is the whole truth or just a mask behind which the retarded individual has learned to hide his true feelings is not easy to decide.

This question came up recently when *Mental Retardation News* was interviewing a young retarded man who appears to have a very well adjusted life, working in Las Vegas. It had been suggested that reactions to the world in general, and his adjustments to his life in particular could be revealing. And they were, because we seem to have found a singularly adaptable young career-oriented fellow in 25-year-old Daniel Wheeler.

---

*Reprinted with permission from *Mental Retardation News,* Feb. 1976, Vol. 25, No. 2, page 8. Copyright 1976 by the National Association for Retarded Citizens.

Wheeler first was an employee at the Opportunity Village (The Las Vegas Association for Retarded Citizens) button factory and he currently is employed at the Golden Nugget Casino, where he recently was promoted from packaging and wrapping to porter. He is married, his wife is pregnant for the first time, and from visible evidence, he has no regrets or bitterness about his life. In fact, he is a public spirited citizen who is on the board of directors of Nevada Advocates for the Mentally Retarded and attends all their board meetings and social functions. He also is a protege advocate George Rogers, who brought him to talk with us.

Daniel appears to have a double mission in life, because he not only has his job and his marriage (to a girl he dated for five years after they met in a special education class in high school) but he himself acts as an advocate for several of his friends at the Opportunity Village Workshops.

"They are sometimes a little irresponsible," his advocate interjected, adding that part of Daniel's duty is to see that they get to the workshop on time, to the bus in time so they won't miss the ride when they are going on an outing, and he even helps to see that they get to church when they want to go.

We talked for a bit about his relationship with George Rogers, his advocate, and Daniel admitted that at first he had been apprehensive. He couldn't understand why anybody would want to sponsor him, but after they had gone to a few baseball games and other functions, he began to warm up to the relationship. It has been a going thing now for the past two-and-a-half years. In fact it has helped Daniel become interested in being an advocate himself.

Neatly dressed in a suit and tie and carrying his hat, Daniel spoke of his career in school.

"I didn't feel any different from anybody else," he stressed, "and all the students seemed to welcome me." He graduated from Sparks High School, in Sparks, Nevada. "I just lived day-to-day and didn't worry about it."

Unlike many of his campanions Daniel has not been content to stay in what he refers to as their "square little world," referring of course to the dimensions and horizons, not a lack of sophistication.

"Too many of my friends just sit in a corner, and don't try to get involved in what's going on," he pointed out.

His hobbies include watching TV, playing records, and going to Sunday School. "That is," he adds, "when I get up in time." He also said, "The more I have my religion, the better life becomes."

He was raised in the Mormon faith by his mother and father and he has three brothers and one sister, all of whom lead normal lives. It is one of his ambitions to better understand the gospel and be able to explain it to some of his friends, who may find it a bit difficult.

As to his relationship with his family, "I keep in close touch with them," he said. "My dad always tried to include me in everything; he never looked down on me."

Daniel's father has worked for the Southern Pacific railroad as an engineer in Arizona for 22 years and during the holidays it has been Daniel's advocate's Christmas present to let him and a couple of his other proteges talk to their parents long distance.

As to the future, Daniel doesn't know just what it holds for him, but he is hopeful. Currently he is working with his advocate on a plan for starting a business using retarded persons in yard maintenance, sweeping, cleaning and watering—something they could do after their workshop hours. He also is interested in art, and in studying cartooning, for which he has marked talent.

"I have also been making speeches," he told us, "going around to local organizations, and telling them how they can help retarded persons."

He admits to some stage fright at first but seems to have become, with time, a reasonably polished speaker. He feels that now he is happily "in the middle," working as a liaison between his retarded friends and the outside world. Apparently a shade more articulate on paper than he is in person, when applying as an advocate to the Nevada Advocacy group, he wrote the following:

"This is what I think I can do. I can help the advocate board by my ability to talk on the level of the trainees and understand their problems. I also can understand and make some of the trainees understand what to do about their problems and hang-ups. I will learn and help in the best of my knowledge. This is what a trainee benefits from an advocate. A trainee has someone to turn to for advice when there is no one around to help. THEY HAVE SOMEONE TO LOOK UP TO WHEN LONELY OR DOWN. The trainees have fun with an advocate by going places, doing many things with their advocate. WHAT IS AN ADVOCATE? They are a group of people helping these trainees have a good time and give them advice on many things and problems they might have."

That is Daniel Wheeler, a young man with a positive attitude towards life and a desire to help improve the lives of other retarded persons like himself.

Danny's story has much in common with those of other young people who have completed public and private school programs that were designed to build on strengths and to minimize limitations (Dinger, 1961). The central task is to bring that kind of high quality education into all schools for all who can benefit from it.

David's Story

Too often the story of an institution's failure to perform its idealized role is emblazoned across the headlines of the daily tabloid, but this is a different story, the story of one institution's success with one client.

Born at Madigan Army Hospital, Tacoma, Washington, the 3rd of March 1956, David was the second of six children born to his parents. David, a 3 lb., 8 oz. baby was born prematurely after a pregnancy of only six and one half months. His early development, both intellectually and physically, was slow. He sat up at one year, walked at three, and began to speak at five. After unsuccessful attempts at school in Germany and in Denver, Colorado, David was admitted to the State Home and Training School at Grand Junction, Colorado on November 30, 1964 at the age of eight.

Almost 11 years later, a confident young man, David was released from the Training School to seek his place in the world, not as he entered, but as an ambitious youth ready to face success or failure on his own.

During the course of his 11 years at the School, David progressed through numerous training and therapeutic programs, both with the institutional school and in the local public school system. David, who attended Grand Junction High School, is one of a small number of institutionalized persons who have scored a touchdown for a state championship caliber football squad.

One of David's earlier adventures was as a Scout, when he was selected to attend the National Jamboree, traveling to Idaho in the process. David later became a member of the State Home and Training School's Jaycee chapter, the first organization of its kind to be based upon the campus of a residential school for the developmentally disabled.

David's family has maintained a close interest in his progress through the Training School, often contacting David by telephone and arranging for visits to various family members from as distant a place as Georgia and California.

At the time of graduation in the Spring of 1975, David had participated in the school district's "Work Experience-Study Program" and had improved both his work and academic skills. His teachers estimated his reading level at between the 3rd and 4th grades and his arithmetic skills at the 5th and 6th grade level. He had completed Driver's Education, earned letters in football and track, and had been selected as the "Spirit King Award" recipient and reigned over one of the school dances. He had also been recognized as an outstanding local student by one of the local banks. His formal educational program, which began in the institution, progressed far beyond what was thought possible when he was admitted in the mid 1960's.

David's participation in the Work Study program included work activities as a grocery carry out clerk, a diswasher at the fraternal lodge, and as a clean-up man for a local drug store. With the money earned at these various endeavors, he has opened a private checking account and is making his own purchases in the community.

A few weeks prior to his release from the Training School David expressed his great desire to become totally independent and a realization that he has much to learn in order to become so. He stated a reluctance to brag about his achievements but also pointed out that many students in "Special Education" can surprise others if given the chance to show their abilities. He spoke of his long range goals of working in construction or as a grocery stocker or cashier.

David has not yet achieved his goal of total independence and is still living in a somewhat restricted environment, that of a group home. He has, however, been able to move himself out of the institutional setting, both by his own efforts and that of the Training School staff and community programmers. He will have his successes and he will have his failures in the months and years ahead, but David Jones' story is one worthy of notice. (Smith, 1976, pp. 7-8)

David Jones, like Danny Wheeler, illustrates how powerful motivation and education can be in instances of slow cognitive development.

MODERN CONCEPT AND SIGNIFICANCE OF MENTAL RETARDATION

If teachers are called on to define mental retardation, they might well say it is primarily a condition of slowed cognitive development, which suggests the need for certain kinds of instruction, rather than anything else of educational import. The instruction needs to be matched to cognitive level and interest.

What can be said of the various subclassifications of mental retardation from this instructional point of view? Are they useful? In general our answer is "Yes." The test of usefulness for the educator is whether these aspects of classification are helpful in allocating or matching lessons to instruction.

The long recognized historical classifications do have contemporary meaning. They have something to say to the educator, but they should not be expected to say too much. We much prefer, in the daily work of education, to make more direct instructional assessments in the domain of the curriculum, indicating what is next in the sequence of learning. Only occasionally will it be necessary to make the grand prediction about the long course of an individual's development, and that, we believe, should be done only *very* cautiously. Realistic long range planning needs to be done, certainly. The descriptions of mental retardation by levels serves a useful purpose in that context.

From this viewpoint, it is the child's cognitive development that is of primary, central, and day to day concern to educators. Individualized educational procedures that target on that characteristic can and should be designed without reference to labels that levels of retardation can easily become. That, it is hoped, will soon become a prevailing practice.

Definition of Mental Retardation

It is a sign of more constructive thinking about human differences that many changes have been made or suggested in the definition of mental retardation in recent years. Currently, the broadest consensus across professions seems to have been reached in this statement, often called the AAMD definition:

> Mental retardation refers to significantly sub-average general intellectual functioning existing concurrently with deficits in adaptive behavior, and manifested during the developmental period. (Grossman, 1973, p. 11)

Even that widely used definition rests on a number of assumptions that appear questionable to many. But they differ on what should be done about it. Bijou (1966) considers intelligence, as historically defined, to be an unnecessary concept when talking about mental retardation. Even the term *mental* may be superfluous. It is his proposal that

> developmental retardation be treated as observable, objectively defined stimulus-response relationships without recourse to hypothetical mental concepts such as "defective intelligence". . . . From this point of view a retarded individual is one who has a limited repertory of behavior shaped by events that constitute his history. Retardation is not conceived of as a symptom. (p. 2)

On the one hand, there are educators and other professionals who consider any definition of mental retardation unnecessary and potentially damaging because of the negative attitudes and limited expectancies its use can engender. On the other hand, there are educators and other professionals who believe that a categorical definition delineating the characteristics and bounds of a condition named mental retardation is fundamentally important to scientific progress in education and the other helping professions as well as being a basic necessity for legal and social welfare policy and administration.

The particular criterion variables in the AAMD definition around which those polarized views turn are very important to teachers because questions about the variables really reflect contemporary educational concerns of major magnitude. The final determination of how matters will be resolved hinges to a large extent on how teachers react to them and help to guide others to think about them.

We recognize the broader social applicability of the AAMD definition, and for that reason we believe teachers should understand it well. However, as we indicated earlier, we consider the concept of variable rates of cognitive development, which can influence and be influenced by the teacher's instruction, to be more useful in education!

Meaning of the Criterion Variables

For the AAMD definition, subaverage intellectual functioning is considered to be present when an individual earns an intelligence test score more than two standard deviations below the test's mean. The test must be an individual one, administered by a professional person competent to do so, and it must be a test that is appropriate for the individual. That is, if the person being examined is blind or has defective vision, the test must make little or no demands on vision and the test administrator must have had training in its use with blind or partially seeing persons. For another example, if the person being examined is of Mexican-American background, with Spanish the initial and home language, the test should be one with accommodations for that built in, and the examiner must have competence in testing persons of such background. In short, the test must be valid, accurate, and fair and so must the examiner, with respect to the individual being tested.

For the AAMD definition's purpose, the period of development begins with conception and concludes at the end of the 18th year. That is, of course, a technical and arbitrary matter; if mental retardation occurs later, it can sometimes be indistinguishable from that which occurred before. For instance, if a 15 year old youth were injured in an accident or had an illness that destroyed a significant amount of the central nervous system essential for cognition, and if the same thing happened to a 19 year old, the results could probably not be distinguished. Yet for definitional purposes the developmental period is limited to the period between conception and the 18th year.

Adaptive behavior, in the AAMD frame of reference, includes coping satisfactorily with the ordinary events of growing up or maturing. It is shown in how successful one is in school and in taking care of one's personal life and needs. Impairment in adaptive behavior can be detected *in part* by below average progress in school achievement, as measured by appropriate tests. Appropriateness, as the word is used here, has essentially the same boundaries as it does for intelligence testing; the assessment needs to be valid, accurate, and fair for the person being tested. Moreover, the person being tested should first have had a reasonable opportunity to learn under the tutelage of sympathetic and professionally able teachers.

Another essential area to be checked before one can be truly said to have an impairment in adaptive behavior is the social development sphere. For this purpose, a test like the Vineland Social Maturity Scale (Doll, 1953) is best used. Again, the same precautions about validity, accuracy, and fairness must be observed. If the child or youth being assessed is deaf, for instance, adjustments must be made in expectancy about typical communication skills development. Other adaptations are needed when physical conditions limit mobility.

The criterion for impairment is not stated as specifically as that for "subaverage" in the intelligence section of the definition. The judgment must be made with great caution and with due consideration of the danger of deciding that the individual's adaptive behavior is impaired, unless one is sure that the individual under consideration has had ample opportunity for remedial help and that it has not been effective. In other words, conclusive evidence of impairment in adaptive behavior that has its roots in the person's own makeup is hard to obtain and it will differ at different ages and in different cultures. Every step must first be taken to assure that any observed impairment is not the result of lack of opportunity to acquire suitable behavior. The American Association on Mental

Deficiency's Adaptive Behavior Scale may be used to help arrive at an objective assessment (Fogelman, 1975).

Mental retardation cannot be identified conclusively, however, simply by a combination of tests of intelligence and adaptive behavior in the developmental period. A low intelligence score *can* be the result of biases that escape the immediate attention of even well qualified examiners. Low scores on academic achievement tests *can* occur in the same way. The same is true for adaptive behavior ratings in the spheres of social, personal, and vocational activity. So, even if all three criteria are met, the assessment must be considered inconclusive until and unless determined remedial efforts are given a thorough trial and prove fruitless.

Degrees of Mental Retardation

Mental retardation is usually spoken of as having four degrees—mild, moderate, severe, and profound. Most retardation is mild. The proportions diminish and the profound degree is least common. The degrees are not clearly separable; one merges into the other. Though their boundaries are not sharp or finite, the four degrees have traditionally guided how educational specialists and other concerned professionals have talked about mental retardation.

Teachers from kindergarten through secondary school need to be knowledgeable about the names given to levels of retardation, how the levels were derived, and what they mean to practitioners in the health and welfare professions. Teachers may be called on to interpret the commonly used levels of retardation to parents, other children, other professionals, and to lay groups.

Table 6-1, Levels of Adaptive Behavior, tells something about what the four levels were intended to mean about potential for attainment during three periods of life. Though developed more than two decades ago (Sloan & Birch, 1955) the brief behavioral statements in Table 6-1 still enjoy wide acceptance as baselines for thinking about the adaptive behavior of persons with mental retardation.

The broad acknowledgement of the rationale in Table 6-1 is illustrated by its appearance in a major publication from the office of the US Secretary of Health, Education, and Welfare (*The Problem of Mental Retardation,* 1969). Also, a number of other writers employ the same four levels with minor changes in language.

As Dunn (1973) said about the four levels in the table,

Clearly there are no sharp distinctions between persons falling on either side of the various demarkation lines. However [these]...general descriptions...have emerged over the years as having more meaning for persons involved in behavioral (educational, psychological, social, vocational)

TABLE 6-1
Levels of Adaptive Behavior

Level	Preschool age (0-5) maturation and development	School age (6-21) training and education	Adult (21) social and vocational adequacy
Mild	Can develop social and communication skills; minimal retardation in sensorimotor areas; rarely distinguished from normal until later age.	Can learn academic skills to approximately 6th grade level by late teens. Cannot learn general high school subjects. Needs special education, particularly at secondary school age levels.	Capable of social and vocational adequacy with proper education and training. Frequently needs supervision and guidance when under serious social or economic stress.
Moderate	Can talk or learn to communicate; poor social awareness; fair motor development; may profit from self help; can be managed with moderate supervision.	Can learn functional academic skills to approximately fourth grade level by late teens if given special education.	Capable of self maintenance in unskilled or semiskilled occupations; needs supervision and guidance when under mild social or economic stress.
Severe	Poor motor development; speech is minimal; generally unable to profit from training in self help; little or no communication skills.	Can talk or learn to communicate; can be trained in elemental health habits; cannot learn functional academic skills; profits from systematic habit training.	Can contribute partially to self support under complete supervision; can develop self protection skills to a minimal useful level in controlled environment.
Profound	Gross retardation; minimal capacity for functioning in sensorimotor areas; needs nursing care.	Some motor development present; cannot profit from training in self help; needs total care.	Some motor and speech development; totally incapable of self maintenance; needs complete care and supervision.

Note. From A Rationale for Degrees of Retardation, by W. Sloan and J.W. Birch, *American Journal of Mental Deficiency,* 1955, *60,* p. 262. Copyright 1955 by the American Association on Mental Deficiency. Reprinted by permission.

interventions than either the conventional three categories or Heber's five level system. (p. 70)

The conventional three categories refer to the very early use of the terms *moron, imbecile,* and *idiot* and to their more recent derivatives, such as the expressions *marginally dependent, semidependent,* and *dependent.* The reference to a five level system is to a terminology and classification monograph edited by Heber (1961) for the AAMD and since revised by Grossman (1973) into a four level arrangement similar to the original by Sloan and Birch.

Thus the short behavioral phrases in Table 6-1 reflect the prevailing style of thinking about expectations for mentally retarded persons. The illustrative milepost statements indicate the general view of what the status will be at certain ages of retarded persons who are tagged mild, moderate, severe, or profound.

The expressions in Table 6-1 do not mirror contemporary preferred practices. Two qualities of the statements prevent that. One is the apparent rigidity of the expectations and the other is the limiting fashion in which they are phrased. If new behavioral statements were to be inserted they would, for instance, emphasize that someone who now fits the severe level might, if given proper personalized education, move to the moderate or mild level. Preferred practice would also alter such expressions as "Cannot learn general high school subjects" to "Can learn useful components of a variety of general high school subjects if given time and individualized instruction." All in all, the influence of today's knowledge about the potentialities that can be developed in children and youth would result in a more optimistic tone about expectations.

In addition to being aware of frequently used expressions like those in Table 6-1, teachers will need to work with other professionals who use their own special terminology of mental retardation. Sometimes, too, the same or similar terminology is used with different meanings attached. To help clarify that situation a number of other designations of levels of retardation are shown in Table 6-2, Levels of Mental Retardation as Variously Stated.

It can be seen from the table that there are from three to five levels in use. Moreover, the same number of levels may be arranged differently. Some intelligence quotient levels are included in one but not in another system. The same terms may vary widely in the intelligence ranges they include.

There is no need, of course, for everyone to settle on one set of terminology about levels and to standardize their meanings. What serves the important purposes of the National Association for Retarded Citizens may be inappropriate for the equally important but different

TABLE 6-2
Levels of Mental Retardation as Variously Stated[1]

Kirk, 1972, p. 164, and Hewett & Forness, 1974, pp. 77-78	Heber, 1961, pp. 58-59 (Grossman, 1973, p. 18)[2]	Dunn, 1973, p. 71[3]	National Association for Retarded Citizens	World Health Organization	American Psychiatric Association
Borderline or slow learner (80-90)	Borderline (63-83)	Mild (55-65 to 70-80)	Marginally dependent (50-75)	Mild subnormality (50-69)	Mildly mentally deficient (70-85)
Educable (50-55 to 75-79)	Mild (52-67)	Moderate (30-40 to 55-65)	Semidependent (25-50)	Moderate subnormality (20-49)	Moderately mentally deficient (50-70)
Trainable (30-35 to 50-55)	Moderate (36-51)	Severe (15-25 to 30-40)	Dependent (below 25)	Severe subnormality (0-19)	Severely mentally deficient (0-50)
Custodial or totally dependent or profound (25-30 and below)	Severe (20-35)	Profound (below 15-25)			
	Profound (Under 20)				

[1]Most sources did not specify information on the intelligence test constituting the reference point for the intelligence quotients. Exceptions were Dunn, Heber, and Grossman. Absence of such information opens another source of variability in meaning, since such tests differ among themselves as to the comparability of intelligence quotients derived from them.

[2]Grossman uses the same levels as Heber but omits the highest, "Borderline."

[3]Dunn's adaptation of Sloan and Birch (1955).

purposes of the World Health Organization. What *is* needed is awareness that these terms and numbers have no intrinsic meaning and that they are potentially misleading when used out of context. Educators and other professionals need to come to terms with the terms, recognize them, understand them, and apply them with sensitivity, professional competence, and objectively, not dogmatically and arbitrarily.

Impermanence of Mental Retardation

The fact that an individual is found to be low in rate of cognitive development does not mean that the rate cannot be changed. In fact, from its outset, a primary purpose of special education has been *the correction and the amelioration of mental retardation in children and youth.*

In contemporary recommended phraseology, that purpose would be better described as "enhancing and furthering a developmental process, primarily cognitive." It would be, therefore, no different in principle from special education for gifted and talented pupils.

Today's concepts, too, hold that the person whose cognitive (mental) development is slow needs a program of educational tasks "matched" to his or her mental level. But mental level itself is usually a target of the educational effort, too. Even if the main intent is to enhance some other aspect of development (such as work habits, attitudes, motor skills, or social skills) it will be necessary to use procedures that take account of and match the pupil's level of cognitive functioning and that help improve cognition itself.

Today's commitment to the individualization of education thus makes it increasingly clear that the traditional concepts and terminology of mental retardation, as such, are less and less relevant for instruction. Yet it is necessary that all professional educators understand the dynamics of the condition as it is currently imbedded in the social and medical sciences.

It frequently happens that a child who is found to be mentally retarded (in the traditional sense) is provided for a period of time with special education to supplement and complement regular education and is thus helped to overcome the impairments in learning, maturation, and social adjustment earlier present. The improvement following schooling is often so substantial that the individual moves into society with enough vocational, social, and personal competence to maintain individual, civic, and family responsibilities with no more outside assistance than anyone else. In those instances there is no longer any justification for considering the person to be mentally retarded.

In other cases the fact of mental retardation in the traditional sociolegal sense (AAMD definition) may not change as a consequence of education, but the degree of retardation does. Thus, some pupils' retardation will be ameliorated to a socially significant degree by persistent instruction with a good match between lessons and cognitive level. The pupils may learn to be productive economically in relatively sheltered employment. They might come closer to achieving adaptive behavior in the range of normality and learn to live more fulfilling lives with less need for supervision and assistance.

All of this testifies both to the efficacy of special education and to the resilience of the human organism. It does not deny the seriousness and the reality of developmental lags and limitations. Neither does it hold out unfulfillable promises about increasing the capacities and accelerating the learning rates of pupils unrealistically. Rather, it offers the prospect of helping many more school children and youth toward the fullest self realization of which they are capable.

Causes of Slow Cognitive Development

What is known about the origins of mental retardation can be stated in three broad categories.

First, some mental retardation is based in *organic or physical causes*. The resulting retardation is mainly in the severe and profound levels and the causes can appear before, during, or after birth. This group aggregates 10% to 15% of persons who are mentally retarded. It includes retardation resulting from chromosomal disorders, inborn errors of metabolism, infections during the fetal period, and such other factors as prolonged high fever in illness and loss of access to oxygen.

Second, some mental retardation results from *severe stimulus deprivation* beginning in early childhood and continuing into the early school years. The following experiment illustrates this category.

Recently fifty-eight 15 month old Black baby boys from District of Columbia poverty areas were engaged in a study to see how they would respond to cognitive stimulation. Two approximately equivalent groups were formed. The stimulated group, 28 in number, started with an average intelligence quotient of 105. The other group, who were to proceed as a control without any special intervention, began with an average intelligence quotient of 108.

Eight women college graduates with inner city experience were given three months of training and assigned as tutors. The cognitive stimulation was done in home visits of 1 hour daily, 5 days a week, for 15 months, by which time the infants had reached 3 years of age. The stimulus content included conversation with the child, teaching new words, showing and discussing pictures, singing and playing records, reading to the child, taking walks, helping work simple puzzles, and coloring. Families could cooperate if they wished and were encouraged when they did.

By age 3 the average intelligence quotient of the stimulated group remained the same, 105. The control group's had declined steadily from 108 to 88, a total of 20 points below what it had been 15 months earlier. The study's director, Earl S. Schaefer, attributed the difference to the lack of daily stimulation, which emphasized linguistic, reasoning, and observational stimuli of a cognitive nature (National School Public Relations Association, 1970). This is not an isolated study, but rather one that points in the same direction as several others (Garber, 1975). Lack of suitable stimulation in very early childhood can create mental retardation in children who begin life with average intelligence. Also, a number of studies strongly suggest that if the early childhood opportunity for cognitive stimulation is lost, it may never be entirely regained through later remedial efforts.

There are limits on the positive, upgrading effects of externally imposed stimulation. These vary from individual to individual. The only sure way to discover an individual's limit is to enrich experiences until the rate of development does not accelerate with added stimulation. If it is done in a consistently warm, sensitive, and observant situation, there seems to be no way youngsters can be harmed by it.

On the other hand, there seems to be no limit to the extent to which stimulus deprivation can have negative, retarding effects. That has not been explored scientifically in human infants and young children, for obvious reasons, but cases on record of extreme child abuse support the notion that early and continued deprivation can have a profound and lasting decelerating impact on human development.

Third, some mental retardation is *a natural consequence of the way human intelligence is distributed* in the species. Some proportions of human mating happen to produce offspring whose capacities rank them at the lowest levels of intelligence and some at the highest. The range in any sizable family of children typically spans a wide spectrum of capacities and the lowest reaches sometimes include the mild, moderate, severe, and profound levels of retardation.

There is a great deal of work going on to increase knowledge about the first group mentioned, those based in organic or physical causes. There are now about 200 known specific organic or physical causes, and more are being discovered each year. Even so, known physical or organic reasons account for not more than 15% of the condiiton.

So far as the second and third groups are concerned, there are a great many unresolved questions. If as yet undiscovered biological factors are implicated in causing much of the condition at the mild and moderate levels, there is little indication of that today. It is not yet possible to sort out which cases are instances of the second and of the third group with any degree of general satisfaction. The only reasonable tack is to assume deprivation plays a part and try to correct it. Also, the environment-heredity aspect of the matter is obfuscated by other factors that are related and often equally clouded; namely, race, economic level, previous condition of servitude, cultural differences, language differences, prior education, stimulation deprivation, and social class. Birth order and the spacing of children have both been shown to be correlated with degree of intelligence, too.

For students who wish to pursue these matters further as they relate to causes of mental retardation, references are given in the topical bibliography at the end of the chapter. Any well educated person is interested in knowing about the various forms of mental retardation and being informed about theory and speculation as to their causes. But from the teacher's position, for about 90% of children and youth with slow cognitive development there is nothing to distinguish them in appearance or character except their limitations in cognitive functioning and personal-social adequacy compared with other individuals of the same age. Moreover, there appear to be no educational procedures or materials that are more applicable to children with one form of retardation than another.

Prevention of Mental Retardation

A great deal of mental retardation can be prevented. Bartram (1974, p. 12) stated: "It is possible to bring about more than a 50 percent decrease in mental retardation if priority is given now to implementing what is already known about prevention of mental retardation and other handicapping conditions." The assertion by Bartram is accompanied by 15 examples of specific steps that would need to be taken to reach the goal he sets. Teachers should be aware of the following possibilities for prevention in order to influence the community and school to hasten the day when the proposed steps materialize.

> *Rubella.* Women who are susceptible to and contract German Measles during pregnancy frequently have babies with multiple defects, including mental retardation. Testing . . . and vaccination costs less than five dollars per woman. All children should be immunized for German Measles.
>
> *Metabolic Disorders.* Screening tests can be done cheaply early in life for phenylketonuria (P.K.U.), Galactosemia and maple sugar urine disease. These are rare conditions, but are treatable if detected early.
>
> *Maternal Age.* Pregnancy in the adolescent and in the premenopausal woman is associated with a higher incidence of prematurity, Down's Syndrome, and other forms of mental retardation. Health education, family planning, amniocentesis in selected cases followed by genetic counseling, would encourage pregnancy during the relatively low-risk years of 20 through 35.

Iron Deficiency. Iron deficiency and other anemias are very common complications of pregnancy and contribute to prematurity which is associated with mental retardation in the infant. Iron deficiency anemia is easily detected and treated.

Malnutrition (and obesity) are common problems in the United States. Inadequate intake of protein, vitamins and minerals during pregnancy results in inadequate development of the fetus, particularly of the brain. There is ample protein to go around, but it is not adequately distributed to or consumed by pregnant women and young children who suffer most from malnutrition.

Radiation. The critical amount of radiation to produce damage to the gonads and to the fetus is not accurately known, but it would be relatively easy to adequately screen all persons exposed to x-ray machines and to stop atomic testing around the world.

Poisoning. Children and perhaps adults' brains are damaged by lead, carbon monoxide and many other poisons. Lead in paint that might get into children's mouths is being controlled to some degree, but little is being done to control lead in the exhausts of gasoline engines. Inhaled vapors are recognized as an increasing cause of poisoning.

Rh Factor. Rh and other blood incompatibilities can cause jaundice and brain injury to the newborn child, but appropriate and adequate treatment will prevent most damage.

Immunization. Children can be safely and cheaply immunized against many of the contagious diseases which are occasionally complicated by brain damage.

Accidents. Accidents, largely in the home, are the leading cause of death between 1 and 15 years of age and for every death, a dozen or more children are permanently disabled. Falls, burns, gunshot wounds and drownings are largely preventable.

Health Education. Health education (which includes sex education and family planning) starting almost at birth and continuing through the human learning period will lead to better understanding and use of a variety of health services that are already available which, when used, will lead not only to a happier and a more normal life, but also to few individuals with developmental disabilities.

Abused and Battered Children. Many children who are abused by parents or other caretakers suffer permanent physical, mental, and emotional damage. The dynamics of child abuse are now fairly well understood, but as yet little is being done to anticipate or prevent such tragedies. If given priority, preventive as well as therapeutic programs could be developed and implemented.

Diabetes. Children of diabetic mothers are potentially susceptible to brain damage during pregnancy. Potential damage can be minimized by special care during pregnancy not only by the obstetrician, but also by help from a physician skilled in the management of diabetes. Such services, where not available, can be supplied on a regional basis. (Bartram, 1974, pp. 12-13)

Teachers and other members of the education professions often are called on to serve on boards and committees of agencies that can influence public health and welfare factors related to the listed conditions. In those settings, and in professional associations and organizations, educators can do much to combat these root causes of mental retardation and of other conditions which can impede human development.

PREVAILING VERSUS PREFERRED PRACTICES

The changes now sweeping across education have at their heart an altering perspective of the place of the regular class teacher in relation to the exceptional child and in relation to special educators and related support personnel. The double column lists that follow give, in brief, a summary of those modifications in practice that indicate what changes are taking place.

Prevailing Practices	Preferred Practices
1. Children are assessed before or soon after they enter kindergarten or first grade to locate those who may have special educational needs.	
2. The needs assessment spots some pupils who show signs of mental retardation.	2. The needs assessment spots some pupils who evidence developmental lags in understanding, learning power, and language.
3. The regular class teacher refers the pupils to the principal who requests examination by a school psychologist.	3. The regular class teacher requests and receives within a few days consultation from a teacher specialist with child learning problems who assesses each case in cooperation with the regular teacher. But most attention goes to the various domains of development to see where and how the child might best be started on an instructional program.
4. If permission is granted by the parents, the school psychologist schedules a visit to the school to examine the children as soon as possible.	4. The results of the assessments are reviewed by the teachers and the principal with the parents of the children. With their participation a program

Prevailing Practices	Preferred Practices
	plan is developed and, with the agreement of all, is put into effect. This initial plan is to be carried out while the child remains full time in the regular class.
5. The psychologist provides a written report of the results of the examination on each child. If a child meets the state's criteria so far as measured intelligence is concerned, transfer to a special program for mentally retarded pupils is recommended. If not, the psychologist includes in the report suggestions for use by the regular class teacher to correct the condition that prompted the referral.	5. The special educator brings whatever instructional materials the plan calls for into the regular class to augment what is already there. The child's level and rate of cognitive development are taken into account, but no label such as mental retardation is attached to the child. The two teachers decide together how best to share the work of implementing the individual plans. The special teacher schedules periods of time during the week to team with the regular class teacher in the regular class.
6. If the pupil qualifies for special education and if parental approval is given, transfer is made to a special class in the same school, a nearby school, or a separate school. The specialist teacher of mentally retarded pupils then designs an individual program for the child. That teacher has access to supervisors, counselors, speech clinicians, school social workers, the principal, and other specialists on call.	6. The two teachers assess progress and call on speech clinicians, other specialist teachers, supervisors, psychologists, counselors, school social workers, and the principal for additional consultation when they feel it is needed. In unusual cases, and with parental concurrence, one or more of the pupils may be assigned part time or full time to a separate group of children with similar instructional needs. When that provision is no longer needed, the child returns full time to the regular class.

Prevailing Practices	Preferred Practices
7. The individual program may include provision for the child to spend some time in regular classes, if feasible. The most common arrangement is for attendance in physical education, music, and, for older pupils, shop and home economics.	7. The specialist teacher is available for consultation, planning, and diagnostic teaching to other regular class pupils that the two teachers suspect are beginning to show evidence of lags in understanding, learning power, and language at any time during the school year. If it seems advisable for any of those children, the two teachers initiate actions that may lead to special education programing for them.
8. The objective for each child is to carry on a program of education featuring curriculum simplification, with learning geared to a slower pace and with content broken down into finer units. The pupil's achievement goals tend to be set in terms of a mental age expectancy projection. Continuation in the special class until graduation is anticipated, with work-study placement usual in the last year.	8. The objective for each child is to foster development of the educational lags that led to the initial assessment with the expectation that the child may become able to continue with little or no special help in regular progress through school. When the child no longer needs a special education program a teacher-pupil-parent conference is held and, with parental concurrence, special education programing is withdrawn. This may happen at any time the teachers find it is no longer needed, and that could be anywhere from the end of the 1st grade to the end of the 12th grade.

THE BEGINNING OF SPECIAL EDUCATION FOR MENTALLY RETARDED PUPILS

Public day school programs for mentally retarded pupils were initiated as early as 1896 in Providence, Rhode Island (Kanner, 1964). They spread rapidly from that point on.

The lower limit of functional literacy was regarded as the ability to learn to read and write at least at fourth grade level. It was believed that fourth grade attainment would allow graduates to read advertisements, labels, most news, directions, and ballots; carry on simple correspondence; and deal with most legal matters. It was acknowledged that schools traditionally had the responsibility for producing a literate citizenry, and it was therefore not too difficult to get legislators and most professional educators to recognize the need for a "special" kind of education for those mildly and moderately retarded pupils who might, with expert and intensive teaching, attain literacy thus defined.

The acknowledged and systematic introduction of educable mentally retarded pupils into the public schools was made easier for everyone concerned by a number of provisions that seemed wise at the time but some of which are now questioned. The children were taught in separate classes, and often in separate schools.

Thus, regular classes were not disturbed. In fact, some pupils already in school who were not doing well were removed from regular classes and placed in the separate classes. The separate classes were made smaller, so the retarded pupils, who were admittedly more difficult to teach, could have better opportunity to learn. Curricula were modified to meet the particular learning needs of these slower pupils, and their schooling was referred to as special education. That name survived after several others (orthogenic education, opportunity classes, Binet classes, for example) were tried out and dropped.

Teachers with added qualifications were recruited and prepared for the special education of educable mentally retarded pupils. Institutions teamed with schools of education in the various states to prepare teachters, usually in summer courses. The teachers made most of their own instructional materials. None had yet been designed that provided the degree of individualization needed to teach these pupils literacy skills and the rudiments of science, social studies, art, and the rest of the common curriculum. The entire operation was made more palatable to school systems by financial support from the state if and when a local school system started a separated special program that met state regulations as to selection of pupils, size of class, and certification of the teacher.

By the mid 1930's special classes for educable mild and moderate level mentally retarded pupils were solidly established in larger urban centers and in many suburbs and were making their way into the rural areas of the country along with the school consolidation movement. In fact, some legislation in the 1940's made the establishment of classes for educable mentally retarded pupils a condition of state financial support for consolidation.

The Forty-Second Yearbook of the National Society for the Study of Education, a landmark document, established the credibility of the special teacher, the special class, and the special school as the format for special education for exceptional children. It reinforced the movement that tended to separate exceptional children from other children for their education. At the same time the yearbook demonstrated that special education for educable retarded pupils was worthy of widespread public support.

About 1950 pressure began to mount to arrange special education for trainable (severely) mentally retarded children and youth, too. For years those pupils had been systematically sorted out and excluded entirely from the public schools. No other state agencies had taken them in charge for education, either. Large numbers were living at home. Even when they were in state residential schools, it was rare that they received systematic education or training.

Certain communities did respond in very constructive ways, though. In the mid 1950's Pittsburgh, Pennsylvania, had mentally retarded pupils with intelligence quotients (IQ's) between 25 and 50 in regular elementary schools. The children were in groups of 12 and 15 with a teacher and an aide; those who needed to be transported were served by taxis. Their teachers were specialists, but were also full members of the school faculty. In the same building there were classes for retarded pupils in the 50 to 75 IQ range, too. Since IQ does not tell the whole story, there were sometimes transfers arranged by the teachers back and forth between the classes to suit the educational needs of the pupils.

The specialist teachers and their charges found ready acceptance from regular teachers and pupils. The principals were well informed about individual differences and gave strong attitudinal leadership to the parents in the community. Children from regular classes volunteered to help with recreation and as teacher assistants in the special classes.

That kind of arrangement in many of the nation's schools was a precursor to contemporary mainstreaming. Whether or not the arrangements worked was usually not tested in any scientific way. Rather, the day to day reactions of the community, the response of the retarded children's parents, and the informal comments of faculty members were the clues used by principals to measure success.

Since the early moves of the kind just illustrated, there have been efforts to document the consequences of integration in more systematic ways. For severely and profoundly mentally retarded pupils the results are encouraging.

It was mainly parents with severely retarded school age youngsters living at home who began to press the question as to whether their children were being dealt with fairly. Encouraged by parents and reports from various communities, a few state legislatures responded. Others followed; while not making it obligatory, they gave school districts some financial incentive to initiate classes for the severe level of mentally retarded children hitherto classed as uneducable.

This started another layer of separate classes. The new classes accommodated children not thought to be educable, as the expression had been defined almost half a century before to rationalize public schooling for the more able mentally retarded.

Now it was necessary to conceptualize a survival skills level of literacy. It included learning to recognize and react meaningfully to words like *stop, danger, wet paint*. It included imperatives to interpret traffic lights and poison symbols and to recognize and say one's own name and address.

The new growth of classes for trainable children bloomed as separate rooms. They were often in separate buildings and had their own curricula, a separate set of state regulations to guide their location, format and teacher preparation, and enjoyed a separate system of state financial support. In short, a network of professional staffing and operating rules was established for those children labeled trainable that paralleled the one established earlier for educable mentally retarded children. Most of the time there was little linkage between levels and minimal interaction between the two layers of professional educators and teacher aides.

Thoughtful special educators usually tried to house the two kinds of classes near each other in the same school buildings, recognizing that the cleavage between the two was often not as evident in the pupils as it was in the organizational structure. But such arrangements, desirable as they were in theory, too often faced the practical factor that previously existing regular classes occupied the most desirable classroom space and the new special classes had to be located wherever room could be found that met state and local fire, lighting, space per pupil, and safety standards.

Present Status of Special Education

In the early 1970's the parents of mentally retarded pupils won legal victories that sharply accelerated the growth of educational services for their children. Tired of pleading with school officials for the right to education for all children and youth with mental retardation, they went to court. A landmark consent agreement in Pennsylvania* made it mandatory for the public schools to supply appropriate special education. The initial favorable response by the court was followed by similar

---

*In the U.S. District Court for the Eastern District of Pennsylvania. *Pennsylvania Association for Retarded Children, Nancy Beth Bowman, et al. Plaintiff v. Commonwealth of Pennsylvania, David H. Kurtzman, et al. Defendants.* Civic Action No. 71-42. Amended consent agreement 14 February 1972.

actions in rapid fire order where suits had been brought in other states (Abeson, Bolick, & Hass, 1975).

The positive court decisions had many ramifications in addition to speeding the rate of growth of special education. The right to education issue was settled, but the ensuing problems were only beginning to appear. Three are of enough importance to highlight in this brief account of the emergence and current status of differences in education for different levels of mental retardation.

First, an additional group of mentally retarded pupils became eligible for free public education. This group, previously regarded as uneducable and untrainable, constituted those children and youth who showed profound retardation. While relatively small in number, they created a new challenge to the educator's orientation to academic schooling. For many of these children the curriculum needed to be expanded to take in matters not previously considered part of American "schooling," such as learning to walk, to roll a ball with purpose, to assist the person feeding or dressing the child, to understand fundamental verbal and visual signals, and to notice and enjoy tones and rhythms.

A second ramification of the court decisions was to introduce and attach some stimulating operational aspects to the expression *appropriate* education. The concept was already understood to refer to individualization—that is, teaching understandable and important content to each child by selected procedures that utilize and enhance that particular child's capabilities. However, the expert educational testimony also persuaded the courts that the most desirable setting in which to carry on that kind of teaching for pupils with mental retardation was in regular classes along with all other children. Separation into special classes or even segregated school buildings was acknowledged as necessary sometimes, to be sure. The burden of proof, though, was to be on those who proposed dividing slow cognitive developing pupils from the other pupils, even for short periods of time during the school day. To be allowed to do so they had to prove it was necessary for sound education, not for administrative convenience.

Third, the courts then ruled that the right to education and to inclusion with regular class pupils that had been determined for children with mental retardation was to be applied with equal force to the education of all other exceptional children and youth. The force of that set of three legal postures combined to generate the waves of change now coursing through all of the nation.

Current Trends in Special Education

Many changes took place to comply with the new expectations that arose from legal decisions about rights to education, due process, and least restrictive alternative. Previously accepted patterns of educating mentally retarded pupils in separate special classes or schools now give way as more and more exceptional children join the mainstream of education with all other children. The principle of inclusion progressively advances into practice. Children and youth are more and more merged for instruction and all other school related activities, which accounts for the term *mainstreaming*. High quality special education is brought to exceptional children to the degree that they need it while they are in regular classes with all other children.

There remain many more or less separate classes for educable, trainable, and profoundly mentally retarded pupils. Also, many separate day schools and residential schools continue. Instructional organization designs that have retarded pupils spending part time in regular and part time in special groups abound, too, under a variety of names such as resource or clinical rooms or centers.

Some such classes and schools are needed now and in the foreseeable future. At the same time there appears to be an accelerating tendency (a) to move children from existing special classes and schools into regular class groups and to bring special education materials, facilities, and specialist staff along with them to form teams with regular teachers and (b) to identify pupils with mental retardation (slow cognitive development), real or suspected, at school entry, and to maintain them in the regular classes with special education support services, thus sharply reducing the flow of new pupils into existing special classes.

If these trends continue, an obvious result will be less need for the special classes as such and a greater need for teachers who are specialists in mental retardation to work in team settings with regular class teachers.

At the same time, it appears that some of the creative concepts that led the early phases of the change from categorical to individualized education now need to be reviewed to be sure that they are broad ranging enough to continue to give guidance to current trends and needs in service delivery.

Sontag (1976) stressed the need for continuous and rigorous reexamination of even the newest concepts about where and how special education may best take place. Quite specifically, he questioned the supposition that *severity of handicap* should be a major criterion for determining the extent to which mainstreaming is feasible.

> I am increasingly concerned with the service delivery models that are in vogue in the special education and regular education communities. In our attempt to provide more special education alternatives for marginally handicapped children, we enthusiastically began to endorse such models as the "continuous" and "cascade." Although these models did propose viable and much needed educational strategies for the marginally involved

child, they offered little—if anything—for the more severely handicapped child. The end result of most of these models has been that the more handicapped a child, the farther he is placed from the mainstream of education.

I suggest that there is little evidence to support the premise that we cannot provide for the more severely and profoundly handicapped child in the regular school building. I propose that we conceptualize a new model—a personnel model that calls for more integration into the regular public school for the severely and profoundly handicapped child. Some school districts have taken the creative and educationally sound step of providing educational services to severely handicapped students in the same buildings that contain non-handicapped students. They have done it, and have not faced insurmountable problems in doing so. An added bonus is that in the process, many normal children and their parents have become aware of, and sensitive to, the problems of handicapped citizens (Sontag, 1976, p. 3)

Another equally apparent need, already present but spurred by Sontag's proposed new personnel model, will be for more regular class teachers who have the competencies to include retarded pupils in their regular instruction, provided that specialist staff assistance and the necessary instructional materials and aids are available as needed.

THE ROLE OF THE REGULAR CLASS TEACHER

Regular class teachers will increasingly have opportunities to take an important part in teaching pupils whose cognitive development is significantly attenuated. That is true for teachers at all levels, from preschool through high school, and vocational school and lifelong learning centers. It holds, also, for pupils of almost all degrees of mental retardation.

The high school or elementary school teacher's question, What can a retarded student learn about my subject? has been turned around. The question now is, What aspects of my subject are most essential and how can they be adapted so they can be taught to mentally retarded pupils? More often than not the second question has some very good answers. Those answers are derived mainly from the principle that through individualized instruction every child can achieve mastery of some important components of the school's curriculum. Individualization means making the content and the procedures suit the child. When that happens, many children other than those who are retarded can be better taught, too.

Teamwork with Specialists

Regular class teachers cannot be expected to do the entire job of individualization on their own. Having a retarded pupil for one period of English, geometry, music, social studies, home economics, or history, for instance, can be very demanding on a teacher's ingenuity and skill. More than one period multiplies the demands. Help is needed.

There are several essential preconditions if regular class teachers are to instruct mentally retarded pupils effectively and efficiently, whether full time or part time, with other pupils. These preconditions are characteristic of successful part or full time mainstreaming; they all involve teamwork in one or more of its many forms.

1. It is essential that there be a teacher trained in the educational implications of mental retardation and other exceptional conditions who is both ready and available to work with the regular teacher as needed. This includes team teaching, planning, and other instruction related activities in the same teaching space or in a nearby area of the same building.
2. The regular class teacher needs to be party to every placement and program decision made about the mentally retarded pupils for whom that teacher has any degree of responsibility.
3. Retarded pupils should be assigned to the regular teacher only with that teacher's prior agreement.
4. Both regular teachers and specialists should have in-service professional preparation for mainstream instruction.
5. It should always be possible for the regular teacher and the specialist teacher to design and to initiate plans for changes in programs and scheduling for the mentally retarded pupils who are full time or part time in regular classes.
6. The regular teacher needs to have ready access to whatever special instructional materials are called for in the mentally retarded pupil's program. This includes help from the specialist teacher and the instructional materials facility staff.
7. Planning and preparation time must be provided and coordinated between the special teacher and the regular teacher.
8. Authority, responsibility, and accountability should be worked out and mutually understood among the regular teachers, special teachers, parents, and principal before the mainstreaming is initiated.

Today it is commonplace for educational policy and practice in school systems to benefit from consultation with teachers. Their influence is weighty enough to assure either program success or failure. It is essential that boards of education and administrators take into account the views of teachers in a spirit of teamwork, not only on direct pupil-teacher interactions but also on curriculum and school organizational matters that relate to the place and role of the school in the community.

It has been shown that regular class teachers and school administrators are willing to try integration of retarded pupils, either full or part time, as the individual instance may require (Zawadski, 1973). At the same time, there are some misgivings. Both regular teachers and administrators are apprehensive that they will not succeed and that both the retarded and the other pupils will receive less than their due if the program design for integration is not mutually planned and does not have the necessary safeguards.

It is because of those important professional considerations that the eight preconditions just listed are viewed as essential. They should be implemented with thoughtful care and in a cooperative spirit by both teachers and administrators.

It is preferred practice today to organize instruction so that retarded pupils and others share regular and special teachers and lessons in carefully planned ways. Teacher-pupil matches are formed to optimize pupil learning and the deployment of teacher competencies. The instructional organization patterns and the terms used to describe them are often new, but the underlying objective is the same: To obtain the best pupil-teacher match, and to do so with the greatest chance of overall pupil benefit.

There is an extremely significant outside-of-class role for teachers, also. Teachers are frequently the main source of trustworthy information for parents about the condition called mental retardation—what it means and what its consequences are for the retarded individual, the family, and the community. In addition, teachers often find it necessary to dispel false beliefs that are passed on by well meaning but uninformed persons.

Teachers find that they need to understand not only the educational implications of mental retardation but also the application of techniques and procedures of individualization. They also need to be able to comprehend the legal, medical, and social welfare connotations of the condition; to relate those connotations to their daily work; to combat the effects of mistaken beliefs; and to teach as a member of a large team both in and out of school so as to shed a new developmental light on what has heretofore been viewed largely in a negative way.

Individualization of Instruction

The quintessence of individualization of instruction is reached when each child has the maximum opportunity to learn. For pupils who show slow cognitive development, effective individualization consists of the proper mix of the same elements required by all other pupils. Curriculum, teaching methods, and instructional materials effectively organized for instructional impact in a suitable setting are the key conditions, whether in kindergarten, 12th grade English, driver education, 5th grade social studies, industrial arts, vocational education, or studio arts.

Curriculum Individualization

Curriculum refers to all that is taught under school supervision. There is no curriculum for mentally retarded pupils that differs completely from the typical. A few curricular elements need so much more emphasis that they may seem unique, and they do require particular skills on the part of the teacher, but only a few.

Background and present status: Educable retarded. The first curricular adaptations for pupils with slow cognitive development dated from the beginning years of this century when separate schools and classes began to be opened. The adaptations were of three kinds, and the pattern then established continued until about 1935 to 1940.

First, *the regular curriculum was slowed down.* To illustrate, the introduction of long division or sentence diagraming might be put off a few years from its usual spot in fourth or fifth grade for 10 and 11 year olds to later years for retarded pupils.

Second, *the regular curriculum was simplified.* For instance, in social studies related to North America the material about Eskimos might be passed over lightly or omitted and the content regarding the United States given more prominence; or, in arithmetic, decimals could be taught only to 2 places because that is all that is necessary for basic knowledge about money.

Third, *the regular curriculum was stretched out.* Because of the slowdown in the flow of introduction of new material and because of the simplification of the material introduced, it became possible to dwell longer on what was being taught, to break it down into smaller parts, and to review it more frequently, more thoroughly, and in more varied ways.

All of these adaptations were useful ones in and of themselves. During that first part of this century individualization of instruction was only beginning to be talked about by most educators. In those rare instances in which it was practiced, it was narrowly interpreted to mean teaching the same things to all pupils, but at slower or faster rates and in more or less simplified form. Little thought had yet been given to either substantive changes in the content itself to match children's differences in backgrounds and interests or to attempts to make learning sets, processes, modalities, or styles part of what might be recognized in children and/or taught to children. Substantive curricular content, skills, and moral-ethical (character) education made up the only content.

Historically, the initial steps toward curriculum adaptation for retarded pupils (slowdown, simplification, and stretch-out) were followed by attempts to formulate unique curricula for pupils who were at different degrees of retardation. The pupils regarded as being educable had curricula designed for them. The content was not to be simply watered down from that for other pupils. Serious efforts were made to match it to the learning characteristics of mentally retarded pupils. Those curricula evolved to the point that it was possible to study and characterize them. For educable mentally retarded children, for instance, Kirk (1972) said:

> In broader concepts, the program should stress the development of (1) social competence, (2) personal adequacy, and (3) occupational competence. Social competence refers primarily to the ability of the individual to get along with his fellow men, that is, his family, his school and neighborhood mates, and other members of the community. Personal adequacy refers to his ability to live with himself in some sort of equilibrium. Occupational competence refers to his ability to support himself partially or totally in some productive activity. (p. 198)

Essentially the same group of children were referred to by Dunn (1973, pp. 164-165) as "children with mild general learning disabilities." He concluded that curricular objectives for them are in four broad areas: "(1) basic readiness and practical academics development; (2) communication, oral language and cognitive development; (3) socialization, family living, self-care, recreational, and personality development; and (4) pre-vocational and vocational development, including housekeeping" (Dunn, 1973, pp. 164-165).

After reviewing the earlier conclusions of Kirk and Dunn, both of whom had also drawn on other key writers on educating children with slow cognitive development (Kirk & Johnson, 1951; Kolstoe, 1970; Smith, R. M., 1968), a summary by Hewett and Forness (1974) concluded that "the focus of special education for EMR children, then is on (1) developing basic academic skills, (2) social competence, (3) personal adjustment, and (4) occupational adequacy" (p. 83).

The summaries are quite similar. They represent the evolution and status of thinking about curricular objectives from about 1935-1940 to 1970-1975. They show that thought had been given to individualization, as the concept came to be better understood. Also, the summaries show the very practical, outcome oriented character that was a large part of curriculum development for all children during the same time span in American education and to which special education curriculum designs may have led. Finally, a clear linkage is observed in those special education objectives to the general objectives of education most widely accepted during the same period: (a) self realization, (b) economic efficiency, (c) civic responsibility, and (d) good human relations (Education Policies Commission, 1938).

The conclusion seems inescapable that the evolution of curriculum objectives for educable mentally retarded youngsters moved with and kept pace with curricular thinking for American children in general. There is nothing essentially unique about the *objectives* that make them special for pupils with mental retardation at this level.

Emerging, however, were other ways of looking at curriculum objectives. They did not deny what had developed, but they added helpful insights because of their difference in perspective.

One of those fresh perspectives suggests that there are two basic skills and that they are necessary in all curricular areas. They are (a) *thinking critically,* being able to assess the realities of a given situation together with the implications, and (b) *acting independently,* making decisions based on realities and following through on the decisions (Goldstein, 1974; Heiss & Mischio, 1971). It is argued that to become an independent adult, the educable youngster with slow cognitive development may have to be taught problem solving methods that apply in generic fashion to academic, personal, social, vocational, financial, and leisure situations.

That kind of thinking can presage a next step in the formulation of curriculum objectives, a step that emphasizes the teaching of processes and the value of teaching those processes to exceptional children and other children together.

Background and present status: Trainable retarded. The distinction between "educable" and "trainable" is difficult for teachers to apply. There never was a sharp dividing line as to how the children functioned day to day, in or out of school. Rather, it was a distinction about the presumed level to which the children could be educated. The ability to attain functional literacy separated the educable and trainable. The dual criteria of gaining bowel and bladder control and functional language acquisition divided the "trainable" and "untrainable."

Actual assignment to either group by psychologists has more often been made on the size of the child's intelligence quotient than on any direct evidence of what the child could or might do. That was particularly the case with young children. There have been variations; some psychologists were more inclined to rational than arbitrary decisions. However, the prevailing intelligence quotient boundaries tended to be: educable—75-50; trainable—50-25; and untrainable—below 25.

It is not surprising, in that context, that curriculum guides for trainable children came into being as quite separate documents from the curriculum guides for educable children (Baumgartner, 1960; Rosenzweig & Long, 1960). The need to identify the more elemental behaviors to be taught to trainable children was evident; it called for some new curriculum specifications. But the new materials were not to be simply downward extensions of already existing curricula for educable children. This is explained by the then prevailing and strongly held belief that a real distinction existed between educable and trainable, and that the distinction was functional and not arbitrary, and therefore had significant value in designing and operating programs.

A summary statement on curriculum objectives for trainable children was set forth by a major scholar of the subject early in the 1970's (Kirk, 1972), which concluded:

> The general objectives of the curriculum for a trainable child are . . . (1) the objective of developing self-care or self-help, (2) the objective of developing social adjustment in the home and neighborhood, and (3) the objective of developing economic usefulness in the home or in a sheltered environment. These constitute the broad goals of the educational program for trainable mentally retarded children. (p. 230)

Shortly thereafter another leader addressed the same question (Dunn, 1973). He first noted that "behavior modification techniques are enabling us to teach more than was previously thought possible to this middle group" (p. 101). Then Dunn called attention to an emerging terminological change: The trainable group was being referred to as semi-independent rather than semidependent, showing what he interpreted as "a subtle but important attitudinal change." In that light, and in view of what he reported as a gradual extension of the intelligence quotient range of this group "upward toward IQ scores of 55, 60 and 65," he said:

> Curricular objectives have been broadened considerably to include the following four rather comprehensive goals:
>
> (1) Self-help, basic readiness, and independent living skills development.
> (2) Communication, language, and cognitive development.
> (3) Socialization and personality development.
> (4) Vocational-, recreational-, and leisure-skills development. (p. 101)

The next year another summary appeared (Hewett & Forness, 1974) that recapped the previous two, but with the difference that it made specific mention of oral language development: "Emphasis is on (1) Oral language development, (2) Self-help skills, (3) Socialization, and (4) Preparation for living and working in sheltered environments" (p. 84).

Reading those objectives out of the context of this chapter would leave one with few clues as to whether the objectives are for bright, slow, or average children. The mention by Kirk and by Hewett and Forness of the "sheltered environment" may be taken as a hint. But even that is indefinite. For which of us does not live in a sheltered and sheltering environment, for the most part? An experience with Outward Bound or a similar survival training program would convince many on that point.

Also, it takes no more than a side by side comparison of these objectives with those for the educable group to show that, out of context, they are nearly indistinguishable. To take the exercise one step further and compare both the sets of objectives with those promulgated for all children by the Educational Policies Commission (1938), namely self realization, human relationships, economic efficiency, and civil responsibility, results in a similar conclusion. In terms of broad objectives there are no educationally significant differences among objectives. The same would be found, too, with the objectives even more recently developed for the education and training of children and youth with severe and profound degrees of slow cognitive development, those who were hitherto dubbed quite erroneously as uneducable and untrainable.

The actual operating day to day instructional programs for these groups do have some differences. The differences are on the same continua, however. Learning to wipe one's nose effectively and politely is on a health and personal grooming continuum with learning to get oneself clean in the shower and to wear clean clothing. Learning to recognize one's name is on a language development continuum with recognizing signs like "Stop" and "Wet Paint" and reading the daily newspaper.

It is not hard to envision curriculum guides that include the whole spectrum of objectives and that supply enough detailed developmental sequences to allow the inclusion of children of all levels of retardation as well as other children. Such guides are emerging. An example can be found in Kanawha County, West Virginia (Birch, 1974, p. 85). When exceptional children with slow cognitive development and all other children are accommodated within the same curriculum guide, it is more realistic to speak of the exceptional pupils' education as being *a part of* rather than *apart from* the principle flow of the rest of public education—the mainstream.

Adaptive Behavior Inventory

Mercer (1974) has undertaken the development of an Adaptive Behavior Inventory that is potentially useful as a pupil-need-referenced curriculum resource. It aims at exploring competency in the four social systems in which the child lives: the family, the neighborhood, the school, and the community.

> In these social systems the number of roles and the level of expectation for performance increases with age. Increasing societal expectations are conceptualized as having three underlying themes: increasing complexity in the nature of the performance expected; the expectation that role performance will be more motivated by internal than external controls; and expanding independence and freedom from adult supervision in role performance. (Mercer, 1974, pp. 172-173)

Mercer has described the Adaptive Behavior Inventory for Children (ABIC) to be used in the 5 to 11 year range. It is administered by asking a prescribed set of questions of the child's mother or other chief caretaker. The questions uncover the child's present social role behavior. According to Mercer,

> When clinicians speak of social adjustment, social maturity or social competence, they refer to an individual's ability to play ever more complete social roles in a progressively widening circle of social systems. As a person matures, the behavioral standards of society become more demanding and the number and complexity of social roles which he is expected to play increases. His ability to cope with these increasing expectations for social role performance constitutes his adaptive behavior. (p. 172)

This statement provokes thought in teachers about the design of curriculum to complement the concept of ever widening circles of personal, vocational, recreational, and other interactions on the part of pupils. It illustrates the linkage between the pupil's present achievements and the pupil's potential for future attainments.

AAMD Adaptive Behavior Scale

The AAMD Adaptive Behavior Scale was designed to encourage the measurement of adaptive behavior as called for in the AAMD definition of mental retardation. The scale allows a detailed assessment of a person's personal and social competencies under the demands of ordinary day to day life. It helps to identify both adaptive and maladaptive behaviors (Fogelman, 1975).

Using Adaptive Behavior Data To Plan Instruction

Teachers may use the information that the Mercer and AAMD scales supply in a number of ways. For instance, if the results are in the normal range for the subject's age, it will be clear to the teacher that the subject is not mentally retarded, despite what other tests might suggest. This is valuable in guiding the teacher's expectations and in parent conferences.

Program planning is another teacher function that can get an assist from the scales' results. The items that are not yet quite mastered can be the subjects for lessons, along with functionally related activities. Teachers and parents can also use scale results to show changes in adaptive behavior before and after instructional programs have been applied.

Scale results can be shown on a profile, and that can sometimes be helpful for interpreting strengths and limitations, objectives of instruction, and achievements to the pupils themselves.

The extension of the right to education to all children and youth with mental retardation created a new demand for curricula focused on the earliest components of human development. Still on the same continua, and still with the same long range objectives, the new curricula needed to delve into very early child development, identify behaviors that should be but were not appearing, and make it possible for the teacher to deliberately foster the missing behaviors. Nowhere else is it clearer that pupils with attenuated cognitive growth often must be deliberately taught what others may be expected to "pick up" through incidental experience.

Typical of the school activities for pupils who begin life in the severe and profound ranges of mental retardation are the items of behavior used in such developmental assessment scales as the Vineland Social Maturity Scale (Doll, 1953) and the Denver Developmental Screening Test (Frankenburg & Dodds, 1967). Cain and Levine (1963) extended and elaborated the Vineland Scale with other useful items for children at these levels, too. When dealing with such elemental behaviors, one has a perfect illustration of the advantage of criterion referenced testing; there is just no other way of showing that a task at this level has been learned than performing the task itself as the test.

The absence of real differences between educable and trainable pupils at the level of educational objectives, plus the concept that their curricular activities are on the same continua, has implications for teacher preparation, too. The justification for the separate instruction sequences for teachers of educable and trainable youngsters is called into question. The curricular similarities support the trend to prepare teachers with competencies to instruct in both regular programs and in programs for all children with slow cognitive development.

The distinctions between degrees or levels of retardation have always been hazy, at best. That is especially true at the presumed boundaries between them, where each really fades into the other. A youngster's actual degree of retardation can be settled only through seeing how far one can get with serious and long term instruction. With those interrelated factors in mind, regular class teachers and the specialists who work with them are well advised to consider any designation of level only temporary and to continue to question the relevance of such levels for education at all. The activities teachers and parents employ with the child should use the curriculum guide to point directions and to assess progress on the way to higher attainment, free of preoccupations about classifications other than those which do relate specifically to pupil needs.

Methods of Teaching

Contemporary applications of social science research to instruction are clarifying the fact that all teaching methods seem to be variations on a few common themes. Important overt differences are seen between what has been called, for example, the project method and what has been called behavior shaping. Underlying each structure, however, are a limited number of common components: the task, the organism, the motive, the instructions, and the criterion.

In a number of school districts teachers have included in their collective bargaining agreements the provision of specific in-service sessions to help them cope more effectively with the instruction of mentally retarded pupils (and other exceptional pupils) in regular classes and in resource room arrangements. In most cases regular or special teachers, often in teams, conduct those workshops. They may be 5 to 30 or more hours long, depending on what is to be covered. The teacher who does the planning and instruction is paid and the participants who successfully complete the courses may count them toward salary increment credit (Birch, 1974).

The teaching methods and procedures for pupils who are slow in cognitive development have much in common with those applicable for a number of other groups of exceptional children and youth. Because of that, a separate chapter (Chapter 9) deals with them as a unit. What follows is confined to those aspects of teaching methods that deserve to be highlighted particularly in connection with exceptional pupils who show slow cognitive development.

There is typically less flexibility of approach to any task among pupils with mental retardation. That sometimes affects performance quite markedly. If a certain key is to be used to open a door and one similar in appearance to it is picked up from a group and tried, the pupil with slow cognitive development will usually tend to go on for a longer time trying to make the wrong key work. If a pupil is taught to respond with accuracy from memory to the question, What is your address? and if, instead, the question is asked, Where do you live? or Where is your home? the youngster with mental retardation is more likely to be unable to reply correctly to the shifted form of the inquiry.

The lesser flexibility illustrated above can also be spoken of as *more rigidity* or *increased specificity* or *preserverative tendency* or *less adaptability,* and each would convey essentially the same concept.

The work of Ziegler (1969) calls sharply into question the assumption that cognitive rigidity is characteristic of mentally retarded children. Instead, it may be that when rigidity appears, it is simply a function of prior training. However, if it appears to be present in a given pupil, Dunn (1973) covered the implications for instruction derivable from this point well.

> The teacher should deal with this "rigidity in changing sets" by pointing out to the pupil why he should shift to another approach to problem-solving. . . .[Those pupils] have more difficulty. . .in dealing with materials that are reversed or otherwise changed from the order in which they were originally learned, suggesting that they either be placed in tasks

where they do not need to reorganize or be taught specifically how to recognize and deal with reordered material. (p. 146)

Certainly teaching the pupils to "recognize and deal with reordered material" is the more desirable alternative, since it leads to an increase in social and vocational adaptability. Such an increase, in turn, is directly related to correcting or ameliorating the person's degree of mental retardation. That needs to be accomplished to the maximum extent feasible for each pupil.

Effective instruction requires that the teacher make doubly sure with these youngsters to plan instructional strategies that begin where the learner is. (The organism and the task must be compatible.) The teacher has to be willing to check to see what the pupil already knows of academic, social, personal, or vocational skills and understandings and start there, rather than start at some arbitrary point determined by a course of study or a textbook. That is true for all pupils, to be sure, but it is of especially great significance for pupils with mental retardation.

Two recently developed instructional procedures hold a great deal of encouragement for teachers attempting to help retarded pupils to develop consistently positive personal-social attributes.

The first instructional approach is through *applied behavior analysis.* It has many other titles, too. A special reference list is included at the end of Chapter 7 to help the teacher learn more about this procedure.

The second procedure is called *moral education.* It depends on small group discussions of specific problems in dilemma form. In moral education, pupils may progress through a sequence of increasingly higher forms of moral behavior as a consequence of acquiring self understanding plus understanding of how society is held together by these civilizing principles.

The applied behavior analysis approach is applicable across all age ranges. It can be used with any group of children, of course. In our judgment it is the method of choice for very early childhood instruction of children with slow cognitive development, and it is probably the most promising approach up to the ages of 9 to 11. At about that age the moral education approach should begin to be effective, too. The reward techniques used in behavior shaping can be utilized in guiding and managing the seminarlike discussions called for by the moral education approach. Also, the moral education approach can bring together, into behavior generalization or principle form, the more discrete pupil actions that usually are the foci of behavior shaping.

The same teaching procedures that are effective with other children are effective with pupils with mental retardation, if:

1. The methods are applied with accommodation to each pupil's state of readiness for instruction.

2. More review and repetition of a varied and interest holding kind are used to help establish retention.
3. Material to be learned is divided into smaller but still meaningful bits, presented sequentially, and then rehearsed in total, with as little change in order as possible.
4. The learning environment is more free of distractions.
5. The teacher quite frequently checks the individual pupil being taught for attention paying or scans the small group for the same behavior.

These five points are consistent with good quality instruction for all pupils. They call for closer and more intensive emphasis on certain details, but not for a strikingly different approach. This is true because children and youth who are slow in cognitive development are more alike than different from other pupils in their educational requirements. At the same time their education, whether in full time or part time mainstream settings, is demanding on teachers. The necessity for teachers to be more than ordinarily attentive to details and to adapt the usual instruction in many ways argues strongly in favor of teamwork with special teachers and attention to moderate pupil-teacher ratios to assure that all pupils may enjoy high quality education.

Instructional Materials

There are now well made instructional materials for mentally retarded pupils for almost all curricular areas. Most are new or adaptations of products that have histories of successful use with other pupils. They make the adjustments needed to accommodate to a slow pace of cognitive growth: small steps, tight sequencing, frequent review, curricular deceleration, and emphasis on academic essentials and vocational training. They allow a longer period of time to reach goals. The materials maintain a slower rate of introduction of more complex materials.

A good illustration of this is the Stanwix House Functional Basic Reading Series (1970). It is really three reading series interlocked. All proceed at developmental rates below the average reader (rates of 75%, 60%, and 50%). The content themes are alike, and all stress vocational objectives. These and many more such materials can be examined in special educational instructional materials service centers.

Much of what has been developed as instructional material for pupils with slower cognitive development rates is incorporated into broader use for other children, too. Pupils of average or higher rates of mental development, too, are often beset by general reading disabilities or by specific learning disabilities. Some of those pupils are recovering, educationally speaking, through their teachers' skilled use of reading series originally designed for use with mentally retarded children and youth.

Learning for pupils with mental retardation is *relatively* more effective when concrete, rather than abstract, materials are used in the process. For instance, learning to make change occurs (reaches criterion) in a shorter time and is more readily retained if it is done with real or play money than if it is done only with written or oral illustrations. The same, of course, is true with other pupils. Pupils with mental retardation usually remain less apt than others regardless of whether concrete or abstract materials are employed; however, they are relatively less disadvantaged when the concrete forms are used.

Organization for Instruction

In working with individuals within a group of school children, teachers orchestrate and conduct one of the most complex of human enterprises. We are concerned here with how a teacher or a group of teachers (working with mentally retarded pupils alone or merged with other pupils) program their instructional activities. It encompasses decision making about what (i.e., spelling, arithmetic, history) shall be taught first or second in the daily schedule; how frequently in the day, week, or year it will be taught; and when and how achievement will be tested. Organization for instruction covers the professional decisions faced in arranging for team teaching, in using paraprofessionals and aides, and in seeing that the right instructional materials are with the right pupils and the right teachers at the right times and under the right conditions. In short, organization for instruction is the generalship and logistics behind the instructional act. Plainly, the more different people, places, and things that are involved the more complicated and difficult the task of organizing for instruction becomes. Those evident difficulties account for much of the appeal of the old paradigm of a pupil on one end of a log and a teacher on the other.

Moving special education for mentally retarded pupils and for other exceptional pupils toward real operational relations with the school system in general obviously can increase the problems of organization for instruction. Such problems, regardless of where they originate, usually end up in the office of the principal unless they are suitably resolved or eliminated. To the pupil's detriment, an easy way to bury such problems is to avoid the designing of teaching arrangements that call for cooperation among teachers. The alternative, of course, is to make high quality organization for instruction so rewarding to all professional persons involved that it is achieved despite personal inconvenience.

There are three points that should be noted especially with regard to organization for instruction of mentally retarded pupils.

1. They often need to be taught deliberately what others "pick up" by incidental learning. That may apply to how to organize books so they

will fit easily into available space, how to use a pencil sharpener correctly, or how to button one's coat against the cold. They *do* learn, however, if given specific, painstaking, and consistent instruction.
2. They are often capable of more and higher levels of learning than may appear to be the case at first. Thus there should be plenty of opportunity to go ahead in any curriculum sequence, whether it be creative activities like graphic arts or sculpture, or driver education and reading comprehension.
3. While acknowledged to be slower starters, these pupils *do* go on learning into the late teens and 20's if given the incentive and chance. Thus, it is important to be so organized as to be able to carry curricular offerings beyond the years usually associated with secondary school graduation.

The key to effective organization for instruction is *planning*. The most fundamental requirements for planning are time to do it and know-how about effective planning procedures. In mainstream situations, where the regular class teacher coordinates planning, that teacher should be provided with both of those fundamental requirements.

School Physical Plant

Mentally retarded children have all too often stood last in line for desirable instructional space in school buildings. An essential ingredient in any solid foundation for individualization of instruction for mentally retarded pupils is a sufficient amount of readily accessible and good quality working space for children and teachers.

By now the means of avoiding or eliminating architectural barriers in schools are well established. Not all separate special education buildings have avoided such obstacles, however, much less ordinary school buildings now standing or under construction. Many children who might otherwise be aided materially by instruction in regular schools are effectively barred from participation by the physical properties of school buildings. Correction of this condition is needed.

The removal of architectural barriers to the general use of a building must be recognized as only an initial step. The larger problem of supplying optimum interaction between instructional requirements and space design and organization remains. Gross evidence of the issue is found in the present knowledge that, on the average, an exceptional child requires twice the square footage of instructional space as other children. Averages do not tell the story well at all, and even measures of variance do not add much; but they serve to highlight the architectural needs that must be considered.

Teachers have discovered that they often have to speak out for themselves and for the children in their charge. It can be particularly helpful, in trying to obtain adequate space and facilities, to share the problems with parent organizations such as the local chapter of the National Association for Retarded Citizens. They can team with teachers in taking strong advocacy roles. This is still needed for those exceptional children and youth who have been neglected and who frequently cannot speak for themselves. (For more detailed information on school physical plant, see Birch & Johnstone, 1975).

Summary

The ingredients just discussed—curriculum, methods of teaching, instructional materials, organization for instruction, and school physical plant—make up the in-school components successful teachers put together to produce the goal of maximum opportunity to learn for each mentally retarded child. In some cases out-of-school services such as transportation, food, medical attention, and community aid and understanding must be developed also.

Today's schools and teachers are certainly better prepared to individualize instruction than were those of a generation ago. But the problem is by no means completely solved. There are still teachers who consistently and uniformly address themselves to the "class" rather than flexibly shifting their focus from the whole class to a small group, an individual, another small group, and back to the whole class, as they guide pupil learning. There are still principals who view maintaining quiet as equivalent to high quality teaching. There are still schools that have totally inadequate instructional facilities and equipment. And there are still parents who contest rather than cooperate and pupils who are not being reached, despite serious efforts on everyone's part. These are part of the challenge.

A PUBLIC SCHOOL PROGRAM IN TACOMA, WASHINGTON

Tacoma, Washington, population approximately 155,000, was the earliest among large cities to begin mainstreaming educable mentally retarded pupils throughout its schools. It started in 1958 as decentralization and progressive inclusion. An important part of decentralization and progressive inclusion is now emerging as a national trend under the name of mainstreaming.

Decentralization and Progressive Inclusion

Completely flexible interaction between regular and special education was spelled out in a 1958 report adopted by the Tacoma Board of Education.

> Decentralization provisions for exceptional children should be made in the public schools . . . exceptional children need to live and learn with

others; separate facilities make this difficult. Our educational philosophy, psychology and practice are calling for an education together rather than apart.

It must be observed that some children, such as the severely involved cerebral palsied child or severely mentally retarded child, need separate and different educational facilities. But even these facilities should have easy access to regular classrooms and children. The emphasis must be on the exceptional child in a general society, insofar as possible.

Many classes for exceptional children will provide distinct advantages for the pupils if the classes can be located within a complex of schools. This complex would include several elementary schools, a junior high school and a senior high school. Progressive inclusion in regular classes at various levels can be accomplished more easily in such a complex.

A decentralized program for exceptional children will have numerous arrangements for these pupils. Most of the special classrooms will be mixed in with regular classrooms. Almost every building will have classrooms for moderately mentally retarded children as well as resource rooms for certain children. . . . (Tacoma-Pierce County Cooperative Study, 1958, pp. 145-146)

A solid structure of educational provisions has been built in Tacoma on the foundations of decentralization and progressive inclusion. Handicapped pupils have ongoing contact with their nonhandicapped peers during their elementary and secondary school years. "Education together rather than apart" is the standard practice. Special education is available in as close proximity to home as possible for all children who need it. Educable mentally retarded pupils in almost all cases can attend the schools closest to their homes.

Progressive inclusion started with the idea that children needing special education should be scheduled into regular classes whenever a regular class teacher could supply instruction equivalent to or better than that in the special class. Exceptional children were to be in close enough proximity to regular classes so that the youngsters could spend from five minutes to most of the day being taught in settings with other children. The concept of progressive inclusion set no fixed amount of time in regular classes for any exceptional child. That was to be individualized. It could change from day to day, depending on the child's needs and the teacher's capabilities.

At first retarded children were sent from special classes to regular classes for program inclusion. That pattern went through a transition and the focus of responsibility changed. *Now the main tendency is for mentally retarded pupils to enter school in regular classes and to continue there.* The regular classroom teacher and the resource teacher determine how much time each pupil needs for instruction from the special education teacher. There is only one school system, and it is for all children.

The regular class teacher accepts responsibility for the handicapped child and knows that help can be obtained from the special education teacher and other school system resources.

In 1961 there were approximately 15 self contained classes for retarded pupils in Tacoma's elementary schools. Few such pupils had classroom contact with other teachers or pupils. There were 15 more classes in junior and senior high schools. Secondary retarded pupils studied home economics, art, music, shop, and physical education mostly with regular class teachers but with limited contact with other pupils.

There are no elementary or secondary classes that fit the 1961 description today. The principles of decentralization and progressive inclusion have produced a functional merger of special and regular education.

In 1973, 75% of Tacoma's 1,400 identified retarded pupils started the school day in homerooms with all other pupils. Approximately 50% of retarded pupils were supplied with the kinds of education they need and can profit from *in regular classrooms most of the school day, every day.* The special education department monitors their progress. Some retarded pupils, perhaps 10% to 15%, were taught entirely by special education teachers. The remaining 35% to 40% received their instruction in regular classes less than half the day.

Flexible interaction between regular and special education is a central factor. Individual children's schedules change as alterations in their needs are noticed by their teachers. The Division of Pupil Services keeps overall responsibility for defining pupil needs in a general sense. But principals, teachers, counselors, parents, and the pupils themselves have broad discretion in adapting local school activities to each pupil's requirements.

Tacoma has deliberately fostered a *quid pro quo* understanding with regular teachers that special education teachers will work also with regular grade youngsters who are having educational problems but who might not be classifiable into one of the special education categories.

It is more and more apparent that objectives for all retarded pupils in Tacoma are more similar to those of regular class pupils than they are different. And more and more retarded pupils are being programed successfully for more and more of the school day with regular class pupils. It is similar for both trainable and educable retarded children. They are programed to a great extent to learning activities with regular classes on individual schedules.

Tacoma teachers and principals point out that inclusion is fostered by four factors that prevail in the school system:

1. *Modified classes* reflect curriculum flexibility at all school levels.
   Ninth grade English, social studies, mathematics, or science for

regular students might each have several options, with different units each quarter, so all ninth grade students take social studies but do not all study the same things during that year. The same is true of other subjects at different grade levels.
2. *Functional classification* is the rule for pupils in need of special education. Children are discussed and planned for in terms of their specific educational assets and liabilities at any one time. Thus, a description like "She reads well at fifth grade level but has number skills and spelling skills at grade 2.5," is the sort of functional statement that is basic for placement for special help.
3. *Management of instruction by objectives* results in highly individualized teaching for all children. Also, teachers plan and work together to mobilize and apply their own individual strengths in terms of the pupil needs they notice.
4. *The "one-ness" of the school system* is expressed everywhere. Teachers, supervisors, principals, and all others point out that "every child is a pupil of School District No. 10. We have only one school system and it is for all children."

The four elements are all considered part of the multiple approaches, the multiple options, and the multiple facilities that make feasible the blending of special and regular education.

Parent Involvement

When decentralization and progressive inclusion were recommended in 1958 there had been broad public involvement in the studies that led to that point. Parents of retarded pupils in Tacoma work with the schools when educational handicaps in their children are called to their attention by school personnel. The emphasis in those discussions falls on what can be done to maximize the child's education. Parents are encouraged to react to individualized educational plans as proposed by teachers and principals.

It is necessary that parents give written approval for their children to enter special education programs. Most contact with parents is in connection with reaching agreement on that matter.

Tacoma began obtaining such written approvals before they were required by the state. Maximum use is made of school social workers, counselors, and school psychologists in direct, interpretive contacts with parents. It is emphasized that the role of the psychologist goes far beyond testing and writing reports. Often the psychologist is the key person in the interpretive session with parents.

Preparation of Teachers

It was recognized at the outset that not all regular class or special education teachers would be immediately ready for the new responsibilities to come with mainstreaming. Short courses and workshops were made available for regular teachers scheduled to have exceptional children in their classrooms, a new experience for both child and teacher. They were conducted in local schools, and the professors were volunteers from the Tacoma professional teaching staff. Tied together as an In-Service Micro-College, 10 class hours equaled one professional credit. Professional credits led to advanced qualifications and increments in salary.

The Micro-College flourishes. A sample from the more than 20 courses offered in one fall term follows (each course was 5 hours long):

Instructional Materials Sharing
Classroom Organization: Scheduling, Room Set-Up, Time
Integrating Children into the Regular Classroom
SST Progress: Slow Learners in the Classroom
How To Interpret Individual Tests (i.e., WISC, Binet)
Individualized Elementary Math
Counseling Techniques in Parent Conferencing
Career Exploration: Junior and Senior High School

Special education teachers are expected to give consultation to regular class teachers not only with respect to exceptional children (by strict definition) but also for regular class children who have learning or adjustment problems. Minicourses directed at helping special education teachers gain skill in giving that kind of technical assistance proved especially valuable.

Colleges and universities in the vicinity of Tacoma feel that the influence of progressive inclusion is a factor in how teachers should be prepared. They know that their graduates will be asked what they know and how they feel about working in the schools where that is the predominant point of view. Teachers are expected to be the prime movers in implementing the school system's philosophy. It is possible, now, for Tacoma to be selective in employing teachers who accept the policy of progressive inclusion.

The Professional Agreement between the Tacoma School District and the Tacoma Alliance of Teachers stipulates certain items closely related to mainstreaming. Staff development activities are to include:

1. Consultant and materials assistance for staff involved in curriculum innovations and change.
2. Workshops and classes to help staff become more aware of the needs of the individual learner and to acquaint them with teaching-learning approaches which will be responsive to these needs.
3. Specific offerings designed for staff needing to meet state certification requirements.
4. Special classes to broaden vocational interests.
5. Workshops and classes to develop more awareness of concerns challenging education of students in an urban society and to improve human relationships.

6. Activities to assist staff in self-evaluation of professional growth.

It is agreed that the district shall develop, with consultation from the constituent organizations, specific in-service and college credit classes for 1972-74. Priority should be given to:

1. Problems of individualizing instruction.
2. Philosophies of behavior in the classroom.
3. Team teaching.
4. Inquiry approach to teaching.
5. Special problems in teaching the disadvantaged. (Tacoma Public Schools, 1972-74, p. 49)

These provisions help to set the stage for precisely the kinds of in-service continuing professional education in skills and understandings called for by progressive inclusion.

Teacher Response

Not all teachers accepted progressive inclusion immediately. Some may not now. In the early days of the movement most teachers, regular and special, were accustomed to separation. Their beliefs were reinforced by the historical division between special and regular education.

Now effective managment of retarded pupils in homerooms and in regular classes is the rule rather than the exception. Regular class teachers ask for and expect to receive helpful consultation from special education teachers with a view to providing the needed education for retarded pupils in their own rooms. Regular classroom teachers seldom suggest now that retarded children be removed completely from their rooms. When that does seem necessary the request is usually made on the basis of a jointly planned educational program rather than on arbitrary considerations.

Functional grouping of children is accepted in principle by Tacoma's professional staff. The Professional Agreements include the statement: "It is agreed that multi-age grouping is a desirable form of school organization" (p. 52).

The flow of pupils between regular and special education teachers is in both directions. There are pupils in regular grades whose academic performance or social behavior puzzles their teachers. Special education teachers respond directly in such cases, giving assistance in diagnosing and recommending remedies to be tried by their regular class colleagues. It is not strictly a one to one exchange; the total school faculty grows to expect all members to share their competencies and resources.

The Professional Agreements could operate to limit inclusion. There are regular class size maximums which, if attained in a given school, could be invoked to prevent assignment of handicapped pupils to those classes. Generally, however, Tacoma teachers and principals practice inclusion under the flexibility allowed by the following additional provisions of the Professional Agreements:

> This maximum class size shall not apply to classes where the staff and administration in a specified school have agreed on variations in curriculum, instructional methods and/or staff organization necessitating a larger class size. (p. 52)

Mainstreamed retarded pupils in Tacoma start the day with all other children in heterogenous report rooms. The retarded pupils are carried administratively on a special education teacher's roll in order to assure accurate accounting for state report purposes. However, approximately three-fourths of the city's retarded children are physically in regular report rooms each morning. They remain with regular pupils for varying portions of the day, leaving only for special instruction that cannot be provided otherwise. This provides strong evidence that the response of teachers to mainstreaming is a positive one.

Results

Decentralization and progressive inclusion are operating principles in Tacoma. The first has been accomplished to the extent feasible with contemporary educational technology. The second, progressive inclusion, does stop short of 100% application, but it is well established, widespread, and growing.

TEACHING MENTALLY RETARDED PUPILS IN RESIDENTIAL SETTINGS

Across the nation there are residential institutions where persons of all ages with slow cognitive development live. Some states own and maintain as many as seven. Private residential schools are operated by nonprofit lay groups and by religious orders. In 1970, the United States had approximately 680 such public and private facilities in operation, caring for a little more than 200,000 residents, or about 1 out of 20 of the nation's mentally retarded citizens (President's Committee on Mental Retardation, 1971).*

It is difficult to estimate how many of those citizens would be in the free public education age range; it may be as many as half. Probably 75% to 80% are in the moderate, severe, and profound ranges with

---

*A source providing names, locations, and admission policies of all such facilities for the mentally retarded in the United States in 1975, by state, city, name, and address is *Directory of Inpatient Facilities for the Mentally Retarded,* available from the Superintendent of Documents, US Government Printing Office, Washington, D.C. 20402, for $2.85 (HE 20.6202:In 7; Sin 017/041/00090/8).

reference to degree of retardation, with the latter two in the majority and growing. The number of residential facilities has been on the increase, too, more than doubling in the 30 years immediately prior to 1970.

The first residential institution in the United States was opened in 1848 in Massachusetts. It had a clear and definite educational purpose: to prepare mentally retarded children and youth for return to the community as self sustaining and contributing citizens. That objective was part of the commitment when others were established, too, and it has never been lost sight of entirely. Yet there were long cloudy periods for the persons in residential schools in the more than a century and a quarter since their inception. The philanthropic, benevolent, and sometimes even altruistic motives that undergirded the early residential school movement were sometimes overshadowed by living conditions that were at best sterile warehousing of humans and at worst actual abuse.

Due largely to the vigilant attention and diligent work of organizations like the National Association of Retarded Citizens (NARC) and a number of professional persons from the ranks of education, the health professions, social work, psychology, and jurisprudence, that situation now appears to be improving. At present there are increasingly exciting and challenging opportunities in and around such centers for regular class and specialist teachers to work with children and youth whose cognitive development pace is slow (Blatt & Kaplan, 1967; Dunn, 1968, 1973; Kirk, 1972; Kugel & Wolfensberger, 1969; US Department of HEW, 1972).

Western State School and Hospital, Pennsylvania

Most education for institutionalized children has taken place in schools built within the institutional complex. Many are quite modern, with good supplies and direction. It should not be assumed, however, that all teachers who educate residential facility pupils do so on the grounds of the institution. In several instances there is a determined effort to blend with regular public schools. For example, at Western State School and Hospital in Canonsburg, Pennsylvania, the public schools of the region operate the educational services for 240 exceptional children who live at the school. In 1975, over 30% attended classes outside the institution, and it was expected that in 1976 as many as 65% would be part of regular elementary and secondary programs. Where it is impossible to place the retarded pupils in a regular school building, temporary classrooms have been set up alongside the school building, with the intent of moving the retarded pupils into the building as space becomes available. The program director, A.C. Sheets, commented:

> We've talked about making these people productive community agents, and their education is surely an important part of their being able to

assimilate. We don't want them to assimilate so well in a separate entity only to find themselves completely confused when we put them into the real world. . . . For all of our exceptional children we have an obligation not only to provide an education, but also to provide an opportunity for each student to develop into a productive, self-satisfied person who is able to find himself in this world of work. (Sheets, Quoted in Grogan, 1975, p. 4)

The public schools cooperating with Western State School provide extensive work experience opportunities, one part of which is in the building trades. It began in 1971. Young people of secondary school age in both the moderate and severe (educable and trainable) levels of retardation are enrolled. They acquire construction skills through renovating old houses and building new ones. The completed structures "are sold to needy families in the area for approximately the cost of the materials." Sheets pointed out that, when students graduate from the building trades program, they not only know the language of the building trades, but are also able to sell themselves to an employer because they have had some positive experience. He reported that as a result of programs such as this, "better than 95% . . . have found employment upon graduation" (p. 4).

Sheets attributed the success of the program to opportunity plus time, saying that "If you give these young people the opportunity or time, time to mature, time to develop, time to experience, they are able to move into areas that heretofore have been reserved only for the normal" (p. 4). On a more philosophical note he has found fault with society for having limited exceptional children more than their exceptionality ever could.

The Western State School and Hospital example is well worth further study because of its community directed thrust and because of its evident record of achievement.

States and communities have not always been engineered to promote the kinds of human accommodations that might be implied from this illustration. More often for persons with moderate, severe, or profound mental retardation, state or private residential schools were conceptualized and operated as completely sheltered and simplified communities that could control and limit the demand intensity and persistence for educational achievement and social and vocational competency, tailoring such pressures to the tolerance limits of the residents.

There are examples of residential facilities for emotionally disturbed persons, for physically handicapped (crippled) persons, and for socially maladjusted persons in the United States and other countries, all with similar purposes, namely, to get their clients ready to participate independently in natural community life, or, failing that, to be contributing members of the sheltered community. To a certain extent residential schools for deaf and for blind children and youth have done the same, though usually not as overt components of their service functions.

There have also been trials of villages planned for persons with exceptional conditions, including mental retardation. The Netherlands has long experience with them. In America, Innisfree Village in Virginia, was reported in 1975 to have "residential and work facilities for about thirty handicapped adults and about half as many non-handicapped co-workers and their children" (US Department of Health, Education, and Welfare, 1975, p. 23).

An innovative example more than 30 years ago was the Southbury Training School in Connecticut. Its originators designed it as a self contained community of communities, with excellent cottage style living centers for the residents, school, recreational facilities, shopping area, good staff quarters in houses, and a staffing pattern calculated to simulate homelike environments and to stimulate initiative.

With few exceptions residential facilities for persons with slow cognitive development have not been able to match the model provided by Southbury, and even Southbury's leaders and proponents find shortcomings they would like to remedy.

Persons in the residential schools often "lost their places" in their home communities simply by being away. They were not in the communities, visible, while growing up; therefore, no accommodation was planned for them. Parents moved or died, marriages broke up, and the family maintained little real contact with the institution. Brothers and sisters matured without fully realizing that a return to the community of a sibling they hardly knew was waiting in their future.

By the same token, leaving the familiar and relatively sheltered institution was often traumatic to the retarded person. The transition process was not well understood and not adequately arranged and staffed.

Group Community Residences

Recently, the early stated goal of return to the community in a productive role has been revived and begun to be realized. The process has developed both inside and outside the area of responsibility of the public schools. Some children and youth of school age are moving out of institutions, as are many persons beyond school age.

It is important for teachers to be aware of both components, however, not only for general information but also because teachers who understand slow cognitive development are being employed by nonschool agencies for posts in connection with the process of normalization (Wolfensberger, 1972), including community living, or asked to be volunteers for positions on advisory committees overseeing the work. The chief reason appears to be that the transition from residential living, with its ever present umbrella of comprehensive custodial care, is recognized as a major learning task (or group of tasks) for the retarded person making the move. It is natural to turn to teachers to analyze the task components; organize them into groups and sequences the learners can more readily assimilate; set up real life or simulations in which to instruct, monitor, and individualize the needed instruction; establish maintenance routines for what has been learned; and be judges of when the learners have satisfied criteria of competence for the tasks required for making successful transitions.

Two forms of community adjustment for transition are common where actual kin are not available or receptive. One is the *foster home* and the other is the group community residence, sometimes called a *halfway house*. Both are needed in many communities. The former is more often needed with children and youth who have not reached their majority. They are taken in by families who agree to treat them as family members, encourage their development, give them schooling, emotional, personal, and social support, and in all appropriate ways *foster* them until, like any other maturing children, they are ready to be independent adults. (The foster home approach, incidentally, is also being used with some success with elderly retarded persons who it is judged would find it a more fulfilling way of life than remaining at the institution. The family centered life objective is the same as for the young people, but it is not expected that the elderly would very often move to independent community living.)

The group community residence literally moves a number of well tested residential concepts off the institution's grounds and into the heart of the community. It has been difficult in some instances to do that, either actually or figuratively. There is often determined resistance from home owners to having a group of 8 to 15 young adult mentally retarded persons move into their neighborhood, either in a newly constructed group residence or into one remodeled from one or more large older existing houses.

The group community residence operates somewhat like a cottage unit within an institution. There are resident coordinators (like cottage parents), usually a married couple, who manage the facility while providing rich opportunities for the residents to acquire home and community living skills leading to increased independence. These include clothing purchase and care, preparing meals, cleaning, money mangement, use of recreation facilities, religious life, conducting courtships and marrying, preparation for child care, attending to one's physical and medical needs, adding to literacy and job skills, voting, and the like. The cottage parents have access to paid professional consultation and supervision, and can put the residents into such contact when necessary. It is common for the residents to be employed initially in diagnostic and skill building workshops maintained for that purpose, and then guided into regular employment, if possible.

Even from these brief descriptions it can be seen that teachers and other educators, who are knowledgeable about slow cognitive development, are in demand to employ their professional capabilities in those enterprises. The foster parents and cottage parents need systematic pretraining and followup instruction by professionally competent persons. Since the bulk of the work is informal education, the design and conduct of that instruction falls naturally to educators with the appropriate background. The same applies to the overall supervision and continuing program development needed. Also, the training programs in the workshops are frequently the products of consultation provided by professional educators, as is the in-service and continuing education of their staffs.

Direct instruction remains, of course, the chief teacher role for the child who resides in the institutional setting. That is true whether or not the institution is reaching out for links with community life for its residents. There are unique opportunities within the compass of the institution. For instance, the teacher can arrange for more access to the pupils' out-of-school time. In a number of cases, late afternoon and evening study time under teacher supervision is negotiated into the professional work situation. Also, in the institutional context the whole child can more easily be dealt with, for the teacher can make direct contacts with the institution's health care, psychological, recreational, and cottage life staff member in regard to pupil problems or problem prevention. Comprehensive environmental control is often more feasible in that setting, making the situation for contemporary behavior shaping instructional procedures applicable in more aspects of the pupil's life space.

Efforts on the part of NARC, AAMD, the Division on Mental Retardation of CEC, and various other volunteer groups and professional associations, plus the institutions themselves, are bringing about constructive changes. Standards have been arrived at by which institutions can be assessed and accredited (Accreditation Council on Facilities for the Mentally Retarded, 1973). It is hoped that educational agencies will do the same for the education components of institutions. The President's Committee on Mental Retardation (1972) has restated and amplified the rationale for residential facilities first made explicit in 1848. The Committee's proposed position is well worth study as a checklist to assess the functioning of institutions. Prospective teachers and others may find the points useful as items to keep in mind when considering whether to take on a professional relationship with a particular residential facility.

SELF CONTAINED SPECIAL CLASSES AND DAY SCHOOLS

Background

Much of today's instruction is carried on in self contained settings for mentally retarded children and youth. Special classes followed residential schools by about 50 years, receiving strong impetus in the first two decades of this century from leaders like Wallin (1924) who planted them in a number of states and major cities during that period.

From the outset, special classes and day schools served a different segment of the population of persons with slow cognitive development than did the institutions. Psychometric procedures (the early translations and applications of the Binet-Simon Scale, other individual intelligence tests devised by Americans, and the group test results on recruits in World War I) were increasingly applied to school children from 1920 on. The results revealed more and more pupils with intelligence quotients sufficiently below the average to be classified as mentally retarded, since at that time IQ and weakness in school achievement were the only criteria applied.

It was soon plain that institutions could not take on that increased load. Also, it was not sensible for some of the children so identified to be moved to residential schools. They had stable families who wanted and needed them at home; many were helpful and productive outside the academic program of the schools. So self contained classes and special schools grew.

The self contained special class was not, at the outset, as distinctively isolated as its name might suggest. Most other elementary school regular classes were self contained at the time. The term reflected a controversy in the 1920's through the 1940's about how elementary schools should be organized for optimum instruction: *departmental* (children moved from teacher to teacher and room to room during the day) or *self contained* (children stayed in one room and had practically all instruction from one teacher). Much of the time the special classes were no more isolated from the rest of the school than other children were. They went to assemblies, walked in the halls, played, ate lunch all at the same times, and had the same opportunities for pupil-pupil interaction outside their own room as other pupils did. Even within their own room there were sometimes other children from the regular classes who, when their work was completed, were privileged to go to the special room to use the tools or craft facilities and weave things on the looms that were standard equipment then.

By the early 1950's in secondary schools, particularly junior high schools, it was common for the slow cognitive developing pupils to attend physical education, home economics, shop, music, and art classes with regular teachers. They spent only three or four periods of a six or seven period day as a group with the special teacher, for core academic work. In some instances they were scheduled individually into specific regular classes because of evident ability in a particular pursuit.

Current Practices

The partial integration practices mentioned are still common. There are, of course, some situations where the separation is absolute. An example is a special central day school to which children are transported from a wide area.

Even when classes are located in regular schools it is sometimes the practice to have separate entry and dismissal times, separate play periods—in short, to deliberately close off the most ordinary opportunities for contact. Except for the case of separate day schools, however, there is a great deal of variation in the amount of interaction between special pupils and special teachers and their regular class counterparts. Thus, when a teacher is considering accepting an offer of employment, this can be a matter of importance to be determined beforehand.

There will no doubt always be some children with slow cognitive growth who will be best served by substantial separation from regular programs, at least for some stretch of time. The need for that is best determined by the professional judgment of a team of qualified teachers. Teachers may be aided in that judgment by consultants, and there should always be parental participation in such an important program decision. Separation as an across the board administrative practice would not be judged appropriate by most parents, special educators, and regular educators today.

Even in cases in which self contained classes appear to be the rule there is an important part to be played by the regular class teacher. That part will become even more important as mainstreaming grows, for then self contained classes will diminish in number and their primary function will alter.

COMPREHENSIVE PROGRAMING FOR PERSONS WITH ATTENUATED RATES OF COGNITIVE GROWTH

The United States is embarked on a total life development thrust for its mentally retarded citizens. Because of its developmental character, that movement contains a major educational component and it will be heavily staffed by educators.

The following eight points give a skeleton outline of what a complete educational design for retarded persons ought to look like:

1. The education of pupils characterized by slow cognitive growth

should be carried on in the same context as the education of all other pupils. Specifically, that means starting to school and being in school in the same classes with all others.
2. The educational program for all children, slow in cognitive development or not, should be of high quality. Each child should have excellent educational opportunities matched to his needs, all day, every day.
3. Professionally qualified teachers should staff every professional teaching position in the school system. Every teacher, in addition to being fully certificated for a specific teaching assignment, should have basic competencies in the education of exceptional children and youth. (Teachers are now being prepared this way in some training institutions, such as Edinboro State College in Pennsylvania. Also, all Teacher Corps preparation programs in the US are expected to include basic competencies for instructing exceptional children in addition to the various primary preparation roles for the teachers in training.)
4. All children with exceptional rates of cognitive development ought to be recognized and well understood by responsible professional persons in the school system. This calls for screening and identification prior to school entrance, plus a system for monitoring the progress of pupils with slow cognitive development. The system used should be designed to serve legitimate educational purposes and should avoid the dangers of labeling and categorizing.
5. There should be a complement of teachers and teacher aides who have made a specialization of the education of mentally retarded pupils. The number should bear a relationship to the number of such pupils identified in the school system, as determined by the regulations governing such matters in that state.
6. The specialists who are competent in the educational implications of slow cognitive development should (a) consult, advise, team teach with regular class pupils, help evaluate pupils, and otherwise participate in parallel in the instruction of such pupils, and of other pupils with whom the regular teacher requests assistance, and (b) should conduct individual or small group instruction with pupils with learning problems. That could be done apart from the rest of the class, when and if that is necessary, but in the same room so far as is possible and, if not, certainly within the same school building.
7. The instructional program for cognitively slow pupils should extend from the preschool years, beginning not later than age 3 years (at parental option) and go on through secondary school, with on the job training and placement being part of the sequence leading to graduation. As soon after birth as low cognitive development is suspected,

the parents, if they wish, should be furnished with guidance for stimulating the child's development at home.
8. Regular class teachers, special educators, parents, and the child, where appropriate, should jointly plan and monitor all elements of the educational program. To do so effectively, of course, they need data and suggestions supplied by support personnel such as counselors, psychologists, and diagnosticians as well as participation and support from administrators and supervisors.

It is apparent from the above list that special education is expected to be truly *a part of* rather than *apart from* the rest of the educational enterprise. That national trend can be read plainly from many indications.

It should be clear that it is the *teacher* who is viewed as the standard bearer and a prime mover in setting forth and implementing educational programs, whether general or specialized. It is more of a leadership position than has been the case in the past. The teacher is seen as expressing views and as exerting guidance and being attended to as first among equals in partnership with parents, administrators, and supervisors.

No doubt the eight points could be extended. Also, many more details could be filled in under each. But if it is allowed to suffice now for the broad outline of a comprehensive educational program for mentally retarded children, it will be added to and enriched by what teachers bring to it in the years to come.

EDUCATION AS PART OF A BROADER GROUP OF SERVICES

In most communities public education first touches children with slow cognitive development when they begin kindergarten or first grade, at age 5 or 6 years. In a few places (and the number is growing) educators and parents begin some form of planned instruction with babies and toddlers. Powerful evidence has accumulated in favor of expanding very early childhood education for all youngsters, and especially for high risk infants (Ramey & Smith, 1977).

In the later years public education continues to age 21 at the most; though, in most cases it stops for mentally retarded youth at about age 17 or 18, as it does for most others. Pupils with lesser degrees of retardation are more and more often completing secondary school, frequently via a work-study curriculum. They are graduated and many have ongoing jobs secured through their work-study experiences.

Pupils with more grave degrees of cognitive attenuation tend to stay on in school until they reach the maximum age allowable, at which point they may obtain further instruction in workshops designed to give added social and vocational skills. If job placements are not feasible, they may stay on in sheltered work conditions, remain at home, or become full or part time clients of state maintained residential centers. The workshop and the residential operations are rarely under the aegis of the public schools, more often being the responsibility of other state agencies or volunteer groups.

It can be seen, then, that the schools influence only a part of the life of a child or youth who is said to be mentally retarded. Retardation is present 24 hours a day, every day.* Characteristics such as need for improved reading comprehension, writing, spelling, speech, and arithmetic skills, which call for adjustments in school, do not go away on Saturdays and Sundays, in the evening, during the summer and other holidays. They impact the child's social, recreational and personal world, too. Schools and teachers, though, have a narrower mission. With few exceptions it is to instruct their pupils during a 6 hour day, from age 5 or 6 to 18 or 21, with no school for the pupils on weekends, holidays or in the summer. So much to do and so little time!

Three agencies most frequently fill in the gaps the schools do not reach for retarded pupils. They are the state bureau of vocational rehabilitation, the local chapter of the National Association for Retarded Citizens, and the county mental health/mental retardation office. The first and third are tax supported; the second is a volunteer service. These are the teacher's, the parent's and the child's out-of-school resources, and they will be the mentally retarded individual's main sources of help after school is completed. Therefore, it is of paramount importance that teacher, parent, and pupil become acquainted with them at firsthand during the child's school years. The following brief descriptions may serve as orientation prior to direct contact.

The oldest of the three is the state bureau of vocational rehabilitation. (The name may differ slightly from state to state.) There is a central office in the state capital and regional and local offices in strategic spots across the state. The work in each state is funded substantially by the US Congress through the Secretary of Health, Education, and Welfare. Staffed by trained counselors, this state agency has responsibility for seeing that handicapped persons have opportunities to become self supporting, contributing workers to the extent that their capabilities will allow. They usually accept clients with mental retardation at age 16 or as soon after that as they are ready to leave school. Services are without cost if parents cannot afford them. Preparation for occupational placement

---

*The President's Committee on Mental Retardation (1971) spoke of "six-hour retarded children," meaning that there were some pupils assigned to special education programs who, out of school hours, were indistinguishable from all other children.

can be interpreted broadly to include training to acquire social and personal attributes as well as direct instruction and practicum on the job.

Next in recency is the National Association for Retarded Citizens (NARC) and its state and local affiliates. Founded at midcentury, it is a volunteer, dues supported organization of parents and friends of mentally retarded citizens. From the point of view of the teacher, the agency supplies many benefits. It establishes and carries on direct services in communities on behalf of retarded children and adults. For instance, it may conduct preschool instruction in the years before public school begins; it may operate recreation facilities year-round for retarded children and adults; it may own or lease space and employ staff for a sheltered workshop; it may promote positive public information messages aimed at building better public attitudes toward individuals with slow cognitive development; and it may mount various other enterprises, depending on the needs uncovered by its members. An important activity is the stimulation of tax supported agencies, including the schools, to do more and better work for and with retarded persons. In 1976 NARC began developing its own national research facility and was considering ways and means to upgrade public school curricula for retarded pupils and the specification of competencies desired in teachers.

The third agency, a relative latecomer to the scene, was established by a federal act in 1965. Each state is encouraged by funds supplied under the act to establish mental health/mental retardation (MH/MR) offices in its counties (or equivalent governmental units). These offices do not give direct services. Instead, they study the local or regional situation to find what services are needed, then attempt to bring these services into being and to see that they are maintained as long as they are required. Their legal mandate encourages the offices to range across education, psychology, medicine, nursing, law, transportation, social welfare, recreation, housing—any area where a justifiable and unmet need can be authenticated by responsible authorities. In the background of this agency there was the seed of a reciprocal relationship with NARC, for that group helped build the legislative strength to enact the bill that was to establish the MH/MR offices. Now the MH/MR offices across the nation rely heavily on NARC to identify unmet needs. MH/MR county offices finance, on a service contract basis, many activities for retarded persons carried on under NARC auspices.

All three agencies work together and with other groups and associations. Teachers have the strong reasons mentioned earlier as incentives to get to know the three agencies well. There is another reason, too. These agencies are potential sources of employment, either full time as educators, coordinators, and directors, or part time in consultation, since they often support substantial educational components over and above those of the public schools.

THE CONTINUING NEED FOR TEACHERS

This *is* a period of special education in transition. But it is more than that. *All the rest of education is in transition, too,* affected by tides and crosscurrents in this nation and others. The need for more elementary and secondary teachers who are competent to work in their regular classes with pupils who show indications of slow cognitive development is one of the predictable outcomes, because that is what has been found necessary in schools already well into the transition. An equally pressing need is for more teachers who are specialists in exceptional child education to team with regular class teachers to enhance individualization of instruction for all pupils in the nation's schools.

Few school systems already have a fully staffed and comprehensive educational program for pupils with slow cognitive development. Most have a partially complete program or they are about to start building a program. The prospects for systematic growth are excellent.

That state of affairs results in a substantial current and projected market for regular class teachers with basic competencies in work with pupils with slow cognitive development as well as for teachers who have made it a specialty. The market extends also to competent special education counselors, administrators, supervisors, psychologists, diagnosticians, and other members of the education professions, as well as to teacher aides and assistants. A bright part of that picture is the opportunity for teachers and others to shape new and emerging programs according to modern and future oriented educational conceptions.

In March 1974, the Bureau of Education for the Handicapped of the US Office of Education supplied the following estimates:

Mentally Retarded Children
Age 0 to 19 years, in the USA	1,507,000
Number Being Served in 1974-75	1,250,000
Percentage Being Served in 1974-75	83%

The US Office of Education used 2.3% as the mental retardation incidence figure for the 0 to 19 year age range. Data on children and youth served came from state education agencies (President's Committee on Mental Retardation, 1975).

The report leaves 17% of the 0 to 19 year old population of persons with slow cognitive development not accounted for except to say that they were unserved at that time. Thus, at a minimum, it can be estimated that approximately one out of six retarded persons in that age range was without appropriate schooling.

Parent groups and organizations of educators will continue to urge that all children, slow in cognitive development or otherwise, receive suitable opportunities for education. State and federal legislative enactments already mandate and support that position. Additional teachers will be needed to close the gap.

SUGGESTIONS FOR STUDENTS AND INSTRUCTOR

1. Visit classes where children and youth with mental retardation are being educated. These should include all degrees of retardation and a range of settings, from separated residential schools to full mainstreaming.
2. Attend sessions of committees that are engaged in planning and reviewing individual educational programs for pupils who are mentally retarded.
3. Go to meetings of the local Association for Retarded Citizens chapter or other parent groups that focus on children and youth with mental retardation.
4. Interview teachers who have specialized in education of retarded pupils; regular class teachers who have retarded pupils in their classes; parents of retarded children and youth and officials of parent associations; principals of schools retarded pupils attend; and school psychologists and diagnosticians who assess retarded pupils and who help plan educational programs for them.
5. Tour a special education instructional resources center to see the array of materials there for teacher-pupil use.
6. Look into early educational intervention conducted with parents and infants in their homes.
7. Learn about the work of the local mental health/mental retardation office.

TOPICAL BIBLIOGRAPHIES
Assessment of Retarded Pupils

Doll, E. *Vineland Social Maturity Scale.* Circle Pines MN: American Guidance Service, 1953.

Doll, E. *Measurement of social competence.* Minneapolis: Educational Testing Bureau, 1953.

Fogelman, G. J. (Ed.). *AAMD adaptive behavior scale.* Washington DC: American Association on Mental Deficiency, 1975.

Lindsley, O. Direct measurement and prosthesis of retarded behavior. *Journal of Education,* 1964, *147,* 62.

Mercer, J.R. Culturalism, pluralism and the standardized testing movement. In G. R. Gredler (Ed.). *Ethical and legal factors in the practice of school psychology.* Harrisburg PA: State Department of Education, 1974.

Meyers, C. E., & Lombardi, T. P. Definition of the mentally retarded: Decision time for the AAMD. *Mental Retardation,* 1974, *12*(2), 43.

Causes of Mental Retardation

Begab, M. J., & Richardson, S. A. *The mentally retarded and society: A social science perspective.* Baltimore: University Park Press, 1975.

Bijou, S. J. A functional analysis of retarded development. In N. R. Ellis (Ed.). *International review of research in mental retardation.* New York: Academic, 1966.

Birch, H., Richardson, S., Baird, O., Horobin, G., & Illsley, R. *Mental subnormality in the community.* Baltimore: Williams and Wilkins, 1970.

Grossman, H. J. (Ed.). *Manual on terminiology and classification in mental retardation.* Washington DC: American Association on Mental Deficiency, 1973.

Robinson, H. B., & Robinson, N. M. *The mentally retarded child* (2nd ed.). New York: McGraw-Hill, 1975.

Stein, Z. A. *Strategies for the prevention of mental retardation.* Bull NY: Academy of Medicine, *51*(130), 1975.

Educational Provisions for Severely and Profoundly Retarded Pupils

Baumgartner, B. B. *Helping the trainable mentally retarded child.* New York: Teachers College Press, Columbia University, 1960.

Brown, A. Integration of trainable students in a regular high school building. *Education and Training of the Mentally Retarded,* 1976, *11*(1), 51-52.

Burton, T. A. *The trainable mentally retarded.* Columbus OH: Charles E. Merrill, 1976.

Cain, L. F., & Levine, S. *Effects of community and institutional school programs on the trainable mentally retarded children.* (CEC Research Monograph Series B, No. B-1). Reston VA: The Council for Exceptional Children, 1963.

Risler, W. P., & Mefford, J. P. Public school education for the severely mentally retarded. *Viewpoints,* 1973, *49*(1), 13-24.

Thomas, M. A. *Hey don't forget about me! Education's investment in the severely, profoundly, and multiply handicapped.* Reston VA: The Council for Exceptional Children, 1976.

Ziegler, S., & Hambleton, D. Integration of young TMR children into a regular elementary school. *Exceptional Children,* 1976, *42*, 459-461.

Followup Studies of Retarded Persons as Adults

Bergman, J. S. et al. *Community homes for the retarded.* Arlington TX: NARC Publications, 1976.

Dinger, J. C. Post-school adjustment of formed educable mentally retarded pupils. *Exceptional Children,* 1961, *27*, 353-360.

Porter, R. B., & Milazzo, T. C. A comparison of mentally retarded adults who attended a special class with those who attended regular school classes. *Exceptional Children,* 1958, *24,* 410-412.

Wolfson, I. N. Adjustment of institutionalized mildly retarded patients twenty years after return to the community. *Mental Retardation,* 1970, *8*(4), 20-23.

History of Special Education for Retarded Pupils

Begab, M. J., & Richardson, S. A. *The mentally retarded and society: A social science perspective.* Baltimore: University Park Press, 1975.

Doll, E. A. A historical survey of research and management of mental retardation in the United States. In E. P. Trapp & P. Himmelstein (Eds.). *Readings on the exceptional child: Research and theory.* New York: Appleton-Century-Crofts, 1962.

Hutt, M.L., & Gibby, R.G. *The mentally retarded child* (3rd ed.). Boston: Allyn & Bacon, 1976.

Itard, J. W. S. *Wild boy of Aveyron.* New York: Appleton-Century-Crofts, 1932.

Johnson, G. O. Special education for the mentally handicapped—A paradox. *Exceptional Children,* 1962, *29,* 62-69.

Jordan, J. B. (Ed.). *Exceptional children at the bicentennial: A parade of progress.* Reston VA: The Council for Exceptional Children, 1977.

Kanner, L. A. *A history of the care and study of the mentally retarded.* Springfield IL: Charles C Thomas, 1964.

Kirk, S. A. *Educating exceptional children.* Boston: Houghton Mifflin, 1972.

Kirk, S. A., & Johnson, G. O. *Educating the retarded child.* Boston: Houghton Mifflin, 1951.

Wallin, J. E. W. *Education of mentally handicapped children.* New York: Harper & Row, 1955.

Labels and Stigma in Special Education for Retarded Pupils

Carvajal, A. L. Predictors of four criteria of self concept in educable mentally retarded adolescents. *Exceptional Children,* 1972, *39,* 239.

Flynn, T. M. The effect of a part time special education program on the adjustment of EMR students. *Exceptional Children,* 1970, *37,* 680-681.

Goffman, E. *Stigma: Notes on the management of spoiled identity.* Englewood Cliffs NJ: Prentice-Hall, 1963.

Goodman, H., Gottlieb, J., & Harrison, R. H. Social acceptance of "EMRs" integrated into a non-graded elementary school. *American Journal of Mental Deficiency,* 1972, *76,* 412-417.

Gottlieb, J., & Gottlieb, B.W. Stereotypic attitudes and behavioral intentions toward handicapped children, *American Journal of Mental Deficiency,* 1977, *82*(1), 65-71.

Hobbs, N. *Issues in the classification of children* (Vols. 1 and 2). San Francisco: Jossey-Bass, 1975.

Iano, R. P., Ayers, D., Heller, H. B., McGettigan, J. F., & Walker, V.S. Sociometric status of retarded children in an integrative program. *Exceptional Children,* 1974, *40,* 267-271.

Jones, R. L. The hierarchical structure of attitudes toward the exception. *Exceptional Children,* 1974, *40,* 430-435.

Mercer, J. R. *Labeling the mentally retarded.* Berkeley: University of California Press, 1973.

Meyerowitz, J. H. Self-derogation in young retardates and special class placement. *Child Development,* 1962, *33,* 443-451.

Monroe, J. D., & Howe, C. E. The effects of integration and social class on the acceptance of retarded adolescents. *Education and Training of the Mentally Retarded,* 1971, *6*(1), 21-23.

Sheare, J. B. Social acceptance of EMR adolescents in integrated programs. *American Journal of Mental Deficiency,* 1974, *78*(6), 678-682.

Trippi, J. A. Special-class placement and suggestibility of mentally retarded children. *American Journal on Mental Deficiency,* 1973, *78*(2), 220-222.

Van Osdol, B. M., & Johnson, D. M. The sociometric status of educable mentally retarded students in regular school classes. *Australian Journal of Mental Retardation,* 1973, *2*(7), 200-203.

Mentally Retarded Pupils with Additional Educational Handicaps

Berry, P. (Ed.). *Language and communication in the mentally handicapped.* Baltimore: University Park Press, 1976.

Dacarie, T. G. A study of the mental and emotional development of the thalidomide child. In B. M. Foss (Ed.). *Determinants of infant behavior* (Vol. 4). London: Methuen, 1969.

Gottlieb, J., Agard, J., Kauffman, N., & Semmel, M. Retarded children mainstreamed: Practices as they affect minority children. In R. L. Jones (Ed.). *Mainstreaming and the minority child.* Reston VA: The Council for Exceptional Children, 1976.

Haring, N. G., & Krug, D. A. Placement in regular programs: Procedures and results. *Exceptional Children,* 1975, *41,* 413-417.

Hurley, R. *Poverty and mental retardation: A causal relationship.* New York: Random House, 1969.

Modern School Programs for Retarded Pupils

Birch, J.W. *Mainstreaming: Educable mentally retarded children in regular classes.* Reston VA: The Council for Exceptional Children, 1974.

Brolin, D. E. (Ed.). *Life centered career education: A competency based approach.* Reston VA: The Council for Exceptional Children, 1978.

Bruininks, R. H., & Rynders, J. E. Alternatives to special class placement for educable mentally retarded children. In E. L. Meyen, G. A. Vergason, & R. J. Whelan (Eds.). *Strategies for teaching exceptional children.* Denver: Love, 1972.

Cegelka, W. J. *Review of work-study programs for the MR.* Arlington TX: NARC Publications, 1976.

Cegelka, W. J., & Tyler, J. L. The efficacy of special class placement for the mentally retarded in proper perspective. *Training School Bulletin,* 1970, *67*(1), 33-68.

Haring, N. G., & Krug, D. A. Placement in regular programs: Procedures and results. *Exceptional Children,* 1975, *41*, 413-417.

Kugel, R. B., & Wolfensberger, W. *Changing patterns in residential services for the mentally retarded.* Washington DC: President's Committee on Mental Retardation, 1969.

Sheperd, G. The education of educable mentally retarded students in secondary schools: A review of the literature. *Oregon University (Eugene) School of Education Curriculum Bulletin,* 1967, *23*(280), 1-31.

Thomas, M. A. *Very special children series: Developing skills in severely and profoundly handicapped children.* Reston VA: The Council for Exceptional Children, 1977.

Tonn, M. The case for keeping mentally retarded children in your regular classrooms. *American School Board Journal,* 1974, *161*(8), 45.

Walker, V. S. The efficacy of the resource room for educating children. *Exceptional Children,* 1974, *40*, 288-289.

People with Attenuated Cognitive Development

Abraham, W. *Barbara: A prologue.* New York: Rinehart, 1958.

Blatt, B. *Exodus from pandemonium: Human abuse and reformation of public policy.* Boston: Allyn & Bacon, 1970.

Braginsky, D., & Braginsky, B.H. *Hansels and Gretels.* New York: Holt, Rinehart, and Winston, 1971.

Buck, P. S. *The child who never grew.* New York: Day, 1950.

Grossman, H. *Nine rotten lousy kids.* New York: Holt, Rinehart and Winston, 1972.

Itard, J. W. S. *Wild boy of Aveyron.* New York: Appleton-Century-Crofts, 1932.

Media

Jordan, J. B. (Ed.). *The CEC Invisible College Conference on the Severely, Profoundly, and Multiply Handicapped* (tape cassettes). Reston VA: The Council for Exceptional Children, 1977.

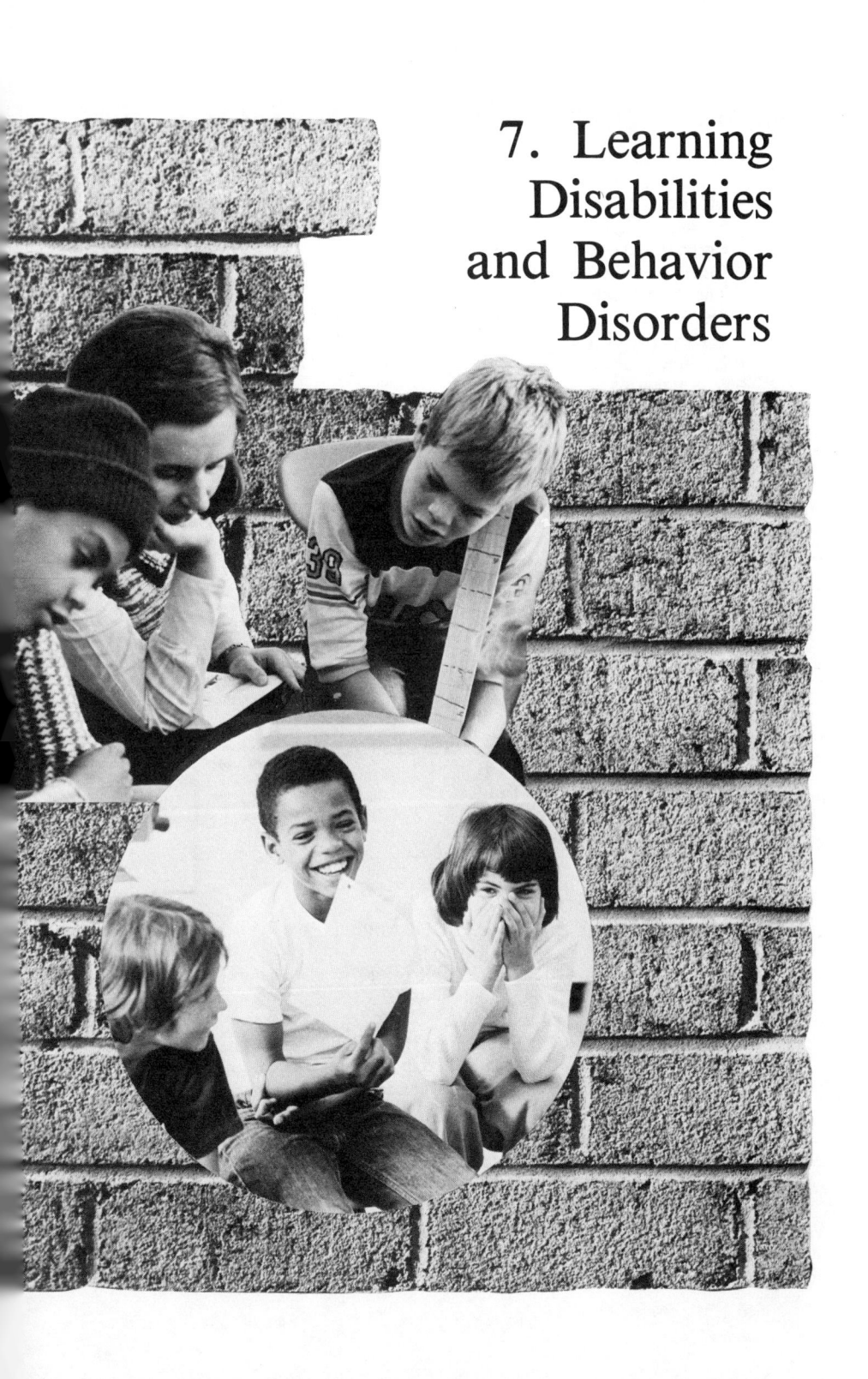

7. Learning Disabilities and Behavior Disorders

CHAPTER OUTLINE

THE CHALLENGE TO EDUCATORS
  Legal Considerations
  Medical Considerations
  Social Welfare Considerations
  Educational Considerations
  Emerging Changes in Terminology
  The Person Called Learning Disabled and Behavior Disordered
THE CONCEPT, TERMINOLOGY, AND SIGNIFICANCE OF LEARNING DISABILITIES AND BEHAVIOR DISORDERS
  Definition of Learning Disabilities and Behavior Disorders
  Summary
PREVAILING VERSUS PREFERRED PRACTICES
  The Beginning of Special Education for Learning Disabled/Behavior Disordered Children
  Theories of Corrective Instruction: Past and Present
    Neurological
    Metabolic
    Psychoanalytic
    Reflective Interaction
    Psychophysiological
    Participatory Responsibility
    Applied Behavior Analysis
    Remedial Education
  Current Trends
THE ROLE OF THE REGULAR CLASS TEACHER
  Teamwork with Specialists
  Special Education in the Regular Grades
  Individualization of Instruction
    Curriculum Individualization
    Methods of Teaching
    Instructional Materials
  Organization for Instruction
  School Physical Plant
  Summary
SPECIFIC PUBLIC SCHOOL PROGRAMS
  Vallejo City Unified School District
  Rochester Primary Mental Health Project
  The Pittsburgh Secondary School Model
COMPREHENSIVE PROGRAMING
  Characteristics of a Comprehensive Educational Program
  Education as Part of a Broader Group of Services
THE CONTINUING NEED FOR TEACHERS
SUGGESTIONS FOR STUDENTS AND INSTRUCTOR
TOPICAL BIBLIOGRAPHIES

THE CHALLENGE TO EDUCATORS

There are two pressing problems challenging educators today so far as children with learning disabilities and behavior disorders are concerned. The first is to see that they receive instruction that will help them. The second is to bring some rational order into both professional and public discussions of what the expression "learning disabilities/behavior disorders" means.

The two problems are interactive; a solution to one is somewhat dependent upon the resolution of the other. It is a formidable task, therefore, to decide which one to address first. We shall start with what learning disabilities/behavior disorders means, as the expression is used in this book.

Pupils who are said to show learning disabilities and behavior disorders are the same children and youth who have been described by the 28 expressions below and who present social and academic school learning problems:

Autistic	Hyperkinetic
Behavior disordered	Incorrigible
Behavior problem	Juvenile delinquent
Brain damaged	Language disabled
Brain injured	Learning disability
Delayed language	Mentally ill
Developmental aphasic	Minimal brain dysfunction
Disruptive/agressive	Minimal neurological dysfunction
Dyslexic	Neurologically impaired
Educationally disabled	Perceptually handicapped
Educationally handicapped	Predelinquent
Emotional blockage	Socially maladjusted
Emotionally disturbed	Subtle neurological impairment
Hyperactive	Strauss syndrome

Children given these labels have two educationally significant qualities in common. First, they do poorly at learning most or all of the skills and other content of the elementary and secondary school curricula, which can be traced in their school records. Second, their deportment in school is out of harmony with how they and other pupils have been taught to conduct themselves. They have not learned or do not practice the personal and social behaviors that are important parts of the human development sequences usually inculcated both at home and in the elementary and secondary school years. Also, their school records show a clear history of that behavior. In short, they learn too little of the academic (cognitive) and the personal-social (affective) school (or home) curriculum to experience reasonable success educationally.

A natural question is, Why? Especially when there may be no hearing or vision or other health problems, when there may be a supportive home, when the schools attended have been good ones, and when there is reason to believe that there is adequate potential for cognitive and affective development?

More will be said about this array of expressions and the matter of "cause" later. It will be seen that educational management of children described as learning disabled/behavior disordered has a set of common themes, that often the children can be helped, and that the labels need be neither bewildering nor frightening for regular class teachers or for parents.

Legal Considerations

Legislatures and courts, notably juvenile courts, play major parts in the lives of many pupils now considered to have learning disabilities and behavior disorders. For those whose personal and social behavior have brought arrest and legal detention, the lawmakers of the various states have authorized detention homes, camps, and a variety of other custodial settings ranging from foster homes to maximum security institutions. The tags society has given to those children and youth include behavior problem, predelinquent, juvenile delinquent, socially maladjusted, and incorrigible.

Teachers may work with these pupils in regular schools, in special classes or day schools, or in residential situations. Whichever is the case, it will be necessary for the teacher to become knowledgeable about lawyers who work with juveniles, probation officers and their work, foster parents and other parent surrogates, and the juvenile court itself. Also, it will be necessary to interpret the educationally significant attributes of these pupils to the juvenile court personnel.

It will be particularly important for teachers to clarify that *only some* of the children who come under the court's jurisdiction are characterized by learning disabilities and behavior disorders. Those who are, of course, should have the special education they need. Also, the great majority of the court's wards, while not learning disabled or behavior disordered, should have the sound regular education they need, too.

A 1967 US Supreme Court decision spotlighted the plight of too many children and youth under juvenile courts in the past. According to Robinson (1974), Gerald Gault was 15 years old when placed in a detention home by a juvenile court. After hearings he was remanded to custody in the detention home for 6 years, the length of time until he would reach age 21.

If the boy had been 18 years old when apprehended and tried, the offense with which he was charged would have carried a jail sentence of no more than two months and a fine of no more than $50.00.

The US Supreme Court reversed the original juvenile court decision. In clarifying the conclusion that due process had been denied Gerald and his family, Justice Fortas wrote:

> A boy is charged with misconduct. The boy is committed to an institution where he may be restrained of liberty for years. It is of no constitutional consequence and of limited practical meaning that the institution to which he is committed is called an Industrial School. The fact of the matter is that, however euphemistic the title, a "receiving home" or an "industrial school" for juveniles is an institution of confinement. . .Under our constitution, the condition of being a boy does not justify a kangaroo court. . . . Against the application to juveniles of the right to silence, it is argued that juvenile proceedings are "civil" and not "criminal". . . [but] the availability of the privilege does not turn on the type of proceeding. . .but upon the nature of the statement or admission and the exposure it invites. (Quoted in Deno, in preparation)

This and related decisions have altered the former operations of juvenile courts so the judge can no longer be a paternalistic dictator, no matter how well intentioned. Children are now entitled to counsel, full participation by their parents, and all the due process considerations formerly reserved for adults.

The realization is growing, too, that youths who run away, who are promiscuous, or who create discipline problems ought not be detained in the same centers that house thieves, arsonists, muggers, and other criminals. The former are *status offenders*—young people who are guilty of actions that would not be against the law if they were adults—as distinguished from those who have actually committed crimes. Judges, probation officers, and other court officials know that separate facilities are needed because many adult criminals started out as status offenders in detention facilities with other juveniles, where they learned the ropes of crime and were led into making it a career.

Modern methods of dealing with status offenders rely on guidance and support as near as possible to the mainstream of society and school. Programs range from immediate family and individual crisis counseling in the troubled home and school to group homes in the community where teenagers can live for extended periods under close but friendly and understanding supervision. Social workers and teachers join in conducting these support activities, with psychodynamic and behavior modification procedures being used with increasing effectiveness.

Another feature of more up to date work with status offenders keeps many juveniles out of the court system entirely. This preferred practice has the children and youth referred directly by police station personnel or schools to a program designed to meet their needs without separating them from their nonoffending peers to any appreciable degree.

Another recent judicial highlight was the court's finding that the state's placement of a child or youth in a special institution carries with it an implicit promise that while there the child will receive individualized special education (*Wyatt v. Stickney,* 1972).

Experienced teachers know that strong pressure mounts to "put away" pupils who persist in disruptive behavior that is unsettling to the regular class and the regular school. For socially maladjusted, incorrigible, delinquent, and similarly labeled youngsters, being put away has meant legal confinement in "reform schools" or other detention facilities. From another point of view, for those pupils termed emotionally disturbed, behavior disordered, mentally ill (and in other contexts, mentally retarded), being put away has referred to some form of hospitalization or mental health management in special schools separate from the regular schools.

The pupil's right to treatment (including specialized education) under conditions of involuntary hospitalization was affirmed by a case in Alabama (*Wyatt v. Stickney,* 1972). The court held that the defendant could not be kept in a mental hospital if the treatment for which the defendant had been admitted was not actually rendered.

These decisions mean that any removal of pupils, no matter how they are labeled, from regular educational settings must be thoroughly substantiated. There must be convincing evidence and competent professional judgment in support of any such projected change. Any legal intervention that limits a pupil's usual freedom to attend a regular school for purported special educational reasons must show unequivocally that it is justified in terms of an improved educational program that can be delivered only in the separated facility. On the other side, if removal is required because of the pupil's illegal acts, the separated facility to which the pupil is removed must provide adequate individualized education.

Permissive and mandatory state and federal legislation in support of special education for pupils characterized by learning disabilities and behavior disorders is of fairly recent origin. It is discussed later in this chapter in association with the historical development of special education for this group of pupils.

Medical Considerations

For a time it was common to assert that certain children had "emotional or psychological blocks" that prevented them from learning. Something *in* the child presumably got in the way. Teachers and parents alike reached out for help to child guidance clinics and to psychiatrists and psychologists who were employed as consultants. Teachers and parents wanted help to break loose the blockage or, at least, to explain it.

How the psychological or emotional block idea originated or what popularized it is not clear, but the currency of the concept gave it a ring of truth. It was and still is widely believed by the lay public that emotional problems cause learning disabilities and behavior problems.

Actually psychiatrists and psychologists report that learning problems more often precede emotional problems. Certainly children sometimes become upset when they do not meet their parents', their teachers', their classmates', or their own expectations for school achievement, but that is seldom the origin of school learning problems. More often the reverse is the case.

Many child guidance clinics employ teachers who are specialists in remedial education, as do special schools for emotionally disturbed pupils. They find the most common need of disturbed pupils is corrective instruction in reading skills. The most frequent reason seems to be that the pupils were not given appropriate individualized reading instruction in the first place.

Psychiatrists and psychologists point out that mental illness health indicators such as emotional tensions, anxiety, agressive behavior, and withdrawl diminish and tend to disappear when school achievement is brought closer to par through remedial instruction. Mental health professionals are among the strongest proponents of improving the capability of regular class teachers to individualize instruction in the regular class. Many psychiatrists, psychologists, and psychiatric social workers have strived to make themselves proficient at teamwork with teachers in order to help them match instruction more closely to each pupil's requirements.

Some physicians take another approach to assisting school personnel and parents to cope with aggressive and hyperactive children and youth. Medications with tranquilizing effects are prescribed to reduce impulsive disruption of class order and to render the pupil more amenable to ordinary instructional routines. It is not uncommon for psychiatrists, pediatricians, and general practitioners to take this same tack in attempting to maintain their young patients in a more manageable state.

Teachers often report that the reduction in overt disorderly behavior due to such medication has an undesirable educational side effect. The cognitive capability of the pupil may be dampened along with the soft pedaling of psychomotor outbursts and the lessening of the general nuisance factor. It is not yet clear whether pharmacological forms of intervention will prove to have long or short term effectiveness in setting the stage for the more fundamental work—the special reeducation that teachers need to do with pupils who show learning disabilities and behavior disorders.

Some of the earliest notions about children now called learning disabled/behavior disordered involved another aspect of medicine, the neurological. Cruickshank and Hallahan (1975) made that point and went on to say:

> Children who have experienced a prenatal, perinatal or post-natal impact on the central nervous system, whether specially diagnosed or assumed, present highly individualized characteristics of perceptual disturbance. It is assumed by a growing number of persons that environmental and nutritional deprivations likewise produce behavior and perceptual characteristics which are like or closely approximate those of children who have a known specific neurological disturbance. The direct relationship on the neurological and perceptual systems is still subject to investigation, but the issue is significantly joined. (p. 496)

In addition to speculating that there is defective physiological substratum implicated in learning disabled/behavior disordered children, Cruickshank and Hallahan proposed that helpful revelations about prevention and correction may come from additional medical and physiological psychology based investigations. They suggested specifically "such areas as physiology, ophthalmology, otology, reaction to color. . . .gustation, olfaction, the tactual modality, and response to thermal change and relative humidity" (p. vi).

The terms that indicate interest in learning disabilities and behavior disorders on the part of physicians, psychologists, speech pathologists, and others interested in neurology include: perceptually handicapped, dyslexic, developmental aphasia, minimal brain dysfunction, neurologically impaired, brain damaged, and others. One of the first publications to trigger this enduring concern was Orton's (1937) book, *Reading, Writing and Speech Problems in Children*.

Probably no potential source of knowledge about learning disabilities and behavior disorders has been more thoroughly explored than professional medicine and its supporting sciences. One educationally relevant result was increased attention to the design of instructional space in attempts to reduce distraction for pupils and to provide them with more opportunity for relative privacy and independence during study. That had positive consequences for all pupils because it gave more impetus to the general move toward individualization of instruction. Another positive influence was to exert and maintain pressure on all concerned to objectify their conceptions of learning disabilities and behavior disorders. That has contributed in no small measure to the recognition of the need for an improved and educationally relevant definition of the condition.

Teachers today find themselves more and more recognized, by physicians and other members of the health professions, as the central figures in dealing with learning disabilities and behavior disorders. The psychiatric, pediatric, and neurologic branches of medicine have been the main groups of physicians to attempt to analyze and deal with learning disabilities and behavior disorders. A number of optometrists have contributed, too, as have some physical therapists. Together their efforts have helped to highlight the importance of the problems of children who have these problems and to provide information that helps teachers create better "matches." As a result it has become clearer that teachers can expect physicians and other health workers to support and supplement individualized educational efforts, the most effective way known today to combat and correct these problems.

Social Welfare Considerations

When children behave in ways that call undesirable attention to themselves or cause other people to wonder about their social and intellectual adequacy, certain results are predictable. Parents become worried and upset. Punishments or sanctions are invoked at home and at school in efforts to produce more acceptable behavior. If the children's behavior reaches extremes, they and their parents become clients of mental health and guidance clinics, the courts, and social welfare bodies, in addition to the helping services of the schools. That is the history of many families of children who show learning disabilities and behavior problems.

Parents are sometimes unfairly derogated for "shopping," that is, going from clinic to agency to hospital to school and back seeking help. Through their own eyes, parents see a healthy child with general development well inside normal bounds. Yet they know that their child has unexplained learning difficulties in school and frequently displays aberrant personal and social behavior without apparent reason. Professional reviews of the wildly different things such parents actually have been told at agencies and clinics during their search for assistance make it clearer why they end up expressing bewilderment and despair.

Social workers, nurses, and others who talk with parents often have to operate from a limited knowledge base, so far as school problems are concerned. They may know little more about schools than what they remember from their own childhood experiences. Also, their orientations are toward their own training, rather than toward professional education. Thus, while they may be willing to give support and constructive advice to parents with learning disabled/behavior disordered children, they cannot do much about the core of the problem, which is how and what to teach the child so the manifestations will diminish and disappear.

Teachers can give first aid to upset and discouraged parents by showing empathy as good listeners, in a professional sense. That helps to assure the parent that the teacher has genuine concern. Also, it gives the teacher an opportunity to sort out useful facts, clues, and hunches about how to personalize education for that particular child.

Frequently teachers are contacted by personnel from clinics and social welfare organizations to supply information or to participate in an out-of-school or an in-school staff meeting regarding a child who shows indications of learning disabilities and behavior disorders. In the past the teacher has tended to be simply a source of information in such situations. The data supplied by the teacher were then integrated into a diagnosis and recommendations by another professional person, usually from medicine or psychology.

Teachers now more often coordinate such situations, by a combination of their own initiative and the expressed wishes of the other professionals. This is because it is recognized that learning disabilities and behavior disorders yield most often to systematic, individualized instruction designed and carried out by a teacher.

Thus teachers find themselves sought out by parents and by the staff members of clinics and agencies in the social welfare sector. They find themselves offered the roles of consultant, integrator of information, and designer of strategy. If accepted, these roles carry added responsibility. To play the parts with integrity and professional competence, teachers need to familiarize themselves with the sociological implications of such roles as well as with many facts about the social welfare sector of their community.

One good way to accomplish both is to learn about community and regional parent organizations and professional groups that focus on learning disabilities and behavior disorders. They can be found in local social agency directories. Every regular class teacher certainly cannot take part in all the parent and professional groups there are. It is more feasible to attend a meeting from time to time, to request that the newsletters and journals of the groups be in the school's professional library, and to follow the news about the work of such organizations. Substantial activity in one local group tends to keep one informed about many of the others.

In the teacher's professional world of today and tomorrow, cooperation with the people who staff both voluntary and tax supported social welfare agencies is essential. Moreover, teachers are finding increased full time or part time employment opportunities in such agencies, either in direct service educational programs or as consultants, advisors, and directors for such programs.

Educational Considerations

Few questions rate higher on the day to day agenda of America's elementary or secondary teacher than what to do about pupils in their classes who lie outside their reach—the low achieving and behavior problem children and youth who are not touched by any of their teaching methods and materials. Whether in disadvantaged central cities, impoverished rural mountains, rich farm lands, or tidy suburbs, teachers are distressed at their inability to make effective educational contact with certain youngsters.

The irritating chafe of one or two disaffected pupils is a constant presence in most classes despite the teacher's success with most children. The particular circumstances may vary from science to driver training, from reading to art, and from home economics to spelling, but some pupils who show learning disabilities and behavior disorders are almost always there. Teachers are united in their desire for some form of help that will let them cope more satisfactorily with the learning and behavior problems those pupils present.

The matter has attracted national attention both in teacher organizations and in other professional and lay groups. The inclusion of learning disabilities and behavior disorders as part of the exceptional child sector in legislation and in court decisions has raised hopes that improvements are just ahead. Teacher organizations have made these problems the subject of resolutions, most calling for increased resources for dealing with them. Not everyone agrees, though, as to what educational steps hold the best promise for solid solutions in the best interests of all concerned.

Serious deterrants currently delay educators, other professionals, and interested lay persons who are trying to encourage the move from prevailing to preferred practices with respect to the instruction of pupils who show learning disabilities and behavior disorders. Success in removing those deterrants calls for a primary commitment to individual pupil development, leadership, and tough minded professionalism on the part of all educators, and particularly on the part of regular class teachers.

First, how can one answer the question, How many pupils show learning disabilities and behavior problems? Replies range now from a huge 25% of all children and youth to the position that it is improper to give a figure because the matter is relative, not really quantifiable, and is a constantly changing phenomenon.

The US Congress wished to help states finance the special education of children with learning disabilities. It was necessary, though, to set an arbitrary amount of funding through Public Law 94-142 because there was no acceptable hard information that indicated how many pupils would really be involved. The Association for Children with Learning Disabilities, likewise, uses a percentage that has little empirical support. However, the Association makes the strong point that it must say something fairly definite about the magnitude of the problem if it is to obtain meaningful support from the general public.

There is no firm knowledge as to how many learning disabled/behavior disordered children and youth there are. Need local school systems await some more concrete figure as a basis for planning? Why not simply count the affected pupils?

That points up a second major deterrant. It is necessary to agree on what one is looking for—what distinguishes a learning disability or behavior disorder—in short, a definition in terms of the characteristics of the children.

There have been several efforts to establish broad acceptance of a definition, but unanimity seems still some distance away. There is no accepted operational definition useful enough to allow an unequivocal count of the children in a school who show such problems. That puts a substantial burden on the professional judgment of both regular teachers and specialists.

There is a third educationally relevant consideration. Some established professional and lay organizations claim prior jurisdiction over some children and youth who are viewed by others as properly belonging with the learning disabled/behavior disordered group. As Cruickshank and Hallahan (1975) noted:

> Since 1963 the term has been extended to include remedial reading concepts, remedial arithmetic problems, emotional disturbances, and a great variety of more esoteric problems. The imprecise use of the term has created communication difficulties among professional people, parents, and legislators. (p. v)

There are valid differences among such important organizations as the International Reading Association, the Association for Children with Learning Disabilities, the American Mental Health Association, and others with respect to categorizing children. Regular class teachers and specialist teachers can help minimize communication difficulties if they try to use pupil specific, instruction specific language among themselves and with parents and other professionals. That should avoid energy waste and should help keep the focus of attention on personalized education for each pupil.

As long as uncertainties prevail regarding the nation's number of children with learning disabilities and behavior disorders, and as long as jurisdictional differences remain unsettled among large lay and professional groups, improvement for regular class teachers in coping with such pupils will be slowed. Language, in this case professional terminology, may be the key to the logjam.

Emerging Changes in Terminology

Communication difficulties stem from lack of agreement regarding the numbers and the definition of pupils with learning disabilities and behavior disorders and from the overlapping responsibilities of various organizations interested in those who display the signs of these difficulties. Some of that confusion is occasioned by emerging changes in terminology.

For example, Dunn (1973) elected in an influential book to rename a a large segment of the exceptional child population. Youngsters who had long been called educable mentally retarded became "children with mild general learning disabilities." Others previously referred to as moderately and severely mentally retarded received a parallel new name, "children with moderate and severe general learning disabilities." Those who had previously been regarded as showing learning disability were differentiated by the addition of the term "major specific," resulting in a third group called "children with major specific learning disabilities."

The use of *specific* traces back to S. A. Kirk's *Educating Exceptional Children* (1962). Kirk had coined the term *learning disability* as follows:

> A learning disability refers to a retardation, disorder or delayed development in one or more of the processes of speech, language, reading, spelling, writing or arithmetic resulting from a possible cerebral dysfunction and/or emotional or behavioral disturbance and not from mental retardation, sensory deprivation, or cultural or instructional factors. (p. 263)

Gearhart and Weishahn (1976) have offered other terminological variants. They wrote of "the learning disabled and mildly mentally handicapped" in the same discussion. The chief characteristic that differentiates the two for them is that the learning disabled child

> must be achieving significantly less than other indicators, particularly intellectual ability, would predict he should achieve. In contrast, the mildly mentally handicapped child is achieving less than his age peers, but there are indications that this is due, at least in part, to lower than average intellectual ability. (p. 234)

For Gearhart and Weishahn, learning disabilities included "dyslexia, dyscalculia, agnosia, minimal brain dysfunction and others," as long as there is a significant discrepancy between the individual's actual performance and apparent ability to perform in thinking, arithmetic, and language arts activities, including oral language. Yet, they recognized delayed speech, which clearly has an inherent discrepancy definition, under another category, speech problems (p. 99). The same discrepancy definition shows up in a group they called "troubled children." They gave as an example: "A child who has experienced considerable failure in oral reading may demonstrate extremes of behavior when asked to read orally before his class" (p. 145).

Gearhart and Weishahn went on to explain the nature of troubled children by saying: "Academic requirements may be unrealistic for the student in relation to his present level of readiness or to his abilities" (p. 145). Thus, discrepancy between actual performance and social or teacher expectation lies at the heart of the identification procedure for speech handicapped and troubled pupils, too, for these authors.

Bateman introduced the discrepancy component of the definition in 1965. In doing so, she enlarged the possibilities for jurisdictional disputes with remedial reading specialists who had for many years been using discrepancy between mental age and reading achievement (expressed in reading age) as the major indicator of what they termed "reading disability." As McIntosh and Dunn (1973) remarked when commenting on this: "Special educators were not only borrowing children from remedial educators but also definitional ingredients" (p. 539).

Also, any identification of learning disabled/behavior disordered children based on a discrepancy between what *is* (i.e., achievement in spelling or reading) and what *ought to be* (i.e., some measure of expectancy such as mental age of achievement in other subjects) is in for heavy sailing today. The reason is the better understanding of what have been called "expectancy indicators." They seem to be chiefly achievement tests, too, under other names (Levine, 1976).

Terminology that leans heavily on physiological-medical concepts continues in the running. It is well exemplified by the recent work of L'Abate and Curtis (1975). They dealt with learning disabilities under the general heading of "borderline biological factors" or "borderline cerebral deficits," linking learning disabilities, emotional disturbances, intellectual retardation, and cultural stimulation in their discussion. They contended that (a) the similar appearing child behavior arises from different groupings of causes; (b) biological and behavioral causes that are implicated can be sorted out and their dimensions specified; (c) causative factors, either biological or environmental, influence each other; and (d) biological factors range on a continuum from zero to overwhelming involvement.

L'Abate and Curtis (1975) took pains to remind their readers that, while a search for causes may have a high priority for some specialists, it is an occupation of questionable import to educators.

> Determining the causes of borderline deficits may become a futile, academic exercise and an indication of unresolved authority and power struggles among those who are interested in exceptionalities in children. Ultimately, regardless of the exceptionality's origin and nature, the special educator should work to cultivate the child's assets and to minimize his liabilities. (p. 63)

Plainly, terminological turmoil is the status at present. That means at least two things for regular class teachers. First, it will be necessary to proceed with caution in talks with fellow teachers, parents, and other professional persons to avoid misunderstandings. Second, there is ample opportunity for teachers, individually and as organized groups, to put their own imprint on what is, in the end, their responsibility. How teachers, regular and special, are moving in that direction will be seen in later sections of this chapter.

The Person Called Learning Disabled and Behavior Disordered

Chris Nassar had always been a "good boy," outgoing and quick. His father, a successful pharmacist, enjoyed Chris, and so did his mother. Two years ago, however, clouds began to mar the school scene.

The second grade teacher had been uncertain about whether Chris should go on or stay another year. He was promoted, but slow school progress persisted. The family's concern mounted along with the third grade teacher's. Chris struggled with language arts skills. His arithmetic computation progress was satisfactory and so was his writing. But he came home with *D*'s, *F*'s and occasional *C*'s in reading and spelling (of course, he could not be expected to spell and write words he could not read). Mischief and disruption in the class were on the rise, too.

At home he was not the same easy going funster. He did not want to talk about school and was irritable in response to his family's often repeated, "What's wrong, Chris?" The notes about misconduct in school grew more urgent. His early promise of achievement and good adjustment had dissolved, replaced by discouragement and evasion. His mother's words about that time were: "I'd say we were worried about him, and upset, too. We were afraid to talk or think about the future."

Chris's personal dissatisfaction with marginal, increasingly weak and unrewarding school performance was growing. The directions appeared to be set toward heightened hostility, truancy, frustration induced aggression, and finally, dropout.

Yet, within a year these conditions were completely reversed. Chris's school attainments satisfied him and his parents. Both could see ahead to using education to help toward competent citizenship and productive adulthood, including pleasure in employment and worthy use of leisure.

How was this magic worked? What happened to shore up Chris's faltering educational development and to establish a firm foundation where there had been serious gaps, slippage, and danger of collapse?

It was not a miracle, though Mr. and Mrs. Nassar might not agree. It was the result of the solid, systematic, professional work of two teachers who joined forces on Chris's behalf. When what they did is outlined in brief, as it is here, it seems too simple. High quality professional teaching does have an appearance of elegant simplicity that belies the energy, concentration, and control it demands of the teachers conducting it.

First, the teachers studied Chris's records and interviewed his parents and his previous teachers. They obtained the parents' approval to have various tests administered to Chris if the test information might help the teachers to discover how to assist Chris. They *listened* to what the parents and other teachers had to say. They probed to get information about what had and had not been done when Chris first appeared not to be responding satisfactorily to instruction.

Second, they asked Chris to talk with them about his school experiences. They were careful to keep this on a positive and nonthreatening plane. They let Chris take the lead and question them, as he wished, regarding the purpose of the discussions and where they might lead. Chris's record had some good spots in it, even a few recent ones. They showed Chris that they were honestly favorably impressed with that part of his record.

Third, they spent considerable time analyzing what the records and interviews had produced. They started with the question, What is the *simplest possible* answer we can imagine to why Chris's educational picture might have developed as it has? It turned out to be inadequate learning of the most rudimentary word analysis skills. If that was what had happened (or failed to happen), and if it had not been subsequently corrected, it would explain Chris's erratic and far below par performance in reading and spelling.

Fourth, they talked with Chris again. They asked him, in private, to read aloud to them from some samples of second, third, and fourth grade texts. When he stumbled on words they watched and listened to see how he proceeded in trying to determine what they were. Then they asked him to tell how he went about trying to unlock the pronunciation of an unfamiliar word. It was true; they saw that he lacked an orderly way of attacking new words. Their empathetic attitude encouraged Chris to talk more about himself and his school work than he had for a long time.

They tried Chris on some nonsense words they had made up, like *stelp, trug, enol, whelgat,* and *wistob*. They taped his efforts and studied them later and confirmed their earlier impression that he was applying a haphazard, self designed set of procedures that were of limited effectiveness in determining how to pronounce a word unfamiliar in print.

The fifth step taken by the teachers was as important as their discovery of what Chris had not mastered. This step was the selection of a working hypothesis about *why* Chris had not mastered word analysis skills. Certainly the records indicated that the earlier grade teachers had taught them, that other children in their classes had learned them, and that Chris had been in school during that time. So it was tempting to think that there must be some other factor—undetected minimal brain damage, an emotional block, a perceptual disability—in the way. And did not his recent record of irritability, poor attainment, and disruptive behavior suggest something like that?

The teachers knew, though, that there were dozens of transitory conditions common to these years that were more likely culprits: fatigue, wandering attention, temporary hearing impairment, concerns about social relations, and many others. They also knew that teachers cannot always monitor their pupils' mastery of skills and content as thoroughly as they would wish. So the working hypothesis they elected to follow, at least for a start, was that Chris could probably have learned good word analysis skills and that there had been unsatisfactory or inappropriate initial teaching.

It is important to notice where the responsibility rested. There was something wrong with how Chris had been taught at the beginning and with the follow-through of that first teaching. At the same time, allocating responsibility was not considered the same as allocating blame or impuning the competence of prior teachers. Most of Chris's classmates had prospered under the same teachers. It was a recognition that teachers, like all professional persons, operate constantly with an acknowledged margin of error.

The sixth step was to plan, put in writing, and carry out a personalized instructional program to teach Chris the word analysis skills whose absence appeared to be playing havoc with his school life. The teachers conferred with Mr. and Mrs. Nassar, explained the special education program they wished to try, and obtained approval to do so. Most of the work was done in the regular class. Chris was helped to work on his own much of the time. An aide and an older pupil volunteer took part, too, under teacher supervision. The Nassars helped at home. Chris kept track of his own improvement on frequent teacher made, criterion referenced tests. At first, rewards in the form of special privileges were often necessary to keep him at the tasks. Success bred increased satisfaction and keeping a chart of improvement became reward enough in itself.

After a few months, the teachers were able to take the seventh and final step. At a conference with Chris, his parents, and the school principal (who had supported them all along) they proposed that the special education program be discontinued because a special program, as such, was no longer necessary. Individualized instruction would continue, but as a normal part of the ordinary course of school events. They did leave the door open to regular class teachers to have consultative aid, if desired, from the special education teacher who had been one of the partners in the whole operation concerning Chris.

This is only one example of the many faces of learning disabilities and behavior disorders and their educational management. Certainly not all work out as smoothly as this one (and it had many rocky stretches along the way). But the principle is there: The great bulk of learning and behavior problems appears traceable to initial instruction that did not attend well enough to a close match between what the pupil needed and what was being taught. Knowing what to do about it, as these teachers did, can turn the problem around.

THE CONCEPT, TERMINOLOGY, AND SIGNIFICANCE OF LEARNING DISABILITIES AND BEHAVIOR DISORDERS

When a teacher teaches and the child does not learn, it is like a marksman who fires and does not hit the target. For a comparison from the helping professions, it is like a physician who carries out a treatment, but the patient does not improve. Certainly the teacher "taught," but like the others illustrated, the teaching "did not work"; it was ineffective.

We think a satisfactory concept of learning disabilities and behavior disorders should start from the position that the *teaching* of the children and youth should hold the center of the stage, not the *characteristics* of the children. We take the view that *how the children are taught* is the most important variable. And there seems to be less and less reason to think that test information about the neurological, psychiatric, intellectual, perceptual, information processing, and personality characteristics of the pupils can be useful in guiding teaching, except in the most gross ways.

In the next sections we will see how this view develops and where it leads.

Definition of Learning Disabilities and Behavior Disorders

The best known definitions in use today focus on the characteristics of the children and say nothing explicit about how the children should be taught. The US Congress definition of children with specific learning disabilities in Public Law 94-142 (Section 5 [B] 4) is an example.

> Those children who have a disorder in one or more of the basic psychological processes involved in understanding or in using language, spoken or written, which disorder may manifest itself in imperfect ability to listen, think, speak, read, write, spell or do mathematical calculations. Such disorders include such conditions as perceptual handicaps, brain injury, minimal brain dysfunction, dyslexia, and developmental aphasia. Such term does not include children who have learning problems which are primarily the result of visual, hearing or motor handicaps, of mental retardation, of emotional disturbance, or environmental, cultural or economic disadvantage.

The characteristics of children embraced by such definitions could exhaust almost anyone's supply of adjectives. In testimony about Public Law 94-142 one congressman noted that there are 53 basic learning disabilities identified by research, that one person has identified 99 minimal brain dysfunctions, and that, "No one really knows what a learning disability is." (*Congressional Record Daily Edition,* 1975).

Clements (1966) tallied the frequency of descriptive expressions in a sample of the professional literature. The following expressions came out at the top, in order, as cited by Hewett and Forness (1974).

1. Hyperactivity
2. Perceptual motor impairments
3. Emotional ability
4. General orientation defects
5. Disorders of attention (e.g., short attention span, distractability)
6. Impulsivity
7. Disorders of memory and thinking
8. Specific learning disabilities in reading, arithmetic, writing, and spelling
9. Disorders of speech and hearing
10. Equivocal neurological signs and electroencephalographic irregularities (p. 72)

The most commonly noted characteristic is hyperactivity. As Hewett and Forness (1974) pointed out, that term carries "the notion of any activity level that is quantitatively above normal and qualitatively different as far as appropriate social behavior is concerned" (p. 72). It is easy to see what that term and the rest in the list mean to regular class teachers and to understand why we and others link learning disabilities *and* behavior disorders. It is also easy to see why one cannot justifiably leave out of this consideration what may be called emotional and social maladjustments.

The major difficulty that has yet to be surmounted, though, is to establish a definition that is really functional for teachers. First, that calls for transforming many items on the list from negative characteristics of pupils to positive instructional objectives. The second step is to link appropriate teaching materials and procedures to the objectives.

> What really matters is that some children simply are not efficient, capable learners in line with their capacity; and since their basic disorders in the learning process persist and can be specified, we try to remedy them quickly. (Hewett & Forness, 1974, p. 70)

We would shift the thrust of that statement from the learners to the teachers. We would say that what really matters is that regular class (and many special) teachers can become more efficient, capable individualizers of instruction for their pupils; and since the individual educational needs of learning disabled/behavior disordered pupils (and all others) persist and can be specified, we would try to match the pace and the type of instruction to them quickly.

Another problem with the congressional definition arises because of its efforts to fence off learning disabilities and behavior disorders from all other school learning problems. One way that is done, for example, is to postulate that these problems are the consequences of as yet undetected brain injuries and anomalies. In that frame of reference, cause of the problem resides in the child, and remediability by the teacher is questionable because its root cause is located outside the educator's domain, in neurology.

Levine (1976) has shown how similar lines of thought in mental health work and in other aspects of public education have been limiting, even self defeating, while excusing the otherwise responsible professional persons from culpability. With that kind of approach, the question of who is accountable has, at best, a vague, feeble answer: "The team."

Turton (in Cruickshank & Hallahan, 1975) highlighted other major problems when commenting on a similar definition to that in Public Law 94-142.

> [It] is not based upon a developmental model or research. It is bound to population categories and is oriented to diagnosis and classification. More importantly, a legislated definition restricts open scientific inquiry directly and indirectly, and brings closure to an issue before it has been thoroughly researched according to scientific methods. The direct restriction is in terms of the funding for programs for research and services. The indirect impact occurs in the influence it brings to bear upon educational and clinical systems to provide services only to certain youngsters. Researchers, teachers, clinicians are then limited in their access to youngsters, thus resulting in a denial of services for children and biased research studies. (p. 310)

Turton's concerns have many serious implications. Of immediate importance to teachers is the possibility that learning disabilities specialists might be prohibited from assisting them with some children who need help but who might not satisfy arbitrary guidelines. In the many successful public school learning disability/behavior disorder operations studied by Deno (1976), a major common feature was the freedom of exchange between regular class teachers and their special educator colleagues. They worked together on any pupil they felt needed them and they were encouraged to do so.

Sometimes a formula is adopted to define learning disabilities. It follows a discrepancy format that has long been used in the identification of underachievement, particularly in reading (See Betts, 1946, pp. 481-484). The basic concept is this: Some presumed measure of expectancy, usually mental age or age-grade level, is contrasted with the pupil's actual achievement, such as reading grade level as measured by a norm referenced achievement test. If the actual achievement is substantially below expected achievement (two grade levels is a common demarkation) the *discrepancy* has been said to denote a reading disability (now also called a *learning disability*).

Such a formula cannot be used where it is obviously not applicable, as in the preschool years.

Often it is recommended that a team determine whether a child has a learning disability. The team referred to is to include the child's regular teacher, a teacher competent to deal with specific learning disabilities, and a school psychologist, speech clinician, remedial reading teacher, or other certified educational diagnostician. The team is appointed by the person responsible for administering special education in the school district.

One of the strengths of this approach to defining specific learning disabilities is that a team is required and that teachers are well represented on it. Also, the team may override the findings of the formula by presenting and agreeing on evidence they consider more significant.

The greatest potential weakness of this approach to a definition is in the discrepancy formulation itself and the tendency of the formula to replace professional insights and reasoning. In too many cases the formula is assumed to be right; if the teachers and others disagree, they carry the burden of proof. The reverse would be more appropriate.

That leads to the crux of the matter. Most pupil behaviors called learning disabilities and behavior disorders are best acknowledged as the consequences of failure to provide enough high quality individualized instruction. The problem does not reside in the child, hidden in some mysterious physiological or psychological recess. It rests squarely in the hands of teachers and its resolution depends on the degree to which they design and carry out personalized teaching.

For us, the usual discrepancy formulation puts too heavy a burden on presumed measures of the child's "ability." We just do not consider mental ability tests worthy of that much confidence in the kind of short range, individual child, academic and social development prediction teachers are thinking about in day to day instruction. Even such worthy tests as the full scale Stanford-Binet Intelligence Test or Wechsler Intelligence Scale for Children (WISC) fall short in this regard; their own subtests and shorter independent tests are even less satisfactory.

These tests, and others like them, certainly have valuable uses. As part of a formula to define learning disabilities and behavior disorders, though, they simply add to the confusion. We find ourselves in accord with Turton (1975), who said:

> When learning disabilities are examined within the child's culture and its academic demands, the responsibility of the professionals becomes one of providing the child with the means to overcome the developmental lag so that he or she has the same social and economic opportunities as do other youngsters. However, within that context, education must provide an appropriate and a quality level of service. . . . The only issue is the competency of the professional and his or her capacity to provide quality service. . . . Professional failure exacerbates and compounds the child's problems. . . . Regardless of the site of treatment, educational setting, or special clinic setting, the approach to the resolution of the disabilities must

be clinical in nature. That is, the assessment/treatment process must be individualized and integrated relative to the child's specific constellation of developmental patterns. (p. 328)

Summary

In 1969, McCarthy and McCarthy said:

> To some, learning disabilities means children with a specific kind of impairment, while to others it is a generic term meaning all those children whose primary problem lies in their incapacity to utilize ordinary school procedures for learning. (p. xi)

They went on to say, "After all, almost all exceptional children could be described, by definition, as having some kind of learning disability" (p. xii).

How, then, might they be sorted out? Will the "true" learning disability please stand up? In broad terms, the following is how the terminology operates in practice.

True enough, deaf and crippled children may have disabilities that interfere to a greater or lesser extent with learning. So may speech handicapped or blind children. But they have not typically been spoken of as having learning disabilities; rather, they have been referred to in terms of handicapping conditions as such. So they are not grouped in the "true" learning disability group.

Another large group of children have been called mentally retarded. Mental retardation has been for a great many educators another name for slow cognitive development plus premature stoppage of the progress of cognitive growth. Thus, it is not a great step to begin to speak of this condition as a general learning disability. It is thought to be characterized, as the term implies, by an across the board limitation, or disability, in learning.

There remain some children whose learning condition cannot properly be viewed as mental retardation. The limitation in learning is not general enough for that. Neither is it traceable to something as overt as impairment of vision or hearing. In short, in some cases there is nothing tangible to which to link some children's poor school achievement. So an assumption is made that their lack of educational attainment results from "a disoriented learning apparatus" (McCarthy & McCarthy, 1969, p. xii). These turn out to be the "true" learning disabilities, if the assumptions made along the way prove sound.

Having sorted this group of children out by a process of progressive subtraction, the next natural questions are, What do they look like? What do they have in common? Much energy has gone into trying to find physiological, psychological, sociological, and educational correlates to tie these children together with common threads. So far the results of those efforts have been, at best, discouraging. The "exclusion" definition leads to agonizing over words rather than to a search for variables that are significant for improving instruction. The residue of the progressive exclusion process is a motley group, heterogenous in practially all but one feature—they have school learning problems. And even those school learning problems are dissimilar from one child to the next. In our view, their most significant common element is that somewhere along the line they have had less than fully effective instruction. Equally important, it appears that it is possible to locate the instructional oversights and to provide individualized instruction that is corrective if attention is targeted on matching the pupil's cognitive state with the instructional material the teacher selects.

The prevailing tendency to date is the adoption of an achievement/ability discrepancy approach in defining learning disabilities and behavior disorders, at the same time limiting the use of identification procedures to pupils who are not otherwise eligible for standard special education programs. The problem is not with the discrepancy concept as such. It is *what* discrepancy is being considered.

Regular class teachers will not find very useful the assumption that there are two different kinds of measures, achievement and ability, even though that assumption is still often employed by specialists when they make discrepancy analyses.

Rather, the discrepancy that regular class teachers will recognize as relevant is that between the child's actual achievement and the teacher's, pupil's, and parents' desired achievement goal. It is with the closing of that gap—step by step, individualized in content and teaching methods in terms of the child's own interests and style and rate of learning—that the teachers are understandably concerned. They want to be able to close the gap for any child who needs it, without having to be concerned about administratively dictated restrictions in definitions of learning disabilities and behavior disorders or about cutting across other established special education categories.

PREVAILING VERSUS PREFERRED PRACTICES

In the left column are summary statements about the common practices of school systems in attempting to minimize or eliminate learning disabilities and behavior disorders among pupils. On the right in contrast, are summaries of procedures that, while not yet common, are used by the most forward looking schools of the nation.

Prevailing Practices	Preferred Practices
1. Screening and diagnostic tests of perceptual and cognitive abilities that are norm referenced are used in attempts to select pupils who are at high risk for learning disabilities and behavior disorders.	1. Teacher observation, criterion referenced educational achievement tests, and informal assessment procedures are used as base information to plan personalized instruction, with minimal reference to comparisons with other students or to diagnostic labels.
2. The major part of the assessment of learning disabled/behavior disordered pupils is done by persons from a district or regional office, on referral by the special and regular teachers, through the principal of the school.	2. The assessment of learning disabled and behavior disordered pupils is done by the special and regular teacher, with the diagnostic help of any others on the local school staff who have skills to contribute. The assessment is coordinated by the regular teacher or a designated local school person. Regional or central office staff with advanced assessment qualifications are used as consultants as needed and often as trainers to maintain and upgrade local school staff members' assessment capabilities.
3. When a child is identified as showing characteristics of learning disabilities and behavior disorders, the child is placed on the special education teacher's roll and the regular class teacher has little or no responsibility for pupil accounting and other functions related to class membership.	3. The identification of a child as learning disabled or behavior disordered is a signal to the regular class teacher that there will be added help of a variety of kinds with the child's education, but all the regular teacher's class membership responsibilities remain intact.

Prevailing Practices	Preferred Practices
4. There is scrupulous attention to the legal requirements for informing parents and receiving their prior consent for program changes. Most communication is by mail.	4. Communication with parents is done in conference whenever possible. Emphasis is on both compliance with laws and regulations and on full parental participation not only in decision making but also in the thinking that leads up to decisions.
5. Pupils presenting the same kinds of educational needs (learning disabilities and behavior disorders) are found under diverse names, ranging from brain injured through emotionally disturbed, and programed primarily in terms of those labels.	5. All pupils presenting learning disabilities and behavior disorders, regardless of labels such as brain injured or disturbed, are under the same school system leadership and programed primarily in terms of their educational needs.
6. Work with learning disabilities and behavior disorders is considered the right and privilege only of those who have specialist training in one or more categorical fields, such as the brain damaged or the perceptually handicapped. There is a sharp separation, for example, from professionals who work with reading disabilities or mental retardation.	6. All teachers and other educators with special training and knowledge about individualized instruction are welcomed onto the team to help plan and implement instruction for children with learning and adjustment problems.
7. Special education teachers are allowed to work only with "identified and enrolled" pupils, at the risk of losing state aid.	7. Special education teachers as a matter of course help to assess and teach some children who are experiencing difficulty but who are not officially on special education rolls.

356 / Teaching Exceptional Children in All America's Schools

Prevailing Practices	Preferred Practices
8. Special education teachers work in their own classrooms or resource rooms with learning disabled/behavior disordered pupils, seldom spending time with regular class teachers and learning disabled and behavior disordered pupils in their regular learning areas.	8. Special education teachers commit most of their time to team assessment, planning, and teaching with regular class teachers and learning disabled and behavior disordered pupils in regular classes.
9. There are annual program reviews and reassessments of learning disabled/behavior disordered pupils to comply with state regulations. They are conducted mainly by personnel from district and regional offices.	9. Annual or more frequent program reviews and reassessments are made by the local school teachers responsible for the pupils. The reviews are part of continuing diagnostic teaching and they frequently go beyond what state regulations would require.
10. A mystique is associated with learning disabilities and behavior disorders, often resulting in uncertainty on the part of parents and teachers as to their own abilities to cope with and help their children.	10. Learning disabilities and behavior disorders are acknowledged to fall clearly within the educator's domain, and there is reasonable confidence on the part of teachers and parents that systematic, individualized instruction will be effective in dealing with them.

The Beginning of Special Education for Learning Disabled/Behavior Disordered Children

Two groups of children and youth were rejected from the outset by the nation's public and private schools. Those who did not learn skills and subject matter were soon eased out. Those who were disobedient and disruptive were quickly squeezed out. When both conditions were present in the same pupil, the rejection mechanisms of suspension, exclusion, dropout pressure, and expulsion joined forces to accelerate the removal action.

The first special education programs in America were organized for just such pupils.

> New Haven, Connecticut, set up a class in 1871 to provide for "scores of contumacious aggressors" who were running wild on the streets and becoming a "public nuisance.". . .Some of these children were truants and incorrigible, but there were also children who did not speak English and children who were mentally retarded. (Cutts, 1955, p. 16)

Despite an occasional effort to design schooling for these truants and other problem pupils, they were, for the most part, moved out of the schools and kept out.

Not all such moves took the children or youth directly into the community at large. Depending on the nature of the pupil's precipitating behavior, there were way stations at which they might stop for longer or shorter periods.

Infractions of social rules deemed serious could lead to the child being judged delinquent, with consequent confinement. Ordinary school work failure, apparently due simply to lack of application, could result in a series of transfers to special education settings outside the principal current of schooling.

Occasionally there was an imaginative intervention. The second child studied in the nation's first psychological clinic by one of the earliest school psychologists may well be the original instance of learning disabilities and behavior disorders performance on record. According to Brotemarkle (1931), Lightner Witmer wrote this report about a child seen at the University of Pennsylvania clinic in Philadelphia.

> The second case to attract my attention was a boy fourteen years of age who was brought to the laboratory of psychology by his grade teacher. He was one of those children of great interest to the teacher, known to the profession as a chronic bad speller. His teacher. . .was at that time a student in psychology. . .; she was imbued with the idea that a psychologist should be able, through examination, to ascertain the causes of a deficiency in spelling and to recommend the appropriate pedagogical treatment for its amelioration or cure.
>
> With this case, in March, the work of the psychological clinic was begun. At that time I could not find that the science of psychology had ever addressed itself to the ascertainment of the causes and treatment of a deficiency in spelling. Yet here was a simple developmental defect of memory; and memory is a mental process of which the science of psychology is supposed to furnish the only authoritative knowledge. It appeared to me that if psychology was worth anything to me or to others, it should be able to assist the efforts of a teacher in a retarded case of this kind. (Brotemarkle, 1931, pp. 334-345)

Happily for the budding profession of school psychology, Witmer was able to locate the source of the difficulty and to do something about it. The teacher had not noticed that the boy had trouble seeing. When Witmer discovered that, it was corrected. Remedial tutoring then brought the boy's spelling up to par.

Witmer's work broke new ground. But other efforts were sporadic and scattered from 1900 through the World War I period. Even the spurt in testing that followed the war was mainly addressed to the study and classification of groups, not to individual diagnosis and corrective teaching.

In the late 1920's, though, the prevention and correction of reading disabilities moved toward center stage in educational circles. Attempts to understand reading and language arts disabilities led to studies of eye movements, lip movements, and other bodily factors and to new teaching methods. Phonics, whole word, configuration clues, and controlled introduction of vocabulary were the sorts of variables related to the latter.

In a few cases as early as the 1930's and 1940's, medical reasons were considered relevant to academic and social problems. Those medical reasons tended to be of two kinds: neurological and psychiatric. The pupils so designated found themselves transferred to neurologically oriented clinic schools interested in brain function or they might become clients of psychiatric or child guidance clinics concerned with strengthening both the pupils' ego functioning and the stability of their families.

This early period is full of the stories of serious minded and determined educators and members of other professions who tried to find remedies for the human wastage they saw. A bibliography topic at the end of this chapter will start the interested student on exploring their ideas. Some, it will be seen, led to today's more effective procedures.

However, the results at the time were not very encouraging. The regular grades annually produced a crop of misfits who became dropouts or push-outs. The special services, whether primarily educational or whether court or medical related, could point to few successful rehabilitants. The numbers of rejects grew, and more and more regular schools and special schools took on the features of holding stations.

It was out of this milieu that the concept of learning disabilities/behavior disorders emerged, only a short time ago. The learning disabilities part of the term itself was coined as recently as 1962 (see pp. 343). The idea itself may be as old as the first primitive teacher who witnessed a pupil/instructional task interaction that did not work out as intended, but its recognition and codification into the education profession's lexicon is of recent vintage.

Theories of Corrective Instruction: Past and Present

In the 1930's, attention began to be drawn to several leaders who were putting forward specific procedures they believed would solve the problems of many of the pupils who had been failing to learn in school and who had also been disrupting the other pupils. Most of these leaders started from theoretical positions and deduced instructional procedures.

In retrospect, it can be seen that some of the proposed approaches had much in common, though that was not so apparent at the time the ideas were presented.

Teachers need to be aware of these different attempts to formulate corrective instruction for children who showed evidences of learning disabilities and behavior disorders. Parents sometimes read or hear about them and bring them up in discussions. Psychologists, social workers, physicians, and other professionals sometimes offer suggestions that relate to their use. In some cases public school systems or private schools are committed to one or another of them. More often, elements of several are combined in an eclectic way.

Eight relatively distinct conceptual patterns can be used to group the various theoretical positions behind the instructional schemes now in operation across the nation. Each, of course, has educational elements, for the intent of each is to furnish a design for instruction. However, the central theory of all but one emerges from other disciplines and professions than education.

Neurological

This approach theorizes that there are actual neuronal cellular defects, deficiencies, malformations, or abnormalities in cell linkage that result in central nervous system functions being improperly performed or not performed at all. These abnormal functions, in turn, are presumed to interact with the individual's environment to cause the learning disorders and behavior disorders. Persons associated with this approach are, for example, Strauss and Lehtinen (1947), Orton (1937), Delacato (1963), and H. Birch (1964).

Metabolic

Certain food additives and preservatives, including otherwise apparently harmless coloring agents and flavor enhancers, are believed by some investigators to be directly implicated in triggering hyperactivity, irritability, and other evidences of learning disabilities and behavior disorders. The precise causative physiological processes are not specified, though certain ones are suspected. The proposed action, of course, is to remove the suspected materials from the diet. Individuals who identify with this concept are Levin, New York Institute for Child Development; Feingold, Allergy Department, Kaiser-Permanente Medical Center, San Francisco; and Conners and Goyette, Western Psychiatric Institute and Center, University of Pittsburgh.

Under the metabolic heading would come, also, attempts by physicians to use quieting or stimulating medications to control or ameloriate hyperactivity, outbursts, temper tantrums, anxiety, panic, withdrawal, negativism, and other extraordinary emotional states. Such management procedures are outside the scope of the education professions. Yet teachers are interested in their potential effectiveness. To date, too little is known about any of the metabolic based management schemes to make definite statements (see also pp. 368-369 later in this chapter).

Psychoanalytic

This point of view attributes the child's learning disabled/behavior disordered behavior chiefly to environmental forces, with the focus on the parents as causative instruments because of their persistent use of improper child rearing practices. Attempts are made to improve environmental conditions and to strengthen the child's ego in constructive ways. Proponents of this viewpoint include Bettelheim (1968), Redl (1959), Morse (1976), and Newman (1967), though there are many variations in the details of their recommended procedures.

Reflective Interaction

We coined this expression to refer to school operated adaptations of the nondirective counseling movement led by Rogers (1951) and Moustakas (1953). This open, warm, permissive within limits, caring, listening, and reflective person to person model, we believe, should include the teacher effectiveness training procedures of Gordon (1974) and play therapy as delineated by Axline (1947).

Psychophysiological

This approach emphasizes behaviors called perception, attending, discrimination, memory, orientation, association, and sequencing. These are assumed to be psychological processes, mediated through vision, hearing, taste, smell, touch, and kinesthetic sensations, or some combination of them. It is postulated that in children with learning disabilities and behavior disorders some of these psychophysiological behaviors are deficient in development. Remediation is aimed at pinpointing and then eliminating or ameliorating the presumed deficits through developmental instruction that matches specific teaching prescriptions with specific deficits. Leaders who have developed a variety of diagnostic and remedial procedures that stem from this common formulation include Cruickshank and Hallahan (1975), Bateman (1965), Frostig (1963), Kephart (1971), Barsch (1967), Kirk (1972), and McCarthy and McCarthy (1969).

Participatory Responsibility

We use this term to cover the teaching procedures offered by leaders like Dreikurs, Grunwald, and Pepper (1971) and Glaser (1965). The aim is to motivate and strengthen responsiveness by involving students in making in-school decisions that affect them and their peers. Presumably, if teachers react with encouragement rather than authoritarian regulation or covert manipulation, children will become skillful and competent at making their own decisions. Also, it is assumed that if those decisions are reached in an atmosphere open to talking and thinking, the student decisions will usually be sound ones, leading to responsible social behavior and academic success, with reduction or elimination of many manifestations of learning disabilities and behavior disorders.

Applied Behavior Analysis

This is the name given to attempts to change human behavior in desired directions by controlling the consequences of the person's present behavior. In simplified form, it operates from the principle that behavior that is rewarded will continue and can be brought to substitute for behavior that is not rewarded. There is a substantial literature that testifies to the efficacy of that principle. Also, there is much evidence that it has valuable educational applications (Homme, 1970; Lindsley, 1972).

Behavior modification is consciously used to some extent by each of the six approaches already described. However, it is employed by them as a tool to help implement the other conceptual approach rather than as an end in itself.

This is, though, an approach to learning disabilities and behavior disorders that has as its sole objective the altering of specific behaviors in constructive ways by means of applied behavior analysis. The goal is simply to reshape existing behaviors that are disruptive, inappropriate, incorrect, or otherwise unproductive into behaviors that are more consonant with desired educational outcomes as set forth in accepted educational goals and objectives. There is nothing more (or less) involved than that. Proponents of applied behavior analysis, as such, as a means of dealing with learning disabilities and behavior disorders include the leaders named above as well as Haring and Phillips (1972) and a number of others. An excellent and relatively brief exposition of this design for teaching is offered by Haring (1975).

Remedial Education

This formulation for the assessment, correction, and future prevention of learning disabilities and behavior disorders has its main roots in remedial instruction. The conceptual structure is as follows:

1. Despite the best efforts of contemporary teaching in regular classes some pupils are not reached, so they do not learn language arts (particularly reading) or mathematics skills or they learn them only partially.
2. The reason for not learning lies mainly with the limitations of the teaching, not the child. Most often the teaching was not sufficiently individualized.

3. The children for whom the regular class teacher's efforts are not sufficient should be noted as soon as possible and consultation should be requested from another teacher who is a remedial teaching specialist.
4. The particular disabilities shown by the child are then identified, corrective teaching plans are made, and remedial teaching is started by one or the other of the teachers or both.
5. The earlier problems are identified and corrected and the more skilled in personalized instruction the regular class teacher becomes through association with the specialist, the closer the whole operation comes to being primarily preventive rather than mainly remedial.

Particularly important is the freedom of the regular class teacher to ask for assistance without fear of reprisal. That point looms large because this formulation puts the responsibility for the child's difficulties mainly on limitations in initial instruction. Professional maturity of a high order on the part of administrators, supervisors, and teachers alike, plus an informed public, are called for if it is to work.

This is an eclectic position, too. It draws on whatever concepts from the other seven approaches might be useful. It takes the position that the great majority of learning disability/behavior disorder behaviors are observed in connection with reading disabilities, so that is a logical place to begin to work on them. Also, most of the remainder of learning disabilities and behavior disorders are held to be associated with learning other language arts and with learning number skills, and it is believed that the same five principles stated here can be extended readily to those areas. Examples of persons who are giving leadership to this position are Birch (1955) and Zigmond (1975).

A great deal of activity still surrounds each of the eight conceptual patterns named above. Our intent in making the groupings was not to imply that they "belong" that way or that there are close alliances among the persons named. In fact, it is desirable that they continue in an open state to encourage the changes that should come as knowledge increases. Rather, we presented the groupings to give the regular class teacher a way of organizing the knowledge that has seemed helpful to us. We hope that the eight groups will be thought of as tentative and in the process of converging as preferred practices emerge and are validated.

Current Trends

A fully satisfactory solution to how to define learning disability and behavior disorder is much needed. It is predictable that the energy of many devoted educators will continue to be invested on that topic because federal and state financial support will be problematic until a widely acceptable and scientifically sound definition appears.

The absence of agreement on a definition keeps disputes and rivalries alive between professional organizations. It results in a proliferation of lay organizations with overlapping concerns. Worst of all, it encourages fractioning and it retards the development of the comprehensive services needed by children and their families.

All that is well recognized among responsible educational leaders. Thus, one of the main current trends is to seek a common ground among various claimants for attention, to reach a set of understandings that will lead to a definition that has both scientific and professional integrity and practical usefulness.

A second current trend of national importance flows from the least restrictive environment principle that was discussed on pp. 24ff. Regular class teachers now have begun to receive the basic preparation and the kind of information about learning disabilities and behavior disorders formerly reserved for teachers who were preparing to become specialists. Competency development is directed more toward coping successfully with these and other exceptional pupils in regular classes.

A third trend moves away from preoccupation with definitions and toward the common instructional needs of children. It suggests that financial support for special education should be on the basis of excellence of total school offerings, rather than simply on a head count of exceptional children assigned to special classes.

Broadening of the scope of the specialist teacher is another discernible trend. In the past the regular class teacher had to look for different specialists, for example, for help with children with specific learning disabilities and for children with general learning disabilities (educable mentally retarded pupils). The shift is toward more generic professional preparation. Many special educators graduating now are prepared to work with exceptional pupils almost across the board. To complement that trend in the preparation of special educators, a parallel ability to accommodate a variety of exceptional pupils is being designed into the professional education of many newly graduating regular class teachers.

THE ROLE OF THE REGULAR CLASS TEACHER

Teachers are the best judges of how human and material resources ought to be deployed within a school to get the best results. If given the opportunity, they will work out how to put together the combinations of people and materials with the optimum potential for productivity. That is well illustrated in Morse's (1976) account of how the helping teacher position evolved in elementary schools with which he was associated over a period of approximately 16 years. His narrative tells a story similar to ones we have experienced in elementary, secondary, vocational, and technical schools elsewhere. The same story seems to hold for colleges, too.

Following is a summary of steps the faculty of a 780 pupil school with 30 teachers took to assure that good accommodations were made to the special needs of children showing learning disabilities and behavior disorders.

1. The majority of the faculty of the school recognizes that there are pupils in most of the classes whose learning disability/behavior disorder characteristics are an effective barrier between them and the teacher so far as instruction is concerned. Teachers discuss this informally and in faculty meetings.
2. They consider the establishment of a separate special class for the pupils whose presence contributes most to the school's problem incidence, both in academic and in school citizenship ways. They review the following points:
    a. If 1 or 2 special teachers were added to the school's staff to conduct 1 or 2 special classes, and 12 to 24 pupils were assigned full time to these teachers, would the present situation be adequately resolved? No, even assigning the maximum of 24 pupils to such special classes would not suffice, because almost every one of the 30 regular class teachers can already identify 2 or 3 pupils with whom they would like help immediately, and there are others, though they do not require help so urgently.
    b. If enough special classes were provided to enroll all the designated pupils, would that suffice? This is not feasible. It is unlikely that the community would feel it could afford to add even 2 or 3 special teachers. Also, placing these youngsters in special classes would not solve the problem for others sure to come along who would have to be put on waiting lists for already filled classes. Moreover, not all these pupils need special attention all the time, or even the majority of the time. What is really wanted is help in the regular classroom "crisis," or better, help in predicting it and preventing it.
    c. The track record of full time special classes turns out to be not very encouraging, anyway, when it is closely examined.
3. The analysis of needs, when thrown against a possible solution by way of special classes, reveals to the faculty that the need and proposed special class solution are not compatible. The requirements of the regular class teachers could be met only to a limited degree through separate special classes. Perhaps clues to what would help could be derived from a closer inspection of the problem itself. The next step in study by the faculty reveals that:

a. There already is a wide range of academic achievement and social behavior in each class. Teachers cope well with most of the range. Most of the pupils gain academically and socially. It is only a few in each class about whom teachers feel incompetent or defeated.
b. Even the most difficult pupils are not that way all of the time. Even the most troublesome and the weakest achievers mesh well into class activities and have friendly, or at least neutral, relationships with other pupils much of the time.
c. Teachers can often predict when to anticipate academic learning or social behavior difficulties with pupils. With that knowledge, teachers have already taken the initial steps, informally, to assess the particular strengths and weaknesses of their most troublesome pupils and have located some of the mismatches between pupil readiness and upcoming learning tasks.
d. Attempts to repress disruptive behavior by harsh words, extra work, temporary removal from the class, ridicule, or other forms of punishment prove to be of no permanent value in reducing the problem.
e. Advice from counselors, psychologists, the principal, or from other teachers is of little practical use. Many teachers already understand the advice; however, what is lacking are the extra arms and legs to put it to use. These staff members are more talkers than doers. Their encouragement and sympathy is appreciated, but it is not a substitute for direct participation in teaching, which they have too little time to do. Even when they do take on a child or a group in the class for a time, it is seldom for long enough or regularly enough for a lasting effect.

4. After that analysis, the regular class teachers conclude that they do need direct in-class and in-school help. Rather than a separate special class or expert but nonparticipating consultants, though, the help should have these characteristics:
   a. The helping person should be capable of working with the emotional and academic problems of all children, and particularly the child who is in, or close to, a crisis. The training of this person should be that of a teacher and a specialist with learning disabilities and behavior disorders.
   b. Help should be present right in the school, not from an itinerant or central office base. And the helping teacher should neither be under rigidly scheduled external control nor tied to a classroom of children. Flexibility for direct and timely cooperative work on call from a regular class teacher should have high priority.
   c. Sometimes the most helpful immediate action might be removal of a child from the regular class for conference or a quiet time under

the visual supervision of the helping teacher. At other times the helper might conduct the regular class, while the problem of a particular child or a small group of children is given the full, concentrated attention of the regular class teacher. At still other times the helping teacher might team with one or more regular teachers to select or prepare individualized teaching plans and to locate the best instructional materials with which to implement them.

d. The actual day to day duties of the helping teacher must grow out of the reality of the specific school, its community, its resources, its pupils, and the competencies and needs of its regular class teachers. The helping teacher needs to be more responsive to the local situation than to restrictive theories, categories, and regulations. There should be freedom to be eclectic within the bounds of professional monitoring provided by the oversight of the local school faculty.

The four step process, with its subordinate points, does not happen in a few days. Often it is a year or more in progressing from beginning to end. Also, it does not move smoothly and evenly. Changes of personnel, community pressures, and other factors can materially alter its pace and its course. Yet, when the regular class teachers on a school's faculty think through together how best to give effective aid to pupils who falter and/or flare up under typical tutelage, the four step model fits the process.

It is important that regular class teachers in elementary and secondary and other schools know and understand how their colleagues elsewhere have worked together to improve the educational management of pupils who show learning disabilities and behavior disorders. It is questionable whether knowing about this kind of process will allow it to be telescoped or shortened because each school's situation will have unique features that will necessitate careful, step by step discussion and resolution. The value of recognizing a process model lies more in the reassurance it gives that such matters have been and can be worked out in an orderly way by regular class teachers and the framework it supplies for planning and implementing the process with optimism.

Teamwork with Specialists

The interest taken in learning disabilities and behavior disorders by various professionals in addition to educators has spawned an array of specialists. That has positive value. On difficult problems it is good to have a lot of help. Also, the breadth of professional interest increases the likelihood that there will be public understanding and support for the schools' efforts to reduce deportment problems and poor achievement. On the other side, though, there is the old saying that "too many cooks spoil the broth." If there is pulling and tugging among specialists for access to children and authority, control, and credit, everyone is the loser. Under those circumstances funds and professional time get dissipated in smoothing out rivalries and diverted from their primary target, the pupils showing learning disabilities and behavior disorders.

Regular class teachers, in either circumstance, serve their pupils best by being open to suggestions and willing to accept help, but remaining in charge, in the professional sense. There are some schools and communities so poor in resources that teachers have little choice but to go it on their own. More often, though, there are choices teachers may make as to which specialists they will use as consultants and whose advice or direction will be taken.

In one community, all of these specialists were already involved or attempting to involve themselves in work with the school system and its teachers regarding pupils with learning disabilities and behavior disorders:

Audiologists	Physical therapists
Neurologists	Psychiatrists
Occupational therapists	Psychologists
Optometrists	Social workers
Pediatricians	Speech clinicians

In addition to those persons who were external to the school system, the following specialists were already in its employ:

Counselors	Social workers
Physical educators	Special educators
Psychologists	Speech therapists
Remedial teachers	

Not only are there many specialists, but there are often conflicting ideas about what needs to be done. The physical educators may offer a course of psychomotor movement education linked to learning spelling or number facts. The speech therapists may put forward a program of language development based on a semantics theory. The physical therapist and neurologist may wish to see a neuromuscular reeducation plan initiated. The psychologist, psychiatrist, and social worker may opt for a behavior modification or a psychodynamic design for remediation. The optometrist may urge that hopes be pinned on eye movement exercises coupled with visual motor perceptual training. And so on, all vying for the pupil's in-school or out-of-school time.

Such well intentioned but differing kinds of approaches bombard the regular class teacher and the parents of pupils who show signs of learning disabilities and behavior disorders. The specialists may all have some degree of well deserved credibility, too.

What is needed is an instructional policy to which teachers can repair. That is the key to appropriate decisions about teamwork with other specialists. When the roles and functions of specialists can be aligned with guidance from established instructional policy, the interactions of regular class teachers with specialists can be much more productive.

Each school system (or local school, if there is decentralized authority) should consciously choose the route it expects to take in work with the learning disabled/behavior disordered pupils. It might be one or a combination of approaches, so long as it is clearly stated and is made a matter of policy. Regular class teachers ought to have major input in connection with the policy formation, so it is consistent with their own professional views.

As an example, one of the most perplexing professional interactions teachers face is with physicians who prescribe medications that need to be taken during the school day. The administration of medication is plainly outside the usual range of duties of a teacher. Yet conditions may arise under which teachers need to react to requests to do so. Grotsky, Sabatino, and Ohrtman (1976) offered the following careful policy oriented procedure for consideration by regular and special teachers in that circumstance.

> Drugs have a definite but limited role in the treatment of students' learning and behavior problems. Drugs can be useful with *some* under *certain* circumstances. Reports vary, but it appears that 30 to 50% of those referred because of disruptive classroom behavior and/or poor academic achievement can be helped by chemotherapy (medication) alone or in combination with psychotherapy, remedial tutoring, or special education programming. Perhaps the most appropriate way to analyze the previous statement is to point out that 50 to 70% of the children referred because of disruptive classroom behavior and/or poor academic achievement do not respond or are not appropriate candidates for chemotherapy.
>
> The procedure under which you may administer medication varies by school district. Check to see if there are established policies for your district. Adhere to these policies, if for no other reason than your legal protection. The following guidelines will aid school systems in dealing with this situation:
>
> a) Written orders are to be provided to the school from a physician, detailing the name of the drug, dosage, and the time interval in which the medication is to be taken. These orders are to be reviewed periodically.
>
> b) A written request is to be received by the school district from the parent or guardian of the pupil, together with a letter from the physician indicating the necessity for the administering of the medication during the day, the type of disease or illness involved, the benefits of the medication, the side effects, and an emergency number where he can be reached. Both letters should be placed in the pupil's file.
>
> c) Medication must be brought to the school in a container appropriately labeled by the pharmacy or physician.

d) The initial dose at school must be administered by the school nurse. If a teacher is to give subsequent medication, the nurse should discuss the medication, including its side effects, with the teacher.
e) The school nurse shall prepare a written statement to the building administrator as to the side effects of the drug, if any, and a copy should be placed in the pupil's file.
f) A locked cabinet must be provided for the storage of the medication. Opportunities should be provided for communication with the pupil, parent, and physician regarding the efficacy of the medication administered during school hours.
g) With the parent's and physician's consent, medication of a short-term duration may be administered by a teacher.
h) The school district retains the discretion to reject requests for administration of medicine.

You will need some information in order to effectively understand and teach a child who is on medication. With written parental permission and through your school nurse, obtain the following information from the child's physician:

a) How does the medication work?
b) What change in the student's behavior can be expected?
c) What effect will the medication have on the child's attention span, memory, motor dexterity, personality, sleeping and eating habits?
d) Does the medication have undesirable side effects?
e) What behavioral and/or motoric reactions indicate that the dosage may be toxic or inadequate for the child's needs?
f) How long will the child have to take the medication?
g) Could the child become physically and/or psychologically addicted to the medication?

The most important aspect of chemotherapy is to understand that the use of drugs does not relieve the physician, parent, and teacher of the responsibility for seeking to identify and eliminate the factor(s) causing or aggravating the problem. (pp. 8-10)

With policy positions such as this one as backdrops, and with the regular class teacher's position a central one with respect to specific instructional decisions about individual children, it becomes possible to sort out and make full use of the special competencies of others. That, in the end, is what is most satisfying to the specialists, too.

Special Education in the Regular Grades

The pattern for remedial instruction in most of the nation's schools has been to schedule pupils out of their regular classes to individual and small group sessions with the remedial specialist from daily to once a week. The intensity depended on the case load of the remedial teacher and the needs of the pupil. The time out of class was planned to interfere as little as possible with activities from which the pupil could profit. That intention missed, however, as often as it hit because of schedule complexities.

Similarly, children with learning disabilities and behavior disorders have usually been scheduled for part time instruction outside the regular class. An area of the school was made the headquarters for one or more specialist teachers. Selected pupils came to learning disability/behavior disorder headquarters for instruction and help with regular class assignments. Visits to that resource room or clinical center were on schedules worked out among the regular teachers, the specialists, the pupil, and often the principal. They, too, attempted to coordinate so the pupils would miss as little as possible of regular class instruction in which they might take part successfully.

In addition, there were understandings among the teachers—regular and special—and the principal, counselor, school nurse, and others on the school's staff that accommodated any crisis. If need be, staff members and other teachers could move as reinforcements to the teacher and pupil or pupils concerned or could accept a pupil or pupils brought to them.

Whether in open space or conventional school plans, in elementary or secondary schools, these arrangements still prevail. Thus the background and the predominant current organization for adapting to the requirements of children who show learning disabilities and behavior disorders remains a partial mainstream pattern. Ways to improve on current practices are illustrated later in this chapter.

Individualization of Instruction

It is not necessary, of course, that individualized instruction be one regular class teacher with one pupil. It can also be one specialist or one peer or cross age tutor with one pupil. As stated earlier, the same instruction may well be exactly what is needed by several pupils. Much individualization, too, can be accomplished by programed and other self instructive materials, with selective monitoring by the teacher or by an aide. Thus, while one to one instruction has a higher yield, a high degree of personalization for pupils with learning disabilities and behavior disorders is feasible without the constant one to one regular teacher-pupil image too often incorrectly associated with the concept (Jenkins & Mayhall, 1976).

Curriculum Individualization

Teaching a child who shows learning disabilities and behavior disorders necessitates starting with something the child can learn. Of course, the same is true of all children. But to achieve success with the child with learning disabilities and behavior disorders it is advisable first to make sure that the match is a tight one between the child and the material or skill to be learned. That kind of close match is more likely if what is to be learned has high interest value, is presented in small, interlocked steps, and is accompanied by reinforcers with high appeal to the pupil. To make such adaptations in what is to be taught it is sometimes necessary to broaden the curriculum or even depart substantially from it. If the history of American colonial times holds higher appeal than the prescribed curriculum on contemporary America, and if high quality, individualizable instructional materials are available for the former, it may well be that much more progress can be made with the child with learning disabilities and behavior disorders by temporarily moving away from what is *supposed* to be taught. The same principle holds for all other components of the usual curriculum. This does not mean, of course, that anything goes. Rather, it means one should exercise professional judgment to help bring into the pupil's orbit curricular content and skill that offer the best chance of successful instruction and learning.

The nature of the content or skill selected to be taught should promise to contribute, also, to improving the child's attention and study behavior. Teachers in high schools and elementary schools need freedom to seek out and use elements from any part of the entire school curriculum in working with children with learning disabilities and behavior disorders. That should be viewed as one of the most important steps on the road to satisfactory accomplishment in the rest of the curriculum.

Methods of Teaching

Haring (1975) commented, "Teaching a learning disabled child necessitates finding a method of instruction which allows the child to learn" (p. 198). He went on to emphasize Becker's (1972) position on the teacher's obligation to find a way to teach each child by saying that

> the idea of the teacher as responsible for the learning of his or her students is gaining momentum as persons applying behavior principles in education show that retarded children can learn to read, disadvantaged children can learn language concepts and reading if they are taught properly, and learning disabilities disappear when more effective beginning reading programs are used. (pp. 198-199)

Observation of regular class teachers who succeed with children despite their problems shows that they have three things in common with respect to their methods of teaching:

1. They make and use plans. The plans are not superficial; they are detailed and specific, with alternatives stated in case the first course of action does not work.

2. They work out objectives (with the child, if possible). The objectives are plainly and factually stated in operational terms. It is easy for both pupil and teacher to know when an objective has been reached.
3. They monitor the child's progress regularly and keep records of it. The records are open to the child but, more important from the standpoint of teaching methods, successful teachers use the data about the child's progress to measure the effectiveness of their teaching and make changes when progress slows or halts.

As to the specific teaching techniques that seem of most value, the majority are variations on the behavior modification theme. This observation coincides with the reports of Morse (1976), Haring (1975), Coloroso (1976), and many others who have set forth descriptions of how effective teachers conduct instruction in the face of learning disabilities and behavior disorders. A runner-up in frequency of use is teaching based on the ego strengthening and controlled acting out elements of a psychoanalytic approach. It is not uncommon to find the two combined.

In our view, the rapidly advancing teaching technology arising out of applied behavior analysis has already become so useful in the everyday work of all teachers that none should be without at least a rudimentary command of it. Employing behavior modification does not commit the teacher to its exclusive use, either. It mixes well with other methods. That encourages teachers to develop blends that suit their unique personalities and preferred teaching styles.

Instructional Materials

Probably no other exceptionality has generated such an assortment of specialized instructional materials. Many of the items whose advertisements promise a lot have had limited field testing or none worth mentioning, while others have years of use under controlled conditions behind them, and data on their effectiveness are available.

For regular class teachers there are four points that may be particularly helpful in weaving one's way through the colorful brochures in search of the precise material to match a child's particular needs.

1. First try whatever is at hand, the usual instructional material employed with other pupils. If adaptation seems to be needed, the special education teachers in the building may be able to suggest how to do that. It is often a plus if children with learning disabilities and behavior disorders can continue for the most part to use the same materials as classmates do.
2. Special education teachers are often quite knowledgeable about instructional materials. The specialist teachers in the local school system may have or know about just the right thing.

3. Many materials are linked to particular points of view about learning disabilities and behavior disorders. Check to see if the items are or can be adapted to the approach that will govern how the child is taught. For instance, for a "process" teaching approach that intends to teach developmentally (a) body image, (b) coordination, (c) perception, (d) association, and (e) conceptualization, see Marshall's (1975) detailed criteria for assessing instructional material.
4. There should be a Special Educational Instructional Materials Center nearby. Such Centers are located regionally. They have samples of materials, many of which have been tried by teachers whose notes can be reviewed. The staff is expert at advising and demonstrating, and materials may be borrowed and used at no cost.

Sometimes, particularly when working on matters such as social behavior and attendance to the learning task, charts and other recording devices become instructional materials of first order magnitude. When these are pupil made and pupil maintained, they can be personalized and become the property of the child when completed.

Organization for Instruction

From nursery age through high school most girls and boys are packed with energy. They even rest in active postures that would tire adults. The extra urge to movement that so often shows in learning disabilities and behavior disorders is added to most children's generally high base line of mobility. In the day's activities, teachers should therefore arrange alternating shifts from sedentary to active engagement in learning tasks. They should allow stretch time and permit unscheduled switches in activities within reasonable limits.

One of the most common points at which class management falters is when group or individual activities change. Serious difficulties can erupt when there is slippage in control as the group shifts from concentration on one set of tasks to another. Kounin (1976) has identified dangerous transition points and has shown how they can become stormy because of ineffective group activating systems. Borg (no date) has developed a set of training procedures from which teachers can acquire class transition management skills.

Pupil control sometimes is threatened unless there is understanding and rapport among the youngsters and between them and the teaching staff, including professionals, aides, and volunteers. Limited or uncertain pupil control makes for a shaky organization for instruction.

Learning disabled/behavior disordered students who are clumsy or awkward can inadvertently jostle others or knock things down and those who are hyperactive can get in the way of others and distract them. These behaviors can excite laughter, anger, or both on the part of the rest of the class.

Yet the poor coordination and overactivity of the learning disabled/ behavior disordered child can be altered only by patient teaching, over a period of time. The teacher needs to ascertain at what level each student is functioning in these respects, as well as in academic matters, and guide the student toward improved performance. If *all* students are helped to recognize the teachers' and pupils' goals in these matters, a solid organization based on understanding can result.

One confrontation every teacher tries to avoid is a program disruption that assumes the proportion of a crisis. Yet regular and special education teachers need to be prepared for them. The management procedures recommended by Grotsky, Sabatino, and Ohrtman (1976) are sound and they can be applied with pupils of all ages.

> A "crisis" involving an exceptional student is really no different from a crisis or problem involving any others in your class. Exceptional students are, first and foremost, persons. They respond to the same value appeal, threats, praise, and support that others do. Here are some things to keep in mind when a "crisis" occurs:
>
> a) A crisis is a disruption in your program. *You* have a choice at this point. You must decide whether the student(s) involved and the issues are important or whether your program is important. If your program takes precedence, mete out whatever consequences you normally would. Be prepared, however, for "spill-over" to occur sometime later that day or week. If the issue is not resolved by you, the student(s) will find some way to resolve it later. This may show up in the form of teasing, name-calling, pushing, fighting, or in some form of resistance to you, e.g., verbal abuse, refusal to cooperate. If you cope with the issue, you must realize that you may or may not be able to resolve it. Whether you do or not is unimportant. The fact that you recognize all students and their needs is important. This is what "building rapport" is all about.
>
> b) Everyone involved in a crisis has his own point of view as to what precipitated and maintained the crisis. Your task is to:
>
> (1) Calmly separate the children involved—physically if need be.
>
> (2) Reassure each child that his/her point of view will be heard completely and without any judgment of right or wrong on *your* part.
>
> (3) Piece the events together sequentially.
>
> (4) Try to arrive at a conclusion. If you have conflicting evidence, you can:
>
>> (a) do nothing;
>> (b) put the children involved "on probation"; or
>> (c) administer whatever consequences you feel are appropriate. The important element here is to be fair. Students can accept differences in treatment as long as the differences are arrived at fairly.

c) A "crisis" can be a learning situation. The others in your class know when you have to deal with a serious problem. They generally will not become disruptive. They may talk among themselves, continue their seat work or projects, or do whatever else you suggest. The atmosphere of "seriousness" that prevails during a crisis is generally sufficient to maintain order in your room. A calm demeanor and stable emotional posture by the teacher also contribute to neutralizing a crisis and reestablishing order. (Grotsky, Sabatino, & Ohrtman, 1976, pp. 4-5).

Children with learning disabilities and behavior disorders are often able to manage themselves better when upcoming events are liked and known or predictable. For that reason there can be merit in soliciting and using their ideas about how to organize for instruction. Experienced teachers often note that they enjoy teaching more after they make adjustments in what had become their routines in order to better manage children with learning disabilities and behavior disorders.

School Physical Plant

A considerable amount of attention has been paid to the impact of the immediate learning environment on the school behavior of children with learning disabilities and behavior disorders. A thorough exposition of the current state of theory and knowledge on the matter is found in Cruickshank and Hallahan's book (1975). In a chapter titled "The Learning Environment," Cruickshank treated thoroughly "stimuli reduction and structure in the actual learning environment of children who have specific types of perceptual disabilities and behavioral characteristics." These children include "those who present evidence of sensory hyperactivity, perceptual-motor dysfunction, attention disturbances, or any combination of these characteristics" (p. 227).

There is a limited amount of hard research evidence on the effects of the physical plant on learning. What there is does not provide convincing evidence that special adjustments are needed. There remains in the minds of many teachers, behavioral scientists, and architects the impression that everyone's learning might profit if it took place in environments that are calm, comfortable, and relatively free of distractions. Teachers should be free to arrange space, furniture, and decorations in ways most pleasing to themselves and the pupils.

Summary

The teacher's chief considerations in helping pupils with learning disabilities and behavior disorders are these: select learning tasks whose mastery the pupils can achieve and find methods of teaching that will assure that the pupils will learn. There is no mystery about how to do that, but it does take time and effort to produce the individualized instruction it requires. Once the two chief considerations are accounted for, proper materials, sound instructional organization, and the appropriate physical plant can assist.

SPECIFIC PUBLIC SCHOOL PROGRAMS

Public schools continue in their shift from the *class* to the *individual* as the basic unit around which special and regular education are planned, organized, and conducted. As that move accelerates, the present cloudy concept of learning disabilities and behavior disorders will be better illuminated. As individualization of instruction changes from theory to reality, it will become less and less necessary to use categorical labels to identify pupils. Rather, *each* pupil will receive personalized education and *every* pupil will be special, in that sense.

Vallejo City Unified School District

Wardlaw (1976) related his experience as principal of an elementary school that moved regular and special education together by attending primarily to designing all instruction for individual pupils. Learning disabilities and behavior disorders are not mentioned specifically. As the model Wardlaw presented becomes established and spreads its influence, such an increase in individualization plus such a reduction in labeling may become the rule rather than the exception.

In Wardlaw's highly personalized and anecdotal account, it is valuable to look for evidence of the step by step process in the summary analysis of Morse's description of how teachers "worked through" a similar problem, described earlier in this chapter. Here it is recounted from the perspective of a principal.

> One of my first teaching experiences was in an elementary school that did have special education classes in the building. I knew that the children were different; I knew that they were labeled handicapped, but they really did not bother me and there was no big interaction. At that particular time in my career (maybe this is a continuing thing), I was really trying to get my act together as a teacher in terms of survival training.
>
> I became a teaching principal—this was a tremendous transition in terms of preparing for a principalship or an administrative position. Then my career took an interesting twist. I became a principal in an economically depressed area, where black students composed 99 percent of the school population. This was before the existence of categorical aid programs; before such programs existed for learning disabilities or educationally handicapped.
>
> I next became principal of an elementary school that housed four different special education programs. They were impaired hearing, visually handicapped, educable mentally retarded, and trainable mentally retarded. These separate programs were a part of an elementary school of

approximately 700 students. Suddenly this program changed. As most of you are aware, housing special education often depends upon space availability within the district. Enrollment shifts then become a major determinator in moving special programs from school to school within the district. As the result of these enrollment shifts, we were left with just one special education program—educable mentally retarded. However, we did supplement the space that was used for the other special education classes by a rezoning measure that increased our minority population. This switch in our student population (1) increased our minority population, (2) reduced the economic level of the parent population that we were serving, and (3) resulted in a much more diverse parent and student population.

It was when we were confronted with meeting the needs of the special program for the educable mentally retarded plus the diverse student population that our efforts toward mainstreaming began.

Now you might ask, What's so important about his background? I don't think it's particularly unique. I'm presenting it because I think there are a lot of principals in California and throughout the country that have a similar kind of background and have had similar kinds of experiences in their administrative careers.

Program Changes Leading to Mainstreaming

I am going to tell you about a mainstreaming program that worked. It worked for our staff. It worked for our parents. It worked for our district. Most of all, it worked for all of our students. Research-oriented people might say: What were your measures? Show us your results. I'm not going to show them to you. I'm going to tell you about some of the results.

One of the first things I need to say for a very political, bureaucratic, parent-related reason is that we increased reading and math scores. That kind of gets us off the hook. You now know that we were paying attention to basic skills. I don't think increased math and reading scores were our most significant results, however. We were also paying attention to student personal and interpersonal growth. We did this by a variety of measures. We did it by opinionnaires and teacher-and student-designed assessment measurements. From a prinicpal's point of view, the following factors were the most important indicators of the success of our program:

–Attendance was improved.
–Office referrals (from classroom and playground) were reduced.
–Bus referrals were reduced.
–Community contact became more positive.

In fact, we had a noticeable increase in parent support. How did we achieve this? Attendance and attitudes at parent-teacher conferences were entirely different. We had an increase of volunteer aides. Parents started coming into the classroom and helping the teacher with instructional tasks. We had a reduced number of phone calls or complaints from parents and from central office personnel.

Another measure of parent support became apparent when we began to get into scheduling changes, such as changing the length of the school day for students, changing the length of the school day for parents, changing our reporting procedures. We had developed stronger and more positive support from parents than we had before we began the project.

What were some of the factors that helped us achieve the results that I've quickly related to you? One of the first things that we did as a school was to examine our general education program. We began to admit that general education was not so hot. In our general education program we were regearing ourselves to meet the needs of our now increasingly divergent student population. So, step one became a recognition that we needed to examine our program.

It's interesting remembering one of the first activities we attempted in looking at ourselves. We contacted Pat O'Donnell who is now Chairman of the Department of Special Education at California State University, San Francisco. He was at San Anselmo at that time. A staff committee went over to his office and had a cup of coffee and asked him if he would provide some inservice training for our staff. We asked him if he would come to Vallejo and help us by presenting a course on the problems and issues of individualization and change. This was before we really got into the whole business of needs assessment. I don't know if Pat fully realizes the implication of his initial survey course on change and individualization for our staff. We followed that course with visits to nearby places such as Napa and Sonoma. We took a look at their existing practices. We reviewed the literature and conducted staff seminars on some of the recent innovations and attempted to apply them to our own school practices.

After the period of inservice training, visits and observations, we tried a special project, developed as a result of studying some of the programs designed by Dwight Allen. We operated a flexible scheduling team-teaching project (FSTP) at the upper grade level, including our educable mentally retarded students in this project; this was our own particular school level effort to keep up with the fad of innovation and change in the 60s.

We ended up with a superdepartmentalized program with minicourses that were unbelievable. There was a heavy emphasis on grouping by academic achievement. We had good academic results and were able to show considerable growth on our achievement test measures. . . . One of the most valuable results from this project was an increased awareness of the diversity of our students and the widely different skill levels indicated by using such measures as standardized diagnostic instruments. Individualization became an impossible task, so we had to stop at that point and reassess where we wanted to go.

At about that time, we were introduced to Madeline Hunter at the University Elementary School (UES) at UCLA. We have been very fortunate to have worked a number of years with Madeline and her staff. We were able to send a number of our staff to UES, and Dr. Hunter was able to come up to our school, where she provided some outstanding staff retraining programs. Emphasized was a program designed to improve teacher competencies; this retraining effort forced us to reexamine our goals for education in relation to individual differences, classroom organization, and classroom strategy. We began to focus on such areas as diagnostic-prescriptive and evaluative approaches for classroom teachers. We began to look at the needs of kids in an entirely different way, more than just improving reading and math. We became concerned with the learning environment and the degree of personal and interpersonal growth. It forced us to reevaluate some of our assumptions about education. How did we feel about differences? What were we doing to promote the uniqueness of youngsters? Were we behaving in a manner that was facilitating or promoting trust and respect? What were we doing about independence and responsibility?

Several important questions related to discipline. Is it separate from instruction? Do you teach math here and discipline over there? Were we caught in a rut of saying, "If we could only get rid of the discipline problem, then we could really improve our math program. We could complete more of our individual contacts in reading." What about humanism? What about increasing the role opportunities for our students? About this time, Dr. Keith Beery came on the scene with Project Catalyst. Project Catalyst is a program based upon Dr. Beery's *Models for Mainstreaming* book funded by the Bureau of Education for the Handicapped. Dr. Beery's main input to our staff was providing assistance for the staff development efforts that were already underway, but with the "mainstreaming concept" in mind. He provided important technical assistance in developing classroom and school level measures for making daily instructional decisions regarding personal and interpersonal growth. Keith not only had the idea but an implementation plan. In his own way he showed us how we might try to heat the ocean a little bit.

Our Model for Mainstreaming

Our mainstreaming project involved eighty students in the 10-12 age group and three teachers (two regular teachers and one special education teacher). We used the multi-age grouping, team-teaching organizational plan; our definition of team teaching (based upon the research of Goodlad and Anderson as practiced by Dr. Madeline Hunter at UES) is a group of two or more teachers who will be responsible for the planning, teaching, and the evaluation of all the youngsters. That doesn't mean that they had equal responsibility for all the youngsters, because we certainly grouped and regrouped according to teacher and student developed criteria.

We assessed each student's learning style, first to determine his degree of student-teacher dependency. We tried to match teacher style to learner needs. We certainly were working toward increasing teacher shared responsibility and competencies so each instructor could be more effective with a wider range of students; therefore, each teacher was teaching all academic areas and as many different skill levels as he could productively manage.

The team viewed its existence as being dependent upon producing a better instructional program. Its members were committed to sharing the richness of the resources that they offered each other. There was a constant questioning of whether their team structure was offering something better than what they had been able to offer as self-contained classroom teachers.

All the usual barriers reported by special education people were problems that we encountered in our project.

–We certainly faced the problem of attitudes of both special and regular education personnel. I felt that it was the number one problem.

–Parent support was a big issue. We were pleased with our improvements.

–Student attitudes mattered very much to us. They helped us value the importance of diversity.

–The level of administrative support one receives can make or break a program.

–Buses can be a major factor. Transportation can control your whole program. You can have all sorts of fine plans, and then they all depend upon the bus schedule.

–Teacher organizations had to be involved. We have teacher organizations in Vallejo, and they have similar kinds of feelings as their colleagues throughout California and across the country. They are a factor to be dealt with, to interact with positively.

–Personnel at other schools was a concern. We were taking a risk in developing the program. Naturally, there was some anxiety regarding our program elicited from personnel at other schools.

–Curriculum revision is a monumental task. Mainstreaming can really open that bag. Some people spend a lifetime working in one particular area of curriculum, but we are talking about revising curriculum for the whole school. I think we made significant progress, but I don't want to infer that we completed the task. We developed some processes for improving our curriculum.

–We had some dropouts. We didn't succeed with all students. There were some parents and some children that did not succeed in our mainstreaming model. We've learned something from it. We now know more ways to help youngsters succeed in a mainstreaming model.

We achieved an entirely new level in understanding ways of evaluating information that's important to us at the school site. We now have instruments for collecting data. In terms of on the firing line, in the trenches, working with kids in the daily situation, we now have better information than we ever had before.

Present Views Regarding Mainstreaming

How do I feel about mainstreaming? I have increased respect for the concept. I believe I have an increased commitment to attempting to achieve a successful mainstreaming model.

However, I now have an increased awareness of the dangers of moving too fast and getting into mainstreaming for the wrong reasons. In our particular model, special education proved to be a resource for improvement. In our particular model we began to value differences as strengths. This is a different point of view from what I hear from some special education people. It is important that special education personnel know that general education is developing a number of programs in the area of mainstreaming. The California Early Childhood Education Program is a tremendous example of trying to promote a diagnostic or prescriptive approach. I think the major implications of the Reform of Intermediate and Secondary Education (RISE) are related to the concept of mainstreaming.

A word to the college people. From a school level perspective, we view colleges as producing better teachers than we've ever had before (teachers for both general and special education). We are delighted with the new young teachers your teacher-training programs are graduating. We are finding more competent, better trained teachers in our district than we've ever had before. That's an exciting situation. So, I think you might want to give yourselves a pat on the back. Your efforts are working for us in a joint way for professional improvement.

In our model, we viewed the principal as the key. So, aside from what college teacher-training programs are producing, one of the real issues that is facing us, in my opinion, is a retraining of administrators. I think some of the things that Bill May, assistant superintendent of public instruction for general education, is involved with in Sacramento, such as the Right-to-Read Program, have to do with school level planning; and that certainly should involve principals and their staffs. Principals will be required to develop staff organization plans in a manner that was not expected previously. The RISE is going to be getting into this area. We are just now beginning to talk about retraining experienced staff. We are now beginning to seriously talk about developing at the district level a whole new dimension of program development.

"The greatest good we can do for others is not just to share our riches with them, but to reveal their riches to themselves." How does this relate to the role of the special education personnel within the mainstreaming concept? From my point of view, based upon our experiences in Vallejo, successful mainstreaming programs include:

- Practices that facilitate and promote uniqueness of all people
- Practices that promote humanism
- Practices that focus on providing specific curricular objectives to meet the specific learning characteristics of the learner

These practices will, in my opinion, increase the need for and utilization of special education personnel at many different levels and in many different roles. (Wardlaw, 1976, pp. 190-196)

Rochester Primary Mental Health Project

Early detection and prevention of school adjustment problems is the objective of a project based jointly in the University of Rochester, the

Rochester City School District, and suburban schools in Monroe County. Called the Rochester Primary Mental Health Project, it deals with three kinds of adjustment-risk indicators that can be observed in children: aggressive-disruptive behaviors, shy-withdrawn behaviors, and learning difficulties. Started in 1957 in one school, by 1976 the operation was part of 25 Greater Rochester schools; about 20 other school districts in the country were using the same format, and the number was growing.

The work began this way. Teachers in kindergarten and the first three grades made systematic observations of everyday behavior on all the pupils with whom they have some sustained contact. There are forms for recording what the teachers note. Parents of referred children were interviewed at home by social workers. School mental health professionals are available for consultation, to conduct group screening examinations, and to assist in planning preventive or corrective actions.

The actual special instruction with pupils is mainly in a one to one child-staff ratio, with occasional small group sessions. Trained and salaried aides, most often recruited from housewives who have volunteered, are given a course of instruction and work in school with the children, under professional supervision. Specific goals are set up in planning sessions with professional staff and parents. The child-aide interaction is aimed at the attainment of those goals. Staff conferences are used to monitor progress, give additional professional guidance as needed, alter initial directions when they are not productive, and close out and reassign cases when help is no longer needed.

Program effectiveness has been tested several times with encouraging results. The probability of school failure for children with incipient learning disabilities and behavior disorders can be markedly reduced at a fairly low dollar cost. That is accomplished, too, while the children remain in the mainstream of education and while regular class teachers and other school personnel grow in competency to cope with potential high risk pupils.

There are a number of detailed case descriptions in the book that describes the Rochester Project (Cowen, Trost, Lorion, Dorr, Izzo, & Isaacson, 1975). They reveal the kind of work done with children by teachers and aides and the results of that work. The case reports range from short term interactions to those that lasted two years or more. They exemplify a psychodynamic style of work with children who show a great range of learning difficulties and aggressive-disruptive and shy-withdrawn behavior.

The Pittsburgh Secondary School Model

The previous illustrations have been based on elementary schools. The next example shows how middle schools and high schools, too, are taking steps in the direction of accommodating the special needs of learning disabled/behavior disordered students. The Pittsburgh model, developed originally for urban secondary schools, has been successfully transplanted to suburban and rural secondary schools in Western Pennsylvania.

Zigmond (1975, 1976) created a model in Pittsburgh, Pennsylvania, for dealing with urban high school students with learning disabilities. This model stresses regular class teacher involvement and maintenance of the pupils in the mainstream. It is staffed by two specialist teachers for each unit, plus a school psychologist. Service is both *direct* to students who spend one or two periods per day in a learning lab and *indirect,* in that consultation is given to regular class teachers so they can help learning disabled pupils in their classes. As Zigmond pointed out:

> The plight of the student with a learning disability is accentuated at the secondary level because curriculum in the secondary school is developed, interpreted and presented by subject matter specialists. These teachers often lack the psychoeducational orientation which is useful for designing alternative teaching and assessment strategies. There is a need for an interpreter, a liaison between the student and the content teacher to help this student "make it" in the mainstream. One resource teacher assigned to each school building works primarily on a one-to-one basis with mainstream content area teachers who have learning disabled students in their classes. The resource teacher helps the mainstream teacher to define instructional objectives and to develop alternative ways of presenting content information and of assessing knowledge. Courses are not watered down but are altered in terms of methods of presentation or methods of evaluation. For example, since curriculum at the secondary level is not ordinarily presented via multi-media or multi-sensory approaches the teacher consultant may recommend to a content area teacher the use of supplementary materials such as film strips or tapes. (pp. 6-7)

In addition to the specialist teacher who devotes time to being a resource for regular teachers in their own classes, there is a learning lab teacher. This is a specialist in the remediation of pupil weaknesses in reading, mathematics, spelling, and writing. The learning lab teacher also determines each learning disabled/behavior disordered student's interests and motivations through informal talks in the learning lab. The information is used to pick instructional materials and teaching procedures most likely to appeal to the student.

During the first month of school the resource teacher and the learning lab teacher jointly visit each regular class teacher, choosing a time such as the homeroom period when there can be some discussion with pupils. The learning lab is described, and pupils may refer themselves for assistance. As the learning lab fills, the time of the two specialist teachers is more and more taken up with their separate duties. They also coordinate with the counselor regarding individual pupil schedules, so everyone who needs that information has it.

The resource teacher also holds a series of in-service sessions for small groups of the faculty. Teachers are paid an hourly rate to attend, since the meetings are voluntary and after regular working hours. The content is based on the needs teachers express. The thrust is to improve the regular class teachers' capabilities to accommodate learning disabled/behavior disordered pupils through individualized instruction.

Acceptance of pupils for special help is based on a team judgment. It is done at a school staff meeting after educational and psychological data have been made available for all concerned to study. At the meeting are the regular teacher from whose class the child comes, the resource teacher, the learning lab teacher, the school counselor, and one or more school psychologists. Together they make the admission decision and set forth the outline of an individualized educational program.

In the meantime the school psychologist had made a visit to the pupil's home, explained the program to the parents, and received permission to do the necessary psychoeducational examinations. After the decision to admit the pupil to a program has been made, the school psychologist is responsible for the due process formalities and for whatever further conferences are appropriate to ascertain the parents' full understanding and agreement.

There is a parent education component with two purposes. One is to explain what the child's teachers are doing, and why. The second is to help parents learn to deal successfully with learning disability and behavior disorder problems that extend into the home, or perhaps originate there, especially child management and control procedures.

The resource teacher also holds weekly meetings with the learning lab pupils. In these sessions pupils are encouraged to discuss the social and emotional stresses of high school life and to talk about post-high-school work and study opportunities, how to improve study habits and test performance, and other topics of importance in clarifying their values and life plans.

Response contingent instruction is an expression used by Zigmond (1976) to denote the particular style of diagnostic teaching found effective with these secondary school students. Instructional material is matched to pupil interests (newspaper sports pages or sports magazines for basketball or football enthusiasts; camera or motorcycle or rock group articles for others). Plans are short range and flexible. What was learned and what continued to maintain interest in yesterday's lesson leads to what is in today's lesson. The results of today's work will determine what is planned for tomorrow.

Though based on informal educational diagnosis in the teaching situation, the instruction is carefully organized. There is continuous assessment of pupil needs based on error analysis. What the pupil wants to be able to do well, but does not (errors), becomes the instructional goal. The pupil participates in that decision. Lesson plans follow and so does the record keeping needed to keep track of progress. Pupils do much of that, too.

The resource teacher, the learning lab teacher, and the regular class teacher team to provide the skills pupils require. They are of two kinds: school survival skills and academic skills. The former subdivide into study skills, behavior control, and teacher pleasing actions. Academic skills include mainly those associated with the language arts and mathematics.

Early experiences with the model highlighted the need for strong and continued emphasis on fast, frequent, and thorough communication among all concerned if the operation were to succeed. The resource teacher reports pupil status weekly to the referring regular class teacher. The whole faculty and administration of the school receive a monthly newsletter on progress in the learning lab. Monthly summary reports are made by the specialist teachers. Parents receive home visits twice a year, during which report cards are hand delivered by teachers.

This program functions in middle schools and high schools, from 6th through 12th grade. It has been in operation since July 1, 1975.

COMPREHENSIVE PROGRAMING

The behaviors that cluster under the umbrella of learning disabilities and behavior disorders seem to become particularly visible in school. They are engendered or nourished by weaknesses and limitations in the instruction pupils receive. Thus, the most desirable kind of comprehensive programing would certainly be that which repairs and strengthens instruction to the end that very few, if any, learning disabilities and behavior disorders occur.

Morse (1976) described how teachers in a school with high problem incidence altered the climate of the school. Increased teacher competence in both psychodynamic and behavior modification procedures led to more personalized teaching and to the introduction of prevention as a major objective regarding learning disabilities and behavior disorders. Haring (1975), writing about a behavior modification teaching approach, said:

> We have found that initial screening and assessment in early childhood is the best prevention possible and also makes remediation of specific learning disabilities an easier task. . . . While individualization of instruction

has been a catchword for many years in education, it is only becoming a real possibility now. (p. 22)

The work of Cowen and his associates (1975), which drew most heavily on psychodynamic procedures, supports the same viewpoint. Zigmond's (1976) secondary design also puts individualization in the forefront.

It should come as no surprise that we encourage emphasis on teaching each child in terms of demonstrated needs as the first objective of comprehensive programing.

Characteristics of a Comprehensive Educational Program

What does a school or school system look like when it is thoroughly capable of dealing with learning disabilities and behavior disorders? What does it have that others do not have? This section lists the main features that, if present, reduce the problems to manageable terms with excellent prospects of success.

First, there should be an initial assessment of each child at the start of each academic year. It should cover reading, language(s), communication skills, computation, and reasoning with numbers. Also, it should cover general health, and, specifically, vision and hearing. Equally important are motor development and personal and social coping skills and understanding.

Second, the initial assessment should be integral to the daily class work, with the teacher participating and coordinating it, rather than seeing it set off as a package of artificial test situations conducted by others. This activity on the teacher's part, working with others, should be an important part of instruction. It should not be regarded as something that interferes with or delays "the real work of the teacher."

Third, while the initial assessment is going on, the teacher should begin to list preliminary program goals for each pupil. The two processes, assessment and program goal setting, should overlap, the latter finishing shortly after the first. The program goals should relate to all three aspects of the assessment, and they should fit the pupils individually.

Fourth, goals should be broad. To help implement them, specific objectives should be drafted. They should be in behavioral terms, and it should be possible to measure the degree of their accomplishment by observing the pupil in action in or out of school. The objectives should be discussed with and agreed to by the pupil, parents, and others who might have concern or responsibility.

Fifth, an instructional plan should be made for each pupil. Where there are essentially the same or similar objectives for two or more pupils, instructional plans should be meshed to allow teamwork and social learning by the pupils and to make efficient use of teacher time.

Instructional plans should be detailed, with step by step phases stated. They should cover time spans from a week or two up to two or three months and, occasionally, longer. The projected times should be specified. Lest this seem like excessive paperwork, an excellent instructional plan often takes one page or less to state.

Sixth, lesson plans should be made to pinpoint the exact learning activities in which pupils will be engaged. Each lesson plan should specify the materials to be involved and how they will be employed, as well as the anticipated pupil-pupil and pupil-teacher interactions expected. These lesson plans, if effective, can be reused with the same or other individual pupils or groups of pupils. They can also be shared among teachers, who often will make minor adaptations in them to suit their own pupils and their own teaching styles.

Seventh, particular attention should be paid at all times to pupil motivation. All school learning is not self motivating. All pupils do not receive home encouragement that makes them want to do well at school tasks. In some situations there are powerful out-of-school influences on pupils that derogate schools. For all these reasons it is necessary to deliberately create and maintain strong proschooling motivation in pupils. An inventory of what is rewarding for each child should be maintained and updated periodically. Teachers should agree as to how rewards might best be used and should employ them to keep pupil motivation high. All the while there should be emphasis on transferring the high positive valence of rewards to the act of learning itself.

Eighth, performance should be measured and progress assessed. Expectation for progress should be stated for each pupil in terms of particular skills, understandings, and knowledge to be attained rather than in terms of grade levels. All measures of progress should be in terms of specific attainments over specific time periods.

It can be seen from these eight points that a high degree of individualization characterizes a comprehensive program. Effective teaching is much more than a series of broadband chalk talks from the front of a room. It calls for planning, diversified staffing, preparation time, and constant evaluation. Teachers need to help get this across to contemporary administrators and program coordinators.

There are still many superintendents and principals who think that their most important interaction with a teacher should be to "stop in and make an observation, preparatory to rating." Many consider a teacher's request for consultation as revealing a weakness. They need to be brought to realize that it is a sign of high competence and professional integrity when an educator, teacher, or administrator, recognizes the need for consultation and takes the initiative to obtain it.

A comprehensive program, therefore, is one that complies with the eight criteria. Equally important, it is one that has understanding, support, and leadership not only from the teachers themselves but also from the administrative structure and personnel of the school system.

Education as a Part of a Broader Group of Services

Earlier in this chapter it became apparent that there are many agencies and professions with proper and legitimate interests in persons with learning disabilities and behavior disorders. These included social welfare, court related, and health related personnel and organizations.

These can be of valuable service to pupils, especially if they ally with teachers and each other to coordinate and concentrate their efforts.

THE CONTINUING NEED FOR TEACHERS

Educational specialization in learning disabilities and behavior disorders continues to enlarge. At present the employment prospects for specialists appear to remain firm, though the rapid expansion of the late 1960's and early 1970's seems over.

Interest is rising in regular class teachers who have an understanding of the kind this book intends to provide. More school systems are seeking regular elementary and secondary teachers who have preprofessional or in-service orientation to pupils with learning disabilities and behavior disorders and who are willing to work in full or partial mainstream patterns with them. The wave in that direction is mounting and it still seems some distance from its cresting point.

SUGGESTIONS FOR STUDENTS AND INSTRUCTOR

1. Visit schools where learning disabled/behavior disordered pupils are being taught in regular classes and through the resource room pattern.
2. Arrange for a panel presentation by persons from the college faculty or local school system on the relations between remedial reading and the instruction of pupils with learning disabilities in the language arts.
3. Work out opportunities for students to help by tutoring in classes that contain learning disabled/behavior disordered pupils.
4. If there is a local association of parents interested in learning disabilities and behavior disorders, students might attend their meetings and learn how these parents perceive their children and their needs.
5. Students might try to locate adults who had learning disabilities or behavior disorders as youth and learn how the grown-ups consider the matter in retrospect.
6. Do pupils in other countries experience learning disabilities and behavior disorders?

TOPICAL BIBLIOGRAPHIES

Applied Behavioral Analysis in Teaching

Becker, W. C. Application of behavior principles in typical classrooms. In C. E. Thorensen (Ed.), *Behavior modification in education*. Chicago: University of Chicago Press, 1972.

Blackham, G. J., & Silberman, A. *Modification of child behavior* (2nd ed.). Belmont CA: Wadsworth, 1975.

Gardner, W. I. *Children with learning and behavior problems: A behavior management approach*. Boston: Allyn & Bacon, 1974.

Glavin, J. P. *Behavioral strategies for classroom management*. Columbus OH: Charles E. Merrill, 1974.

Haring, N. G., & Philips, E. L. *Analysis of modification of classroom behavior*. Englewood Cliffs NJ: Prentice-Hall, 1972.

Homme, L. *How to use contingency contracting in the classroom*. Champaign IL: Research, 1970.

Jordan, J. B., & Robbins, L. S. (Eds.). *Let's try doing something else kind of thing*. Reston VA: The Council for Exceptional Children, 1972.

Leitenberg, H. (Ed.). *Handbook of behavior modification and behavior therapy*. Englewood Cliffs NJ: Prentice-Hall, 1976.

Lovitt, T. C. *What research and experience say to the teacher of exceptional children: Managing inappropriate behaviors in the classroom*. Reston VA: The Council for Exceptional Children, 1978.

Stephens, T. M. *A comprehensive bibliography on mainstreaming*. Columbus: College of Education, Ohio State University, 1976.

Autism—What It Means for Educators

Bettelheim, B. *The empty fortress: Infantile autism and the birth of the self*. New York: Free Press, 1967.

Bower, E. M. *Early identification of emotionally handicapped children in school*. Springfield IL: Charles C Thomas, 1974.

Lovatt, M. Autistic children in a day nursery. *Exceptional Children*, 1962, 28, 103-108.

Stuecher, U. *Tommy: A treatment study of an autistic child*. Reston VA: The Council for Exceptional Children, 1972.

Class Crisis Management

Borg, W.R. *Classroom management* (Protocol materials). Tampa FL: National Resource and Dissemination Center, University of South Florida, no date.

Kounin, J. *Discipline and group management in classrooms*. New York: Holt, Rinehart and Winston, 1970.

Morse, W. C. *Classroom disturbance: The principal's dilemma*. Reston VA: The Council for Exceptional Children, 1971.

Morse, W. C. The helping teacher/crisis teacher concept. *Focus on Exceptional Children*, 1976, 8(4), 1-11.

Parks, A. L. *Behavior disorders: Helping children with behavioral problems*. Austin TX: Learning Concepts, 1976.

Redl, F. The concept of a therapeutic milieu. *American Journal of Orthopsychiatry,* 1959, *29,* 721-734.

Drugs and Learning Disabilities

Bosco, J. J., & Robin, S. S. (Eds.). *The hyperactive child and stimulant drugs.* Chicago: University of Chicago Press, 1977.

Connors, C. Keith. Deanol and behavior disorders in children: A critical review of the literature and recommended future studies for determining efficacy. *Psychopharmacology Bulletin,* 1973 (Special issue), 188-195.

Gadow, K. D. *Children on medication: A primer for school personnel.* Reston VA: The Council for Exceptional Children, 1978.

Grinspoon, L., & Singer, S.B. Amphetamines in the treatment of hyperkinetic children. *Harvard Educational Review,* 1973, *43*(4), 515-555.

Omenn, G.S. Genetic issues in the syndrome of minimal brain dysfusion. *Seminars in Psychology,* 1973, *5,* 5-17.

Dyslexia in Children and Adults

Griffiths, A. N., et al. Leave dyslexics in the classroom. *Academic Therapy Quarterly,* 1972, *8*(1), 57-65.

Vogel, S. A. *Syntactic abilities in normal and dyslexic children.* Baltimore: University Park Press, 1975.

Wagner, R. F. *Helping the word-blind: Effective intervention techniques for overcoming reading problems in older students.* West Nyack NY: Center for Applied Research in Education, 1976.

Emotionally Disturbed Children in School

Bower, E. M. *Early identification of emotionally handicapped children in school.* Springfield IL: Charles C Thomas, 1974.

Bunch, G. Emotionally disturbed children in the regular classroom. *Special Education in Canada,* 1970, *44*(3), 29-33.

Cowen, E. L., Trost, M. A., Lorion, R. P., Dorr, D., Izzo, L. D., & Isaacson, R. V. *New ways in school mental health: Early detection and prevention of school maladaptation.* New York: Human Sciences Press, 1975.

Hewett, F. M. *The emotionally disturbed child in the classroom.* Boston: Allyn & Bacon, 1968.

Pappanikou, A. J., & Paul, J. L. *Mainstreaming emotionally disturbed children.* Syracuse NY: Syracuse University Press, 1977.

Rubin, E. J. et al. *Emotionally handicapped children and the elementary school.* Detroit MI: Wayne State University Press, 1968.

Schultz, J. J. Integration of emotionally disturbed students: The role of the director of special education. *Exceptional Children,* 1973, *40,* 39-41.

Wood, M. M. *Developmental therapy—A textbook for teachers as therapists for emotionally disturbed young children.* Baltimore: University Park Press, 1975.

Hyperactivity and Its Management

Fairchild, T. N. *Managing the hyperactive child in the classroom.* Austin TX: Learning Concepts, 1976.

Grzynkowicz, W. *Meeting the needs of learning disabled children in the regular classes.* Springfield IL: Charles C Thomas, 1974.

Kunzweiler, C. E. Learning for behaviorally disoriented children in regular classrooms in middle schools. *Instructional Psychology,* 1974, *1,* 11-15.

Newman, R. G. The assessment of programs in the treatment of hyperaggressive children with learning disturbances within a school setting. *American Journal of Orthopsychiatry,* 1959, *29,* 633-643.

Learning Problems and Bilingual Children

Ching, D. C. *Reading and the bilingual child.* Newark DE: International Reading Association, 1976.

Ogletree, E. J., & Garcia, D. *Education of the Spanish-speaking urban child: A book of readings.* Springfield IL: Charles C Thomas, 1975.

Simoes, A., Jr. (Ed.). *The bilingual child: Research and analysis of existing educational themes.* New York: Academic, 1976.

Verma, G., & Bagley, C. *Race and education across cultures.* Stamford CT: Greylock Publishers, 1975.

Minimal Brain Dysfunction: Assessment and Management

Bersoff, D. N., Kobler, M., Fiscus, E., & Ankney, R. Effectiveness of special class placement for children labeled neurologically handicapped. *Journal of School Psychology,* 1972, *10*(2), 157-163.

Birch, H. G. *Brain damage in children.* Baltimore: Williams & Wilkens, 1964.

Cruikshank, W. M., & Hallahan, D. P. (Eds.). *Perceptual and learning disabilities in children: Psychoeducational practices.* Syracuse NY: Syracuse University Press, 1975.

Hallahan, D. P., Cruikshank, W. M. *Psychoeducational foundations of learning disabilities.* Englewood Cliffs NJ: Prentice-Hall, 1973.

Ley, D., & Metteer, R. The mainstream approach for the SLD child: A public school model. *Bulletin of the Orton Society,* 1974, *24,* 130-134.

Purpura, D. P. *Methodological approaches to the study of brain maturation and its abnormalities.* Baltimore: University Park Press, 1974.

Strauss, A. A., & Lehtinen, L. E. *Psychopathology and education of the brain injured child.* New York: Grune & Stratton, 1947.

Parents of Learning Disabled and Behavior Disordered Pupils

Love, L. R., Kaswan, J. W., & Bugental, D. B. *Troubled children: Their families, schools, and treatments.* Somerset NJ: Wiley-Interscience, 1974.

McCarthy, J. J., & McCarthy, J. F. *Learning disabilities.* Boston: Allyn & Bacon, 1969.

Southwest Educational Development Laboratory. *Working with parents of handicapped children.* Reston VA: The Council for Exceptional Children, 1976.

People with Learning Disabilities and Behavior Disorders

Axline, V.M. *Dibbs: In search of self.* Boston: Houghton Mifflin, 1965.

Beers, C. *A mind that found itself.* New York: Longmans, Green, 1917.

Bettelheim, B. *Paul and Mary: Histories from truants from life.* Garden City NY: Doubleday, 1961.
Hart, J., & Jones, B. *Where's Hannah?* New York: Hart Publishing, 1969.
Lewis, R. S. et al. *The other child.* New York: Harcourt, 1960.

Visual, Auditory, and Motor Perceptual Training

Barsch, R., *Achieving perceptual-motor efficiency* (Vol. 1). Seattle: Special Child Publications, 1967.
Cunningham, S.A., & Reagan, C.L. *Handbook of visual perception training.* Springfield IL: Charles C Thomas, 1972.
Edgington, R. Public school programming for children with learning disabilities. *Academic Therapy Quarterly,* 1966-67, *2*, 166ff.
Humphrey, J. H. *Improving learning ability through compensatory physical education.* Springfield IL: Charles C Thomas, 1976.

What Reading Disability Means for Pupils and Teachers

Birch, J. W. *Retrieving the retarded reader.* Indianapolis: Bobbs-Merrill, 1955.
Bond, G. L., & Tinker, M. A. *Reading difficulties: Their diagnosis and correction.* New York: Appleton-Century-Crofts, 1967.
Bush, W.J., & Waugh, K. W. *Diagnosing learning disabilities.* (2nd ed.). Columbus OH: Charles E. Merrill, 1976.
Enfield, M. L. *An alternative classroom approach to meeting special learning needs of children with reading problems.* Unpublished doctoral dissertation, University of Minnesota, 1976.
Moyer, S. B., & Newcomer, P. L. Reversals in reading diagnosis and remediation. *Exceptional Children,* 1977, *43*, 424-429.
Spache, G. D. *Investigating the issues of reading disabilities.* Rockleigh NJ: Allyn & Bacon, 1976.
Stromer, R. Remediating academic deficiencies in learning disabled children. *Exceptional Children,* 1977, *43*, 432-440.
Tarnopol, L. (Ed.). *Reading disabilities.* Baltimore: University Park Press, 1976.

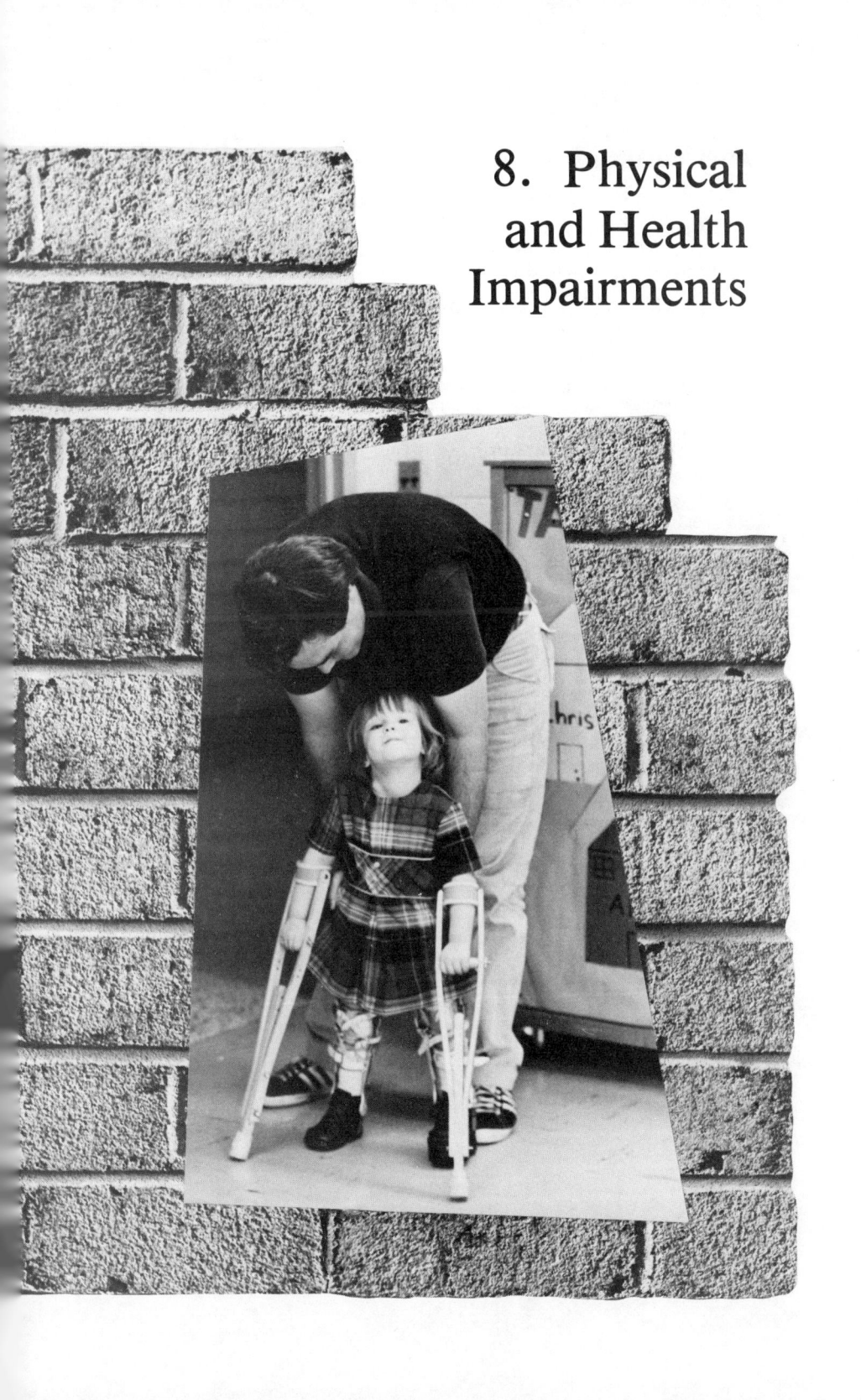

8. Physical and Health Impairments

CHAPTER OUTLINE

THE CHALLENGE TO EDUCATORS
  Legal Considerations
  Medical Considerations
  Social Welfare Considerations
  Educational Considerations
THE PERSON WHO IS CALLED PHYSICALLY OR HEALTH IMPAIRED
THE CONCEPT, TERMINOLOGY, AND SIGNIFICANCE OF CRIPPLING AND HEALTH PROBLEMS
PREVAILING VERSUS PREFERRED PRACTICES
  Guiding Principles for Preferred Practices
  Summary
THE BEGINNING OF SPECIAL EDUCATION FOR PHYSICALLY AND HEALTH IMPAIRED PUPILS
THE ROLE OF THE REGULAR CLASS TEACHER
  Teamwork with Specialists
    Instructional Activities
    Service Activities
    Coordination
    Record Keeping
    Parent Relations
    Professional Development
  Individualization of Instruction
    Curriculum Individualization
    Methods of Teaching
    Instructional Materials
    Organization for Instruction
    School Physical Plant
    Summary
EXAMPLES OF SPECIFIC SCHOOL PROGRAMS
  Village Nursery School
  Holladay Center for Handicapped Children
  Urbain Plavan School
  Marshall-University High School
  Clark County School District
COMPREHENSIVE PROGRAMING FOR PERSONS WITH PHYSICAL AND HEALTH IMPAIRMENTS
THE CONTINUING NEED FOR TEACHERS
SUGGESTIONS FOR STUDENTS AND INSTRUCTOR
TOPICAL BIBLIOGRAPHIES

THE CHALLENGE TO EDUCATORS

Mary F. Ramsey taught primary grades for 5 years, then for 18 years taught physically impaired pupils who were homebound, took a sabbatical leave for a year to visit school programs for physically impaired students, and taught 12 more years at a special public day school for physically impaired children and youth. Her remarks during the following 1976 interview illuminate the changes during a career as witnessed by one "very special" special teacher.

Q. What prompted you to become a special education teacher?
A. Although I was a regular class teacher for five years, my heart has always been in special education. When I was a child I had a sledding accident and I spent two years at home, with no help from the school with my school work. I spent all that time plugging along on my own, and the realization of what it meant to be handicapped always stayed with me. When I had the opportunity to work with physically handicapped* children I welcomed it.

Q. What were some of your first experiences as a special education teacher?
A. Back then, physically handicapped children were always taught at home. I was one of the first teachers of homebound instruction in the city and I drove all over town working with children. I worked with doctors, home-school visitors ("truant officers"), and regular class teachers to get my children back in school. It wasn't always easy, but many children got to regular classes in high school and some went on to college.

Q. Do you have any success stories to share?
A. Oh, my yes! As I said, I always felt that many of my students could be in the public school. I remember one girl in particular who had a number of operations on her face and she was quite upset by this. Even after she had very effective plastic surgery, her doctor routinely signed an excuse for her to be out of school. I tracked down the doctor—literally chased him all over the hospital—and explained to him how important the group setting of regular classes was to her social adjustment. The doctor said he hadn't thought of that, so together we got her back into school.

Q. What were some of your most difficult moments?
A. Back in the 1930's medical technology wasn't what it is today and some of my children died. It was terribly difficult for me when a child died . . . .

---

*In this book we will be consistent in calling these youngsters physically impaired. For educational purposes, physically impaired children and youth are defined as those with crippling conditions, illnesses, or other physical health problems which make some form of special education or school service necessary. Physical impairments primarily involving hearing, vision, and speech are dealt with in other chapters. The remainder are the subject of this chapter; the definition will be amplified later.

Q. What are some of the advantages of teaching special education?
A. Even though as a special education teacher back then I was always bucking the system, I had the opportunity to try more things with my children. Because I was somewhat anonymous I could be more creative. I think that is still true to some extent today.

Q. As a special education teacher did you face any particular problems?
A. I remember that in 1946 or '47 the city was considering cutting out the homebound program. We mobilized parents to write letters—and they wrote some dillies—and we saved the program. And once a colleague and I wanted to make a survey of all the physically handicapped children who had received homebound instruction. We wanted to assess their success as adults. But the board of education refused to pay the postage for mailing the survey forms. There were many administrative difficulties then.

Q. Over the years you've seen successful and unsuccessful teachers. What do you feel accounts for success?
A. When teachers were successful they showed genuine caring and empathy for all children. These teachers were exceptionally creative and they always made the child aware of what he could do.

Q. Mainstreaming, or the placement of exceptional children in the least restrictive alternative of the regular class, is an important issue for special educators today. Does the mainstreaming issue relate to your past experiences?
A. Back in the 1940's, I always thought that many of my students could be in public schools. Children who posed behavior problems tended to frighten the regular class teacher, and the basic problem with mainstreaming back then and today is that teachers are afraid when it comes to handicapped children. They don't know what to expect.

Q. What was the attitude of public school people when you tried to place your physically handicapped students in the regular class?
A. I found then, in the 1940's right up through the 1970's, that often public school people have difficulty accepting handicapped children. But I found that when I myself worked with the regular class teacher and helped her develop the necessary skills, I could pave the way for a more positive reception for my students.

Q. Many regular class teachers resist the inclusion of handicapped children because they say that it takes time from the rest of the students. How do you feel?
A. When I was a regular class teacher in 1938 I had a physically handicapped child in my class for a time. I was afraid and very uneasy about the situation, so I know how the regular class teacher feels. Yet, by and large, that is an unwarranted complaint in my opinion. The handicapped child

has a right to spend some time in the regular class and to get some individual attention from the teacher just as all children do. Possibly as the school population drops, class size will decrease and things will be better for handicapped children in regular classes. I hope so.

Q. If you were a fourth grade teacher today, would you want to work with a handicapped child in your classroom?
A. At this point in my life I could manage it. But I can see how less experienced teachers might be hesitant. Years ago special education teachers made more money than regular teachers. That created a gulf between them that still exists.

Q. What is your opinion of the mainstream movement?
A. The school experience should prepare all children to live well in the mainstream of society. It is our responsibility as teachers to make that happen, and placement in regular settings is one of the best ways I know.

Q. How have you seen special education change?
A. The changes that I see are for the better. Today almost every type of handicapped child is being served, and new programs have begun to include the multiply handicapped. Today in Pittsburgh the gifted, physically handicapped child is being served well.

Q. What are your concerns regarding special education?
A. I am concerned about the right to education laws and their definition of education. I feel that education must be redefined to include self help and independent living skills for the severely handicapped child—and the public must share this attitude. And we need to make a greater effort to train teachers to "educate" the severely involved child.

Q. Do you have any advice to special education teachers who are just starting out?
A. I would strongly encourage special education teachers to get at least one year's experience in the regular classroom. My years as a regular teacher gave me unusual perspective on learning and child development and helped me to be a much better special education teacher. But to both regular and special teachers I have the same message: You need dedication, empathy, creativity, and originality. And remember that confidence comes with years. (Aiello, 1976, pp. 4-5)

The following sections trace in more detail the legal, medical, social welfare, and educational backgrounds alluded to by Ms. Ramsey. They constitute the backdrop against which modern schooling for physically impaired children and youth needs to be seen if it is to be understood.

Legal Considerations

Children, youth, and adults with crippling and other health impairing conditions find that a body of federal and state laws and judicial decisions has grown about them and other exceptional pupils in recent years. Five of the most significant of them follow.

First, access to education increased. A 1971 US district court consent decree held that all mentally retarded children in Pennsylvania must be provided with education at public expense. In the same year a federal district court decision in the District of Columbia extended the principle to all handicapped children (Abeson, Bolick, & Hass, 1975). An explosion of suits in other states attained the same end. While all states had been providing special education for some physically handicapped and health impaired pupils, many others had been neglected because there was no firm mandate to serve them. That is being remedied rapidly.

Second, there is greater access to regular school buildings. The principle of "least restrictive alternative," a part of the aforementioned federal court findings and now embodied in federal laws and many state laws (Abeson et al., 1975), means that special educational programs must be integrated with regular educational programs. The concern is to individualize education for exceptional children and for all other children in the same class or group. For example, the Rehabilitation Act of 1973 (Section 504) prohibits any programs receiving federal funds from discriminating against handicapped individuals. A West Virginia suit, *Hairston v. Drosick, et al.,* rose out of the refusal of a public school to admit an otherwise eligible child to first grade because she was incontinent and had a noticeable limp. The school district had offered the parents of the child three alternatives to the usual admission. But the school district had not made use of a thorough assessment procedure prior to the segregated school placement decision and had not adequately informed the parents or involved them in the considerations leading to the decision. The federal district court ruled for the plaintiff, saying that a school must provide extensive procedural safeguards of the pupil's rights before a handicapped pupil may be assigned to a special school and, then, only as a last resort (American Association of School Administrators, 1976).

Third, public transportation is more accessible. Airlines, railways, buses, and taxis are under legal pressure to devise and implement ways to include in their service individuals who are unable to use conventionally designed transportation. In the spring of 1975, for instance, the Metropolitan Transportation Authority of New York City placed an order for 398 special buses with boarding sections that can be lowered to within 3 inches of the curb to make entering and leaving easier (*The New York Times,* Sunday, May 18, 1975).

Fourth, access to meetings, conferences, and to public buildings in general increased. Government office buildings, restaurants, libraries, theaters, museums, shopping areas—places where people in general might ordinarily go as part of everyday living—are enjoined by a combination of federal and state laws and by new and revised building codes to accommodate handicapped persons. As a demonstration of what could be done, in February 1976 the American Association for the Advancement of Science held its annual meeting in Boston. Physically disabled scientists were encouraged to attend. Hotels and other meeting places installed ramps and other facilities to make the sessions fully accessible. Transportation to an evening concert by the Boston Pops Orchestra was arranged in a bus equipped with a hydraulic lift. Symphony Hall had ramps to accommodate wheelchairs.

Fifth, there is greater access to employment. The Rehabilitation Act of 1973, latest in a series of such acts beginning around World War II, was a bill of rights for handicapped persons. Among other provisions, it established the rights of handicapped persons not to be discriminated against in employment, education, and other sectors of society that receive federal support. Working through state offices and through local schools and other public and private agencies, the Rehabilitation Services Administration helps support handicapped young people and adults on their way to independence through training, counseling, and job placement. These vocational rehabilitation services centered first on crippling conditions and began at age 16. Now they have extended to all human disabilities that might limit independent living, and they interact with school services, supplementing and articulating with public education.

These positive legal considerations and others are a far cry from not so long ago when physically handicapped persons were ridiculed and derogated and were, at best, the objects of a doubtful charity. The legal foundations for real equality of opportunity now are in place. They are interlocked with increased medical knowledge and with changes in the health professions.

Medical Considerations

The major concern of the health professions is increasing life expectancy. That is accomplished in two ways: (a) by preventing accidents, anomalies, and diseases and (b) by limiting the effects of the accidents, anomalies, and diseases that do occur.

Despite the efforts of the professions, however, success is only partial. Each advance in the health sciences, too, is bought at some price such as increased viability of impaired infants. The net result is that every wave of newcomers to kindergarten contains crippled and other health impaired children who need teaching, facilities, and services of special kinds.

Following are given the medical terms that identify those children with special needs who are most often found in educational programs for pupils with physical and other health impairing conditions. In order to discuss these pupils intelligently with parents and health workers, teachers should become familiar with the terms and their meanings.

It is important to point out three things immediately: (a) The names of the medical conditions give few clues to individual special educational needs; (b) only a minority of children with these conditions have any special education needs at all; and (c) there is no educational justification for grouping these children in school by their medical diagnoses. Each of those points will be elaborated later; the emphasis here is on supplying information about medical factors.

- *Allergies*—Adverse sensitivities or low tolerances to specific substances that are not problems to people in general. Reactions may take many forms; the most common are watering eyes, sneezing, nasal discharge, itching, or rash.
- *Arthritis*—Inflammation of a joint, making motion difficult, painful, and limiting its scope.
- *Asthma*—Repeated occurrence of wheezing coughs, difficult breathing, and feeling of constriction because of bronchial contractions.
- *Cerebral palsy*—Several forms of paralysis due to damage to the brain. The most common forms are *ataxic,* shown by marked inability to coordinate bodily movements; *athetoid,* appearing as slow, repeated movements of the limbs; and *spastic,* characterized by abrupt contractions of muscles or muscle groups, producing interference with and distortion of movement. All forms involve involuntary movements, and they appear in various combinations in different body locations depending on the nature and sites of the brain damage.
- *Congenital anomaly*—Any body organ or part existing in an abnormal form from the time of birth. It can include, for example, the whole body, as in dwarfism (unusually small size) or albinism (absence of pigmentation); can be limited to one part (absence of an arm or a leg); can be clefts (cleft lip to palate); or can affect internal parts like the spine or spinal cord (spina bifida), or malformation of heart.
- *Diabetes*—Disorder of metabolism of carbohydrates that is indicated by excessive amounts of glucose in the blood and urine.
- *Epilepsy*—Disorder of the brain sometimes resulting in convulsive movements and periods of unconsciousness of approximately 5 minutes and sometimes in brief lapses (up to 10 seconds) of consciousness or feelings of unreality, dizziness, or semiconsciousness.

- *Hemophilia*—A condition in which the normal blood clotting procedure is defective, with consequent difficulty in stopping bleeding when it occurs for any reason on the surface or within the body.
- *Leukemia*—A form of cancer affecting the balance of cells in the blood and, therefore, the normal functioning of the blood.
- *Poliomyelitis*—A viral infection that can result in the paralysis of body parts or systems, depending on the parts of the central nervous system attacked.
- *Rheumatic fever*—A disease that is characterized by fever, inflammation, and pain around the joints and inflammation of the muscle and valves of the heart.
- *Spina bifida*—An anomaly characterized by a defect in the bone that encases the spinal cord.
- *Traumatic injuries*—Impairments that result from accidents. They include a great variety of conditions ranging through amputations, paralyses, and limitations of body function.

It was previously noted that only a minority of children with these conditions need special education. Friedman and MacQueen (1971) attempted to sort out from the 45,000 children in 6 Iowa counties those whose physical impairments had educational and psychological relevance. They found that approximately 4 children out of 1,000 had such conditions. We have no exactly comparable data on the total number of children with medically significant physical impairments. It is our estimate that for every 20 children with medically significant conditions, perhaps 4 or 5 of them will be in need of special educational programing of some kind. The nature of that programing will be discussed later in this chapter.

Social Welfare Considerations

Teachers who work with crippled and health impaired pupils receive information and help from two kinds of organized volunteer groups. The first is associations of interested citizens whose objective is to assure that proper health, education, and social services are readily available. The second kind of organized volunteer group is made up of handicapped persons themselves.

The former include such organizations as the Muscular Dystrophy Association of America, National Easter Seal Society for Crippled Children and Adults, National Epilepsy League, National Foundation-March of Dimes, and United Cerebral Palsy Associations. Incorporated agencies such as these carry on service and public awareness activities through their national, state, and local affiliates. They prepare and distribute suggestions for teachers and other professionals who work directly with handicapped children. They offer counsel to parents. In a number of cases they distribute curriculum materials to be used in regular grades to help all pupils to understand impairments and to be at ease with their exceptional classmates.

Organized groups of physically handicapped persons also do many of the same things as the above associations, often in cooperation with them. At the same time these groups have thrusts of their own. Illustrative is the work of one local chapter of Open Doors for the Handicapped, which during one month was engaged in the following enterprises:

- Arranged for 45 members and friends to attend a major league baseball game.
- Presented a slide show on Rhodesia, Malawi, Kenya, and South Africa for members and friends.
- Had a meeting of its subcommittee on barrier free design.
- Sent a delegation to the annual state meeting of the Governor's Committee on Employment of the Handicapped.
- Informed members of a scheduled lecture on health care.
- Announced the group would host the first of four regional meetings to identify major problem areas in providing opportunities for the handicapped.
- Took part in and invited local employers to join in a seminar on affirmative action, particularly the regulation that "every Government contractor must prepare and maintain an affirmative action program for the employment and advancement of qualified handicapped workers."
- Had 30 members attend a meeting with a representative of the Regional Office for Civil Rights, Department of Health, Education and Welfare, to learn in detail the implementation procedures for Section 504 of the Rehabilitation Act of 1973.
- Had a delegation attend a reunion at a regional rehabilitation center.
- Gave members information on a new mode of transportation, a pedestrian vehicle, that allows a handicapped person in a wheelchair to load and unload himself unaided. A ramp is part of the machine. It travels over hard surface roads, on sidewalks, up and down inclines, and through gravel, sand, mud, and snow.
- Published editorial comments on the problems associated with being handicapped and a member of a racial minority.
- Published a note speculating that the wavy signature of Rhode Island Governor Steven Hopkins on the Declaration of Independence may have been because of cerebral palsy. On placing the deciding signature on the document he is reported to have said, "My hand may be shaky, but my heart is firm."

The two kinds of volunteer groups also have three other forms of activity in common. First, they engage vigorously in advocacy for impaired children and adults, without regard to the nature of the impairment. Second, they encourage continuing education with respect to impairments for health, education, and welfare professionals. And third, they press both government and private foundations to sponsor research aimed at preventing or ameliorating impairments.

Both regular class and specialist teachers find these organizations to be valuable allies in helping to assure that exceptional pupils and all other pupils obtain high quality education. In addition, such agencies benefit from participation by teachers in their membership and on their advisory committees.

Educational Considerations

From the point of view of instructional needs there is no justification for assembling children with crippling and health impairments into one group for schooling. Actually, no more heterogeneous array of pupils could be found, educationally speaking.

Mullins (1971), one of the first to call attention to this problem, spoke of "untenable groupings." She said:

> Many teachers have reported an I.Q. range of over one hundred points in their classes. It is not unusual to find a gifted child with muscular dystrophy sitting next to a cerebral palsied child with unmeasured intelligence or vice versa. In the same class there may be children with communication problems such as blindness or deafness who may also be physically handicapped. There will often be one so-called "brain-damaged wall-climber." The age range of such a class may extend from pre-puberty through adolescence. (p. 15)

She pointed out that

> The best teachers cannot supply the kind of group cohesiveness and peer motivation essential to social learning in such a heterogenous class. (p. 15)

She called the teacher's task of individualized modification of methods, curriculum, and materials "gargantuan."

What brought such youngsters together initially in special classes were noneducational considerations. First, many needed to be transported if they were to attend school at all. It was more convenient and economical to transport them all to one central place. Second, many required frequent and intensive occupational, physical, and speech therapy, plus medical consultation and nursing and dietary supervision. It proved more feasible to group those therapies and related health services in one place and to bring the pupils to them. Third, many of the pupils could not manage stairs and many used mobility aids such as crutches, walkers, and wheelchairs. To design and construct one school building to accommodate those factors seemed far less a problem than to make all existing and future school buildings barrier free. So transportation; professional, health related care; and architectural accessibility were the factors responsible for the original tendency to cluster crippled and other health impaired pupils in their own special schools or classes.

Even with special transportation and facilities it was not feasible to move some children. Self evident examples were those in traction or iron lungs. Also, there were always some children who could be accommodated in their local schools with modest adaptations. By the late 1940's it had become customary to speak of a need for a spectrum of six types of school settings essential for adequate educational opportunity for physically and health impaired pupils. These were:

1. *Regular class adjustments* for pupils who can do the work of the regular school if minor adjustments in such things as seating, scheduling, and instructional materials can be made.
2. *Special day classes in regular schools* for pupils who can attend a regular school but who need a specialist to teach them all or most of the day.
3. *Special day schools* for pupils who need a school building and equipment totally adjusted to their needs.
4. *Homebound instruction* for pupils who must remain at home either in bed or with extremely limited activity for periods of time long enough to interfere seriously with their education unless special teaching is brought to them at home.
5. *Hospital instruction* for pupils who must be hospitalized for medical treatment on a 24 hour per day basis for enough time to constitute a major interruption in education and yet who are well enough for instruction.
6. *Residential schools* for pupils who are undergoing long term convalescence or rehabilitation that necessitates living in a specialized setting adapted for that purpose.

These arrangements are still as important as ever. All have been changing in one significant way, however, since the middle and late 1940's. They have moved into closer contact with regular education, while maintaining the special qualities needed by the exceptional children and youth they serve.

An early pacesetter in the move toward inclusion was the Rancho Los Amigos Rehabilitation Center for Children (Wendland, 1972). The Center was among the first to arrange with a local school district to receive physically impaired pupils into its regular grades while the children lived at the Center in order to receive medical and other services they needed.

Technological advances, ingenious teachers, and helpful classmates brought even homebound pupils into closer contact with regular school activities. Home-school telephone hookups became generally available in the early 1950's. The child at home was able to participate in class and teacher dialogues, listening and responding and asking for attention by flashing a light on the in-class sender-receiver. Teachers adapted by talking about what they were putting on the chalkboard or about the visuals they were using. Classmates carried the portable telephone apparatus from room to room and plugged it in. Other classmates carried books and assignments to the child's home and back, thus also maintaining a thread of direct social contact.

There have been abrupt fluctuations in the nature of the physically and health impaired population that make use of the above facilities. That is because of changes in health care, some of which were mentioned earlier. When special schooling of this kind began, for example, it catered to pupils with "lowered vitality." Improved nutrition, the almost complete abolition of childhood tuberculosis, and surgical procedures that effectively repair heart anomalies in the first few months of life are the kinds of influences that brought marked changes in the proportions of such pupils. At one time, the most common of the crippling conditions was poliomyelitis. Vaccines have sharply reduced its incidence. At the same time cerebral palsy, which leaves children with much more complex educational problems than polio did, has come to the forefront as the most prevalent crippling condition seen in special education programs.

Today's education for children who are physically impaired and who have health problems is projected, therefore, against four main considerations.

First, it is, educationally speaking, an "artificial" grouping of children because there are no common threads of special instructional needs that provide a rationale for bringing them together.

Second, a spectrum of administrative or operational school settings has come to be recognized as needed for these pupils. The spectrum ranges from extraschool situations like the home or the hospital through various levels of integration within the orbit of the schools.

Third, there is a growing trend to move physically and health impaired pupils into their local schools for all their education, special or regular. That direction was initiated more than three decades ago. It has accelerated sharply in the contemporary context of court decisions and laws that press for implementation of the least restrictive alternative principle in educational programing for all exceptional children.

Fourth, major changes have taken place in the makeup of the pupils classed for educational purposes as physically handicapped and health impaired. The alterations are related to changes in health care, for the most part, though some (the inclusion, for example, of pregnancy and child abuse) reflect modifications in social attitudes and behavior, too.

This amalgam of background educational conditions, when joined with the legal, medical, and social welfare factors enumerated earlier, poses a formidable set of educational challenges. The following sections will be devoted to showing how regular class teachers and the specialists who work with them are responding to those challenges.

THE PERSON WHO IS CALLED PHYSICALLY AND HEALTH IMPAIRED

The very heterogeneity of this group makes it impossible to limit our discussion to two or three individuals. But some feel for the range and the intensity of the school and daily living crises they must surmount can be found in the following three stories. The first is about Kelly Segars of Toledo, Ohio; the second is about Lisa Blumberg of Winchester, Massachusetts; and the third is about Alan King of Yakima County, Washington.

Lack of Pain No Pleasure for Kelly

Toothaches, stubbed toes and all of childhood's bumps and bruises are meaningless to her. The word "hurt" really isn't in her personal dictionary.

Put together, the pages of her medical history are as thick as two volumes of any encyclopedia—even though she's only eight years old.

She's Kelly Segars of Toledo, Ohio, a sparkling child with a mischievous twinkle in her eye. Kelly is unusual in that she has a congenital insensitivity to pain. This unique handicap doesn't provide her with the warning system that pain gives to each of us. As a result, Kelly's first active years were filled with accidents. She broke bones in her legs without feeling any sensations, cut herself as all children do, but was totally unaware. Normal childhood injuries thus became seriously aggravated and were noticed only when Kelly's mother was able to actually see physical signs of abnormalities. By the time she was six, being in the hospital was a way of life. By that age she had already had eight operations.

The abnormal amount of hospital attention plus her physical insensitivity to pain of any sort helped create behavioral and emotional problems for Kelly both at home and in school. For example: How do you cope with a child who can stand barefoot on a hot radiator to get her way?

Kelly's complex situation led her to be excluded from school and play situations with other children her age.

Through a relation Kelly's story came to the attention of Anderson Industries of Toledo, Ohio. The company set aside some funds to help her through the Maumee Children's Society. After visits to several facilities throughout the country, Mrs. Segars chose the Home For Crippled Children because of its national reputation in comprehensive child care.

Kelly entered the Home in December, 1973. Like all Home For Crippled Children's children or young adults, Kelly was assigned a coordinator responsible for supervising a comprehensive rehabilitation program designed to fit her special needs and to return her to her home community as quickly as possible.

According to Kelly's coordinator, Mrs. Beate Vogl, "The main thrust of Kelly's program here was to give her as many experiences of normal childhood as possible which included accepting limits and decreasing her hyperactivity."

Kelly was reinforced for using her eyes and her mind to replace pain as an aid to keeping herself safe.

Equally important factors in Kelly's program at the Home were helping her Mother learn some behavior management skills and also helping her feel more at ease with the burden of Kelly's physical impairment without being overwhelmed.

Less than a year after her admission to the Home, Kelly was readmitted to school in Toledo. Mrs. Segars reports Kelly is doing well in reading and her behavior continues to be acceptable.

"It was a great relief for Kelly to receive such valuable training to deal with her particular handicaps. The problem is not as overwhelming as it once was and I definitely feel the Home For Crippled Children was a turning point for both Kelly and me," Mrs. Segars says. (Urbanowicz, 1975, p. 182).

Lisa Blumberg, who was born with cerebral palsy, tells how her handicap effected her education and makes recommendations for mainstreaming exceptional students.

The Case for Integrated Schooling*

Although I have an obvious and, in some respects, limiting physical disability as a result of having been born with cerebral palsy, I have always attended schools with nondisabled students. Through six years in public schools, private schools in two different locations and college, I have had good times and bad times, but I have always been glad that I have been in regular schools. I feel that I benefitted academically, emotionally and socially from having gone to regular schools rather than to special ones.

One of the biggest decisions parents of a child with a physical or sensory disability will ever have to make is deciding on the type of schooling their child should have. Because disabled children are individuals with individual needs, it is ridiculous to think that there is one universally correct decision. There are, no doubt, some physically or sensorially disabled children for whom special schools may indeed be the best answer. However, I think that too often children who should be in regular schools and would do well there are sent to special schools for reasons that are ill-founded or unjustified.

---

*Reprinted from THE EXCEPTIONAL PARENT magazine, copyright© Psy-Ed Corporation, 1973, Room 708 Statler Office Building, 20 Providence Street, Boston, Massachusetts 02116.

Mechanical Problems Solvable

Often the roadblocks that seem to stand in the way of a disabled child attending a regular school are not real or can, with a little ingenuity, be circumvented. A child who does not write legibly can do his written work on a typewriter. A child who walks very slowly should be able to arrange to leave each class two minutes early so he can get to the next one on time. Recently, I heard about a girl with polio who was discouraged from going to the neighborhood school because there were three steps down to the cafeteria and she could not manage steps unassisted. Apparently, it did not occur to anyone that another student could help her down those three steps or, alternatively, if worse came to worse, she could eat lunch in a classroom.

I also know of an instance where a deaf student was advised not to apply to a full-fledged college despite the fact that she had always done well in school. This was because she could not take notes in class since she read lips; when she put her head down to write, she would not be able to see what the instructor was saying. Three solutions to her problem immediately come to my mind. First, she could copy another person's notes after class. Second, she could provide someone with carbon paper so that their notes could be automatically duplicated for her. Third, and perhaps this is the best solution since it lets her be completely independent, she could just jot down topic sentences and then immediately after class write down everything else of importance that she remembered. This, after all, is what many psychologists and social workers do who must keep detailed records on their patients and yet do not want to write in front of them. I say all this only to show that in so many cases, all it takes is a little thought or inventiveness to solve the mechanical problems presented by a disability.

Teasing

Parents may be hesitant about sending their child to a regular school for fear that the other children will ridicule him for his disability. From my experience, I can say this fear is basically unfounded. In elementary school, for example, my classmates were all surprisingly accepting of me and I had many friends. My disability was, in fact, rarely mentioned to me by children who knew me. When it was mentioned, it was virtually always just a matter-of-fact acknowledgement of it rather than any expression of hostility towards me. Like most children, I was sometimes teased but usually this teasing was only a gesture of friendliness. I would have felt left out if I had not received it. Also, the things kids teased me about were almost always unrelated to my disability. For example, in sixth grade kids used to make fun of me because I would not tell anyone my middle name.

I cannot truthfully say that all through school I have always been "just part of the gang." In my high school years especially, I think my disability did put some distance between my classmates and me although this was no doubt partly due to my growing awareness of myself and my disability.

However, although many of my relationships have been more superficial than I would have liked, for the most part I have gotten along well with people in school.

Helpful Friends

I have found that the others in the class are usually willing to offer at least minimal assistance to a disabled student. My friends have always helped me in countless small ways. In high school, for example, someone normally carried my books for me when we changed classes because I could go up and down stairs more easily and get to my next class faster if I was not carting along a load of books. The one thing that a disabled student should remember is to ask different people for help rather than the same one over and over so that nobody is ever unfairly burdened.

Therapy at School?

One reason advanced for making use of special schools is that the child will be able to receive various kinds of therapy there for his disability. However, this therapy takes place during the school day so that the amount of academic time a child receives is less than he would receive in a regular school. This, if nothing else, puts the child in a special school at an educational disadvantage. I am not knocking the value of therapy but I think parents should look for it elsewhere than at school. When I was younger, I received speech, physical and occupational therapy weekly at an orthopedic hospital. Sometimes I did have to leave school half an hour early to get to it, but this cut into my school time was minimal.

I think that sometimes the most therapeutic thing, at least for a physically disabled child, is to be confronted with real life situations. Today, stairs are absolutely no problem for me. As long as there is a railing, I can go up and down flight after flight without thinking twice about it. This is because I have always been in places where I have had constant practice with them. At first, in school, I needed other people to help me manage stairs. But then, as I gained more experience, I became able to go up and down them by myself. I can almost guarantee, however, that if I had gone to special schools that were only on one level and had had my experience with stairs confined to the model steps in a physical therapy room and to the old tried and true stairs at home, I would not have gone up and down stairs unassisted to this day.

Teacher Assumptions

A child with a disability in a regular class will probably be categorized by the teacher as a disabled child. However, the teacher will probably make no assumptions about the class as a whole. When he or she is teaching the group, the disabled child in the class will receive instruction unclouded by any prejudice the teacher has against the disabled. As long as the teacher is speaking to the whole group, the disabled child will, in effect, be treated as a "normal" child, and this is all to the good. In a special school, on the other hand, the teacher will see the entire class as "handicapped," "special," "disabled" or whatever he or she chooses to call them. Even a relatively broad-minded teacher will have some assumptions, be they positive or negative, about the disabled and will teach the class accordingly.

In other words, a disabled child in a special class will be receiving instruction geared to disabled children, based on the premises the teacher has about them. It may be thought that those who work with people with disabilities are far less prejudiced against such people than most people, but from my experience, this is manifestly not so. Many teachers who have never had a noticeably disabled person in the classroom before have treated me as far more of an individual than have many of the therapists with whom I have come in contact. (Of course, stereotyping the nondisabled who work with the disabled is as wrong and as narrow-minded as stereotyping the disabled. I do know of therapists and special educators who are sincere in what they are doing and have enlightened views about the disabled.) Thus, parents should be aware that a disabled child in a regular school may in fact be less a victim of categorization than a disabled child in a special school.

Playing with Friends

For younger children especially, friendship with the other children in the neighborhood is extremely important. A disabled child will far more likely be accepted in the neighborhood play group if he attends the same school or at least the same type of school as the other children. He will less likely be seen, both by others and by himself, as overwhelmingly different if he has a bond of commonality with them. Contacts and familiarity in school will help in socialization after school. As a child, most of my friends' talk revolved around school happenings. If I had gone to a special school, I would have been barred from most of these conversations. Sending a disabled child to a special school creates a further distinction between him and the neighborhood children. Also, since a child usually must travel some distance to a special school, he may get home later than the other children and simply not have time to play with them. If the neighborhood children do not know him or only see him very infrequently, they may indeed be hostile towards him.

Fear of the Unknown

It is human nature that people tend to fear or be suspicious of types of people with whom they do not have frequent interaction. A disabled child in a special school is surrounded by other disabled children. He may come to fear children who do not have disabilities because of his limited contact with them. Brush encounters with nondisabled children may only serve to reinforce this feeling. Fear is apt to communicate itself. When nondisabled children perceive that a disabled child fears them, they are apt to be hostile toward him, and so a vicious circle is begun.

Unless a person with a disability is expected to lead an unbelievably narrow life—working in sheltered workshops, having only disabled friends, etc.,—he will at some time or other have to start dealing with the nondisabled world. It will be much easier for him to start dealing with it in early childhood than later on when fear and self-consciousness may have built up. I am sure that many people who have gone to special schools make the transition from a disabled world to the nondisabled world very smoothly, but countless others may never make this transition successfully. Also, if a person has gone to a special school, he may wrongly believe that he cannot function in the nondisabled world. I think this is a real psychological danger of special schooling.

Beneficial to All

The disabled child is not the only one who benefits when he attends a regular school. Nondisabled children will be far less likely to build up misconceptions about the disabled if they have them as classmates. People who have gone to school with a visibly disabled person and who have seen him experience much of what they have experienced and seen him respond to things in almost exactly the same way as they have will be far less prejudiced than someone who has never had real contact with anyone disabled.

Many of my college friends tell me that they were uneasy with me when they first met me. I resent this, but I cannot really blame them because I am the first person with an obvious physical disability most of them have ever known. It is no wonder that they are at first as unsure of my reactions as they would be of a Martian's. However, if throughout school they had had one or two disabled children in their classes, I think they would have been far more comfortable in relating to me or any other disabled person.

Exposing nondisabled children to children with physical or sensory disabilities can only make them more accepting of all kinds of people. It will provide them with living proof that people with limitations in some areas do have talents and abilities. I think that prejudice against the disabled will only begin to be eliminated when significant numbers of disabled children go to school side by side with nondisabled children.

I am glad I have attended regular schools. I believe that sending a disabled child to a regular school is good for the child, for the others in his class and, indirectly, for disabled people as a whole. It is the goal of many people to someday see persons with disabilities fully integrated into society. What better and more necessary place to start than in the schools? (Blumberg, 1973, pp. 15-17)

Following is the story of Alan King, who was born with cerebral palsy.

Each One Can Learn

Alan King was born 18 years ago with cerebral palsy. He cannot walk or speak. The only muscles he can accurately control are the muscles in his left foot.

Yet Alan now enjoys communicating with others. He is a registered voter in Yakima County, Washington. He has a job delivering mail from his wheelchair, at the school where he learned his present skills.

Before Alan began his self-help and academic program at the Department's Yakima Valley School nine years ago, he spent most of his time in bed. He was limited to a positive or negative motion in responding to questions. Like the 150 other severely disabled residents of the school, he needed highly individualized treatment.

Joe Fram, the school's superintendent, says Alan has one of the best attitudes he's ever seen; his disability is not holding him back, and the institution isn't either.

In years past, people as extensively handicapped as Alan were given little more than custody. That has all changed. Yakima Valley School staff work closely with specially trained teachers from the Selah School District to provide continuity in a total program specifically tailored for each student.

Alan's program began with intensive self-help training to determine his capabilities and goals. Perhaps his most difficult problem at first was simple communication. Staff and teachers can recall spending hours with Alan just trying to figure out exactly what he wanted or needed.

About four years ago Rita Stilwater, a teacher at the school, opened the door to communication for Alan by introducing him to the Bliss Language System. This system is composed of some 100 basic language symbols which, in combination, can convey any meaning. Charles Bliss created the system while a prisoner of war during World War II, hoping it might become an international symbol language. The Ontario Crippled Children's Center adapted it several years ago for use by non-verbal cerebral palsy patients. Stilwater obtained the adaptation for Alan.

A metal frame was attached to the foot of Alan's wheelchair. The frame holds six rollers covered with Bliss symbols. Alan asks and answers questions by moving his left foot along the rollers to the symbols needed to express his thought. With the Bliss System enabling him to communicate, Alan's academic progress was accelerated dramatically.

Like other students who demonstrate good scholastic progress, Alan became eligible for employment at the school. And he didn't have to take a civil service examination to get the postman's job he now holds. Every afternoon he reports to the mailroom for items to deliver on his daily rounds. Pushing his wheelchair in reverse with his left foot, he carries the mail in a pouch attached to the back of the chair. Everyone at the school knows Alan's job, and all maintain he is very conscientious about his work. He makes few mistakes, and receives a modest salary for his services.

When Alan turned 18, some staff took him to the Yakima County Auditor's Office where he registered to vote. He plans to study the field carefully before he declares a party affiliation and casts his ballot in a regular election.

Stilwater says Alan will soon be ready to leave the school. She hopes he will go to the Interlake nursing facility in Seattle, where persons with cerebral palsy can become part of a specially designed sheltered working environment.

Fram says programs at Yakima Valley School are constantly being modified and individualized, with staff and teachers working cooperatively toward maximum competence for each student.

"A physically disabled person is not necessarily mentally disturbed," he says. "Among our residents you'll find the same variety of personality characteristics as in any population. We temper our work with compassion, understanding and patience. We care about the residents here as individuals, and we do our best to meet their complex needs." (State of Washington Department of Social and Health Services, 1976, pp. 11-18)

Kelly's situation is a striking example of the crucial part a residential center can play. In this case intensive and relatively short term training readied a child to return with self confidence and with the necessary coping skills to be successful in a previously incompatible regular school. Moreover, Kelly's overtaxed mother found help toward becoming a more competent parent through aid from the same agency.

Lisa's report about herself helps to lay to rest some of what she calls "ill-founded or unjustified" beliefs about the need for separate and highly specialized elementary and secondary schools or classes, at least for many physically handicapped students. Self knowledge, understanding nonhandicapped people, and being understood by them rate high in importance and are more readily attainable if one attends regular schools, in her view.

The story of Alan King highlights the difference nine years of individualized education can make, even after nine earlier years of near vegetation in bed. This kind of dramatic move from virtually complete dependency to almost full self maintenance shows the power of personalized instruction in the hands of competent teachers.

THE CONCEPT, TERMINOLOGY, AND SIGNIFICANCE OF CRIPPLING AND SPECIAL HEALTH PROBLEMS

Definitions of exceptional conditions that have acceptance over a wide range of responsible organizations and agencies appear in Handbook VI of the US Office of Education's State Educational Records and Reports Series (Putnam & Chismore, 1970). The Handbook gives the following meanings for these key terms:

> Crippled—Individuals with a physical impairment of a type which might restrict normal opportunity for education or self-support. This term is generally considered to include individuals having impairments caused by

a congenital anomaly (e.g., cleft palate, clubfoot, absence of some member, etc.), impairments caused by disease (e.g., poliomyelitis, bone tuberculosis, encephalitis, and other neurological involvements which may result in conditions such as cerebral palsy or epilepsy, etc.), and impairments caused by accidents (e.g., fractures or burns which cause contractures, etc.).

Pupils with special health problems—Pupils identified by professionally qualified personnel as having—either permanently or periodically—less than the usual amount of strength, energy and endurance and hence may need appropriate modifications in their educational programs. Such a condition might result from chronic illness or environmental causes, e.g., diabetes, epilepsy, cardiac disease, and lead poisoning. (p. 319)

Definitions of physical conditions, like those listed here and earlier in this chapter, do make a fair start at identifying youngsters who might need highly individualized teaching. What is much more needed by teachers, though, is a unifying concept related to education, some way to think about all these manifestations of impairment that can be related directly to educational needs. How does *impairment* relate to *handicap*, especially *educational handicap*?

Stevens (1962) was one of the first to spell out the differences among *impairment, disability,* and *handicap,* and to show the linkages between their physiological, psychological, and educational manifestations in a way useful to teachers.

According to Stevens, *impairment* is the physical defect itself, the actual condition of the tissue. Examples would be the absence of fingers, a severed nerve, a port-wine nevus (a "birthmark" of purplish colored skin on the face), diabetes, or cardiac disease.

Disability is different from impairment in that it is not a matter of tissue. Instead, it is a matter of function. It is literally a lack of some ability. It is a limitation of the behavior directly dependent upon the impairment. To continue to use the same illustrations, a disability associated with absence of fingers is, in a general sense, lack of digital dexterity. More specifically, there would be disability associated with ordinary writing or typing. The severed nerve is an impairment that could result, for instance, in a flaccid hand, producing the same disability that the absence of fingers did. Diabetes can produce unconsciousness. Cardiac disease inhibits energetic activity. The port-wine nevus, however, could not be considered to give rise to a disability, for no functional failure or limitation is associated with it. So impairments can exist without disabilities.

Sometimes, for primarily psychological reasons, individuals find themselves unable to carry out some ordinary bodily movement. Perhaps the back is bent forward and cannot be straightened, as in camptocormia, a form of hysteria appearing most often in soldiers. The affected individual walks with apparently great difficulty. Yet there is no actual tissue impairment. All the skeletal and neuromuscular equipment essential for an upright posture is intact and in good working order. But the bent back syndrome continues. That is an example of a disability without an impairment being present.

A *handicap,* then, is measured by the extent to which an impairment, a disability, or both gets in the way of normal living, including acquiring an education. Handicap is highly personal, for it is the name for an individual's own reactions to the presence of an impairment or disability. The central concept of handicap is this: It consists of the individual's own interpretation of the impairment and the individual's ability to live with that interpretation. Many people have impairments and disabilities. Only some people are handicapped because of them.

Understanding these differentiations is of prime importance to teachers for four reasons. They demonstrate, for one thing, that handicap is not an inevitable accompaniment to impairment or disability. Does Lisa Blumberg have a handicap? Tim Feiock (Pennsylvania State Education Association, 1975) lost the use of both legs as a result of spinal damage in a violent motorcycle accident. Though in a wheelchair he has a full time regular position as a teacher at Canton Elementary School—a physical education teacher! Is Tim handicapped?

A second reason for becoming conversant with these differentiations is that they form a foundation upon which a teacher can build interpretations for counseling exceptional pupils and other pupils as well. Such a foundation is of practical value when conferring with parents. The distinctions can be explained to them, and their knowledge of the differences can help them deal with their children in more rational ways.

The third reason this concept is important for teachers is its value in working with other specialists. Physicians, typically, focus their concerns on the impairment itself.* They try to correct or ameliorate the tissue problem. Physical therapists and occupational therapists attend mostly to the disability. They help the child to gain or to recover as much function as possible through practice. They assist the youngster to learn to use prostheses and to master daily living skills whose acquisition might otherwise be jeopardized because of the impairment. Counselors work with the child chiefly in developing a sound self concept and a positive feeling of personal worth and self determination. That bears directly on the child's interpretation of any actual impairment and it attempts to strengthen the child's ability to live as an effective person with that

---

*Physicians who are members of the small but growing speciality called rehabilitation medicine can be counted upon to take a broader view, interesting themselves in psychological, social, educational, and vocational factors in the case in addition to medical factors.

interpretation. The teacher's work interrelates with the tasks of the other professionals just named. The impairment-disability-handicap construct provides a conceptual framework for cooperative and coordinated professional interactions.

The fourth reason, the most important of all for teachers, is that this conceptual model can help them see how to formulate and coordinate individualized education programs for pupils in terms of minimizing handicaps, regardless of the pupil's impairment, as such. Teachers, therefore, bend their efforts toward helping the pupils acquire and stockpile educational assets that can be employed both immediately and in the future to blunt the thrust of impairment and to reduce or remove the weight of any handicap.

PREVAILING VERSUS PREFERRED PRACTICES

In other chapters the material under this topic appears in a double column. Prevailing practices are listed to the left, paralleled by alternative preferred practices.

The status of special education for children with crippling and health disabilities does not lend itself well to that form of treatment. That is due to the previously mentioned heterogeneity of this collection of pupils and to their great variety of service needs, apart from education. (Service needs refer, for example, to health care and therapies, food, transportation, school furniture, personal hygiene, and social work. Two children may require virtually the same instruction and curriculum but differ greatly in their service requirements. The reverse may be true, too.) There are also so many ways in which both service and educational needs are being met that it is questionable if modal "prevailing" practices as such can be validly identified.

This section, therefore, consists of six principles that can aid in establishing whether or not a given practice is a preferred practice. That is, a teacher can look at a practice and at the principles and ask the question, Is the practice in harmony with these principles, not in violation of any of them? A positive response should encourage one to rate the given practice as "preferred."

Guiding Principles for Preferred Practices

The first principle is that *regular school classes are the initial placements of all children who do not present insurmountable transportation problems.* This means that if transportation to a special school is feasible, it must also be feasible to a regular school. If the regular school presents architectural barriers, they should be removed. If attendant and aid services are needed by the pupil and are available in a special school or class, they should also be made available to the regular school in order to support the child's attendance there. In short, special education staff, facilities, and support services that make attendance feasible in a special school or class should be redeployed to make the same available in the regular class setting.

Another way to accomplish this is to convert the special school to a regular school by redistricting attendance areas and adding instructional space, if that is necessary. This allows the special school to take on a new role, with its predominant pupil population one that does not require special education. For an example of how this move was made by a special school for deaf pupils, see Chapter 11, the Lexington School.

Second, *keep schooling a continuous and full time process adjusted in intensity to the child's vitality level and reaction speed.* If a child needs to be admitted to a hospital, education should follow the child there. The criterion as to whether to provide teaching should be whether the child is able to take instruction, not how long the hospital stay will be. The decision about whether the child is ready for teaching, and the amount of teaching, should be a joint one of the physician and the specialist teacher. Also, therapies and medical examinations and conferences should seldom interrupt the child's school day, but should be scheduled before or after school or on weekends. As will be seen in the next principle discussed, the slowed physical pace of many pupils causes their school program to move at a lower than typical rate. It should not be decelerated any more by nonschool matters that ought to be arranged outside of regular school time.

Third, *the pupils should attain self regulation with regard to exertion and scheduling of activities.* Many of these pupils, while still quite young, are required by their physical condition to husband their strength and to budget their energy output. Others, while having as much sheer energy as any child, simply cannot move themselves with the speed and coordination that intact bodies and brimming energy banks allow for other pupils. It is preferred practice, according to this principle, to give youngsters opportunities to test themselves. All children should be given free rein to find out for themselves about the effects their disabilities have on their daily lives, if there are any.

These two anecdotes from Mullins (1971) are relevant:

> A mildly cerebral palsied boy from a small town was assigned to a classroom for the physically handicapped on the ground floor of a neighboring city school. The teacher (in the new classroom) said she could not integrate him into her intellectually limited class since he had superior intelligence. "When he is bored," she said, "I just have him run upstairs to the library to get some books." If he can run upstairs, why is he in the special class? (p. 15)

> Two hemaplegic boys, who play football after school, are assigned by their doctor to a small high school for disabled students. They, and some

of their classmates, have begged for a transfer to their neighborhood schools, but neither school officials or the physicians have been willing to consider modifications. (p. 15)

The same reasonable monitoring that any child needs should apply for those with crippling and health impairments. Overprotection should be avoided.

Fourth, *organize educational programs in terms of the pupils' educational needs; match both short and long range instructional designs to the pupils' own cognitive rates, their learning styles, and their present and projected educational achievements.* Adherence to this principle (which was discussed earlier) is incompatible, for example, with organizing classes specifically for children with cerebral palsy or any other such category. The only thing such children have in common is a medical diagnosis that tells little if anything about their educational abilities and requirements. Likewise, it is a violation of this principle to group children because they all need physical therapy, even though they represent a variety of medical diagnoses. Full compliance with this principle calls first for making decisions about each child's educational program and school placement just as though there were no crippling or health impairment present. Then, it calls for adjusting that program and that school setting until it takes into account any impairment the child has. Often it proves a less formidable task than it seemed at first. For instance:

> Jake Cappa, a teacher in the Riverview School District (near Pittsburgh, Pennsylvania), and father of a son suffering spina bifida, said a cooperative school board and understanding parents and teachers have effected changes for handicapped children. One grade was moved from the second to the first floor, another grade was moved to a different building, and the library and music room have been moved downstairs.
>
> "These things have made our son a normal student. He's accepted," Cappa said. (Rosensweet, 1976, p. 9)

As a teacher and a parent, Cappa's comments show appreciation for flexibility on the part of his colleagues, the kind of flexibility that encourages teachers to invent solutions that are practical and that cost little or nothing to achieve. The impact of such solutions, though, can be immense with regard to making it possible for children to live normally and to carry out their tasks and responsibilities on their own.

Fifth, *make technology the servant of pupils and teachers.* Making this principle operational requires two kinds of action on the part of the regular class teacher and specialist teacher team. One is to assure that every technical aid of established value is available for use in regular schools by children who need them. If, for instance, those two teachers conclude that a mechanical page turner or some adapted paper and a paper holder are needed to make it feasible for a pupil to work in the regular class, those materials should be supplied by the school district.

The specialist teacher should have up to date knowledge about those and similar items of educational technology. That teacher, too, should have immediate access to the items and should be able to assist the particular pupil and the regular class teacher in becoming skilled in their use.

The second kind of action needed to operationalize this principle goes further. Teachers must form cooperative relationships with engineers, psychologists, and other scientists who work at the interface of machines and people. To illustrate:

> A student at the University of the Pacific School of Pharmacy at Stockton, California, has developed a device that makes written communication possible for a Lodi girl who has been unable to write for some 12 years.
>
> Laurence R. Upjohn of Carmel, a senior pharmacy student studying electro-physiology, has developed a device to allow 29-year-old Cass Moreland to activate a special typewriter by using the frontalis muscles in her forehead.
>
> Miss Moreland, who suffers from congenital cerebral palsy and is unable to speak, has been confined to a wheelchair since birth. Her only form of written communication was an especially designed typewriter that she could activate with her shoulder muscles—until surgery in the early 1960's made this impossible. Despite these handicaps she has completed high school and attended enough classes at Delta College to be a sophomore at the local community college. However, her inability to write had prevented her from going much further through college.
>
> When Dr. Howell T. Runion, director of the electro-physiology unit at the UOP School of Pharmacy, found out about the problem facing the girl the current project began.
>
> The small box that Upjohn constructed serves to amplify the electrical activity from the movement of the girl's eyebrows—via electrodes placed on her forehead with a band and wired to the box. This allows the girl to activate a switch and control panel and thus use the specially designed typewriter.
>
> "There is electrical activity in all of our muscles, and in the situation facing Cass we had to come up with the proper electronic equipment to magnify the impulse from the muscles in her forehead," explained Runion, who has been studying the relationship of electronics to physiology and pharmacology for the past 15 years.
>
> For Miss Moreland, the device is a slow process of written communication, but it does allow her to convey her thoughts in written form. "Cass has been able to adjust to the new device with a minimum of training time and now has a slow but viable method of communication," explained Upjohn. "This will allow her to complete her college education," he added. (US Department of Health, Education, and Welfare, 1976, pp. 11-12)

This is certainly a unique and highly complex writing assistance device. The machine may, at the moment, have limited generalizability when compared, for example, to the Bliss symbols. The focal point, though, is that Cass Moreland, and every other crippled or health impaired child or youth, has the right to as full an education as her cognitive reach will allow. For that, it sometimes is necessary to go to extraordinary lengths to open channels through which full education may be delivered.

Sixth, *provide expert educational assessment, instruction, and counseling all along the way.* This principle emphasizes the everyday working partnership regular class teachers should be able to have with specialists. Because of the often mentioned differences among pupils called crippled and health impaired, expertise in assessment, instruction, and counseling are not always found in the same consultant. To design a high quality school and schooling for a kindergarten child of slow cognitive development with muscular dystrophy is widely different from counseling and helping plan education for an 11th grade honor student and athletic star whose recent injury resulted in a permanent paralysis from the waist down.

Top quality education, especially in the mainstream, calls for easy and direct access by regular class teachers to all the requisite specialists to consult on cases like these, on a person to person basis. This is necessary if proper matches are to be created by the teacher between the exceptional pupil's needs and the educational plan drafted for that pupil. Some of these specialists include:

Special education teachers	Vocational rehabilitation counselors
Speech clinicians	Psychiatrists
Social workers	Pediatric neurologists
School psychologists	Orthopedists
Instructional supervisors	Occupational and physical therapists
School principals	
School counselors	

Regular class teachers who have instructional responsibility for crippled and health impaired pupils need to know what kinds of help are available from such specialists and need opportunities to work with them in collegial relationships. Then there is increased assurance that preferred practices will be reflected in the personalized educational activities formulated for pupils.

Summary

Preferred practices, by their nature, are front-runners, well ahead of typical practices. Regular class teachers and their special education coworkers, however, should be aware of the characteristics of leading practices. In considering employment, in negotiating for improved work situations, and in designing educational plans for exceptional pupils, it is the preferred practices that should set the standard toward which all professional activity is directed. Thus, teaching facilities, state and local regulations, and plans for new developments in each should be examined as to whether they are consonant with the six principles discussed.

THE BEGINNING OF SPECIAL EDUCATION FOR PHYSICALLY AND HEALTH IMPAIRED PUPILS

The reasons special education began as it did for these pupils is obscure. Wallin (1955) pinned down the following dates and places for some subgroups:

Orthopedically handicapped	1899 or 1900	Chicago
Pretuberculosis or malnourished	1908	Providence
Epileptics	1909	Baltimore

Pupils with these conditions had not all been out of school until the times listed. Some were in regular classes, probably more or less satisfactorily adapting. Some who were also mentally retarded, deaf, or blind might have been found in special residential schools that opened for the three groups between 1817 and 1900. Wallin's dates and locations are for the first special day classes. Aside from the dates and places, however, the motives and rationales for separate classes have not been searched out and published.

Mobility, including transportation, has always been fraught with problems for persons who were crippled or who had limited vitality. It can be speculated, then, that the parallel between the growth of special, centralized schools for physically and health impaired pupils and the increased ease of mechanized private and public transportation during the period from 1900 to about 1935 was no coincidence. Add to that a spurt of medical knowledge about the use of braces during and after World War I and the increase in mobility that knowledge permitted, and it becomes clear how it became feasible to bring groups of physically and health impaired pupils together for their education. These conditions, coupled with a growing "service" orientation among citizens and an economy that could easily support it, may account for the steady increase in special schools and classes for physically and health impaired children and youth in the first 35 years of this century.

After World War II a sharp turn in the tide was noticeable—a turn away from separate special schools and classes. Fewer separate facilities were built, and more schools were constructed to accommodate all exceptional pupils.

Two other moves were taking place simultaneously. Throughout public education the long accepted but seldom practiced creed of individualized instruction was being made an operational reality. Also, the enormous new space age technology was being applied to create prostheses and implants that closely approximated the functions of real arms, legs, hands, feet, hearts, joints, and arteries. The same technology, too, was creating motorized personal transporters that markedly extended the impaired child's or adult's range of independent movement.

These moves were interactive, influencing each other. They were also linked with increased civil rights awareness and with a widened view of rehabilitation. The broader view emphasized more private sector employment and more preparation for independent living on the part of physically and health impaired clients, as well as other clients.

A number of school systems were actually demonstrating the feasibility of integrated education for exceptional pupils of all kinds. A notable example was Minneapolis, whose approach is described later in this chapter.

Thus, the court decisions cited earlier in this book came during a period when school programs for the physically and health impaired were more prepared for change than most. With few exceptions, the mainstreaming of physically and health impaired pupils had already begun and it continued in an atmosphere of cooperation from all concerned.

THE ROLE OF THE REGULAR CLASS TEACHER

Teamwork with Specialists

Earlier in this chapter there was given a list of specialists to whom regular class teachers need access if there is to be optimum education under either full or partial mainstream conditions. The most important is the teacher-colleague who is a specialist in work with exceptional pupils. The common forms of teamwork between the two are listed and illustrated here.

Instructional Activities

The regular class teacher takes the lead in arranging instructional activities, with the specialist teacher a participating partner. Activities may include assessment of educational needs; obtaining specialized instructional materials; designing the psychoeducational match that guides both what is taught and how it is taught; personalized instruction in tutoring, small group, or total class settings; developing instructional plans and schedules; helping select and train peer tutors and helpers; and guiding the work of employed aides and volunteers.

Service Activities

The specialist teacher ordinarily has chief responsibility for attending to service activities, though the regular class teacher should take part in making plans and decisions. Also, some of these activities may be done by the school administrator; others may best be delegated to aides and helpers, with both teachers taking part in monitoring the work. Included are arranging pupil transportation; scheduling therapies; proper use and maintenance of braces, crutches, and wheelchairs; obtaining and maintaining special instruction related equipment such as standing tables and page turners; and having special purpose ramps, handrails, and the like made and installed. The latter might be temporarily necessary, for instance, if the class is putting on a play and the stage needs adapting so a physically impaired pupil can take part in the production as an actor or as a stagehand.

Coordination

Under this heading comes the work of the specialist teacher in receiving pupil referrals from regular class teachers or others; processing such referrals; contacting community social and medical agencies; being a liaison with other regular or special schools regarding transfers, promotions, and other matters; participating in various staff meetings; and interfacing the pupil with vocational rehabilitation services. The special teacher and regular teacher relationship here is mainly one of maintaining an effective two way flow of information between themselves and significant others. School social workers often play important roles in coordination, too.

Record Keeping

The two teacher team periodically updates their own in-class records of pupil plans and progress. That is a joint activity behind which there is discussion and agreement on what should become part of the record. The same is true both for the report card (or whatever other form the regular achievement report to parents takes) and for teachers' entries in the school and central office cumulative folders. Usually the regular class teacher has final responsibility for these items. For data about medicines, prescribed physical activity routines and limitations, and for other medical treatments, the specialist teacher or school nurse makes the entries.

Parent Relations

Wherever possible it is advisable for the regular class teacher and the specialist teacher to confer as a team with parents. That helps to assure accurate communication. It can serve, also, to strengthen the parent's resolve to follow through at home with school related procedures the two teachers recommend. Beside reporting school progress to parents, the teachers can often obtain useful information and suggestions from them. Joint discussions with parents, too, can often help to open out-of-school social activities and recreation to physically and health impaired pupils, especially where parents tend to overprotect them.

Professional Development

Regular and specialist teachers find it valuable to attend in-service education sessions together, particularly if the sessions give them practice in the professional roles they have to play in real life. The same is true for professional association meetings and conferences where both can receive updates on research and on technical advances.

The regular class teacher should expect the teamwork to extend generally to any children whose reactions to instruction are puzzling, not just to those who are identified as physically and health impaired. The specialist teacher's skills will be applicable to many, if not all, of the pupils the regular teacher has difficulty reaching alone. Thus, most of the specialist teacher's typical day will be spent in regular classes in cooperative assessment and instruction with regular teachers.

Individualization of Instruction

Assessment uncovers the specific and general educational needs of pupils. Teachers prepare instructional plans based on the educational needs revealed by assessment. The tightness of the match between the two, plus the thoroughness and skill with which the plans for teaching are executed, determine the quality of pupil attainments. Taken together that is the definition of effective individualization of instruction.

That kind of personalization for pupils with physical and health impairments requires attention to all of the elements that make up their schooling; the process is considered here.

Curriculum Individualization

Physically and health impaired pupils very seldom need to be taught material that is outside the curriculum of all other pupils. Mullins (1971) highlighted that point vividly with an illustration of twin brothers, one with spina bifida, who have attended three grades together in their local school. Since what is taught in school is largely cognitive, with less emphasis on the affective and motoric, the major portions of typical curricula need no substantive changes. There are, of course, matters that do call for adaptation or particular emphasis. Examples are the teaching of:

- *Habits of planning*—Retracing one's route unnecessarily is too time and energy consuming for children and youth whose supply of those commodities is less than average.
- *Choosing the essentials*—Most pupils can carry along an additional book just in case it is found to be required later. Not so for pupils who

need one or both hands to help with movement and who may already be carrying a heavy brace.
- *Mobility training*—All children have to learn how to travel with increasing independence. Special added instruction is required when only certain routes, buses, buildings, and streets are sufficiently barrier free to use and when weather changes pose extraordinary hazards.
- *Health habits*—The basic instruction in health takes on special meaning when functionally limiting physical and health impairments already exist. For example, brushing one's teeth, which for a young child may be a quickly performed task under adult pressure, can be an extremely complex and time consuming operation for a youngster whose arms and hands are impaired or missing. From the point of view of safety, pupils with diabetes need instruction in the prevention of coma. Epileptic pupils who are liable to seizures or to brief blank periods must have instruction in the management of those incidents.
- *Physical education and recreation*—This curriculum is the one that most frequently needs alteration. Happily, physical educators themselves have long recognized that need. They have devised ways to help pupils with physical and health impairments to acquire and maintain superior levels of general fitness through individualized programs termed *adaptive* physical education. This gives special attention to body alignment, posture, and to the adjustments needed to facilitate pupil participation in recreational sports such as bowling, fishing, and golf.
- *Handwriting*—This curriculum may require changes, too, for pupils with hand or coordination difficulties. Some will be able to attain competence in writing if templates and line guides continue to be used whenever needed and if more simple and larger letters are substituted for those pupils conventionally learn. Others may have to bypass handwriting altogether, except for learning a signature, and do all their writing on standard or modified typewriters.
- *Socialization and self development*—This part of the curriculum refers to what students learn in school about cooperation, respect for individual rights (both personal and property), consideration for others, their own strengths and weaknesses, and the generally accepted values of the child and adult worlds in which they live. These and related matters make up what some call the affective curriculum. The continued presence of physically and health impaired pupils among other pupils encourages this learning in a real life setting both for the exceptional pupils and their classmates, an opportunity that can contribute to positive mental health for both.
- *Other curricular areas*—Vocal music may be extremely difficult for pupils with slowed speech and distorted articulation due to cerebral

palsy. Studio arts may require adaptations in technique and media for pupils without the use of hands and arms. Playing wind instruments may be too dangerous for pupils with weak arterial walls or asthma. Chemistry experiments may have to be adapted for youngsters still learning how to manipulate objects by means of prostheses. Wood or metal shop machinery may require added safety devices and special signs and fixtures. Calculators may have to be supplied in mathematics classes. Relevant adjustments may need to be made in all other curricular components, too.

These examples indicate that the adaptation, whether in arithmetic and the language arts, in the social and natural sciences, in the health and physical development areas, or in the creative and performing arts must be very personalized. The need for such adaptations should be the subject of careful review by teachers, at least annually, for each child. The general rule is that curricular adaptations ought to allow these pupils equivalent access to content and skills with other pupils of like levels and rates of cognitive development.

Methods of Teaching

The teaching methods described in Chapter 9 are applicable to pupils with physical and health impairments. There seem to be no teaching methods that are uniquely proper only for these pupils. There are, of course, pupils in this group who range widely in rates of cognitive development. For those, the teaching techniques particularly applicable to the retarded or gifted ought to be employed. Equally, for those who have vision or hearing impairments or who show learning disabilities and behavior disorders it is advisable to use teaching procedures to match those conditions. The teacher who works with these youngsters, then, is helped most by acquiring a grasp of the broadly generalizable methods in Chapter 9, as well as those more particularized methods just noted.

Instructional Materials

Concern here is with arranging for the child to be able to use instructional materials with ease. A child in a wheelchair may have difficulty using the ordinary chalkboard, reaching the globe, or manipulating a large dictionary. Some need stands for textbooks, plus mechanical page turners. As part of a physical therapy routine, some pupils ought to stand for a large part of the day. Others are faced with even more complicated problems.

What has been said about teaching methods applies here with equal force. Actual special instructional materials are not usually necessary. The problem is to achieve a comfortable and efficient interface between the pupil and the regular class material the pupil has to use. This calls for contrivances that bring those materials under the pupil's control. Many have already been invented, and specialist teachers are familiar with them. In conference with the regular teacher (and often with suggestions from regular class pupils) these devices can be designed and their construction arranged.

Organization for Instruction

As noted earlier, this is the logistic phase of teaching. It means, quite literally, getting it all together—scheduling, pupil attention, correct materials in proper sequence, assignments of work to aides and volunteers—in an orderly way, so effectiveness of instruction is enhanced. (It has a parallel in medicine—the preoperative check of all equipment, supplies, personnel, positioning, and patient condition before the crucial action starts.) And, as the situation changes, as so often happens in a class, it calls for reorganization on the spot with minimal confusion or lost motion.

On the average, a physically or health impaired pupil and the associated special equipment takes up twice the floor space of an ordinary child. Changing a pupil's position can often be a major undertaking. These and related considerations are prevented from becoming serious problems when regular class teachers make use of their specialist teacher colleagues for advice on tactical management and when fellow pupils and aides or volunteers are prompted as to how they might help expedite such matters. Once routines are established it becomes possible, with little difficulty, to make flexible variations in them.

School Physical Plant

The nation's elementary and secondary schools, designed for typical pupils, effectively bar many exceptional children and youth from attending them. The same is true of most colleges, public or private. Moreover, well qualified teachers with physically limiting conditions are often kept out by the same architectural barriers. There are parents, too, with physical and health impairments who cannot come into their nonhandicapped children's schools.

New construction, open to exceptional persons, is appearing, and remodeling is achieving the same result. There are guides for architects and school planners that show the way to a barrier free environment (Birch & Johnstone, 1975).

There is more to the matter than getting rid of built-in barriers, important as that may be. Three projected themes for the physical plant of today and the future are:

1. Common architectural barriers to total building use by the handicapped can be eliminated.
2. Subtle space adjustments can be arranged to produce significant positive impacts on quality of teaching and learning.
3. School building design should maximize the opportunity for handicapped children to stay in the mainstream of education. (Birch & Johnstone, 1975, p. 9)

Regular class teachers and their specialist associates can move these themes forward by exerting their personal influence, by working with community groups, and by making them part of teacher organization objectives both in state legislation and in collective bargaining. In the meantime, regular class teachers can encourage and support common sense adjustments such as those mentioned earlier in this chapter in connection with the stories of Lisa Blumberg and Jake Cappa.

Summary

The individualization of instruction takes on added dimensions when it is viewed in the context of pupils with physical and health impairments that call for special educational approaches. The optimum match between a pupil's needs and the pupil's prescribed educational plan can call for (a) curricular emphases, (b) a variety of teaching methods, (c) adapted instructional materials, (d) special attention to how instruction is organized, and (e) modest to major school physical plant alterations. All of these can be achieved for most pupils while they are in full or partial mainstream programs, if there is a sound, working partnership of regular and special education teachers, as well as appropriate consultation from other specialists.

EXAMPLES OF SPECIFIC SCHOOL PROGRAMS

Moves toward partial or full mainstreaming for physically and health impaired pupils can be detected in a number of communities in the past three decades. Significant changes in social behavior are seldom smooth flowing and uniform across a nation so complex as this one. So it is not surprising to find examples of school programs at different stages of progress toward social and scholastic integration of exceptional and regular pupils.

The schools described here were chosen to indicate various degrees of involvement in mainstreaming at different age and grade levels, and they represent several localities. Each has qualities that will be of interest to regular class teachers and to their special educator colleagues.

Village Nursery School

In the following report, Elizabeth J. Pieper,* Director of the Village Nursery School in Amsterdam, New York, tells about ways to ready regular class pupils to welcome classmates with physical and health impairments. It is well, while reading it, to think about how the exceptional children might be prepared, too, and how parents might also be brought into the situation.

Preparing Children for a Handicapped Classmate*

More and more often, handicapped children are being integrated into regular classroom settings. As a teacher who may now (or in the future) have handicapped children in your group, you will want to be knowledgeable and competent in meeting their special needs.

But to successfully build their self-image, you must first help other children to develop healthy and positive attitudes toward them. One way to do this is through a thoughtfully conceived program which is both enjoyable and instructional, and which leads to deeper understandings of the nature of physical limitations. Following are suggestions and goals which might be included in such a program.

Your first goal should be to promote the acceptance of handicapped children as individuals, more like than unlike other children, and to encourage their participation in regular group activities.

Explain the nature of certain limitations to students and encourage them to probe these handicaps with perceptive questions. Whenever possible, have students try to imagine themselves in a handicapped child's place. Would they like to feel isolated? Inferior? As you are trying to improve attitudes, present children with *facts*. Talk openly about the causes of some of these handicaps. Point out the aids available to disabled children such as wheelchairs, braces, crutches; services such as physical and occupational therapy; and architectural modifications to accommodate them, including ramps, handrails, adequately wide doors (or curtains instead of doors), low kitchen counters, and so on. Disabled children do have abilities. Emphasize what they *can* do. Try some of the following activities to carry through these suggestions.

- Borrow wheelchairs and crutches so that children may use them. Many children enjoy "wheeling around." Some handicapped children

---

*Reprinted from INSTRUCTOR, Vol. 84, No. 1, Copyright© August/September 1974 by The Instructor Publications, Inc., used by permission.

Elizabeth Pieper is also the producer of "The Able Disabled Picture Kit." For more information on this kit, which contains cartoons and pictures depicting disabled people in everyday activities emphasizing their abilities and normalcy, write to the author, RD 1, Ridge Road, Scotia, NY 12302.

even do "wheelies" with their chairs or have races as other children do with their bicycles.
- "Three-legged" races and "potato sack" races give children the idea of physical limitation. And a wheel-barrow race is one competition in which many paralyzed children can participate (even excel).
- Use books, records, and films to lead to deeper understandings. *Amahl and the Night Visitors,* an opera by Gian Carlo Menotti, for instance, is particularly suitable for the Christmas season. Discuss such recordings or dramatizations once they are finished. Ask, "If you were an actor and you played the part of Amahl, how would you show that you were lame?" (Let youngsters experiment and demonstrate their answers to this question.)

Another good example is *The Prince and the Pauper* (Disneyland Records). You might ask such questions as "Who remembers what Tom Canty's father did to make it seem as if Tom were crippled? Why did he do this? Do handicapped people do that today? Have you seen a Cerebral Palsy Telethon? Is that the same? How is it different? What do you think about this?"

If your children express feelings of pity, or helplessness and inability to work on the part of the handicapped, accept this without moralizing. Don't say, "We shouldn't pity them," for example. Instead, you might pursue the topic with more questioning.

"Do you know anyone who is handicapped? Does he work? Does he take care of his home? Does he have a hobby?" Give children examples of people who have disabilities yet lead productive lives. For example, I know a woman who is confined to a wheelchair yet holds a fine position as a nurse; a teacher who is blind; and paralyzed men who can still swim or fly airplanes. If children find this hard to believe, have them enact the situation. How might a handicapped person get into a plane? Slip a lightweight rubber band around each child's ankles to remind him that he cannot use legs. Now have him show how he would lift himself into the plane using only his arms. Talk about the many different activities in which the disabled can participate.

One young woman who visited our class answered the children's questions very naturally. When they inquired how she became disabled, she told them she had had polio as a child. (It is good to reassure youngsters that this will not happen to them, in situations where this would be honest.)

"Can you feel?" they asked.

"Yes, but some people can't. They have to be careful not to burn themselves with a cigarette, iron, and other hot objects and materials."

"Can't you move your legs?"

"No, not the way you can. But I lift them with my arms."

"Doesn't that make you feel sad?"

"No, not anymore. I can teach school, play the piano, sing with my friends, and drive my car. My house is the way I like it. Most of the time I am happy just as other people are. Sometimes I'm sad—but everyone is sad once in awhile."

Other materials you might use with children are the books *Mine for Keeps,* by Jean Little; *Apartment Three,* by Ezra Jack Keats; and *Fly, Wheels, Fly,* by Harriet Savitz.

- Invite one or several handicapped persons to talk with your youngsters. It is essential that they be well adjusted and acceptant of their disabilities. Many of the independent young people I know are interested in helping younger disabled children. They are also concerned that other people begin to understand and accept them as individuals with special talents of their own. Still, the physically impaired are often quick to realize that they must explain away noticeable difficulties before others are able to "go beyond" and view them as they really are.

- If possible, have a physical therapist visit the class, too. He can explain how he helps children become more independent, demonstrate techniques, and show some of the equipment used. The therapist might also tell ways in which children can help individually. (Usually a handicapped person is taught to ask for help if and when he needs it.) The advantage of constructing low buildings with some ramps or elevators instead of stairs, having a van equipped with a hydraulic life or ramp to transport children might also be discussed.

- If a child in the class has a temporary disability such as a broken leg, make constructive use of the event. You might initiate a thoughtful discussion with remarks such as, "Can Sally do everything today she could do last Thursday?" "What can't she do? (Can she go to the library with us?)" A child may suggest that she cannot play kickball. "What about kickball, then?" "Is there some way Sally can be part of the game?" Someone may suggest that they play a different game in which she can participate or have "free" play so that she won't feel left out. Other children who are permanently disabled are sometimes content to keep score, figure averages, and so on, while others are just as content to fall right out of their wheelchairs if need be to hit the ball!

- Often, able-bodied people have misconceptions of what are suitable activities and vocations for disabled persons. Help children to make realistic suggestions about what Sally can really do. After a week passes, ask, "Did you notice Sally's cast more today or the first time you saw it? Is everything different about her because of her leg? Do you feel different in any way, Sally? Did you like it better when you could do more things? Is it harder to come to school now? What about children who are permanently handicapped? Do you think it would be better if they came to school or had home teachers?"

- Assembly programs, sports exhibitions, special movies, musical concerts, and so on, would make good joint activities to which you could invite children from a special school. You might also work out some kind of creative exchange program with a special school. For example, some schools have swimming pools or vocational workshops which would intrigue youngsters from regular schools. There might be ways in which to integrate some classes on a permanent basis—"busing" in such cases could be a real plus.

Once you start thinking along these lines, you'll be able to plan for more elaborate ideas. Many of the traditional reasons for separating physically disabled and healthy children will become obviously invalid to you. The reasons may have been a "smoke screen" for the real fears people are not sophisticated enough to face. Besides doing untold emotional damage, they are needlessly costly. The same basic psychology applies to all human beings whether their different characteristic is short stature, red hair, blemishes, or paralyzed legs. Everyone needs to be accepted for himself, to be valued, to be allowed to serve as support and inspiration to others. (Pieper, 1974, pp. 128-129)

Holladay Center for Handicapped Children

The Holladay Center for Handicapped Children, a part of the Portland (Oregon) Public Schools, is a short term day school linked to a regular elementary school. It is a splendid example of the movement toward the preferred practice of bringing special education and necessary ancillary services into regular schools. The public information statement issued by the school system says:

> The classrooms at Holladay Center are ungraded and self-contained. They are divided into preschool, primary, intermediate, and upper levels. To provide for special instructional and physical needs, each class is staffed by a teacher and an aide. Depending upon enrollment, more than one classroom may be designated for the same level. Age, skill development, severity of handicap, and personal development are criteria for movement from one class to another. The highest level students are assigned to the team room with two teachers and two aides. Teachers of music and art supplement the program in each classroom.
>
> The educational objectives and curriculum parallel those of regular elementary classrooms, even though special education methodologies are employed. A multidisciplinary approach affords classroom reinforcement of therapeutic efforts in such areas as language and speech development, initial writing and typing skills, and self-help skills. Also, the therapists largely determine and often design or make the adaptive equipment used in the classroom (electric typewriter and keyboard guards, typing mitts, pencil holders, head and mouth stylus, enlarged manipulative materials, cutout tables).
>
> When a child has reached a satisfactory level of development in all areas, he will be considered for integration into our adjoining elementary school before full-time integration into a neighborhood school.
>
> If a child continues to profit from our educational and therapeutic program until age sixteen, he may continue his learning in a setting commensurate with his abilities.

This is a fine illustration of a "first generation" mainstream model for pupils of this kind. It is a giant step away from the entirely separated special school and a distinct change in the direction of progressive inclusion.

Urbain Plavan School

Similar in concept to the Holladay Center is Urbain Plavan School in Fountain Valley, California. It was designed for regular school pupils as well as those with cerebral palsy, polio, birth defects, accident caused limb losses, and other physical and health impairing conditions. It is described as follows:

> The school, which opened in 1973, was planned and built specifically to integrate orthopedically handicapped and typical children.
>
> Since moving from one activity to another requires considerable effort by handicapped children, the school was designed for maximum circulation efficiency. This was achieved by an irregular oval-shaped building in which four distinct elements surround and feed into a fifth element—an 8,100 square foot central learning center. The four basic elements are an administration section, classrooms, a special services section for handicapped students, and a music platform and storage facility. The focus of the complex is inward with eleven circulation paths leading to, through, and out of the learning center.
>
> Although one section of the school is devoted entirely to handicapped students, no real boundaries exist. Orthopedically handicapped children participate in all regular activities.
>
> Ninety-six handicapped children attend the school along with 330 typical children in pre-school through eighth grades. The teaching staff consists of ten teachers for typical children, eight teachers and eight teacher's aides for orthopedically handicapped children, two learning center coordinators and two aides, one teacher for educable mentally retarded children, and one speech therapist.
>
> The normal children attending the school are drawn from a "walk-in" area immediately surrounding the school site. The orthopedically handicapped children come from four cooperating school districts.
>
> Some of the special orthopedic equipment in the school includes electric parallel bars, balance beam, rocking beam, rocking boat, walking rails, bicycle exerciser, foot placement ladder, triplex pulleys, punching bag, shoulder wheel, finger ladder, wrist roll and a standing tilt table. There is also a training bedroom for daily living skill adaptation, a training bathroom, training kitchen and hydrotherapy room.
>
> The orthopedically handicapped section of the school also functions as a full-time clinic. Parents can bring children here for doctor's examinations, consultation and therapy. A separate reception and waiting room with an outdoor play area serve these parents and children. (Russo, 1974, p. 25-38)

The next illustration concerns a secondary school. It, too, furnished educators with an early prototype.

Marshall-University High School*

Full regular school integration for physically and health impaired pupils, plus partial or full scholastic mainstreaming, has long been characteristic of Marshall-University High School in Minneapolis, Minnesota. It represents a "second generation" concept, one in which special education and support services are included in the school rather than appended to it.

To the casual observer it is an ordinary city high school—large, an old but well kept building, and a student body from a variety of ethnic, racial, and socioeconomic backgrounds. Exceptional pupils, however, start each day in Marshall-University's regular report rooms. Their daily schedules parallel those of all other students. Elevators, hand rails, and similar aids are available. Regular class teachers have at hand the special equipment and materials needed to accommodate individual pupil needs.

Physically handicapped high school students attend Marshall-University Junior and Senior High School when they require the specialized services of a combined education/health and medical support component not available at other West Metropolitan area high schools. Health/medical support services include hydraulic lift bus transportation to and from school, use of the building elevator to reduce fatigue and/or to eliminate stair walking, and the aid of daily living activities of two licensed practical nurses supervised by a certified school nurse.

All exceptional students in the Marshall program are integrated with the rest of the student body for general education academic subjects. Two resource teachers work with the students and general education teachers to ensure that the students understand and fulfill expectations of their course instructors and the course requirements. Course modifications are instituted only as required by the needs of individual students. Students whose physical conditions call for major course modifications may take as substitute courses: Adaptive Physical Education, Adaptive Typing and Business Skills, Adaptive Industrial Arts, and Adaptive Foods.

A work program at Marshall provides courses in work orientation, attitudes, and prework skills. Work placements within the school are available to some students while others participate in work experience outside of school. Work orientation is an essential component of the school program for physically handicapped students. The amount of student involvement is determined on an individual basis, as a number of students are college bound and require a full program of academic instruction.

---

*This description was developed from material kindly supplied by J. H. Bisek.

The Division of Vocational Rehabilitation (DVR) initiates individual casework services during the students' junior year, with definite plans and responsibilities determined before the conclusion of the senior year. The DVR Coordinator then continues to assist the student in pursuing suitable vocational/educational goals until employment is located.

Other physically handicapped junior and senior high school aged students who do not attend Marshall-University because they are capable of full participation in their home schools with special educational programing may be involved in one of the prevocational or vocational training programs available in the West Metropolitan area (Special Rehabilitation Center, Minneapolis Rehabilitation Center, Sister Kenny Institute, Cooperative Special Rehabilitation Center, and the United Cerebral Palsy Center).

The Marshall-University High School format for integration is applicable to preschool, elementary, and middle school settings, also.

The guiding influence wielded by a strong policy, intelligently applied, shows in the next and concluding report.

Clark County School District

Attempts to integrate physical and health impaired pupils into the regular school program began in Clark County, Nevada, in 1958 (Marr, 1969). At the time of Marr's report there were 70,000 pupils in 85 schools in the district. Of all the known physical and health impaired pupils only 52 were enrolled in the district's separated special facility for the physically and multiply handicapped. Marr (1969) stated:

> The tough rules of entrance (to the separated special school) have caused regular school personnel, pupil personnel services, community health agencies, etc., to jointly develop a cooperative approach to the solution of the problem of the physically handicapped in a regular school program. A Las Vegas "gamble" that has paid off! (p. 2)

In order to qualify for special school admission the candidates must require an amount or a kind of care or handling that simply cannot be managed even in a well equipped and well staffed regular school. Thus, the pupils in the special school are those who would otherwise have to be taught at home or not supplied with public education at all.

Summary

The spectrum of educational settings described earlier is still necessary for balanced programs. It is plain, however, that advances in social and educational philosophy and technology are moving the fulcrum so that more weight is directed toward bringing needed special education and services to exceptional children while they remain in regular class groups.

COMPREHENSIVE PROGRAMING FOR PERSONS WITH PHYSICAL AND HEALTH IMPAIRMENTS

Education for physical and health impaired pupils has to be seen as one important part of a complex of developmental support systems aimed at maximum normalization. Obvious other parts are those that deal with health services, home and family living, religion, social services, vocationally oriented training, and recreation.

To be sure, these are interactive systems. Education overlaps to some extent with each of them and each overlaps with the other. And they should support each other. But it is essential that teachers recognize and impress on others the following two principles.

First, educators and education cannot justify expending significant amounts of funds and staff time on matters other than education as such. That means, for example, that funds should come from health sources for physicians, nurses, therapists, and other health services, even though they are carried out on school children in school settings. When teachers go into hospitals to work with children, they are usually paid by school systems from education funds. When physicians and other health professionals work in schools, the support should come from health funds. There is too little financial support for schooling as it is to allow some of it to be expended for other purposes, however worthy.

Second, school time should be devoted to schooling. Teachers have too little time with most children to work in all the instruction that is needed, so no time should be given up to nonschool activities. This principle translates into moving therapy time, for instance, into what is normally out-of-school time. The same is true for pupil medical diagnosis, family counseling, recreation, and other activities that often impinge on the time teachers have with their physical and health impaired pupils.

Comprehensive programing is necessary. Teachers must help to see that it happens, but not at the price of shortchanging education. What is needed is balance.

THE CONTINUING NEED FOR TEACHERS

Possible roles continue to expand for teachers who understand physical and health impaired persons. Regular class teachers who have basic knowledge about special education can expect to find employment opportunities on the increase as the wave of mainstreaming spreads.

SUGGESTIONS FOR STUDENTS AND INSTRUCTOR

1. Arrange for students to work part time as volunteer teacher assistants in regular classes that include physically and health impaired pupils.

2. A pair of students might "adopt" a child who is going to need to remain at home or in a hospital for an extended time, but who can receive education during that period. It would be valuable in such items as the first two if the students kept logs of their experiences and discussed them with the instructor and classmates.
3. Set up simulation exercises in class to show the adaptations needed for crutches, walkers, wheelchairs, braces, and a variety of other conditions.
4. Have students write educational plans for pupils who need adaptations in (a) curriculum, (b) instructional materials, (c) organization for instruction, and (d) physical plant. In each instance try to use an actual child.

TOPICAL BIBLIOGRAPHIES

Orientation of Regular Classes to Pupils with Physical and Health Impairments

Billings, H. K. An exploratory study of the attitudes of non-crippled children in three elementary schools. *Journal of Experimental Education,* 1963, *31,* 381-387.

Buchanan, R., & Mullins, J. B. Integration of a spina bifida child in a kindergarten for normal children. *Young Children,* September 1968, 339-344.

Dibner, S., & Dibner, A. *Integration or segregation for the physically handicapped child?* Springfield IL: Charles C Thomas, 1973.

Pell, D. M. Teacher acceptance and perception of behavior transferred from special to regular classes. *Dissertation Abstracts International,* 1973, *33*(8), 4209-A.

Pieper, E. J. Preparing children for a handicapped classmate. *Instructor,* 1974, *84*(1), 128-129.

Rapier, J. et al. Changes in children's attitudes toward the physically handicapped. *Exceptional Children,* 1972, *38*, 219-223.

Richardson, S. A. Children's values and friendships: A study of physical disability. *Journal of Health and Social Behavior,* 1971, *12*(3), 253-258.

People with Physical and Health Impairments

Agrault, E. W. *Take one step.* Garden City NY: Doubleday, 1963.

Berg, N. A. *Wednesday's child: A tale of love and courage.* Philadelphia: Muhlenberg Press, 1966.

Douglas, W. *Of men and mountains.* New York: Harper & Row, 1950.

Gallico, P. *The snow goose.* New York: Knopf, 1941.

Jones, R. The acorn people: What I learned at a summer camp. *Psychology Today,* June 1977, *11*(1), 70-81.

Lukens, K., & Panter, C. *Thursday's child has far to go.* Englewood Cliffs NJ: Prentice-Hall, 1969.

Schary, D. *Sunrise at Campobello.* New York: Random House, 1958.

School Adaptations for Physically and Health Impaired Pupils

Abeson, A., & Blacklow, J. *Environmental design: New relevance for special education.* Reston VA: The Council for Exceptional Children, 1976.

Aiello, B. *Places and spaces: Facility planning for handicapped children.* Reston VA: The Council for Exceptional Children, 1976.

Anderson, R. Mainstreaming is the name for a new idea. *School Management,* 1973, *17*(7), 28-30.

Birch, J. W., & Johnstone, B. K. *Designing schools and schooling for the handicapped.* Springfield IL: Charles C Thomas, 1975.

Calovini, G. *The principal looks at classes for the physically handicapped.* Reston VA: The Council for Exceptional Children, 1969.

Green, P. (Ed.). *One out of ten: School planning for the handicapped.* New York: Educational Facilities Laboratories, 1974.

Hawkins-Shepard, C. (Ed.). *Making it work: Practical ideas for integrating exceptional children into regular classes.* Reston VA: The Council for Exceptional Children, 1978.

Molloy, L. The handicapped child in the everyday classroom. *Phi Delta Kappan,* 1975, *56*(5), 337-340.

Mullins, J. B. Integrated classrooms. *Journal of Rehabilitation,* 1971, *37*(2), 14-16.

Weishahn, M. W., & Mitchell, R. Educational placement practices with visually disabled and orthopedically disabled children—A comparison. *Rehabilitation Literature,* 1971, *32*(9), 363-366.

Workshop

Ward, M. J., Arkell, R. N., Dahl, H. G., & Wise, J. H. *Everybody counts! A workshop manual to increase awareness of handicapped people.* Reston VA: The Council for Exceptional Children, 1979.

9. Emerging Trends and New Partners

CHAPTER OUTLINE

INTRODUCTION
DISSEMINATION OF KNOWLEDGE AND COORDINATION OF ROLES
    The Emergence of Collaborative Models
    Diagnostic-Prescriptive Teacher
    Resource Teacher Model
    A Consulting Teacher Model
    The Crisis Teacher
    Collaborative Early Intervention
    Summary of Collaborative Roles
NEW ROLES FOR OTHER SCHOOL PERSONNEL
    School Psychologists
    The School Counselor
    School Social Workers
    Other Working Partners
MODIFICATIONS IN THE LARGER SYSTEM
    The Individually Guided Education System
    The Job Corps Program
INSTRUCTIONAL PROCEDURES USEFUL FOR ALL STUDENTS
    Basis of Effective Teaching
    Teaching Approaches
        Undercutting: Beginning a Little Below Where the Child Is
        Using Direct Experience
        Helping the Child Set the Pace of Learning
        Employing Principles of Reinforcement Systematically
        Giving the Child Choices
        Encouraging Constructive Divergent Thinking
        Giving Children Chances for Leadership
        Using Peer Instruction
        Using Pupil Feedback
        Giving Prompt Feedback to Pupils
        Moving from Familiar to Unfamiliar
        Modeling Behavior
        Using Reviews Meaningfully
        Helping Pupils Learn How They Learn
        Limiting Extraneous Stimuli
        Invoking the High Interest/Low Difficulty Principle
        Being Consistent
        Observing the Child Closely
PREVAILING VERSUS PREFERRED PRACTICES
SUGGESTIONS FOR STUDENTS AND INSTRUCTOR
TOPICAL BIBLIOGRAPHIES

INTRODUCTION

In the preceding four chapters we have dealt with four of the traditional categories of exceptional children: mental retardation, giftedness, learning disabilities, and physical handicaps. We have urged the view of mental retardation as attenuated (or low rates of) cognitive development, and of gifted as accelerated (or high rates of) cognitive development. So-called "learning disabled" children, according to our view, respond poorly to initial instruction provided in basic subjects (the cultural imperatives) and, thus need especially intensive or different methods of instruction; and physically handicapped children have needs that, except for varying architectural and facility modifications, can best be understood in terms of learning problems.

We accept the viewpoint of many experienced teachers that children in these four categories of exceptionality are really not educationally distinctive and that they do not require separate educational programs and separately or distinctively prepared teachers. This point of view is more and more seen in the merging of formerly separate teacher training programs for the four groups. Traditionally, of course, arbitrary criteria have been invoked to screen children into separate categories. For example, children with IQ's between 50 and 80, as measured on one or another test, have been called the educable mentally retarded. IQ tests have been used in a more complex way to estimate different academic or grade expectancies for children with different scores and then to calculate each child's discrepancies on the basis of what is expected for him. For example, the following formula has recently been suggested to identify severely learning disabled children (*Federal Register,* Nov. 29, 1976, p. 52407):

$$\frac{CA\,(IQ + .17) - 2.5}{300} = \text{severe discrepancy level}$$

According to this formula any child whose actual grade score in reading or other basic subjects is below the established criterion would qualify as a case of severe learning disability. According to its initial proponents (the idea was later withdrawn), children identified by this formula would, if served in special education, qualify their local school districts for special financial aids.

Procedures based on expectations, however, are always haunted by the will-o'-the-wisp that all children are already performing exactly as "expected" if only we knew enough to set up accurate expectations for them. If some children are capable of higher achievement under different conditions, then we have the logical problem of expecting different achievement levels under different circumstances, which makes the concept of expectancy ambiguous.

Actually, the traditional categories represent merely simplistic surfacing systems. Too often, unfortunately, they have been accepted as the basic organizing concepts of special education. This attitude has been especially evident under the "two box" arrangements discussed in Chapter 1. There is little if any empirical support for the differentiation of instruction for educably mentally retarded (EMR) children, who are identified in one way, and learning disabled (LD) children who are identified in another way. Even less support is indicated for the creation of separate environments and separately trained teachers for the various categories of children discussed in the preceding chapters.

Alternatives to the delivery of special education services in categorical terms have been found to be both possible and practical by many school systems, as the following account illustrates:

> In a cooperative school district, created through the consolidation of three small rural districts, school buses for years had criss-crossed the country roads, carrying EMRs to their special classes and LDs and EDs to their special centers. Finally, the school board asked the superintendent to examine the situation to see whether all of the travel was really necessary. The result, after careful study, was a very much revised special education program. The criss-crossing of buses came to a near halt; a great deal of retraining for both regular and special education personnel was undertaken, and changes were made in the roles of school psychologists and many other specialists. Parents and other members of the community, who were involved in the decisions all the way, supported the changes.

In a sense, this chapter expands on the story of this community. Discussed are patterns of service that have evolved to eradicate the excessive categorization and labeling of children and to eliminate the unnecessary duplication of bus routes and schooling arrangements that were developed to keep all the categorical stations properly occupied and managed.

DISSEMINATION OF KNOWLEDGE AND COORDINATION OF ROLES

In part, what we are talking about here are problems in the dissemination of knowledge and the coordination of roles. Consider, for example, all of the kinds of knowledge that are relevant to the solution of exceptional children's problems in the important area of language development, a topic of primary concern to almost all of special education. The total domain of language development includes innumerable subdomains, which are represented schematically in Figure 9-1.

As indicated on the left side of the schema, one can mediate between the needs of the schools and this knowledge domain by preparing and employing any one of several kinds of mediators (e.g., speech clinicians,

Emerging Trends and New Partners / 443

FIGURE 9-1
The Total Domain of Language Development, Its Subdomains,
and Two Ways of Dealing with Needs of Regular Class Teachers

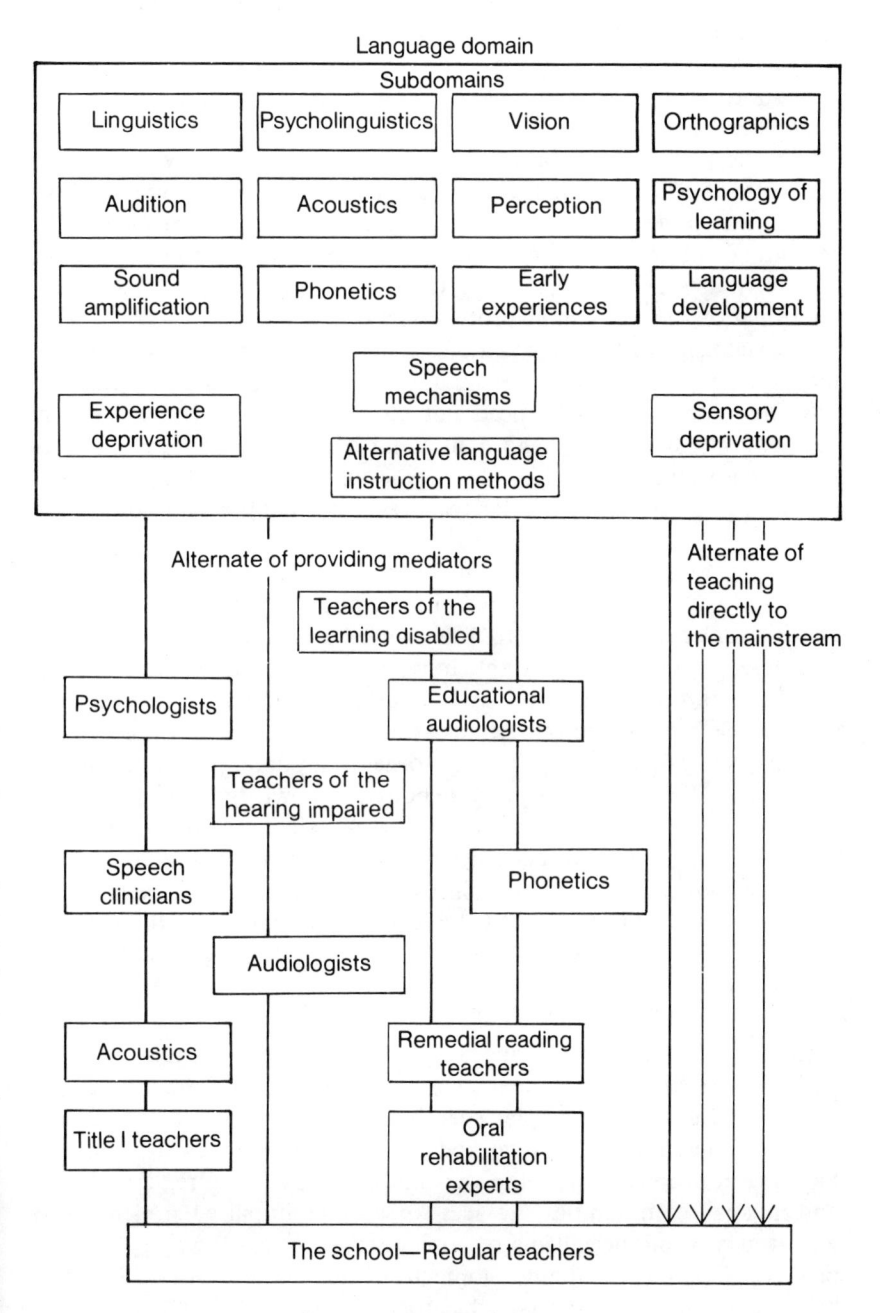

Language domain

Subdomains

- Linguistics
- Psycholinguistics
- Vision
- Orthographics
- Audition
- Acoustics
- Perception
- Psychology of learning
- Sound amplification
- Phonetics
- Early experiences
- Language development
- Experience deprivation
- Speech mechanisms
- Sensory deprivation
- Alternative language instruction methods

Alternate of providing mediators

- Psychologists
- Teachers of the learning disabled
- Educational audiologists
- Teachers of the hearing impaired
- Speech clinicians
- Phonetics
- Audiologists
- Acoustics
- Remedial reading teachers
- Title I teachers
- Oral rehabilitation experts

Alternate of teaching directly to the mainstream

The school—Regular teachers

educational audiologists, remedial teachers) who would be expected to have backgrounds in language studies. Unfortunately, the preparation of such mediators is often narrower than one would wish, which reflects the failure of specialized university faculties to achieve appropriate interactions.

Schools are expected to employ specialists to deal with language problems because the language development of children is very important. The kinds of specialists considered necessary can be many when children are categorized and placed accordingly because the commonalities among the children's problems are not recognized. Thus the problem of providing specialized service often becomes very complex. It is no wonder that school boards are driven to ask for some more effective coordination of roles among professional staff.

The right side of the schema indicates that one alternative is to provide more thorough preparation of regular teachers in as many domains as possible. The preparation need not all be at the preservice level, of course; some can be through continuing education. Colleges and universities as well as local school districts should be responsible for increasing the competencies of regular teachers in as many broad domains as possible.

Another strategy, and one highly favored here, is for specialists employed by the schools to have broad training themselves—as in language problems—and then to function as trainers of regular school personnel. It might be more apt, however, to describe this last strategy as one of *sharing* expertise between specialists and regular classroom teachers. Sometimes, in our enthusiasm for adopting new concepts and changing old procedures we tend to forget that public school teaching is a profession that is based on a large body of knowledge, much of which is derived from experience and that every specialist must function within the context of that knowledge. Perhaps the most rewarding experience for all school personnel in a mainstream situation is that teachers and specialists have broken out of their isolation to experience the stimulation of sharing and working together.

The Emergence of Collaborative Models

Various prototypes of collaborative efforts between regular teachers and specialists began to emerge in special education in the early decades of the century. For example, speech clinicians developed an itinerant service model in which they worked part time directly with students who had speech problems while the students were enrolled in regular classes; and in some communities, services for visually impaired students took what today would be called a resource teacher form. However, the most productive period for the development of new models of collaboration between regular and special educators was the 1960's (Deno, 1973).

Descriptions of several of the significant models that emerged during that time follow.

Diagnostic-Prescriptive Teacher

The George Washington University program for teacher preparation was one of the earliest to commit itself to a noncategorical and collaborative mode of operation (Prouty & McGarry, 1972). The diagnostic-prescriptive teacher (DPT) is an

> educational diagnostician-consultant to regular-class teachers in the development of appropriate instructional and socialization experiences for children who are viewed as posing problems in learning and/or behavior. (p. 47)

DPT programs operate without categorical labels for children and with the explicit intention of limiting the demissions of children from regular classrooms. The program operates through the support and collaboration offered by DPT's to regular classroom teachers, following a 10 step process.

1. Referral: The classroom teacher submits a written referral—a simple, one-page form—of the child seen as posing problems. An anecdotal description of the problem and a summary of the referring teacher's efforts to that point to adapt the program to the child, are required.
2. Observations: The DPT observes the referred child in his regular-class environment one or more times.
3. Referral Conference: The DPT confers with the referring teacher to update referral information, clarify their respective roles and responsibilities in the case, and arrange suitable times for the referred child to come to the DPT's room for diagnostic teaching.
4. Diagnostic Teaching: Informal, small-group work is conducted by the DPT with the referred child to determine successful teaching techniques and materials based on the child's needs and strengths.
5. Educational Prescription: A written educational report is prepared; it recommends well-defined techniques and materials to the referring teacher and describes in detail their use with the child.
6. Prescription Conference: Explanation and open discussion of the Prescription with the referring teacher result in modifications that are mutually agreed upon and culminate in a schedule for demonstration by the DPT.
7. Demonstration: The DPT takes over the referring teacher's class to demonstrate elements of the Prescription in the total class environment.
8. Short-Term Follow-Up: The DPT makes periodic visits to the referring teacher's room to offer suggestions, provide encouragement, and give demonstrations as they are needed.
9. Evaluation: The referring teacher completes a single-page evaluation form 30 days after receiving the Prescription, indicating progress to date.

10. Long-Term Follow-Up: The DPT continues periodic checks with the referring teacher. Only when *both* DPT and referring teacher view the child's progress as satisfactory is the case closed. (pp. 49-50)

Resource Teacher Model

A great many schools in recent years have implemented what may be termed a resource teacher model of special education services. The description of one such program (Johnson & Grismer, 1972) follows:

A large inner city school that operated five special classes for educable mentally retarded, learning disabled, and hard of hearing pupils was made the object of change efforts involving movement toward a resource model. A special education teacher who had experienced the changeover from special class to resource program model in a smaller school was assigned to gradually work toward the new model in this large and complex school. The effort was launched in the primary grade levels in the first year and extended to intermediate grades in the second year.

A large double classroom space was assigned to what became known as the resource center. In the beginning, the resource teacher worked with regular and special teachers and gradually assumed a strong role in the study of children and in case management. The school principal, who had promised his support before the project started, was a strong, constant source of encouragement and assistance. Little by little, the resource center was built up into a primary resource for specialized instructional materials for the whole building.

A student support team was created, consisting of the resource teacher, a psychologist, a school social worker, the principal, the regular teacher, and parents. Any teacher may request the team's services. Usually, a child whose school progress or adjustment is problematic is asked to come to the resource center for about half an hour each day for two to three weeks; during this period all necessary examinations are conducted. At the end, the student support team meets to consider all facets of the situation—child, school, home—and specific goals are developed for the child's educational progress. In addition, the roles of all the teachers and others who are involved in the child's program are delineated.

Very often, children are scheduled into the resource center for 30 to 90 minutes per day for especially intensive and systematic instruction. A wide variety of materials and procedures are available in the center so that a good possibility exists of "matching" the child's needs.

The resource center gradually grew to the point where it employed three special education teachers. One had a background in work with hearing impaired children and, thus, was able to give leadership in certain management and instructional procedures for such children, and the other teachers also had particular strengths. Over time, the three shared their expertises and each became capable of operating any part of the total program.

In addition to the direct instruction of children for limited periods, the resource teachers spend much time consulting with regular teachers and helping to install enriched and alternative programs in regular classrooms. The resource center and special education teachers serve also as a crisis center for pupils and classroom teachers when a child's behavior becomes extremely disruptive or the child is out of control in the regular classroom situation.

The effect of this resource teacher program has been to broaden the capacity of the school as a whole to deal with exceptionality. The number of children sent to special classes has been reduced to less than that required for a single class. While the resource center serves about 35 to 40 children per day, over a year it serves more than twice that number. The educational progress of all children in the building is monitored much more closely than in the past, parents are fully engaged in the planning of educational programs for their children, and regular teachers are given immediate and substantial support for serving the children in their classes who have learning problems or are gifted.

A Consulting Teacher Model

A somewhat different role for a special education mediator is typified by the consulting teacher model. The most distinctive feature of this approach is that the consulting teacher, although always a skilled teacher, does not engage in the *direct* instruction of pupils; the role calls for *indirect* instruction in that the consulting teacher functions almost exclusively in consultation with regular teachers. One of the best examples of this model is in Vermont where a cooperative project among school districts, the State Department of Education, and the University of Vermont has been in progress since the late 1960's (Fox, Egner, Paolucci, Perelman, & McKenzie, 1973).

The Vermont program operates through consulting teachers who are called in by regular teachers whenever children are identified as not making adequate progress in school learning. The consulting teacher helps the regular teacher to apply the principles of applied behavior analysis and individualized instruction. Steps in this process are:

1. Referral by the regular teacher, which includes specification of the particular academic difficulties or social behaviors that are of concern.
2. The agreement by regular and consultation teachers on specific behavioral *targets.*
3. Determination of the child's entry level in the target areas.
4. Specification of instructional objectives, including conditions for assessing progress.

5. Developing teaching/learning procedures and implementing them.
6. Arranging environmental consequences (reinforcements).
7. Evaluation of procedures and progress toward objectives.

A unique feature of the Vermont consulting teacher model is the systematic preparation of consulting teachers at the University and the authorization of these teachers to act as continuing agents of the University in the field to teach approved courses. Through this linkage of the University and an increasing number of the state's school districts through consulting teachers, a constant exchange of information, instruction, and live data is maintained.

There are several features of great importance in the consulting model: (a) it tends not to be categorical in orientation to pupils; (b) it strongly emphasizes modifications of the regular school environment to accommodate exceptional students, rather than the removal of such students to separate places; (c) it places great emphasis on the training of personnel of all kinds and recognizes that much of this training must go on at inservice levels; (d) it provides for the continuing interaction of local school districts, the State Department of Education, and the University department of special education; and (e) it is planful, gradually spreading across the state in a systematic, prespecified form.

The Crisis Teacher

One of the earliest forms of collaborative, noncategorical support by special educators for regular teachers is provided by the helping teacher or crisis teacher model (Morse, 1976). A fundamental concept of the model is that regular teachers do not need help with exceptional students all the time, but in moments of crisis intensive help is needed by both teachers and pupils.

This model, in contrast to the Vermont consulting teacher model, (a) emphasizes direct assistance to pupils, (b) has an eclectic approach to intervention strategies, (c) is concerned with the prevention of problems as well as their remediation, and (d) tends to be broadly concerned with the total life space of the child rather than targeted on specific discrepancies or deficits. In general, the emphasis by the developers and advocates of this model has been on improvement in self concepts, human relationships, and self management. The model requires a great deal of collaboration by the helping teacher and regular teachers, which is certainly a far cry from traditional "two box" operations.

Collaborative Early Intervention

In general, special education has given far too little attention to early interventions that are designed specifically to reduce the incidence rates of later severe problems. There follows a description of a program that has had early intervention as a specific goal and, at the same time, illustrates new collaborative roles for special educators and regular teachers.

All elementary schools in the Bloomington, Minnesota, public school system formerly used the same basal reading program, which followed the whole word analytic approach. Accommodations to individual differences in this regular program were made mainly by the broad grouping of pupils into ability groups and by differential pacing and repetition for mastery.

The special education department helped to install a different approach for the primary grades. Synthetic rather than analytic, the new approach included the use of multisensory material/techniques and highly systematic instruction, basically, an Orton-Gillingham approach (Enfield, 1976).

The program was initiated by sending special project teachers into regular first, second, and third grade classrooms where they demonstrated the alternative methods and helped teach those children whose initial responses to the district's regular program were inadequate. After two or three weeks, the regular classroom teachers usually were able to take over the alternative approach; but special education staff continued to return to the classrooms to help out with new lessons, materials, or techniques, and to consult with the regular class teachers when requested.

Several characteristics may be noted about this program:

1. The children remain in the regular class at all times.
2. The special education staff work directly in the regular classes.
3. The purpose is to create a more diverse set of options in the mainstream setting.
4. Much emphasis is given to the preparation of regular teachers to handle the alternative methods.
5. No child is ever labeled as learning disabled or by any other term.

Remarkable results have been achieved by this program: (a) The numbers of children scoring low on reading tests have been reduced sharply; for example, as compared with earlier years, the proportion of children falling below the 25th percentile on nationally normed reading tests was reduced by 71% in the first year, and by 83% and 85% in the following years. (b) The percentage of children districtwide who were below grade level in reading fell substantially; for example, at the second grade level, the percentages below grade level fell from 36 to 25 on reading vocabulary and from 49 to 35 on reading comprehension. (c) The numbers of children receiving specialized tutoring in the categorical special education program was reduced approximately by half; and even more remarkably, the waiting list for such programs was eliminated. (d)

The cost of the new program was less than half that of a traditional tutoring program. (e) Among the regular teachers, 96% agreed that the program should not be discontinued. (f) All (100%) of the school principals agreed that the program had been successful in their buildings. (g) More than 90% of the parents whose children were in the program wanted it continued; only 1% said that they would not like to have their children continued in the program (Enfield, 1976).

Fortunately, the Minnesota State Department of Education has been willing to support this outstanding collaborative effort by special and regular educators through its reimbursable special education program. The school system's new way of delivering special education services does the obvious thing required of any profession: It provides specialized services at the first sign of difficulty. Thus, more children are given the opportunity for successful learning experiences; and the number of serious casualties, who usually are dealt with too late and in the context of great discouragement and anxiety permeating the life of the child and the family, is reduced. Fortunately, also, the special educators in this project evaluated their efforts carefully and, on this basis, were able to assist the school board in making its judgments. The board has been persuaded of the value of the program and has installed it in all the schools in the district.

The Bloomington program exemplifies a great many of the principles this book is intended to convey:

1. It has been a courageous effort led by well informed people.
2. It illustrates a major point of mainstreaming practice: The major efforts must go into program development and into really changing the regular class environment, rather than just into moving children about or assessing them in some new way.
3. It stretched many of the special education rules and regulations that, perhaps, would not have been permitted in many places or, at least, would not have qualified the project for special education support. By not categorizing and labeling children, the project did not fit the usual patterns of one teacher working with a limited number of children in a special setting, and it focused on many of the functions of regular teachers.
4. The program has established a good record for helping children, and it is the obligation of the administrators who make the rules and the laws to catch up with and offer strong support for this kind of effort.

Summary of Collaborative Roles

The five emerging role models for special educators described here all involve collaborative working relationships with regular teachers. They are by no means the only models available and, indeed, even these models are constantly changing with time and with the needs of different schools. But the programs illustrate approaches that are essentially noncategorical in the traditional sense, proceed directly to the analysis of the child's problems by shaping individual plans for each child, maintain most exceptional children in the regular class environment, give the regular teacher immediate in-school help to deal with children who have special needs, and emphasize the advanced preparation of regular teachers and other school staff members for greater child focused professional performance.

In a sense, each of these models proposes a solution to the problems of knowledge dissemination and of role coordination. From the broad domains of knowledge relevant to the education of exceptional children are drawn the knowledge and skills that are most useful in school practice. Instead of mediating the knowledge and skills through a variety of narrowly categorized specialists, attempts are made to mediate through generic workers who have been selected and prepared with great care and who, themselves, engage in continuing training efforts. See Figure 9-2 for a graphic representation of a training based system.

FIGURE 9-2
Responsibility of Institutions of Higher Education
(IHE) for Knowledge Dissemination

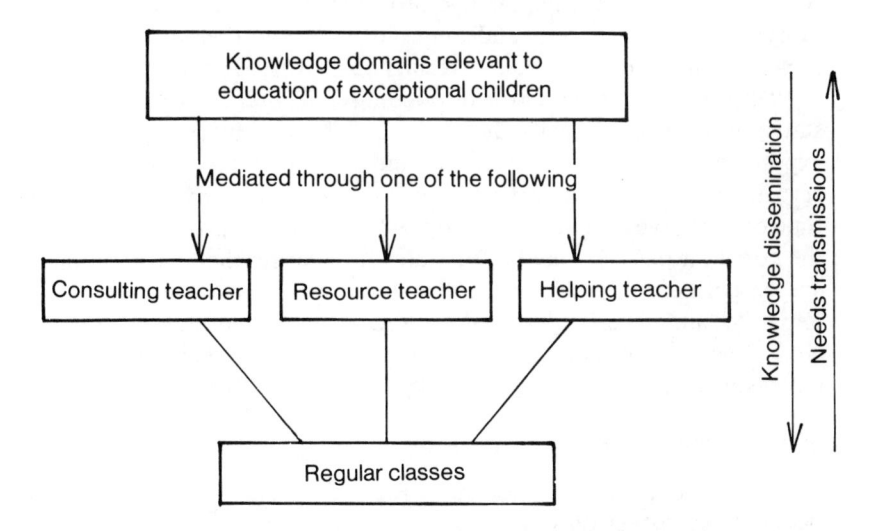

In considering the total system, it is possible to differentiate roughly among the responsibilities of various agencies for training activities, although collaboration among the agencies for training is always desirable. In general, institutions of higher education may be said to have primary responsibility for identifying and synthesizing the knowledge from relevant domains in order to train mediators for school situations. This responsibility is accomplished, in part, through preservice education and, in part, through continuing education activities.

Higher education's responsibility for knowledge dissemination is indicated in Figure 9-2 by the arrow pointing downward on the right side of the schema. Provisions should be made also, of course, for transmissions in the opposite direction, from daily classroom experiences through mediators to university personnel, so that the knowledge domains and the training efforts of university personnel are enriched by practical field data.

The sociology of school staffing has been made much too complex by the addition of too many specialists. Schools cannot employ all the specialists who might be needed; and even if they were affordable, deploying them would be too complex a task to be feasible. Thus, we can anticipate that the schools will employ and the institutions of higher education will prepare more and more special educators for more generic roles. A corresponding change will follow in child study and classification procedures; and crude, simplistic, and often demeaning categories and labels will no longer be the starting points for special education.

The implementation of more generic, collaborative models of special education raises difficult questions for teacher certification and program funding. A few states have made provision for more generic certifications (e.g., Massachusetts and Pennsylvania), and there are indications that many more will do so. The results of a DELPHI survey, conducted in 1973, demonstrated that the responding state directors of certification, state directors of special education, and leaders in special education expect the numbers of different kinds of special education teacher certification to be reduced from about seven or eight (the average at the time of the survey) to about four by 1983. One might predict that by then the common pattern may be for states to offer teacher certifications in speech correction, teaching the visually impaired, teaching the hearing impaired, and generic special education, the latter representing a merger across the now common areas of educable mentally retarded, emotionally disturbed, and learning disabled (Reynolds, 1973).

NEW ROLES FOR OTHER SCHOOL PERSONNEL

Like special education teachers, regular teachers frequently have occasion to work with other school staff members to serve exceptional children. These other staff members include school psychologists, school social workers, school counselors, and many other specialists. Brief descriptions of the changing roles of the three pupil personnel workers follow.

School Psychologists

School psychologists are a diverse group. Their competencies range from minimal qualifications in psychometrics to a broad and encompassing training in psychology and education. Traditionally, school psychologists have served as the gatekeepers of special education by making categorical certifications to meet the requirements of state departments of education for the placement of children in special classes.

Many of the developments in special education over the past decade have had the effect of devaluing the limited psychometric functions of school psychologists. Much of the traditional testing, such as the administration of the Stanford-Binet Intelligence Test or the Wechsler Intelligence Scale for Children and the classification decisions of psychologists have been discredited by the courts and dismissed as useless by many educators. The judicial and social demands for nondiscriminatory assessments present a great challenge to both school psychologists and educators. How can we identify the children who need help and provide that help without compounding the children's differences or making them suspect in the eyes of their peers? The serious efforts to answer this question have led to the investment of substantial energies in reconceptualizing the functions and role of school psychologists. As a result, the following topics are receiving new examinations and emphases:

1. Applied behavior analysis and contingency management.
2. Nontest (observational) assessment procedures.
3. Developmental assessment.
4. Psychoeducational diagnosis.
5. Teacher education, on topics such as individual assessment, systems procedures in individualization, behavior management, and use of peer tutors.
6. Ecological analysis and interventions.
7. Developmental education; for example, moral and ego development and social skill development.
8. Group processes.
9. Language development.

Day to day, the school psychologist often works closely with special educators, such as the resource teacher, and the regular class teacher. The psychologist and special educator usually try to learn how a given pupil functions by making observations of the youngster's characteristic activities in school or schoollike situations. Some of the observations are informal, that is, in the classroom while instruction is going on. Sometimes school psychologists stand in for the teacher or assist the teacher for part of one or more days to get a "hands on" sense of the teacher's concerns.

Teachers may help psychologists and other specialists gain insights into children's problems by simply arranging for them to listen and watch during periods of instruction. The more psychologists and special educators can see and hear at first hand, the more background they will have for using their particular special talents to help teachers.

Another important activity of the school psychologist and special educator is the collection and integration of relevant information on children with learning problems. Such data include the permanent records of a child's previous schooling; current achievement test scores; teacher grades, on both report cards and informal tests; records of parent contacts; notes made by the teacher or other personnel; summaries of staff conferences; and other test records and observations. It is not enough, of course, just to gather such raw facts and records. They must be collated, analyzed, and summarized. Usually the teacher has done some of the work. The school psychologist or special educator picks up the task at the point the teacher has reached and carries it forward.

Another part of data collection is initiated and carried out directly by the school psychologist and special educator. It consists of administering tests to the pupil, interviewing the pupil and, perhaps, family members, employers, community agency personnel, and other involved persons. Frequently, testing is complemented by diagnostic instruction of the pupil. Many psychologists consider such instruction to be more revealing than testing.

The teacher is in a central position throughout these data gathering activities. In a figurative sense the teacher is the quarterback, attentive to all the action, calling huddles when necessary, conferring with individual players, making sure that every necessary move is made and made correctly, and directing the whole effort toward the correct goal—the solution of the instructional problems that engendered the consultations in the first place. But the teacher is not omniscient and the school psychologist and special educator are not wizards; thus, all of their earnest efforts sometimes come to naught. More often, however, when they confer and discuss the ideas that evolve from their analyses, a plan of action can be designed and the teacher can try it out with the pupil. And that is the real objective of all of their work.

So far, the focus has been on the situation in which a pupil presents an instructional problem. But the teacher, school psychologist, and educational diagnostician need to work together in other situations, particularly when:

1. A plan of action for a particular child has been tried and is not productive.

2. A plan of action for a particular child appears to have been fully effective and the teacher wants another assessment of the child's progress to check that impression.
3. A parent wishes to review a child's status and records and the teacher feels that the specialists should participate in the review.
4. The teacher wants to know more about some of the instruments and procedures that are used by the psychologist and the diagnostician.
5. The teacher has developed a new approach to a particular instructional problem and wants help to evaluate it.
6. The teacher becomes concerned about individual or group behavior and wishes consultation on how to interpret and adapt to it.
7. The teacher wishes to be informed about or trained in some aspect of psychology or its application to classroom situations.

The list is not exhaustive; it shows that there are a great many instances in which teachers and their colleagues can aid each other. It is equally obvious that professional specialists and teachers are of little use to each other and to pupils unless they agree on their roles, coordinate their work, and act with a high level of integrity and consideration toward one another. As a member of the education professions, each can be a model for others in that regard.

The School Counselor

In many schools the functions of school psychologists and of special educators may well be performed by school counselors. However, counselors tend to be engaged in work with all students and often are not as readily available for intensive collaborative work with teachers on the problems of exceptional students.

One of the continuing important functions of counselors is to give leadership in the schools on topics of career development and career education. Preparation for employment is central to career development, and counselors usually are able to offer leadership in this aspect of student development and planning. This involves helping to develop effective instruction on career topics in all curriculum areas, and helping students to develop the self understanding that is essential to planning career goals.

A second topic, which is emerging unevenly in different parts of the country, is deliberate psychological education. Some counselors increasingly are turning their attention to curriculum, in such subjects as English and social studies, as a medium for facilitating the personal growth of students. For example, in literature instruction, efforts are made to structure the programs so that human developmental trends can be shown and the development of social roles for young women can be highlighted (Sprinthall & Erickson, 1974). In social studies, students are taught the techniques of developmental studies by interviewing persons of different ages on critical topics; the purpose is for the students to learn to see their own "problems" in developmental perspective. Direct instruction can include moral development, using the techniques of Kohlberg, and counseling and teaching skills, such as effective listening and reinforcement. Such deliberate psychological education can be an important means of facilitating the personal development of students and, in particular, of enhancing their ability to deal with differences among their fellow students (Mosher & Sprinthall, 1971).

School Social Workers

Recognizing that the problems of many children can be solved only through the cooperation of parents and teachers and that sometimes a broad array of community resources must be involved, many urban school systems have employed social workers to serve as general coordinators of school-community and school-parent efforts on behalf of children.

Overly close working relationships are not necessarily desirable between school and home. It is not uncommon, for example, for some parents to become excessively concerned about their children's academic achievements and, therefore, to exert constant, unrelenting pressures at home. When teachers and social workers observe a 10 year old boy who has yet to make his first real progress in reading, they often find that his parents are compounding his difficulties. The parents may try to tutor the boy at home in sessions that merely fatigue and exasperate them and make the child feel that he is a total failure. Such homes do not provide the loving, supportive refuges that children need. As part of the school's total plan of remediation for such children, the social workers may be called on to help the parents to learn to separate themselves from school concerns and to focus instead on their children's other needs.

In other cases, the problem may be to establish relationships with parents who completely dissociate themselves from their children's difficulties in school. These parents, who may have had difficulties in school themselves, often distrust teachers and other personnel, and they may prefer "closed door" policies both at home and school. The communication problem may be heightened if the cultural values of the family and school personnel differ.

The problem is to achieve a balanced degree of school-home-community interactions (Litwak & Meyer, 1967) that permits effective communication about and planning for children whose educational progress is in doubt. Sometimes, school social workers need to work through community organizations, such as settlement houses, voluntary associations of neighborhoods or cultural groups, health and welfare agencies, or others to achieve contacts with the family and to begin planning for the child.

School social workers may be the first contact for teachers in some schools when special studies of children must be undertaken and the involvement of parents and other community agencies in the process is essential. In other schools, these social work functions may be performed by the school principal, a psychologist, or a special education supervisor.

Other Working Partners

Potentially, the teacher has many other collaborators to call on to serve students with exceptional needs. Some are employed by the schools, such as counselors, nurses, and special education supervisors; others may be employed in the community but are available for consultation, such as physicians, audiologists, optometrists, and clinical psychologists.

Teachers often have had less experience in face to face consultation with the broad array of specialists in the schools and community than these specialists have accumulated in their work. Consequently, it is often helpful, when broad ranging studies and consultation are involved, to provide for teachers at least one person who will help represent the classroom situation. For example, a school principal or school social worker, after having become thoroughly familiar with the classroom situation of the teacher and child, may join in the broad interprofessional staff meetings to help to develop plans for a child.

As studies of children proceed through the efforts of many specialists and consultants, they must not overlook the fact that it is usually the teacher who spends the most hours with the child during the long school year. Other than the home, the school is the most important environment for children developmentally, and it is the teachers who shape this environment. It is essential that all professionals who engage in the study of children with school difficulties work within the context of so aiding the teacher that the practical result, in turn, will be to enhance every child's development. The teaching-learning situation managed by teachers must be the central focus of the collaborative efforts of psychologists, social workers, audiologists, physicians, and others who consult with the teacher. The teacher, and those who work with teachers, must recognize the teacher's central, coordinating role. Teachers should insist, we believe, on being accountable for carrying out educational plans only when they have had a significant role in drawing up the plans. Teachers often need help, but they need it in forms that can be clearly translated into the realities of instructional process.

MODIFICATIONS IN THE LARGER SYSTEM

In earlier sections of this chapter, some of the new roles that are being developed by special educators, school psychologists, school social workers, and others are described. The development of these roles is important for teachers because it is based on new conditions for planning and implementing new kinds of programs. The entire structure of school as a social institution and of role relationships within the school is changing.

The Individually Guided Education System

Another aspect of change that has important implications for the teaching of exceptional students is the broad change now occurring in many schools in the systems of service delivery. The following description of an elementary school that organized itself according to the individually guided education system, which was devised by the University of Wisconsin Research and Development Center on Cognitive Learning (Klausmeier, Quilling, Sorenson, Way, & Glasrud, 1971; Klausmeier, Rossmiller, & Sailey, 1977), is an example.

The teachers who had been in age-grade classrooms reorganized themselves into three units (A, B, and C). Grades no longer exist. Children who in most schools might be in grades 5 and 6, for example, are in Unit C.

The several teachers in each unit work together on the total program with each having a specialty. For example, one teacher leads in science, another in math, a third in language, and so on. One teacher serves as unit leader.

A variety of methods and materials for instruction is organized in each content field so that, for example, students can work individually or in small groups and can vary their rate of progress. The scheduling of instruction is organized to give every teacher time for planning and development of instruction. (Teacher aides and parents are used to this end.)

Subject matter consultants and pupil personnel specialists are called in at propitious times to work with the whole staff to solve problems or to assist in developmental work.

Criterion/domain oriented assessments are widely used to specify what individual children are ready to undertake in their studies. The assessment system is coordinated carefully with the particular instructional objectives that have been set in reading, arithmetic, and other subjects.

Parents are given every opportunity to learn about the new instructional system and they are engaged in helping processes at many points. Report cards have changed quite dramatically to reflect specific achievements as well as relative progress in the various subjects.

Children who formerly were placed in educable mentally retarded and learning disabled special education classrooms are now part of the regular stream of instruction in the schools. The special education teachers work with the clusters of teachers in the several units to provide particularly intensive studies and plans for the children who seem to have most difficulty.

Obviously, exceptional children who attend a school that has gone on the individually guided education plan, or some similar system (Talmage, 1975), are in a much different situation than those who attend most schools. The regular teacher who serves in an individually guided education school or one that has fully developed such a system for individualizing instruction, is in a far better position to meet the particular needs of each pupil.

The individually guided education system is essentially a method for the management of instruction. It can be adapted to varieties of objectives and instructional materials. However, specially adapted sets of materials are now becoming available for use in broad systems-oriented programs. In a development that is collateral to the individually guided education system, the staff of the University of Wisconsin has produced a special set of reading materials called the *Wisconsin Design for Reading Skill Development*. This is a management system for individualizing reading. By using the system, the teacher can identify the scope and sequence of a pupil's skills.

Skills are defined in terms of behavioral objectives and progress is measured by criterion referenced tests. The materials include six components and a teacher's resource file. There is a card for each component with a hole punched out for each skill in the component. The skill is taught and the test is taken. The cards of pupils who have passed the test are notched so that the hole is opened to the edge of the card. When the teacher is ready to review that skill, the whole group of cards is placed on a long wire through the hole representing that skill. Then the teacher shakes the wire, the cards remaining on it belong to pupils who need further instruction in that skill. Only these students are retaught the skill using suggestions from the resource file.

The teacher can have several different skill groups going at one time by using learning centers, individual work sheets, or whatever the needs of the children suggest. The system can be used with any basal series or the individualized reading approach, in which students choose their own reading material, and the teacher never has to teach skills to students who already have mastered them. Students work only on those skills in which they have weaknesses. Those who do not need reteaching move on to other activities. No one is held back or pushed forward in the mastery of a skill.

The Job Corps Program

Another example of a systems approach to reading for older students is provided by the General Educational Development (GED) Reading

Program of the Job Corps, which was developed by the US Department of Labor. Boys in the Corps learn to read factual materials that are normally presented in high school. The program deals simultaneously with reading as a skill and the various subject matter fields of secondary education.

The material is arranged in the order of increasing difficulty. A boy begins reading at the 9.0 grade level and completes the program at the 12.0 level. A series of screening and unit tests are given. When a screening test is passed, the pupil goes directly to the unit test for that study unit. If a pupil fails the screening test, the next step is to read booklets for that study unit before taking the unit test.

A student reads only about the subject matter the screening test shows he does not know. In learning the subject matter, the student is also improving his ability to read.

The program, individualized and self pacing, includes 24 units and 125 booklets. Students have from one month to two years to complete the program. Some students complete one booklet per day while others complete a whole unit of study in that time. Some are able to skip reading booklets. Students who are self motivated do well on their own. Those who have certain skill deficiencies may have problems with the method; teacher assistance is provided when it is needed.

The program is not recommended for group instruction, only for individualized teaching. The literature contains reports on several modified reading programs that have been patterned on the Job Corps program so information on this approach is readily available.

In both of the above examples, students proceed to advanced topics only when they have mastered the prerequisites. As noted elsewhere in this volume, such carefully systematized approaches to learning as the mastery approach (Bloom, 1968) seem particularly important for students of low academic aptitude or those whose initial responses to instruction in a skill are minimal (Burrows & Okey, 1975; Tobias, 1976).

In increasing numbers of communities, there is not only an ongoing renegotiation and realignment of regular education and of special education programs, with all of the role changes that this activity implies, but also the installation of broad, schoolwide programs to deal with individual differences. These systems are not simply ability grouping, like the systems so common in the 1930's, or tracking systems, like the systems that were discredited in the 1960's. They are systems of a different order that depend on domain oriented assessments, clear specification of objectives for instruction, careful management of instruction in accordance with what seems to be optimal for the individual, and remarkable changes in the roles of teachers. The role changes involve more collaborative modes of work among teachers, which allow for some specialization and time for developmental work on instruction. The context for the education of handicapped and gifted students is remarkably different and promising when it is part of a system that is committed to effective education for all students. Special educators have a special commitment in this context.

INSTRUCTIONAL PROCEDURES USEFUL FOR ALL STUDENTS

A fact that has become clearer in recent years is that the same principles, procedures, and techniques of teaching nonhandicapped children are often useful with many different kinds of exceptional children. That is a basic assumption of this chapter. We reject the notion that distinctly different instructional procedures are necessary for children in the several traditional special education categories. Most of the teaching approaches, for example, that are effective with speech handicapped pupils or so-called mentally retarded pupils also work well with emotionally disturbed, blind, or other exceptional pupils. Considerable crossover from one group to another is possible in ways of teaching exceptional children effectively.

Another fact that has recently become more widely recognized is that many principles, procedures, and techniques of teaching, which were first created or used for the instruction of exceptional children, are just as effective for regular class pupils. Actually, for years many regular class teachers have been following teaching approaches very similar to those used by their special education colleagues, and with rewarding results.

This is not to say that there are no forms of instruction particularly appropriate for certain exceptional children. Specialized forms include, for example: mobility training, braille, and other forms of tactual approaches for blind pupils; breath control and delayed sound feedback for pupils who stutter; and speech reading, sign, and manual communication for deaf pupils. But these are not methods; they are technical skills that are of limited use for regular class pupils, although they are essential for the appropriate exceptional children. Some of the other specific instructional needs for exceptional pupils are described in the chapters devoted to specific exceptionalities.

The instructional principles, procedures, and techniques designed chiefly for exceptional children make up only a small portion of the instructional approaches that are used by special educators. The largest portion are applicable to a much broader population. To paraphrase Lester Myer, an early leader in special education, "What is good for special children is often especially good for all children." Nowhere is this axiom better demonstrated than in the application to regular class pupils of teaching approaches that were originally proposed for children with special learning needs.

Basis of Effective Teaching

In both regular and special education, the basis of effective teaching is to "understand the problems and deal with them in terms of the child in a special environment as arranged by the teacher. Discussions which fall short of that level are mere rhetoric or emotion" (Reynolds & Balow, 1972, p. 365). We believe this principle applies with equal force to all pupils and we emphasize that in implementing the principle the teacher is the central professional figure.

Gage (1972) summarized the research on effective teaching in terms of four teacher characteristics: warmth, indirectness, cognitive organization, and enthusiasm. Each characteristic is open to a range of interpretations, it is true, but we take all to mean a combination of lively, friendly interest, a style of interaction that includes considerate listening and adapting to others, a rational, planful approach to one's daily tasks, and an infectious zeal for whatever is undertaken. To produce those qualities all day every day is a tall order, to be sure, and most of us fall short of that goal occasionally. Nevertheless, these characteristics are known to be associated with effective instruction more often than not.

American educators who visited modern British schools analyzed them to locate the teaching-learning factors that differentiated the innovative primary schools from their traditional counterparts. The visitors identified the following instructional practices as those that seemed to make school more interesting and satisfying (they are listed in order of frequency of identification):

1. Stimulation and reward of the pupil's curiosity by the teacher when the curiosity was directed toward appropriate objects, activities, or information.
2. Secure and relaxed, often home-like, environments that nurtured and responded educationally to probing from the children.
3. Frequent use of parent and community resources in varied ways.
4. Capitalization on the incidental motivations of children arising from the interests and curiousities engendered by their self-directed and free activities.
5. Many different instructional materials covering a wide range of topics and difficulty levels.
6. Arrangement and re-arrangement of the instructional space to help children in the changing class activities.
7. Encouragement of pupil imagination in educationally constructive ways.
8. Use of child interactions to promote social growth in pupils. (King-Stoops, 1974, p. 215)

Much dependence on the professional judgment of the teacher is evident in making these factors work. In the first one, for instance, the teacher's understanding and insight provide the criterion for what is meant by the key word *appropriate*. The same is true in each of the following factors. In the last one, the teacher is relied on to know what interactions to select for use and how to use them and to know what is the correct social growth objective to aim at next for each child. Nowhere is the great responsibility and sound judgment expected of the teacher better illustrated than in the selection and management of instructional practices.

Teaching Approaches

Each professional teacher should find his or her own instructional style that combines effectiveness and comfort. This is not to imply that every teacher must labor alone through trial and error to rediscover the principles of instruction, or that there are fixed, set, guaranteed ways of dealing with pupils that can be used automatically by the teacher. The road to the development of a productive personal teaching style is also a road to self realization, self knowledge, and self esteem—the road to responsible professional freedom.

The critical qualities can be cultivated, and it is worth the attempt to achieve them. So, too, the following teaching approaches can be made part of a repertoire of professional skills and abilities. This series of descriptive statements about teaching procedures can be called "pointers" on how to teach. Each is based on research and theory. Reference to the supporting documentation is kept to a minimum to save space and increase readability.

None of the procedures has the quality of a magic wand. Each requires thought and effort to apply. Teaching procedures are building blocks that can be used to construct truly individualized education for both exceptional and regular pupils. Using the pointers also can increase teaching productivity and lead to the professional and personal satisfaction of a job well done.

When you observe master teachers, see how many of the procedures they use. Try them in practice yourself. As we said, teaching is something that you do.

Undercutting: Beginning a Little Below Where the Child Is

A teacher should start to teach well within the range of a pupil's present skills and understandings, rather than at the limit (Betts, 1946; Birch, 1955). If a child's reading comprehension is at grade 3.5, the day's reading should start with material at grade 3.0 and move on to more challenging material after a few assured early success experiences. If the new material's difficulty level begins to upset the youngster, the teacher should drop back a little until the reader regains confidence.

The same procedure can be followed in more complex learning tasks, such as filling out tax forms or balancing a checking account. It applies also to pupils who are learning important self help behaviors, such as washing and drying hands or buttoning coats.

Many exceptional children and youth experience more than a fair share of failures in the ordinary course of life. The cumulative effect of too frequently finding oneself unable to do what most contemporaries succeed at is demoralizing. Worse, it breeds an expectation of failure. Undercutting is a sound tactic to combat such expectations in the context of a school lesson. It gives the pupil a running start on a success paved road by raising the level of self expectation just prior to the assault on the next task. If the instructional sequence that follows is then matched to the pupil's capacity and deliberately seeded with "easy spots" to maintain the pupil's self confidence, the child's level of self expectancy will be confirmed (rewarded) often enough to keep the learning on an upward course. In the long range, if that tactic is used consistently and kept realistic (not overprotective), it becomes a strategy for altering the pupil's total behavior. If internalized, it can be a step toward a more success oriented outlook on life in general.

Some children, of course, function inconsistently from day to day. For example, there may be days when a child is completely unable to attend or respond to teacher instructions; another child may be able to mobilize all resources to work at a high mastery level only occasionally. In such cases, the teacher may wish to consult with a special education teacher or psychologist for help in designing systems by which the teacher can recognize the child's signals and determine what is appropriate on any given day in order to work toward greater attentiveness and responsiveness. Hewett (1968) has suggested a sequence of educational goals that may be considered both in undercutting and in development; the sequence is: attention, response, order, exploratory, social, mastery, achievement. Thus, in applying the principle of undercutting there will be occasional cases of extreme difficulty even under the best of circumstances that call for teamwork by the staff of a school.

Using Direct Experience

Many widely recognized approaches to instruction build on the potential value of past pupil experience in helping the teacher to determine where and how to begin instruction. Indeed, the process of instruction can be made more interesting if the pupil is engaged in "hands on" experiences rather than being confined to a passive observer role. Methods of teaching that contrast active and passive learning roles follow:

Pupil as Active Participant

Discussion, pupil led
Experience story reading
Free expression
Dramatic play
Discovery
Independent study
Research
Problem solution by pupils

Pupil as Passive Participant

Demonstration by teacher
Lecture by teacher

There is a great difference between the arbitrary assignment by a teacher of a topic to be investigated and the recommendation by a teacher of a topic from a list of three or four generated by a pupil. There also is a great difference between a solely textbook determined approach to social studies and one based on actual, local community issues, as unearthed by pupils. When the focus is shifted from the ideas of the teacher and the textbook to the preoccupations of the pupils, the hackneyed expression "meaningful" takes on reality.

In a small Texas city, children of middle school age addressed the question of how to develop a school playground that would be appealing and adaptable to exceptional children. With the aid of their teachers, the children studied the special recreational needs of blind, deaf, and other physically impaired youngsters who are traditionally identified as requiring special education. Teacher Corps volunteers helped the project through to the actual development and "grand opening" of the playground. In a short time, regular class pupils abandoned the "regular" playground for the new one, and joint play with exceptional pupils grew. The collaboration continued and the originators of the project—pupils and teachers—discovered more about human likenesses and differences and their meaning for social interaction than could ever have been gleaned from passive participation in textbook and lecture lessons.

Helping the Child Set the Pace of Learning

Even very young children sometimes have a surprising degree of awareness of their own best pace for taking in new experiences. That self knowledge grows in usefulness as the children have more opportunities to set their own rates on learning tasks. Therefore, teachers are well advised to help pupils become aware of their own performance characteristics.

"How long shall we plan for this activity to take?" is preferable to "This assignment is due by tomorrow at noon." The question, after discussion, may lead to the same end as the declaration, but it has been answered in terms of pupil participation and commitment.

Factors related to pupil requirements (e.g., problems of mobility, slowness in writing, speech impairments, printed material needing to be transposed to tape or braille) sometimes influence learning pace significantly. So do factors extrinsic to the pupil, such as the relative difficulty of the learning task, other assignments and time commitments, and the adequacy and availability of teacher or tutorial assistance.

Three outcomes are to be looked for:

1. The pupil learns to estimate accurately how long it will take to accomplish any new learning task.
2. The pupil learns to set a personal learning pace that will accomplish a task within a reasonable margin of error.
3. The pupil will learn to identify and practice techniques for advancing the pace of learning while maintaining standards of comprehension and retention.

Teachers can employ charts and intermittent rewards to help pupils foster the first two outcomes. The third may be better encouraged by verbal reinforcement for positive accomplishments..

Regular teachers may wish to consult special education teachers for assistance in designing instructional systems for students who have particular difficulties in the pacing of instruction and learning. The special education teacher might help, for example, by installing detailed systems for the day to day timing and charting of children's progress or by differentiating spaces or environments according to the rate of behavior expected or by rewarding the timely completion of assignments.

Employing Principles of Reinforcement Systematically

Teachers who work with pupils with special needs find the procedures developed by applied behavior analysts very useful. A number of such schemes are based upon the basic work of Skinner (1968) in the facilitation of learning. The schemes may differ somewhat in emphasis but all have the following elements in common:

1. A pupil's specific behavior is chosen for attention. It can be any behavior from learning an addition combination or carrying a tune to proper fingernail hygiene or using polite language.
2. Systematic attention is given to reinforcing the pupil's desired behavior when it occurs. The teacher who is not familiar with the basic principles of reinforcement should carefully study materials on the optimal conditions for achieving and maintaining rate changes (Haring & Phillips, 1972; Haring & Schiefelbusch, 1976).

3. Systematic records are kept on the pupil's progress toward mastery of the desired behavior, and reinforcements are changed as necessary to maintain progress and attainment.

These procedures have the virtue of being readily applied by teachers, singly or in teams, and by parents under teacher guidance. Thus, they supply a promising way for teachers and parents to work together to produce pupil behavior that is identified as desirable.

The Premack principle (Premack, 1959) is a special case of operant conditioning in which the learning activities themselves can be used as positive reinforcement. Desirable learning activities are scheduled to follow immediately and as a positive consequence of the desired behavior on a less desirable learning task. For example, if a child who loves music is allowed to go to music acitvities as a consequence of good performance in mathematics lessons, which are valued less highly by the child, the result should be a better rate of performance in mathematics. All teachers want to encourage the love and practice of learning for learning's sake. The Premack principle is a behaviorist parallel to that philosophical goal of liberal education. The principle can be made operative in a variety of school settings and with all kinds of pupils at all levels.

The application of behavioral principles is a topic in which teachers may frequently wish to involve special education teachers or school psychologists as advisors and consultants. The consultant often can help make observations in the class to pinpoint the behaviors that need to be influenced, to establish the rates at which they appear, and to design systems of reinforcing change. The most frequent failures in applying the procedures result from inconsistency of any degree and not keeping systematic records. The use of a consultant to help install a workable system for dealing with extreme behaviors that need either to be accelerated or decelerated is highly recommended.

Giving the Child Choices

The variety of stimuli in today's world makes it imperative that children learn during their school years to make intelligent choices. Happily, to give pupils opportunities for choices is often a helpful way to motivate them to improved achievement. One way is to arrange the day's activities so that each pupil can select a personal daily schedule, as long as all parts of the day's work are accomplished. Such self scheduling gives needed practice to pupils who tend to be disorganized. If options are presented carefully, a few at first and more as the child learns to handle them, the teacher will be able to observe the pupil's progress in self management. The pupil's choices can devolve on *what* is to be done, *when* things are to be done, *where* the activity is to take place, *with whom* the work is to be done, and sometimes, *whether or not* to take on the task at all. It is fundamental, of course, that the teacher monitor very closely the pupil's decision making tasks and performances to be sure that the youngster is not overwhelmed, on the one hand, or, unchallenged on the other hand.

Another way to construct a learning environment replete with opportunities for practice in how to make wise choices is to use contingency contracting. The pupil and teacher agree that if and when a certain task is accomplished the pupil will then be free to do one of several other appealing things. Contingency contracting can be used with more than one pupil at a time, too. Sometimes an entire class may be involved.

Offering choices is realistic and effective. It parallels experiences in out-of-school life. It helps pupils to learn to depend on their own judgment. It gives pupils conscious daily experiences in self control and in the management of their own affairs. And it has the further advantage of giving teachers opportunities to guide pupils, rather than coerce them, and to observe how pupils grow in the assumption of responsibility.

Occasionally, some students should be given freedom just to take time out, to plan disengagement from school tasks for a while. Special spaces for time out are sometimes necessary also for children who have episodic periods of incapacity to engage in learning activities. Teachers may wish to consult with special education teachers or school psychologists in thinking through and planning the use of time out as a student choice.

Encouraging Constructive Divergent Thinking

Many children appear to lose their imaginative abilities during the school years. Constructive imagination is a wholesome quality, and it may well be the precursor of adult artistic, literary, or scientific creativity. The conscious ability to think in divergent ways is important in its own right for problem solving in childhood and youth. The nation needs adults who can invent ways to keep abreast or ahead of the problems spawned by our burgeoning civilization. Thus, all school children, exceptional or otherwise, should be encouraged to develop the ability to engage in productive divergent thinking.

Teachers can take deliberate steps to foster positive forms of creative thinking in all aspects of the school curriculum. There is no child, young or old, high achiever or low achiever, who cannot profit if the following procedures become a part of each teacher's daily repertoire of instructional behaviors:

1. Planning a "what if" element in every lesson. What if suddenly no one in the world could see colors? How would that change our lives? What if the average temperature of the world rose 2 degrees for a year? What if the South had won the Civil War? What if no one in the world could hear? What if there were no insects? What if Columbus had not received backing for his explorations?

2. Checking each lesson plan, homework exercise, and test to see that there is a balance between questions that have only one satisfactory answer and questions that allow the pupil to reason through to alternative appropriate responses.
3. Encouraging each child, at least once a day, to introduce a divergent thought into whatever is being studied.

These three procedures should not preclude situations in which only one answer is correct. The world is full of such situations. It would be a disservice to overlook teaching pupils the kind of convergent thinking that is needed in those instances. What is wanted is equal time for acquiring skill in and learning to value the constructive divergent thinking upon which so much of each pupil's future might depend.

There are some students who have great difficulty in accepting assignments or structuring from anyone in positions of authority; they have extraordinary need to design their own approaches to schooling. Perhaps they will eagerly read widely on broadly framed topics and happily engage in creative discussions about them, but resist and resent directions by teachers to converge on particular knowledges and skills. Adolescents who drop out of regular schools and then enroll in street academies or school within a school arrangements may be seeking more opportunities for divergent and creative thinking. These students often are best served by encouraging them to explore and to create on their own if, for whatever period of time, they are unable to tolerate a more balanced convergent and divergent educational diet.

Giving Children Chances for Leadership

A graduate student completed making a brief presentation to the other eight students in the seminar and led a spirited half hour discussion on the topic. The student then asked the instructor, "How did it go? How did I do?"

"Don't you know?" asked the instructor. "Can't you tell from what you saw and heard?"

"No. That's the first time in my whole school career that I ever did anything like that!"

A number of recent studies have revealed that (a) the great majority of talking in elementary and secondary school classes is done by teachers and (b) the overwhelming majority of all questions in those classes are asked by the teachers. The consequent advice for teachers is to set up more situations in which the teacher is a listener and responder rather than a talker and questioner.

Leadership is a subtle matter, often no more than a feeling by the person who is before the group. Pupils who are comfortable in leadership roles are those who have had practice in leading, under teacher guidance, and who are leading because they are acknowledged to be ready for the role by the rest of the group.

Leadership skills range from the knowledge of parliamentary procedures, which are essential to the conduct of formal meetings of established organizations, to personal control, to the mastery of such techniques as brainstorming. The elements of these skills are important to all pupils and, especially, exceptional pupils. The skills originate and develop best in classes where the teachers do not monopolize the informal leadership opportunities by doing all the talking and asking all the questions.

Using Peer Instruction

Children learn a great deal from each other and retain what they learn at a high level. Teachers can harness that pupil power and return it to even more effective use.

In one school, fifth and sixth grade pupils voluntarily give part time service as teacher assistants in the third and fourth grades. They flip flash cards to reinforce arithmetic combinations or reading sight vocabulary, and tutor one, two, or three of their younger schoolmates at a time. In another school, musically talented pupils join with the music teacher in coaching aspirants to the school band, orchestra, chorus, and smaller instrumental and vocal units. In secondary schools, pupils serve as laboratory assistants in biology, chemistry, and physics; as assistant instructors in physical education, dance, and art studios; and as theme readers for less advanced composition classes.

The activities are not all teacher generated. Three husky fifth graders stopped the principal in the cafeteria one day, and one said, "We'd like to be the stage set up team for assemblies, Mr. Williams. Just let us know what you want moved."

A high school junior volunteered to a physical education teacher, "I'll help you for one hour a week in the adaptive physical education classes if you will teach me something about fencing."

Pupil to pupil instruction need not be exploitative. Both pupils ought to realize the advantages, as should their parents. Older, emotionally disturbed pupils gain self confidence through reading stories to kindergarteners. Gifted students, while helping to teach others, extend and apply their own knowledge. High school pupils, who "buddy" with deaf students by sharing class notes and rechecking the correct comprehension of assignments, receive special instruction in efficient note taking. Other secondary pupils assisting pupils who use crutches and wheelchairs in movement or in carrying books obtain credit toward extracurricular activities awards. Moreover, many of the helpers engage in reciprocal academic tutoring with the same pupils.

Additional potential benefits include the development in pupils of empathy, willingness to listen, and rudimentary counseling skills. The responsibility for helping others can become more real to the pupils who participate, too. Equally important, young people can sample the activities, problems, and satisfactions of the professional educator, and a more knowledgeable pool of potential educators can result.

Teachers may wish to consult with their special education teacher or psychologists for help in setting up training systems for students who have agreed to participate in intensive tutoring exercises with handicapped students.

Within the same class or across class or age groups, peer instruction is more and more recognized as desirable and advantageous. It can be a substantial instructional tool if it is planned and developed by teachers, pupils, and parents.

Using Pupil Feedback

Most teachers look informally for pupil reactions and use them to sense when things are or are not going well in a lesson. Highly skilled teachers have developed the ability to stand outside themselves and to make relatively dispassionate assessments of their performances. That quality of consciously using oneself as an instrument to guide and mediate learning by others may be the key characteristic that separates the journeyman from the artist in teaching.

Pupil feedback comprises the external data needed by teachers to help determine the worth of what they do. To collect the data informally is of value, but the feedback data are much more useful if they are collected systematically. Then the ordered data can be combined by teachers with their subjective impressions and, together, they form a basis for decisions about next steps.

The most widely used device for obtaining pupil feedback is the test. Pupils should be tested frequently, and the tests should be criterion referenced. Washing hands before eating, for instance, is not really learned until it is part of a pupil's regular day to day behavior; correctly answering a true-false question is an inappropriate criterion. Similarly, marking the correct tense of a verb on a multiple choice test does not assure that the child will use the correct tense in writing or speaking; observation of everyday usage is the proper test because it refers directly to the criterion.

Teachers often find it useful to discuss with pupils what forms tests should take and when they should be administered. Even in the earliest years children are surprisingly perceptive about what they need to learn and how mastery should be tested.

Regularly, too, the input of pupils should be sought regarding the relevance of what is being taught. For instance, eight pregnant inner city teenagers were drawn into a discussion of how they wanted their babies to talk when they grew up. In the inner city argot? In the stylized form of the television commentator? Like admired contemporary personalities? Out of the discussion emerged a new appreciation for the boundary crossing capability, the broader life opportunities to be expected from the versatility arising from a command of both inner city and cosmopolitan language, in written and oral form. It was a short step then to more participation by the pupils in self testing, monitoring their own and each other's speech, and then writing.

Modern instructional systems (i.e., individually prescribed instruction or individually guided education) have built-in checkpoints to supply feedback from pupils to the teacher. The procedures are even more helpful when the teacher supplements them by informal observations and the ideas of pupils.

Giving Prompt Feedback to Pupils

Another characteristic of some contemporary instructional systems (i.e., Distar or Plan*) is that information on performance is rapidly returned to pupils. There is substantial evidence that the shorter the time lapse between action and reaction, the more learning is facilitated.

It is helpful for pupils to see their progress charted, whether in learning foreign language vocabulary, novels read, staying in one's seat, making a set of bookends, or mastering spelling words. Charting seems often to serve as a reinforcement. Although it can be maintained by the teacher, aide, or a pupil who is "chart coordinator," the chart seems to work more effectively if the learner makes the periodic and cumulative entries.

Whether charts or other visual displays play a part in pupil feedback, it is crucial that the entire response system be domain rather than norm oriented. Pupils gain the most if they can see progress against their earlier achievements rather than against a norm—an external criterion made up by averaging the achievements of other pupils.

Moving from Familiar to Unfamiliar

In some respects this procedure is a way of saying, "Individualize in-instruction," but it goes deeper than that. Pupils frequently are not aware of the important linkages of tasks they have learned to the seemingly new learning tasks that confront them. Hence, expressions like, "Begin where the learner is," take on a special significance.

Teachers who probe carefully are sometimes surprised at what pupils know and what they are able to do. A 9 year old Mexican American boy

---

*Distar and Plan are highly developed instructional systems. (See Engelmann, Osborn, & Englemann, 1969 and *Distar Orientation,* 1971.)

appeared very deficient on intelligence and achievement tests, even when examined in Spanish by a sympathetic person. He could read and write less well than most second graders. Yet he held his own with much older pupils on the school playground, and he organized a small but tough group that he led like commandos. Delving into his background showed that since he was 6 years old he had hawked cigarettes in a Mexican border town, exacted tribute from other street children there, and maintained himself in that human jungle, with only a tenuous relationship with a home and a mother who was preoccupied with her own survival. It can be assumed that the Spanish in which he was examined at school bore about the same relationship to his natural language as midwestern American does to Louisiana Cajun.

The first step for the teacher is to find out where the pupil is, educationally speaking. That calls for sensitive probing and listening. Once it has been ascertained what is *familiar* to the youngster, the teacher then can help build a bridge to what is familiar to the other pupils. That calls for taking small steps, at least at first, and reinforcing them strongly. Once started, however, the network that ties unfamiliar to familiar can expand geometrically, at whatever rate the child proves capable of maintaining.

Obviously the special education teacher and other consultants can help in special instances of children who require detailed study in order to determine where they are in background and skills. It may be helpful for the school social worker to study the home background and cultural context from which the student comes; and the psychologist often can help specify the cognitive functioning and language or other achievements that need to be considered in trying to "match" child and program.

Modeling Behavior

Children tend to imitate adults and other children they admire. They mold their own behavior to conform to the examples of others they observe to be successful. Knowledge about this phenomenon can be turned by teachers into a strong and versatile instructional tool, especially when it is combined with an understanding of the power of positive reinforcement.

Teacher A felt that Mary Adams and Andy Cameron were fine examples of how pupils should behave, both academically and as school citizens. Teacher A often stated this opinion to other pupils, frequently suggesting that it would be well if all of them were like Mary or Andy.

Teacher B considered Joline Whetsell and Tony Renzulli to be the best illustrations of studious and well mannered pupils in the class. Sylvia Roof and Billy Jones were the opposite. Teacher B arranged the class as often as feasible so Sylvia and Billy could see Joline and Tony. She also had figured out what things Sylvia and Billy liked to be allowed to do in school that were acceptable in the class context. These activities became rewards, although the teacher said nothing about them to the pupils. She also picked out the behavioral objectives for Sylvia (raising her hand for attention rather than interrupting others) and Billy (keeping his hands at rest on his desk rather than tapping with a pencil or poking the child in front).

Joline and Tony consistently did what the teacher wanted Sylvia and Billy to do, and they generally liked doing whatever the teacher asked. From time to time, not on a regular schedule, the teacher asked Joline and Tony to do what she knew that Sylvia and Billy liked doing. Also, whenever Sylvia or Billy achieved, for even a short time, the objectives set for them, the teacher smiled or made a small favorable comment, quietly, to them. From time to time, but not always, when either Sylvia or Billy performed as desired, the teacher told them they could do one of the things they liked. When Sylvia and Billy had become habituated to the behaviors set as objectives, the teacher then moved on to do the same with other desired behaviors. Joline and Tony were kept in view, also, and Sylvia and Billy saw them being rewarded for desirable deportment.

Teacher A recognized the situation for what it was, but did not deal with it effectively. In fact, the approach taken could be expected to worsen the behavior of some pupils who found undifferentiated teacher attention rewarding.

Teacher B deliberately set out to accomplish two broad goals: (a) to guide Sylvia and Billy toward identifying and using certain other pupils as models and (b) to embark on a series of systematic moves to help Sylvia and Billy to find increased satisfaction in more acceptable academic behavior. The odds are good that Teacher B would make substantial headway toward those goals.

The teacher, of course, is a model of major dimensions. If a teacher habitually shouts at children it can be predicted that loud talking and shouting by the pupils will be reinforced. If a teacher is calm and speaks directly in a well modulated tone, that example will tend to be taken by the pupils. In other respects, too, the actions of the teacher tend to reappear in the pupils.

Using Reviews Meaningfully

Successful teachers use reviews frequently to remind pupils of what they have already learned. Opportunities to repeat and thus to see and feel one's own achievements build and strengthen self esteem.

There is a delicate and constantly changing balance between what pupils can achieve at certain stages of development and what is beyond them, and the sensitive teacher monitors that balance carefully. Thus, the review of past lessons is helpful if it results in building up in pupils a feeling of positive accomplishment, not failure. This feeling of accomplishment can motivate pupils to keep on trying in order to achieve that rewarding feeling again.

Review should be regular, meaningful, and focused on recent learning. When it includes fundamentals that were learned earlier, the association between those fundamentals and recently learned material should be made explicit. A good way to make review meaningful is to encourage pupils to teach what they have learned to others. Also effective is allowing committees of pupils to invent new ways of review, or incorporating reviews into such activities as dramatic play, games, or publications. Almost any kind of review works, providing it is meaningful and regular and pupils are aware that they are reviews.

Helping Pupils Learn How They Learn

For at least the past half century, elementary and secondary school curricula have included content from such sciences as mathematics, biology, chemistry, and physics. Although the behavioral sciences for many years have been required studies for teachers and other educational personnel, only recently have they been included in the course offerings of public schools. In many secondary schools now, psychology is being offered as a secondary school course, frequently accompanied by laboratory activities.

However, the content of psychology is such that it need not always be taught formally. There are many potential advantages for all children, whether handicapped or not, in acquiring insights into how and under what conditions learning takes place. Learning about learning (a) gives pupils a realistic understanding of and perspective on their own cognitive, affective, moral, and motoric development; (b) explains interpersonal differences in style or approach to learning; (c) makes pupils more knowledgeable participants in arranging their own learning experiences; and (d) furnishes pupils with a base for understanding the concept of development as it relates to different ages and stages of growth.

The purpose of encouraging elementary and secondary pupils to learn how they learn is more than to provide theoretical knowledge, important as that can be; it is to help the pupils to make the theory operational, in parallel to the professional work of the teacher, and to increase their skills in managing their own learning and relating to others.

Limiting Extraneous Stimuli

Industrial engineers consistently emphasize the importance of keeping work places safe and efficient by preventing the intrusion of unnecessary and distracting objects or materials. The same principle holds in general for the teaching-learning space of teachers, aides, and pupils. The elimination of clutter in the classroom increases the effective use of the space in the room, focuses attention on the specific task of learning, and reduces the amount of distraction from that task.

An uncluttered environment does not mean that a Spartan one is desirable. Nor does the reduction of distractions demand the closeting of pupils away from each other to a noticeable degree. Rather, it is a call for the simple, uncomplicated, and orderly organization of a classroom by both pupils and teacher that permits the conduct of group or individual activities under conditions of mutual respect and consideration.

Competing noises, strewn objects, garish and clashing colors, and strong light contrasts make for testiness and irritation when anyone, especially an exceptional child, is trying to concentrate on a meaningful responsibility.

Invoking the High Interest/Low Difficulty Principle

Children aspire to accomplishments beyond their social development levels or physical capabilities. The 2 year old wants roller skates; the 3 year old wants a two wheel bike; and the 11 year old wants to drive a car or work in a supermarket. A normal part of growing up is learning to tolerate the discrepancy between desires and reality.

School can be a tragic experience, however, when even the usual textbooks for the child's age and grade are beyond his or her reading capabilities. Thus, perceptive teachers have found ways to break the usual one to one relation between high interest level and high difficulty level. Some feasible ways to foster learning by invoking the high interest/low difficulty principle follow.

First, at every grade level books are now available that have been especially rewritten to maintain the high interest of the original but to sharply reduce vocabulary and sentence complexity. These books include elementary readers, history and other texts, and literary works of all descriptions.

Second, pupils with limited reading ability usually have normal hearing comprehension. Thus they can make use of the books that have been recorded for blind persons and they can study through hearing the same material their classmates study visually. Moreover, if the specific material needed is not available on tape, other students, aides, or community volunteers often are willing to record it.

Finally, advanced students, too, frequently are willing to share what they have learned through reading with students for whom reading is not available as a channel for learning.

Limited reading ability is less of a bar to achievement when procedures such as these are used. They make it possible for remedial instruction to go on without building up excessive pressure in pupils and delaying their progress in the rest of schooling.

Being Consistent

Successful teachers have learned that pupils, aides, parents, and colleagues function better when they know what to expect. Consistent behavior permits people to plan their behaviors with the certainty of what the consequences will be.

Assuring the appropriate personal-social behavior of pupils is a concern for all teachers. Pupils themselves have reported, time after time, that one of the most powerful influences on their behavior is the teacher's example.

Consistency is important to establish and maintain a sound working relationship between teacher and pupils in a self contained classroom. It is even more important now because of two growing phenomena. The first is instruction in open space, where teachers interact with each other more and with a wider range of pupils. The heightened importance of consistent behavior in such a situation can readily be appreciated. The second new situation arises out of the regular classroom teacher's new role as the captain of the team that integrates exceptional children in regular classes. Consistent professional behavior by the teacher-leader can be the keystone to effective team operations in mainstreaming.

Observing the Child Closely

Educational diagnosis (or assessment) is inextricably intertwined with instruction. In fact, educators increasingly recognize that the most satisfactory way to gain insight into a child's learning problems is to try to teach the child a skill in a standardized situation and to make observations while doing so. If the teacher attends to how the child responds— the child's feedback—enough information is present to indicate how the instructional situation should be modified or revised to maximize the child's ability to learn. Thus, the teacher must use all teaching for diagnostic assessment and be observant of the child's approach to task, wavering of attention, or any blocks to progress.

PREVAILING VERSUS PREFERRED PRACTICES

Longstanding systems for the categorization and placement of pupils and teachers into narrow groupings under labels such as educable mentally retarded, learning disabled, and emotionally disturbed are beginning to break down. In part, this grows from the difficulties and resistances encountered in such classifications and labels, but also from the complication of having more specialists than can be employed and managed effectively in a highly decentralized school system.

What is emerging in the place of narrowly based special classes is a set of more generic special educators who usually offer some direct instruction to exceptional students along with consultation and team teaching conducted with regular class teachers. Roles of school psychologists, social workers, and other specialists are also in a period of rapid revision, again emphasizing supportive and consultation functions with regular teachers. In all of the changes it is increasingly appreciated that many of the specialized functions carried by special education teachers, psychologists, and others can be "given away" through training to regular teachers and that much of what has been found useful in work with exceptional students is equally useful with *all* students.

This summary is concluded with a brief set of contrasts of prevailing and preferred practices.

Prevailing Practices	Preferred Practices
1. States issue as many as eight different kinds of special education certificates.	1. States issue only three or four special education teaching certificates, leaving the negotiations about more specialized competencies between teachers and their employing school districts.
2. The typical local school might employ as many as five or six different kinds of special educators.	2. The typical school employs one generic special educator who works closely with regular teachers and such other specialists as may need to be called in.
3. Institutions of higher education prepare numerous specialists for school employment with little regard for the complexity of the employment situation in local schools.	3. Institutions of higher education prepare generic workers for the schools who can mediate between IHE's and local schools over broad knowledge and skill domains.
4. The modal administrative format of special education programs is the categorical special class.	4. The modal administrative format for special education is the well supported regular class, plus a resource room or system.

Prevailing Practices	Preferred Practices
5. The school psychologist performs mainly psychometric functions in service to the state required categorical classification and placement system.	5. The school psychologist is occupied mainly in programmatic development and training, plus some amount of direct study of pupils and school and home situations—using a broad range of observational and assessment procedures.
6. Preparation of personnel for individualization of educational programs is conceptualized and implemented mainly in terms of studying individual learners.	6. Preparation of personnel for individualization of educational programs gives attention both to learners and broad systems and programs of education.

SUGGESTIONS FOR STUDENTS AND INSTRUCTOR

1. Visit local programs for exceptional children that are conducted on a noncategorical model. There may be resource rooms, for example, where you can check on the extent of "categorizing" of pupils in connection with their placement.
2. Check the definitions and categories for exceptional children and of special teacher certification in your state; observe changes that may have occurred recently. Discuss these topics with officials in your state department of education.
3. Consider for your setting all of the resources you have relating to language development problems of children. Observe how closely interactive they are. Do the audiologists know the linguists? And do they work with the speech clinicians? Who is called on for consultation in the difficult cases—say of a hard of hearing child? Does the training of special education consultants and teachers draw from broad areas?
4. Collect data on the reading abilities of a number of pupils. See if you can classify them reliably as learning disabled, educable mentally retarded, "remedial case," etc. What differences would it make if you had categorical classification?
5. Conduct interviews with school psychologists, counselors, and social workers to get their conceptions of their roles and how they see their roles changing. What changes seem to be indicated by new federal laws and recent court decisions?

6. Check into Kohlberg's ideas of moral development and the linkage to cognitive development.
7. Visit or conduct interviews in connection with peer tutoring or cross age tutoring programs being conducted in your community. Consider how such programs might be made a part of mainstreaming without being exploitative.
8. Secure training materials (see Appendix B) for use with regular teachers and review films, filmstrips, or other materials concerning new roles of special educators or other staff members. For example, see filmstrips on roles of consulting teachers, resource teachers, and other specialists included as part of the Principals' Training Program (PTP) created by the Texas Regional Service Center No. 13, Austin, Texas.

TOPICAL BIBLIOGRAPHIES

Noncategorical Approaches in Special Education

Deno, E. N. (Ed.). *Instructional alternatives for exceptional children.* Reston VA: The Council for Exceptional Children, 1973.

Hobbs, N. *The futures of children: Categories, labels, and their consequences.* San Francisco: Jossey-Bass, 1975.

Reynolds, M. C. & Balow, B. Categories and variables in special education. *Exceptional Children,* 1972, *38*, 357-366.

Reynolds, M. C. *Futures of education for exceptional students: Emerging structures.* Reston VA: The Council for Exceptional Children, 1978.

Mainstreaming in the Broader Community

Brolin, D. E. (Ed.). *Life centered career education: A competency based approach.* Reston VA: The Council for Exceptional Children, 1978.

Caplan, R.B. *Helping the helpers to help.* New York: The Seabury Press, 1972.

Passow, A.H. The gifted and the disadvantaged. *The National Elementary Principal,* 1972, *51*(5), 24-31.

Rosenblum, G. (Ed.). *Issues in community and preventive mental health.* New York: Behavioral Publications, 1971.

(See also Topical Bibliographies, Chapter 1)

Contingency Management

Becker, W. C., Madsen, C. H., Arnold, C. R., & Thomas, B. A. The contingent use of teacher attention and praise in reducing classroom behavior problems. *Journal of Special Education,* 1967, *1*, 287-307.

Buys, C. J. Effects of teacher reinforcement on elementary pupils' behavior and attitudes. *Psychology in the Schools,* 1972, *9*, 278-288.

Haring, N. G., & Philips, E. L. *Analysis and modification of classroom behavior.* Englewood Cliffs NJ: Prentice-Hall, 1972.

Jordan, J. B., & Robbins, L. S. (Eds.). *Let's try doing something else kind of thing.* Reston, VA: The Council for Exceptional Children, 1972.

Lovitt, T. C. *What research and experience say to the teacher of exceptional children: Managing inappropriate behaviors in the classroom.* Reston VA: The Council for Exceptional Children, 1978.

Systems for Individualizing Instruction

Jordan, J. B. (Ed.). Progress by partners in step, Special Issue on IEP. *TEACHING Exceptional Children,* 1978, *10*(3).

Musgrave, G. R. *Individualized instruction: Teaching strategies focusing on the learner.* Boston: Allyn & Bacon, 1975.

Thorenson, C.E. (Ed.). *Behavior modification in education* (72nd yearbook of the National Society for the Study of Education). Chicago: University of Chicago Press, 1973.

Weiner, B. B. *Periscope: Views of the individualized education program.* Reston, VA: The Council for Exceptional Children, 1978.

(See also Appendix B)

Divergent Thinking

Callahan, C. M. *What research and experience say to the teacher of exceptional children: Developing creativity in the gifted and talented.* Reston VA: The Council for Exceptional Children, 1978.

Dellas, M., & Gaier, E.L. Identification of creativity: The individual. *Psychological Bulletin,* 1970, *73*(1), 55-73.

MacKinnon, D.W. The nature and nurture of creative talent. *American Psychologist,* 1962, *17*, 484-495.

Renzulli, J.S. Talent potential in minority group students. *Exceptional Children,* 1973, *39*(6), 437-444.

Torrance, E. P. *Discovery and nurturance of giftedness in the culturally different.* Reston VA: The Council for Exceptional Children, 1977.

Torrance, E.P. *Guiding creative talent.* Englewood Cliffs NJ: Prentice-Hall, 1962.

School Psychology

Bardon, J.I., & Bennett, V.C. *School psychology.* Englewood Cliffs NJ: Prentice-Hall, 1974.

Fein, L.G. *The changing school scene: Challenge to psychology.* New York: Wiley, 1974.

Herron, W.G. *Contemporary school psychology.* Scranton PA: Intex Educational Publishers, 1970.

Holt, F.D., & Kicklighter, R.H. *Psychological services in the schools: Readings in preparation, organization and practice.* Dubuque IA: W.C. Brown, 1971.

Consulting Processes

Berlin, I. Learning mental health consultation: History and problems. *Mental Hygiene,* 1964, *48*, 257-266.

Caplan, G. *Mental health consultation.* New York: Basic Books, 1971.

Parker, C.A. (Ed.). *Psychological consultation: Helping teachers meet special needs.* Reston VA: The Council for Exceptional Children, 1975.

10. Speech Problems

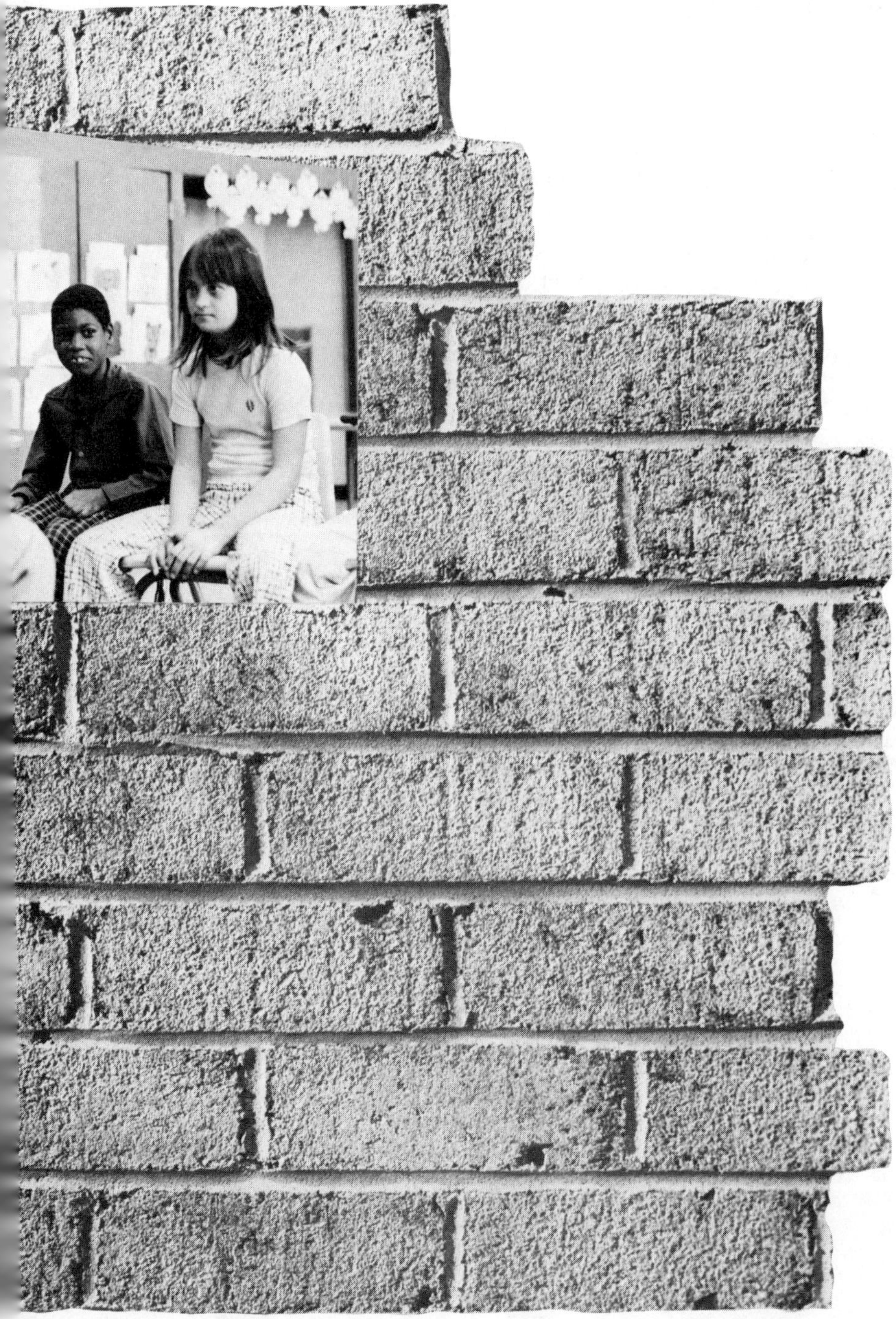

CHAPTER OUTLINE

THE CHALLENGE TO EDUCATORS
    Medical Considerations
    Educational Considerations
THE REGULAR CLASS TEACHER AND A CHILD WITH COMMUNICATION PROBLEMS
SPEECH CONCEPTS AND TERMINOLOGY AND THEIR SIGNIFICANCE
    Definition of Speech Defect
    Typical Forms of Speech Problems and Their Correction
        Stuttering
        Slow Mental Development
        Articulation Defects
        Voice Problems
PREVAILING VERSUS PREFERRED PRACTICES
THE BEGINNING OF SPECIAL EDUCATION FOR PUPILS WITH SPEECH PROBLEMS
    Present Status
    Current Trends
SPECIAL EDUCATION IN THE REGULAR GRADES
    Individualization of Instruction
        Curriculum Individualization
        Methods of Teaching
        Instructional Materials
        Organization for Instruction
        Summary
    A Specific Public School Program
COMPREHENSIVE PROGRAMING FOR PERSONS WITH SPEECH PROBLEMS
SUGGESTIONS FOR STUDENTS AND INSTRUCTOR
TOPICAL BIBLIOGRAPHIES

THE CHALLENGE TO EDUCATORS

Communication through speech is so fundamental for most people they seldom think about it. But for persons without clear, pleasant sounding, unhesitant speech, talking can be an exercise in agony.

> The other boys in school used to call me "stuttercat" and imitate me whenever I came to school. At first I always managed to be tardy and to stay after school to avoid them, but my folks got after me and then I began to fight with them. I got to be a pretty good fighter, but the bigger boys licked me and the teacher punished me when I hit the girls. I still hate girls. (Van Riper, 1963, pp. 41-42)

> Even when I was a little girl I remember being ashamed of my speech. And every time I opened my mouth I shamed my mother. I can't tell you how awful I felt. If I talked, I did wrong. It was that simple. I kept thinking I must be awful bad to have to talk like that. I remember praying to God and asking him to forgive me for whatever it was I must have done. I remember trying hard to remember what it was, and not being able to find it. (Van Riper, 1963, p. 61)

> The most wonderful thing about being able to pronounce my sounds now is that people aren't always saying "What? What's that?" I bet I've heard that about fifty thousand times. Often they'd shout at me as though I were deaf and that usually made me talk worse. Or they'd answer "Yes" when that just didn't make sense. I still occasionally find myself getting set for these reactions and steeling myself against them and being surprised when other people just listen. (Van Riper, 1963, p. 72)

Problems of speech appear in approximately 1 out of 20 children. They occur with little regard to socioeconomic condition, family, sex, race, rate of cognitive development, or the presence of other exceptionalities. The fact that they may crop up almost anywhere, coupled with their potentially devastating personal, social, and academic consequences, as well as their substantial numbers, make the prevention and correction of speech problems one of education's major challenges.

Medical Considerations

Professionals who concentrate on speech problems have developed a point of view, a terminology, and a place for themselves among the "helping professions." However, they maintain a close alliance with dentists and physicians because some of the more complex speech problems are closely linked with medical and dental conditions. As will be shown later, speech clinicians also have a close relationship with the education professions.

The great majority of speech problems are developmental and are not tied to physiological abnormalities. This is the place, however, to briefly describe the six major kinds of medically connected speech problems that regular class teachers may find themselves working with in collaboration with speech clinicians in elementary and secondary schools.*

1. *Central nervous system (brain) damage.* Injury to the brain before or after birth, from whatever cause (accident, stroke, tumor, illness) can reduce the capability to produce intelligible speech, even though the ability to think may not be appreciably impaired. The ability to understand the speech of others may be absent or limited, too, from the same presumed cause. Childhood or developmental aphasia are expressions sometimes used to denote such speech problems.
2. *Cerebral palsy speech.* This faulty, slow, slurred, and difficult to understand speech is associated with the poor voluntary control of muscles characteristic of persons with cerebral palsy. There is no set pattern of speech disparities. It is related to the particular form and degree of the cerebral palsy, and that varies from person to person.
3. *Cleft palate and/or lip speech.* Some babies are born with a split in the roof of the mouth and/or the upper lip, leaving an opening between the mouth and the nasal cavity. Sometimes in this deformity the gap goes to the soft palate, which may be divided or missing. The difficulty in closing the nasal and oral cavities from each other during speech makes the formation of certain speech sounds, such as /s/, /t/, or /f/ particularly difficult, even following high quality surgical repair of the cleft plus remedial speech work. Dental abnormalities of teeth and gums likewise complicate articulation. Since 99% of these children have middle ear disease in the early preschool years, patterns of fluctuating hearing loss are frequently found. That, too, can inhibit learning correct articulation and can slow down or delay language development.
4. *Deformities.* Occasionally children are born with other deformities of the mouth, nose, tongue, or throat, or such deformities may result from accidents or from surgery necessary to correct other conditions. A consequence may be difficulty in producing certain speech sounds because of the structural changes in the speech organs.
5. *Slow cognitive development (mental retardation).* Language and speech are cognition linked. Slow cognitive development, therefore, can be expected to parallel slow grammatical, syntactical, and conceptual development. If cognitive development is substantially slowed, incorrect speech sound production, too, may continue into the teens and adult years.

---

*There are serious speech and language problems connected with hearing impairments, too, which are dealt with in Chapter 11. Also, the medical considerations regarding language problems associated with learning disabilities are found in Chapter 7. Speech clinicians have important roles to play in both of those situations.

6. *Stuttering (or stammering)*. This refers to involuntary stoppages or pauses that frequently and noticeably interrupt the flow of speech and that are irritating to the speaker and the listener. Stuttering is also termed disfluency or nonfluency. There are medical points of view some speech clinicians share that link stuttering to psychiatric or neurological conditions. Many other speech clinicians, though, attribute it to learned patterns of behavior.

These six medical and dental conditions include the speech problems that are most difficult to improve or correct. Fortunately, they are also among the least frequent of all speech problems. The most frequent, called articulation problems and voice problems, will be described later, when approaches to the remediation of all speech defects are discussed.

Educational Considerations

The improvement of speech has long been an important goal of elementary, secondary, and higher education in Western civilization. The vocational implications of effective speech today, from actor to lawyer to minister to senator, salesman or sportscaster, are significant. The personal and social values of good speech in conversation and discussion are evident, whether in the family, among friends, or in the community. Its utility in everyday survival is undisputed in a culture that increasingly employs such technology as dictation equipment, telephone conferences, citizen band radios, and tape recorded messages to increase the range and variety of oral communication. A well modulated, expressive, and easily understood voice is an unquestionable asset.

It is understandable that parents and teachers are in accord that speech should be an important part of the curriculum. Also, it is easy to understand why parents show serious concern if their children's speech does not appear to be developing in what they consider a normal way.

Like reading and writing, speech is every teacher's business, from the primary grades through secondary school graduation. The way the regular class teacher models excellent speech, gives recognition for its proper use by pupils, and provides individualized instruction leading to better speech—these have general acceptance as key educational considerations.

Now another role is rapidly shaping for the regular class teacher, one that in the past had been reserved for the specialist only. As Hull and Hull (1973) noted, this new trend means that

> the selection of any child for individual therapy away from the classroom would be made only after all other possible alternatives had been explored and rejected. The primary goal is to keep the child with a communication problem in the mainstream of education as much as possible. . . . This is

seen as a truly cooperative effort on the part of the teacher, the speech clinician, and any other team members involved. (p. 300)

What the Hulls noted as a new trend in 1973 has now become public policy in the United States. That policy is to include the special education of children with speech problems in the same domain with regular class instruction. How regular and special teachers join forces to carry out that policy successfully is the main thrust of the following discussion.

THE REGULAR CLASS TEACHER AND A CHILD WITH COMMUNICATION PROBLEMS

The implementation of a new policy can be a bumpy road at first. That is especially true if there is less than adequate preparation for the new responsibilities.

This real life story, written by Linda East, a first grade teacher at Altavista Elementary School in Virginia, tells how one determined regular class teacher mustered the support to cope successfully with what at the outset seemed an impossible situation and, in the process, helped to show how similar situations might be better prepared for in the future.

A Mainstreaming Success Story*

I've always found it helpful as a teacher to jot down a few first impressions of children after their parents brought them by to enroll in my first grade class. My first impression of Bill seemed normal enough: brown skin, short curly black hair, large almond-shaped brown eyes filled with wonder, terribly shy but terribly excited.

His mother was a large dominating woman with eyes like Bill's that seemed to be busy looking past you as she spoke. "I'm afraid you're going to have trouble with Bill," she said. "He's never been away from home, so he may not know how to act. Didn't send him to kindergarten. I was scared the noise of so many children would upset him. Say hello to Miz East, Bill."

A soft "low" came from Bill, who clung tightly to his mother's hand. As they left, she added an afterthought, "Oh, and Miz East, you may have to help Bill when he goes to the bathroom."

The next day was to be a sudden awakening as to just how much I would have to help Bill. Besides not being able to use the bathroom by himself, Bill couldn't eat by himself (he chewed one pea at a time); nor could he speak comprehensibly, walk properly, go up or down steps, run, or jump. When asked a question, he mumbled a stream of unrelated sounds. Bill spent most of the first three days crying in my lap as I tried to organize a new class of diverse and demanding first graders.

---

*Reprinted with permission from *Today's Education,* the journal of the National Association, November-December 1976, p. 71.

I quickly rushed in every specialist I could reach, the principal, and a videotape crew to film Bill in the classroom and on the playground. The tape was sent to some specialists I couldn't reach.

Their verdicts were very discouraging, and I learned nothing new. He obviously needed special education. *But* mainstreaming meant Bill must remain in my room the entire school year, spending only 10 minutes at the end of each day with a learning disabilities teacher. A speech therapist worked with him twice a week for short periods of time, too.

Each day as I worked with the class, I struggled desperately to make every minute of Bill's time a learning experience. Every evening, I cursed the idea of mainstreaming and wondered what kind of thoughtless people could have instituted such an impossible program.

At lunchtime it was necessary for me to feed Bill. After a week of not eating lunch myself, I decided I would try to teach Bill to feed himself each lunchtime until one of the pupils had finished eating and could take over for me. It became apparent that I wasn't going to be Bill's only teacher—the classroom was filled with 24 eager instructors. And they put all they had into teaching Bill to walk, talk, eat, go to the bathroom by himself, run, jump, go up and down steps, and play.

As weeks went by, miracles began to happen, and each day I went home with a glowing account to give my husband. "Bill learned to say 'lunch tray' today." "Bill learned to eat a forkful of mashed potatoes today." "Bill learned to jump from a small chair today."

Bill demonstrated one skill the first week of school which astounded me and which was to be the basis for further learning experiences. He loved the record player and learned to operate it himself after only one lesson. I realized that if Bill could work the record player by himself, he could learn to do other things as well. By the second month of school, not only could Bill turn on my cassette player, he also could set it up, record his own voice, play the tape back, and listen to it. The wonder and smiles on his face delighted me. I recorded simple songs and stories for him to listen to over and over.

At Show-and-Tell time, Bill always mumbled his stories and songs. No one understood anything he said, but the whole class listened attentively to see if he would use one of the words they had taught him. Our big reward finally came at Christmastime, when Bill stood before the class and sang "Jin'le Bells Jin'le Bells Jin'le Bells" over and over again. The class broke into spontaneous applause, and my eyes filled with tears.

By the end of the school year, Bill had learned to speak in short, comprehensible sentences. He could read 10 words and recognize three numbers. He ate by himself, sang songs, walked up and down steps, and ran races.

As for mainstreaming, I learned a big lesson that year: Only a classroom full of "normal" children could have set the examples Bill needed to improve his faulty speech and coordination.

Epilogue: In the end, I volunteered to keep Bill in my classroom the following year. He learned to speak coherently, count to 20, recognize letters and sounds, read through three levels of Ginn, retell stories, and make up his own songs. His attention span increased to 40 minutes.

My deep thanks go to his mother, who worked closely with me, and to his speech, special education, and special reading teachers. Most of all, though, my thanks go to all of Bill's fellow classmates, who set such good examples for him. (East, 1976, p. 71)

The following are some items to notice in Ms. East's story:

- Use of notes to record impressions of children at entry.
- Call for consultative aid from the principal and from specialists.
- Immediate check on possible help from specialist teachers: learning disabilities specialist and speech clinician.
- Use of peer teaching, starting with lunch and leading to other things.
- Determination of Bill's cognitive potential by informal assessment, namely, learning to operate the record player.
- Setting of short range objectives and rewards for their attainment.
- Objective record of Bill's accomplishments.
- Increased understanding and ability to maximize use of parent, regular teacher, and specialist teachers team.
- Acknowledgement of helper roles of regular class pupils.

It may be useful to imagine how an in-service education unit could be developed that might have helped Ms. East or other teachers to manage such situations. What should be included? Why? What roles should the principal and specialist teachers play, if any? Parents? How, when, and where should the in-service be conducted?

This is a beautiful illustration of a teacher's high caliber competence in the face of an extremely difficult professional challenge. It points up how regular class pupils will react when they see that their teacher is a model of helpfulness. It shows how direct interaction can build positive character in both exceptional children and their "normal" companions. It is an example of the intelligent use of consultative services and of teamwork between regular and specialist teachers. The mainstream conditions under which Ms. East found it necessary to work were less than optimal. But her approach, the decisions she made, and the spirit with which she worked are superb evidences of preferred practices.

SPEECH CONCEPTS AND TERMINOLOGY AND THEIR SIGNIFICANCE

Three concepts call for definition when one thinks about the emerging interactions of regular class teachers and speech clinicians. The concepts are speech and language development, speech improvement, and speech correction and they take on a new significance in today's climate of inclusion. Regular teachers and clinicians are coming to recognize that they both have much to contribute to each of these activities and that they should share responsibilities for them, though in different degrees.

Speech and language development is the acquisition of increasing ability to understand and produce oral language. It begins at birth and can continue throughout life. During the school years deliberate efforts are made to foster speech and language development in pupils by such activities as teaching new words, correct pronunciations, and forms of oral language such as questions and exclamations. This teaching is based on sequential guidelines in printed curricula and textbooks.

Speech improvement is the enhancement of the quality of already existing speech. It starts informally in the preschool years when parents monitor their children's oral language and encourage increased clarity, appropriate volume, accurate expressiveness, logical organization, proper temporal sequencing, and correct sound production. Speech improvement in the school years continues those activities and uses oral reading, acting, discussion, debate, role playing, and the like as vehicles. This instruction, like that for speech development, is integral to the language arts curriculum, though it overlaps into other curricular and extracurricular sectors.

Speech correction refers to the remediation of oral speech patterns that are so markedly deviant that they interfere with communication to a significant degree. The deviant speech in need of correction is differentiated from that which is imperfect because it is still in the normal developmental sequence. Hence, speech correction is applicable only to significantly deviant speech patterns that are fixed or are becoming fixed in the person's day to day speech behavior.

Regular class teachers and speech clinicians can help each other in all three of these important functions: development, improvement, and correction. Figure 10-1 represents the sharing of professional knowledge and responsibilities. There is an approximately equal division with respect to speech improvement. The regular class teacher carries the major burden with respect to speech development. The same is true for

FIGURE 10-1
Regular Class Teacher and Speech Clinician's Sharing of Responsibility

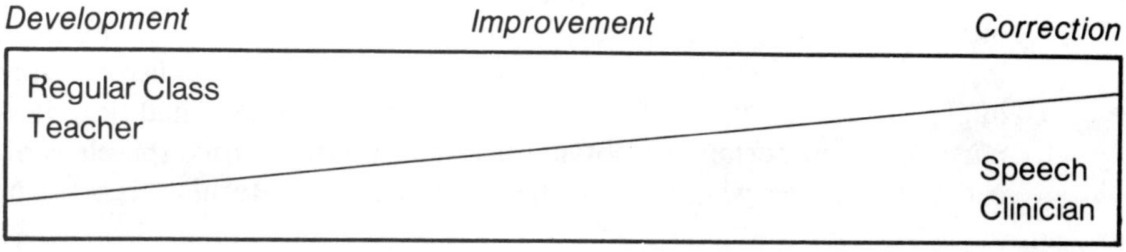

Development	*Improvement*	*Correction*
Regular Class Teacher		Speech Clinician

the clinician with respect to speech correction. There is no sharp dividing line, no solely held territory. The pupil can always look to both for help in any of the three.

Definition of Speech Defect

Like the definitions of deafness and blindness and other conditions in this book, this definition is an educational one. It does not concern itself with the physiology of the speech organs. Rather, it is "product oriented"; the speech that is produced is the center of attention for definitional purposes. Following are definitions of defective, satisfactory, and good speech.

Defective speech interferes with communication; it lacks intelligibility. It causes the speaker to be uncomfortable and maladjusted. Defective speech attracts more attention to the speech sounds and accompanying mannerisms than to the content of what the speaker is saying.

Satisfactory speech transmits communication without distortion. It produces little or no affective reaction in the speaker. The content of what the person is saying is conveyed with little or no distraction from mannerisms or unusual speech sounds.

Good speech enhances the communication without distortion. It gives the speaker positive feedback through hearing and sight that the intended affective tone is accompanying the message. Accuracy and clarity of speech sounds, in addition to the use of appropriate face, hand, and body movements, add to the force and fullness of the message being communicated.

In short, if speech cannot be readily understood, if it is upsetting to the person speaking, or if it causes distraction or negative reactions from the audience, it is a speech problem. Thus, the definition is entirely functional.

The teacher's first concern, of course, is to help the pupil with defective speech to learn to produce speech in as normal a manner as possible. For all pupils, too, the teacher's objective is to help them to attain and use good speech in everyday life.

Typical Forms of Speech Problems and Their Correction

Speech problems that tend to be associated with medical conditions were introduced earlier. Those related to cerebral palsy or other presumed brain damage, cleft palate, or other deformities do not display what might be called typical forms, despite some common qualities. It is particularly important to obtain early consultation from speech clinicians in instances where any of these are suspected. Regular class teachers, school psychologists, and counselors will probably not see enough such cases to assess them adequately without direct help from a speech specialist. Well designed corrective work often produces fine results in cleft palate speech and in some of the other conditions, too.

Stuttering

Stuttering is more likely to have come to the attention of regular school personnel. Even the most conscientious work has not been substantially successful in correcting disorders of speech rhythm. There is, however, general agreement on two principles to follow to help pupils keep nonfluency in check and to be full regular class participants.

First, know that conflict or excitement tends to increase stuttering behavior. This does not mean one should overprotect nonfluent children, keeping all stress or exuberance out of their lives. Rather, it means that one should expect and not be surprised by what happens to their speech under such conditions. Also, it means that one should help nonfluent children and youth to learn to consciously control their own activity and emotional states while talking.

Second, treat children who stutter like all other children. Call on them. Give them opportunities to ask questions and take the time to listen. Do not fill in words for them any more than for any other child. Be a model for the stuttering pupil's classmates.

Slow Mental Development

Slow mental development is usually paralleled by slow speech development. Speech and language stimulation is the recommended procedure in such cases. It has two components, quantitative and qualitative. The first is aimed at increasing the sheer amount of meaningful verbalization. The second focuses on raising the level of accuracy and variety of the pupil's oral expression. Applied behavior analysis procedures have shown great promise in both components of speech and language stimulation.

Speech clinicians and regular class teachers, working at speech and language stimulation as a team with parents and aides, can prove important in the lives of a pupil who shows slow cognitive development. When speech is stimulated, language growth is most likely promoted, too. A child's amount, accuracy, and variety of oral language is frequently a manifestation of growth in cognition. Thus, the impact of successful speech and language stimulation can be heightened cognitive development for the child. The effect may be pronounced on some children, particularly those whose home and family lives have been relatively void of such stimulation.

Articulation Defects

Articulation defects are the most frequently found speech problems in school age children and youth. They are most common in the early elementary school years, though some persist into the secondary and college years. Articulation defects fall into three classes:

1. Omissions of certain sounds, such as "I ike ou" for "I like you."
2. Substitution of one sound for another, like "Acwoss the wibew" for "Across the river."
3. Distortion of sounds, like "srimp" for "shrimp" or "schtop" for "stop."

These three types of speech errors have been studied thoroughly and there are proven methods of correcting them. The errors themselves seldom result from physiological factors. Instead they appear to be developmental in origin in the sense that a particular part of the child's step by step acquisition of normal speech fixated instead of moving along toward the next developmental point.

For instance, it is part of the normal speech development process for kindergarteners to sometimes say "bawoon" for "balloon." But if by the end of second grade or the beginning of third grade that substitution continues, it is a sign that corrective work is probably needed.

The analysis of an example can help illustrate this point more fully. Johnny came to first grade with a Band-Aid on his index finger one morning in October. He held it up for the teacher to see and said, "I tut my finder on a thoup tan. Mommy wapped it up. It will det be er thoon, Mommy thay."

The teacher knew that Johnny's cognitive development was superior because of how quickly he adapted in school and because of how readily he had learned daily routines. But his speech was often difficult to understand. What to do about it?

First, take note of Johnny's speech errors.

*T*ut for *c*ut
Fin*d*er for fin*g*er
*Th*oup for *s*oup
*T*an for *c*an
*W*apped for *w*rapped

*D*et for *g*et
Be er for be*tt*er.
*Th*oon for *s*oon
*Th*ay for *s*ay

The next step is to look at the errors Johnny made in the light of the sequence in which the correct use of sounds tends to develop in young children.

Before starting kindergarten, children usually have good command of these sounds in oral communication:

/w/ as in *we, one, water* /m/ as in *me, mad, mother*
/b/ as in *baby, bat, bug* /p/ as in *paper, pop, pole*
/h/ as in *hop, hair, hat*

In kindergarten and first grade it is natural for some pupils to be still learning to use these sounds correctly:

/y/ as in *you, yes, yet* /n/ as in *nut, knife, new*
/d/ as in *day, bed, doll* /t/* as in *toe, hit, batter*
/ng/ as in *ring, thing, singer* /g/** as in *big, getting, gas*
/k/** as in *can, ink, tack* /f/ as in *fall, leaf, offer*

During second grade a number of pupils will be gaining increased control over these sounds:

/v/ as in *vase, stove, five* /th/ as in *bathe, father, this*
/sh/ as in *shoot, shine, dish* /l/ as in *lot, limb, bill*

By the end of third grade almost all children should be using these sounds properly in everyday speech:

/th/ as in *thin, three, bath* /s/*** as in *soap, mess, biscuit*
/z/ as in *zero, hose, his* /r/* as in *rain, rip, over*

When seen in the perspective of these lists, Johnny's imperfections (noted by an asterisk for each occurrence) are revealed to be normal, natural ones in terms of his current development, rather than defects calling for immediate correction.

Johnny seems to have no difficulty with the sounds most pupils make easily by the beginning of first grade. There is some difficulty with three "first grade" and two "third grade" sounds.

Johnny should not be reprimanded or teased for his manner of speech. He ought not be singled out in any way nor told that his speech is incorrect or defective. At this point, individual corrective exercises are not the most appropriate approach, either. The regular teacher's skills, augmented by consultation by a speech clinician, are best directed at helping Johnny improve his speech in the context of speech and language development activities with the whole class. The first grade sounds are the ones to emphasize in this speech improvement activity.

One of the advantages of the suggested sound groupings by grades is that they let teachers know where to begin. They are not hard and fast timetables. If anything, they are conservative. The sounds that are listed by grades can be linked to the sequence of the phonic elements introduced in the basic reading series; teaching one can then reinforce the other. Other related illustrative material can be found in Birch, Matthews, and Burgi (1958).

For the most frequent special problems, the articulation errors, there is a three step sequence that has a good record of effectiveness in remediation.

First, be sure the child *hears* the error. This often requires ear, or auditory, training to help the child learn to notice how the correct and incorrect sounds differ. Masking one's mouth with a card, the sound can be made correctly and incorrectly, in isolation and in words, to see if the child catches the differences. Tape recordings of sounds can be used, too. The speech clinician can suggest many interesting ways to conduct auditory training. Children can help each other. It is fundamentally important that the child become able to hear the correct sound made by someone else and to distinguish it from other sounds. Some sounds can be readily seen and felt, too. It helps if the child can see and feel the error and the correct sound and note the differences.

Second, be sure the child can *produce* the sound correctly. Once the youngster can *hear* the sound, it is possible to use a tape recorder, for instance, to allow an auditory comparison between the actual sound the child produces and a correct model. Then the child can be brought, through successive approximations, to say the sound acceptably. Again, speech clinicians have identified many ways to motivate interest in achieving the correct response. Practice should continue until the pupil produces the target sound acceptably on almost every attempt.

Third, move the newly acquired correct sound into everyday speech and fix it in the pupil's spontaneous language usage. The first two steps do not result in automatic accomplishment of the third. A large amount of highly motivated and closely monitored repetition is needed to establish a new or revised speech habit.

This three step outline of a teaching method can be fleshed out and individualized in planning sessions in which the particular child's characteristics are taken fully into account. Potential physical and environmental factors that might cause the articulation error should be investigated, also. For instance, is the child's hearing in the normal range? Do the child's parents or other frequently seen adults make the same articulation error, providing a constant model? The speech clinician, too, can suggest high interest instructional materials and procedures for use both in the regular class and by the parents at home.

Voice Problems

Voice problems are difficult to describe in an objective way because what is considered strange or objectionable by one person may be intriguing or distinctive to another. Even their classification is uncertain. For instance, it can be questioned if rate is actually a voice problem, though we include it here. Among the five types of voice problems (quality, rate, flexibility, volume, and pitch) the first in frequency is quality. Included in this problem are voices that are so nasal, harsh, or breathy that they interfere with communication. Rate problems refer to dragged out, prolonged speech or the converse, extremely quick, clipped, staccato speech, either of which is so pronounced as to diminish intelligibility. A flexibility disorder is exemplified by a flat, uninterrupted monotone that is difficult to attend to. Volume refers to a too loud or too soft voice for the situation. Pitch has reference to a voice that is too high or a very deep voice that is too low in terms of the musical scale.

Abrupt changes in a pupil's voice may signal a medical problem. The appropriate move is to call such a change to the parent's or school nurse's attention.

In general, voice problems are so idiosyncratic that the regular class teacher should seek consultation with a speech clinician before attempting any corrective steps. The one principle to be mindful of in the meantime is to model considerate and acceptant behavior for other teachers and classmates.

PREVAILING VERSUS PREFERRED PRACTICES

On the left are listed practices that are usually found in speech improvement and correction programs in today's schools. On the right are preferred practices. While not frequent, the preferred practices are successful approaches found in schools that are showing the way to others.

Prevailing Practices

1. Annually the speech clinician screens kindergarten or first grade pupils by taking them, one at a time, to a small specially equipped room where speech articulation, rhythm, and voice tests are administered. Special speech testing and instructional materials are available in the speech correction room.

Preferred Practices

1. The speech clinician teams with the regular kindergarten or first grade teacher to assess speech and language status and plan and conduct speech and language improvement for the entire class. The clinician notes which pupils provide excellent speech models, the developmental status of each pupil with regard to language and speech production, and any serious aberrations in their speech or language. This is done informally in the regular class during the general speech and language instruction.

Prevailing Practices	Preferred Practices
2. The clinician selects certain pupils, perhaps five or six from a room, for weekly or semiweekly correction lessons. These pupils leave their regular class and return to it on a regular schedule, going to the speech clinician's room for their special instruction. There they are taught individually or in groups of three or four with similar speech problems.	2. The regular class teacher and the speech clinician jointly plan and carry out improvement and corrective procedures as an integral part of the language arts component of the regular curriculum. Pupils with all degrees and kinds of speech problems are helped as a matter of course, individually or in small groups, in the context of regular class work.
3. Occasionally the clinician and the teacher have brief hallway talks about how the children designated as having speech defects are progressing. Sometimes the clinician gives suggestions for regular class help. When a child's speech is sufficiently corrected, the regular visits to the speech correction room taper off to a maintenance schedule and finally to discharge.	3. Clinicians have the needed special equipment and materials for speech and language testing and corrective instruction in regular classes for use by the clinician or regular teachers. The latter are shown by the clinician how to do basic speech assessment and corrective instruction. Occasionally it is necessary to move a child to the speech clinician's room for more intensive work, but not regularly. All pupils have been oriented to the speech correction room. It is also used from time to time for teacher planning sessions, parent conferences, and individual or small group tutoring.
4. The same pattern is followed through all the elementary, middle, and secondary schools whether open space or traditional in design. Some pupils continue to receive corrective attention for several consecutive years.	4. This pattern continues through high school. Where the child moves to more than one teacher, the closest team partner with the clinician is the language arts teacher, though the other teachers are kept informed and shown how

| Prevailing Practices | Preferred Practices |

to help. In open space schools the clinician may team simultaneously with several teachers who are jointly responsible for larger groups of pupils. Coordination is accomplished through the team leader, but the principles illustrated above remain the same.

The total time spent by the clinician is not different in either the prevailing or the preferred practices. The latter does reduce or eliminate some of the "dead time" occasioned by back and forth movement of pupils and clinician from regular class to special speech correction room. If teacher aides are available they can be used to good effect in either approach. The preferred practices also encourage participation by the speech clinician in planning and carrying out the whole language arts curriculum. That is an advantage because speech clinicians often are among the best informed faculty members regarding linguistics, oral expression, and the developmental aspects of human language. The frequent presence of the clinician in the regular class encourages that person's participation in assessing other language related learning problems, while making speech improvement and correction as natural to all pupils as the improvement and correction of arithmetic. A case load of names can be maintained under the preferred practices, and it can be used for administrative purposes without obtruding into the pupil's awareness.

THE BEGINNING OF SPECIAL EDUCATION FOR PUPILS WITH SPEECH PROBLEMS

Variations from typical speech have drawn attention to themselves for centuries. It can be surmised, too, that efforts to make speech more "normal sounding" started as soon as those variations attracted ridicule or, in other ways, detracted from the speaker's social acceptance.

One of the earliest references to public school provisions in the United States was reported by Lance (1976). He found evidence that a New York City public school initiated speech correction in September 1908. The pupils with speech problems attended a class conducted by a teacher who had prior preparation in helping children overcome speech problems. The superintendent of schools is quoted as saying: "The experiment . . . demonstrates that the attempt to cure serious speech defects, which interfere with success and satisfaction in life is possible and well worth while." The original source Lance (1976) located is McDonald (1915, p. 88).

During the first quarter of this century private schools that taught elocution abounded. Many of them also undertook the correction of speech problems in both children and adults. The public schools were able, with special education fundings, to employ more speech correctionists (as they were then called) as teachers. Centers to prepare these speech correction teachers grew rapidly in number in the second quarter of the century and well into the third. The preparation tended to specialize and become separated from that in dramatic and forensic speech. At the same time, elocution schools lost ground, all but disappearing by mid-century.

Simultaneously, speech problem specialists' participation in hospital, medical, and dental clinics increased. This was related to a revival of interest among the health professions in correcting or ameliorating such conditions as cerebral palsy, cleft palate, aphasia, mental retardation, hearing impairments, and autism. The habilitation or rehabilitation of children and adults with those conditions involved the development or restoration of useful speech, hence the heightened need for speech pathologists and clinicians. Financial support administered by federal and state rehabilitation agencies and private organizations made training and employment feasible.

Public schools quickly moved to a procedure for delivering speech correction services that is still the prevailing mode. Variously called an "itinerant," "helping," or "consulting" teacher model, the pattern is for one speech clinician to work in more than one school, selecting and instructing those pupils judged by the clinician to be most in need of and most likely to profit from one to one or small group corrective work.

Present Status

Speech clinicians who are most helpful in elementary and secondary schools today direct their activities along three paths. They correct speech defects, prevent the occurrence of speech defects, and foster the development of good quality speech for all pupils. There is still a much heavier weight on the first of those three functions. However, in the present situation a movement toward a more even balance among all three activities can be observed, accompanied by closer day to day linkage to the work of the regular class teacher. The last is most noticeable in language arts activities.

Under prevailing practices, a regular class teacher may find a speech clinician in the same school one to three days per week, depending on the size and type of school. Early in the term most effort is devoted to screening and testing to determine which children will be officially placed on the clinician's case load. A schedule is then made by the clinician. For instance, with four schools the weekly schedule might look like this:

Day	Morning	Afternoon
Monday	School A	School B
Tuesday	School C	School D
Wednesday	School A	School B
Thursday	School C	School D
Friday	Consultation and testing	Planning and materials development

The Monday through Thursday schedule is usually made up of 20 to 30 minute individual or small group lessons in the speech clinician's room with children with similar problems who are drawn from one or more classes. As can be seen, Friday is reserved for new admissions, discharges, conferences with teachers and parents, and other obligations. The regular class teacher and the clinician find some opportunities to confer and to work together within this kind of schedule, but the chances are limited.

Speech clinicians may see from 75 to 150 pupils or more per week. The estimated modal tendency is 75 to 80. Such case loads, plus the school to school time and the regular class to speech room and return time combine to limit the hours for constructive interactions between the clinician and regular teacher.

There are many variations on the schedule just illustrated. One, for instance, puts the clinician full time for several weeks into one or two schools, then another one or two, then another, then back around the schedule, for the term. Called a block schedule, it is an attempt to concentrate and use segments of time with more efficiency and effectiveness.

Current Trends

The strengths and weaknesses of these approaches to clinical speech services are evident. If the objective is simply to get clinicians together on some regular basis with children with speech problems, an approach through schedule and case load manipulation may prove fruitful. But if real weight is to be given to preventing speech problems and to enhancing the speech and language development of all pupils, it is the different nature of the objectives that must be examined. The way the clinician's time is used can then be related to the work to be done with regular class teachers toward accomplishing those objectives. That approach can be observed in some of the emerging trends projected here.

Like school psychologists and specialist teachers of gifted, retarded, or learning disabled pupils, speech clinicians now see how important it is to "give away" many of their closely guarded skills to regular class teachers. This trend encourages regular class teachers (and often parents or aides) to help pupils in ways previously reserved for the speech clinician. Research in the early 1950's indicated that parents, working at home under the guidance of speech clinicians, produced significant, positive changes in their children's speech. Bradley (1976) commented that such findings should not surprise us, in view of the fact "that mothers, without any specific training, have been helping 80 to 90% of the population acquire and use language skills by three years of age, in every cultural and socioeconomic setting" (p. 1).

Alvord (1977) described how seven Iowa speech clinicians prepared and supervised nine communication aides to work with pupils who showed articulatory disorders that required correction. The aides achieved results with their pupils equivalent to what speech clinicians attained with similar pupils, in a comparable amount of time and with high maintenance of results. The cost-effectiveness gain was appreciable. Equally important, a marked increase in clinician time availability was noted. How that time can best be used now becomes a matter of real concern, where before it had been only an academic question. (An earlier study in the same direction was reported by Alpiner, 1968.)

Another trend is to extend the preparation of speech clinicians so that they are also qualified as regular class teachers and as specialists in the instruction of children with learning disabilities/behavioral disorders, slow cognitive development, hearing impairments, or other exceptionalities. It is plain that a clinician who is also a specialist in learning disabilities and behavior disorders or a regular class teacher might well be employed to great advantage in a wide ranging role in one school building, even one with a small enrollment. Multiple certification, or "generic" certification combining several specializations, is attracting more and more attention.

Speech clinicians find themselves drawn into more participation in the basic elementary and secondary school programs. Ainsworth (1965) encouraged that move early. Other leaders (Hull & Hull, 1973) have also pressed for the more complete integration of clinical speech work and the rest of the school's programs. The speech clinician's point of view can be helpful to all pupils, especially if injected during curriculum planning and program individualization design.

A complementary trend is toward deeper involvement of regular class teachers in speech remediation for individual pupils. That involvement touches the whole range of types and severity and ages in which speech problems appear. Applied behavior analysis studies have spotlighted the significance of modeling and the value of planned reinforcement schemes in changing speech patterns. The work of Bandura (1971) and others pointed out the role observational learning can have in pupil acquisition of skills and understandings. The regular class is a more favorable staging area for the application of such learning principles than is the separated one to one setting or small speech problem group in which the speech clinician has ordinarily worked. And the regular class teacher is the more logical implementer of such principles, though they may well be planned jointly and their outcomes assessed jointly with the speech clinician.

The tendency to expand public school admission practices to include children with highly complex academic learning, personal management, mobility, and communication problems has been mentioned in other chapters. This response to "right to education" mandates brought with it more encouragement to offer speech development and improvement instruction to pupils who had not generally been reached by those services. One result is an accumulation of evidence that speech work can bring about significant changes in the language capabilities of pupils with slow cognitive development and other developmental disabilities such as autism and cerebral palsy. Here, too, the "giving away" of professional-technical procedures makes much more progress possible. Bradley (1976) said in this connection:

> Speech pathologists have found one thing to be most critical. They must be willing to share their techniques with teachers, child care workers, parents and students who can assist them in the development, stabilization, and generalization of goals appropriate to the handicapped individual's present level of functioning. (p. 3)

A trend of great significance to regular nursery and kindergarten-primary teachers is the two pronged thrust of speech clinicians toward the early childhood years. Not long ago, when clinical speech work was almost entirely corrective, it was common to hear it said that youngsters under 7 or 8 years old were too young to benefit from the assistance of the speech clinician. Now that the potentialities of speech improvement and language and speech development are better understood that statement is less often heard. Instead, two things are happening. First, developmental and improvement speech and language procedures are being used with babies and toddlers and their parents in home based or center based operations. Second, above the newborn to 3 year old age group, speech clinicians are pairing with nursery and kindergarten-primary teachers to foster general speech development and to improve the quality of already present speech. This trend can be found both in programs especially for young handicapped children and in programs that include all young children.

Thus, these kinds of current trends have been identified:
1. More emphasis on speech and language development and improvement, rather than sole attention to corrective work.
2. Recognition of the need to "give away" professional-technical skills to colleagues in order to allow everyone's work to be more effective.
3. Broadening of professional preparation for both regular class teachers and for speech clinicians.
4. Closer teamwork with regular class teachers and with the general school curriculum.
5. Expansion of clinical speech instruction to handicapped pupils who present the most complex educational problems.
6. A new service emphasis thrust toward the earliest preschool and the early school years for all children.

These are not all the trends that could be identified, but they are important ones. If they are attended by a sensitivity to the need for high professional standards and the need for thoughtful evaluation, they could result in superior service to a large portion of the pupils who need it.

SPECIAL EDUCATION IN THE REGULAR GRADES

The most common practice of the past has been to take the child with a speech problem completely outside the mainstream class to a separate special room for special speech instruction. That practice still prevails. Some school districts are showing, however, that it is feasible most of the time to arrange a less restrictive alternative, namely, to bring the speech clinician's help to the pupils who need it while they are in the regular class. Thus, regular class teachers can expect the work of the speech clinician to move step by step into the current of education's mainstream. That is a pattern that is in keeping with "appropriateness" of education under the present national public policy. Since it has already been shown to be operationally realistic, its spread can be anticipated.

Individualization of Instruction

Speech problems occur throughout the school age range, in boys or girls of all backgrounds and temperaments in the company of any or all other exceptionalities, and among pupils who show no other exceptional conditions. That array of possibilities helps to explain why no one pattern of instruction fits all situations. There are, however, a number of guidelines that regular class teachers and their colleagues will find useful as they shape individualized programs of instruction.

Curriculum Individualization

Speech has a major place in the language arts curriculum along with reading and the other verbal communication skills. Like the rest of the language arts, it progresses through a sequence of higher and more complex skill stages as the child grows and matures. And, as in reading and the other communication skills, children learn at different rates and sometimes fail to progress at all, despite serious efforts to help them.

When that happens, it soon becomes evident that the impact of inadequate speech ricochets across the rest of the school's curriculum. Talking about science or social studies becomes more difficult. Asking questions in shop or health class calls attention to the defective speech. No part of the school curriculum is unaffected.

Thus, when the school mobilizes for corrective action regarding a speech defect, all components of the curriculum should be thought of as resources. If music or art activities, for instance, are not enlisted in support of the remedial speech plan, they may not be neutral and thus might inadvertently thwart the carefully designed corrective reinforcement of appropriate speech, for instance, during reading and arithmetic instruction. The prime principle of curriculum individualization for corrective speech, therefore, is to involve all elements of the school curriculum in the remedial effort in a coordinated way, while keeping the central focus on the language arts.

For speech development and improvement, curriculum individualization is important, too. However, the same degree of attention to it is not needed as in instances of defective speech.

Methods of Teaching

As mentioned earlier with regard to stuttering, there is no widely accepted instructional method with a consistent record of correcting or ameliorating the condition. Two caveats (p. 493), thoughtfully applied, will minimize the frequency of stuttering, though, and that is a desirable goal.

For other types of speech problems (pp. 493-497) the teaching methods follow in principle the same general format, namely, (a) that the pupil, can be helped to become aware of the problem, (b) learn what might be done about it, and the (c) attempt to make the correction a part of every day oral communication so that it becomes habitual. There is increasing use of applied behavior analysis to implement those steps.

Instructional Materials

A rich array of well tested materials can be found to support all aspects of speech and language instruction. Speech development is an intrinsic part of most contemporary language textbook series in both elementary and secondary schools. Speech improvement materials are widely used. An example of a carefully designed set is The Best Speech Series,* which includes workbooks for kindergarten-primary regular classes to help improve use of the six most frequently misarticulated sounds in American English, plus lesson guides for teachers and parents. (See also, Byrne 1965; Goldman & Lynch, 1971.) For speech correction, these materials and many others can be examined (and often borrowed) from Instructional Materials Centers. (Check with state education agencies for the locations of these centers.)

Organization for Instruction

Regular class teachers find four factors related to speech programs that influence how they regulate daily class activities. First, if pupils are being withdrawn from the class to attend therapy sessions, that means certain children will be away from 1 to 5 times a week for 15 to 30 minutes at a time. Regular class plans must be adjusted if the impact of those absences is to be minimized. Second, if the speech clinician and the regular class teacher are to confer and plan about the pupils with speech problems, time must be built into the week's schedule for that. Third, where the regular class teacher should carry on specific, individualized activities for children with speech problems to complement the time out of class work with the clinician, those must be woven into the day's fabric. Fourth, in cases in which the regular class teacher and the clinician spend time in team teaching, both in the same class, the scenario for space allocation, pupil grouping, materials availability, and timetable calls for arrangement.

Aside from these four main contingencies, there will be occasions when the regular class teacher will wish to sit in on or participate in a therapy session at the clinician's room, or when both will wish to confer with parents, the principal, or with other specialist colleagues. All in all, organization for effective instruction requires considerable tactical ingenuity, particularly when the regular class teacher interfaces with a speech correction system that removes children from regular classes for short time periods on an irregular schedule during the week.

Summary

It is in curriculum, teaching methodology, instructional materials, and organization for instruction that the individualization necessitated by speech problems is most urgent. No physical plant adaptations or ancillary service needs arise from dealing with speech problems as such.

---

*An adapted set was also designed for children with slow cognitive development. Both are available from Stanwix House, Inc., 3020 Chartiers Ave., Pittsburgh, PA 15204.

However, it is reemphasized here that speech problems do appear, and usually with greater incidence, in connection with all other exceptionalities. Hence, wherever other exceptional children are found in school, the staffing pattern and related arrangements should include speech clinicians.

A Specific Public School Program

At the beginning of this chapter the story of Bill, a first grader with limited speech and a number of other problems, was related. His teacher, Ms. East, made telling use of every resource she could muster. The validity of her professional insights and of her actions could be seen in the aftermath. That story illustrated the present state of the art in much of the country and it showed what intelligently applied effort can effectuate under prevailing practices.

As the following description of another school program unfolds, think about how a Bill and a Ms. East might interact in these different circumstances. Would the principles governing the teacher's actions change? Would there be differences in the details of the two stories? Would the outcomes change?

Richardson, a rapidly growing Texas community near Dallas, had approximately 36,000 pupils in its elementary and secondary schools in 1976. Beginning in 1968-69 with discussions about bringing special education and regular education together, and at the same time decentralizing the school system's operations in general, there has been a steady march toward accomplishing both those goals.

Every child who enters a Richardson kindergarten can expect to meet and talk with a speech clinician along with the kindergarten teacher as part of the day to day experience in the regular kindergarten class. There are 21 elementary schools in the system. Each has a full time speech clinician on the faculty. They spend the first 60 days of each term with regular teachers in kindergarten classes working at diagnostics and individualized program planning.

Ten years ago Richardson's then much smaller number of clinicians would have been waiting for referrals by teachers regarding children with speech problems. At that time case loads were 90% articulation errors.

Today the clinicians' functions are much more extensive. What they are called, speech and language therapists, tells part of that story. So does the average case load: about 70 children, of whom only about 5% have articulation problems. Nearly 90% are pupils who present *language* problems and with whom the therapists frequently work in small groups in the context of the regular class.

The thorough backgrounds in language of the therapists in Richardson principally bolster the kindergarten-primary language curriculum, though two full time clinicians and half time of another are assigned to service high schools, too. There is cooperation, not overlap, between the therapists, regular class teachers, and other special educators who work in the same settings as resource teachers. Sometimes, when it is advisable to pull one or more pupils out of a regular class for specialized instruction, the therapist may work in the same room as a resource teacher.

For most of the work that is specific to speech as such—articulation, voice, stuttering, and the like—pupils are taken from the regular class to a separate therapy room in their school. Richardson's pattern in this, though, is one of intense concentration aimed at speedy results. Ordinarily, arrangements are made with the regular class teacher for a regular one period per day schedule with the therapist. Progress in correction is usually so apparent that the regular class teacher and other pupils in the class can notice changes and take real satisfaction in giving supplemental support to the pupil. Also, the therapist makes periodic personal reports to the regular teacher.

This school district conducts prekindergarten classes, too, beginning at age 3, for children who, by that time, can be seen to need some form of special education. Many of them are showing speech and language problems, in addition to other problems. In these noncategorized early childhood groups there are speech and language therapists who team teach with other specialists. All work is done in the class setting itself.

In their language instruction in regular classes, the therapists tend to work with small groups selected because of basic language problems and language development needs. They attend to aspects of language that underlie reading, writing, spelling, listening, and speaking, rather than attempt to teach in those curricular areas directly. The therapist and regular teacher make assessments based on actual samples of the pupil's writing, speaking, and other language behavior. Sometimes clinical language tests are used, but much of the assessment is based on the day to day language production (or lack of it) of the pupil.

If a pupil's writing performance is inadequate, it may come out in the assessment that the youngster cannot say, either, what the assignment asked for in written form. The speech and language therapist may trace this linguistic lack to foundational weaknesses in the pupil's conceptions about morphology or semantics. Then, using material from the regular class social studies texts, spelling lists, preprimers, or whatever is in use by the regular teacher, the therapist helps the pupil to develop and strengthen the ability to understand the nature of whatever the inhibiting condition is and to learn how to overcome it. Sometimes a third professional, perhaps a resource teacher, works with the same pupil on remedial reading, for instance, in concert with the language therapist and the regular teacher.

The consultative help of a speech and language therapist makes its way to the regular teacher through a fairly typical referral process. It usually begins with the regular teacher pointing out to the counselor that a pupil is experiencing difficulty. From there it moves quickly through the Texas Admission-Review-Dismissal Committee process. When special educational assistance is no longer needed, that same committee officially disengages the support linkages that had been put in place earlier by the regular-special educator team, and the speech and language therapists move to the next cases. Actually, the process is much less mechanical than it might sound. Within the school, everyone is in some sense a teacher of language and speech and that helps establish and maintain a rapport among the faculty that encourages an easy informality and a continuing and mutual concern shared by regular and specialist staff with regard to all pupils, with or without speech and language problems.

Richardson's plan is not fully described in the above summary. It also includes many other forward looking practices. Richardson and a number of other communities in Texas and other states have made serious efforts to determine the value of innovative practices. Those described here have been in operation long enough to allow their merits to be tested in the hard court of community acceptance.

COMPREHENSIVE PROGRAMING FOR PERSONS WITH SPEECH PROBLEMS

The public schools of the nation are coming closer and closer to fulfilling the obligation to correct or ameliorate defective speech among all school age children and youth. Services for speech correction and improvement in the schools promise to encompass, by 1980, pupils from 3 to 21 years old.

Since in some children speech problems are present or begin during the third year of life, a comprehensive school based program ought to have a staff of clinicians actively seeking and beginning corrective and preventive work at that early age. In addition, certain speech problems can begin at any time in life. Therefore, a truly complete program must have the staff and facilities to bring corrective instruction to pupils in elementary, middle, high schools, and technical schools. Moreover, there needs to be *enough* staff so thorough and intensive corrective activity can be carried on for all who need it as soon as they are located and as long as it is required.

The public schools, though, are not the only agencies that should take part if truly comprehensive coverage is to be assured. Some speech problems show themselves even before age 3. Some occur during middle adulthood and others are associated with aging. Health, rehabilitation, higher education, and social welfare organizations, public and private, have parts to play, too, for individuals not reached by the public schools.

Full programing, also, must have a public information component so it will be known, and it must be free or within reasonable reach as to cost. The potential for all of that is here at present. The education professions, jointly with the other helping professions, can be instrumental in changing that potentiality into an actuality.

SUGGESTIONS FOR STUDENTS AND INSTRUCTOR

1. Are class members from different geographic regions? Is it possible to distinguish them by their speech? What are the distinctive characteristics? Are they speech defects?
2. Make tape recordings of conversations with preschool and primary age children. Play them and have others try to estimate the ages of the children.
3. Make your own articulation test by collecting pictures that can be used for speech stimulus materials by asking the child, "What is that?" or "Tell me what is going on in the picture." Be sure to have all sounds represented in initial, medial, and final position.
4. Compare the order and time of introduction of sounds in a primary reading series that uses a phonic word analysis approach with the order of learning of sounds given in this chapter. Why is this an important thing to do?
5. Make a tape recording of your own voice in which you pretend you are talking with parents about their child's achievement. Ask other students or the instructor to listen to it and make suggestions for improvement in your own speech.
6. Arrange to visit a school where you can observe teamwork between a regular class teacher and a speech clinician.
7. Volunteer to be a student aide for two or three weeks with a speech clinician. Keep a log of your activities and make a report to the class about the experience.

TOPICAL BIBLIOGRAPHIES
Modern School Programs for Speech and Language Impaired Pupils

Alvord, D. J. Innovation in speech therapy: A cost effective program. *Exceptional Children,* 1977, *43,* 520-525.

Bradley, D. P. Expanded speech pathology services. *Prise Reporter,* June 1976, 1-3.

Dopheide, W. R., & Dalenger, J. Improving remedial speech and language services through clinician-teacher in-service interaction. *Language, Speech, and Hearing Services in Schools,* 1975, *6,* 196-205.

Freeman, G. G. *Speech and language services and the classroom teacher.* Reston, VA: The Council for Exceptional Children, 1978.

Fudala, J. B. Applied awareness: Speech improvement in an elementary classroom. *TEACHING Exceptional Children,* 1973, *5*, 190-194.

Gray, B. B., & Barker, K. Use of aides in an articulation therapy program. *Exceptional Children,* 1977, *43*(8), 534-538.

Rees, N. S. *I don't understand what you mean by comprehension.* Paper presented at the annual meeting of the American Speech and Hearing Association, Las Vegas, Nevada, 1974.

Spollen, J., & Ballif, B. L. Effectiveness of individualized instruction for kindergarten children with developmental lag. *Exceptional Children,* 1971, *38*(3), 205-209.

Persons with Speech Problems

Caudill, R. *A certain small shepherd.* New York: Holt, Rinehart and Winston, 1965.

Henry, N., *King of the wind.* Chicago: Rand-McNally, 1948.

Johnson, W. *Because I stutter.* New York: Appleton, 1930.

Speech and Language Problems among Minority Children

Anastasiow, N.J. & Hanes, M.L. *Language patterns of poverty children.* Springfield IL: Charles C. Thomas, 1976.

Jones, R. L. (Ed.). *Mainstreaming and the minority child.* Reston VA: The Council for Exceptional Children, 1976.

Simoes, A. Jr. (Ed.). *The bilingual child: Research and analysis of existing educational themes.* New York: Academic, 1976.

Theories and Methods in Clinical Speech and Language

Aaronson, D. R., & Rieber, R. W. *Developmental psycholinguistics and communication disorders.* New York: New York Academy of Sciences, 1975.

Birch, J.W. Matthews, J., & Burgi, E. *Improving children's speech: Teaching exceptional children in every classroom.* Cincinnati: Public School Publishing, 1958.

Hammill, D. D., & Larsen, S. C. The effectiveness of psycholinguistic training. *Exceptional Children,* 1974, *41*, 5-14.

Hull, F. M., & Hull, M. E. Children with oral communication disabilities. In L. M. Dunn (Ed.). *Exceptional children in the schools.* New York: Holt, Rinehart, and Winston, 1973.

Morehead, D. M., & Morehead, A. E. (Eds.). *Normal and deficient child language,* Baltimore: University Park Press, 1976.

Schiefelbusch, R. L., & Lloyd, L. *Language perspectives—Acquisition, retardation, and intervention.* Baltimore: University Park Press, 1972.

Van Riper, C. *Speech correction: Principles and methods* (4th ed.). Englewood Cliffs NJ: Prentice-Hall, 1963.

The Training of Speech and Language Clinicians

Ainsworth, S. The speech clinician in public schools: "Participant" or "separatist"? *American Speech and Hearing Association,* 1965, *7,* 495-502.

Bradley, D. P. Expanded speech pathology services. *Prise Reporter,* June 1976, 1-3.

Dopheide, W. R., & Dalenger, J. Improving remedial speech and language services through clinician-teacher in-service interaction. *Language, Speech, and Hearing Services in Schools,* 1975, *6,* 196-205.

Media

Aragon, J., & Marquez, L. *Spanish Americans—Language and culture* (cassette). Reston, VA: The Council for Exceptional Children, 1973.

Smallwood, G., & Taylor, O. *Black language—Black culture* (cassette). Reston, VA: The Council for Exceptional Children, 1973.

11. Hearing Impairment

CHAPTER OUTLINE

THE CHALLENGE TO EDUCATORS
  Legal Considerations
  Medical Considerations
  Social Welfare Considerations
  Educational Considerations
  Emerging Changes in Terminology
  The Person Who Is Called Hearing Impaired
THE CONCEPT, TERMINOLOGY, AND SIGNIFICANCE OF HEARING IMPAIRMENT
  The Language Process
  Defining Hearing Impairment
    Audiometric Classification
    Educational Classification
  Hearing Loss Conditions that Influence Education
    Nature of the Hearing Defect
    Degree of the Hearing Defect
    Onset of the Hearing Defect
    The Hearing Impaired Child's Cognitive Development
    The Nature and Amount of Stimulation Provided
PREVAILING VERSUS PREFERRED PRACTICES
THE BEGINNING OF SPECIAL EDUCATION FOR HEARING IMPAIRED PUPILS
  Recent Past and Present Status
  Current Trends
    Principles of Successful Mainstreaming
    Common Elements of Successful Programs
    Oral and Total Communication Programs
    Changing to a Mainstreaming Policy
THE ROLE OF THE REGULAR CLASS TEACHER
  Teamwork with Specialists
  Special Education in the Regular Class
  Individualization of Instruction
    Curriculum Individualization
    Methods of Teaching
    Instructional Materials
    Organization for Instruction
    School Physical Plant
    Summary
COMPLETE AND PARTIAL MAINSTREAMING PROGRAMS
  Public Schools
  Residential Schools
COMPREHENSIVE PROGRAMMING FOR PERSONS WITH HEARING IMPAIRMENTS
    Characteristics of a Comprehensive Educational Program
    Education as Part of a Broader Group of Services
    The Continuing Need for Teachers
  SUGGESTIONS FOR STUDENTS AND INSTRUCTOR
  TOPICAL BIBLIOGRAPHIES

THE CHALLENGE TO EDUCATORS

More and more hearing impaired children and youth in America are receiving larger and larger portions of their education in regular preschool, elementary, secondary, and college classes. Special and regular educators, working as teams, have been finding increasingly practicable ways to bring high quality individualized instruction for hearing impaired pupils into regular classes. The chief purpose of this chapter is to provide the information and concepts necessary for teachers, with the support of other specialists, to teach hearing impaired pupils as full time or part time members of regular class groups.

The chapter begins with information about hearing and the problems engendered by auditory defects. It then goes on to illustrate how hearing impairments can affect education and how those effects can be overcome or minimized by teachers and other members of the education professions working together with other specialists and with parents.

It is especially important to recall the contents of Chapters 6 and 7 while studying this chapter. The full range of rates of cognitive development are found among pupils with hearing impairments, of course. The hearing impairment, however, can interfere with normal language development, which in turn can inhibit mental growth. As we shall see, the teacher of hearing impaired pupils has the triple task of fostering cognitive development, helping the pupil attain language competence against severe odds, and providing ability matched instruction in the regular curriculum at the same time.

Legal Considerations

Impairment of hearing calls for unique considerations in legislation and in the courts. For instance, since hearing impairment can interfere with the normal course of language and speech development many states have legislated free public education for deaf children beginning as early as 2 years of age so that special teaching can take place during part of the crucial period when hearing children typically learn to understand and to use oral language and speech.

Hearing impairment can be an effective barrier to employment, also. For that reason federal and state laws equalize job opportunities through medical services, counseling, special training, and placement services for hearing impaired persons seeking employment. For those who are involved in litigation and who need assistance with communication, trained interpreters are supplied.

Parts of this chapter were excerpted, adapted, or condensed from *Hearing Impaired Pupils in the Mainstream,* by J.W. Birch, published by The Council for Exceptional Children, Reston, VA, 1975.

It is not essential, of course, that teachers and other educators be intimately familiar with all these laws and regulations. It is important to know that they exist, however, so individuals with hearing impairments can be referred to the proper sources for the assistance to which they are entitled. Moreover, the legal determination of "deafness" or "hard of hearing" are not usually made in the same way as they are for educational purposes. As will be seen, legal definitions, and many of those used in other professions, tend to focus on the disabling nature of the condition, whereas educational definitions emphasize the individual's developmental needs that can be met through professional instruction.

Medical Considerations

In order to interact intelligently with members of the health professions, regular class teachers should understand the hearing sense and the elements of its operations. This is helpful, also, in talking with the pupils themselves, with their parents, and with special educators and other colleagues.

The outer portion of the ear is its visible part, but there are several other complex components of the hearing system that are not readily seen (Figure 11-1). The purpose of the external ear is to collect sound waves and channel them inward through the ear canal where they strike the eardrum.

FIGURE 11-1
Cross Section of the Hearing Mechanism

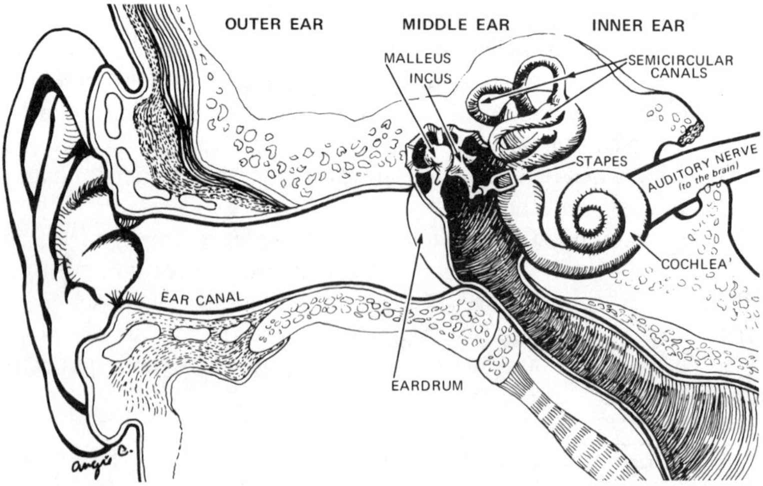

The middle ear houses three bones called, because of their shapes, the hammer, anvil, and stirrup (malleus, incus, and stapes). They transmit, as mechanical, jointed levers, the sound waves from the eardrum to the other end of the middle ear to a membrane called the oval window. The middle ear contains air, with the pressure regulated through the eustachian tube, whose other end opens into the throat.

The inner ear (the labyrinth) contains fluid. The sound waves reach the oval window by mechanical transmission through movements of the three bone linkage. The movements of the oval window set up waves in the liquid of the inner ear. It is here that the sound waves activate the auditory nerve. Its thousands of end fibers are attached to the roots of tiny hairs in the liquid. The hairs are stirred by the sound wave patterns in the liquid, energizing the nerve ends to form the sensation of sound. The component parts of this complex organ are illustrated in Figure 11-1. It allows one to trace the process of hearing through the reception of the sound waves at the outer ear through to the excitation of the ends of the auditory nerve, which might be spoken of as the recognition of a sound signal. The actual perception of the sound and its integration into comprehension and memory are central nervous system functions that are not as well detailed or as well understood.

The drawing of the human auditory mechanism (Figure 11-1) shows a number of especially vulnerable points (the drum and inner ear). Teachers need to be aware of these points in order to understand the nature of different types of hearing loss and to help safeguard all pupils from common dangers to normal hearing.

Anything that prevents the movement of sound waves into and through the outer ear and the middle ear obviously creates an impediment to hearing. Children have often been warned: "Put nothing smaller than your elbow into your ear." Yet all manner of debris finds its way into the outer ear, sometimes causing scratches, infections, punctured eardrums, which in turn can cause permanent damage.

The middle ear is often invaded by infection causing agents from the throat and nasal passages via the eustachian tube. Mostly these attacks are fought off by the body's natural defenses, with only minor discomfort during the time and no lasting harm done. But frequent repetitions of middle ear infections, if not correctly combatted, can bring about scar tissue and other changes that reduce the flexibility of the joints of the three bones whose job it is to transmit the sound waves, making it difficult or impossible for them to perform their appointed functions.

The inner ear, too, can be the victim of agents of infection carried through the lymph. They can damage the nerve ends or the hair cells in the cochlear region. Some drugs used in controlling infections elsewhere in the body are suspected of producing degenerative changes in the inner ear structures. Also, there is evidence that inner ear malfunctions can be associated with prolonged exposure to high intensity sounds, whether meaningful or noise.

There are auditory perceptual anomalies that are attributed to the central nervous system, too. Autism is one illustration. (It, and others, are discussed under learning disabilities in Chapter 7.)

At each step of the way, from where sound waves enter the ear all the way to the brain where they somehow join the store of personal data as percepts, it is possible to interrupt hearing, and that means interrupting the lifeline of language and communication. Disease, accident, noise pollution, genetic variations, medical side effects—these appear to be the main causes.

Teachers and other educators should look to physicians and audiologists to ascertain the causes of hearing losses and to suggest what educational implications the causes may have. It is then the educator's responsibility to integrate that information with other relevant information to design and conduct the educational programs needed by individual pupils.

It is not the primary obligation of teachers to attend to the health of school age children. Teachers, by training, are not prepared to do so. The responsibilities of parents certainly include looking after the health of their children. In the public sector that responsibliity devolves on the nation's public health physicians and nurses and on the private physicians who have families as their clients. Yet, as concerned citizens and as observant persons who have daily contact with the country's young people, teachers do watch from their unique vantage point for early warning signs of child health problems.

In school, these are indications that justify calling a child to the attention of parents or of the school nurse or physician because of a possible hearing problem.

1. The child appears to strain to hear, including leaning toward the speaker and cupping the ears with the hands.
2. The child asks to have comments or questions repeated and then gives correct responses.
3. The child shows speech inaccuracies, especially dropping the beginnings and endings of words.
4. The child is frequently confused during discussions, even though evidently trying to participate.
5. The child has running ears, soreness, or aches and frequently rubs and scratches the outer ear canal.

When these conditions are seen, teachers are justified in calling them to the attention of parents and school health authorities. The result may well be the prevention or correction of a hearing loss that could have a devastating effect on the child's educational development.

Social Welfare Considerations

There is a long history of vigorous action in the United States by groups of deaf and hard of hearing adults on their own behalf.

Hearing impaired persons have been exploited in a number of ways. They are underemployed, too often needing to work at jobs below their levels of actual training. They have been the objects of crude jokes, and they have been preyed on by unscrupulous merchants.

Through social and political action oriented clubs and associations, however, hearing impaired persons have successfully helped each other in matters ranging across such areas as employment, recreation, education, insurance, and legislative lobbying. Some writers on the sociology and social psychology of hearing impairment speak of these groups as making up "the deaf community."

Also, America is dotted with volunteer organizations, often called speech and hearing associations, which tend to be amalgams of professional persons, parents of hearing impaired children, public spirited lay citizens, and hearing impaired adults. These organizations employ professional staffs to conduct public information campaigns on prevention of hearing defects, provide free hearing tests, act as direct assistance or referral agencies for hearing impaired persons, conduct demonstrations of education or other services they believe their communities need and act as advocates for hearing impaired persons in whatever ways their boards of directors consider relevant and necessary.

Both of these forms of social welfare action groups are strong and useful resources for teachers when there is a need for direct help in planning, tutoring, interpreting, and other instruction related matters. For broader considerations, such as helping to form and guide the policies and practices of state and local education agencies, they can have important roles, too. These agencies are also potential employers of teachers in the various service projects they conduct.

Educational Considerations

The proportion of children and youth who have hearing impairments that make some form of special education necessary is probably a little less than 1 out of every 100 pupils. In areas of low socioeconomic conditions the proportion may go to 1 out of 50, and it may be limited to 1 out of 200 in high socioeconomic situations. Adequacy of health care and general nutrition and the occurrence of accidents tend to be more common where incomes are low, and one of the results is impaired hearing. The reverse is true where incomes are high.

Regular hearing tests and examinations of the ears and throat should be part of growing up. Prevention or prompt correction of hearing problems is important both for educational and for medical reasons.

Table 11-1 gives an idea of what proportion of preteen school children have been found with various levels of difficulty in hearing. It can be seen that the more serious the problem, the smaller the proportion of pupils who are affected.

TABLE 11-1
Effects and Prevalence Data for
Decibel Levels and Degrees of Hearing Loss[1]

Decibel loss in speech range[2]	Degree of handicap	Ability to understand speech	Prevalence in percent
0-25	Insignificant	No difficulty	98.25
26-40	Slight	Problems with whispers or soft speech	1
41-55	Mild	Consistent problems with normally loud speech	0.5
56-70	Marked	Loud speech often not understood	0.2
71-90	Severe	Understands only strongly amplified speech	0.05
91-	Extreme	Maximally amplified speech not understood	

[1]Material in this table should be taken as approximations applying to preteenage school children. The data and concepts were drawn and adapted from Davis and Silverman (1970), and McConnell, in Dunn (1973).

[2]The ranges in this column can be thought of as the average for the better ear.

Teachers will find that it is possible to predict in only the most general ways how many hearing handicapped there will be in a given school or class from data such as those in Table 11-1, or the relative degrees of their losses. Actually the pupils in each school and class should be examined for hearing acuity each year. Teachers should also ask that there be provision for medical and audiometric examination in between the scheduled routine examinations whenever they believe there is reason to think something interferes with or threatens a pupil's hearing.

It is not news to educators that communication between pupil and teacher and from pupil to pupil is absolutely necessary if effective instruction is to go on. The better the communication, the more efficient and productive the instruction can be. Anything that interferes with communication is likely also to detract from the quality and pace of the instruction.

We shall see that communication is the core educational consideration with hearing impaired pupils. It is a central consideration not only because of the hearing impairment itself. Rather, it is the negative impact the impairment can have on the normal development of the most common medium of communication, oral language, which is at the heart of the matter. That is why educators and their helpers in psychology, linguistics, audiology, and speech pathology have spent so much energy over the years attempting to improve the teaching of language in all of its ramifications to hearing impaired persons.

Meager language or total absence of language is one of the chief characteristics of deafness when it has existed from early childhood and when it has been unattended, educationally speaking. Some other exceptional conditions in children have somewhat the same characteristics. Teachers need to know about them to avoid being misled as to what educational procedures to apply. When uncertain, teachers should use additional professional assistance from colleagues in determining the true nature of the situation. Some of the other conditions that are accompanied by communication behavior resemble those of pupils with hearing impairments.

Mentally retarded children typically have limited oral language development. It is possible to use informal checks on hearing to assist in making a distinction. If teachers are uncertain, school psychologists and audiologists can help in differentiating the two.

Aphasia, which literally means total absence of speech, can occur in young children. So can *dysphasia*, or very limited language production. The cause is not well understood, but one thing is certain—it is not the consequence of impaired hearing. Aphasic or dysphasic children usually have fully adequate hearing, audiometrically speaking. Consultation with a teacher of children with learning disabilities or with a public school psychologist familiar with learning disabilities and with deafness can be of aid in making the distinction and in planning appropriate educational programs.

Sometimes children who are quite withdrawn speak very little or not at all. Also, they are occasionally so inattentive that they resemble children who do not respond because they cannot hear. Such youngsters may become so detached from their surroundings that they show no reaction to even the most extreme stimulation, be it sound or light. They may appear not to hear, even at normally painful sound levels. If there is reason to think that mental illness may be the root of uncommunicative behavior, it is advisable for the teacher to seek consultation with a teacher of emotionally disturbed children, with a school psychologist who has had experience with markedly disturbed pupils, or with a child psychiatrist.

We shall return later to the matter of hearing impairment, its potentially limiting effect on education, and how regular class teachers and specialists are working together to instruct such children. Now, though, it is advisable to clarify the concept of mainstreaming as it applies to hearing handicapped pupils and to become familiar with some technical terminology.

Emerging Changes in Terminology

The technical expressions used in the education of hearing impaired pupils are coming into more common use by regular class teachers. That is necessary if there is to be adequate professional communication by the team referred to below.

Mainstreaming

Mainstreaming means that children who need special education are receiving it on a high quality level and that it is being brought to them while they enjoy the personal and social advantages of life in regular school classes with all the other youngsters of their age and neighborhood. It means that high quality regular education is going on, too, and not being interfered with for other pupils. Further, it means that the regular class teacher coordinates and is assisted by a staff of special educators, aides, and others. Together they make up a team whose central concern is topflight instruction for exceptional and regular children alike.

Mainstreaming for deaf and hard of hearing pupils is coming to mean that special schooling is blended from the outset with regular schooling with other children in regular classes. Simply putting hearing and hearing impaired children together is not enough. Proximity is not the same as integration.

The regular class teacher has always been the central professional person in the education of the great majority of American children. Mainstreaming maintains that principle.

Properly administered and adequately supported, mainstreaming for hearing impaired pupils is welcomed by regular class teachers. They find their own professional horizons expanded. They discover that the added staff and instructional resources for the hearing impaired children in their classes are frequently helpful with some of their regular class pupils who seem to be having learning problems.

Educators of deaf and hard of hearing pupils have always been guided by the desire to help their students attain full personal, social, and vocational membership in society on equal terms with all other people. Until recently, the only accepted way of trying to bring hearing handicapped persons into the mainstream was to start them young and supply intensive special education in special schools or classes through the preschool and elementary years. Then, during the secondary, technical school, and college years, some of the deaf and hard of hearing youth were encouraged to attempt to attend schools with hearing students.

It is different now. Mainstreaming has that same goal, but it moves in a quite different way. It starts from the premise that the great majority of deaf and hard of hearing children can be educated from the outset in the school's mainstream and that they should be part of the school's mainstream, socially and personally, from the preschool years all the way through the formal education years. Thus, deaf and hard of hearing children are expected to be educated from the start in the mainstream of life. They function from the beginning as a part of the regular school like all other children, rather than having to begin on the outside and try to win their way into an educational and social setting where all the other children already are. This was predicted by McConnell (1973) when he wrote: "The rapid increase in early detection, infant and preschool education, and day-class programs of higher quality should result in greater numbers of children able to join the regular education system" (p. 379).

Adherents of starting exceptional pupils separately, and gradually introducing them to the mainstream, often see little merit in the approach that starts all pupils together. The opposite is true, too. Sometimes each group reacts as though the other approach simply did not exist. That is unfortunate. Any evenhanded description of today's education for hearing impaired children and youth must attend to the two extremes, to the many graduations that spread between them, and to the direction of today's trends.

Not all hearing impaired children are served best by full mainstreaming. Some profit most from partial mainstreaming. Some, at least for a time, are best separated completely for intensified special teaching. When mainstreaming is the policy and the practice, the decision is made in the following way.

The parents and child are encouraged toward enrollment in an augmented regular nursery, kindergarten, or first grade, as the case may be. It is a regular class that is also organized, equipped, and staffed to maintain hearing handicapped pupils as full, participating members of the group.

If it is found after reasonable trial that the augmented regular class cannot satisfactorily meet all the needs of the hearing impaired child, then consideration is given to another placement. That change to another placement, if needed, would not be to total separation. Rather, it might be on a part time schedule to a resource room or a clinical setting or to full special education staffing while the child remained in the same regular school in visual contact and in a substantial and meaningful degree of social contact with the other pupils.

Progress toward integrating hearing impaired pupils has been slow. Each gain has been hard won by devoted educators, parents, and the young people for whom they have striven. Now, in the United States, the many isolated success stories about mainstreaming are coming together into recognizable patterns and are being acknowledged as preferred practices. The problem that remains is to move those preferred practices into becoming prevailing practices of today and tomorrow.

Technical Terms

Many hearing impaired pupils will be wearing *hearing aids* while attending classes with hearing children. Some may wear one for each ear. The aid may well be a curiosity to the hearing pupils and a concern to the regular class teacher. Here are some suggestions for understanding what a hearing aid is and does and how to capitalize on the regular class pupil's curiosity.

First, the regular class teacher can ask the special education teacher to demonstrate two or three different hearing aids and to explain how they work. By trying one on and listening, it will be seen that hearing aids are basically similar. There is first a device for picking up sound (a microphone). Second, there is a mechanism for making the sound louder (an amplifier). And third, there is a part that delivers the amplified sound to the hearing impaired person (earphone or speaker). The whole thing is energized by electrical batteries, resulting in a relatively lightweight yet powerful instrument.

The regular class teacher can also reach an agreement with the special education teacher and the child's parents, if appropriate, on these and any other matters of concern:

1. Hearing impaired pupils who come to your class will be prepared, to the extent their ages permit, to take responsibility for ordinary care of their hearing aids and will know how to use their aids.
2. The special education teacher will be on call to help with trouble shooting occasioned by problems with any aids.
3. The special education teacher will notify you if there is to be any change in how or when a child is to use an aid.
4. You will keep the special education teacher up to date on how the child is complying with the prescribed use of the aid.

Second, the regular class teacher can make constructive use of the natural curiosity of the hearing pupils about aids by asking the special education teacher to prepare one or more lessons for the class on the background, functions, and operation of hearing aids. The approach can be through physical science, social studies, biography, psychology, or any or all of those avenues. Naturally, the level of complexity would need to fit the capabilities and interests of the hearing pupils. Children of nursery and kindergarten age, for example, tend to be less distracted by such matters as hearing aids worn by their companions than are older children.

The teacher can join the pupils in learning about hearing aids. Practice with them in locating and trying out the volume controls and the off/on switch. Learn how to test the batteries and to replace them. When you see a child with an aid with which you are unfamiliar, ask the child or the special education teacher to explain to you how it works.

Perhaps the special education teacher or the school nurse will be willing to demonstrate an audiometer (a device to test hearing) for the class and explain how it works. That could extend the pupils' knowledge and increase their understanding of their own hearing and of how to protect it.

Hearing impaired (or hearing handicapped or auditorily or acoustically impaired or handicapped, used as synonyms) is a very broad term. It includes both deaf and hard of hearing—all kinds of hearing problems that may interfere with schooling in any way. Pupils called "hearing impaired" do need special education, but it is not possible from that term alone to know what kinds or amounts of special education might be needed. A widely accepted definition of *hearing impairment* is a hearing disability that may range in severity from mild to profound and that includes the *deaf* and *hard of hearing*.

Deaf means the absence of hearing in both ears for all practical purposes. For education, the time when the loss of hearing occurred is significant. If hearing was absent at birth or totally lost by the end of the first one or two years of life, the normal foundations for language that the hearing infant learns are missing. That means that language must subsequently be taught through special education means. Special educators have still not found fully satisfactory ways to do that well for all children. Thus, if children have no usable hearing during the first year or two of life, they suffer the maximum educational handicap that hearing impairment can impose.

Deafness is a serious problem, of course, whenever it happens, but the later in the childhood years that deafness occurs, the better equipped special educators are to minimize its negative impact on school learning. A major professional association has defined the condition this way: "A *deaf* person is one whose hearing disability precludes successful processing of linguistic information through audition, with or without a hearing aid." (American Association for the Deaf, October 1975, p. 509)

Two other terms, *audiometric deafness* and *hard of hearing,* should be understood, also, in relation to the word *deaf.* Audiometric deafness simply means that the amount of hearing loss a person suffers is beyond a certain point, as measured by testing with an audiometer. It is a way of expressing "deafness" in quantified terms.

Hard of hearing refers to hearing impaired individuals who had sufficient hearing during infancy to acquire the foundations of language without special teaching. Many such persons need special education because of imperfections in their language development and because they have limitations in learning communication skills such as speech, reading, and writing. However, special educators have excellent procedures that work effectively with most such youngsters. A formal definition of this condition is as follows:

> A hard of hearing person is one who, generally with the use of a hearing aid, has residual hearing sufficient to enable successful processing of linguistic information through audition. (American Association for the Deaf, October 1975, p. 509)

Special education teacher is used here in a generic sense for any educators, other than regular class teachers, who have some form of instructional responsibility for the hearing impaired child. It encompasses such titles as: teacher of the deaf, speech clinician, teacher of the hard of hearing, teacher of the hearing impaired, speech therapist, resource teacher, liaison teacher, itinerant teacher, and academic tutor.

Ameslan, or American sign language, is a separate and distinct language. Signs represent concepts, not words. As in English, where a word represents a concept (i.e., time), in Ameslan a sign represents a concept (i.e., a finger pointing at a wrist watch or the place where a wrist watch should be, if being worn). Ameslan is a form of manual communication.

Manual alphabet refers to an alphabet with a one to one relationship of finger positions of 1 hand and the 26 English letters (see Figure 11-2). Using the manual alphabet, English words can be spelled and sequenced into sentences as a direct substitute for English speech or writing. Punctuation can be shown, also.

The Person Who Is Called Hearing Impaired

These incidents from the lives of Peter Brawley and Dr. James Marsters show that the hearing impaired are creative, contributing persons. They also suggest that the educability of hearing impaired persons is too often underestimated.

A Product of Miracles

The following remarks were made by Dr. H. C. Evans, Jr., President of Lees-McRae College, Banner Elk, N.C., to heads of school for the deaf at a banquet held in Greensboro last summer:

"I had been taught that a person with a severe and long time hearing impairment could, with a high motivation, secure the equivalent of a 10th grade education through a proper and individual high school education.

FIGURE 11-2
The American Manual Alphabet (As Seen by Finger Speller)

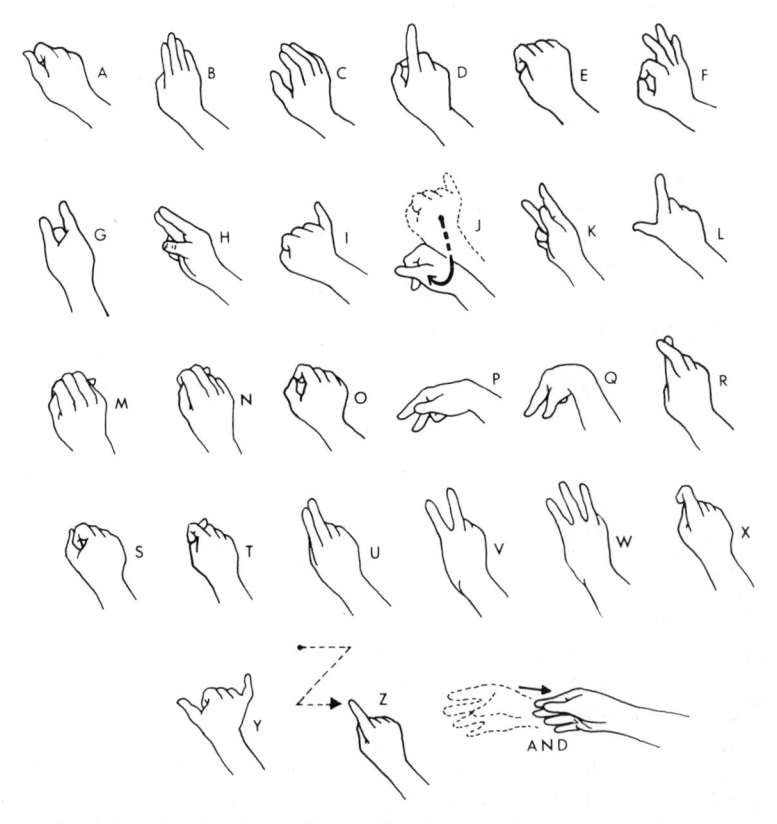

Source: L. J. Fant, Jr., *Say It with Hands.* Washington DC: Gallaudet College Centennial Fund Commission, 1964, p. 1. Reprinted with permission.

For this reason, when our Admission's Committee called to my attention the application of a Peter Brawley of Winston-Salem, I immediately responded that I felt admission to Lees-McRae College would place him in an impossible position and, thus, would be unfair to him. Our admission's policy for Lees-McRae is very open but never to the point of intentionally bringing a person on campus who cannot conceivably succeed here and in a senior college. We consider our major mission to prepare a student for success in a strong academic senior college.

"Peter, some days later, walked into my office accompanied by his father and was very unhappy about the decision and asked for a trial period. His determination was apparent. Having had many personal experiences with the deaf communicating through sign language, I was amazed at Peter's ability to communicate through voice, even though both of us had to work very hard to achieve full communication.

"Two years later Peter Brawley received the first standing ovation for an individual student which I have ever witnessed during my 15 years as a college teacher and administrator. He had not only done it, he had done it well and there were very few dry eyes that day when this brave and remarkable young man marched off the stage toward success in one of the finest senior colleges in the south.

"With no question in my mind, Peter came to Lees-McRae College a product of miracles, the miracle of a family which understood and accepted and never questioned, at least openly to Peter, and the miracle of the Clarke School for the Deaf where Peter gained the academic confidence to take a handicap and make it a stepping stone.

"Lees-McRae College will always be richer by having given Peter Brawley a chance to prove that its president's generality about the abilities of a deaf high school graduate just don't work out very well in some specific cases."

(Peter is now a Senior at the University of North Carolina in Chapel Hill.) (Clarke School for the Deaf, 1976)

Teletype Phone Network Helping Deaf Reach Out*

A Pasadena dentist, who has never heard a spoken word, has made it possible for 14,000 deaf people to carry on conversations over the telephone.

Dr. James C. Marsters inspired the development of a communications system that combines the telephone with the Teletype machine.

Deaf persons "talk" to one another by punching teletypewriter keys. Their messages are carried from one teletypewriter to another via the telephone.

An orthodontist, Marsters, 51, is one of only three totally deaf persons in this country ever to become a dentist.

Since birth he has lived in a world of complete silence. Yet, like many born without hearing, he has learned to master speech, using words he has never heard himself. He "hears" others by reading lips.

"A telephone for those deprived of hearing is often a matter of life and death," Marsters explains.

"Imagine waking up at 2 in the morning and finding your wife having a heart attack. You are deaf. You run to a neighbor and start pounding on his door.

"The neighbor has no idea who's at the door. He shouts—'Who is it? Who is it?' You can't hear him, you don't answer. He doesn't open the door. He doesn't know who it is.

"What do you do? You are stuck.

---

*From *The Los Angeles Times,* December 7, 1975. Copyright© 1975 by the Los Angeles Times. Reprinted by permission.

"Multiply that by 1,000 times. It gets serious. You can't reach out when there's a need to reach out."

In 1963, Marsters sought out Robert Weitbrecht, a deaf astronomer and electronics engineer.

"I was so frustrated trying to use the telephone," recalled the dentist. "I had heard of Bob Weitbrecht's expertise in electronics. So I flew up to San Francisco to talk with him and see if we could come up with a telephone for the deaf.

"We worked together for months and finally came up with the equipment we now have.

"Teletype machines were being phased out by the telephone companies, Western Union and other firms and being replaced with computers. We found a way to put the Teletype machines to work for the deaf."

The two men formed an all-deaf owned and operated company, Applied Communications Corp., headquartered in Belmont in the San Francisco Bay area. Marsters is president and Weitbrecht is vice president of research and development.

Out of their research came the Phonetype, a device that converts telephone signals into teletypewriter signals and vice versa.

When the phone rings in the home or office of a deaf person who has a teletypewriter and Phonetype, lights go on and off.

If a person is both blind and deaf, fans go on. The deaf-blind person uses a Braille teletypewriter.

When the phone is lifted off its cradle and placed on a recess in the Phonetype—a small black box—the teletypewriter is activated.

Then a message from the caller begins to appear on the receiver's teletypewriter. The message is punched out by the caller.

The person receiving the message responds by punching out his message on his teletypewriter keyboard. And the conversation goes back and forth throughout the length of the call.

In 1968, the Marsters-Weitbrecht project was given a boost when American Telephone and Telegraph Co. agreed to donate surplus Teletype machines to deaf people through the Alexander Graham Bell Association for the Deaf, Inc. (Alexander Graham Bell's wife was deaf.)

That same year, Marsters, Weitbrecht and others from the National Association of the Deaf and the Alexander Graham Bell Association for the Deaf formed Teletypewriters for the Deaf, Inc. (TDI), a nonprofit organization.

TDI buys teletypewriters and receives donated ones. TDI and Marsters' firm work together to place teletypewriters and Phonetypes in homes of the deaf.

It costs a deaf person $100 to have the teletypewriters brought to top working condition, delivered and installed, and $155 for the Phonetype. The deaf person becomes sole owner of the equipment.

There is a great need for additional machines.

Teletypewriters for the Deaf published its first directory of people with teletypewriters and Phonetypes in 1968. There were 174 listings. Today the directory carries more than 14,000 listings. (Hillinger, 1975)

THE CONCEPT, TERMINOLOGY, AND SIGNIFICANCE OF HEARING IMPAIRMENT

Standard modern practice with newborns and infants includes efforts to determine if there are any defects in their hearing. Such examinations are continued by up to date pediatricians at regular and frequent intervals. From the medical point of view, the obvious reason for these early checks is to identify and correct, if possible, any auditory defects.

There is an equally important educational reason. If infants have significant hearing losses in the speech-sound range, and if they do not receive special instruction, they will become victims of the most serious educational handicap an otherwise normal human can have.

- We learn to speak because we can hear.
- We learn to understand the speech of others because we can hear.
- But, more fundamentally, we learn that there is such a thing as language, and we learn how to employ language to communicate because we can hear.

It is a serious matter that a congenitally deaf child, without special instruction, cannot *say* his name.

It is also serious that the child does not really *know* his name. *But it is most important and most serious of all that he does not know that there is such a thing as a name.* It is that most fundamental lack—absence of the most elemental concept of language—that is the core of the educational problem. It is language in all of its ramifications that the child must be taught.

The Language Process

Language comes naturally to infants and toddlers who can hear and who are not otherwise handicapped in such a way as to prevent it. The expression "comes naturally" needs elaboration. The process, stripped down to its essence, is illustrated in Figure 11-3.

Speech sounds are produced by A, the adult. (See solid line.) They enter the ears of B, the baby, and are perceived, that is, transmitted to the brain and recorded there. Sounds that are produced by B, the baby (see dotted line) are transmitted to the adult's ear, who already knows language and can compare the baby's sounds with known (to the adult) words or approximations of words. When the baby produces a sound that is close to that of a word, the adult often repeats it back, delightedly, or otherwise shows pleasure selectively in favor of wordlike sounds.

FIGURE 11-3
The Language Process

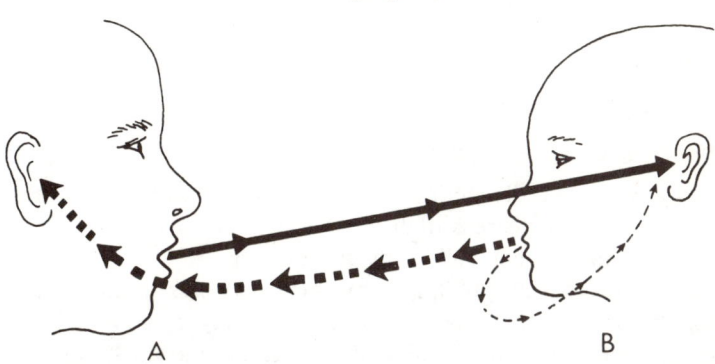

A   B

Thus, the baby is aided in forming and repeating and becoming skilled at producing the sounds of the adult's language.

The baby's hearing is already involved importantly in the transaction. If the baby could not hear, or heard imperfectly, there could be no perception of the adult's sounds in the first place. In the second place, there could be little or no knowledge of the meaning of the adult's reactions to sounds produced by the baby.

There is another role hearing plays in very early life, too. When the baby utters sounds they are heard through the baby's ears almost simultaneously (see line of dashes). Thus the baby's hearing provides the added capability of self monitoring of speech sounds. Given the assumption that the baby has the remembered perception of an adult produced sound, it is now possible for the baby to practice alone and to find satisfaction in matching sounds uttered to those remembered.

The crucial role of adequate hearing in all of this is plain. Without hearing on the baby's part there is a gap in the line of oral-aural communication and a similar gap in the monitoring line.

Much more could be said about this process. The way meanings get attached to spoken sounds along the way was not mentioned. The fact that normal language development is very swift moving in the earliest years is another factor not discussed here. And there are other points of significance to a fuller understanding of how language is acquired and perfected. But the essential fact being emphasized is that adequate hearing in the speech range is a fundamental requirement for normal language development. Its absence can cause one of the most devastating cognitive and communicative disabilities to which humans can be heir.

Hearing is important also for learning about music, about the sounds of nature, and for a multitude of other reasons, including safety, in our world.

Fortunately, there are ways to ameliorate the impact of deafness on the general development of the child and the child's education, specifically. They will be noted later.

Defining Hearing Impairment

Audiometric Classification

One way to make a distinction between deaf and hard of hearing pupils is by the different degrees of hearing they have that can be measured through an instrument called an audiometer. A widely used cut off point indicates that deaf children have hearing losses greater than 90 decibels in the better ear and that hard of hearing persons have hearing losses not that great. That is an audiometric definition. It is in terms of hearing as measured in decibel units by means of an instrument that emits tones of different frequencies at controlled loudness levels to test what one can hear.

It is evident that one child may be audiometrically deaf (91 decibels) and another child may be audiometrically hard of hearing (90 decibels). Yet, practically speaking, there is really not enough variation between the two insofar as hearing is concerned to make an educationally significant difference. Thus, it is not feasible to use the audiometric classification as a valid predictor of how an individual hearing impaired child might react to language instruction or achieve in school.

Educational Classification

A second way to make a distinction between deaf and hard of hearing pupils is in terms of how they learn language. As indicated earlier, children with little or no hearing in the first or second years do not learn language in the natural, informal way most children do. They can be regarded as educationally deaf. The hard of hearing children are those who have significant hearing losses but who learn language in the usual way, though in some instances imperfectly.

This distinction in terms does not necessarily mean that one can expect higher school achievement from one than the other. Nor does it indicate where the child's education should take place. It does mean that by using this kind of grouping one can predict that deaf pupils will usually need more special teaching to acquire language arts skills than will hard of hearing pupils.

Northcott (1973) alluded also to the problem of definitions that tend to imply prophecies about personal development, social behavior, or about where and how hearing impaired pupils ought to be educated. She indicated that she prefers the definition: "A hearing impaired (deaf or hard-of-hearing) individual is a person who requires specialized education because of a hearing impairment" (p. 9). Explaining why, Northcott said,

> The general term *hearing impaired* is used deliberately because it is relatively neutral in emotional content; it does not arouse automatic prediction of the level of personal, academic or social performance that will be achieved by any students whose hearing loss may range from mild to profound by audiological assessment and audiogram. (p. 2)

Further, She said,
> There is ample evidence in current literature and research that the terms *deaf* and *hard of hearing* are diagnostically and psychologically unsound as a basis for judging how well a hearing impaired child will perform in the classroom. The focus today is on labeling not the child but the supplementary services and resource personnel...required to assist the child and his family. (p. 5)

In 1975 the Conference of Executives of American Schools for the Deaf, jointly with the Convention of American Instructors of the Deaf, published the most recent authoritative statement on definition. The report offers these general definitions:

> *Hearing Impairment.* A generic term indicating a hearing disability which may range in severity from mild to profound: it included the subsets of *deaf* and *hard of hearing.*
>
> A *deaf* person is one whose hearing disability precludes successful processing of linguistic information through audition, with or without a hearing aid.
>
> A *hard of hearing* person is one who, generally with the use of a hearing aid, has residual hearing sufficient to enable success for processing of linguistic information through audition. (p. 509)

For the most part, we have used these definitions in this book. Also, the Ad Hoc Committee's several recommendations on the use of definitions in education and research are reflected in our use of terms. In particular, for educational consideration, we have emphasized the importance of this distinction the Committee made:

> *Prelingual deafness:* deafness present at birth, or occurring early in life at an age prior to the development of speech or language.
> *Postlingual deafness:* deafness occurring at an age following the development of speech and language. (p. 510)

This report also supplies useful operational definitions that relate specifically to the mainstream concept:

> *Full integration* means total integration into regular classes for hearing students with special services provided under direction of specialists in in educational programs for deaf and hard of hearing.

Partial integration means taking all classes in a regular school, some on an integrated basis and some on a self-contained basis.
Self-contained means attending classes exclusively with other deaf and/or hard of hearing classmates in regular schools, special day schools, or special residential schools. (p. 510)

The concepts embodied in these 1975 definitions are light-years in advance of those that appeared only a short decade before. That observation is reinforced by the Ad Hoc Committee's indications that full integration can be feasible and appropriate for some pupils with any degree of hearing impairment, so far as "present-day implications for educational settings" are concerned (p. 510).

Hearing Loss Conditions that Influence Education

The educational influences noted below stem from five factors. Technical advances have resulted in corrective procedures through which all of the five factors have come increasingly under control.

Nature of the Hearing Defect

The first question is whether the hearing defect is in the speech range. There are many sounds such as the bass horn or the rumble of distant thunder that are lower than most human voice sounds. Even total loss of hearing for those low sounds interferes very little with hearing for ordinary conversations. The same is true for sounds higher than those usually used for talking. Examples would the tones of a piccolo or the shrill of a whistle. True enough, it is an inconvenience to miss those kinds of sounds or to hear them imperfectly. Loss of hearing of that kind does carry with it some educational problems that call for special instruction. However, the most serious special educational problems arise when there is a hearing loss for the sounds ordinarily made by the human voice in conversation.

Degree of the Hearing Defect

The second important factor is the degree of the hearing defect. Assume that the child's hearing loss cuts across all or most of the speech range. If so, and if the loss is complete or almost complete, nothing that is said by a teacher or by any other person will be heard. That closes oral communication off entirely—a most serious problem, since a great deal of teaching and learning depends on hearing and responding to what is heard.

If the hearing loss is total, an ordinary hearing aid will have no value. It would be like offering ordinary glasses to a totally blind person. However, if the hearing loss is not quite total, sometimes specialized hearing aids can be helpful. But as with vision, if only a little remains, amplifying devices (hearing aids) cannot be expected to work miracles. At best, they can allow the child to hear a little more, though what is heard will usually be quite distorted. That is because all the sounds of the environment are made louder, not just the voice of the person speaking. And it is much more difficult to "listen to" something specific, shutting out the rest, than it is to "look at" something specific and attend to nothing else.

If the hearing defect is a relatively limited one, however, a hearing aid can be of great value. It can make practically normal functioning possible for some pupils. It takes real effort, though, to learn to use a hearing aid well. Also, it takes practice to sustain good hearing aid use and the hearing aid itself needs regular care and maintenance. All of that must be made part of the child's special education.

Onset of the Hearing Defect

The third factor of major significance is when the hearing defect started. If a 15 year old youth loses all or most hearing, it is a matter of real importance and concern both from an educational point of view and for other reasons, too. Yet it is not at all as serious, from any point of view, as losing all or most hearing while an infant or toddler, or as serious as being born with that condition. The 15 year old, other things being equal, has permanent assets that the infant will to some extent be denied, despite the most expert efforts to help attain them. Here is a list of some of those assets that very early profound or severe hearing impairment make it extremely difficult for a person to achieve:

1. Knowledge of one's native language.
2. Clear oral speech.
3. Understanding of the oral speech of others.
4. Ability to read with speed and comprehension.
5. Understanding of abstract concepts.

All of the 5 assets the 15 year old would have gained to an average degree in the normal course of events. Becoming deaf at that age would not take any of those achievements away except the third. With the others present, acquiring reasonable proficiency at lipreading (speechreading) would not be an insurmountable task.

But imagine beginning life with no means to make contact with others through sounds! When one recognizes that adequate hearing is the key to all five of the above qualities, the importance of the age at which hearing was lost becomes clear.

The three factors named so far all have to do directly with how hearing impairment can affect the educability of a child. The relationships of these three factors can be summarized in the following statements:

1. The more the sounds in the speech range are blocked out by the hearing impairment, the more serious the special education problem.

2. The nearer the hearing impairment to complete loss, the more serious the special education problem.
3. The earlier in childhood the hearing impairment started, the more serious the special education problem.

There are two other important factors still to be discussed. They are also of prime significance for special education, even though they do not relate directly to the defective hearing. Instead they are concerned with the pupil's intelligence rate and complexity of cognitive development and the instruction the youngster receives in the very early years. Since it is well recognized today that proper stimulation in the early childhood years can have a positive effect on cognitive development, these factors are often linked.

The Hearing Impaired Child's Cognitive Development

The pupil's cognitive development affects the response to special education. This is the fourth of the five major influential factors.

The more intelligent the hearing impaired youngster is, the higher the probability that language, speech production, understanding of speech, ability to read, and the understanding of abstractions can come close to being normalized through special education. For that reason (as well as for social and personality reasons) it is important to take a positive and dynamic attitude about the cognitive development potentialities of hearing impaired children.

One can easily underestimate the intelligence of hearing impaired youngsters. To those who are unfamiliar with the effect of hearing loss, such children are frequently thought to be mentally retarded. Therefore, it is fundamentally important to get the professional opinion of a school psychologist who has experience in working with hearing impaired children and with special educators of the hearing handicapped. Anything short of assessment by that kind of psychologist is likely to result in a false impression that can lead to serious and permanent curtailment of the child's educational opportunities. Often young hearing impaired pupils need weeks or months of patient work by the school psychologist and teacher, acting as a team, before the full extent of the child's intelligence can be brought out. Taking that time, if necessary, can be the most important investment ever made on the child's behalf.

The Nature and Amount of Stimulation Provided

The fifth factor of major significance is the kind and amount of stimulation the hearing impaired individual has received. It is well known that babies born without hearing begin to babble in the first months of life just as hearing babies do. That soon stops, however, unless it is encouraged by the adults around the baby. Similarly, in older children, language comprehension will tend to deteriorate when a hearing loss develops. The speech quality of the person whose hearing is leaving will also deteriorate. However, if regular, conscious efforts are made to encourage the baby's babbling and other kinds of striving for communication and to bolster and maintain the older child's language development and speech quality a great deal more can be accomplished toward minimizing the special education problems associated with hearing loss.

Thus, two more summary statements can be added to the three listed previously.

1. The hearing impaired child will be more likely to profit from special education if a dynamic view is taken of intellectual potential, with continuing efforts being made to reveal, develop, and employ the child's cognitive capabilities.
2. Early, orderly, and regular stimulation of language comprehension and communication can maximize the constructive impact of special education.

PREVAILING VERSUS PREFERRED PRACTICES

Probably no aspect of special education draws on so many different professional participants, has turned up such a variety of educational methodologies over the years, and still has maintained its separate identity as a specialization. Those conditions made it more than ordinarily difficult to spell out the 12 statements below.

Yet there are two broad moves we can identify, around which the preferred practices are coalescing. One is a pragmatic view that says that teaching a system of language in the earliest childhood years is of overriding importance. Let us teach a system, then—any system we can—and build refinements later.

Second, let us not debate about the role of the residential school. Some still look on it as an elitist center for the most able of the most hearing impaired to be educated. More commonly, though, its new position is emerging as a regional resource, a research agency, a training promulgator and a school specializing in work with hearing impaired pupils with the kinds of complex educational problems which defy solution in the mainstream. The residential school, we believe, will remain and grow in strength as it takes on new roles such as these and others, perhaps, which cannot yet be envisioned.

Prevailing Practices	**Preferred Practices**
1. Children with severe to profound hearing impairments are detected, for the most part, in the first year or two of life. Mild to moderate hearing losses tend to be located later, usually at or shortly after admission to regular kindergarten or first grade.	1. Educators join with the health professions to obtain staff and facilities for routine and repeated screening from birth through the preschool years, emphasizing that early discovery allows early educational intervention, and the earlier education can start, the better the chances are for fully successful education and normalization.
2. Otologists, audiologists, nurses, and psychologists are the contacts parents tend to have when they are learning about their children's hearing impairments and beginning to make plans for them.	2. Teacher specialists in very early childhood education (birth to 3 years) representing the local school system work directly with parents from the time the hearing loss is discovered, coordinate educational planning, and make use of otological, audiological, and psychological findings in doing so. The parent has a tie to regular and special educators from the local school system from the time the hearing loss is found. Care is taken to match learning tasks to the child's rate and level of cognitive development.
3. Educational guidance in the preschool years emphasizes the desirability of sound amplification and of intensive auditory training by audiologists or speech and hearing clinicians in one to one or small group clinical settings.	3. Preschool educational guidance stresses participation with hearing children and their families in all normal developmental activities while using sound amplification and receiving intensive auditory training from qualified specialists.
4. The local school system becomes aware of the existence	4. The local school system accepts responsibility for all as-

Prevailing Practices	Preferred Practices
of most of its preschool hearing impaired children when they reach legal school entry age. Preschool educational programs, where they exist, tend to be operated by volunteer agencies.	pects of preschool education for hearing impaired pupils from the time the hearing loss is discovered and employs qualified educators to conduct the needed special and regular education. Volunteer groups are welcomed as helpers in conducting programs, in supplying services that supplement education, and as innovators in suggesting and demonstrating new directions the schools might take to make program improvements.
5. Parents are confronted in the preschool years with the question of which form of instruction—oral or total communication—to choose for their severely or profoundly hearing impaired child. Acceptance of one tends to separate the child and parents from contact with children and adults who espouse the other. Professional persons take sides in sometimes acrimonious conflicts over the opposing form of instruction.	5. Parents are given objective information by school system staff about differing forms of instruction. They have options about which form they elect for their children and may transfer from one to another at their own initiative. School systems have qualified staff who work together effectively across forms of instruction.
6. Free public education for hearing impaired pupils with severe and profound losses is available in a few states from as early as the condition is detected and in several states beginning at age 2. Many states have not yet arranged for schooling for these children before standard admission age for all children.	6. Education for all hearing impaired pupils is free and public, beginning at any age hearing impairment is found.

Prevailing Practices

7. At the time of formal school admission parents in rural and small town settings usually have the option to send their severely or profoundly hearing impaired child to reside in a boarding school or to attend a special class that calls for a daily bus ride to a different school from that attended by the rest of the family. In a large number of cases the same is true of parents who live in large cities and suburbs.

8. Children with mild to moderate hearing impairments usually may have special education from speech therapists in their local schools. The therapists ordinarily take the child out of the regular class to give 20 to 40 minutes of corrective and remedial language and speech instruction each week, and to monitor the child's use of any hearing aid that might be worn. They advise regular class teachers about favorable seating for the child and stay alert for any other special needs the child might have. There is little or no direct contact with parents. Often the speech therapist's training and experience with hearing problems is limited or nonexistent; in some cases, however, the therapist's preparation is excellent.

Preferred Practices

7. Teachers and aides supply instruction in the homes of very young children, if parents wish. When mature enough to go to school, hearing impaired pupils attend regular classes in the local school or a nearby regular school to which they are transported and the special education they need is brought to them in the regular class context. Clinical otological, audiological, and psychological work, if needed, is done mostly outside regular school hours.

8. Educational programs are individualized. Plans are prepared in writing by a team and are coordinated by the regular class teacher. Specialist teachers work with children in the context of the regular class rather than removing them, in most instances. Parents take an active part in preparing program plans and give their approval to them.

Prevailing Practices	Preferred Practices
9. The great majority of hearing impaired pupils of all degrees of hearing loss are separated from the outset for instruction from regular classes and other classes for part or all of each day, all year long. Relatively few severely or profoundly hearing impaired pupils (deaf pupils) move into the mainstream for any of their formal elementary or secondary education.	9. Special educational help outside the regular class is given when needed, and may extend to periods of full time attendance at residential schools. Generally, however, full time or most of the time mainstreaming is the case.
10. Many, perhaps the majority, of speech and hearing specialists and teachers of the hearing impaired have training or experience only in their specialties. Regular class teachers only occasionally have backgrounds that ready them for helping hearing impaired students in their regular classes.	10. Specialists who have advanced preparation in the education of the hearing impaired or in speech and hearing are drawn from a pool of professional educators who have training and successful exerience as regular class teachers. Also, the regular class teachers in the school system have had in-service training to prepare them to instruct hearing impaired pupils in the mainstream and for coordinating and using the help of specialists upon whom they might call.
11. Most special classes, day schools, and residential schools have some but not many facilities for hearing impaired children with additional exceptionalities—giftedness, social or emotional maladjustment, mental retardation, other sensory or physical problems—from the point of view of staff	11. Resources are available in the school system or special class or residential school and can be readily mobilized to accommodate multiply exceptional pupils, and the attitude is favorable toward doing so.

Prevailing Practices	Preferred Practices
preparation, physical plant, curriculum adjustments, and instructional materials.	
12. Liaison between regular elementary and secondary education and special day classes and schools for hearing impaired pupils is minimal. There is little mingling for professional, educational, or social reasons between the staffs or the pupils of the two.	12. Specialists in the education of hearing impaired pupils view themselves as close working colleagues of regular class teachers. They meet together frequently on professional and on educational matters concerning themselves and their pupils.

THE BEGINNING OF SPECIAL EDUCATION FOR HEARING IMPAIRED PUPILS

The beginning of education of children who are deaf or hard of hearing in the United States is identified with techniques and procedures imported from Europe. The first record of a manual alphabet for the deaf is the 1620 publication of Juan Pablo Bonet, in Madrid. Another Spaniard of the same period, Jacob Rodrigues Pereire, added sign language to Bonet's manual alphabet. That gave deaf persons an additional means of expression which, when coupled with the manual alphabet, allowed a full range of communication which could also compete with speech for speed and accuracy (Wallin, 1924).

Pereire is also credited (Wallin, 1924) with bringing attention to the possibilities of lipreading, which has evolved into the broader concept now called speechreading. That concept involves obtaining meaning solely from the lip and other natural facial and bodily movements that occur when a person talks. It, plus throat vibrations that can be felt, formed the basis of what is now called the oral method of teaching language to hearing impaired persons.

In Paris, a public school for deaf pupils was founded in 1755 by the Abbé Charles Michel Del'Epée. There, teaching was by the manual method. At about the same time a school that used the oral method was started in Germany by Samuel Heinicke. Thus the two distinct methods still in use today for teaching language to deaf children were formally inaugurated in the mid 18th century in Europe.

The European work moved to the United States by way of Scotland. Thomas Hopkins Gallaudet from Hartford, Connecticut, had heard of the work of Thomas Braidwood, an oralist, in Edinburgh. Gallaudet went there to observe and then went on to France to study the manual method. In 1817, Gallaudet returned to the United States and opened what is now the American School for the Deaf in Hartford.

The movement spread and there are now residential schools, day schools, and integrated programs all across the country. Edward Minor Gallaudet, Thomas' son carried on after his father's developments, leading to what is now Gallaudet College in the District of Columbia, a federally sponsored college for deaf youth.

Alexander Graham Bell's invention of the telephone in 1876 was a landmark, too. His interest in the education of deaf children led to application of the same principles in the development of amplifiers and ultimately to the modern hearing aid. Those inventions opened the door to increased and more effective use of oral instruction.

The history of education for deaf pupils now appears to be moving into a new phase. More deaf pupils are beginning their education with hearing pupils and progressing through school in the same classes, and educational approaches developed for them are benefitting hearing pupils as well.

Recent Past and Present Status

Methods of teaching language and communication, increased interest in sign language, improvement of school achievement, and increased interest in hard of hearing pupils characterize the recent past and intrude on the present. They are discussed briefly here.

Two methods in recent years have contended for dominance in teaching hearing impaired students: manual and oral. There are many variants of each of the two main methods. Much professional thought and energy have been consumed as a part of this contention.

Total communication, which combines both, is currently receiving much favorable attention. That is probably due chiefly to recent research findings. Suppes (1974) provided a succinct current review of the research. One of Suppes' summary remarks is very germane:

> It is hard to think of an area (methods of teaching) in which really careful and extended experiments would be of more use, for there is a long tradition of support of each position. Until recently, the oral position was probably the dominant one, but in the last few years there has been an increasing interest in and respect for what has been achieved by manual methods beginning with the very young child. (p. 145)

It is not our intent to take an "either-or" position on methods or systems of teaching communication. We leave that for solution on the basis of the research evidence that is accumulating.

More and more special and regular educators are becoming fluent in manual communication. The same is true of pupils, whether or not they have impaired hearing. The growth in use of sign language stems from three sources.

One is the conscious promotion of the growth of total communication, which combines the use of oral speech, speech reading, sign, and the manual alphabet in teaching deaf pupils.

Second is the increase in the proportion of deaf and hard of hearing pupils who attend regular classes. Given that daily close contact, hearing pupils and their regular teachers find it interesting, useful, and not difficult to learn sign. In a number of cases it is taught as an in-service unit for teachers who wish to acquire the skill.

Third is the more and more frequent translation of television news and feature presentations into sign by superimposing a signing person in a corner of the screen. This has markedly increased the access of those programs to persons who can understand sign. At the same time it has made knowledge of sign more valuable to all hearing impaired individuals. Further, the increase in public visibility of sign language has gone a long way toward increasing public understanding and acceptance of manual forms of communication. Another related result is that those who use sign and manual alphabet are less objects of curiosity.

Over the past several years there has been a steady increase in the proportion of hearing impaired pupils who attain standardized achievement test scores equivalent to those of hearing children of the same age. (Office of Demographic Studies, 1973). That upward trend is important because deaf and hard of hearing pupils tend to be educationally retarded when compared to hearing pupils and when compared to their own potentialities as judged from measures of mental development. The educational retardation has been substantial; it was 3 to 4 years for deaf pupils and 1½ to 2 years for hard of hearing pupils in 1970-71. Despite the significant amount of educational retardation of hearing impaired pupils on the average, though, there are more and more with achievement at or above par.

Actually, the school achievement of hearing impaired pupils can best be predicted in the same way it is done for other children. The two best predictors are (a) past performance and (b) intelligence tests. Past performance in school work is an excellent indicator of what to expect in school in the future if there have been no important changes in the child. Intelligence tests, too, are good predictors. However, they must be tests that are especially adapted for hearing impaired children and, as indicated earlier, the tests should be administered by school psychologists who are familiar with the tests and with the education of deaf and hard of hearing youngsters.

It can be educationally disastrous for hard of hearing children if they are grouped with deaf children, unless the instruction is highly individualized. Otherwise, the hard of hearing child, who ordinarily could move faster and farther in language development, is held to the slower language development pace more typical of the deaf. One of the advantages of mainstreaming that starts in the earliest years is that the hearing impaired pupil, whether educationally deaf or hard of hearing, has predominantly hearing pupils as models and can develop educationally as rapidly as individual endowments will allow. It is essential that each hearing impaired youngster be provided with an individually designed educational plan in writing, with close attention to matching tasks and cognitive level and rate, and that it be followed and updated regularly.

Current Trends

The teaching of language, the concern for achievement, and the other matters that were listed as professional preoccupations in the preceding section continue. They are merged, however, in the growing interest in teaching hearing impaired pupils together with other pupils.

During 1974-75, an investigation of successful mainstream programs in the United States was conducted (Birch, 1975). The procedure included on-site observations and interviews of regular class and special education teachers, all of whom had experience with hearing impaired pupils in full or partial regular class programs. Parents, pupils, aides, supervisors, and administrators were interviewed, too. One focus of the investigation was the question: What does it take to make mainstreaming effective? That query was pursued from the point of view of teachers and others who deal directly with hearing impaired pupils and from the point of view of those responsible for school organization and administration.

Principles of Successful Mainstreaming

"Successful" programs were defined operationally. They were usually situations where mainstreaming had a history of more than 5 years duration, where it was schoolwide or school-system-wide, and where all concerned—board of education, teachers, administrators and parents—were in support of continuing in the same direction. (That is not to say the programs were problem free. In most of the case illustrations given in the report of the study the current problems were noted, too.)

In all instances the summary reports written from the interview data were returned in draft form for verification. Corrections were made as indicated by the local persons responsible for reviewing the written reports.

Here, in brief, are the principles found necessary for successful mainstreaming:

Principle 1: Apply a preteach/teach/postteach strategy.
Principle 2: Teach toward hearing world participation.
Principle 3: Have a planned, organized, systematic approach.

Principle 4: Have unified and consistent commitment and direction.
Principle 5: Bring special education into the regular class.

Each principle is explained and illustrated below.

Principle 1: Apply a preteach/teach/postteach strategy. When this principle is in operation, there is a close, cooperative instructional team relationship between the regular class teachers and the special teachers of the hearing impaired. Each hearing impaired student's achievement is closely monitored so there is a maximum chance for initial and continued success in regular classes. Further, the preteach/teach/postteach pattern carries on until the hearing impaired child becomes less and less dependent on it and more and more able to dispense with all or most of the preteach and postteach phases. Then the pattern changes from one of regular application of the preteach and postteach phases to one where the hard of hearing or deaf student seeks help from the special teacher only as the student feels it is needed. An important personal growth objective has been reached when that degree of independence is successfully shown by the hearing impaired student. The teachers, too, must learn when to let go.

With that background we turn to an illustration. It could apply to either an oral or a total communication language instruction base. With minor adaptations it could be generalized to a residential, day, or regular public or private elementary school.

Assume that fourth or fifth graders are studying *Robin Hood*. The regular class teacher's lesson plan calls for (among other things) discussion of a thought question: Why did Robin Hood and his men believe that they could not expect to receive justice at the hands of the Sheriff of Nottingham? The special teacher of the hearing impaired, as a matter of course, would have reviewed the lesson plan with the regular class teacher during part of an earlier planning period. The pupils would have had a homework assignment on Robin Hood.

The special teacher would meet the hearing impaired boys and girls for a 20 minute period sometime before their regular class and go through the upcoming lesson with them. The special teacher might find that some of the children are not clear as to the meaning of the word *justice*. Other hearing impaired children who do know the meaning of *justice* might have difficulty with other expressions. The special teacher would have the children discuss the terms with each other, monitoring the exchange to assure that the concepts are clarified. When the special teacher is satisfied that the hearing impaired pupils are ready to enter into the regular class teacher's instructional period on equal terms with the hearing children, the preteaching is concluded.

The hearing impaired pupils then attend the regular social studies or literature class that is studying Robin Hood. (It is understood that the regular class teacher and the other pupils have previously been oriented to having these deaf and hard of hearing pupils in the class.) If the special teacher has noted one or two matters that should have particular attention in the lesson for certain children, they are passed on to the regular teacher by a short note or a brief chat as the class is taking up.

At the conclusion of the regular class the regular teacher reports any special problems encountered with the hearing impaired pupils. These are passed on by a short note, checks or comments on a checklist, or a personal chat, or they may be transmitted by the pupils themselves. The special teacher then takes whatever action is necessary in the postteaching session, depending on whether it is a behavior problem, failure in communications, a lack of preparation or background, or whatever.

The postteach time period with the special teacher can be used flexibly. Its initial portion may be needed to top off the previous regular class lesson. Its latter portion might be employed to preteach key material for the next regular class lesson. Also, material related to more than one regular class lesson can be included in the same period. Other variations are possible, too, depending on the needs of the hearing impaired pupils.

This sequence of three teaching components (preteach/teach/postteach) forms an instructional principle that is practiced in successful mainstreaming situations. The actual day to day details of application of the procedure vary. Some arrangements are highly complex; others are simple. Some appear informal and others are tightly structured and regularized. Some use time before or after the usual school day; some do not include all of the regular school program in the hearing impaired pupils' curriculum; some use parents, volunteers, buddies, or paraprofessionals in the process. But careful observation and analysis reveals that the preteach/teach/postteach principle is operative in mainstreaming programs which work effectively.

Principle 2: Teach toward hearing world participation. This principle makes the goal of participation in the hearing world the focus of 100% of the instruction of the hearing impaired child. Every moment of the child's school day plus much of the child's out-of-school time is taken up with planned instruction toward that goal.

It is not a pressure cooker situation, however. The teaching is usually fun for the child. There is no unusual anxiety or excessive demand for performance. Learning is enjoyable and everyone participates.

Also, everyone teaches. That includes parents, aides, supervisors, regular class teachers, special educators, principals, social workers, psychologists, playground assistants—everyone who has contact with the child.

There is no time or place for babysitting during the school day, or before or after school. If hearing impaired children are in the charge of an aide, they are not left to haphazard, aimless idling. The aide has a definite responsibility for practicing, with each child, some skill or ability that is being consciously developed. The same is true for parents, real or substitute. There is a plan for each child and everyone who has contact with the child knows what that plan is and accepts responsibility for furthering each child's education in an orderly and measurable way toward hearing world participation.

There are times for fun, for games, and for unstructured romping. These are arranged so that hearing impaired youngsters also learn important attitudes and behaviors under pleasurable conditions.

An aide in one school said that "the deaf like to play by themselves." To prove the assertion, the aide pointed across the room to a group of 7 or 8 nursery-kindergarten hearing impaired children who were bouncing and swinging and climbing and whirling together on several pieces of indoor play equipment. There were two hearing children in the room, also. One was off alone in a corner painting at an easel. The other was at the periphery of the group of hearing impaired children, occasionally trying to enter part of the play, not quite making it, and retiring to the outside edge of the group again.

Earnest efforts were being made at that school to begin integration of hearing impaired children with others, but the principle, "teach toward hearing world participation" was not in full operation. The effort toward mainstreaming was failing and those responsible did not know why. They had not conceptualized the principle fully, so they were not clear as to the implementation needed. They did not have understanding and participation by everyone. After several days of observation, these were the specific gaps in implementation that became apparent.

1. Aides did not understand the integration effort because it had not been described and explained to them adequately.
2. The aides had not been given roles and responsibilities in the implementation of integration.
3. Written plans were not available to the teachers or aides to help them determine what to do with the pupils under their charge.
4. The aides did not really understand why the hearing and deaf pupils were there together.
5. Neither the hearing impaired nor the hearing pupils knew why they were together at that place and at that time.
6. The aides were frequently alone with the children for more than an hour with no supervision before, during, or after that period from a professional educator.

7. The aides initiated no communication with any of the children. Neither did they encourage any communication the children initiated between themselves or with the aides, except to stop disputes or misbehavior.

The concepts central to this principle were being violated. Everyone was not teaching toward hearing world participation. Precious time for the children was slipping away.

Some of the children were having fun, to be sure. And all of the children, as well as the aides, were certainly learning, but they were learning the wrong things. The deaf children were learning to ignore hearing children of the same age. The hearing impaired were learning to live beside but not with the deaf and hard of hearing pupils. The aides were learning that their nonguidance and noninvolvement were completely acceptable to their supervisors, for none made any efforts to get them to change. The aides' regular reward of money came every month. The intermittent rewards of smiles and friendly greetings came from superiors whenever the superiors' uncertain schedules brought them into fleeting contact with the aides. (Incidently, the aides were not alone in that behavior. Many teachers, parents, and supervisors were uncertain about the same matters.)

Successful application of this principle calls for positive, planned action rather than laissez faire inaction. Effective mainstreaming requires not only understanding on the part of all concerned. Even commitment is not enough. Understanding and commitment must be translated and expressed 100% of the time in the day to day, the hour to hour, the moment to moment teaching activities of all who are in contact with the hearing impaired pupils.

Principle 3: Have a planned, organized systematic approach. This principle says that there is a design to the mainstreaming effort, a grand strategy into which all the bits and pieces can fit. It is planned, which means that a document or statement setting forth the plan is readily available. It also is organized. That means there is a discernible structure and that individuals have assigned responsibilities in connection with the program. Moreover, those responsibilities are accompanied by the authority necessary to see that the responsibilities are carried out. Further, the approach to mainstreaming is an orderly one, following some system.

In some schools or school districts, mainstreaming activities have not gotten beyond reflecting the individual interests of principals or teachers or of individual schools. One community had a substantial portion of its hearing impaired children mainstreamed in the elementary grades. Continuity into the secondary years was lost, however, because there was a plan only for the elementary school phase. The children who had been mainstreamed in elementary schools often found themselves placed in special classes in junior and senior high schools, for no clear reason. The program design did not carry through.

Neither did policy, authority, or responsibility, for that was equally divided between elementary and secondary administrators who had differing points of view. It was a classic case of good ideas and worthy efforts losing their impact because of faulty planning.

This principle needs to be applied with maximum rigor in large and complex school systems, though it is necessary in even the smallest, least complicated school situation. The principle gets excellent support when the state department of education promulgates detailed program guidelines. The state guidelines can be used by local schools as a framework upon which to draft a document that is specific to the community.

There is one ever present danger, however, to spelling out and publishing the grand design for mainstreaming activities: that the plan, once crystallized, becomes inflexible. Therefore, while there should be a document that outlines the school's plans available to all, it also should be updated periodically. With that provision, the plan can serve both as a reliable anchor and a motivating guide.

Principle 4: Have unified and consistent commitment and direction.
Where mainstreaming was a healthy and vigorous program the groups that formed the power base of schools were together in their belief in the correctness of mainstreaming as the preferred pattern for special education. The board had adopted policies that emphasized it. New schools being planned or constructed and schools being remodeled made provisions for the inclusion of regular and exceptional children. Personnel policies provided for employing teachers who were sympathetic toward integrating handicapped pupils. The school system offered in-service education courses on team teaching and consultation between regular and special educators. Organization that represented teachers in collective bargaining had often negotiated into their contracts clauses that specified recognition of factors involved in maintaining sound special education for exceptional children in regular classes. These examples, as well as others, show unity of commitment through evidence of the implementation of that commitment.

Equally important is unified and consistent direction. The schools that were experiencing serious problems in trying to get mainstreaming established sometimes lacked power structure commitment. But even more often they were without someone who was clearly in charge of implementation. Nothing can slow movement in a program of this kind more than divided and inconsistent authority. On the other hand, each smoothly operating and thoroughly implemented mainstream program had one person who clearly possessed both the authority and the responsibility for the program's management. The supervisory styles of those persons varied and so did their management behaviors. But one thing was certain: They and everyone else involved recognized who had been delegated the right to guide the program and where accountability for its proper conduct rested.

Principle 5: Bring special education into the regular class. This, like the first principle, says a great deal about the alterations in what teachers do when mainstreaming becomes a major pattern of special education. Certainly, to operate special education within the structure of the regular class and the regular school ultimately spells change for the most regular class teachers and teachers of hearing impaired pupils.

In 1970-71, only about 6 or 7 out of 100 hearing impaired pupils were being taught in regular classes, with help from specialists as needed. About 4 others out of every 100 were in special classes part time and in regular classes part time. Together they totalled about 10%. The rest, approximately 90%, were in self contained classes, special day schools, or residential schools, with the latter alone accounting for 45 or 46 out of every 100 of the total (Office of Demographic Studies, 1973). Yet in that same year some school districts of the nation had close to 100% of all hearing impaired pupils integrated with hearing pupils, with many being fully mainstreamed.

The gap between 10 and almost 100%, if it is closed in the rest of the nation's school systems, means potentially wrenching changes in the professional lives of many teachers who are now working in residential schools, special day schools, and self contained special classes, to say nothing of the regular class teachers who will also be called on to make changes. Fortunately, enough has been learned from those teachers who have ventured into the central current to engender confidence that it can be done by others without serious hardship.

Special education has been brought into the regular class by public schools and private schools, by residential schools and day schools, by elementary schools and secondary schools, by large school systems and small ones, by technical schools, by nursery schools, and by colleges. There is almost no end to the inventive variations on how it is done.

Common elements of successful programs. Despite the extensive variations, in all cases where approaches to mainstreaming have worked well there are certain operational commonalities regarding the teachers, pupils, and facilities.

First, *teachers are given options.* No regular class teacher is forced to receive handicapped pupils into regular classes. No special education teacher is pressured to become a member of a mainstream team. It is expected that full mainstreaming will rarely be the sole special education organizational model found to be needed in a school system. Therefore, there will continue to be opportunities for teachers of the hearing impaired who prefer to serve in a self contained class arrangement or as a resource room teacher. Special residential and day schools, too, will continue to be important in the foreseeable future, though the nature of their pupil population and their function probably will change appreciably.

Second, *inclusion starts early.* Full mainstreaming is initiated for all hearing impaired children just starting to school, usually at nursery or kindergarten level. For example, 4 to 6 hearing impaired pupils may start to school the first day in September with a regular complement of nursery or kindergarten children, perhaps 20.

Third, *the staffing is appropriate for the setting.* Typically, a staffing unit for the nursery school just mentioned would be four full time people; one regular teacher, one teacher of the hearing handicapped, and two aides. That would be no more staff than would be required if the two were separated.

Fourth, *in-service training precedes program changes.* Staff members would have satisfactorily completed in-service training covering procedures, observations, and practical experience. In the training sessions they would practice working as teams, including the aides, and would learn techniques for effective use of parents and older school children as volunteers working on schedules. Another major focus of the training would be to increase the feeling of interdependence within the team, through learning to accept each other's judgments and ideas and learning to work out mutually agreeable ways to arrive at decisions by which everyone will abide. This is emphasized because up to this point teachers have been relatively independent in the private worlds of their own classrooms, answerable chiefly to some higher administrative authority. The team learns interdependence and decides for itself how the captain or quarterback role will shift under different circumstances. Also, the team expects to be given less direction from the school administration, understands that the team's decisions are paramount in what will be done with children, and accepts professional accountability for that.

Fifth, *needed facilities and materials are on hand.* The teaching space is equipped and supplied with all that is immediately required and there are ample additional resources on call.

Sixth, *specific teaching plans are made.* There is an individual instructional plan for each child, designed, understood, and kept up to date by the team members.

Seventh, *teaching responsibility is shared.* The members of the various teaching teams each take part in instruction, sometimes dividing the group and sometimes working with the entire group. The teacher of the hearing impaired, having special knowledge of language development, may do individual or small group work with hearing pupils who the team members feel need it. Some of the hearing impaired pupils are often instructed along with others by the regular teacher or the aide while the special education teacher prepares for a lesson or does individual tutoring. The tutoring could be with hearing impaired pupils and regular class pupils who are having problems, too.

Eighth, *separation from the regular class is minimal.* Hearing impaired pupils rarely leave their class to go separately to some special activity in another part of the building. Instead, the special activity, the special equipment, and the special personnel to conduct it, be it auditory training or whatever, is brought to them and conducted in a section of the regular teaching space. Thus everyone in the class and on the team may be visual participants and comprehend the special activity as part of their work and responsibility.

Ninth, *each team meets on a regular basis as a committee.* The school principal frequently presides. A parent, the school's eduational diagnostician or school psychologist, and any others attend as needed. Each hearing impaired youngster's record is reviewed periodically. If continued full mainstreaming seems too much for the child, arrangements are worked out for a resource room or some other placement until whatever prevents full mainstreaming is corrected if it can be. The same committee functions to consider admissions (i.e., perhaps a hearing impaired child moves into the school attendance area) and dismissals (when the pupil no longer needs a special education program).

For any specific school situation, the concepts illustrated in the nine points above would remain valid; only the details would change. The principle of bringing special education into the regular class, to whatever extent special education remains needed, rather than taking children out for it, would continue intact.

Oral and Total Communication Programs

Mainstreaming is being carried on effectively in oral teaching programs and in total communication programs. There is one fundamental difference between the two approaches. The oral method requires that the pupil learn lipreading (speechreading) and oral speech as the only means of communication in face to face situations, whether with hearing persons or deaf or hard of hearing persons. No gestures or movements are allowed other than those ordinarily used by hearing persons to supplement ordinary conversation.

The total communication approach also teaches the pupil to become skillful in lipreading and in oral speech. In addition, this method requires that the pupil learn proficiency with communication by the manual alphabet (finger spelling) and by sign language. The manual alphabet allows the user to employ finger movement to literally spell out words and sentences, including punctuation, for the receiver to read. The sign language used in total communication is a more detailed one that makes use of positions and movement of the hands and arms in relation to each other and the rest of the body to convey concepts, including things, places, actions, emotions, quantities, prefixes, suffixes, and other nuances of language. The manual alphabet and sign language are used by the person speaking, with the manual alphabet being used to supplement the information conveyed by signs where necessary, such as in proper names. Teachers and pupils who are listening observe the speaker's lip and facial movements, the signs, and the manual spelling.

Children who are educated by the oral approach can attend regular classes if they are skillful in oral language and lipreading and if their scholastic achievement is comparable to that of at least some of the hearing pupils. The same is true for pupils prepared by the total communication approach, for those pupils have had the opportunity to acquire oral language and lipreading competencies too.

In some instances hearing children and their regular class teachers deliberately learn manual communication and sign in order to better communicate with the hearing handicapped pupils who have been prepared through total communication procedures. Both regular teachers and hearing pupils appear to be able to acquire sign and finger spelling skills rapidly.

Some school systems offer parents the option to choose the method to be used with their child. In that case it is necessary to keep the hearing impaired pupils in the two programs separated. Otherwise the children in the oral group tend to learn to use sign language and finger spelling from those in the total communication group and to use them for manual communication.

Changing to a Mainstream Policy

Changing to a mainstream policy and practice is a step by step affair rather than an overnight move. It calls for phasing out present practices and phasing in new ones.

Three foundation blocks are essential. First, the five essential principles stated earlier must be made operational, or be ready to be made operational. Second, an orderly transition scheme must be formulated and must be understood by all concerned. Third, the pupils in currently functioning special education and regular education programs must have their educational requirements met and their programs safeguarded from disruption.

Assuming that the school or school system is ready, in terms of the above foundation elements, here are eight actions that need to be taken. They can be used as a checklist.

1. The chief administrator (usually the superintendent) makes public statements in support of a policy of mainstreaming.
2. The board of the school or school system enacts a policy statement committing it to mainstreaming.
3. A memorandum of understanding is exchanged between the state education agency and the school or school system, specifying whatever agreements are necessary about regulations, financing, and accounting ability.
4. The superintendent and other administrators work out, with regular and special teachers, the changes in staffing patterns and responsibilities that will be entailed. Teacher organizations, especially those that are recognized for collective bargaining, are involved as key partners in these discussions.
5. Cooperative arrangements between and among schools or school systems are negotiated, where such arrangements are needed.
6. Advice and consent are sought from the parents of both the regular class and the hearing impaired pupils who might be involved. It is advisable to do this through already existing parent organizations for general consideration of the proposed plan *before* the policy is acted on by the board.
7. In-service programs of continuing education are designed and scheduled for regular and special education teachers and for the principals, supervisors, and the pupil personnel workers who will be touched by the changes.
8. The understanding of other community agencies serving hearing impaired pupils should be sought, and coordination with them should be arranged as needed.

The necessary moves certainly will be implemented in different ways and will have different weight in different situations.

In some states local school districts may need to take the lead in the face of limited cooperation from the state level. Private schools, a number of which practice mainstreaming, will have somewhat different priorities among these points. The same is true of state or state related residential schools. Also, the order in which the actions take place may well differ. In some situations, it has been the teachers, supervisors, or parents who have provided the initial motive and push that started mainstreaming. Sometimes it has been the head administrator, sometimes state leadership, and sometimes community organization pressure that has started the move. Whatever way the move is begun, it is essential to include at least the eight checkpoints just given.

THE ROLE OF THE REGULAR CLASS TEACHER

At first mainstreaming means extra work. It means extra work for the regular class teacher, the special education teacher, and the regular school principal—it means extra work for everyone, including the hearing impaired child involved.

The extra work is of two kinds. One is new work, such as the added lesson preparation and the increased chalkboard use called for from the regular class teacher. Another kind of extra work is the work required to change. The special education teacher and the regular class teacher have to learn to become a team. That change, from their former relative isolation from each other, takes work because it means altering established patterns of daily professional behavior.

Where mainstreaming has worked out well, the extra work incident to getting the program under way has been made rewarding. High quality in-service programs have been offered, many with credit for advanced degrees, advanced certification, and recognition toward salary increments. Teacher aides have been furnished. New or remodeled teaching space, modern instructional materials, added audiovisual aids and other improvements that make teaching more satisfying have been supplied. Teachers of regular classes have had access to more help from supervisors. Also, they have received direct on-site consultation and assistance with regular class pupils from the special education teachers who work with them, frequently right in their own classes. A number of special and regular class teachers find that the challenge sharpens their teaching skills and techniques.

Teamwork with Specialists

Diversification of professional job functions plays an important part in effective mainstreaming as well as in the various forms of part time integration that, while short of full mainstreaming, do bring hearing impaired pupils into some contact with other pupils. When a child receives instruction, direction, and assignments from more than one teacher, confusion and conflict can easily arise. That is particularly true for young children. Opportunities for misunderstanding are increased, of course, when children have the kinds of language and communication limitations imposed by defective hearing. Thus it proves important that there be clear and consistent role definition for the professional persons who are responsible for the various parts of mainstream schemes.

Following are examples of some statements of responsibility for certain professional positions that could be specific to mainstream team members.

Counselors (regular) are responsible for counseling services for all pupils, including hearing impaired pupils. They may use assistance from specialists, but they use the help as consultation and do not turn over counseling as such to those specialists.

Principals (regular) have authority and responsibility for special education as well as regular education in the school. They have a chief voice in selection and assignment of teachers and placement of pupils, and they are expected to use consultation from specialists in the school and on central office staff, but do not delegate decision making to them. Principals are expected to employ teacher committees and parent participation in planning and organizing individualized education for all children in the school, with particular attention to exceptional children.

Regular class teachers have the first voice in day to day decisions about educational programs for all pupils, including handicapped pupils assigned to a regular class. They have access to assistance from specialists on school and central office staff and have the authority to direct and supervise work of teacher aides assigned for fixed periods of time. They may call and arrange meetings of teacher committees concerning pupils in the class, with the concurrence of the principal. Regular class teachers may deal directly with parents, with the concurrence of the principal, or may make parent contacts through the school social worker or counselor.

Teachers of the hearing impaired help regular class teachers who have hearing impaired pupils on their class rolls. They preteach and postteach hearing impaired pupils from regular classes. They are also expected to accept referrals from regular class teachers for assessment and aid in planning instruction for regular class pupils who may be in need of special education. They serve on teacher committees and arrange for, and make available to regular class teachers and hearing impaired pupils, special instructional materials. The provide orientation and continuing education to regular class teachers regarding teaching hearing impaired pupils.

A number of others (i.e., school psychologists, school social workers, and various supervisors) could be added to the list. But this should be sufficient to show that mainstreaming involves some tasks not common to special education as it is traditionally conducted, and that different responsibilities devolve to the professional persons who participate.

One of the reasons for the emphasis on keeping pupil accounting and related responsibility clearly in the hands of regular education personnel is to make sure that the hearing impaired pupils maintain and increase their skills in pursuing real world resources. In the end, this should reduce the need for a special counseling centers or similar services for hearing handicapped persons. It should make the use of such services not a matter of habit for hearing impaired persons, but rather it should strengthen their independence of those services. Another reason is to prevent mainstreaming from becoming a fraud, with only the surface appearance of inclusion, while really all the education of the hearing impaired child is conducted in regular schools, but by specialists, with regular education personnel as onlookers or bystanders.

There is also a real need for the reorientation of specialists in the education of the hearing handicapped to assist them in working in new relationships with regular school personnel. Only a few have had training and experience in joint professional consultation woth other teachers from other educational specializations and with members of other professions; yet, that is a significant new skill required of them. The same is true of participating in committee decision making and team teaching. Thus there remains an important unfulfilled need for reeducation material for persons now prepared only for special education for hearing handicapped pupils in classic settings.

Special Education in the Regular Class

In every mainstream effort, whether full or partial and whether in elementary or secondary schools, all persons concerned should (a) know what is going on, (b) have opportunities to make suggestions and ask questions, (c) believe that their input is being used, and (d) have real options about the manner in which they participate. Two program characteristics, therefore, are highly significant. First, in-service study is needed and it should be based on what teachers and other staff say they need to know. Second, participants should take part in planning how the instruction should be organized and scheduled.

Concerns expressed about mainstreaming are similar in principle to those mentioned frequently in connection with other proposed changes in educational procedures, but they also have unique qualities. Here are some of the most common questions.

1. Will all hearing handicapped pupils be dumped into regular classes?
2. Can regular class teachers communicate with and teach hearing impaired pupils?
3. What will become of special education?
4. Can hearing impaired children do the work of regular classes?
5. What evidence is there that mainstreaming will work?
6. Will hearing impaired pupils be a drag on the regular class?
7. Will the costs skyrocket?

8. Will hearing children accept deaf and hard of hearing youngsters socially?
9. Don't regular class teachers already have too much to do?
10. Doesn't the hearing impaired child deserve full time attention from specialists?
11. Will the parents of either group, hearing or hearing impaired, agree?
12. Who will have final responsibility for the hearing impaired child's achievement?

These queries give strong clues about what in general to cover during orientation and in-service activities. They need to be particularized further by needs assessments directed to the specific faculty groups for whom the in-service training program is to be designed.

Reading and study are valuable means of giving in-service preparation. In addition to this book and that of Northcott (1973), there are a number of other publications, films, and filmstrips that can help as texts and library resources.

A ready-made package designed by Project NEED (Bitter, 1974) supplies an example of a sound base around which either a strong preservice or in-service unit may be constructed. It contains nine major modules, each a filmstrip with a tape cassette of narration. The material orients not only regular class teachers, but also administrators and the families of hearing impaired pupils. The nine topics include:

1. *Language*—Concepts of language development and techniques for upgrading language.
2. *Classroom management*—Causes of problems and ways to deal with undesirable behaviors.
3. *Reading*—Special help with teaching reading to hearing impaired children.
4. *Peer orientation*—Helping hearing handicapped pupils to relate to hearing classmates, and the reverse.
5. *Classroom communication*—Facilitating speech reading and conducting auditory training in the regular class.
6. *Family orientation*—How the family may assist in the school and the community.
7. *Speech*—Maintaining and improving speech quality in regular classes.
8. *Administrative guidelines*—Key elements such as organization and teacher selection, central to sound program management.
9. *Hearing aids*—Operation, troubleshooting, and minor repairs.

The nine main modules are supplemented by an introductory booklet, narration guides, and two related pamphlets. If the NEED package is buttressed by material that is specifically responsive to the actual local situation, it should prove very beneficial in either total communication or oral settings.

There are at least two other in-service packages that can be of real value, too. One is called *An Experience in Deafness* (Paul, undated). A second is *Hearing-Impaired Formal Inservice Program*, prepared by Nober (1973).

Individualization of Instruction

Bruce (1973) said:

> Integrated educational settings for the hearing impaired range from those that offer mere physical proximity with hearing pupils to those in which the hearing impaired children are completely independent of supportive personnel. A child may be integrated as early as 0-3 years or as late as high school age. The effective implementation of integration is dependent on the quality of personnel, equipment, transportation, and curriculum. (p. 213)

We would add only that the school physical plant and methods of teaching, too, need attention if instruction is to be properly individualized.

Griffing (1970) made the point that certain hard of hearing children would be well served in regular classes. Northcott (1973) went further by stating that there are hearing impaired children who, "although the unaided audiogram may indicate a hearing loss ranging from moderate to profound" (p. 3), are appropriately placed in regular classes. She requires only that children have these qualities:

1. Active utilization of residual hearing and fulltime hearing and utilization, if prescribed.
2. Demonstrated social, academic, cognitive and communicative (auditory and oral) skills *within the normal range of behaviors* of hearing classmates at a particular grade level.
3. Intelligible speech and the ability to comprehend and exchange ideas with others through spoken, written and read language.
4. Increased confidence and independence in giving self-direction to the tasks at hand. (Northcott, 1973, p. 3)

Yater (personal communication, 1974) agreed that criteria such as these are certainly appropriate, but that they need not be fully attained before the hearing impaired child is moved into the mainstream. She made the point that it is more difficult for pupils to reach those high levels of achievement while associating only with other hearing impaired pupils. Therefore, it is sometimes advantageous to move a hearing impaired pupil into mainstream education and to also furnish heavy doses of special education training and support in that context. The hearing impaired child can thus benefit from the examples and the socialization and the practice with hearing pupils under controlled conditions because the special education teacher works in tandem with the regular class teacher.

Curriculum Individualization

The curriculum content that needs the most adaptation for hearing impaired pupils is obviously that which depends on accurate hearing. Music is a concrete example. But there is no curriculum content hearing impaired pupils cannot learn in a meaningful way.

Comparable ability and attainment. Special education has not yet developed procedures for assuring that all hearing impaired youngsters reach achievement equal to hearing children of the same age and intelligence. However, a great many do attain that level of academic development. In mainstreaming programs, deaf and hard of hearing pupils are approximately equal to their hearing age mates in reading speed, reading comprehension, spelling, arithmetic fundamental operations, and arithmetic problem solving. They are not necessarily up to their hearing age mates in oral language production or in comprehension of oral language. In mainstream programs the hearing impaired pupils use many of the same textbooks and other resources such as maps and dictionaries as their hearing classmates of the same age and grade placement.

Relevant student characteristics. According to Caccamise (1974) there are six key concepts about hearing impaired students that need to be understood by all regular school personnel who will participate in the individualization they need under partial or full mainstreaming.

1. Hearing impaired youngsters, despite their language handicap, are the mental equals of other youngsters.
2. Many hearing impaired adults live richly meaningful and socially productive and fulfilling lives now. The number who do so can be increased through better education.
3. Most hearing impaired children can be taught to read silently, to write, to spell, to master arithmetic, and to achieve in other school subjects as well as other children their age.
4. Hearing impaired children and youth show approximately the same kinds and number of behavior or mental health problems as do their hearing peers.
5. From the point of view of education, hearing impaired pupils have three kinds of learning problems that are unique to them and that call for special teaching:

Language. Learning that there is such a thing as language and acquiring enough understanding about language to be able to use it in thinking and in gaining proficiency in communicating with others. Specialists in education of the hearing impaired call that "acquiring a language base."

Communication. Learning to carry on efficient and effective communication with other persons with hearing handicaps and with the general run of hearing persons. The latter is quite difficult for most persons to achieve.

Substitution. Learning to use vision and other senses to compensate for not being able to hear auto horns, sirens, barking dogs, violins or saxophones, rustling leaves, running water, or other common sounds.

6. Most hearing impaired children can be taught to overcome the three kinds of learning problems they have. Modern teaching know-how is making that possible for hearing handicapped children while they attend regular school classes. Accomplishing that is what mainstreaming is all about.

Among the early suggestions about what to look for when considering whether to move hearing impaired pupils into regular class instruction were those of Hayes and Griffing (1967). They attended particularly to hard of hearing pupils, while the criteria of Northcott (1973) and Yater (1974), mentioned earlier, took in all hearing impaired pupils. We have followed the outline of the Hayes and Griffing (pp. 237-238) characteristics, but absolve them from responsibility for the content because we have expanded their material with our own views and extended it to include the full range of hearing impaired children and youth.

It is advisable to review these guidelines (or similar local ones, if they exist) in each instance when a pupil now in a separate program is being considered for movement into partial or full mainstream activity. These points are especially important where hearing impaired pupils have not been mainstreamed before. The first such efforts should always be planned to give as much assurance as possible of a satisfactory outcome.

1. The student's attainments should be within the range of those of the hearing pupils in the content and skills in which they will be doing any group work. Since language arts skills are called on in almost all other school work from arithmetic to zoology, particular attention should be paid to the ability of the student to take part in language, reading, writing, spelling, and conversation. Superior reading and understanding of the conversation of others may compensate for less satisfactory expressive skills, or the reverse. Also, being in a regular class can motivate speedy improvement in the skill

with which some hearing impaired pupils use their communication capabilities.
2. Does the hearing impaired pupil have adequate social and emotional maturity? Remember that regular classes have a range of social and emotional behavior among the regular students. The issue is whether the regular class teacher, having learned through observations and from the special teacher's reports about the hearing handicapped youngster's typical behavior in a group, feels the child can be fitted in with the regular class friendship groups and cliques. (Where possible it is a good idea to begin mainstream activities at the start of a term, so the hearing impaired pupil has the opportunity to be assimilated while such social units are in the formative stages.)
3. Does the student attend and follow directions well? Familiarity with the way the regular class teacher conducts instruction can allow the special education teacher to help the hearing impaired pupil sharpen the necessary attending skills.
4. Independence, self confidence, and determination to succeed are important. Some hearing impaired pupils are really able to perform well, but lack the self confidence to desire regular class placement for themselves. With encouragement from their teachers, hearing impaired children may find in the regular class the kind of positive experience that bolsters confidence in themselves and helps them face the next of life's challenges with more assurance.
5. The hearing impaired pupil should have intelligence within the range of that of the regular class pupils. There is no reason why mainstreaming should be reserved for hearing impaired pupils of average or higher learning ability. The range of learning ability in a regular class includes hearing youngsters below the average. Also, mentally retarded or gifted hearing impaired pupils should have the opportunity to take part in special education programs with hearing mentally retarded or gifted pupils if other appropriate criteria are met. (Such programs are found more and more in the mainstream, too.)
6. It is preferable that the age of the hearing impaired pupil be within 2 years of the average age of the group of hearing pupils. The child's chronological age is important, but if there is reason (i.e., if the child is unusually large or small or unusually gifted or talented) the 2 year age limit should be disregarded.
7. Not all regular class pupils can be counted on to treat the rest of their classmates with respect and consideration. The introduction of a new child into an already formed class certainly tends to create tension among existing social units in the class. The child with a hearing impairment needs to be readied for that and it is possible for the teachers, special and regular, to prepare the regular class for the new

child to a certain extent. But hearing impaired pupils should not be denied integration solely on the ground that respect and consideration will not be forthcoming immediately from every one of the regular class pupils.
8. The regular class teacher should have proper background, preparation, and knowledge. If the regular class teacher is well motivated and willing to try, that receptive attitude deserves equal weight with the teacher's understanding of the problems faced by a hearing impaired student.
9. The placement should not push class size beyond agreed on limits. Experience in many different parts of the country indicates that it is seldom necessary to reduce regular class size to accommodate hearing handicapped pupils so long as the total class size, including the children with hearing impairments, does not exceed the typical class size for that school system.
10. Proper amplifying equipment should be on hand and the regular teacher should understand its operation.
11. Hearing impaired pupils are helped when they have constructive support from their parents. Thus the parents should be aware of and willing to play their roles well. But the absence of such support (or even the absence of parents) need not hold an otherwise ready pupil out of the mainstream. Some school districts have worked out special boarding arrangements with parent surrogates to assist in the afternoon, evening, and morning. Others have helped to find high quality temporary foster homes in the neighborhood of the regular school that the hearing impaired child is to attend.
12. The hearing impaired child feels willing to move to the more demanding placement and knows how to call on additional resources when needed.

These 12 suggested criteria are intended to be flexible. Teachers and the pupils themselves are best able to judge who can qualify for consideration for integration. As a general rule, pupils need more opportunity to test themselves, rather than to be shielded from contacts with regular classes.

Methods of Teaching

Suggestions and information for the regular class teacher. Following is a group of "teacher to teacher" comments and suggestions. Most came directly from professional educators who had already included hearing handicapped pupils in their regular classes. All agreed that at first they had been apprehensive. They found their worries diminished if they kept these guidelines in mind and tried to use them. They also found that there

Hearing Impairment / 565

are specific and well organized methods for teaching language and communication and that they could rely on their specialist colleagues to apply them. For the rest, however, it was a matter of minor adjustments in standard procedures, relatively easy to learn.
1. It is better, for understanding, to be near the hearing impaired child. That applies to the child's understanding of the teacher or other pupils, and it applies to the teacher's or other pupil's understanding of the child.
2. Hearing aids make sounds louder, but not necessarily clearer. They are usually quite helpful, but not the whole answer to helping children understand.
3. Particularly with young children, check from time to time to be sure hearing aids are working.
4. Place the hearing impaired child for each teaching session so there is face to face visibility of the teacher's speech movements. The child should be free to change position or seats, as needed.
5. Use your own natural gestures to supplement oral presentations, without exaggeration.
6. When using films, make use of captioned films as often as possible. The sound is supplemented by printed material on the film. The special education teacher can help you get these. Regular class pupils can profit from the combination of sound and print, too.
7. When referring to something in the room, point to it, nod in its direction, glance at it, or walk over and touch it. If discussing something in the room, manipulate it, to the extent possible, to synchronize with what is being said.
8. Use supplementary pictures and diagrams whenever possible. As in the case of captioned films, the special education teacher may be able to show you how to get pictures, diagrams, and other instructional materials that have been developed especially for use in teaching hearing handicapped pupils. These same materials can often help in instructing the hearing pupils, too.
9. Write (or print) key words, expressions, or phrases on the chalkboard or use an overhead projector.
10. Take care not to talk when your face is turned to the chalkboard while you are writing, or when your face is turned down to see your notes, or when it is hidden by a book or papers or by your hands.
11. Help your students keep the general noise level of the class down in situations where a hearing impaired pupil may need to listen to and understand conversation or instructions. The hearing aid makes *everything* louder, so it gives no particular advantage under generally noisy conditions. Noise is no problem, otherwise. The hearing impaired child can turn off the aid.

12. Hearing impaired pupils sometimes need special help in learning how to be quiet and not disturb hearing pupils by unknowingly making noises. Special schools for deaf and hard of hearing pupils are often among the noisiest of education settings.
13. In learning to read, hearing impaired pupils are sledom helped by phonic word analysis as much as they are by instruction that emphasizes visual clues.
14. When showing films or slides keep enough light on in the area so the hearing impaired pupils can see the faces clearly when the teacher or narrator makes comments.
15. Hearing impaired students cannot take notes while they watch the faces of their teacher and fellow students. If note taking is necessary, one way to help is to give all students copies of the teacher's notes. Another way is to arrange for two hearing students to make carbon copies of their notes to give to the hearing impaired classmate. (Two students' notes work better than one; less will be missed.) Another essential thing for the teacher to do to help is to share the key ideas of the lesson with the special teacher of the hearing handicapped so the ideas can be used in the preteaching and postteaching sessions. It is helpful, also, to use a buddy system in which regular class students take turns reviewing their notes orally with the hearing handicapped student in planned study sessions. That, of course, can help the hearing buddies, too, for it is a fine form of study for them.
16. Expect hearing impaired pupils to accept the same responsibilities for considerate behavior, homework, and dependability as is required of others.
17. Reach an agreement with the pupil, the special teacher, and the parents, as the case may be, on what achievement is projected, both short and long term.
18. Schedule regular and frequent communication with the special education teachers who have preteaching and postteaching responsibilities and who work on special problems. Preparation for and reinforcement of regular class work calls for close teamwork. The guidance of the regular class teacher is needed by the special education teacher in knowing what particular help each hearing impaired pupil most needs.
19. The majority of hearing impaired pupils still have some hearing. They usually have been fitted with hearing aids and taught to use their remaining hearing. (Such instruction is called auditory training.) Encourage them to wear their aids.
20. Speak to the child. Call the child's name when asking for attention. Touching or tapping the arm or shoulder should not be necessary, any more than with other pupils.

21. Even with the best of aids and auditory training, hearing handicapped children can miss many speech sounds. Get the special education teacher's advice on how to help the child recognize (see) sounds that are not heard and to make the sounds correctly when speaking. Classmates can learn to help, too, and they frequently become very good at it. The same is true in aiding the hearing handicapped child to monitor voice quality.
22. Remember, hearing children can tell how loud their own voices are, and how expressive, because they can hear themselves. This is not so for most hearing impaired pupils. You and the other pupils can find out from the special education teacher how to reinforce good expression and how to help maintain appropriate voice volume with hearing impaired pupils.
23. Orient new hearing pupils who join your class to what you and the other regular class pupils already know about hearing loss, hearing aids, and the rest. Other pupils can help do that, too.
24. Everyone may profit from time to time from being reminded that hearing impaired children have acquired an almost incredible skill. They "see" what others hear, and when they speak they do so without hearing the sounds of their own voices.
25. Talk to hearing impaired pupils in full sentences. If you are not understood, say the whole sentence again or rephrase the same thing in a new sentence. Avoid using just single words. It is easier to grasp content or meaning in context than from isolated words.
26. Some pupils, including hearing impaired pupils, have learned to look attentive and to appear to be understanding when they are not. Once in a while direct a question to each of the hearing impaired pupils to assess whether they are really tuned in on what is being taught.
27. When making assignments, write them on the board or have them duplicated for distribution to all pupils.
28. Outlined lesson steps on the chalkboard or in duplicated form can be helpful.
29. Use your own natural, normal teaching voice.
30. Give hearing impaired pupils the same opportunities to make reports orally as other pupils get. But let the hearing impaired pupils have more notice and time for preparation so the special education teacher can participate and help make it a more rewarding and enriching experience.
31. Remind the hearing pupils in the class to speak in complete sentences, to enunciate clearly, and to turn in the direction of the hearing impaired pupils.
32. Ask for opportunities to observe how the special education teacher works with hearing impaired pupils. Note teaching approaches you

might be able to use in the regular class. Get the special education teacher to explain the rationale behind the teaching methods used. Knowing the rationale for an approach makes it easier to develop an adaptation of it without losing the underlying idea.
33. Keep in mind that your attitude is quickly caught by your pupils and they will tend to adopt your way of behaving and feeling about hearing impaired pupils.
34. Make sure the hearing handicapped pupils learn any special "in" words or expressions used by the regular class or by children in the school's neighborhood. Making and maintaining a local dictionary of such terms can be a class project of general value.
35. Light can be a problem in lipreading. The speaker's face should be clearly visible. Also, it is difficult to lipread when there is a strong light behind the speaker (window, sun, lamp).
36. When a hearing pupil is explaining something and you are not sure the hearing impaired child is catching what is being said, try interspersing your summary statements about what the hearing child is saying while the explanation is going on, if you can do so without bothering the child who is speaking. Or you can question the hearing impaired child to check on comprehension.
37. Share your short and long term teaching plans and objectives with the special education teacher and with any others who are working with the hearing impaired child inside or outside your class.
38. Visit classes and schools for hearing impaired pupils when you have the opportunity. Invite special education teachers into your class to observe what you are doing. They will sometimes have helpful suggestions if you ask for them, and they are very much interested in how hearing impaired pupils are doing in your class.
39. Try to be as consistent as you can about daily routines and requirements, particularly when a new hearing handicapped pupil is entering your group. That will limit communication problems, especially while the process of getting acquainted takes place.
40. Give the hearing impaired child encouragement and help in making child to child contacts that can lead to friendships in the regular class.
41. Check regularly on the match between the pupil's rate and level of cognitive development and the educational tasks now offered, plus those sequenced ahead for that pupil.

These suggestions are directed primarily to the regular class teacher. Many of them are relevant also for regular school principals and other administrators and for regular school supervisors. A review of the items by the special education teacher, too, would have value both to update and to clarify them for the local situation and to make sure that the special education teacher understands and concurs in what is being said to the regular class teacher.

No list can encompass all it takes for a regular class teacher to be effective with hearing impaired pupils in regular classes. It just is not possible to make a list that long and comprehensive. The best a list can do is call attention to instructional adaptations other teachers have found useful. The rest, of course, is a matter for the individual teacher to deal with in terms of professional competencies, insights, judgments, and imagination already possessed.

Suggestions and information for teachers of hearing impaired pupils. The work of the special education teacher under conditions of partial or full mainstreaming is different than in traditional programs. Following are suggestions for that new situation.

1. Concentrate on using the hearing impaired child's time to maximum advantage for teaching. Avoid having four or five pupils as merely onlookers while you interact with only one. Use aides, volunteers, peer helpers, independent study, and every other resource possible to maintain an individualized learning activity for every hearing impaired child all the time. Help the regular class teacher do that, too.
2. Plan to help the regular class teacher from time to time with regular class pupils who have learning problems. Keep top priority on hearing handicapped pupils, but use your competencies to give a hand with assessment, teaching materials, and other ways to make the regular class teacher's load a little lighter.
3. Insist on good manners from hearing impaired pupils. The regular teachers and the pupils' parents will appreciate it and you will be building habits useful in later life.
4. Expect to follow stipulated school hours and to be available before and after school and during part of the lunch hour to help students and regular class teachers.
5. Plan to attend building teacher meetings called by the principal or others.
6. Check with regular teachers at least once a week and more often if needed to be alerted to areas of student weakness where preteaching or postteaching can help.
7. Make a brief checklist for integrating (regular class) teachers to use to let you know about individual pupil problems and progress.
8. If a hearing impaired pupil is neglecting assignments or if the regular class work seems too much, be the first to notice it. Suggest remedies to the regular class teacher, including temporary removal from the regular class, if necessary.

9. Keep possible sources of regular class teacher irritation to a minimum. For example, remind hearing impaired pupils about lunch money, monitoring hearing aids, neatness, being quiet when moving from one part of the room to another to hear better, and the like.
10. Be sure the integrating teacher is invited to parents' meetings and to social affairs such as picnics with hearing impaired pupils and their families.
11. Be especially careful with first year teachers. Try to bring them into frequent contact with experienced regular class teachers who have been successful with integration.
12. Be alert to the problem faced by substitutes. If for yourself, try to have clear lesson plans ready. Prime the pupils; ask a colleague to be ready to help the substitute. If for a regular teacher, make it a point to stop in for a short chat. If you have seen substitutes who worked out well, suggest that they be invited back.
13. Detail for each hearing impaired child what is expected in emergencies such as fire, accident, or other unusual occurrences. It is especially important that the child know what the regular class teacher expects under such circumstances.
14. Coordinate lesson plans, objectives, texts, and references with the regular class teacher.
15. Arrange for an adapted schedule when a child needs it (i.e., fourth grade for arithmetic and fifth grade for reading).
16. Contact the parents of your hearing impaired charges regularly and in case of special need. For the latter, remember to make use of any or all of the following who might be able to advise or assist: school psychologist, school nurse, regular counselor, supervisor, regular teacher, secretary, reading specialist, vocational rehabilitation counselor, principal, teacher aide, other special teacher, and other pupils.
17. Join staff and in-service sessions for regular teachers to keep in touch with developments.
18. Go along on regular class field trips and arrange for regular classes and teachers to share in yours.
19. If appropriate in your program, offer to teach regular class teachers to sign and to use the manual alphabet. Do the same for regular class pupils and for the family of the hearing impaired pupil.
20. Regular class teachers sometimes have misconceptions about handicapped children. Take appropriate opportunities to supply correct information. Setting up a small professional library of selected materials for regular class teachers helps in this and in other matters, too.

The 20 items make up a list of things which special education teachers have said they need to consider in adapting to settings where hearing and hearing impaired pupils are merged for teaching.

Instructional Materials

The design of instructional materials to help hearing impaired pupils has concentrated, naturally enough, on the language arts. The most widely used item is called the Fitzgerald Key (Fitzgerald, 1954). It uses a set of visual symbols and sentence examples that can be used to encourage accepted grammatical construction in oral and written speech. To monitor the system such questions as "Who?" "What?" "Where?" and "How many?" are cued in visually.

Adding printed captions to modern instructional or entertainment films has proven a helpful use of contemporary technology for assisting deaf pupils in learning. Started in 1958 through federal funding support, it has allowed the accumulation of a substantial library of such films available for loan.

The federal support originally allocated for captioned films has broadened greatly. It now embraces educational media development on a national scale, development work in programed instruction, educational television, personnel training, and equipment for use not only in schools but also in the homes of hearing impaired persons. One of the recent developments is the adaptation for home use of teletype and telephone systems to allow communication by print rather than spoken word between hearing impaired persons or with hearing persons.

Other impressive technological advances are being made in the way the low frequency and limited residual hearing of most hearing impaired pupils can be enhanced and used to help them acquire language. Hearing aids can now capture and convert between the low frequencies and higher levels to improve audibility, for example. It yet remains for relatively fail proof miniaturizations to be made practical, but that may not be far away.

While not originally designed for hearing impaired pupils, books written with high interest appeal and low vocabulary loading have been found useful. They maintain motivation and bypass limited reading abilities. Thus, their use encourages gains in concepts, understanding, and information despite the limiting impact hearing impairments can have on general language development.

Access to these and other specialized instructional materials can be made available in any community. The local special education personnel should be familiar with nearby resources and those distributed from national centers. Regular class teachers should also ask for consultation from their specialist colleagues to learn about materials with which they might not be familiar. It is important to keep in mind, too, that regular class teachers often find they can make effective use of some of these devices and materials with children other than those for whom they were originally intended.

Organization for Instruction

Despite the variety of professional persons usually associated with programs for the hearing impaired, organization for instruction need not be complex. The regular class teacher and the educational specialist are the two leading figures in contact with the child, so they must arrange their time together. If translators are employed, as is common in situations using total communication, their participation needs to be scheduled where and when it can be most effective.

Certain points are of special importance. Hearing impaired pupils need to be where they can see what is going on and especially what the teacher is saying. Be sure that consideration is part of all lesson plans. Take full advantage of the possibilities in a buddy system and encourage older pupils, regular or exceptional, to help in the instruction of younger pupils. Get to know the hearing impaired pupils under ordinary, nonstress conditions. That will help when it is necessary to deal with them if conflict or discipline situations arise.

School Physical Plant

Student welfare and safety need special attention when hearing is defective. Teachers will want to familiarize themselves and their pupils with visual fire and other alarm signals and will want to be certain that the school administration has done a thorough job of installing and maintaining them.

Announcements over the school public address system or by other oral means may well be misunderstood or unnoticed. It is well to assure that they are given in writing, or, when appropriate, by translation for hearing impaired pupils.

Moveable seats and permission to move at will from place to place in the class should be arranged. There should be a central headquarters for translators, too, for times when there might be an emergency and precise communication is at a premium.

Summary

Hearing impaired pupils can take part in all aspects of regular education. Usually only minor adaptations are needed for them. Sometimes those adaptations turn out to be beneficial for all. An example is the football huddle, used originally by deaf players so opponents would not see their manual talk while setting up the next play.

As in the case of communication in the huddle, the great bulk of curricular adjustments, special teaching methods or materials, and other accommodations relate to some aspect of the language arts. Given the staff and facilities, those accommodations can be arranged so a substantial degree of mainstreaming can be attained from the very beginning of school.

COMPLETE AND PARTIAL MAINSTREAMING PROGRAMS

Hearing impaired pupils are now mainstreamed successfully in the widest array of schools and school systems. Partially or fully, mainstreaming is carried out under strikingly different conditions, ranging from massive, school-system-wide endeavors with extensive professional and paraprofessional support services to instances of a single hearing impaired child, the regular teachers and principal of one school, a helpful supervisor, and the child's parents. In all cases, the focus is on assuring that the hearing impaired child obtains high quality special education in the context of regular schooling.

This section contains summaries of integrated school programs in a variety of settings. They range from large to small, from local units to intermediate units, and they are located in different sections of the United States.

Public Schools

Monroe County, Michigan (Ida School District)

Between 1955 and 1957 the nine school districts of Monroe County arrived at a mutual agreement to educate their deaf and hard of hearing children themselves. The centrally located community of Ida became the locale. The first class, a small preschool age group, opened in 1957. Almost 18 years later, in the spring of 1974, there were 90 known hearing impaired pupils among the 36,000 school children in the county. All but 2 of them were in the Ida based program. These 2 were at the state residential school because their parents, who were deaf, had asked for that placement.

The hearing handicapped pupils are educated in the regular school buildings on the elementary-intermediate-high school campus at Ida. They are transported daily from all parts of the county, which is shaped roughly like a 40 mile square.

Monroe County's 1957 decision did not call for bringing children back from the state residential school. Instead, its purpose was to locate hearing handicapped youngsters as early as possible, help get training under way in the preschool years, and offer parents and children an alternative. The enrollment increased each year. The great majority of parents elected to continue at Ida. The enrollment is now spread proportionately across all grades, and the quality of the program attracts parents with hearing impaired pupils to move into the county, though no efforts are made toward that kind of recruitment.

The program has had the same supervisor since it was started. The 14 staff members and supervisor are employed as part of the Ida School District staff. They feel as much a part of the school system as do the regular class teachers. They take administrative guidance from the regular elementary, intermediate, or high school principals, depending upon where they are assigned.

Hearing impaired pupils are scheduled into regular classes individually, after review by all personnel concerned. Regular class teachers, with very few exceptions, consider hearing impaired pupils to be "theirs" as much as any other pupils. (Incidentally, integration of pupils with hearing defects led the way to the same attitude towards mentally retarded pupils. Their separate classes were phased out in Ida in 1972.)

The hearing impaired pupils who are enrolled divide as follows: 70%, educationally deaf; 30%, hard of hearing. *Multicaps* (often used to designate pupils with more than one educationally significant handicap) make up about 15% of the total. Handicaps other than hearing include cerebral palsy and other crippling conditions, partial vision, emotional or social maladjustment and mental retardation. The school population comes almost entirely from lower to middle class blue collar families that make up much of Monroe County.

There are 130 teachers and usually 5 to 6 sections of each grade or subject in the Ida system. A regular school system of that size is desirable for mainstreaming for three reasons. First, the hearing impaired pupils can be scattered, with not too many in one regular class. Second, there are alternatives if one placement does not work out. Third, the program for the hearing impaired, even a countywide one like Monroe's, is not so large when compared with the rest of the school system that it overbalances.

Once hearing impaired pupils join the centralized program in the Ida district, the pupils tend to stay on in the Ida schools for integration rather than return to any of the other eight districts in which they may live. The reasons are clear. They make friends among the regular Ida students and teachers and they have ready access to special help.

There is a great deal of social interaction at school, and large numbers of the regular pupils come to school by the same buses, so there is hearing pupil companionship. Boys and girls with hearing impairments take part in intramural and interscholastic athletics; during 1974 one was a cheerleader and another was on the student council. Both curricular integration and extracurricular social proximity build the feeling in the hearing handicapped pupils that the Ida schools are their schools.

The Monroe County teaching method is entirely aural-oral. It relies heavily on the early development of a large reading and understanding vocabulary. There is no track that turns to manualism if children do not appear to be able to acquire oral communication skills. For such youngsters, reading and writing get more emphasis, and much individual tutoring is provided.

The Special School District of St. Louis County, Missouri

This Missouri county school system bordering on the city of St. Louis is a comprehensive intermediate unit for special education. With its own staff and many of its own buildings, it serves most of the handicapped children of the 25 school districts of St. Louis County other than the city of St. Louis.

It is administratively and legally separated from the home school districts of the hearing impaired pupils it serves. However, the special district establishes and carries on mainstreaming in many of the local school classes that the pupils would normally attend if they were not hearing handicapped. In the special district the term *integration* is preferred to *mainstreaming*.

Before integration began, hearing impaired pupils were transported to a central building, which is still used to house some classes for children with hearing impairments beginning at nursery level. Also, it is headquarters for an infant education program. Babies under 3 years of age do not come to the school for instruction, but their parents come on a periodic basis for group guidance. Special school district staff members go regularly to each home to demonstrate educational procedures to be used by the parents with their deaf babies.

In 1967 and 1968 integration moves for hearing impaired pupils were stepped up because a group of pupils ready for it were received from Central Institute for the Deaf. The school progress made by some of the children was of such high quality that their teachers thought the youngsters might achieve as well or even better if they could be moved to regular classes, provided that the hearing impaired children and their regular class teachers could have support from special education teachers serving in the regular schools.

Now there is integration from nursery through secondary school. Approximately 200 attend regular classes in 141 different schools. The 200 pupils are the full responsibility of the local school districts. Hearing clinicians from the special school district provide support service. Not all hearing impaired pupils attend school with hearing children, but that is the goal.

At nursery level, starting at age 3, there is half day integration. At age 4, children judged ready can become fully integrated, or mainstreamed, at kindergarten level.

Staff members referred to as hearing clinicians go to schools with integration programs and work with the regular class teachers. Clinicians may be employed with preparation as speech therapists, educational audiologists, or teachers of the deaf and hard of hearing. Whatever background they begin with, they receive highly concentrated orientation to the new role of support and consultation and team teaching with regular class teachers.

Transfers of pupils to regular classes are usually made at the beginning of the term each fall. Thus the hearing impaired child enters a new class at the same time the rest of the pupils do. The move is preceded by a number of preparatory steps, beginning often in the middle of the previous year. The hearing clinicians have major roles in the preparation. They work with the special class teachers to arrange tests (ability, achievement, audiological). They check on the readiness of the hearing impaired child's local school to accept the pupil. The teachers most likely to have the child are given orientation to the program itself and to the individual child. Orientation includes print materials, conferences, visits to special classes, opportunities to talk with other regular class teachers who have had hearing impaired pupils, and discussions with the child's parents. These are more than "get acquainted" conversations. The clinician's case load is 10 to 12 children. Meetings with parents are 2 to 3 times per week. They cover common understandings on the parent's roles in teaching, the educational objectives for the child, and plans for continuing contacts.

It is the prevailing point of view that hearing impaired pupils should enter the educational mainstream early. A few years ago there was a tendency to delay integration for certain pupils, perhaps on the supposition that they might need to develop better communication skills or achieve more social maturity. It is now recognized that socialization and communication can be developed most effectively in a real life hearing world under the tutelage of the regular teacher, special teacher, and parent team.

Both the oral teaching method and total communication are used in the St. Louis County Special School District. Integration takes place under both.

Tacoma Public Schools, Tacoma, Washington

Tacoma was the first major city school system to make the mainstreaming of handicapped pupils a matter of policy. The term *progressive inclusion* was coined to indicate that the instructional programs and social interactions of handicapped and nonhandicapped children and youth would be merged, while high quality standards of education would be maintained for both. The Tacoma Board of Education enacted the policy and the staff began implementation (1958). In several categories, including the hearing impaired, the decision to integrate was a joint one with the rest of the schools of Pierce County surrounding Tacoma. Thus the public school program of Tacoma also serves hearing handicapped pupils from Pierce County. Additional information on the progressive inclusion concept and about how it works with educable mentally retarded pupils is found in another recent publication on mainstreaming (Birch, 1974).

Until 1971 Tacoma's hearing impaired pupils were taught by the oral method. In that year it was decided to add total communication as an option. By 1974 there were 8 teachers and about 30% of the pupils in the oral track and 13 teachers and approximately 70% of the pupils in total communication. Responsibility for monitoring the educational development of hard of hearing youngsters is held by the speech and hearing therapists, while instruction of the deaf is in the hands of teachers of the deaf and their coordinator and supervisor. There is an easy flow of interaction between the two groups and cooperative work with individual students is frequent.

The major source of referrals to Tacoma's preschool for 3 year old hearing impaired children is the Speech and Hearing Clinic at Mary Bridge Children's Health Center. The clinic conducts infant and toddler training, using total communication. That training blends into the same approach used in the Tacoma preschool at the Downing Elementary School. Parents who elect to send their preschoolers to Downing do so with the understanding that they may opt to have the children moved into an oral track after the preschool years if they wish.

The 3, 4, and 5 year old hearing impaired pupils are housed in a modern early childhood suite connected by a corridor to the hearing kindergarten and primary grades. The hearing impaired children are not maintained in age groups, but are mixed because the children are encouraged to relate to each other in terms of developmental levels. They may move from group to group as activities change; the same child may be at different levels in socialization, language, or motor competencies.

One of the special education teachers has a signing and manual alphabet class for 5 regular primary teachers and several playground attendants, lunch room assistants, and custodians. A teacher of the hearing impaired has kindergarten and first grade pupils along with hearing handicapped pupils twice a week for story reading time. The children are generally integrated for physical education and art. On individual schedules certain hearing impaired primary pupils are in regular kindergarten activities and regular first grade reading groups.

Integration increases as the children move upward through the grades. By junior or senior high school it is almost 100% for many, and by seventh grade most pupils have attained sufficient independence to use school passes on city buses.

Inclusion at junior high level is explained to parents by teachers of the hearing impaired who make home visits. Slide presentations are used to illustrate to parents what secondary school will be like and what will be expected of their sons and daughters.

Both oral and total communication pupils are integrated for some courses in secondary schools. Regular class teachers who are most successful at it are those who do most of their teaching through individually paced instruction, with much written or printed self instructional material. Reverse inclusion is utilized, too. Teachers of the hearing impaired, for example, teach classes in German, photography, or Northwest history; several hearing handicapped youngsters are scheduled into the course, with regular class pupils making up the rest of the section.

Junior high school regular class teachers were asked in a number of interviews about their experiences with having hearing impaired pupils in their regular classes. This comment by a teacher who had had three different hearing impaired students in various regular classes ranging from 27 to 35 enrollment is a fair example of the responses.

> It takes a little longer and a little more of my attention at the start of a project to get all matters clearly understood. But they appear to make up for that by working just a little harder than the average student does. I enjoy them and they seem to enjoy me. Moreover, they are wonderful examples for the rest of the students of how striving and perseverance can overcome a handicap. And after the term is underway a while there are days I forget there are deaf people in my class.

Active participation by the special education teachers in the life of the school is reported to be a significant influence on the acceptance of progressive inclusion. Teachers of the hearing impaired help in coaching track teams, sponsoring and preparing high school yearbooks, teaching sections of health classes, instructing regular teachers and pupils in the manual alphabet and sign language, coaching the school chess team, and performing countless other tasks, thus making themselves part of the mainstream of the school. Their enthusiasm for their work with hearing impaired pupils rubs off on others.

A recurring question from some quarters about the special education teacher's role in progressive inclusion goes like this: "Since you are a specialist, shouldn't you be spending all your time with the hearing impaired pupils you are especially prepared to help, rather than giving part of your time to children who have no hearing problems? Also, shouldn't the hearing handicapped pupils be full time under the instruction of specialists like you, rather than be taught by regular class teachers who lack your preparation?"

Teachers of deaf and hard of hearing pupils in Tacoma are firm in their support of cooperative work with regular class teachers and pupils, and that feeling is reciprocated by regular class teachers. They all make these points in response to the above queries.

1. Sharing classes and instruction increases the scope of worthwhile experiences for all pupils, hearing impaired or not.
2. The regular class teacher acquires some of the skills of the specialist when they work together.
3. The team of regular and special teacher can offer more to the child than either alone.
4. Some of the special skills of the teacher of the hearing impaired are applicable to children who have similar language related learning problems even though they do not have hearing losses.
5. Teamwork increases mutual understanding among teachers and reduces the likelihood of class size discrepancies creating conflict. Each comes to appreciate the real problems dealt with by the other, and superficial comparisons are understood for the oversimplifications they are.
6. The special education teacher's perspective is kept in balance by regular professional contact with hearing pupils.

Simi Valley Union School District, Ventura County, California

Simi Valley lies northeast of Los Angeles in the mountain region of southern California. The Union School District includes 40 square miles of rolling country dotted with clusters of middle income homes of workers who commute to nearby Los Angeles and Orange Counties daily, where the aerospace industries, for example, are major employers. Among the 68,000 population of the district are 1,500 police officers who work for the city of Los Angeles and the Highway Patrol. Simi Valley itself is relatively limited in tax base, having only a few light industrial activities and no other major sources of employment.

The school district houses 25,000 pupils in 24 elementary, 4 junior, and 2 senior high schools. The program for hearing impaired pupils serves the eastern half of Ventura County. The maximum bus ride time for hearing impaired students is 75 minutes one way.

In 1967 an oral special education plan was started. It operated for 3 years and in 1970 was changed to a total communication system, which continues as the only public school approach available.

From the outset Simi Valley elected to carry on the instruction of hearing impaired pupils in the mainstream of regular education. California's current Master Plan for Special Education fosters the mainstream concept, and Simi Valley is developing its program in that favorable context.

If 4 hearing impaired infants (age 6 months to 3 years) are located and enrolled in a planned program of education at home, a teacher can be assigned from the public schools. Two such infants had been identified and others were being sought. In the meantime, it is possible for the hearing handicapped infants and their families to come on a regular basis to the schools for nursery-kindergarten education (ages 3 to 5) and to obtain educational advice and direction from the teachers there.

An unusual arrangement supported by adult education makes it possible to blend hearing impaired and hearing children at ages 3 and 4 before public school kindergarten is ordinarily available. A nursery for hearing children is maintained as part of an adult education course aimed at improving the parenting skills of their mothers and fathers. By mutual agreement between the regular nursery teacher and the special teacher of hearing impaired children, and with full cooperation from the parents in both cases, team teaching and combined education was started in 1974. Parents of the 4 enrolled hearing impaired pupils orient the hearing parents. All, including the regular class teacher, are becoming familiar with sign and finger spelling.

In the primary and intermediate grades team teaching is used increasingly to provide the setting for integration. The majority of teachers of the hearing impaired have credentials for regular class teaching. That includes two elementary teachers who are deaf. While not a requirement, dual certification is considered very desirable.

Teachers of hearing impaired pupils instruct regular class pupils along with their deaf and hard of hearing charges. Regular class teachers select students in science, social studies, and reading to go to the special education classrooms for those subjects. Children are matched for those instructional groups by age and by reading levels. Hearing impaired pupils average the same reading comprehension and speed scores as their hearing age mates, and the range is similar.

Approximately half of the hearing impaired youngsters in the total enrollment are considered educationally deaf. They are sharing in the mainstreaming at preschool and elementary levels. However, the impact at the junior high level is new, and it has not yet reached strongly into the senior high school. Itnerant teachers and resource teachers at the latter levels have mounted thorough preparatory activities that include:

1. Orienting principals and counselors about the California Master Plan for Special Education and its emphasis on inclusion.
2. Alerting principals and counselors to hearing impaired pupils who are on their way to being promoted to junior or senior high schools.
3. Capitalizing on the assets of hearing impaired pupils already in the high schools.
4. Organizing and conducting beginning and advanced classes in sign language and manual alphabet for regular class teachers and pupils.

5. Offering to make faculty meeting presentations about how regular faculty can help as team members in teaching hearing impaired pupils.

In junior and senior high schools, basic and advanced courses for credit are offered for regular students interested in sign and finger spelling. The courses include principles of audiology, prevention and care of defective hearing, and human problems related to deafness. At one comprehensive senior high school with 2,250 enrolled, there are 32 hearing students in the basic course and 19 in the advanced one. There are 8 hear- hearing students in the basic and advanced courses of sign and finger the thrust of the recently begun program penetrates the high grades. The hearing students in the basic and advanced courses of sign and finger- spelling comprise a pool of "buddies" for note taking and joint study for new hearing impaired students and interpreters to work in regular classes which include hearing impaired students. As a potential fringe benefit, 8 of the high school students in the advanced class have announced their intentions to become special education teachers.

In teamwork between regular class and special education teachers, these are items that the cooperating faculty in Simi Valley noted:

1. The regular class teacher needs to get to know the hearing impaired pupils well. The special teacher can help in this and save the regular class teacher's time by giving the regular class teacher relevant data in written summary form and by updating it periodically.
2. The school nurse can be a powerful ally who can inform the regular class teacher and pupils about any aspects of hearing loss that might be of concern.
3. The regular class teacher should be asked about any particular weakness the hearing impaired pupil is showing, so that the ininerant teacher can take corrective action.
4. The special education teacher should plan with the regular class teacher so the hearing impaired pupil's schedule is disrupted as little as possible when it is necessary to remove the child for special tutoring.
5. The special teacher should let the regular teacher know that the pupil's school program can be altered any time circumstances and the good of the pupil seem to warrant it.
6. Regular teachers should be involved as much as possible in local admission and dismissal committee determinations.

The Simi Valley program was serving approximately 75 pupils in 1974, and growing. Moreover, as one of the high school principals pointed out, success with hearing impaired pupils had opened the way to plans for similar inclusion of visually impaired and physically handicapped pupils.

Lawndale, California, Los Angeles County

Lawndale is the school system headquarters for a 12 district intermediate unit serving a school population of 176,000. The unit is administered from the office of the Superintendent of Schools of Los Angeles County. The dozen suburban school districts, some bordering the city of Los Angeles, range from one of the poorest in terms of tax base for education to the wealthiest in California.

There are 180 hearing impaired children in the program. Those who attend special school programs are scattered among 8 different sites in various school districts. Hearing impaired pupils who are transported to special programs away from their neighborhood schools are not necessarily sent to the nearest special program. Instead, decisions are made about placement on the basis of which one is the most appropriate for the child's abilities and needs.

The formal preschool program begins with toddlers, from 8 months to 3 years. Infants have no organized program under public school auspices; parents who request assistance are referred to private agencies. Beginning at 4 years, there is systematic, planned integration. Head Start programs cooperate to make that possible. Integration continues in kindergarten and through the elementary and secondary school years.

The nature and the amount of inclusion depend on the speed and thoroughness with which each hearing impaired child acquires a substantial language base. The nature of the inclusion may be social, educational, or both. The amount varies from 10% to 90%. Decisions about the integration prescription for each child are made by a teacher-parent-principle committee, with regular and special class professional faculty and staff participating.

Mainstreaming is approached from resource rooms. Such rooms are located in elementary schools in which enrollments range from 600 to 750, approximately. The resource room sites are distributed to keep the ratio of hearing handicapped to hearing pupils 1 to 15 or fewer in order to minimize the chances that any hearing class might be asked to include more than 2 deaf or hard of hearing pupils.

The 1974 Lawndale Cooperative Unit staffing complement included 35 teachers of the hearing impaired, 30 aides, 2 audiologists, 1 psychologist, 2 speech therapists, and 1 principal to coordinate and supervise. The intent is to have a one to one ratio of teachers and aides, with no teacher having responsibility for more than 6 hearing impaired pupils.

Once a pupil shows, in the judgment of teachers and parents, the competence to ride the currents of regular classes, a plan is made to return that youngster to the neighborhood school. The pupil is monitored in the neighborhood school by an itinerant teacher; that teacher offers from 1 to 5 hours support time per week, as needed, to maintain the pupil in the mainstream.

At the same time, the teacher of hearing impaired pupils helps the regular class teacher with hearing children who may be having learning problems. For example, the special education teacher might be tutoring a hearing impaired pupil in mathematics 30 minutes a day. The regular class teacher might identify 2 or 3 hearing pupils in the class who need similar instruction. The special teacher would, with the agreement of the regular teacher, tutor them all together in the regular classroom, in a resource room, or in another part of the building.

Another way the teacher of the hearing impaired assists the regular class teacher is by locating and bringing instructional materials to supplement those of the regular teacher. Still another way is by teaching the entire regular class for a period from time to time, perhaps to allow the regular teacher to attend a professional meeting, confer with a parent, or give intensive individual attention to one pupil.

The Lawndale Cooperative Unit began with an oral approach to language and speech teaching. In 1969 total communication was inaugurated, and it is now the predominant way of language and speech instruction. Both tracks were maintained out of consideration for those who wished to continue under the oral approach. Thus by 1974 total communication had had time to become well established only in the earlier grades.

The financing of the 12 district program is from the county level. Teacher salaries, instructional materials, transportation, special furniture and equipment, rental for rooms, and other costs are financed by the county. Thus, local districts are usually not unwilling to cooperate for financial reasons. While this system of funding does have problems, it can be a boon to encouraging cooperation on the part of the regular class teachers. If a hearing impaired student is spending time in a regular class, the local district is paid additionally for the portion of the average instructional cost that pupil's time in the regular class represents. In several cases the local school superintendent earmarks that particular payment from the county and turns it over to the elementary or secondary school to be used to enhance its program in general. In such cases, regular class teachers recognize a direct benefit to the school's regular program stemming from the integration of deaf and hard of hearing pupils.

Of the 180 hearing impaired pupils on the register, slightly more than half would be classed as deaf for educational purposes. Of those who are deaf, approximately half are in some degree of academic integration, some as much as 90% of the school day. Almost all are active participants in social integration.

Chicago Public Schools, Chicago, Illinois

The Alexander Graham Bell Elementary School was constructed with the idea that hearing impaired and hearing children would go to school together. During the half century since it opened, that has been its major mission.

There are approximately 850 pupils enrolled from nursery through the eighth grade. Deaf children account for about 165 of that number. Hard of hearing pupils were assigned for integrated education to another elementary school several years ago. In addition to the deaf children there are 40 partially seeing pupils at A. G. Bell. They, too, have opportunities for inclusion in regular classes.

A. G. Bell's high ceilinged, three story, squarish building is at 3730 North Oakely in a middle and lower middle socioeconomic level community. Hearing impaired pupils are bused there mostly from Chicago's North Side. The pupil population of hearing handicapped represents the European, Middle Eastern, and (more recently) the Latin American heritages of that part of the city.

Educational programs similar to A. G. Bell's are found in schools in other parts of Chicago. They are located to serve hearing impaired pupils within reasonable transportation distance.

As a matter of schoolwide practice there is educational and social integration in physical education, at recess, in auditorium activities, in swimming, in class governance, and on the playground. The same is true during the daily late afternoon dancing, corridor games, and quiet table games sponsored by the staff as recreational activities for the pupils.

Hearing impaired pupils start in a nursery at age 3. In a typical group there may be 8 pupils, 1 teacher of the deaf, 1 child welfare aide, and 2 fifth or sixth grade student volunteers. The latter are nominated by their teachers and appointed by the principal. A school "letter" can be earned by accumulating sufficient points for such services. The students may be hearing impaired or not.

Since classes for hearing children begin with kindergarten for 5 year olds, the nursery age deaf pupils have less opportunity for integration with other children than they do in later years. There are get-togethers with hearing kindergarteners, however, for movies, stories, and similar activities in which the age discrepancy does not pose problems.

In 1971 the language instruction program changed from oral to total communication. Because of a long tradition there remains a strong oral influence, with sign and manual alphabet used along with it.

Integration began at the A. G. Bell School in the 1950's. It has grown steadily, and currently it is found in many forms. Parents of hearing impaired children continue to move into the attendance area of the Bell school to assure that their youngsters will have maximum opportunity to use the school's resources.

For pupils who are found early and whose development is not complicated by multiple handicaps, blending into regular kindergarten and first grade can usually begin immediately. The special and regular teachers share responsibility. By the middle or upper grades many are integrated for most academic subjects. All deaf children in the upper grades are integrated for mathematics, science, and reading unless they have handicaps in addition to deafness which preclude that kind of schedule.

In-service courses have made most special teachers proficient in total communication. Those teachers may, in academic classes, have 8 deaf pupils plus 10 or 12 hearing pupils with achievement at the same grade level. The key difference between that arrangement (called *reverse integration*) and the regular hearing class is that the teacher of the deaf uses sign and finger spelling along with normal speech. Approximately 85% of the special teachers have dual certification qualifying them to teach both regular classes and classes for the hearing handicapped.

A strongly positive attitude toward deaf children characterizes the regular class teachers at Bell. Teachers considered for assignment in the regular program there are informed about the nature of the faculty's team efforts on behalf of deaf students, and they are advised what to expect. It has been possible to maintain high quality regular class staffing with teachers who are responsive and flexible. Chicago's teachers are historically well organized as a collective bargaining unit. The integration of deaf pupils has not been a matter for specifications in the agreement and has not been a source of grievances. Regular class teachers are in favor of high quality special education and view integration as part of it.

Within two blocks of the A. G. Bell School is one of Chicago's most distinguished technical secondary schools, Lane Technical High School. With 6,000 students, a well maintained plant, and sophisticated facilities, it admits only pupils who complete eighth grade in the upper third of their classes. Lane's technical curricula—art, pre-engineering, science/mathematics, engineering drafting, and music—all have thorough academic foundations, with the result that they can satisfy college preparatory requirements. The school is coeducational.

Two teachers of the deaf staff a resource room at Lane Technical High School. They and their aides are contact points for the Lane counselors and teachers who work with deaf girls and boys attending. One-third of A. G. Bell's graduation class of hearing impaired youth have been accepted at Lane each of the last several years. The remainder went to other Chicago schools. Of the students who move to Lane approximately half would be classed as educationally deaf by the most strict interpretation. These youngsters are found in all areas of the curriculum except music;

they typically carry full loads, using the resource teachers only when faced with serious difficulties.

The Bell population has been changing. In 1973-74 a survey revealed that 44% were multiply handicapped. As noted earlier, Latin American families were on the increase. Spanish speaking parents come to the school to learn total communication from Spanish speaking faculty members. Also, it is more and more frequent that deaf children are not found until age 7 or 8, having been kept at home in educational neglect by their parents. The majority are in families that recently moved to Chicago.

As a standard practice at Bell there is now a weekly staff conference on the hearing handicapped students because the problems have become more complex.

In at least partial response to the increasing complexity of problems presented there has developed a unit called the Non-Categorical Clinic. Its staff is 2 teachers, an educational therapist, and a welfare attendant. One of the teachers is a specialist in education of the deaf and the other in language and speech. Pupils presenting extraordinary problems come to the Clinic about 2 hours per day. They are assessed and taught diagnostically by the staff on a one to one basis. They work up to full time school attendance, moving into the regular classes as their instructional problems are resolved.

The integration of hearing impaired pupils in the Chicago schools is part of a broad policy. In-service workshops have encouraged elementary and secondary principals in that direction. Also, schools can be allocated more teachers if they establish integrated programs. Principals work with PTA's and other community groups to foster increased understanding of the advantages of blending regular and special education.

Residential Schools

Signs of both increased interest and more attempts to arrange integration are reported from residential schools. Craig and Salem (1975) surveyed 75 United States residential schools, asking about integration practices. Of the 75, 39 said some integration was being practiced; 22 responded to a second inquiry, which went into more depth about integrative practices.

From Craig and Salem's study it became clear that approximately half of the nation's residential schools have made some moves toward integration. Almost a third of the total, 22 of them, have programs they felt were developed enough to describe.

For the actual number of residential school students being integrated, the scene appears less bright. The 22 schools giving extensive reports said that a total of 410 students took part in some form of integration. In 1970-71 there were approximately 18,700 hearing impaired pupils in residential schools. Thus, based on those figures, a little more than 2% (2.3%) of the residential school population of hearing impaired pupils were experiencing integration at the time of the Craig and Salem study.

The study contains data, also, about the nature and purposes of integrative procedures currently in use. Thus it is a valuable source of information about the state of the practice in residential settings.

Lexington School for the Deaf, New York City, New York

Lexington, a private residential and day school in the Borough of Queens, New York City, has an illustrious history of service to hearing handicapped children and youth. In recent years the school has made five major moves which, taken together, keep it in the vanguard of contemporary advances in the integration of deaf and hard of hearing persons in the everyday world. All of Lexington's hearing impaired pupils take part in school planned integrated socialization, recreation, or sports programs. Not all participate in formal education integration, but that is an overt goal and more students attain it each year, as will be seen as the following five steps are described.

First, there has been steadily growing emphasis on making full time transfer to hearing schools an attainable goal for more hearing impaired pupils, and for doing so earlier. It had been recognized that occasionally children who were educationally and objectively (audiometrically) deaf had sometimes in the past achieved full and practically independent mainstream standing. Special schools and classes thus gave up their best students, in terms of academic achievement and communication skills, to the regular schools. While everyone was pleased at the progress of those few individuals, many of the professional persons in the special schools were not happy at the loss of the leadership of that elite student group.

The Lexington faculty has taken a step ahead by opening the transfer potential to many more pupils. Two nearby New York City public elementary schools and several private and parochial elementary and secondary schools are partners in a placement network within walking or very short transportation time of the Lexington campus. A staff of external liaison and consultant personnel from Lexington know the principals and teachers of the participating schools well. They usually begin a year in advance to prepare parents, teachers, and pupils for the first trial placements, scheduling hearing impaired pupils from one period to most of a day in the regular class in which there is most probability of success. This component of the integration thrust reaches more and more pupils.

In the 1973-74 school year teachers referred between 55 and 60 new candidates out of Lexington's 380 total to the program coordinator for consideration. Followup data convinces staff, parents, and pupils that the program pays off. Also, it is not an either-or matter. Students may return to full time at Lexington, and some find that best. The door is always open and it can swing in either direction.

The second component began in 1957. It is integrated vocational education for secondary students who, after parent-student-guidance counselor conferences, choose that option. Each year about 35 deaf students attend regular business, technical, and vocational schools where they study and train with normally hearing classmates. Beginning in 10th grade with 2 hours per day off campus, by 12th grade it is full time off campus, culminating in job placement.

The third large element in the school's multifaceted approach is a kind of reverse integration. Early in 1970, Lexington Board adopted the policy of operating as a private school for hearing pupils, beginning at nursery age, in addition to serving the same purpose it always has for the hearing impaired. In the fall of 1974 the initial second grade opened, to mark four levels: nursery, kindergarten, first, and second grades in operation, covering ages 3 through 7. Each class has both hearing and hearing impaired pupils, about 17 to 20 of the former and 5 to 8 of the latter. A masters degree level teacher of the deaf is in charge. A second teacher prepared at the bachelors degree level in elementary education serves as assistant, and aides are available as necessary. The teacher of the deaf has also had training and experience with hearing pupils. The two teachers work together, individualizing instruction for all pupils while all remain together as a class group. Evaluations made internally and by outside experts during the last 3 years have shown that both hearing and hearing impaired pupils receive a superior education.

The neighborhood of the Lexington School has high quality public, private, and parochial schools. Yet there is a waiting list of hearing pupils whose parents are willing to pay Lexington's competitive tuition to have their youngsters attend school there and be taught along with deaf and hard of hearing children.

The fourth major component in the grand scheme of normalization starts with babies. Hearing impaired infants need sound and language stimulation. Infants with normal hearing are aided in mental development by perceptual motor stimulation, too. In the spring of 1974, Lexington had 29 newborn to 3 year old babies brought regularly to its Infant Center. Five hearing babies were also in attendance, and along with their parents were receiving instruction and guidance addressed to fostering mental and emotional development. At the same time the hearing infants are ever present models of normal child development against which the staff and parents can measure the progress of the hearing impaired babies.

By 1974, some of the first group of infants had progressed through the program to nursery school age. Thus the infant program has been linked both to the regular school placement program and to the reverse inclusion program because some hearing impaired children moved from the infant group into each of the two programs.

The four interlocking programs mentioned so far are carried out in the context of the fifth, a broad complex of socialization-recreation-community services conducted by the school. Teenagers and adults from the neighborhood use the playing fields, gymnasium, swimming pool, meeting rooms, and auditorium of the school. Before, during, and after school, and in the evenings, Lexington has hearing groups from churches, Boy and Girl Scouts, Y's, athletic associations, social clubs, and other organizations using the school's facilities. In turn, hearing impaired young people and adults have opportunities to be part of those groups at the school and in their off campus activities. Also, the school operates an adult education program and a hearing and speech clinic for the community. In addition, steps have been taken to increase the proportion of residential pupils who live off campus. The school staff has been successful in locating very acceptable hearing foster homes within easy walking to transportation for some hearing handicapped residential students. Other students, under staff supervision, live in small group homes in the neighborhood. Thus, educationally integrative activities take place in a setting totally committed to normalization.

Though a private school, Lexington cooperates with the New York State special education program to serve an allocated section of the state. Thus there is not a selective intake policy. Approximately 45% of the students are multply handicapped. All pupils, on completing school, either continue their education, move into full time jobs, or, in the case of some of the multiply handicapped, enroll in sheltered workshops.

Lexington's many moves toward life's mainstream for its pupils have called for other changes before and during implementation. Faculty and staff orientation was one. Another was financing. A third was parent participation and support. However, the foundation is an avowed objective to make the school a real service center with a philosophical position resting on the oral teaching approach. All rationales for specific changes were based on the principle that oral teaching's root purpose is to bring hearing handicapped persons into normal contact with the rest of the world's people.

Western Pennsylvania School for the Deaf, Pittsburgh, Pennsylvania

The first objective of integration arrangements at Western Pennsylvania School has been to ready students for postsecondary education with hearing students. Therefore part time regular class attendance began in the upper secondary years.

In 1968 agreement was reached with a nearby public high school to permit selected students from the Western Pennsylvania School to enroll in certain classes. The students chosen were those who were being counseled to apply for admission to colleges or technical schools after completing 12th grade. The primary purpose was to simulate and solve problems such as those hearing impaired students might encounter in higher education.

The experience of attending class in the regular high school was expected to have two other advantages, also, whether or not the hearing impaired students went on to higher education. The large public high school could maintain a much more varied curriculum than could the Western Pennsylvania School, making a wider selection of courses available to the hearing impaired pupils. The second advantage was the opportunity to acquire increased skill in relating to hearing peers in the classrooms, halls, cafeteria, and other areas of the high school.

To increase the likelihood that the latter interactions would occur, two deliberate moves were made. Only one or two hearing impaired pupils were assigned to any one class, thus making it difficult to form a separate clique of such pupils. In the cafeteria, the regular high school counselor encouraged hearing students to join those with hearing impairment for meals.

The secondary school part time integration outreach of the Western Pennsylvania School has been extended to the public technical school division of another nearby community. Also, whereas integration was originally open to senior year students, it has since been extended to junior year hearing impaired students. The details of the process used to arrange secondary school integration and the criteria for pupil selection were reported by Salem (1971).

The secondary school integration move had been made with college guidance in mind. Careful selection plus the application of intensive and personalized counseling led to increased numbers of applications to hearing colleges. The hearing college attendance trend is now quite noticeable among Western Pennsylvania School graduates.

Many of the colleges in the Pittsburgh region had little if any experience with students who were educationally deaf when the first applications from such students began to arrive. Knowing that, Western Pennsylvania School officials went to the colleges and offered to be available for the kinds of help and support needed, should the colleges admit hearing impaired students. Thus the applicants could be assessed by admission committees using the same criteria as for hearing students. By 1974, 32 students had participated in public secondary school integration and later attended college. Of them 17 (53%) attended hearing colleges, the majority near enough to Pittsburgh to allow ready consultation from Western Pennsylvania School staff. Twelve of the hearing handicapped students went to Bethany college in West Virginia. Followup reports of students to date have been encouraging.

The Western Pennsylvania School's longest and strongest integration efforts have been at the college and the immediate precollege periods. However, integration is now beginning in the early grades, also. Some hearing children attend the nursery for hearing impaired pupils at the school. A first and second grade class with their teachers from the School for the Deaf go to a nearby public elementary school for two periods daily.

The staff of the Western Pennsylvania School is performing a significant national service, also, by researching integration practices in all of the residential schools for the deaf in the United States. Since almost half of America's hearing impaired special education pupils (45.5% in 1970-71) are educated in the nation's state, private, and parochial residential schools, research and dissemination of findings on approaches to mainstreaming in those schools is of great national import.

The Western Pennsylvania School for the Deaf, a private nonsectarian school, cooperates with the Commonwealth of Pennsylvania by serving in the role of a state residential school for western Pennsylvania. Its instruction is oral, with a combined system available to students who prove to require it. Of the 1973 graduating class 38% had multiple handicaps. The school had an enrollment of 516 in the fall of 1974, with 20% being day students.

Utah State School for the Deaf, Ogden, Utah

A statewide educational system for hearing impaired children and youth has its headquarters in Ogden at the State School for the Deaf. Operating administratively as a form of intermediate unit, the State School represents the state education agency of Utah as the provider of special education for Utah's hearing impaired pupils in the State School itself and in the public school districts of the state. Hearing impaired children and youth in public schools are registered with the State School and provided educational services by faculty and staff in the employ of the State School, with two exceptions.

The first exception was a temporary one for children in the age range from birth to 5 years. These infants, toddlers, and preschoolers were located and given developmental guidance through a special project staff. In 1975 that program moved into the orbit of State School administration. Some 3 to 5 year olds are now grouped in nursery and kindergarten settings under State School auspices.

The second exception is one that promises to continue and to grow. It consists of those deaf and hard of hearing pupils who are competent enough to cope with full time regular school schedules without support from the professional faculty and staff of the State School program. In such instances the local school district monitors the progress of the pupils and buttresses them if necessary with aid from district employed speech and hearing clinicians or teachers of the hearing impaired. Such pupils now number approximately 100, most having attained fully integrated status during the junior or senior high school years.

The Utah program is integration oriented. Therefore, there are increasing numbers of hearing impaired pupils in the mainstream. That continues to be a goal for the approximately 275 deaf or hard of hearing young people now on the Utah State School's registry.

The administrative and supervisory staff of the state system make arrangements with local school systems to conduct special education for the hearing impaired pupils enrolled there and in nearby school systems. Rooms are rented, faculty specialists are supplied, instructional equipment and materials are brought in, and pupil transportation is provided. Personnel policies and management procedures applied by the State School authorities are designed to merge the faculty, staff, and the educational activities for the hearing handicapped into those for all other pupils in the local elementary or secondary school.

Only a few, perhaps 5 to 15, hearing impaired pupils are allocated to any one school building, depending on the total enrollment. A common pattern is to maintain a separate nursery group of hearing impaired children. Then a kindergarten class may be in one elementary school, a first grade in another, a second grade in another, and so on through the elementary years, with classes of the hearing impaired in more than one grade in larger elementary schools. Children in those classes continue in the same school, with their special education teachers changing from year to year. At the secondary level the class of hearing handicapped pupils with one special teacher includes several grade levels.

Beginning with the kindergarten there is much integration with hearing pupils. It increases in each succeeding grade. It is engineered somewhat differently from class to class, of course, because of personal variables among both pupils and teachers. But the trend is clear. Integrated time in kindergarten may vary from 10% to 25% per child. By senior high school it may range from 30% to 90%. Integration time is often different from pupil to pupil in each grade. Also, there is a steady attrition in numbers of pupils registered on the roll of the State School program as one goes higher through the grades. More and more hearing impaired youngsters are judged ready to move to full time into the mainstream, with responsibility for their education shouldered entirely by their school districts of residence, where speech and hearing therapists monitor and aid in their progress.

Parents and pupils have a choice from the outset to have either an oral or a total communication style of language and speech instruction. The The latter is a recently instituted option. At present approximately 70% of pupils are being taught orally. The two approaches are kept separated at the level of teacher-pupil and pupil-pupil contact by operating them in different, though often neighboring school districts. Since transportation is by taxi, there is little pupil-pupil contact in that process. There is, however, close coordination at the professional administrative and supervisory level, with consideration for transfer from one instruction grouping to the other always open.

Elementary, junior, and senior high principals, vice principals, and counselors are enthusiastic about the effect on the other pupils of integrating hearing impaired pupils. They say the practice provided a focal point to bring students together to make sure that their school will do its best for the handicapped students. The latter are regarded as models of good study habits, school citizenship, and examples of what an individual can do to maintain equilibrium and to move ahead despite hardships.

Faculty members are generally favorable to bringing hearing impaired pupils into the regular schools. Their views were sought in faculty meetings before beginning integration, where feasible. It was made clear by the principals that faculty and staff cooperation would be requested regarding regular class integration and that no such assignment would be made final without a trial period and ample opportunity to consider the regular class teacher's reaction.

Following is a letter illustrative of those given to teachers to help orient them to hearing impaired pupils.

Dear Teacher:
If you have never had a deaf or hard of hearing child in your class before, don't be too nervous about it. If you don't understand his speech at first, tell him. He'll try again: he's more used to his problem than you are.
We would hope that you would be thoughtful of his handicap, but we would hope that you would NOT make excessive concessions for him or give him grades he doesn't deserve because he is the "poor deaf kid."

He has been placed in classes that we think he can handle. If he can't, he will be withdrawn or we will give him some help—but this is our problem, not yours.

The term "deaf" can cover a multitude of hearing losses. But hearing impairment is like a color. You can see a dozen various shades and call them all red, even though not one of them is the same color. So with "deaf" children. Some hear better than others, in many gradations—and their speech and use of language will be better or worse depending upon the amount of hearing they have.

Here are a few comments about *lipreading* that you might not have thought of.

1. Lighting is best if it hits the speaker's face. It is impossible to lipread a person who is standing with his back to the window so that the glare is blinding.

2. Don't expect the student to lipread beyond 8 to 10 feet.

3. Lipreading is easiest straight on or at a 45 degree angle.

4. Talk normally. Don't exaggerate the mouth movements out of recognition. Don't slow down and string out single words. That's just as hard to lipread as too rapid a rate. Slow down a little in phrasing if you wish, but a good moderate rate is best.

5. Natural gestures are fine but excessive motion of the head or arms, or pacing back and forth makes words difficult to catch.

6. Chewing movements—gum, candy, a pipe or pencil, etc.—make it hard for a deaf child to know where the chewing ends and the speaking begins.

7. Flickering lights are distracting, as are any movements around a deaf child. He is conditioned to respond to light, movement, and vibration to make up for his lack of hearing.

8. Sunglasses are distracting probably because they create two black holes which catch the eye and then movement is reflected in them.

9. Lipstick helps. Apparently it frames the lips, making them easier to read.

10. Lipreading is tiring at the best of times, but stripes, dots, spots, or tops of brightly colored or patterned fabric make it that much harder.

11. As far as seating is concerned, it depends on the kind of class you run.

    A. If it's small enough for a semicircle, place the lipreader on the end with his back to the light so that he has the whole group in his view and is not fighting the glare.

    B. If you use the lecture method, place the deaf student near the front in the middle or on the window side so that the light is at his back.

C. If there's a lot of class response the deaf child has trouble locating the speaker, and by the time he does, the recitation is half over. If the students raise their hands or stand up before starting to speak, that extra second gives the deaf child time to locate the speaker and start to lipread.

12. As a check—talk to yourself in a mirror and see how you look.
    Do you move your lips excessively?
    Do you move them at all?
    Do you talk out of the side of your mouth?
    How well could you lipread yourself?
    Would you like to have to watch that shirt for a solid hour?

13. In talking privately to him, if he does not understand you, there may have been phrases that were hard to lipread or a word which was unknown to him. So it is best to rephrase yourself to simplify the language.

14. You may not always understand him. If not, tell him. You will get used to him after a while. If he makes errors in his language structure, give him the correct pattern to repeat the practice.

On the whole you will find these children pleasant and a little naive. Their speech may be stiff and their language a bit disordered, but they are excited about being in the "hearing" school.

We want these students to succeed in this foray into "hearing" school. Thank you so much for this important work with us. If there is anything we might be able to do to help you with a hearing impaired student or any other student, please let us know.

(Signed)

Total communication pupils are accompanied to regular classes by interpreters when necessary, as determined by their oral communication skills; some attend classes without interpreters. Interpreters are assigned, when needed, to groups of three or four hearing impaired pupils.

The teacher's speech is repeated by the interpreter through sign, finger spelling, and nonvocalized speech. The pupils may speech read the teacher directly or use the interpretation, the latter being available in a steady flow from the interpreter, who usually stands just outside the direct line of sight from pupils to teacher. The interpreter watches the teacher, too, because often what the teacher says must be conveyed in the context of what the teacher is doing at the same time.

Interpreters are not teachers. They are expected to be experts in total communication, however, and they are given an orientation to public school operations before being assigned. They quickly learn the idiosyncracies of pupils and teachers. Sometimes they do more than straight, literal translation by offering alternative phrasing or synonyms when hearing impaired students do not know the words the teacher uses. On some occasions the special education teacher takes a turn at acting as an interpreter.

Whether in oral or total communication, decisions about regular class enrollment follow the same pattern. Planning and projecting is done in the spring. Parents are involved. Regular and special education teachers and coordinators weigh and balance pupil assets. The school principal moderates the process. Possibilities are reviewed with the pupil. The whole procedure is usually informal, but clear understandings are reached and mutually agreeable conclusions are achieved. The same kind of process and spirit are found when any change in a hearing impaired pupil's school program is considered.

Regular class teachers with hearing impaired pupils in their classes offered the following ideas, based on successful experience:

1. It is best in secondary schools if schedule changes for hearing impaired pupils are determined sufficiently in advance to allow the pupils to start with the regular class at the beginning of the term.
2. In regular elementary and secondary schools there often are students, teachers, secretaries, cafeteria workers, custodians, and others who have been raised with deaf brothers, sisters, parents, or other relatives. Use these natural resource persons to help others learn to appreciate and work with hearing impaired pupils.
3. Technical vocabulary can be the highest hurdle for hearing impaired pupils. Regular teachers of mathematics, ceramics, geography, photography, mechanical drawing, or any other subject with a technical language often need to check to be sure the terms and expressions are understood by deaf or hard of hearing pupils.
4. Eye contact by teachers with hearing handicapped students can give valuable clues as to when the students are in need of special help as discussions or other oral activities go on in class. It helps with behavior control, too.
5. Hearing pupils can gain in personal growth by helping classmates or younger children who have educational problems because of hearing loss.
6. In elementary or secondary schools the special teacher of hearing impaired pupils may often arrange with one or two other teachers to divide their classes and take 10 to 12 hearing pupils in with the hearing handicapped children. Each teacher ends up with a small class, allowing more individualization. And the special teacher conducts an integrated class.
7. Avoid unnecessary pressure on hearing impaired youngsters when they first join a hearing class. Instead, use the "undercut" approach

—try to give them tasks at which they can succeed, thus strengthening their self confidence at this crucial time.

Principals, counselors, and coordinators who were interviewed agreed with the above suggestions. They are equally applicable whether the school system's orientation is toward an oral approach, total communication, or both.

Transportation by taxi for hearing impaired pupils is legislatively authorized in Utah at public expense. The 1973-74 cost was 34 cents per pupil per mile. That amounted to $5.80 per pupil per day and totaled $1,043.00 per pupil per year.

COMPREHENSIVE PROGRAMING FOR PERSONS WITH HEARING IMPAIRMENTS

Teachers, as much or more than any other professional group, find that their work takes on a communitywide orientation. They must know local and regional cultural norms and standards. They operate constantly with the living, growing progeny of all components of the citizenry. They recognize, perhaps more than any other group, that the schools are part of a larger whole.

Because teachers truly have a need to know the broader context in which they work, this section traces the outlines of that wider world. First, the key characteristics of a comprehensive educational program are presented. Second, the variety of services that impinge on education is discussed.

Characteristics of a Comprehensive Educational Program

Some elements of preferred practices in the education of children and youth who have hearing impairments are listed earlier in this chapter. They should be part of a comprehensive educational program, certainly, and they need not be recapitulated here. There are, however, 10 additional characteristics needed to assure that programs are truly comprehensive and that they overlook no legitimate educational rights of the pupils in question. Both regular and special educators experienced with education of hearing impaired pupils and with mainstreaming recommended these points for inclusion.

1. Assure that there is a solid commitment from the board of education and the community. It should be firmly based (a) on understanding of the rationale for the program and (b) on confidence in the staff.
2. The supervisor or coordinator of the program for the hearing impaired should help in interviewing applications for regular class teaching posts, and vice versa. That is valuable for initial orientations and to avoid taking on new staff members who would resist working toward integration.

3. A school-system-wide 5 year program plan should be made and updated each year. It should be both systematic and consistent. The program should stay on the course initially agreed on, changes being made only as needed and only after full consultation with all concerned.
4. Administrative and instructional leaders should be aware that they are models for all the staff in the effort to foster the attitude that "we can do something for this kid."
5. Teachers can become overburdened. A monitoring system should be operating to watch for the tendency to overload a willing teacher. Administrators should intervene *before* that happens.
6. The school system's integration policy should be publicly announced and discussed and should be implemented in collective bargaining negotiations, if there are such, with teachers and others. It should be prevented from becoming a focus for grievances by foresight in reaching agreements on class size, placement procedures, special education responsibilities, and related matters and about how the understandings will be implemented in practice.
7. There should be laws and regulations that work out the costs with local districts, intermediate units, and the state so no district is hurt by moving to an integrated program.
8. The rationale for the program should be explained to substitute teachers, to new faculty and staff, and to new families moving into the school district.
9. Arrangements should ensure there are not real inequities in workload between regular and special teachers. Their work is not the same, but each should understand the other's and recognize the balancing factors that make them equivalent.
10. In-service and continuing education should be an ongoing reality. It should be based on periodic needs assessments among regular and special teachers to determine topics for training workshops.

These items may well be universal. That is, they may apply to all programs for exceptional children, not just those for pupils with hearing impairments.

Education as Part of a Broader Group of Services

What was said in earlier chapters about this topic should be reviewed and applied to persons with hearing impairments. There are gifted and talented individuals and there are mentally retarded individuals among those who are hard of hearing or deaf, so the material in chapters 5 and 6 applies. Also, two of the agencies previously named, the Mental Health/

Mental Retardation Agency and the Vocational Rehabilitation Agency, are there to supply needed services that are outside the school's scope to hearing impaired persons or their parents who request them.

Almost every community also has volunteer health and welfare agencies that interest themselves in hearing loss and in preventing or ameliorating its associated problems. These organizations' services range, too, across all age groups. When one adds to that the groups of hearing impaired persons who band together for their own personal and social purposes, it can be seen that there is a network of agencies, of which the school system is one.

In some places there is a more or less formal council of representatives of all such agencies. They meet from time to time to let each other know of new developments, to seek consultation from each other, to talk and express joint positions on mutual concern, and to help assure that some community or individual needs are not escaping attention. Such a council and its individual members can be very supportive of the regular and special teacher's efforts.

The Continuing Need for Teachers

A steady demand has existed for the past decade for qualified teachers of deaf children and youth. Graduates in 1975 and 1976 were locating positions with little difficulty. Regular class teachers who understand and can work with mainstream programs for hearing impaired pupils can expect to be favored for employment in forward looking school systems.

The rapid growth of interest in the very early childhood years suggests that there may be a sharp acceleration of demand for teachers for that population. McConnell (1973) stated:

> The goal in the parent-infant program is to develop a program of instruction for young hearing impaired children and their parents, to be carried out in a home environment, allowing for incorporation of language and auditory training into the more normal routine of home activities. (p. 291)

He went on to point out that:

> The success of the program for children under three which stresses early use of audition in acquisition of language is dependent not only upon highly skilled and competent teacher-counselors but also upon close coordination between the teacher and the audiologist. (pp. 391-393)

This kind of program, which begins with babies before 6 months of age, suggests that there will be a need for teachers who combine knowledge of very early child development with the competencies to teach deaf children.

At all points in the regular schools, including vocational education, it appears that there will be need for teachers who specialized in the education of the deaf plus others who, while not specialists, are knowledgeable about accommodating to such pupils while carrying on regular grade instruction.

SUGGESTIONS FOR STUDENTS AND INSTRUCTOR

1. Acquaint students with the National Theatre of the Deaf (see Stratton, 1976).
2. Arrange for some deaf young adults to visit socially with your class.
3. Have students visit schools in the region that exemplify the full range of educational settings, from residential school to regular school.
4. Arrange for hearing parents of a deaf child to be interviewed by students.
5. Make it possible for students to spend a day assisting a teacher of deaf pupils. Do this in special schools, in special classes, and in full or partial mainstream programs. In the latter, the students can assist both the regular class and the specialist teachers.
6. Set up a demonstration of a psychologist making an assessment of a deaf pupil.
7. Arrange for students to have hearing tests using an individual audiometer.
8. Use swimmers' earplugs, earphones, or muffs to reduce the sound students hear and have them try to converse on unfamiliar topics to obtain some feel for the plight of hearing impaired persons.
9. Ask an otologist or an otolaryngologist and an audiologist to explain their specializations to your students.
10. Suggest that pairs of students join in watching television newscasts with the sound off, then tell each other what they thought was being said. Use a third student to monitor the telecast with sound and to be a judge of the accuracy of the other two. Do the same thing with a soap opera episode.
11. Arrange for students to visit the various community agencies that are organized by or on behalf of persons with hearing impairments and learn about their local objectives and activities.

TOPICAL BIBLIOGRAPHIES

Educational Intervention with Preschool Age Hearing Impaired Children

Connor, L. E. Mainstreaming a special school: Lexington School for the Deaf, NY. *TEACHING Exceptional Children,* 1976, *8,* 76-80.

Kennedy, P., et al. Longitudinal sociometric and cross-sectional data on mainstreaming hearing impaired children: Implications for school programming. *Volta Review,* 1976, *78,* 71-81.

Northcott, W. The integration of young deaf children into ordinary educational programs. *Exceptional Children,* 1971, *38,* 29-32.

Pollack, D., & Ernst, M. Learning to listen in an integrated preschool. *Volta Review,* 1973, *75,* 359-367.

Hearing Impaired Students and Higher Education

Birch, J. W. *Hearing impaired children in the mainstream.* Reston VA: The Council for Exceptional Children, 1975.

Fellendorf, G. W. Hearing impaired graduates of regular schools. *Volta Review,* 1973, *75*(2), 232-255.

Stuckless, E. R., & Enders, M. A study of selected support services for postsecondary deaf students in regular classes. Rochester NY: National Technical Institute for the Deaf, 1971.

History of Education of the Hearing Impaired

Craig, S. B. Fifty years of training teachers of the deaf. *School and Society,* 1942, *56*(1449), 301-303.

Davis, H., & Silverman, S. R. (Eds.). *Hearing and deafness* (3rd ed.). New York: Holt, Rinehart and Winston, 1970.

Kirk, S. A., & Lord, F. E. (Eds.). *Exceptional children: Educational resources and perspectives.* Boston: Houghton Mifflin, 1974.

Assessment and Measurement

Avery, C. B. The education of children with impaired hearing. In W. M. Cruikshank & G. O. Johnson (Eds.). *Education of exceptional children and youth* (3rd ed.). Englewood Cliffs NJ: Prentice-Hall, 1975.

Davis, H., & Silverman, S. R. (Eds.). *Hearing and deafness.* (3rd ed.). New York: Holt, Rinehart and Winston, 1970.

McConnell, F. Children with hearing disabilities. In L. M. Dunn (Ed.). *Exceptional children in the schools.* New York: Holt, Rinehart and Winston, 1973.

Stillman, R. D. *Assessment of deaf-blind children: The Callier Azusa Scale.* Reston VA: The Council for Exceptional Children, 1976.

Modern Elementary and Secondary School Programs for Hearing Impaired Pupils

Avery, C. B. The education of children with impaired hearing. In W. M. Cruikshank & G. O. Johnson (Eds.). *Education of exceptional children and youth* (3rd ed.). Englewood Cliffs NJ: Prentice-Hall, 1975.

Bitter, G. B., & Mears, E. G. Facilitating the integration of hearing impaired children into regular public school classes. *Volta Review,* 1973, *75*(1), 13-22.

Coleman, P. G. et al. Severely hearing impaired child in the mainstream. *TEACHING Exceptional Children,* 1975, *8,* 6-9.

Craig, W. N., & Salem, J. M. Partial integration of deaf with other hearing students. *American Annals of the Deaf,* 1976, *121,* 63-68.

Griffing, B. L. Planning educational programs and services for hard of hearing children. In F. S. Berg & S. G. Fletcher (Eds.). *The hard of hearing child: Clinical and educational management.* New York: Grune & Stratton, 1970.

Hemmings, I. A survey of units for hearing-impaired children in schools for normally-hearing children. *Teacher of the Deaf,* 1972 *70*(416), 455-466.

Nix, G. W. (Ed.). *Mainstream education for hearing impaired children and youth.* New York: Grune & Stratton, 1976.

Northcott, W. The integration of young deaf children into ordinary educational programs. *Exceptional Children,* 1971, *38,* 29-32.

Owsley, P. J. Can a residential school program students into public schools? *Volta Review,* 1973, *75*(1), 28-31.

Salem, J. M. Partial integration at the high school level. *Volta Review,* 1971, 73(1), 42-46.

Strattner, M. J. Deaf and hearing children learn together—An Australian model. *Young Children,* 1974, *29*(4), 321-332.

Yater, V. V. *Mainstreaming of children with a hearing loss: Practical guidelines and implications.* Springfield IL: Charles C Thomas, 1976.

Persons with Hearing Impairments

Burlingame, R. *Out of silence into sound: The life of Alexander Graham Bell.* New York: Macmillan, 1964.

Josephson, N. *Edison, a biography.* New York: McGraw-Hill, 1963.

West, P. *Words for a deaf daughter.* New York: Harper & Row, 1970.

The Hearing Impaired Child's Parents

Dale, D. M. C. *Deaf children at home and at school.* Springfield IL: Charles C Thomas, 1967.

Garrett, C., & Stoval, E. M. A parent's views on integration. *Volta Review,* 1972, *74*(6), 338-344.

Katz, L., Mathis, S. L., & Merrill, E. C., Jr. *The deaf child in the public schools: A handbook for parents of deaf children.* Danville IL: Interstate Printers and Publishers, 1974.

Kroth, R. L. *Communicating with parents of exceptional children.* Denver: Love, 1975.

Kroth, R. L., & Scholl, G. T. *Getting schools involved with parents.* Reston VA: The Council for Exceptional Children, 1978.

Workshop

Ward, M. J., Arkell, R. N., Dahl, H. G., & Wise, J. H. *Everybody counts! A workshop manual to increase awareness of handicapped people.* Reston VA: The Council for Exceptional Children, 1979.

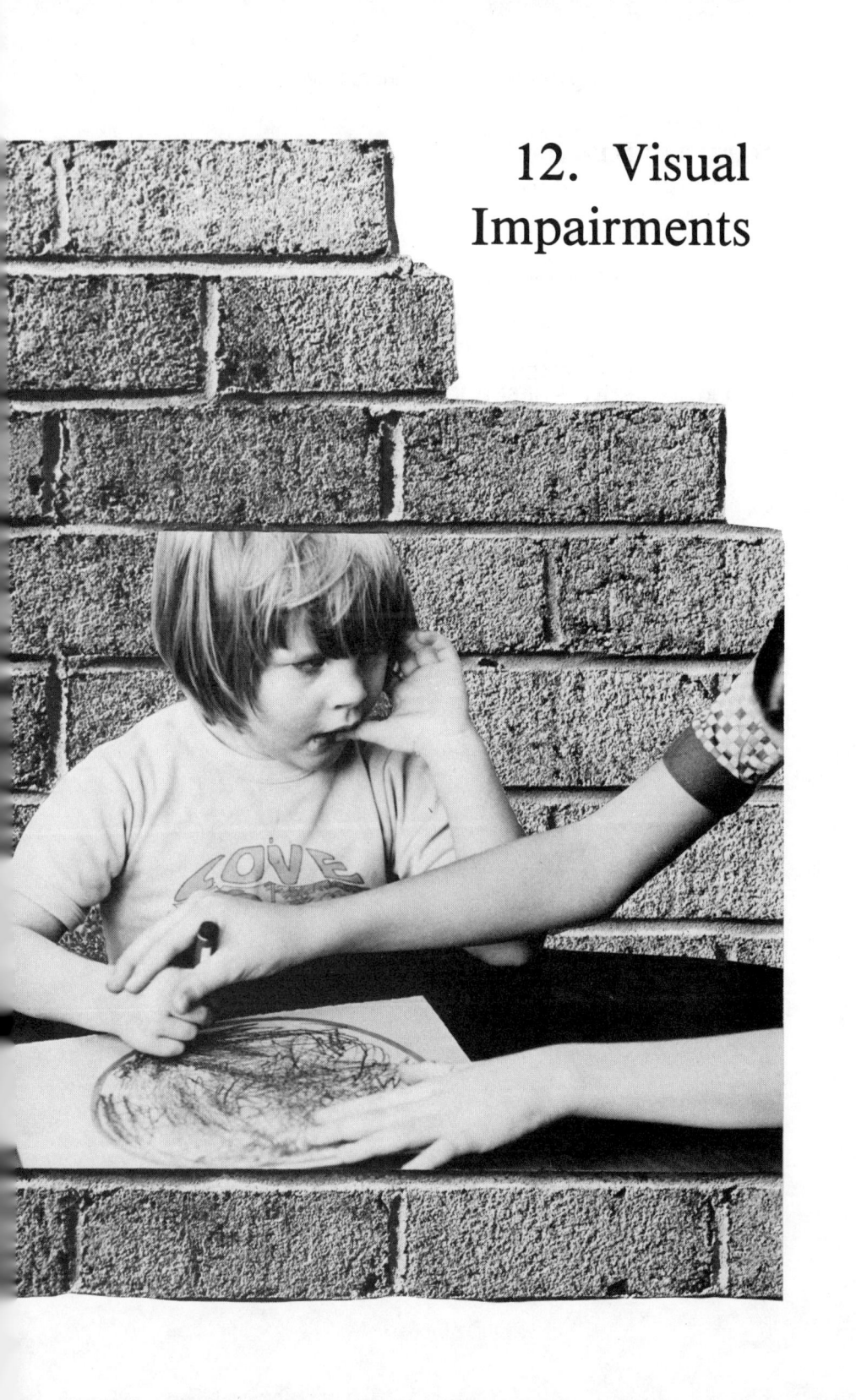

12. Visual Impairments

CHAPTER OUTLINE
THE CHALLENGE TO EDUCATORS
  Legal Considerations
  Medical Considerations
  Social Welfare Considerations
  Educational Considerations
    Case Studies
    Educational Handicaps of Vision Impairments
THE BEGINNING OF SPECIAL EDUCATION FOR STUDENTS WITH VISION IMPAIRMENTS
PRESENT STATUS OF SCHOOL PROGRAMS
THE ROLE OF THE REGULAR CLASS TEACHER
  Teamwork with Specialists
  The Special Teacher of the Vision Impaired Student
  A Case Study
  Some Areas of Concern to Regular Teachers
  Special Supplies, Equipment, and Services
CHARACTERISTICS OF A COMPREHENSIVE EDUCATION PROGRAM
PROSPECTS FOR THE FUTURE
PREVAILING VERSUS PREFERRED PRACTICES
VOLUNTEER ORGANIZATIONS
SUGGESTIONS FOR STUDENTS AND INSTRUCTOR
TOPICAL BIBLIOGRAPHIES

THE CHALLENGE TO EDUCATORS

The odds are increasing that regular class teachers will encounter a student with a severe visual impairment sometime during their careers. Earlier than for most other handicapping conditions, special and regular education teachers demonstrated that by working together they could provide the specialized education needed by students with visual impairments totally within the regular class or with removal for limited periods and purposes. The movement to enroll visually handicapped children in regular classes and to maintain them there with whatever special supports may be needed has spread widely throughout the nation's schools. Thus, it has become increasingly common for regular teachers to know and serve children who have significant visual impairments.

Visual defects occur in about 20% of the general population, but the majority are corrected with prescriptive lenses. Highly significant, noncorrectable visual impairments are found in only about 1 student in 1,000 and only about 3 out of 10 of such visually handicapped children are considered to be blind for educational purposes. A much higher proportion of serious visual impairment is found among older persons, particularly those beyond age 65.

Legal Considerations

In early spring of each year when Americans file federal income reports and pay taxes for the preceding year, they probably notice the spaces on the forms that authorize a special tax exemption for the blind. This is but one of a broad set of categorical provisions made by law for persons who have visual impairments (e.g., special financial aids, services, and exclusive eligibility to conduct certain small businesses, such as snack stands, in large post offices and other public buildings). The major beneficiaries of these provisions are those visually impaired persons who fall within the definition of blindness that is most widely used in this country. The definition is not medical but legal or economic. It was written into the Social Security Act of 1935, primarily for the benefit of aged persons; since then, however, it has become the basis for a broad range of categorical programs.

> Blindness is. . .visual acuity for distant vision of 20/200 or less in the better eye, with best correction; or visual acuity of more than 20/200 if the widest diameter of field of vision subtends an angle no greater than 20 degrees. (National Society for the Prevention of Blindness, 1966, p. 10)

It should be noted that this is strictly a *legal* definition, one that identifies categories or classes of persons for certain legal purposes. When we turn to educational planning or other purposes, the classification problem is totally different.

It is important to note that the legal definition of blindness includes not only persons who are totally blind, that is, unable to distinguish light from dark or with no perception, but those who have some vision—severely visually impaired though it may be—in one or both eyes. By definition, then, the legal term *blindness* is not synonymous with *total blindness*.

In order to establish the eligibility of individuals to participate in the federal-state aid to the blind program, state agencies were required to adopt a definition of visual loss expressed in terms of ophthalmic measurements. Most states, consequently, adopted the Social Security Act definition completely or with more liberal modifications.

The Social Security Act definition is also followed by most other agencies, official or private, that provide aid or services to blind persons, such as eligibility for income tax exemption, talking books from the Library of Congress, special teaching materials (braille and large print) from the American Printing House for the Blind, and state service programs.

The term *partially sighted* is often used for that larger group of individuals whose vision in the best eye after correction is somewhere between 20/70 and 20/200 (legal blindness). The person with 20/70 vision can read at 20 feet printed letters 1¼ inches high; the person with 20/200 vision can read letters 2½ inches high at the same distance. Anyone with 20/400 vision or worse cannot read letters of any size at 20 feet, yet such a person may be able to function as a sighted person educationally by reading pages of normal type at the usual distance, or closer, with the aid of special lenses.

A relatively new legal consideration, affecting persons with vision impairments (see Chapter 1), is that educational institutions and employers who receive federal funds in any form—and most do—may not discriminate against handicapped applicants solely on the basis of the handicap. The law involved is part of the federal government's Rehabilitation Act, particularly section 504 as amended in 1973. In effect, this Act adds the handicapped to the affirmative action agenda, already busy on issues of race and sex discrimination, of almost every school, college, and business establishment of the nation. The details of regulations are just emerging now, but it is likely that the definitions cited here will be used.

Medical Considerations

Physicians are usually concerned about classification of visual impairments according to cause (etiology), prognosis, and possible treatment. Thus, medical classification differs from those of the financial adviser, social worker, or lawyer who may be concerned about legal rights, social services, or financial considerations.

For about a decade following World War II, an unexpectedly large number of young children were found to be suffering from progressively deteriorating vision or blindness; otherwise, the children showed a normal distribution on other traits. These were the retrolental fibroplasia (RLF) victims who, after birth, had been placed in incubators with high oxygen concentrations. Upon removal from the incubators, the immature blood vessels in their eyes gorged, ruptured, and caused blindness. The cause and cure were discovered in 1954 and remedial action followed quickly in most communities. After about 1959, the number of RLF children moving into kindergarten and the primary schools dropped sharply. Many of the RLF sufferers now are young adults who are in advanced phases of their education or seeking employment opportunities.

Currently, visual impairments are increasingly coincident with other impairments so that fully half of the children with impaired vision can be described as multiply handicapped. One probable cause is the medical advances that make it possible to keep alive newborns who have suffered trauma or some type of adversive prenatal influence. Diseases are another important cause. Rubella (German measles), for example, leaves in its wake large numbers of multiply handicapped children, especially when it occurs in women during the first trimester of pregnancy. The last epidemic of rubella in the United States, 1964 to 1966, is estimated to have produced 30,000 children with visual and other concomitant impairments.

Most children with severe multiple handicaps, those who are both blind and deaf or both blind and very slow in cognitive development, for example, are usually served in special school settings. Special units are sometimes established within residential schools or in community settings where a spectrum of specialists can combine their resources to serve these complex children.

For the most part, children with vision impairments who are enrolled in regular school programs present a pattern of normal variations on traits other than in vision. Some of them may be slow in academic progress, some may need help by the speech clinician, some may exhibit worrisome emotional problems, but there is no clear pattern for all.

Most children with severe visual impairments are easily discovered at birth or in infancy. As in the case of many of the handicapping conditions, however, not all are easily detected. Careful observation by parents and examination by physicians are essential in the early years of life, but elementary school teachers can join in watching for such characteristics as the following:

Appearance

Red rimmed eyelids
Swollen eyelids
Crust near lashes
Frequent sties
Red or watery eyes
Eyes in constant motion
Crossed eyes or one eye turning in and the other eye out
Eyes that cross when the child is tired
Eyes with pupils of different sizes

Behavior

Blinks constantly
Rubs eyes often
Tends to have eyes crossed when reading
Tries to brush away blur
Seems overly sensitive to light
Stumbles or trips over objects
Holds book too close or too far away when reading
Frequently changes distance of book from near to far as he reads
Shuts or covers one eye when reading
Tilts head to one side when reading
Screws up face when reading
Frowns when trying to see distant objects
Thrusts head forward in order to see an object
Holds body tense when trying to distinguish distant objects
Becomes inattentive during reading lesson
Reads only brief periods without stopping
Shows reversal tendencies in reading
Tries to guess words from quick recognition of a part of a word in easy reading material
Tends to lose the place on the page
Confuses *o* and *a*; *e* and *c*; *n* and *m*; *h, n,* and *r*; *f* and *t*
Reads less well the longer he tries
Wants to play when he should read
Has short attention span when doing chalkboard, bulletin board, or map work
Shows lack of interest during field trip discussion
Has poor alignment in writing
Cries frequently
Becomes irritable over work
Has frequent temper tantrums (Calovini, undated)

Any child may exhibit one or more of these characteristics or behaviors at different times for different reasons, but when some of the behaviors or signs are present day after day under the same circumstances, the teacher should follow the school procedure for referring the child for an eye examination.

By age 4 or 5, standard screening devices such as adapted Snellen Charts or telebinocular instruments can be used to screen for vision problems. In general, these procedures tend to overrefer, that is, to suggest more problems than will be confirmed by an ophthalmologist. A high rate of false positive (referring more children for examination than have vision problems) is preferable to a large number of false negatives (failing to refer children who actually have significant vision impairments).

In most states and communities, screening programs are conducted cooperatively by schools, health departments, and various voluntary agencies, such as local affiliates of the National Society for the Prevention of Blindness. The importance of effective screening programs cannot be overemphasized. Sometimes the results will not bear heavily on school programs but they will be critical to medical or ocular corrective treatments bearing on the long term health and development of the child.

Social Welfare Considerations

People with vision impairments, particularly those considered to be blind, have been the object of a great many social and welfare programs. A distinction insisted on by some blind persons is between programs *for* and *of* the blind, as in the case of the prestigious American Foundation *for* the Blind, which draws interest and resources from anyone who wishes to join in efforts for improving opportunities for the blind, and the American Council *of* the Blind, an important leadership agency and advocacy group consisting only of blind persons.

Associations of several kinds have been effective at many levels in securing better schooling for children, services for parents, opportunities for both sheltered and competitive employment, public transportation, recreation, legal services and protection, housing, and health services. Leaders in the various associations typically give much time and attention to public education, to improving the general public understanding of the blind, and to advocating for their members before legislatures and other policy making and administrative bodies.

Teachers of children with visual handicaps frequently will have contact with organizations of parents of visually handicapped children who monitor carefully the extent and quality of schooling and other services provided for their children. Another type of common interaction is with volunteer groups who read for blind students or translate into braille the assigned reading materials. In Minnesota and many other states, for example, a strong women's volunteer group has given endless hours of service in "brailling" reading materials for blind students; in addition, they have worked with the state correctional agencies to teach braille skills to female prisoners who then assist in the brailling of school books.

Often, this coalition of a volunteer women's group and imprisoned women to serve handicapped children has led to long lasting supportive relationships for the women when they leave prison.

A particularly important program for preschool children with vision impairments and their parents is offered by welfare agencies. Social workers, employed in or through specialized networks of state and local offices, help to locate and register, at the earliest possible ages, children with significant vision impairments, and then to provide them and their parents with all needed services, such as medical help, parent training, and preparation for schooling. The children of families receiving strong and effective services in their early years have considerably better chances of profiting from schooling later.

Educational Considerations

For educational purposes, the reconsideration of classification is an important matter. As noted earlier (Chapter 2), classification systems must take account of the purposes for which the classifications are made; that is, the classification should be functional. Educationally, children are considered to be blind when they must be taught to read by using braille, the Optacon,* or other means that do not involve sight. Partially sighted students, for educational purposes, are those who have significant vision problems that require some special adjustments in instruction but, nevertheless, can be taught to read print of regular or large size. These classifications are the only two that are educationally functional; they are determined by the pupil's preferred mode of reading.

Deciding whether a child is educationally blind or partially sighted, in the sense of requiring a special mode of reading, is by no means simple. The decision should not be made solely on the basis of a medical report, the legal definition, or an ophthalmic measurement. Some children with visual acuity measuring 20/400 may need braille while others will be able to read clear print quite adequately; the differences among such children are complex.

Whether a particular child is taught to read print or braille may well depend on many factors other than visual acuity, such as intellectual ability, motivation, family support, availability of expert professional help on the use of low vision aids (e.g., magnification devices), competency and attitudes of local teachers, presence of secondary handicaps, preferences of the child and other significant persons, and prognosis for

---

*The Optacon is an instrument that scans print materials electronically and raises the orthographic features. Literally, the print is raised and, hence, can be distinguished and "read" by feel. However, braille is by far the most common form of reading by educationally blind students. Systems using auditory signals transformed from print are being studied but are still in the experimental stages.

improvement or deterioration of vision. Some of the decision variables are characteristics of the child but others are characteristics of the total life situation. Finally, the decision on whether a child needs accommodations for visual impairment in an instructional program may depend on actual trials within the school situation, although even then the child's needs will not be static and the programs planned for the child will require changes with time and experiences.

Case Studies

Consider the following case illustrations. The first is concerned with arranging education for a partially sighted child whose vision is in a period of change; the second case involves a child who has some vision but who will need braille instruction.

Judy. Judy was 8 years old and in the third grade. Judy's teacher asked the special vision teacher to come to the building to help in making plans for Judy. The teacher felt that Judy was not seeing as well this year as last and was beginning to drop back in her school work. After their cooperative study of the child, the two teachers wrote the following report:

Background information. Right eye 20/70, left eye 20/70. Judy had a cataract washout in her left eye a while ago and cannot see in that eye. She also said her eyes ache sometimes. The parents have reported to the teacher that Judy sees the eye doctor regularly and that she will receive a new prescription very soon. They believe the new glasses will improve her vision. She is expected to have surgery on the other eye in January. The teacher finds no evidence of any learning disability. Judy has not been given an individual intelligence test but is believed to be of above average ability.

Evaluation. Although she tried very hard, Judy had a great deal of difficulty in performing most of the functional visual tasks presented at both near and far points. Glare bothered her; she was able to see better when the material was held up at an angle. She claimed both the print in her regular reader and the large type print presented were easy to see. However, she read poorly in both mediums but seemed to have less actual difficulty in *seeing* the large type.

Discussion and recommendations. We can hope that the new prescription and anticipated surgery will help to solve Judy's problems in seeing. However, it is our impression that she can benefit now from the use of a reading stand, perhaps a marker, dark lined paper and at least some of her books in large type. The dilemma of dittos can be solved at the present time by the teacher continuing to darken them.

It is also our impression that difficulty in reading may be caused by the difficulty she is experiencing in seeing and the possible subsequent lack of experience in reading. Hopefully the large type will add encouragement for her to read. Even though it is difficult for her, she should continue to learn to read and to use her eyes.

It should be expected that Judy's ability to see may be inconsistent. If she can see and prefers to use regular materials at times she should be allowed and even encouraged to do so.

Debbie. Debbie, aged 5, is a potential braille student who has been attending a day care center 7 hours a day while her parents work. Following is a portion of a report prepared by the day care center teacher and a special vision teacher of the local public schools who will help plan for Debbie as she enters kindergarten next year.

The center has had a short period of structured kindergarten readiness skills each day. Much time has been given to free play with toys indoors and out, walks to parks and nearby playgrounds, small group activities, and nap time. The school's director ably set the pattern of treating Debbie as a normal child, and this has carried over to the teachers and other children. She has not been pampered or given special privileges.

She is an extremely verbal child and appears to be very capable of learning. She has excellent orientation and mobility skills considering that she apparently has "light perception only" vision.

The many behavioral objectives worked on this year have included the following skills: meaningful language development; object identification, discrimination, and classification; self care; math readiness; sensory listening and smell; and large muscle coordination including running, skipping, jumping, and galloping. In addition, specific skills used in kindergarten such as cutting, pasting, folding, and coloring have been worked on.

Two areas of concern with her are her habit of very frequently rubbing her eyes (even when walking) and a tendency to frequent illnesses. She has taken a long nap each day at Learning Tree.

Recommendations and future plans. First, Debbie will be receiving day care in her neighborhood even after she enters kindergarten. She will be taking the same school bus as the neighborhood children. Second, a vision teacher plans to be in her school two times per week next year which would include time for direct tutoring, preparation of special materials, and interpretation of needs with teacher.

One year later Debbie's kindergarten teacher and the consulting vision teacher made the following report.

The behavioral objectives planned for Debbie this year for the special tutorial sessions included: braille readiness, orientation and mobility, handwriting, self care skills, and classroom maintenance needs.

Debbie completed through Book 14-E in the Lippincott reading readiness series. Appropriate portions from each book were selected, brailled, and read in the resource room. She was also a part of a reading group that emphasized listening skills. Many reading readiness games from the classroom were adapted in braille. She has been able to successfully match, recognize, and recall all of the upper and lower case braille letters and has mastered beginning sounds. She has effectively blended sounds for beginning reading as a part of this series.

Many of the math readiness games from the "Work Jobs" book that were in the kindergarten room were readily adapted in braille and first taught in the resource room and then used in the kindergarten room. The daily calendar program was also prepared in braille as well as experience stories.

Debbie has moved freely within her classroom, to the tutoring rooms, and in the physical education program. She is unafraid and has a keen awareness of herself in space. Self care assistance has been minimal with shoe tying receiving the greatest emphasis. She generally is responsible for her own routine classroom needs.

Manuscript writing of her first name was a goal that was recently attained through the use of a number of tactile aids. Nearly all the craft projects planned by the kindergarten teacher required no special adaptations to be meaningful.

Debbie's mother has been able to attend the meetings planned by the vision team for parents of a young visually impaired child and has applied for Talking Book and braille book services from the regional lending library.

A concern in preschool was frequent illness and tiredness. This was not evidenced this school year.

Recommendations and future plans.

1. Debbie has experienced much success in a unique, challenging year of kindergarten. It would be likely that this will continue in grade 1. She will need the services of a vision teacher on a daily basis. In addition to direct tutoring, additional time will be needed to prepare materials and interpret her needs with her classroom teacher.
2. A successful method "to erase" the habit of eye rubbing has not been found. Debbie is aware of it and is able to talk about it, which may be a start.
3. She evidences a healthy attitude about her impairment but, as would be the case with many other blind children, she needs assistance in interpretation of social situations and awareness of her own social impact.

Educational Handicaps of Vision Impairments

In general, children with vision impairments who are enrolled in regular school programs tend not to have significant complicating or secondary conditions. Their major problem, to put it bluntly, is that they do not see well. Obviously, reduced vision limits their environmental experiences, mobility, spatial orientation, and the acquisition of behaviors that are learned by imitation.

Vision coordinates most of our sensory impressions of the environment around us. Although it is true that children with little or no vision can use their touch and hearing to become familiar with the sound and feel and features of some objects and persons, there is much that cannot be learned just from feel alone, such as a bird in flight, a small insect, colors, different kinds of cars, or the moon and stars, or from sound alone, such as the song of a bird (which tells nothing of its size or coloration), a person's voice (which tells nothing of appearance or behavior), or running footsteps (which could indicate a person fleeing from something or jogging).

We also use sight to acquire concepts by relating the coordinated information received from our senses to the meaning of words. Young sighted children, for example, quickly learn to distinguish between the appearance of a truck and passenger car, a fire engine and a police car or ambulance, and even between the makes of their family's and a neighbor's cars. No one teaches them the concepts of the different vehicles; they develop them from the evidence of their senses and the words for the vehicles. Children without sight may learn to distinguish the sounds of the different vehicles, but they are unable to form the same concepts sighted children have of them.

Because a great deal of a young child's learning is derived from imitation, the blind child cannot see to imitate, for example, smiles, frowns, chewing motions, the placement of feet on stairs, the use of tableware, clapping hands. Children with very low or no vision usually must be taught such behaviors deliberately. Blind children, seldom aware of the possible range of facial expressions and their significance, do not know that they too are capable of expressing emotions facially. Thus, blind children's faces tend to be immobile, to be "silent," not because they lack feeling or are not responding, but because their learning has been limited. Furthermore, blind children do not learn by imitation that they should turn their heads to look at a speaker or to speak to someone; without explicit teaching to move their heads, blind children may give the erratic impression of speaking to space.

The lack of environmental stimulation leads young blind children to develop what are known as "blindisms," that is, forms of self stimulation, such as turning the head rapidly, rocking back and forth, or poking their eyes with their fingers. Most blindisms decrease with age, however. Young children with only light perception will often "light play," that is, they will look directly at a light source while they move their hands and fingers back and forth very close to their eyes. Unfortunately, sighted persons who do not understand the reasons for the behaviors are often disturbed by them and sometimes misinterpret them as evidence of emotional disturbance.

While blind children display the same range of mental and emotional disturbances as other children, they tend to be free of personality problems on the whole.

Partially sighted persons, perhaps because they bestride the worlds of both the seeing and the blind, "tend to be less well-adjusted than either the blind or the seeing" (Lowenfeld, 1973, p. 55). In a way, they are subject to frustrations that are unknown to the sighted and the blind. Although they have sight, seeing requires effort and strain and may be efficient under some circumstances but not others. Such persons, for example, may be able to see very well at close range; yet, they may not be able to stand close enough to read a street sign or the name of an approaching bus; if their fields of vision are very limited, they may give the impression of confusion as they try to integrate bit by bit all the information in a new environment; and if they have difficulty with light, they may be blinded on entering a brightly lighted noisy room or unable to read the menu in a darkened restaurant, for example.

It is not uncommon for partially seeing children with very low vision to be misunderstood because of slow reactions or confused responses to some environments. In a brightly lighted, noisy cafeteria, a new classroom, or a room in which the furniture has been moved about, or on a sunny playground where running children and shadows blur and shift, for example, partially seeing children may have difficulty organizing their perceptions of what is around them. Their slowness, a response to a situation that is not visually clear, may be interpreted as a sign of mental retardation when adults are unthinking and impatient, and the interpretation may lead to depriving the children of help they need. More importantly, the interpretation may result in an educational program that is inappropriate for the child.

Visually impaired children, whether blind or partially seeing, may be additionally handicapped by the emotional attitudes and misconceptions of the adults in their environment. The limitations of a visual impairment and the reactions of adults to the limitations sometimes combine to slow the social-emotional maturation of the blind or partially seeing child. If these children seem immature, it may be because they have not had as wide a range of experiences as other children. They may have been held back from what are considered normal developmental experiences by their lack of vision, fears, or the fears of parents or teachers. Sometimes too little is expected of visually impaired children in terms of achievement or social behavior; the result may be that they have not developed a concept of themselves or a set of behaviors that are suitable for their age group.

The fairest and most accurate statement about children with visual impairments is that they vary greatly. They are not all of a kind; they cannot be described in terms of averages or norms, and no common set of expectations can be made for them. They need and deserve to be known individually.

THE BEGINNING OF SPECIAL EDUCATION FOR STUDENTS WITH VISION IMPAIRMENTS

Prior to the 18th century, handicapped children and primarily those with visual impairments, were generally regarded in Western societies as marked by divine displeasure. Frequently, they were the victims of massive neglect because, in part, they tended to be concentrated among the poor and, in part, it was widely believed that they could be neither educated nor trained. It was not uncommon for such children to be set adrift by their families during hard times; if the children were fortunate, they became wards of charitable institutions.

Valentin Haüy, remembered in France as the father and apostle of the blind, experimented with the training of a blind boy and discovered that he could be taught to read embossed letters. In 1784, Haüy courageously opened a school with 12 blind pupils in Paris and proved his educational methods. Subsequently, he established comparable schools in Russia and Germany, and by the end of the first decade of the 19th century, schools for the blind were flourishing in almost every European country. Within another two decades, the movement spread to the United States. During the years 1832 and 1833, three private schools for the blind were founded: the New England Asylum for the Blind (later, the Perkins Institute and Massachusetts Asylum for the Blind), the New York Institution for the Blind, and the Pennsylvania Institution for the Instruction of the Blind.

Although the pattern of residential schools for the education of blind children was solidified as the various states established publicly supported institutions, the shortcomings of such schools were generally recognized.

Residential schools continued to be the primary mode for the education of blind children until well into this century and they continue to have importance even into the 1970's. It is important to recognize that residential institutions were a natural response to a social problem not a response to the developmental needs of children. However, as carefully coordinated parts of a total system for education of children with visual impairments they have important functions to perform.

Haüy's experiments with embossed letters led to a number of attempts to refine his system. For blind readers, the plethora of methods limited their access to books until the worldwide adoption of the braille system. Louis Braille (1809-1852) was blinded at the age of 3 and became first a pupil and then an instructor at the Institution des Jeunes Aveugles in

Paris. There he developed the system of embossed writing that bears his name. Essentially, braille is a code based on a cell of three embossed dots in each of two vertical rows. By varying the placement and number of dots in each row, braille provides all the letters of the alphabet and the numbers 1 through 10 (the letters *a* through *j*). Additional variations of placement and added cells permit the notation of all punctuation signs and the end of communications. Braille is read by passing finger tips across the braille figure in left to right order, as in sight reading.

As it is used in the United States today, braille consists of two forms: full spelling (English Braille Grade 1) and contracted braille; the latter consists of the first form plus 189 contractions and short-form words and is known as English Braille. The alphabet and numbers 1 through 10 are illustrated in Figure 12-1.

FIGURE 12-1
The Braille Alphabet and Numbers

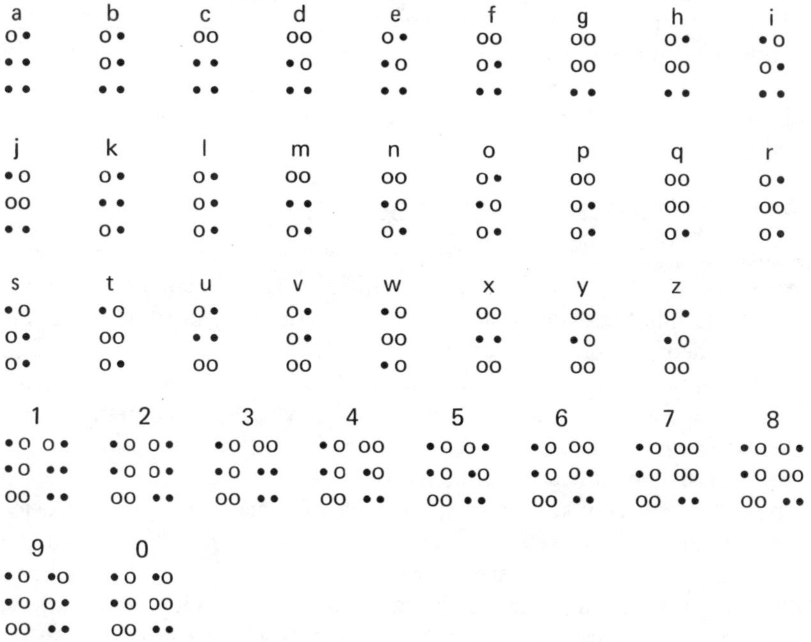

a	b	c	d	e	f	g	h	i
o●	o●	oo	oo	o●	oo	oo	o●	●o
●●	o●	●●	●o	●o	o●	oo	oo	o●
●●	●●	●●	●●	●●	●●	●●	●●	●●

j	k	l	m	n	o	p	q	r
●o	o●	o●	oo	oo	o●	oo	oo	o●
oo	●●	o●	●●	●o	●o	o●	oo	oo
●●	o●	o●	o●	o●	o●	o●	o●	o●

s	t	u	v	w	x	y	z
●o	●o	o●	o●	●o	oo	oo	o●
o●	oo	●●	o●	oo	●●	●o	●o
o●	o●	oo	oo	●o	oo	oo	oo

1	2	3	4	5	6	7	8
●o o●	●o o●	●o oo	●o oo	●o o●	●o oo	●o oo	●o o●
●o ●●	●o o●	●o ●●	●o ●o	●o ●o	●o o●	●o oo	●o oo
oo ●●	oo ●●	oo ●●	oo ●●	oo ●●	oo ●●	oo ●●	oo ●●

9	0
●o ●o	●o ●o
●o o●	●o oo
oo ●●	oo ●●

World War II was a watershed in the education of the blind. Veterans who lost their sight in the services refused to resign themselves to lives of sheltered inactivity. They demanded training in mobility and orientation so that they could maintain broad contacts in their communities; and they sought out vocational training that would equip them for lives of economic independence. At the Hines Veterans' Hospital near Chicago, mobility and orientation techniques were developed and soon veterans were in training there. Orientation training* (to help in maintaining sense of direction and place) and mobility training (e.g., the use of white cane techniques—tapping ahead of oneself to check for elevation change and obstructions) were essential to independent life in the community. Intensive training for independence spread to other veterans' facilities and then into the training of teachers. Pioneers such as Georgie Lee Abel and Katherine Gruber, then of the American Foundation for the Blind, led the way in spreading the developments into teacher preparation centers and schools during the 1950's so that visually impaired children could begin to profit from the new techniques.

In schools for the blind, the excesses of basket weaving and piano tuning paraphernalia began to be shunted into storerooms and broader programs for vocational education were organized. And in an increasing number of communities, the regular schools began opening the richness of regular classes, shops, and laboratories to visually impaired students. Most important, perhaps, the veterans and their advocates helped to change attitudes toward, and to open up new vistas on, the potentialities of visually handicapped persons. There is still much distance to go before blind and partially sighted students are well understood and well educated.

PRESENT STATUS OF SCHOOL PROGRAMS

Currently, school programs for students with visual handicaps are organized in a variety of ways. In a qualified way, they can be summarized by the familiar cascade of administrative arrangements (see Figure 12-2). The students enrolled in regular classes and schools with little or no special support (Level 1, Figure 12-2) tend to be the older ones who have had excellent earlier instruction and who have achieved a high degree of self sufficiency. The service continuum shows the various instructional and environmental arrangements that can be organized to meet the individual needs of students with a range of visual impairments. At least two qualifications need to be mentioned, however, in interpreting the cascade; they tell of mixed forms of service. First, many residential schools have come to serve as day schools for their communities or regions as well. Second, increasingly students who are domiciled at residential schools actually go from their residence into nearby community day school programs. Because of these, the meaning of the cascade has changed considerably in recent years.

---

*Specialists who teach orientation and mobility to the blind are sometimes called peripatologists.

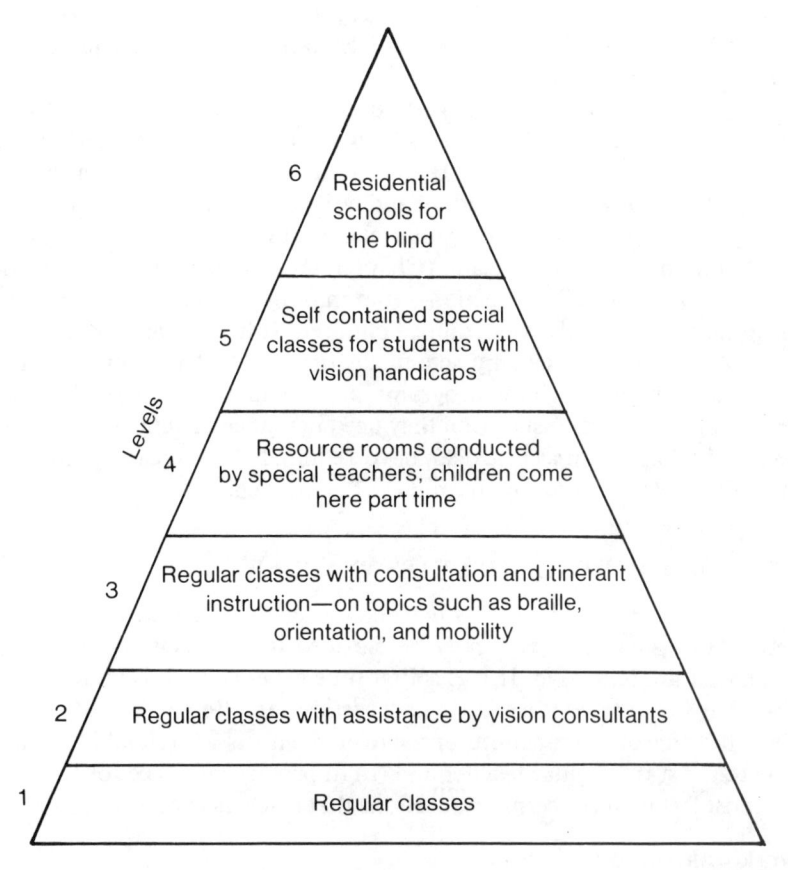

FIGURE 12-2
Cascade of Services for Vision Handicapped Students

- 6: Residential schools for the blind
- 5: Self contained special classes for students with vision handicaps
- 4: Resource rooms conducted by special teachers; children come here part time
- 3: Regular classes with consultation and itinerant instruction—on topics such as braille, orientation, and mobility
- 2: Regular classes with assistance by vision consultants
- 1: Regular classes

All levels and varieties of service delivery have value and should be available as alternatives in a community, region, or state. A child may require a number of different services over the entire period of schooling. For example, at the primary school level a child may need extensive help from a resource teacher who can provide intensive instruction in braille; later on, the student may need only occasional itinerant services to develop and maintain compensatory skills; and for brief occasional periods the student may need to go to the residential school for intensive instruction in daily living skills and for experience with other blind persons with whom models for learning and adjustment can be shared.

However, the place where education is provided is far less important than the quality of the instruction. It has been demonstrated clearly that much of the specialized instruction formerly offered to students only in specialized environments can be brought down the cascade from isolated centers and into the regular school environment. The area of vision impairment was one of the earliest to demonstrate that the necessary specialized skills usually can be taught in regular classrooms or by cooperative arrangements, and that the children can be maintained in regular classrooms most of the time.

Only a decade or two ago, it was not uncommon in many states to see blind and partially sighted students almost automatically referred to and placed in residential schools. However, a countertrend has grown to bring instruction in braille reading and writing and other special subjects into the resource rooms and regular classrooms of community schools. Thus, the instructional cascade (Chapter 1)—the moving down on the cascade of specialized instruction—is exemplified to a high degree in the programing of visually handicapped children. It has become the prevailing practice in a great many school districts to start visually impaired children in regular school programs and to maintain them there by delivering the special instruction they need in that environment or nearby resource rooms. These practices have required the increasing involvement of regular teachers in programing for these children.

THE ROLE OF THE REGULAR CLASS TEACHER

It is not uncommon for regular teachers, when they first learn that a student with visual handicaps may be enrolled in their classrooms, to be somewhat apprehensive. If it is a first time experience, it is understandable that they are concerned. In this section, an attempt is made (a) to describe some of the functions of the team members who should be available to assist the regular teacher and (b) to provide guidance for some of the most frequent concerns or questions that teachers express.

Teamwork with Specialists

In addition to school principals, counselors, psychologists, speech clinicians, and remedial teachers who frequently team up with regular teachers, some other personnel are likely to be involved in specific ways that relate to vision impairments when a student with such problems is enrolled in the regular class. The roles of specialists may vary considerably from community to community, and the places where they work may vary, but their functions are likely to include common elements. The special teacher of the vision impaired, especially, tends to provide a common set of skills and expertise in all school systems.

The Special Teacher of the Vision Impaired Student

Teachers who are prepared in specialized training programs and certified for instruction of visually impaired students may be employed as consultants, itinerant teachers, resource teachers, or teachers in specialized settings; they also may serve in supervision and administrative roles. Regular teachers can expect vision teachers:

1. To provide special materials, such as braille, large print and recorded materials, braille writers, typewriters, braille slates, and magnifiers.
2. To help develop proper use of special equipment (such as those listed above and others, such as the abacus, special maps, tape recorder, and records).
3. To assist in the assessment of students and to make referrals for further studies, as needed.
4. To monitor general progress and specific problems and needs as each student with visual handicaps proceeds through the school program.
5. To participate in team planning sessions.
6. To advise and counsel parents and teachers.
7. To organize reader and brailling services.
8. To teach students in orientation, mobility, and the use of residual vision.

An especially informative study of the functions of the itinerant teacher or teacher consultant of children with visual handicaps has been reported recently from Pennsylvania (Moore & Peabody, 1976). Participating in the study were 66 teachers serving children from preschool through secondary schools; on the average they were serving about 19 students each. The following functional description of a typical itinerant teacher in Pennsylvania provides a rough summary of the working day of the specialist most likely to be teaming with regular teachers on behalf of visually handicapped children.

> In an average week, the teacher spends 19¼ hours in direct instruction of children, 1½ hours consulting with regular classroom teachers, 2¼ hours in procurement and construction of materials, 2 hours in consultation with parents, other professional personnel, volunteers or community agencies, 2½ hours in administrative duties (reports, meetings, etc.) or collecting information on referrals, and 5¼ hours driving in addition to driving to the first school in the mornings and home from the last school in the afternoons.
>
> The teacher is serving children in an area considered to be predominantly suburban-urban. Most referrals come from school nurses, classroom teachers and principals. Services which are available to the children and parents, in addition, include psychological testing, remedial reading services, vocational counseling, and perhaps social work counseling. The teacher is responsible for the procurement of materials for the children with whom he/she works.
>
> Nineteen children are on the teacher's total caseload and the teacher collects medical information and information from school records, such as age, grade, and/or reading level, for all of them. Eleven of these children are elementary visual learners, six are secondary learners, one is

either a pre-school visual learner, or a severely multihandicapped visual learner who is in another special program, and one is a non-visual learner, most probably at the secondary level. Only thirteen of these children require regular service; eight of the elementary visual learners, four of the secondary visual learners, and the one non-visual learner. Six children are visited infrequently during the year for checking only.

For all eight of the elementary visual learners who require regular service, the teacher consults with the classroom teacher and school nurse; assesses visual functioning of the child, and interprets medical information and visual functioning of the child to the regular classroom teacher. . .*

Had conference with teacher on needs of a new visually handicapped student entering her class. (Effective)

Was unable to be at a school when teacher was available for conference. (Ineffective)

Had conference with teacher on uses of large print under certain conditions. (Effective)

Was unable to convince administrator of the total facets of the program. (Ineffective)

Had conference with student and teacher on completion of daily assignments. (Effective)

Tried to interpret medical form for partially seeing sixth grade student for principal. (Ineffective)

The teacher observes seven of these children in the school classroom and consults with the principal and parents. . .

Had home visit with mother to reassure her and explain school program; results changed child's feelings and he improved in school. (Effective)

Tried to convince school district that a child should be brought home from residential school even over parents' protests. (Ineffective)

Had conference with mother on kinds of behaviors that would be expected of her child as he changed from an elementary classroom to a large junior high. (Effective)

Advised parents not to have their first grader learn braille until absolutely necessary in spite of doctor's recommendation; two years later child is still doing well with large print. (Effective)

Could not get teachers to accept same quality of work from students as from normal students. (Ineffective)

---

*Italicized statements were taken from teachers' reported "effective" and "ineffective" Critical Incidents as classified in an earlier study.

Was unable to show school personnel and parents of slow learner who has repeated twice that child should not be placed two years ahead because of physical maturity; she could not do work and now is being taken out of school each afternoon for vision retraining at a hospital. (Ineffective)

The teacher assesses the reading skills and teaches reading to five of the children. . .

Made evaluation of student; discovered she was well below her level and placed her in a special reading class. (Effective)

Worked with student at school district's insistence although girl did not want any help and resented being taken from class. (Ineffective)

Examined picture of a rainbow with a partially seeing fifth grader who could not see a real one and whose reading assignment required her knowing what one was. (Effective)

Could not motivate second grader during a reading lesson. (Ineffective)

The teacher, in addition, locates and procures materials and assesses and teaches listening skills to four of these children. . .

Prepared copies of poorly done ditto sheets for a partially-seeing student to use. (Effective)

Supplied books which were never unwrapped. (Ineffective)

Obtained books for student as extra reading in science. (Effective)

Delivered books and materials during week prior to first day of school. (Effective)

Delivered large print book which was not used because copyright was different; book contained only slight differences in text. (Ineffective)

Ordered large print books for student at M.D.'s recommendation; student refused to use them. (Ineffective)

Taught listening lessons, use of tape recorder, and notetaking. (Effective)

Obtained copy of large print achievement test which teacher had had the partially seeing student take in regular print. (Ineffective)

Three of these children also require assessment of mathematic skills and teaching in mathematics, assessment of study skills, social skills and independence in travel. For these three, the teacher also consults with the school psychologist and provides guidance toward personal and social adjustment. . .

Provided reinforcement in working simple math problems to a visually-hearing impaired slow learner. (Effective)

Worked with child only once a week on math; attribute lack of success to working with child only once a week. (Ineffective)

Helped clarify some conceptual problems relating to math of a second grader. (Effective)

Accompanied class on a field trip and described sights to the visually handicapped student in the class. (Effective)

Took child for walk to see things and play with bugs, leaves, seeds, etc. (Effective)

Tested student with Slosson test; hadn't been done for six years. (Effective)

Provided alternative materials to a ditto sheet emphasis in math study. (Effective)

Worked with uncooperative student twice a week for one hour at insistence of school district. (Ineffective)

One of the children, in addition, requires instruction in utilization of low vision, preparation of special materials, and instruction in study skills (use of library, readers, recordings, etc.) and motor skills.

Arranged for partially seeing student to use films and remote control projector for supplementary materials. (Effective)

Enlarged typing drills on 3M transparencies for use by several students with an overhead projector. (Effective)

Had English book done in large type. (Ineffective)

Used playing ball to improve eye-hand coordination. (Effective)

For all of the secondary visual learners, the teacher collects medical information, consults nurses, guidance counselors and classroom teachers. . .

Had conference with guidance counselor in junior high on services to be provided for a new partially seeing student. (Effective)

Discussed personal Army experiences with a junior high counselor. (Ineffective)

Worked with teacher who taught students as a class, not as individuals. (Effective)

Observed gradual visual loss in student; referred student for eye exam through parents—detached retina. (Effective)

The teacher, for at least three and perhaps four of the children who required regular service, suggests environmental modifications, (seating arrangement, lighting, etc.) to the regular classroom teacher, assesses visual functioning, consults with the principal or other administrator, and locates and procures material. . .

Worked with guidance counselors and teachers to alert them to problems of a visually handicapped student and to enlarge materials he would need. (Effective)

Presented partially seeing student with large print books in front of some of her classmates; she refused them—she didn't want the others to see them. (Ineffective)

Recommended use of talking books by student for supplementary work in history. (Effective)

Ordered and delivered books to student who then refused to use them. (Ineffective)

The teacher observes two of these youngsters in the school setting, assesses study skills and provides guidance toward personal and social adjustment...

Taught student how to write friendly letter and to address envelope. (Effective)

Tried to get mentally ill high school student to go to Mental Hygiene where he had been previously referred. (Ineffective)

Taught personal typing to partially seeing student and noted attitude change. (Effective)

Had several discussions with a high school student about drugs and alcohol. (Effective)

Answered questions on birth control asked by a 16 year old partially seeing girl about to be married. (Effective)

Was forced to go over homework with student when what he needed was remedial work. (Ineffective)

Read to student without knowing purpose of assignment. (Ineffective)

Served as sounding board to relieve student's emotional, social and educational problems. (Effective)

For one child, in addition, the teacher assesses listening ability, social skills and reading performance, teaches study skills and teaches the child about vocational opportunities, after consultation with the school psychologist.

Helped student to decide to attend the vocational technical school. (Effective)

Failed to convince student to stay in school and school to let student in vo-tech curriculum. (Ineffective)

Arranged for another student in vocational rehab to discuss advantages of rehab program with student in high school who had rejected being referred and receiving services. (Effective)

Made referrals to Bureau of Visually and Physically Handicapped. (Effective)

For the one secondary non-visual learner, the teacher collects medical information, locates and procures materials, consults with the classroom teacher, vocational counselor, nurse, guidance counselor, principal and parents...

Had teacher-principal conference to persuade them to include blind student in spring fashion show. (Effective)

Had conference with administration to arrange for admission of a blind student into a technical school computer programming course. (Effective)

Brailled history test for student who was made exempt from final. (Ineffective)

Arranged for administration of College Boards for 11th grader braille student—involved conferences with counselor, principal, and proctor. (Effective)

Encouraged blind student to submit her poems to a national children's magazine—published. (Effective)

Failed to convince "newly blinded" adolescent she needed to learn braille. (Ineffective)

Gave materials to volunteer along with directions as to format; work was not done properly and had to be redone. (Ineffective)

The teacher also assesses independence in travel and social skills, arranges for readers, and teaches the child the use of tangible aids and how to independently acquire materials...

Arranged for braille student to have reader service to prepare her for debate team; did some research myself for student and brailled information for her use. (Effective)

Provided tangible aids to a blind geometry student but teacher moved not to use them. (Ineffective)

Used cut-out figures with blind student to teach geometric shapes and their superimposition. (Effective)

Felt ineffective in trying to help blind student create graph for required problems. (Ineffective)

For the one child who may be in a pre-school or in a program for severely multihandicapped children, the teacher will, on a regular basis, observe the child in the school setting, assess visual functioning, consult with the parents and classroom teacher and interpret medical information and visual functioning, and suggest environmental modifications to the classroom teacher...

Tried to suggest projects for a teacher to use with a non-verbal very active partially seeing boy in a trainable class. (Effective)

Could not make trainable parents of trainable child understand my purpose in coming to talk with them. (Ineffective)

Used counting frame to teach blind retarded homebound boy about money; frame became toy; should have used money. (Ineffective)

> *Devised system of using poker chips as money to reward retarded blind child for his success in working two place addition problems. (Effective)*
>
> *Gave guidance department of a school district a push to get their mentally retarded student in vocational technical school despite his first rejection by the vocational technical school. (Effective)*

In addition to these regular services, the teacher will, on an infrequent basis, review referral materials, periodically review children not requiring regular services, make referrals to appropriate persons for auxiliary service needed for the children, review placement of children in other programs, and participate in recommendations for placement of children in other programs. Perhaps she/he may, very occasionally, conduct in-service programs for school personnel or make speeches for community organizations such as Lions Club, Kiwanis, etc.

> *Set up program with town women's club to provide social enrichment for blind students. (Effective)*
>
> *Tried to find student who moved five times in seven weeks. (Ineffective)*
>
> *Arranged for local Lion's Club to purchase a tape recorder I had recommended for a needy blind student in high school. (Effective)*
>
> *Gave opinion on placement of a second grader—fail him; child repeated, improved, and no longer is on program. (Effective)*
>
> *Spent time evaluating first grader whose visual acuity was later to be reported as 20/40. (Ineffective)*
>
> *Talked a youngster and his parents into submitting to surgery which they previously had avoided and thereby helped a child see well enough to go off program. (Effective)*
>
> *Spoke to class on blindness at teacher's request. (Effective)*
>
> *Arrived at school to discover my student was absent. (Ineffective)*
>
> *Typed and composed letters which could have been done by a secretary. (Ineffective)* (Moore & Peabody, 1976, pp. 56-64)

A Case Study

Georgeann, a 13 year old student with both a severe visual impairment and some orthopedic problems, had been assisted through a full year by regular teachers and a consulting vision teacher. The following summary report, written by the vision teacher, will illustrate some of the kinds of day by day activities this involves.

> The objectives in the academic areas for Georgeann included the following: Effective use of slate and stylus, introduction to Grade III braille, typing, review of abacus, writing her signature, writing and evaluating her own short term educational goals, and interpretation of maps, charts, graphs. Time was also spent learning to listen and learning to consistently use conversational posture.

She practiced taking timed dictation on the slate and stylus. Her speed and efficiency have improved to the point that she can use the slate and stylus for note taking. While working on the slate and stylus some Grade III braille was introduced. After learning several of the short forms in Grade III she began making up her own abbreviations and stated that her own method was just as effective. Formal instruction in Grade III braille can be continued if she desires. At this time she does not see the need. Since Georgeann can use the slate and stylus effectively with her own techniques, continuing formal instruction is not essential.

Georgeann types most of her work for the classroom teacher. Her speed, format and accuracy are acceptable. She was having difficulty in using quotation marks and knowing when to indent for paragraphs. These problems have been resolved, and various typing formats were reviewed over the year.

She can set up and work math problems including problems with fractions on the abacus. She did need a short review on the procedure for setting up multiplication and division problems. The concept of place value as it relates to fractions, percentages, and decimals is confusing to her and she is now working on it in math.

She can write her name in cursive form within the signature guide and she can use the check template. She has used the raised letters from the Optacon and identifies them easily.

A United States atlas and an African atlas have been provided for her. One hour was spent reviewing the keys to the atlas and she now uses them independently.

Georgeann has gone through tape 16 in the "Listening Improvement Series No. 789." Excerpts from texts were read to her and she identified the facts and opinions in each passage. Together we have gone through several exercises in Academics III and IV from the listening activities file. Her listening skills within a group seem to have improved.

Everyone in the class sets his own goals. At the beginning of the year Georgeann began setting up weekly goals for herself. At first they were very broad and very difficult to accomplish in a week's time. Through work in her accountability group Georgeann's goals have become more directed. She now puts her goals on a time table for the week and is much more successful in accomplishing them.

She has received three hours of orientation and mobility evaluation and/or instruction per week for two months.

The evaluation found a very dependent student capable of travel only inside the classroom or home. To get around in the school building required sighted assistance. This travel was also found to be extremely slow and inefficient.

This evaluation found that the full range of orientation and mobility will be necessary over the next several years if she wants to be able to travel outside routes with complex intersections, etc. A complete course of instruction requires approximately 250 hours of sequential and intensive instruction.

This instructor recommends continued orientation and mobility instruction through the summer. Instruction will need to continue during the school years or until she can master the skills and travel commensurate with her travel abilities and attitudes.

Recommendations for next year. Direct service by the vision teacher three or more times a week.

1. She will need assistance in the classroom maintenance and material preparation. At least at the beginning of the year the vision teacher will need to discuss weekly goals with her and encourage her to set her goals for the quarter at an earlier date. She needs encouragement to follow through on her quarterly goals.
2. She has had difficulty with some math concepts and as something new is introduced she may need some assistance in interpreting it.
3. She will need help in orientation and mobility over the summer and next year as indicated above.

The regular class and special teachers may come into contact with the following people and should be familiar with each specialty: The *ophthalmologist* is a physician who, in addition to basic preparation in medicine, has undertaken special studies and qualifies as a specialist in problems of the eyes. The *optometrist* is a specialist who is trained in optics, measurements of visual functions, and prescribing corrective lenses; he also may be able to prescribe low vision aids (magnifiers) and training in their use. The *braillist* is a person, sometimes an employee of the school and sometimes a volunteer, who prepares necessary school materials in braille form for use by blind students. Much commercial school material is available in braille and more is provided through the American Printing House for the Blind; but there are always needs for help in producing materials needed in a specific local context.

Some Areas of Concern to Regular Teachers

As soon as regular teachers become aware that a student with visual impairment will come to their class a partnership should be established with the vision teacher to learn about any special adjustments in program and special equipment that may be required and to make general plans.

An early concern—in the case of blind children—will be introducing them to the spaces and places they must know. It may be helpful to take a bit of extra time at the beginning to walk with the children through the routes to be traveled to various parts of the classroom and around the school areas to which they must travel, such as lavatories, exits, shops, gym, lunchroom, special rooms, and the principal's office. Special alerts should be given to obstructions and danger points, such as drinking fountains and staircases. Visually impaired children will need to be alerted when changes are made in the routes or in room arrangements. The special vision teacher will consult and assist in orientation activities and often will offer direct instruction on the use of the white cane and other mobility activities, but much can be done without difficulty by regular teachers.

In travel and orientation and in all other activities the aim is for independence. Once the child has formed a cognitive map of the school and made a good start on independent travel, it is important to expect consistent independent performance. Overprotection is a great disfavor.

As soon as possible the child should travel even outside the school in an independent way, using the same means of transportation as other children of the building. There have been occasions when all children with visual impairments were carried to school in private taxis or by special buses and occasionally this may still be required; but, in general, such arrangements are not necessary and should be minimized.

Students with vision impairments need vigorous physical activities as part of their school program, just as other students do, unless there are special reasons for limiting activities for health reasons. The vision teacher will be able to suggest ways of integrating the child into regular physical education activities and some of the adaptations that can be made. It is important for students to learn the rules of common games—even those they may not engage in regularly—and the principles of fair play.

It will be helpful if one place can be provided where the child can store necessary special equipment and remove it for use as needed. Taking care of the equipment and storing it carefully and consistently should be the child's responsibility.

Teachers who face their first experience with a child who has severe visual impairments will often be apprehensive about the attitudes of the other children. Will they be unkind or overprotective? The best prediction is that the "other" children will carry the same attitudes into their relationships with the child who has vision problems as they observe in the behavior of the teacher. Children tend to be realistic; they enjoy helping a classmate who genuinely needs help but they dislike dependency. The teacher can help them to understand their new classmate by giving them facts about the situation, including causes of and the nature of the child's impairment and of the special materials and equipment that may be used.

In general, standards of behavior, classroom duties and privileges, and work assignments should be the same for the child with vision impairments as for all others. The regular teacher may wish to help other teachers in the building understand what the expectations are. Grading need not be a special concern either. Hopefully, all children will receive individualized instruction according to their developmental needs; in such a context, the child with visual impairments need not be nearly so "different" as first anticipated.

Few changes in curriculum are required specifically because of vision impairment, although it is necessary sometimes to use special materials (e.g., large print books or braille materials). It may be necessary to devise special substitutes for "visuals," but the vision teacher can help with this. Fellow students are also quite ingenious in designing substitutes for "visuals," for example, use of string diagrams (string glued to paper) to replace visual mathematical charts. It may be necessary to use a special reader service, volunteers who read (directly to the student or on audio tapes) for the student. If a student uses braille, the vision teacher assigned to work with the regular teacher—and possibly a specially trained aide or volunteer—will help to prepare assignments and tests and translate the student's braille responses. Some regular teachers begin to learn braille, perhaps reading it visually rather than by touch, but it's not a necessity that braille be mastered by them.

What has been said of the regular school program can be said as well of the extracurricular program of the school. With careful preplanning and a few modifications, the student with visual impairments can profit from every type of activity: field trips, student government, debate, music, publications, athletics, and others.

Often there are special scheduling needs to be faced, so that the vision teacher can offer the specialized instruction the student might need. Quite often school systems offer special intensive training programs in summer months on braille, orientation, and mobility and thus avoid excessive interruption of the regular flow of school work during the academic year.

It may be advisable to ask one or two other students to take responsibility for assisting the student with visual impairments in case of emergency. For example, although most students with vision problems can perform quite adequately in fire drills or emergencies, it may be wise to have a special arrangement for assistance if needed. Teachers will wish to check their liability coverage for emergency situations and for regular school activities that have dangerous aspects, but there need be no serious problems on this count.

Does it all really work? Usually progress is quite adequate. Indeed, programs in regular schools for children with vision impairments frequently become the source of feelings of great pride and satisfaction by teachers, administrators, and parents. But, of course, the story is not always one of unmixed progress. Appraisal must go on constantly and when difficulties occur, changes are indicated. Even with best efforts, problems sometimes mount to serious proportions and a major change in program may be required. Perhaps, for a time, a program outside of the regular classroom will be required.

Special Supplies, Equipment, and Services

A variety of specialized equipment is used in the schooling of handicapped students. There follow a brief description and discussion of some of the more common items that are used with students who have vision impairments.

Large print books are used with children whose partial sight is of such a nature that they cannot read ordinary print but can discriminate larger letters and words. In general, there is a tendency to underestimate the child's ability to read ordinary print. Large books are a considerable inconvenience and, therefore, should be used sparingly. With experience in reading, a student's dependence on large print usually lessens.

Because braille calculation processes in mathematics are long and slow, the *abacus* is useful for blind pupils. It speeds math processes. Sighted children also enjoy using the abacus.

The *braille writer* is a special device, somewhat smaller than an ordinary typewriter, that is used to produce braille print by mechanical processes. Basically, it consists of a spacing bar and six keys that correspond to the six dots of the braille cell; the keys can be pressed simultaneously in any combination to produce the desired cell constellation. It is commonly used by blind persons early in elementary schools and as a continuing aid through school and life.

The *slate and stylus* are the equivalent for blind pupils of the tablet and pencil for sighted persons. The equipment consists of a lap board, special braille paper, and a slate (a template with spaces corresponding to dots and cells of braille). The student uses a hand stylus to punch the dots in each cell, which is obviously a slower procedure than the braille writer. The slate and stylus often work well for spelling tests, short answer assignments, recording assignments, and many other classroom chores.

A great many students with visual impairments use *reader services,* which come in various forms. Volunteers frequently are needed simply to read aloud to students; they may be classmates (if they meet the criterion of age, they can be paid for their services by the state) or other members of the community who have organized themselves to provide systematic reader services. In other cases, readers may put materials on tape recorders or on radio. The Library of Congress provides nationwide services through so-called "Talking Books," recordings of outstanding books that are often read by well known figures, and blind persons can obtain the records from regional depositories. In some states, special recordings are made for occupational groups, such as blind lawyers. In at least one state, reader services are provided by radio, using the side channels of a public FM radio network. A special agency (Recording for the Blind, Inc.) provides recordings of materials for blind college students.

CHARACTERISTICS OF A COMPREHENSIVE EDUCATIONAL PROGRAM

How can the characteristics of a comprehensive program for students who have visual handicaps be summarized? The following brief list includes elements of the necessary school program and extends to some of the necessary related services; it indicates the variety of activities to which school board members and other community leaders must make a commitment if excellence is to be achieved in this important field.

1. *Early education.* Preschool education programs should be available to each child as early as needed. Most often the child can be enrolled in a regular preschool program, but some children, after an initial trial in a regular class, may need help in special centers.
2. *Parent education.* As soon as vision impairments are identified it is important to provide services to parents, to give them information on child care, health care, training procedures, resources available to the family, schooling possibilities, general expectations, and like matters.
3. *Individualized school programs.* Children with visual handicaps need appropriately individualized programs. With the current trend toward the individualization of education programs for all students, the program for the visually handicapped student requires little additional organization.
4. *A well oriented regular school staff.* Students with visual handicaps can be mainstreamed successfully when regular teachers, school principals, and other school staff members are selected, oriented to, and trained for mainstreaming functions.
5. *High quality leadership by specially trained vision teachers.* High quality programs for children with visual impairments need well informed and skillful special teachers for consultation with regular class teachers. Such specialists often team teach regular class pupils as well as give direct instruction to visually handicapped students.
6. *Materials and equipment.* Fortunately, much of the necessary braille, large print, and other material and equipment required by children with visual impairments is readily available at little or no cost. A full supply of what is needed when it is needed in the program of each student requires management and organization, and that is one sign of a comprehensive school program.
7. *Good models.* Students with vision handicaps, like all children, require good models in regular classes at all levels of the school. They should be both nonhandicapped and handicapped, children and adults, to help to structure the children's own self perceptions and lives.

8. *Good counseling.* Students with vision impairment, like other children, may need expert help in building an understanding of themselves in terms of strengths, weaknesses, patterns of satisfying activities, and aspirations, and help in making career plans. Full service school systems have counselors who understand and work effectively with visually impaired pupils in both elementary and secondary schools.
9. *Screening.* Careful, systematic vision screening is an essential part of the school program.
10. *Coordination of school and health services.* Children with visual handicaps need high quality, regular care from physicians so that the condition of their eyes and visual functioning are well understood and all necessary treatments are offered. Health professionals have much to contribute also in preventive programs, screening programs, parent education, and consultation with school personnel. Coordination with health professionals is a key concern for educators who serve children with visual handicaps.
11. *School followup.* Too often students with vision impairments have completed secondary schools only to encounter a real letdown in further education, employment, and social life. There is a great need for forward looking planning at secondary levels and for the mobilization of optional continuation programs. Community agencies can play an important role in followup programs.
12. *Statewide coordination.* Local programs for students with vision impairments often are insufficient if regional and statewide resources are uncoordinated and unavailable, or if programs do not comply with state standards. Good programs for visually impaired students depend on good communication with state offices.

PROSPECTS FOR THE FUTURE

As a field for professional preparation and service, visual impairment is not large; however, it presents outstanding opportunities for the trainee who seeks good preparation. There are about a dozen top quality teacher education programs in the country. Students who complete programs in these centers find good employment. Special need exists for trainees who will prepare themselves to work with multiply handicapped students, including the deaf-blind. Several special centers exist for the preparation of orientation and mobility instructors (peripatologists). A critical need exists for researchers who will give attention to the pressing problems in this field.

Opportunities are emerging for persons who undertake truly broad preparation in special education and who are in a position to assume support roles across a variety of the traditional categories of handicapped children. For example, a teacher might prepare to conduct a *general* resource room in a school and to serve children who need braille or other specialized forms of instruction as well or, for example, students who have learning disabilities or are hard of hearing.

PREVAILING VERSUS PREFERRED PRACTICES

As in previous chapters, a list of prevailing and preferred practices in educational programs for students with visual impairments is presented. The topics covered do not comprise a comprehensive statement of present programs; rather, they represent a contrast in particular domains in which it is believed progress can and should be made in the near future.

Prevailing Practices	Preferred Practices
1. Children with visual handicaps are mainstreamed for academic instruction, but social mainstreaming is often lacking.	1. Attention is given to both academic and social mainstreaming.
2. Mainstreamed children with visual handicaps lack identity with other visually impaired persons.	2. Children with visual handicaps are educated mainly with sighted children, but they are also provided with significant experiences with other visually handicapped persons.
3. Children with visual impairments are taught mainly by one special vision teacher in cooperation with one or more regular teachers.	3. The school principal, parents, and all teachers work together to plan the educational program.
4. Special education teachers encourage regular classroom teachers to send handicapped children to resource rooms for much of their instructional needs.	4. Special education teachers learn consultative skills so that they can help regular classroom teachers to mainstream the handicapped children in practice as well as theory.
5. The program for students with visual impairments is mainly academic.	5. Emphasis is given to social skills and development as well as academics; special out-of-school arrangements are made as necessary for experience

Prevailing Practices	Preferred Practices
	and training in social areas and daily living skills.
6. Few carefully designed support programs are available for postsecondary students with vision impairments.	6. Vocational schools, colleges, and graduate schools modify admissions and develop strong support programs for students with vision impairments in mainstream programs.
7. Residential schools for the blind operate often as comprehensive alternative programs.	7. Residential schools become integrated elements of total state programs, serving specific needs, such as programing for severely multiply handicapped students or offering short term training on special topics for students otherwise enrolled in mainstream programs.

VOLUNTEER ORGANIZATIONS

As school services for visually impaired children have grown dramatically during the past two decades, so have the volunteer services for these children. In fact, many volunteer transcribing organizations began because of the needs of teachers who found themselves with visually impaired children and no instructional materials.

Each state has numerous small groups of transcribers and transcriptionists who record materials for schools. They also work for visually impaired adults who are either enrolled in colleges or universities or engaged in some professional or business activity. For many of the groups, state organizations coordinate the work. A sizable number are affiliated with national groups, such as the Library of Congress, the American Printing House for the Blind, the National Braille Association, and National Recording for the Blind (see Appendix A).

One of the most gratifying experiences for professional workers is to observe the highly motivated work of literally thousands of transcribers who devote time and energy to the production of appropriate reading material for visually impaired children and adults.

SUGGESTIONS FOR STUDENTS AND INSTRUCTOR

1. Obtain a Snellen Chart, telebinocular, or other devices for vision screening and conduct tests on yourselves or others; or have all per-

sons in your group remove their prescription glasses and demonstrate the variability in visual functions that exist.
2. Study the vision screening procedures being used in the schools of your community and participate in it, if possible.
3. Invite one or more blind adults to discuss their educational experiences as related to vision.
4. Collect a set of the special equipment used in instruction of students with visual impairments and try them.
5. Under careful supervision, spend a few hours with blindfolds on; try to travel without sight in your accustomed environment. Start in the center of a gymnasium, make turns on the direction of another person, and then check your orientation.
6. Visit classes or schools that enroll visually impaired students for observations and discussions.
7. Talk with parents of visually impaired students about family experience in dealing with services and needs they have experienced.

TOPICAL BIBLIOGRAPHIES

Attitudes Toward the Blind

Lowenfeld, B. (Ed.). *The visually handicapped child in school.* New York: Day, 1973.

Lukoff, I.F. et al. *Attitudes toward blind persons.* New York: American Foundation for the Blind, 1972.

Marsh, V., & Friedman, R. Changing public attitudes toward blindness. *Exceptional Children,* 1972, *38,* 426-428.

Scholl, G.T. The education of children with visual impairments. In W.M. Cruikshank & G.O. Johnson (Eds.). *Education of exceptional children and youth.* Englewood Cliffs NJ: Prentice-Hall, 1975.

People with Visual Impairments

Davidson, M. *Louis Braille, the boy who invented books for the blind.* New York: Hastings House, 1971.

Braddy, N. *Anne Sullivan Macy—The story behind Helen Keller.* New York: Doubleday, 1933.

Keller, H. *The story of my life.* New York: Doubleday, 1954.

Dickshoff, J. *Milton on himself.* New York: Oxford University Press, 1939.

Chevigny, H. *My eyes have a cold nose.* New Haven CT: Yale University Press, 1946.

Mobility and Oreientation

Blakeslee, A. Blind baby "sees" with echo device. *Los Angeles Times,* June 22, 1975.

Hanninen, K.A. *Teaching the visually handicapped.* Columbus OH: Charles E. Merrill Co., 1975.

Hill, E., & Ponder, P. *Orientation and mobility techniques.* New York: American Foundation for the Blind, 1976.

Whitstock, E.L. Orientation and mobility for blind children. *New Outlook for the Blind Children* 1960, *54*, 90-94.

Classroom Procedures

Brothers, R. J. Arithmetic computation by the blind. *Education of the Visually Handicapped,* 1972, *4*, 1-8.

Duker, S. (Ed.). *Teaching listening in the elementary schools.* Metuchen NJ: Scarecrow Press, 1971.

Foulke, E., et al. The comprehension of rapid speech by the blind. *Exceptional Children,* 1962, *29,* 134-141.

Martin, G. J., & Hoben, M. *Supporting visually impaired students in the mainstream: The state of the art.* Reston VA: The Council for Exceptional Children, 1977.

Recreation

Buell, C. E. *Physical education for blind children.* Springfield IL: Charles C Thomas, 1966.

Nezol, A.J. Physical education for integrated blind students. *Education of the Visually Handicapped,* 1972, *4,* 16-18.

Trevena, T. M. Integration of the sightless child into regular physical activities. *Journal of Health, Physical Education and Recreation,* 1970, *41*, 42-43.

General

Barraga, N. *Visual handicaps and learning: A developmental approach.* Belmont CA: Wadsworth, 1976.

Hanninen, K. A. *Teaching the visually handicapped.* Columbus OH: Charles E. Merrill Co., 1975.

Napier, G., Kappan, D.L., Tuttle, D.W., Schrotberger, W.L., & Dennison, A.L. *Handbook for teachers of the visually handicapped.* Louisville KY: American Printing House for the Blind, 1975.

Workshop

Ward, M. J., Arkell, R. N., Dahl, H. G., & Wise, J. H. *Everybody counts! A workshop manual to increase awareness of handicapped people.* Reston VA: The Council for Exceptional Children, 1979.

13. Emerging Programs

CHAPTER OUTLINE

THE GROWING CONCERN FOR ALL CHILDREN
EARLY CHILDHOOD EDUCATION
  Historical Background
  Very Early Childhood Intervention
    The Brookline Early Education Project
    The Tucson Program
    The "Saturday School" Program
    Program Comparisons
    The Western Illinois Program
    Implications of the Extension of Very Early Intervention
    Head Start Mainstreaming
CHILD NEGLECT AND ABUSE
  The Challenge
  Theories and Models
  What Teachers Can Do
    Legal Systems of Reporting
    Signs of Child Abuse and Neglect
    Hunger
    Educational Adaptations for Abused and Neglected Children
    Teaching Better Parenting
DRUG HANDICAPPED LEARNERS
  What Teachers Can Do
  Rehabilitation of Addicts
SCHOOL AGE PARENTS
  Early Patterns of Schooling
  Weaknesses in Traditional Approaches
  A Modern Approach to Education
  General Background
SUGGESTIONS FOR STUDENTS AND INSTRUCTOR
TOPICAL BIBLIOGRAPHIES

THE GROWING CONCERN FOR ALL CHILDREN

A significant component of the mainstreaming movement, which may be overlooked in the day to day urgency of complying with judicial and legislative mandates, is a more humane conception of children and our obligations to them. As a people, we have long been concerned with the physical welfare of children and youth; now, however, that concern has been expanded to include their psychosocial development and opportunities for better lives. The extent of our present concern is exemplified by the programs that are emerging for those young populations who, up to this time have been on the fringes of society: high risk preschool children, drug handicapped learners, school age parents, and neglected and abused children. As the rest of this chapter indicates, the principles of mainstreaming are part of a much broader concept of child care than classroom placement.

EARLY CHILDHOOD EDUCATION

Historical Background

Teachers who graduated from training programs in the 1950's heard little about early childhood unless they were enrolled in a preprimary or primary major. During the 1960's, more consideration was being given to the early years of children in teacher preparation programs as public awareness of the importance of early education was heightened as a result of the federally funded Head Start program and related educational projects whose targets were 3, 4, and 5 year old children, especially those who were either members of economically poor families, physiologically handicapped, or both. By the 1970's, interest in early childhood education reached its present height. A contributing factor was a new rationale.

Early childhood instruction for exceptional children during the 1950's and 1960's, had a pragmatic base. It just seemed to "make sense" to start working earlier to educate children who were blind or deaf or had congenital crippling conditions such as cerebral palsy. For children with emotional problems, nursery school was prescribed, mainly when it was necessary to relieve a home situation or to maintain the children in a therapeutic setting for long stretches of time. Children without evident problems attended nursery school if their parents worked outside the home or if the home itself was a potential source of problems. A relatively small number of children were also enrolled in private nursery schools because their parents viewed the experience as valuable for their children's development.

Kindergarten, as an educational experience, was growing in general acceptance during the 1950's and 1960's but attendance was not yet universal. It was considered to be a potentially helpful, although not really necessary, transition from home to school.

The inconsistency in midcentury of the pragmatic approach is well illustrated by the fact that some exceptional children actually were denied early education on the grounds that they were not mature enough to profit from it because they required dressing, toileting, and other physical care that usually was not supplied in the preschool. Whether the child might be able to gain intellectually or socially from the preschool curriculum was seldom considered.

The new rationale for early childhood education began to receive widespread attention in the 1960's and 1970's. This rationale held (a) that educability itself could be furthered through properly planned early experiences and (b) that economically and socially disadvantaged and other handicapped children in particular could be aided by such experiences. By the middle 1970's, that rationale had strong, if not unanimous and conclusive, evidence to support it. Within the same period, other arguments began to emerge: (a) that similar, properly planned early experiences might well be valuable for the personal, social, and intellectual development of *all* 3 to 6 year olds, and (b) that it might be well to start educational efforts at birth or shortly after. These points of view were being advanced in the context of working with and through parents in their homes as well as in day care centers, nurseries, and kindergartens.

Very Early Childhood Intervention

The Recent surge of interest in the earliest childhood years has high promise for improving the chances of exceptional children. The central thrust of the movement is to insure that children get off to a good start. Educational procedures are carried out with infants and toddlers in the home by parents with guidance from specialists. The purpose is three fold: to help babies and their families to live fuller and happier lives together from the outset; to prevent or minimize the development of problems that have their roots in the first three or four years of life; and to increase the chances for satisfactory future schooling and wholesome later life patterns.

Well conducted very early education programs are in effect, here and in other countries. They hold out the likelihood of fascinating new roles for teachers of both regular and exceptional children, in addition to refining the roles such teachers already play and will continue to play in today's schools and communities.

Most very early education projects take as their major aim the provision of resources, support, and information to parents in their roles as teachers of their young children. In such diverse places as Brookline,

Massachusetts; Bogota, Columbia; Tucson, Arizona; Auckland, New Zealand; Gainesville, Florida; Bratislava, Czechoslovakia; Ann Arbor, Michigan; and Washington, D.C., evidence of the usefulness of such activities is being established. Many projects are conducted under the auspices of the public schools, and all employ staff who operate as teachers of both parents and young children.

The Brookline Early Education Project

The Brookline, Massachusetts, project, which is described here in some detail,* provides an example of the potential of these projects for creating some national and international guidelines for very early childhood educational intervention strategy and tactics. Brief items about other places are also included to indicate the quantity and quality of project operations.

In Brookline, the program to improve the quality of early education and to reduce educational handicaps started in 1973. From the beginning, a link was established and maintained with physicians concerned with child health, particularly the prevention, early detection, and management of medical problems in young children.

Initially, the program enrolled 225 families in which a birth was anticipated; participation started a few months before the birth and continued through the beginning of conventional schooling. The project went outside the school district in order to include appropriate proportions of Black and Spanish speaking families. The purpose, of course, was to allow generalizations to be made more readily for the rest of the United States.

Participation is voluntary. The only criteria for enrollment are that the parents expect a baby and have no definite plans to move from the area within a 5 year period. Program activities begin immediately with general information and guidance for parents in response to their questions. The first activity involving babies is an examination two weeks after birth at a neighborhood Brookline Early Education Project (BEEP) center. A psychologist, public health nurse, and pediatrician look at the child's development and condition in general; in particular, they search out any signs that may presage educational handicaps. At this early stage it is necessary to presume that any departure from the normal range of

---

*This summary is based on direct observations, written materials, and discussions with project personnel. Dr. Donald E. Pierson, formerly an elementary school principal in Brookline, is the project director. Dr. Robert L. Sperber, superintendent of schools, initiated the program with consultation from Dr. Burton C. White, director of the Preschool Project, Harvard Graduate School of Education. The project historian is psychologist Dr. Elizabeth H. Nicol. For a published description of the project, see Pierson (1974).

infant behavior, whether social, sensory, or motor, deserves attention for the child's total welfare. Except for major conditions like deafness, blindness, and overt bodily anomalies, it is not feasible to attempt to separate medical and educational problems in such young organisms; aberrations in development are alarm signals for educators and physicians alike.

Subsequently, the infants are examined at 3½ months, 6½ months, 11 months, 14½ months, 24 months, and 50 months. The usual pediatric examination is supplemented by neurologic, physical, and mental assessments. Anything suspicious is followed up in further study by specialists. For example, if speech appears to be delayed, if there is uncertainty about whether the child hears or sees adequately, or if the child is not relating to other people appropriately, special educators, audiologists, speech clinicians, or other professionals work in an educational-diagnostic manner with the child until (a) the basis of the problem seems clear and (b) an educational corrective or ameliorative program is established. Teachers discuss with parents the particular patterns of their children's development. They help parents to understand and adjust to a child's developmental spurts and lags, to encourage the spurts, to respect the lags, and to assist the child in overcoming the latter. They also aid parents in maintaining equanimity in the face of temporary periods of unusual behavior.

Naturally, each examination and staff review adds to and enriches the understanding of the children. More and more, as behavior differentiates, educational programs are organized to emphasize social behavior, self help behavior (e.g., dressing or eating), language understanding and production, visual and auditory perception, personal control, and other combinations of motor, affective, and cognitive learning.

It is all too easy to think of BEEP as simply a downward extension of day school, with parents depositing children in some kind of a central facility that is half school and half child care center. But that is not the BEEP design. The BEEP operation emphasizes bringing increased understanding and actual hands-on assistance to parents in their own homes with their own children. However, when parents come to the project center to take part in seminars, their children receive expert "babysitting" services.

Pierson (1974) described BEEP's aim and intention as follows:

> The aim of the BEEP educational program is to help each child experience the best possible beginning in life by providing resources for the parents in their roles as teachers of the young child. The intention is to increase parental understanding of child development and to focus on the design of home conditions that encourage the child's emerging abilities.
>
> BEEP does not seek to accelerate or force children's development. Instead, its educational philosophy is oriented toward assisting the family

in arranging for each child an environment rich in resources and in opportunities for...exercise...of natural talents. (p. 33)

BEEP is not an experiment to determine whether its provisions are good for children; rather, it demonstrates the application of the positive evidence accumulated by earlier investigations (e.g., Hunt, 1961; Schaefer, 1972). It is trying to learn the level of intensity at which the principle must be applied to achieve acceptable results and the costs.

> Families are randomly assigned to one of three program levels, which vary in cost...and from which other communities can later choose the one most appropriate for their needs. The three programs differ in the amount of scheduled contact between BEEP staff and parents. One program involves frequently scheduled seminars and home visits, as often as every two or three weeks; a second program has less frequent seminars and home visits, about once every four to six weeks; the third has no formally scheduled seminars or home visits.
>
> In all levels each family is assigned a teacher, who has an academic background in child development and who is also a parent, to be the liaison between BEEP and the family.
>
> Aside from the program intensity variation, all three programs provide similar basic educational services to all participating families. For instance, the families may:
>
> ☐ call upon their specially assigned teacher...
>
> ☐ drop in at the Center whenever they like bringing along their children who will be cared for by trained staff in a specially equipped play room
>
> ☐ explore the materials about early childhood that BEEP has gathered together in its 'resource center'
>
> ☐ borrow books, pamphlets and toys
>
> ☐ view films and videotapes on child development topics and on other aspects of childhood
>
> ☐ attend special events such as films on home safety, workshops on toymaking, and speakers from a variety of fields related to child development
>
> ☐ use BEEP's free transportation service to and from the Center
>
> ☐ learn about other resources for young children that exist in the Boston area—recreational, educational and medical. (Pierson, 1974, p. 134)

The Tucson Program

Other communities have taken different routes to attain similar goals. In Tucson, Arizona, for instance the mother of each newborn child is the initial contact point. In the city's hospitals, after a child has been delivered, the mother receives on her first meal tray a small booklet containing a greeting from the board of education to the parents and child and a welcome to the prospective new pupil. The booklet points out that the parents are expected to be as concerned about the baby's intellectual, social, and emotional development as they are about the the baby's health and physical development, and the parents are urged to work closely with their physician regarding the latter and with the schools to maximize the former. A telephone number is given for the parents to call if they have questions or concerns. Also, they are told that someone from the schools will make a personal contact about two weeks after the mother and child return home, if the parents have not initiated a contact in the meantime.

The initial contact leads, if the parents wish, to periodic home visits by a trained aide, who is one of several giving help and guidance to parents under the supervision of a professional teacher. The staff also conducts informal discussions that take place, more often than not, in the kitchen or living room of a home with three or four neighborhood mothers, while an aide and/or older family member takes care of the babies.

The program is conducted in family appropriate languages: English, Spanish, and the common Indian languages in the Tucson region. Sometimes the initial contact is made through direct conversation rather than print, with parents unable to read and with some Indian parents whose languages do not have well established written forms. Also, initial contact efforts extend beyond hospitals for children born in homes. The teachers and aides, therefore, are challenged by differences in customs, languages, literacy, cultures, and family life styles, in addition to the usual professional and paraprofessional matters. The teachers and aides themselves come from different backgrounds. Teamwork is a key factor to their success, however.

The Tucson program has curriculum materials for use in the early years, and a lending library is operated for parents. Specialists are called in for consultation and activities for families are generally similar to those described for the BEEP. The main differences lie in the contact procedure, the adaptations to the setting and population, the use of homes for meetings, and the substantial use of trained aides under supervision.

The "Saturday School" Program

A unique "Saturday School" program in which exceptional children make their school start in the context of mainstreamed early childhood offerings is conducted by the Ferguson-Florissant School District in Missouri. High effectiveness coupled with low cost characterizes this operation which starts with 4 year olds. Called Saturday School, it is a home-school arrangement which each year draws 700 pupils, 75% of the target population, at a yearly per pupil cost of $230.

Children go to school three hours on Saturday morning or afternoon. Mothers and fathers are totally involved, on prearranged schedules, as parent-teachers at school and home, as planners, and as aides, all under professional guidance. Preschool teachers meet on weekdays in different homes with three or four neighborhood children. Parents and siblings are encouraged to join in.

Close to 15% of the 4 year olds in the program received special education and services. Precipitating conditions ranged from minor lags in motor skill to major coordination, language, and behavior problems.

All handicapped pupils were mainstreamed in the regular Saturday classes. Teachers spent time, too, in each handicapped pupil's home showing parents how to apply activities specifically designed to match the child's needs.

The first cohort of Saturday School children were in grade 4 in 1977. In every grade along the way they scored higher than students with other preschool experience on standardized achievement tests and significantly higher than classmates with no preschool preparation. When the progress of the handicapped children who needed special attention was checked it was found that:

1. The majority were functioning well by the end of the Saturday School year.
2. Of those with learning disabilities, 85% retested at age level by the end of the first year.
3. Children with emotional problems evidenced marked improvement in behavior and adjustment.
4. Seven out of eight of the children whose test scores were initially in the retarded range moved out of that range.
5. Former Saturday School students with diagnosed learning disabilities improved more each year than did classmates without preschool training.

Teachers, parents, and pupils in this St. Louis County community are pleased with Saturday School, consider it a success, and want it to continue.

Program Comparisons

The several programs discussed here have a major common characteristic: They are comprehensive. *All* children are their target population. The assumption is that it is essential to start with *all* children and to monitor their growth very carefully if one is to be able to locate each child who may prove to need special attention. This approach, properly applied, should produce such results as the following:

1. All children who may need special education because of giftedness, talents, sensory defects, motor problems, emotional problems, slow cognitive development, speech anomalies, or any other reason will be identified.
2. These children will be located early, as soon as available procedures allow.
3. Early identification will permit equally early intervention, to do what is needed about the condition and to provide the best start for the child's education, self concept, and future life.
4. The longer a condition persists without appropriate special education being applied, the more time consuming and costly it is to obtain favorable results. Therefore, early location and intervention should result in a lower cost-effectiveness ratio. In other words, effective special education should be less costly per child because it is applied earlier when the situation is more amenable to change.
5. Parents will be spared of the concerns and anguish that tend to mount as they see their exceptional children grow older without adequate attention to their talents and without substantial improvement in their coping abilities.
6. A higher state of mental health should be found in the exceptional children themselves, and in their siblings and peers, because positive stimulation and continuing special education in the earliest years become a familiar part of life at the time attitudes and understandings are formed.

Other early intervention programs are conducted, commonly, by medical or public health agencies and public welfare agencies. Many of the programs are *comprehensive in design,* in the sense that they seek to locate all exceptional children, but they are *limited in scope,* in that they do not take in the whole population of a community. For example, a comprehensive program for high risk families might include only those with one or more exceptional children among earlier progeny or in the extended family. Other scope limitations might be income or location.

Some other very early intervention systems focus on one kind of exceptionality. For instance, agencies for the blind, the deaf, the cerebral palsied, or the emotionally disturbed may mount campaigns and conduct clinics to find, in the very early years of life, babies and toddlers who fall into the specific groups they serve. Such efforts are *restricted* to certain exceptionalities, although the scope, in terms of population served, may be communitywide, countywide, and, sometimes, statewide. The agencies may be governmental, such as the New Jersey Agency for the Blind, or volunteer, such as the Pittsburgh (Pennsylvania) Association for the Blind. In each case they employ staff to help locate newborn children with limited vision or blindness. Once the children are located, their parents are supplied with continuing advice and counsel on how best to help their visually impaired child adapt and acquire independence. The identification efforts of specialized agencies frequently uncover other kinds of exceptionalities; in such instances, of course, the parents are referred to an agency that can better assist them. Teachers frequently are the best sources of advice on such referrals because they tend to be familiar with all the services for exceptional children of all kinds.

The Western Illinois Program

Program models are also available for rural communities. One, in western Illinois, covers a geographical area of 3,300 square miles, including five counties with a total population of 120,000. Initially, a pilot program was operated in one county from January to August 1975 to identify and project the needs for the five county area. In September 1975, specific guidelines were adopted and all five counties began to participate.

A developmentally based evaluation instrument to use with the children was put together from selected items borrowed from several infant scales, intelligence tests, and developmental checklists. The conglomerate instrument was called a Skill-Log (Corson & Makowski, 1975). Its 200 items assess six aspects of development: gross motor, fine motor, language, social, self help, and cognitive. The tasks selected for the Skill-Log are in sequence for normal development from 0 to 3 years of age, but without reference to specific chronological ages. A visual representation of each child's developmental status can be shown keyed to each aspect of development.

Children referred to the Western Illinois Association program for 0 to 3 year olds are given the Skill-Log, and those with developmental delays are enrolled, if the parents wish. Instructors of infants spend the first few sessions in each home administering the Skill-Log and acquainting themselves with the child's learning style and parental expectations. Using the completed Skill-Log as a base, the instructors then plan yearly goals for each child. These long range goals are discussed with the parents whose suggestions are added. In planning specific lessons for the biweekly home visits, the instructors design specific sets of lesson plans that will eventually lead the children to mastery of the long-term goals. Lesson plans are also written for parents to carry out during the days the instructor does not visit. The parent lesson plans are highly specific; they describe step by step exactly how a parent should present a task to a child. A simplified chart on which to note the number of successful trials accompanies each lesson plan.

At the beginning of each home teaching session, the instructor shows the parent the lesson plan for that day and discusses the rationale behind the planned activities. Together, the parent and instructor instruct the child and evaluate his or her performance. At the end of the session, the instructor demonstrates the parent lesson plan for the week, shows the parent how to mark the chart, and indicates how many times a day the task should be taught. The instructor then observes the parent carrying out the lesson and they discuss possible problems or adaptations in the different steps. At the end of the week, parent and instructor go over the chart to decide if the child is ready for a new task or if a further breakdown on the same task is needed.

All lesson plans and charts are cataloged and filed for future reference and they are available to parents and other staff members. In addition to the parent lesson plan, a set of Work Bags was developed to aid parents in teaching new skills to children. Each Work Bag is a one concept teaching kit designed to help teach one task from the Skill-Log. The bag contains all the materials necessary to teach the skill and a card with detailed instructions for several "games" aimed at enhancing that skill. The Work Bags are explicit and comprehensive; they can be left with the parents to use separately or in conjunction with the weekly lesson plan.

Since there are a great many social skills that cannot be taught in a one to one tutorial relationship, a diagnostic-prescriptive classroom was established to allow interaction among the children and to provide prescriptive feedback on goals and lesson plans to instructors. Because the geographic area served by the program is fairly extensive, it was not practical to establish a daily classroom schedule. Instead, bimonthly classes are held for small groups of children and their parents at a centrally located classroom. During the diagnostic classes, instructors and parents plan and conduct small group activities, supervise free play, and try out new activities with the infants.

This setting also provides an arena for other support staff (hearing, vision, speech, physical therapy, and psychological) to observe the children, to assist the instructors in planning future lessons, and to talk with parents in a relaxed atmosphere. Parents seem to enjoy the opportunity to meet other families, discuss common problems, and have access to a variety of specialists in other fields of child development.

Implications of the Extension of Very Early Intervention

Very early intervention systems are demonstrating their worth as they grow in comprehensiveness and scope. From the standpoint of regular and special education teachers, the extension of early educational intervention has the following important implications:

1. There should be more teaching positions in the early childhood range as state educational policies show increased concern for and added acceptance of responsibility for the earliest years of life.
2. Teachers working in early education settings today are establishing the prototypes for the cities, towns, and rural areas that plan to start programs.
3. A shift in public school resource allocation toward the early years can be anticipated.
4. Added resources will be needed; if a redeployment of resources occurs to any substantial degree, the effectiveness of later education may be threatened.
5. New curricula will be developed, particularly for the very early years. They will not necessarily be simply a downward extension of present preprimary and primary curricula.
6. Encouragement will be given to certain curricular position shifts now partly under way. Examples are (a) teaching conversational competence in foreign languages and (b) teaching skills such as swimming in the very early childhood years instead of in secondary schools.
7. The health, social welfare, and education professions will be drawn even closer together to share responsibilities, along with parents, for overall management of the developing child.
8. Community and state agencies and the education, health, and social welfare professions will move away from the present stress on correction to increased investment of energy in prevention.
9. The training of educators will be extended, with more substantive knowledge and understanding of the earliest years for all professional teachers.
10. Scheduled educational services for young children will relate more to their needs and the time available patterns of their parents than to present nursery and kindergarten schedules.
11. The expected national growth in number of child care centers for working parents will be accompanied by an increased demand for educational programs in all such centers, so they will be more than physically safe parking lots for babies. The result will be a sharp upsurge in the demand for qualified educators to operate the educational component of such centers, with special consideration for the exceptional children in the group.
12. Major changes in the substance, placement, and sequencing of curriculum content and skills instruction in the elementary and

secondary schools may well be needed in the future because of experiences with the very early education of children.

These programs do not mean that the essential nature of childhood is being changed or that "school" is being imposed to the exclusion of the joys of childhood; rather, they mean that a partnership of thoughtful parents and knowledgeable teachers are applying reliable, new knowledge that is helping their children to reach fulfillment. The knowledge is being applied earlier and more scientifically rather than leaving the children to the often not so tender mercies of chance.

Head Start Mainstreaming

The Head Start program recently has become an important source of information about the mainstreaming of handicapped children. In 1972, amendments to the Head Start law stipulated that at least 10% of the children enrolled should be handicapped. The intent was to give handicapped and nonhandicapped children a chance to live and learn together.

Klein (1977) summarizes the Head Start experience in mainstreaming as follows:

> Observations of early childhood programs indicate that even the most severely impaired children can benefit from integrated preschool programs. Head Start staff members who have worked with handicapped children as part of their regular program believe firmly that mainstreaming is beneficial to both handicapped and normal children. Parents of both normal and handicapped children have expressed very positive attitudes toward Head Start in general, and particularly toward efforts on behalf of the handicapped. Most parents of disabled children in Head Start report that the program has had a significant impact on their children. These observations reinforce the belief that handicapped children should not be isolated. Mainstreaming is difficult, but its impact can reach far beyond the child and the immediate situation.
>
> Handicapped individuals have become increasingly vocal in the past few years. They are cognizant of their rights to education, employment, information, and all the other things associated with a full and useful life. Whether these rights are attained and how they are used are dependent on the motivation, goals, and abilities of the individuals concerned—all factors that are influenced by early experiences. The formative years may determine whether individuals are boxed in by the things they cannot do or whether they focus on the things they can do. Reaching out requires a kind of realism that is nurtured in the world of the nonhandicapped where the individual has the opportunity to know and observe many people without visible disabilities.
>
> If handicapped persons have the right to share the world of the normal, we as educators have a responsibility. We are obligated to try to help children develop the outlook and skills which may enable them to function effectively in spite of a handicap. What better place to start than in a preschool group? (p. 9)

CHILD NEGLECT AND ABUSE

The Challenge

The following case history was drawn from an actual account; it has been fictionalized to disguise the location and the persons involved, but the reported facts have not been altered.

> Eastburg, South Columbia. The parents of a 9 year old Venida Township boy who died of pneumonia last month in a padlocked bedroom in his home have been arrested on charges relating to the death.
> Lewis and Helen G_____, of 4625 Fifth Avenue in the Bolton Heights section of the township, were arrested Friday night and charged with aggravated assault, recklessly endangering another person, simple assault, and endangering the welfare of children.
> They were arraigned by Magistrate Edgar Kirk in Venida Township. He set bond at $25,000 each and scheduled a hearing for Wednesday.
> Police said Lewis G_____'s bond was posted by a friend and he was released, but his wife is still in County Jail.
> The death of the boy, Lewis Jr., brought expressions of disgust from outraged neighbors. Two reports of child abuse against the parents had been filed earlier with Child Welfare Services.
> Lamont Carpenter, Venida Township police chief, said his office received numerous calls from people claiming the boy had been abused and beaten.
> The phone calls, the condition of the body, and knowledge of past child abuse cases against the parents prompted Carpenter to ask county detectives to investigate.
> Police were notified by the boy's grandmother, who lives near the G_____'s residence, at about 11 a.m., Nov. 11.
> The boy, who was found lying face up on his bedroom floor, was pronounced dead at the scene by a doctor at 11:15 a.m. The coroner's report noted that the body showed bruises and abrasions.
> When the police arrived at the home to take reports they noted that the father at first refused to get out of bed to give them any information. They also noted in their report that while they were in the upstairs bedroom with the body the mother was downstairs watching television.
> A special investigator for the coroner's office, Ramon Gomez, said the boy's room was without a light fixture and was padlocked from the outside. Gomez said there were no toys in the room, no sheets on the bed and an empty dresser. The windows were nailed shut.
> An investigation revealed that on February 15, 19____, the boy, who was 2 years old at the time, was treated at Standish Mountain Hospital for three fractured ribs and bruises. X-rays showed the fractures were in the healing stage.
> Five days later a doctor at the hospital filed a child abuse report with Child Welfare Services. The report noted the boy's "over-all weakness and malnutrition." When questioned by the doctor the parents denied any knowledge of the abuse, police said.

A second child abuse report was filed against the parents with Child Welfare Services on April 8, 19_____, when the boy was three. This time the report came from St. James' Hospital where the boy had been taken for treatment of an eye injury.

The boy was admitted with abrasions of the forehead and right side of the face. A more thorough report revealed the boy had "slow motor growth development and was in a state of depression."

Doctors removed a cataract from the boy's injured eye and on April 30, he was discharged and taken to Suiza Shelter in Mulvahill Township. The report also noted that the boy had not yet learned to walk.

A month later Lewis Jr. was transferred to another Child Welfare Services facility in Portford and in September, 19___, he was released to foster parents on a temporary custody basis.

Twenty-three months later, on August 28, 19___, he was returned to his natural parents by Child Welfare Services. Case workers reportedly made periodic checks on the G_____'s, for the following nine months, and then apparently stopped.

One detective investigating the case said, "The boy was taken from the foster parents and sent to hell, where he remained until he died."

Gomez said the boy's father told police the youth was acting up at the dinner table the night before he died. The father reportedly got up from the table, punched his son, threw him against the wall and beat him with a board.

The father told police he ordered the boy to his room and later that night said he heard the youngster coughing and gasping for air. The father told police he did not go into the room to check on the boy.

The mother, in a statement to police, said her son had been suffereing from a cold and had a fever. The day before he died she gave him two cold water baths in an attempt to lower the fever. Police said a doctor had not been called to treat the boy's cold.

Two days after the boy died Child Welfare Services, with court permission, went to the G_____'s residence and took away two daughters who were living in the home. There were no reports of the girls being abused, police said.

The actions in this story are repeated more than 800 times every day in the United States. Martin (1973) estimated that 50,000 children die from child abuse each year and 250,000 more are abused and live. It is not always easy to detect the difference between abuse and neglect.

Not far from the hospital room of her grossly neglected two-month-old infant, Sherry (fictitious name)—a 16 year-old mother— is convalescing from an attempted suicide. The attempt was, in part, triggered by Sherry's separation from her baby, ordered by court and hospital authorities in the District of Columbia.

In the fall of 1973, the infant was brought to the hospital and was diagnosed as suffering from severe diaper rash. The young mother had aggravated the rash by bathing it with an acid solution which caused burns on the baby's skin. In terms of height and weight, the baby was underdeveloped. Her eyes had been washed with milk and she had been fed solid foods. Bruises were also found which indicated physical abuse such as hitting and slapping. A "medical hold" was placed on the infant and court action was scheduled for January, 1974. Following this, the young mother attempted suicide.

Later, in working with Sherry, doctors found her to be very intelligent. (She had been an "A" student while in school.) They also learned that the pregnancy was unplanned and unwanted and that Sherry had been abandoned by the baby's father three weeks before her scheduled delivery. She also revealed that her own mother had beaten her when she was a child.

Doctors in the case were initially reluctant to characterize Sherry's treatment of her baby as intentional abuse. Most of the damaging practices described seem to be the result of ignorance. The young woman apparently did not know appropriate child care techniques and did not understand the extreme vulnerability of her child. (Dell'Amore, 1974 p. 3)

National concern for neglected and abused children has mounted in recent years. The Kempe (1973) report, showing that more than 60,000 children were seriously abused in the United States in 1972 has served to alert many professionals and the general public to this apparently growing problem. A more recent report by Nagi (1975) suggested that the problem may be 10 times larger than Kempe has suggested. Yet the phenomenon is far from recent. It can be taken as a sign of an advance in civilization that our sensitivity to the problem is heightened and that efforts are growing to face and combat it. Abandoning unwanted children was once common in many cultures (Hurt, 1975) but interest in child advocacy has grown to the point where it is clearly recognized that children have rights of their own and that they should be removed from homes in which they are maltreated.

Theories and Models

A variety of points of view have been advanced to help understand the phenomena of child neglect and abuse. Some believe that the explanation, and presumably the treatment, should focus on the psychiatric problems of the parents (Parke & Collmer, 1975). Unfortunately there is little evidence to suggest that parents who abuse their children are homogeneous on any set of traits. However, it is widely held that many abusing parents were themselves the object of early mistreatment (Green, Gaines, & Sandgrund, 1974).

Other theorists advance a sociological perspective that focuses on the extent to which an adequate "social support system" exists for parents (Bronfenbrenner, 1974). According to this view it should be possible to construct predictive or high risk indexes concerning the likelihood of child abuse or neglect and enable the community to launch preventive programs.

Still other theorists suggest that characteristics of children, for example, the irritating quality of an infant's crying, may interact in complex ways with stressful conditions weighing upon parents to precipitate abusive behaviors. Many theorists connect child abuse to the widespread acceptance of violence in our society, in entertainment, on television, and in control behavior. The use of corporal punishment in schools suggests that personal aggression is an acceptable mode of behavior control (Zigler, 1976).

What Teachers Can Do

Teachers have three functions to perform with regard to this national problem: (a) to identify and report instances of child neglect and abuse; (b) to see that neglected and abused children do not lose out on education as a result of their other misfortunes, and (c) to teach each new generation the child rearing principles and practices that will act as preventive measures for the future.

Teachers, school psychologists, counselors, and others who come in frequent contact with children have opportunities to form an early warning network. Such an alarm system can pick up signs, report them, and often avert tragedy.

Legal Systems of Reporting

All of the 50 states have systems to expedite the reporting of suspected abuse and neglect of minors. The Pennsylvania procedure is an illustration.

The state law requires the reporting of suspected cases not only by school personnel but also by physicians, nurses, dentists, hospital employees, day care center workers, and others whose employment brings them in close contact with children. The mandated procedure is that a written statement be filed with the local county welfare agency. When reports are made in good faith, the persons reporting are protected from legal reprisals; if the reports are unfounded, those reporting are notified and all pertaining records are destroyed.

Pennsylvania's "Child Protective Services Law" became effective in November 1975. It provides an initial report channel, the "Child Line," a toll free 24 hour telephone service with a multilingual staff. Reports can be made by any citizen, and they may be anonymous. The calls may not substitute, though, for the written statements required of persons in the named professions. Calls on the Child Line are noted and the data are fed to appropriate county welfare agencies for action. Investigations are made and suitable actions are taken.

Signs of Child Abuse and Neglect

Evidences of abuse and neglect may be signaled by the child's appearance or behavior, parental behavior, or some combination of the three. The following lists of signs are highlighted in Pennsylvania's public information material on the subject.

- Does the child often bear bruises, welts or burns?
- Does the child complain of beatings or other maltreatment?
- Is the child usually unclean or is his clothing consistently torn and unwashed? Is the child often dressed inadequately for the weather?
- Is the child underfed? Does the child complain of hunger, going to bed hungry, or missing meals because of punishment?
- Does the child linger at neighbor's homes at mealtime?

Child's Behavior:

- Is the child constantly crying?
- Is the child extremely fearful?
- Does the child frequently miss school?
- Is the child left unattended or allowed to wander about on his own?
- Is the child running around the neighborhood at odd hours? Is the child frequently not allowed (locked out) into his own home?
- Is the child emotionally disturbed due to family breakdown or serious illness, with the parents neglecting or refusing to secure medical care and treatment?
- Is the child forced to take over adult responsibilities, such as a six-year-old in charge of younger children or preparing meals for the family?
- Is the child exposed to degenerate conditions in or out of the home?
- Is the child overworked or exploited?

Parental Behavior:

- Do the parents leave small children unsupervised or at home alone?
- Does the parents' excessive use of alcohol or drugs interfere with the care of the child?
- Are the parents disinterested when approached about problems concerning the child?
- Does the parent administer unusual punishment such as excessive shaking of the child, locking the child in a room or closet, or using objects such as belts or cords to strike the child? (Pennsylvania Office of Children and Youth, 1976)

Unless such conditions are reported, children will continue to be killed or permanently injured, physically and emotionally. Parents and other adults will be encouraged to lash out at children out of warped personalities, ignorance, and the frustration that flows from the inability to cope with problems.

Hunger

A particularly worrisome aspect of child neglect is hunger. Hunger increases nervousness, irritability, and inattentiveness in pupils. Those qualities appear as disinterest and lack on concentration and they can contribute to failure to learn. Long term malnutrition is accompanied by lethargy resulting from a general low energy level. Children whose nutritional needs are simply neglected or those from families with little money and little health care can be profoundly and adversely affected by the poor nutrition that often accompanies those conditions.

It has been estimated that about one-fourth of all American school children go to school without having eaten breakfast. Even if they get sufficient nutrients later in the day to sustain them, a skipped breakfast can result in hunger pangs and depleted energy by midmorning.

An early part of the assessment of any school learning problem should be a probe into general nutritional level as well as meal intake regularity. The school nurse can be helpful if asked to check the child's appearance and eating habits. It is often necessary to verify the situation by actual contacts with the family, too. Children, and especially older children, may be unwilling to reveal home conditions of which they think school personnel may not approve.

It is a safe guess that poor general nutrition and improper eating habits are the sole culprits in many school learning problems and that they aggravate others. When hunger saps a child's ability to attend and concentrate, the result can resemble mental retardation, learning disabilities, poor hearing, or withdrawn behavior. Since improper nutrition and food intake habits are amenable to correction, it is desirable that they be checked out early in the assessment process and be changed if necessary.

Educational Adaptations for Abused and Neglected Children

As might be expected, these children present a great variety of educational characteristics. They may come from the well to do homes of business or professional parents or from abject poverty. The parents may be young or old, well or poorly educated (in the academic sense), and of any race or religion. The children themselves may have records of doing well or poorly in school. Sometimes school has been a haven or refuge; other times, it has added to the child's problems because of failure and rejection by other pupils and staff.

Regular class teachers should be encouraged to start an informal educational assessment with any child who displays one or more of the signs of abuse and neglect listed here. The assessment should be made whether or not the suspected case is reported to local or state authorities. It would be advisable to ask a special teacher to join in the initial informal assessment. The special educators likely to be most helpful are those with particular knowledge about slow cognitive development, learning disabilities, and behavior disorders. We have only our own observations to support this impression, but we believe that (a) youngsters who show those characteristics early in life are more frequent targets for adult violence and (b) cognitive development and orderly personal-social development are particularly vulnerable to the wanton and irrational attacks that characterize much of such abuse.

The educational procedure of choice, then, becomes the by now familiar one of establishing the best possible match between the child's needs, as determined by the assessment, and the instructional program. Concomitantly, the involvement of parents in developing and agreeing to an individualized educational program may open the door to a better understanding of the home situation. Teachers should show warmth and acceptance for abused and neglected pupils; at the time, the teacher may be the only adult in whom the child can consistently place confidence.

Teaching Better Parenting

Regular class teachers have a huge stake in the effectiveness of the nation's parents now and in the future (Martin, 1973). When teachers and parents together help youngsters to establish self control and thoughtful consideration of others, the results are favorable for the future of those children both as parents and as well educated people. So one place for teachers to concentrate is on the pupils now in school. Sequential instruction, from the earliest years to graduation, in attitudes and behaviors conducive to a mature and mentally healthy personal and social life is probably the best assurance that neglect and abuse of children will diminish and disappear.

Another pressure point to concentrate on is with the parents of children now in school. Continuing education and counseling for these parents have important places in the mission statements of public and private schools. Parents are almost always interested in becoming more helpful and skillful with their children than they now are, especially parents of exceptional children. The last point can be particularly important in the context of neglect and abuse because exceptional children are noticeable among those so treated. Many volunteer groups, such as local chapters of the National Association for Retarded Citizens, sponsor training sessions for parents. For parents in general and parents who are already strongly motivated, there are increasing numbers of learning opportunities that can be of value.

Resources to help the chronic child abuser are growing, too. In 1976 there were approximately 300 local chapters of Child Abuse Anonymous in the United States. When fathers and mothers recognize in themselves the conditions that trigger episodes of child abuse, preventive support is only a telephone call away. In a model similar to that of Alcoholics

Anonymous, this organization's members aid each other by distraction, positive modeling, peer counseling, and professional help when needed. Teachers may locate nearby chapters by telephoning the local public welfare office, social services clearinghouse, or asking the school social worker.

The most promising preventive measures through improved parenting are imbedded in very early childhood intervention systems. (See an earlier section in this chapter.) Early intervention models have in common that *they establish and maintain relatively frequent and regular contacts with the parents of young children in a framework of friendly interest and support.* This is the key to prevention of most child neglect and abuse and to its prompt detection if it does occur.

Better parenting, then, can be approached along at least four paths: (a) sequential instruction of the parents-to-be while they are in school, (b) in-service education for the parents of current school age youngsters, (c) referral of abuse or neglect prone parents to agencies designed to reeducate them, and (d) guidance of parents in the earliest weeks, months, and years of their children's lives, as part of the new move toward very early childhood education. Each approach has the potential for enhancing opportunities to provide the regular or special education children need and to do so under conditions of close cooperation between school and home.

DRUG HANDICAPPED LEARNERS

A survey that sampled United States youth about their key problems (Gallup, 1977) found that the highest rank was given to drug use and abuse. More than one-fourth of American young people (27%) called it a major problem. Seven percent said the same about alcohol use and abuse. While the survey permitted multiple answers, it is probably a fair estimate to say that close to one-third of teenagers feel these two conditions combined make up the biggest problem facing their generation.

The continued use of drugs, alcohol, and narcotics may produce irreversible nervous, muscular, digestive, and circulatory system damage. Even occasional use can result in disturbed mental processes and the loss of control of behavior. In connection with motorbike or automobile operation and in sports such as swimming, boating, skiing, skating, snow scootering, and surfing, even a small amount of alcohol, tranquilizers, amphetamines, barbiturates, hallucinogens, or narcotics sharply increases the hazards of serious injury or death. The danger is not only to the user but also to innocent bystanders. (Armor, Polich, & Stambul, 1976).

No one has exact figures on the abuse of alcohol and drugs by school age children and youth, but the numbers are substantial—probably

Emerging Programs / 661

above one million. Because of efforts by pupils and parents alike to hide the facts of addiction or abuse and to deal with their consequences outside usual educational, public health, legal, and social agency channels, the actual incidence, prevalence, and rate of change are not known.

What Teachers Can Do

The same reluctance to acknowledge the problem has kept both parents and their children ignorant about drugs, alcohol, and narcotics. Children who are emotionally unprepared to handle a confrontation with users may be easy converts to the idea that it is "the thing to do." The fact that the escape provided is fleeting, deluding, and ultimately deflationary eludes them until too late. It is only recently that schools have been enlisted in the correction of the situation. The school's stratagems listed here, are familiar but their application to this problem is relatively new.

- Make school an exciting and fulfilling place for each pupil so the likelihood is reduced that "kicks" will be sought through drugs, alcohol, and narcotics.
- Provide students with more authentic information. Since experimentation with drugs often begins before adolescence, start the educational activities in elementary schools (e.g., Stoll, 1974). Materials are available from the National Institute on Alcohol Abuse and Alcoholism, National Institute on Drug Abuse, National Clearinghouse for Drug Abuse Information, National Institute of Mental Health, and Education Commissions of the States. Locally, teachers can locate resources through county mental health and mental retardation offices.
- Seek family counseling services on behalf of children who are seriously disturbed by their parents' or other family members' use of alcohol or drugs.
- Improve the preparation of teachers. Funds for adding to teacher competencies are available from the federal government through the Drug Abuse Education Act. The support sometimes comes directly from the National Institute of Mental Health and the US Office of Education. Other funds have been channeled through and added to by states.
- Think of educational offerings as multidisciplinary. Use resources from the community and the region such as lawyers, narcotics agents, pharmacists, physicians, agencies such as Alcoholics Anonymous, and rehabilitated drug addicts.
- Bring the educational effort to a strong focus at the ninth grade level and maintain its vigor through the rest of the secondary school years. Arrange for educational services to follow and maintain the participation of dropouts.
- Establish an emergency center in the school system where students may

be taken if they are discovered to be actively experiencing a drug episode. The center staff should also provide emergency help on a self referral basis for students who consider themselves in danger from drugs.

- Orient staff, students, and school patrons to possible indications of drug abuse. Use these indicators with sensitivity but *use them* to help in location and referral of drug, alcohol, or narcotic abuse:

    Regular wearing of sunglasses, even indoors, to hide dilated pupils.
    Long sleeved clothing worn at all times to cover needle scars on the arms.
    Marked changes in appearance over a short time.
    Sharp drop in quality of school work and in dependability regarding completing assignments.
    Temper tantrums that originate suddenly with apparently little provocation.
    Drowsiness or sleeping in classes.

Exceptional children are not exempted from the ignorance, curiosity, and social pressure that appear to be important factors in triggering drug, alcohol, and narcotic use. Both regular and special teachers, therefore, should be familiar with the problem in order to talk about it knowledgeably with pupils, both in class and individually. Open and honest teacher-pupil communication is one of the best assurances that pupils will feel that they can talk without fear of their confidences being violated, that they are not inviting punishment when they reveal problems, and that they will be listened to, understood, and helped.

Scare tactics have no place in the direct interaction of teachers, parents, and pupils regarding drug, alcohol, and narcotics abuse. Instead, inservice and adult education should help both teachers and parents to understand the situation more fully and to react sensibly when faced with such problems in young people.

Rehabilitation of Addicts

The rehabilitation of youthful alcoholics and students addicted to drugs is a task far outside the capability of the schools. Certainly, though, teacher organizations and school boards ought to help agencies that have the responsibility. One way is to adopt policies and develop practices that result in dealing with affected pupils intelligently and constructively, such as driving pushers away from the school environs and educating teachers and parents to do a better preventive job. Perhaps most important, though, are the models that teachers, parents, and other pupils represent. If pupils in trouble are helped by the people around them in school to learn to live as well adjusted citizens—people who are "turned on" by their own lives without need for the highs, jolts, and dependencies engendered by alcohol, drugs, and narcotics—the schools will be making their best contribution.

SCHOOL AGE PARENTS
Early Patterns of Schooling

The traditional pattern of educating school age parents had three characteristics:

1. Mothers-to-be were excused from school as soon as the condition was known and home instruction was provided.
2. If the mother returned after the baby was born, it was usually to a standard program in a different school.
3. Nothing was done to change the father's school status.

That pattern prevailed until between 1950 and 1960. It made little difference whether the parents were married, so far as how the public schools educated them, though marriage did make a difference in their social acceptance. Beginning about 1960, a number of school districts took more constructive steps, especially for school age expectant mothers. The most common decision was to establish a special center with the following features:

1. Pregnant girls who wished to continue to attend school were supplied with transportation to the center.
2. The center was either located apart from regular school buildings or in a separated section of a regular school.
3. The curriculum was extended by prenatal and marriage counseling and intensive child care instruction.
4. The usual curriculum was restricted to core academic subjects because the centers were not ordinarily equipped for laboratory sciences, business practice, physical education, art, and music.

Girls who elected to attend the centers did so until giving birth. Afterward, they were allowed to return to regular schools if they wished and circumstances permitted. Often, they returned to a different regular school than the one attended previously or to an evening high school, if one was available. It remained uncommon to provide any alteration in the educational programs for school age fathers.

Weaknesses in Traditional Approaches

In 1973 a school law expert began a series of articles that were influential in revealing the inequities of home teaching and special centers and the prevailing educational practices and in turning education for school age parents in a new direction (Nolte, 1973). Nolte reported that the restrictive school board policies guiding the education of pregnant girls dated from an era when pregnant women were expected not to appear in public, much less attend public schools. The policies, aimed at protecting the health of the mother and at discouraging marriage and pregnancy among students, did not work and did not stand up under court challenges.

School officials are not competent to judge whether school attendance constitutes a health hazard to pregnant girls. Moreover, competent medical personnel do not believe that it does. Also, to deny a pregnant girl education either as a punishment or an example is unjustifiable, as far as the courts are concerned. Such action infringes on the right to due process and the right to equal protection under the law. Attempts to prove immorality, disruptive behavior, or danger to the welfare of other students simply on the basis of an unmarried, pregnant girl's presence in school are very difficult to substantiate, especially as a basis for a general policy of exclusion. Also, when schools have tried to limit the participation of pregnant students in extracurricular activities, the courts have lifted the restrictions.

Some actions of school boards or school administrators seem arbitrary, capricious, and unreasonable, even without the intervention and interpretation of the courts. In one instance, a high school principal would not permit a 17 year old unmarried mother to run for homecoming queen because "only virgins can run for homecoming queen." Two other girls, high school graduates in another community, challenged the board of education's decision to keep their pictures out of a high school yearbook because they had become pregnant in their senior year. One had been senior class queen and the other, Future Farmers of America queen (*Sharing*, 1974).

Nolte (1973) concluded that there is no legal question but that schools should be just as open to students who are pregnant as to all other students. In addition, there are sound reasons for adding to the usual curriculum and for individualizing instruction to satisfy the special educational needs occasioned by pregnancy.

Home instruction, the traditional pattern, has weaknesses, some of which follow:

1. It is not as complete as inschool instruction. The teacher is with the pupil only a few hours per week. Laboratories, practica and libraries are not available.
2. Class discussion, working on projects with other students, regular school hours, supervised study, and access to teachers and others to ask questions are not routinely provided in home teaching.
3. At a time when emotional problems may be present, the girl is removed from contact with friends in the same age group and may feel isolated, even abandoned.

4. Fear or embarrassment may prevent requests for home instruction. Girls may be too concerned about themselves or the inadequacies they feel characterize their homes.

Special centers, too, have drawbacks. Some are similar to those connected with home teaching.

1. As noted earlier, special centers often do not include the comprehensive curricular and extracurricular opportunities of regular schools.
2. Students are separated from potentially supportive friends among the student body and the faculty.
3. Aggregating students for educational purposes simply on the basis that they are all pregnant is grouping based on an educationally irrelevant criterion.

A Modern Approach to Education

Today's preferred educational practice is to afford each school age parent-to-be or parent two options: (a) to attend a special center or (b) to continue (with facilitated attendance) at their regular school.

Garmezy (1975) described how one district moved to assure that pregnant girls and young mothers might continue their education in their regular school. She described the program's purposes as to:

Enable student mothers to remain in their regular school;
Provide them with practical information and supervised experience in child care and parenting;
Provide their children with individualized care in a safe and stimulating environment. (p. 4)

Minneapolis had operated, since 1961, a separated program for pregnant girls and young mothers. It was found that increasingly these pupils wanted to continue their schooling where they were already enrolled. In 1971 that was made possible in a pilot secondary school in order to determine what would need to be done to make it feasible elsewhere.

Extrapolating from Garmezy's (1975) report, certain characteristics could be found to exemplify preferred practice in maintaining pregnant girls and young mothers in their regular school programs and in personalizing education to suit their needs. The focus here is on secondary schools. Although the age range of pregnant girls takes in some 11 and 12 year olds, the numbers in the school age group do not loom large until ages 13 and 14. Where younger girls are involved, of course, they should have opportunities to continue in regular schools, too. The preferred practices extrapolated from Garmezy are as follows:

1. Home economics facilities should be equipped and staffed for day care, including food service, for infants and toddlers during the

school day. A staff-child ratio of one to four is suitable, although service should be provided even if only one child needs day care. (The service may be extended to married teachers and other staff, if desired, on a fringe benefit or paid basis.) Basic equipment extends from diapers and cribs to toys and indoor play areas. The day care service should be free to pupil-parents and available until the mother's graduation.
2. Pupils should have prenatal counseling and postnatal instruction in parenting skills. If permission is obtained from the parents of children in day care at the school, other pupils, boys and girls, may participate in their care as part of the home economics curriculum.
3. The city or county public health service should furnish medical supervision as needed. A public health nurse should be detailed from that service to work at the school, with the amount of time dependent upon the number of babies involved.
4. The fact of pregnancy or motherhood should not be allowed to overshadow the pupil's continuing need for individualized education matched to cognitive level, learning style, interests, and present achievement, like all other pupils.
5. Transportation should be supplied, if needed, to and from school.
6. Recognition should be given to the needs and rights of both fathers and mothers, whether married or unmarried.
7. Mothers should have appropriate opportunities to feed and play with their children during the school day.
8. The entire professional and support staff of the school needs orientation to the program long enough before it is started to allow questions to be raised and answered, and to allow everyone at least to make progress in working out their moral and ethical feelings about it. Some help on the latter is in the next subsection.

General Background

Annually, in the United States, more than 210,000 births are recorded to mothers between 12 and 18 years of age. The number has been increasing by about 3,000 annually. The increase is connected with the growing population in that age group rather than a rising rate of pregnancy.

Girls who become pregnant during school age come from all socioeconomic classes and from both public and private schools. All races, all religions, and all parts of the country, rural and urban, are represented. The pregnancy is not typically the consequence of a casual or fleeting relationship. Ordinarily, the mother and father have known each other at least a year and their strong feelings for each other were present substantially before the sexual relations began (Howard, 1975). The parents usually are close to the same age, come from the same socioeconomic backgrounds, and achieve about the same in school; and neither is typically more worldly-wise than the other. Pressure to initiate the sexual relationship may have come from either partner. When it does take place it is most often in the context of two individuals who are embarking, for the first time, on an interpersonal relationship they both consider serious.

A generation ago, most teenage mothers gave up their infants, whom they never saw, for adoption. But that is no longer the case. A 1973 estimate (Nolte, 1973) indicated that 85% of the school age girls who give birth each year keep and raise their children.

Agencies dealing with school age parenthood are turning more attention to fathers, also. There is evidence to justify the belief that many very young fathers wish to take the actual father role with their babies (Howard, 1975). Of the others, most will want a future marriage in which they will have true father roles. So the long range goals for young fathers are not essentially different from those for young mothers:

1. To complete schooling and acquire the competencies to maintain independence in competitive society.
2. To learn how to be a worthy parent.
3. To acquire maturity in personal and social behavior.
4. To be a contributing and stabilizing force in family life.

It is a fact of life that teenage parents are and probably will continue to be part of every community. In earlier days, the unmarried parents and their child were objects of scorn, punishment, or both, and these attitudes still are not uncommon. However, many people realize that traditional responses to the problems of school age parents and their offspring have been inadequate, and thus a new look is being taken at young families.

There are as many individual variations among teenage parents as among any other segment of the population. Adolescents range all the way along a developmental continuum from childhood to adulthood. Age is only a general guide. Early maturity in one area may not be paralleled in others, whether affective, motoric, or cognitive. It is misleading to think of schoolage mothers and fathers as a homogeneous group.

The new approach, therefore, musters services on an individualized basis to provide the additional measures of support that are needed by young fathers and mothers. They include information, practical help, counseling, job guidance, loans, and personalized education. The consequences can only better individual and family life for young parents and give a better life start for their children.

SUGGESTIONS FOR STUDENTS AND INSTRUCTOR

1. Check with your state department of education and welfare (or county offices) for information on the extent of provisions for exceptional children in early childhood education programs and for early parent consultation.
2. Investigate the provisions of law in your state regarding child abuse and neglect and the extent of compliance with the laws you locate.
3. Visit one or more agencies in your community that serve young people who have chemical dependency problems.
4. Check local programs for teenage parents against the criteria suggested in this chapter for forward looking programs. Check also on trends in births out of wedlock and placements for adoption by teenage parents.
5. Investigate programs offered in local secondary schools on problems of drug and alcohol use.
6. Visit and/or become volunteers in early education programs.

TOPICAL BIBLIOGRAPHIES

Early Childhood Education for the Handicapped

Gallagher, J. J. (Ed.). *Application of child development research to exceptional children.* Reston VA: The Council for Exceptional Children, 1975.

Hunt, J. M. The psychological basis for using preschool enrichment as an antidote for cultural deprivation. *Merrill-Palmer Quarterly,* 1964, *10,* 236.

Jordan, J. B., Hayden, A. H., Karnes, M. B., & Wood, M., Eds. *Early childhood education for exceptional children: A handbook of ideas and exemplary practices.* Reston VA: The Council for Exceptional Children, 1977.

Karnes, M. B., & Lee, R. C. *What research and experience say to the teacher of exceptional children: Early childhood.* Reston VA: The Council for Exceptional Children, 1978.

Karnes, M.B. How one nationally validated early education program meets the mandate of Public Law 94-142 and assists others in replication. *Center,* 1977, 3(1), 1, 7-9.

Karnes, M. B., Teska, J. A., & Hodgins, A. S. The effects of four programs of classroom intervention on the intellectual and language development of 4-year-old disadvantaged children. *American Journal of Orthopsychiatry,* 1970, *40,* 58-76.

Snyder, L. Appolloni, T., & Cooke, T.P. Integrated settings at the early childhood level: The role of retarded peers. *Exceptional Children,* 1977, *43,* 262-266.

Chemical Dependency

Armor, D. J., Polich, J. M., & Stambul, H. B. *Alcoholism and treatment.* Santa Monica CA: Rand Corporation, 1976.

A family response to the drug problem. Washington DC: US Government Printing Office, HE 20. 8268: F, 21/2, 1976.

Drugs and personality. Washington DC: US Government Printing Office, HE 20, 8214, 14, 1976.

Gadow, K. D. *Children on medication: A primer for school personnel.* Reston VA: The Council for Exceptional Children, 1979.

Teacher Training

See resource list, Appendix B of this volume.

Teenage Parents

Howard, M. *Teenage pregnancy and parenthood.* New York: Seabury Press, 1975.

Klerman, L.V., & Jekel, J.F. *School-age mothers: Problems, programs and policy.* Hamden CT: Sinnet Books, 1973.

Nolte, M. C. Why your school board should review and (probably) remake its policy toward pregnant school girls. *American School Board Journal,* March 1973, 23-27.

Child Abuse and Neglect

Kline, D. F. *Child abuse and neglect: A primer for school personnel.* Reston VA: The Council for Exceptional Children, 1977.

Thomas, M. A., Ed. *Children alone: What can be done about abuse and neglect.* Reston VA: The Council for Exceptional Children, 1977.

Media and Workshops

Child abuse and neglect: What the educator sees (multimedia). Reston VA: The Council for Exceptional Children, 1977.

McCaffrey, M., & Tewey, S. *We can help: Specialized training for educators on the prevention and treatment of child abuse and neglect.* Reston VA: The Council for Exceptional Children, 1979.

Thomas, M. A. (Ed.). *The CEC Invisible College Conference on Child Abuse and the Exceptional Child* (cassette tapes). Reston VA: The Council for Exceptional Children, 1977.

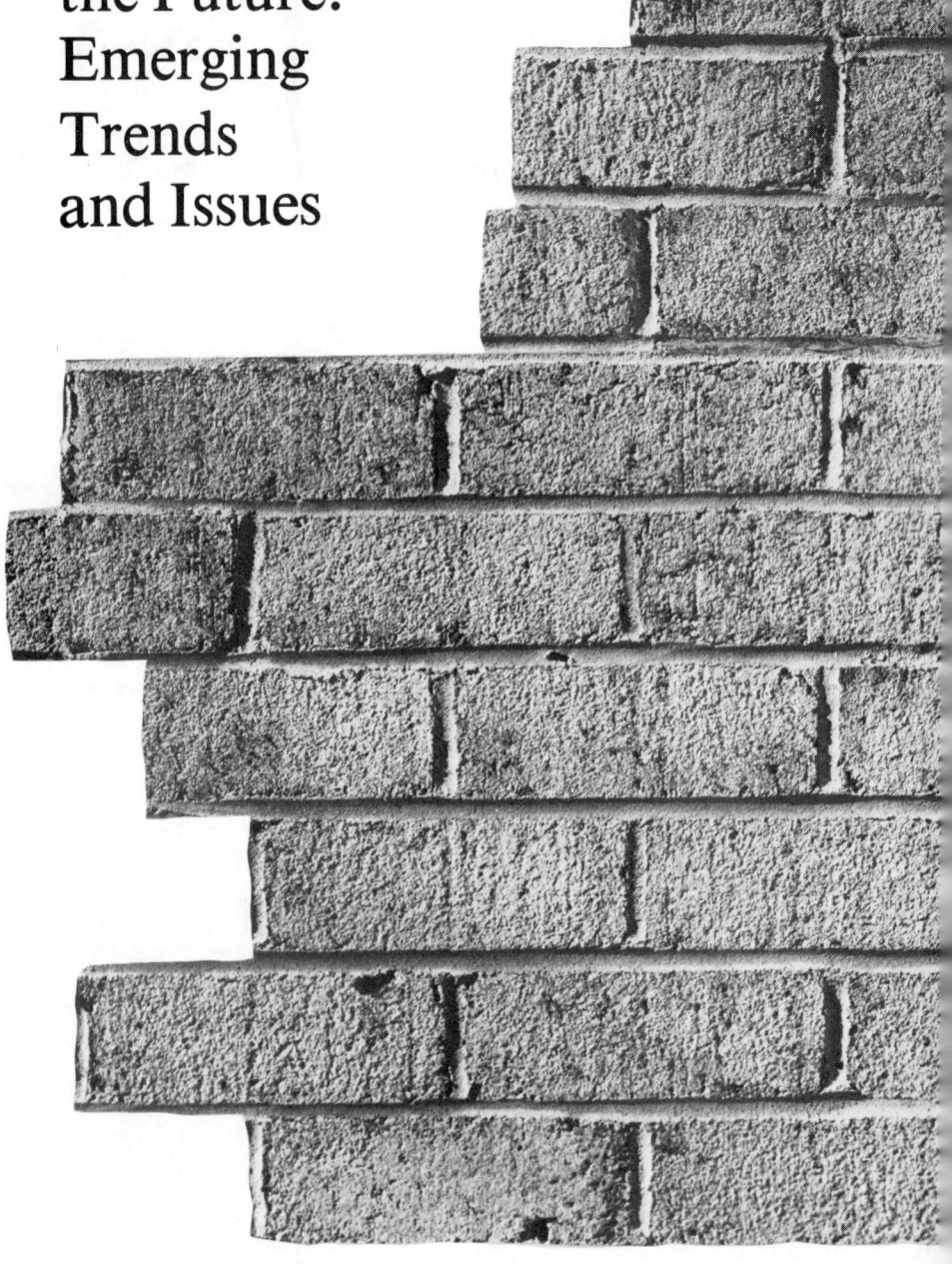

14. Facing the Future: Emerging Trends and Issues

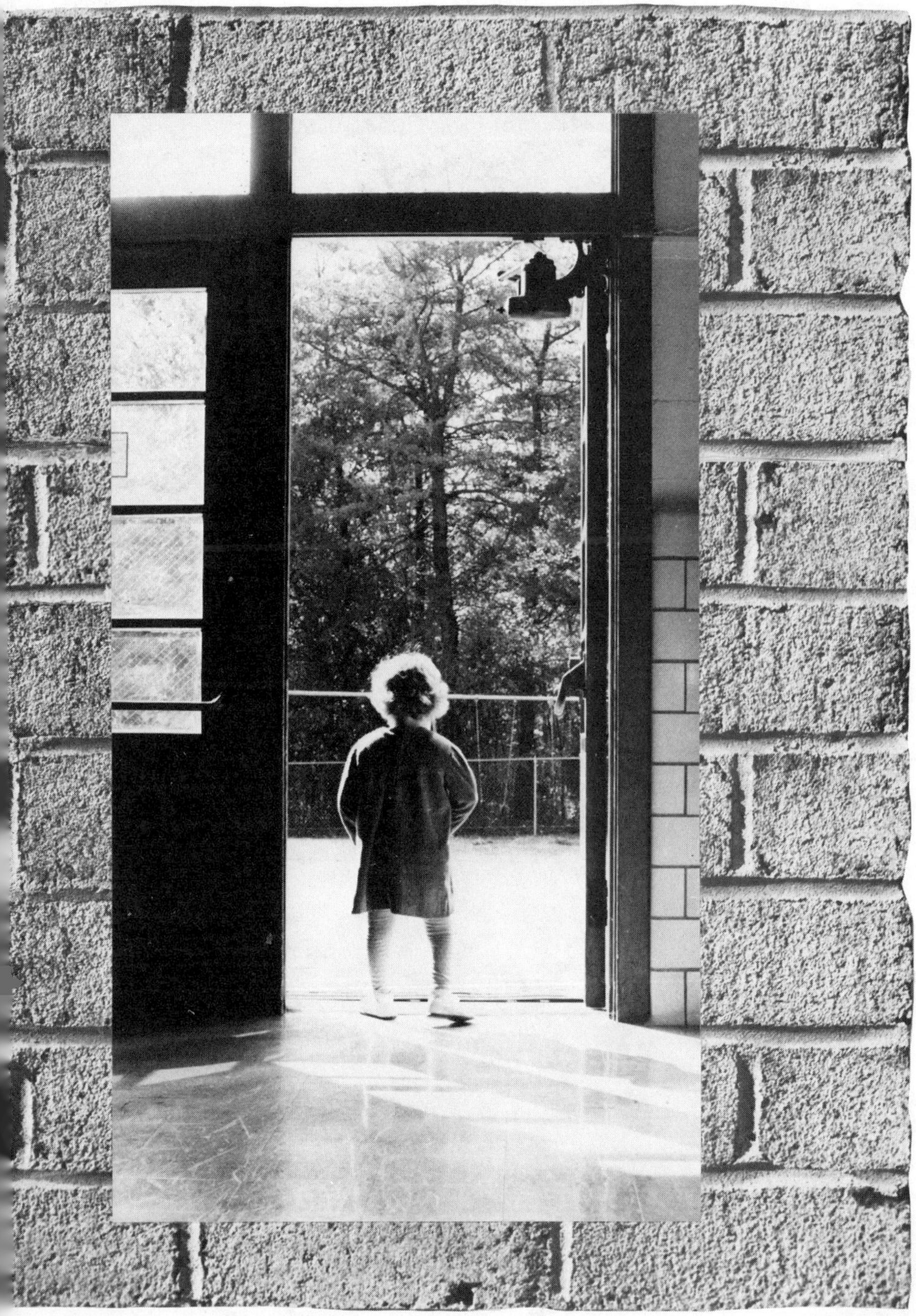

CHAPTER OUTLINE

CURRENT CHANGES IN THE SCHOOLS
CURRENT PROBLEMS IN THE SCHOOLS
    The Large Cities
    Funding
    Private Schools
    The Distribution Problem
    Commitment
    New Relationship with Remedial Specialists
    New Relations with Programs for Disadvantaged Children
    Categorizing—Labeling
    Disjunction of Diagnosis and Instruction
    More Process Than Is Due
COLLECTIVE BARGAINING AND EXCEPTIONAL CHILDREN
LOOKING TO THE FUTURE
    The Schools of the Future
    In-Service Education
CHANGE PROCESSES
CONCLUSION
SUGGESTIONS FOR STUDENTS AND INSTRUCTOR
TOPICAL BIBLIOGRAPHIES

CURRENT CHANGES IN THE SCHOOLS

The preceding chapters of this book describe some of the important changes that are currently occurring in our schools. Basically, these changes, which are subsumed under such terms as *progressive inclusion, mainstreaming, right to education,* and *decategorization,* reflect shifts in our society in attitudes toward minority groups and atypical individuals. As with many social developments, governmental recognition was spearheaded by the judicial system and then followed by state and federal legislation. Thus the series of adjudications from 1954 to the present led to the passage in 1975 of congressional legislation (Public Law 94-142) that mandates for every child the right to education and for handicapped children the right to appropriate education. Although educational practices in this country have long been evolving toward these goals, the advancement of these principles by the Congress and state legislatures has forced the acceleration of the process.

Whenever change is demanded of established institutions such as schools by outside forces, disruptions are inevitable. Thus, currently, education is in a period of transition. Old certainties are being challenged and entrenched roles and functions are under redefinition. At the same time, new problems have surfaced and old ones have taken new forms. Many educators have become so preoccupied with observing the new laws and regulations and resolving the immediate questions that they tend to have a fragmented view of the present and future of education. We can see where we have come from but not, clearly, where we are or where we are headed. What will schools be like in the future, for example, when all the present trends and issues reach their logical conclusions? In this final chapter, we have tried to answer this question as best we can.

It has been said that all we know is of the past but our decisions determine the future. Therefore, it is fitting that we should focus on present problems and issues that appear to hold strong portents for the future development of public school operations. Although the following discussion is based, admittedly, on personal experiences and interpretations, it may provide the stimulus for more educational personnel to make their own analyses of the present and projections for the future.

CURRENT PROBLEMS IN THE SCHOOLS

The problems and issues discussed in this section, although recognized for some time, are closely related to the changes in schools demanded by the new laws and regulations. Some are part of the societal shifts that led to the new legislation; others are consequences of those shifts.

The Large Cities

In 1973, the 23 largest cities* enrolled in public schools somewhat over 10% of the children of the nation. These same cities had 30% of the children who qualified as disadvantaged (as defined in certain US Office of Education programs). The lives of many children in the cities are in disorder, especially the high proportion from minority groups (Blacks, Chicano, Indian). Minority group children have been placed in special classes for the educable mentally retarded at two to four times the rate for the placement of White children. Special education stations have been used also, more often than not, as places to isolate "disruptive" children so that order can be kept in regular programs, rather than as distinctly specialized education centers for carefully diagnosed children. Minority group parents and professionals have rebelled against the special placements and the resulting negative labels, and they insist on integrated programing for their children. But if difficult children are returned in large numbers from special education to regular classes, the teachers may resist unless strong, supportive arrangements are made.

Undoubtedly, it would be desirable to undertake massive new programs to individualize instruction in the regular classes of the large cities and to use special education personnel in support roles, but the funds and other resources—leadership, vitality, commitment, and trainers—needed for the change are too often lacking. Indeed, the largest cities are those with the most serious financial problems and those most likely to reduce educational expenditures. They have relatively little capacity at this time to mount the desirable retraining and support systems. In the meantime, residential institutions are returning to the cities many children who are mentally ill, retarded, or adjudicated delinquent.

There is little doubt that we have crowded a large proportion of children with serious problems into large urban centers that are themselves in disorder and that, in turn, magnify the disorder in the lives of children. These youngsters have too few stable and constructive supports in their lives. They and their life situations should be the focus for the best resources of special education. But the fact is that, so far, many state departments of education and institutions of higher education operate as if they were largely unaware of the distinct and massive problems of special education in the cities.

There are a few signs that the cities themselves may organize new forces with which to "bootstrap" their own repairs (Reynolds, 1975). For example, the city of Minneapolis has shown considerable strength in its programs for handicapped students; Boston schools, despite great

---

*In 1973, there were 23 city members of the Council of Great Cities. These observations are made mainly on the basis of date on the Council cities.

difficulties with desegregation, have managed to effect a major reorganization of special education programs (Johnson, Gross, Reynolds, & Nash, 1975); somehow, Philadelphia has surmounted the difficulties of the *PARC* decision and has organized a great many new programs for severely handicapped students, and mainstream programs appear to be progressing (Young, 1976). The Dallas public schools are showing much vitality, in services to children and in training programs. The Council of Great Cities has organized a special technical assistance system to aid member cities in the development and transformation of their special education programs. The schools, of course, cannot deal with the economic sources of the children's difficulties but they can provide the opportunities for the children to break old discouraging patterns.

Funding

Always a problem, the funding of specialized school programs looms now as a larger and, to some extent, different challenge. The courts are ordering new developments for special education but they can provide no money; they only have the power to direct. Not surprisingly, many state legislatures and the congress seem reluctant to change their agendas and budgets at the behest of the courts. There is much rhetoric about "full service goals" but the dollar gap between legislated authorizations and appropriations remains enormous. The result is that special educators are directed to initiate new programs just as fund raising has become a severe problem. Thus they are forced into the position of arguing for the reallocation of insufficient local funds.

State and local authorities often appear to be more interested in holding down taxes, even though it means slighting the needs of special education along with other aspects of education, because votes against the handicapped are no longer political suicide. It is a great difficulty for school leaders in many states and a cruelty to many children that, as institutions for the mentally ill and retarded are being required to return children to the communities, corresponding shifts of funds to the local schools, which must bear the brunt of the exodus, are not being made. There is a tragic lack of broad policy development and planning so that what happens in one part of a total system for serving the handicapped is often unconnected with other parts.

Another very great difficulty is that as programs emerge for the integration of special education with mainstream programs, as interchanges of children between specialized and regular school stations are being developed, the eligibility of the schools for state special education financial aids frequently becomes uncertain; that is, in many states the special education aids are categorical and are available only when specific children have been labeled and placed into specialized programs other than the regular classroom. If the handicapped or gifted student is served in a broadened mainstream without being labeled, the local district often is not recompensed by the state. Since preschool programs seldom involve "set-aside" stations for exceptional children, they seldom qualify for categorical special education funds. Thus, a most unfortunate deterrent is introduced into the school situation: School leaders may wish to accommodate handicapped children in the mainstream, but they are rewarded only for maintaining isolated program formats.

To a degree, special education now suffers the same problem as health. For example, public monies or insurance programs usually cover costs for hospitalization (special placement) but not for home treatment (mainstream) and careful attention to health (education) there. Consequently, people are sent to hospitals and children to special classes and special schools because money for program support can be obtained in no other way. Our policies on programs and funding are at cross purposes. Eliminating the difficulty in the case of special education is likely to be difficult because in most states the basic unit for "payoff," the unit that triggers the dollar flow, is the individual child who is labeled in a category and placed in a special program. That approach may not be viable for much longer; it will have to be replaced by funding systems that deal with a different unit if we are to fulfill the judicial mandates for mainstreaming.

If schools are to develop a broad continuum of services that do not all require the categorization of handicapped and gifted children in traditional niches, it will be necessary to define new units for documenting the work of special educators. Categorizing, labeling, and listing exceptional children, and then using the size of the roster as the measure for the public financial support for programs, are unnecessary and defeating. The public outcry against such practices is mounting. The key changes must come in both legislation and regulations.

Part of the answer may lie in shifting the basic reimbursement unit from the child to the specialized teacher or other professional worker, and then permitting them to be employed in whatever capacities will enhance the opportunities for children with exceptional needs. An alternative procedure is to fund broadly framed programs or major program components. Hobbs (1975) envisioned a system in which costs of "requirements of service" for specialized program components could be reimbursed to local districts from state and/or federal treasuries, and computerized systems would help to ease the accounting difficulties. Examples of these alternatives are beginning to emerge in several states. The master plan, which was initiated in California in the mid 1970's, for example, offers special state financial support for major programmatic units rather than for children in categories. In Minnesota, a state special education reimbursement system has dealt with the "necessary personnel" as the basic unit for many years. In any case, the definition, dissemination, and acceptance of new units, other than child in category, is likely to be a major challenge to special education for some time (Bernstein, Kirst, Hartman, & Marshall, 1976).

A subtle but potentially devastating funding problem is the general loss in recent years of development and broad support system funds. The Education Professions Development Act, for example, which in the late 1960's and early 1970's provided federal funds to support innovative training and, indirectly, new service models, has been stripped of its authorization and resources. In the long run, this lack of developmental funds will impose severe limitations on the generation faced with establishing new concepts and leadership in special education.

Under Public Law 94-142, which is rapidly becoming the dominant determinant of the federal role in special education, priority of concern is given to severely handicapped students, especially those who, in the past, have not been in schools. Many of these students cannot be enrolled in integrated or mainstreamed school programs. But the law also stresses the importance of educating handicapped children with nonhandicapped children whenever feasible. It remains to be seen whether the dollar flow under Public Law 94-142 will go only to programs for the severely handicapped or whether a significant part of the funds will flow to mainstream programs. It is axiomatic, then, that school programs follow the dollar flow; that is, if the federal dollars fail to flow to mainstream programs the development of mainstream programs will flounder.

A fundamental funding question, of course, is just what proportion of the total child population shall be the concern of special educators. The parallel question is how much the public is able and willing to pay for under the special education rubric. There are increasing numbers of signs that legislators want to put a "cap" or some kind of rational control on special education expenditures. At this time, the common percentage claimed for "handicapped" is about 10% to 12% of the total child population with the "gifted and talented" adding approximately another 3%. Some persons would stretch the percentages; others would contract special education services and dedicate the field only to the most severely handicapped and the most highly gifted children, perhaps aggregating to only 4% to 5% of the general child population. The assumption made here is that, at least for the near future, the contemporary special education thrust, in addition to taking clear and definite leadership in providing programs for the "most exceptional of the exceptional," will need to supply a large proportion of the energies, commitments, and skills necessary to serve the many other pupils with special needs. It is mainly in the latter aspect of the special education mission that new relationships with regular education must be negotiated. Further, it is assumed that special educators themselves will need to lead the way in setting limits in programmatic costs.

It can be argued that society will tolerate large dollar differences in the investments made for the education of children who have special needs and of other children only when the numbers of exceptional children involved are relatively small, much as extraordinary costs are tolerated for individuals in a hospital and for medical care as long as the numbers involved are small. There are concerns in Congress, state legislatures, and boards of education that the most expensive forms of education not be extended needlessly to an excessive number of children. The assumption made here is that one of the ways of protecting services for pupils with the most extraordinary educational requirements—which are often expensive—is to provide effective early education and well supported mainstream education for students who have special needs. In any case, costs will be high; but expenses could go out of sight and programs into disfavor if special stations for education are allowed to become too large. It should not be anticipated, we believe, that school costs will go down as mainstreaming policies are implemented; but caution in claiming ever increasing special education budgets seems to be a necessity. Basically, the problem is one of public policy, of priorities for how public monies should be expended. Educators, as citizens, should not neglect their obligation to help to determine these priorities.

Private Schools

One convenient way for local schools to comply with "right to education" directives is to send difficult children to private schools. Although the policy creates no programmatic disturbances at local levels, it is beset with many difficulties. Chief among them is the unfortunate removal of the children from home and community supports. If the movement in this direction is great, costs can be enormous, as they now are in several states, and political forces can develop that place all of special education out of control. Powerful, well meaning advocates for private schools easily could use their resources and the due process mechanisms to build a new private school system in the nation and, in the process, deprive the local day schools of the energies and resources necessary to develop broad and effective programs for exceptional children.

Sometimes a special version of the medical model emerges in which psychiatrists or other noneducational specialists virtually control referral and admissions to private schools. The whole system can be turned to the advantage of relatively affluent families—those who can secure private diagnoses and maneuver through the necessary steps of referral and placement. There is evidence, in some places, that public payments for expensive private schools tend to be used to preserve racial segregation.

Exceptional children need all the help they can get and some of it, appropriately, comes from the private sector. There are excellent private schools and many other forms of private contributions to the education of exceptional children. We have a great need to make visible the examples of healthy interaction between public and private programs for exceptional children but, equally, to expose and oppose unhealthy operations and trends.

The Distribution Problem

Special education services always have been maldistributed, but never so obviously as now when the courts and Congress direct that all children be served. One key facet of the distribution problem is that specialists tend not to go to certain high need areas for employment. For example, it is difficult to place highly trained teachers of braille and mobility in rural areas where only a small number of widely handicapped children need services and a major portion of the specialist's time is spent in traveling. Somehow, better methods of recruitment, placement, and use of specialized personnel must be found so that the obligation to serve children in normal environments can be realized, even for those in remote and rural areas. The most logical solution is a wider distribution of special training among regular class teachers.

The major implementing changes in this domain may have to occur in the colleges. Somehow they need to direct their training efforts to people who will serve where they are most needed. But equally important, specialists in speech correction and the teaching of blind or deaf pupils, for instance, will need to be willing to "give away" their skills and agree that at least the basic elements of their specializations can be made part of the preparation of all teachers. The sharing of expertise could result in the preparation of a corps of broadly trained teachers who, with supportive help, could deliver a wide spectrum of specialized instruction and leadership. A deeply committed and resourceful person so prepared could work in rural areas, and through special support systems (e.g., more specialized consultation through a computer linkage, video discs, or other technologues), the teacher's competencies could be stretched to accommodate the additional needs of the child.

One other possible solution may be for federal and state officials, in concert with teacher organizations, to organize a hierarchical system in which personnel needs are specified for whole states or broad regions, and the corresponding training functions are allocated to institutions of higher education. The recruitment, training, and placement of trainees would be monitored and evaluated according to how well personnel needs were satisfied, even in rural and other areas of specific need. There are some signs of movement in this direction through the encouragement of coordinated voluntary programs among colleges and state departments of education by federal officers in the awards of training grants.

A different approach may be to shift some of the training funds, which now are awarded to colleges, local schools, and agencies to permit them to purchase specialized training for personnel according to their needs. It could be assumed that they would recruit, select, and support the training of indigenous teacher candidates, those who are firmly committed to return with their specialized skills to the communities sponsoring them. Another probable effect would be to draw collegiate training resources out to communities where they are needed for on the job training. This plan would force more college departments of special education to "package" and "export" their training for on-site use.

Technological developments (e.g., the miniaturization of electronic devices and the video disc), improved communication (e.g., remote access computer terminals), and improved transportation will help to create new opportunities to deliver diverse educational programs, even for pupils in remote areas.

Commitment

Many persons whose positions are powerful enough to give them strong influence on education are doubtful of some of the emerging principles and practices of special education. For example, some school administrators do not accept easily the ideology represented in the "right to education" principle. Teachers' associations and unions are not always enthusiastic about the mainstreaming trend in school and community life, probably because it involves fewer referrals out of, and the return of some exceptional children to, regular classes, which is viewed as a threat of disorder and deterioration in the learning environment for other pupils. Some leaders feel that commitments to new forms of special education should wait until research and evaluation processes are further along and we have better evidence for whatever action is taken. Further, some minority group parents are skeptical of special education in any form.

Part of the answer to the commitment problem may come with the dissemination of information on the many promising new models by which exceptional children are provided with special education services in mainstream school and community settings and in which special educators form closer partnerships with the regular school personnel to create improved learning environments for all children. Demonstrations of such new practices and retraining programs are essential. With effort, there undoubtedly can be progress in winning commitment to the necessary developments, however large and formidable the problem may seem, in implementing the policies of our society now expressed in court decisions. Special educators can contribute by giving careful attention to problems of evaluation so that deliberations about the formats of special education programs are as informed as possible. Somehow, leading general administrators and lay persons, such as members of boards of education, must be persuaded that the integration of exceptional children in regular school programs is feasible and practical as well as an ethical and a judicial requirement. These influential persons must be educated also in the purposes of mainstreaming as a social movement and not as an excuse to increase class size without increases in special personnel.

New Relationships with Remedial Specialists

In recent years, many of the long standing programs of remedial instruction in reading and mathematics have become the responsibilities of special education under a "learning disabilities" banner, partly, one suspects, because more money is available for special education. A set of similar programs has operated, since 1965, under Title I of the Elementary and Secondary Education Act (ESEA) to provide a great deal of tutoring in basic subjects to children who have shown poor responses to early instruction. Except for the distinctive administrative structure required for ESEA programs, much of the instruction it supports could well be conducted within either a special education or a remedial instruction framework.

Congressman Quie (Republican, Minnesota) introduced in the Congress (1970) a proposal to fund special programs for children, without regard for categorical distinctions, who score low on criterion referenced tests in basic academic skills, that is, it would not matter whether the low scoring child is educable mentally retarded, gifted, a remedial case, learning disabled, or whether the parents are rich or poor. Only the child's progress in basic skills would determine eligibility. That kind of action on a broader front seems a promising step. Separating children into categories that are created by notions of "process disorders," sometimes said to be the problem of learning disabled children, or according to patterns of discrepancy analysis, as in defining remedial cases, just does not hold up in careful analysis. Each child would be carefully studied, but would not be classified in the traditional special education categories to be provided with whatever extra help is needed, temporarily or permanently.

School leaders might justifiably raise serious questions about the current necessity of supporting so many different streams of activity on behalf of children with learning problems in each school. There are so many different patterns of financial support and accountability, different forms of teacher certification, and recurring patterns of "applications" for support, often followed by long and anxious waiting periods for "approval," that the climate for many programs is far from desirable. We hope that new relations will be established among the several programs so that a more unified service to children becomes possible. To achieve this unity will require difficult changes in professional organizations, teacher preparation and certification, and funding provisions.

New Relations with Programs for Disadvantaged Children

The negative attitudes toward special education in the urban ghettos is not a revulsion against specialized school programs; indeed, more specialized programs that focus on basic needs of children are demanded. The attitudes, rather, reflect an intolerance for simplistic and degrading labeling systems and what appears to be the rejection and isolation of many minority group children in special settings. Parents of the minority community and many others see the reformation of special education programs as an aspect of the long standing civil rights movement.

As special educators join with regular teachers and help to install systems for the individualized instruction of all students in basic skills, there is reason to hope for good acceptance by all parents in the urban community and elsewhere. The acceleration of this acceptance will depend on the extent to which special educators seek counsel and mutual assistance from leaders in minority group education and direct themselves with a sense of high urgency to the problem of urban education.

Special educators have had an awkward time since 1965 in clarifying how they wish to relate to programs for the "disadvantaged" under the Elementary and Secondary Education Act, in part because it was felt necessary to distinguish specialized programs for the handicapped from those serving "other" children. Again, the kind of simple, straightforward proposal offered by Congressman Quie—to support improved education for children whose learning is not progressing adequately—seems refreshing and right. Ultimately, the distinction between programs for the disadvantaged and special education programs sought to be blurred if not eliminated in favor of programs that serve the special needs of individual children. The distinction between Title I, remedial education, drug education, and special education, and many other narrowly categorical programs, each with its separate administrative officers and state or federal regulations, has created a veritable jungle of problems. However, the strong trend toward programs in which learners are served according to their individual needs will force important amalgamations among the various categorical programs.

Categorizing—Labeling

The categories still used in many places for the labeling and placement of handicapped children do not serve anyone well. They do not "carve nature at its joints" or even fulfill their ostensible purposes. The labels—retarded, disturbed, and defective—narrow rather than broaden children's opportunities. Educators, we believe, should avoid crude classifications and focus on children and concentrate instead on assessments of children that are meaningful for instructional purposes. As we open up the special/regular educational boundaries, there is good reason to rethink and revise our classification systems. Is it really necessary to continue to label children in traditional categories to win political support and to insure accountability? In our view, any but a negative response is short sighted and threatens the long term development or services for children.

There are many voices speaking to special educators these days of the necessity of dropping the degrading, nonfunctional categorical systems of the past. The President's Committee on Mental Retardation (1969) titled one of its recent major reports *The Six-Hour Retarded Child*. Its implication is that educators are the only ones who find it necessary to apply the label mentally retarded to many children. Following the *Larry P. v. Riles* (1972) court case, the numbers of children labeled educable mentally retarded in California schools declined sharply. Witness the apparent inability of the profession to satisfy itself or the Congress about a definition of learning disability. Public Law 94-142 called upon the Commissioner of Education to supply the US Congress with a definition of learning disability. At the time of this writing, efforts to supply the definition have been abortive.

The fact is that there is no clean and clear way to delineate the population of handicapped children by attending just to certain attributes of the children themselves. Many children are handicapped only in situuations that do not accommodate their needs. The required focus of attention is broader than the child in the classroom and should encompass the school and family situations. This broader ecological framing of the problem requires delineation of new systems of classification.

It can be argued, of course, that the traditional categories and labels may be necessary, that they serve important social and political purposes, and that they thus need to be preserved—especially as a means of rallying special interest and support by legislators and administrators. Hobbs (1975), in two contrasting passages of his important work on the classification issue, stated the problem as follows:

> Categories and labels are powerful instruments for social regulation and control, and they are often employed for obscure, covert, or hurtful purposes: to degrade people, to deny them access to opportunity, to exclude

> "undesirables" whose presence in some way offends, disturbs familiar custom, or demands extraordinary effort. (p. 11)

On the other hand,

> categories and labels may open up opportunities for exceptional children, facilitate the passage of legislation in their interest, supply rallying points for volunteer organizations, and provide a rational structure for the administration of governmental programs. (p. 13)

We cannot long have it both ways, maintaining simplistic categories while denying their utility. There is an urgent necessity for an educational program for legislators, administrators, teachers, parents, and others to elevate everyone's awareness of the need for a more sophisticated conceptualization of the classification problem.

It should be possible to say to legislators, parents, and others something like the following:

> There are children whose cognitive development is problematic, some who do not respond well to the ordinary or modal forms of instruction and others whose behaviors for whatever reason seem erratic, disturbing, or at least nonattentive to school tasks. In times past, for such children, we've used various categories and labels such as mentally retarded, learning disabled, or emotionally disturbed; and we've even been caught up in systems that congregate special groupings of such children.
>
> But now we're discovering more promising approaches to developmental problems. In the process, we see the necessity of much more detailed and broader classification systems, encompassing not only the child but his/her life situation as well.
>
> So, while we recognize that terms such as "mental retardation" or "emotionally disturbed" or "learning disabled" have been and continue to be organizing concepts for much social action, legislation, parent groups and even professional associations, we urge all concerned to understand that these terms need no longer be the starting points for special education programs. There is no special merit in sending children off to isolated classes and centers for instruction by separate categories. Instead, the study of children and of their life situations is now proceeding to finer points, all of them oriented to improving the instructional programs offered to the child in the regular school environment. And as we attend in this different way to children formerly thought of in narrow categorical ways, we can spread attention to other children as well, many of whom may not have been well served in our schools yet who did not fall within the traditional categories.

By a strategy such as this, we can hope to extricate ourselves and the children we serve from the confinements of an outdated categorical system without sacrificing the great concerns and resources that are needed if all children are to be served well in the schools.

Disjunction of Diagnosis and Instruction

Mainstreaming implies a major effort to decentralize both diagnosis and instruction, that is to incorporate both in the functions performed in ordinary school buildings rather than to keep them in special centers under the jurisdiction of special centralized teams. When diagnosis is performed in remote places and instructional prescriptions are then delivered at long distance to teachers who are to be accountable for implementing the prescriptions but have had no part in writing them, there is great risk of default on all of the promises made to the children. We propose that the preferred practice be to work toward a highly decentralized diagnostic and instructional service that involves the personnel who are accountable for implementation. This means developing more capacity for diagnosis and specialized teaching in every school facility and using highly specialized staff members for consultation and training functions—and only occasionally as staff in separate facilities to which teachers make referrals.

More Process Than Is Due

There is some danger that in the name of due process schools may find themselves implicated in much *more* process than is due. Teachers and parents, we hope, generally will be able to work together constructively, creatively, and informally to design programs for handicapped children, and the formalities and adverse features of due process will be reserved for only the most difficult problems of decision making. When there is much distrust in a community, there may well be excesses of regulation and due process. So much time and resources could be consumed in regulatory matters that too little would remain for the important business of improving the services for the children at issue. For example, the history of the juvenile justice movement of the past two decades has been described as mostly a very expensive story of promises unfulfilled; diagnosis, treatment, and education undelivered; and bureaucratic machinations mounted to overpowering levels. There could be a similar tale in the next decade in special education if we do not construct effective means for coordinating school-home efforts and keeping "processes" clear, well disciplined, and focused on the purposes of enhancing equal and appropriate opportunities for the education of all children.

At the time of this writing many professionals are involved very deeply in working out systems that can be applied at local and state levels in meeting the innumerable demands of new federal laws (mainly Public Law 94-142 and Section 504 of the Rehabilitation Act). Involved are systems for prior notification to and approval by parents before any child assessment takes place, similar parental assent on diagnosis and plans, open reviews of all data on children, team meetings of professionals and parents to work out individual education plans. Educators are busy educating one another on due process, individual educational plans, hearings and appeal processes, monitoring files, and like matters. It would be comforting if one could believe that all of this activity would lead to truly creative problem solving by the significant parties in each child's life, and it may do so; but a large part of the content and procedure seems oriented to mere compliance with regulations or the law—"staying clean" on the requirements.

Commenting on developments in one state, Reynolds (1975) noted the following:

> The final development of regulations in the state I visited are all that I feared and more. For example, regulations specify the kinds of stamps to be used in mailing formal letters to parents about the plans envisioned for their children; and they specify the number of days that must elapse between stages of due process actions. The regulations cover virtually every legal problem that could possibly arise among schools, school personnel, and parents and children but, in my view, they reflect little vision of the ways in which significant persons might come together creatively to shape environments that will useful and helpful to children. I believe that adherence to the detailed regulations of that state will consume the energies and distract the attention of special education leaders at all levels. It is predictable that the best of their leadership will leave the state rather than succumb to such a system. Some children and parents no doubt need and will profit by all the formalities of the procedures. But my guess is that many more will be frightened by the process. The professionals who submit to this kind of blitz of paper and process will be alienated from their clients and greatly disheartened. (pp. 62-63)

Commenting generally both about the new state-federal partnership and about regulations for implementing Public Law 94-142, Shedd (1977) said this:

> A civil war has broken out in this country; battle lines have been drawn and shots fired. It is being waged in our schools and government offices with pupil survey forms, USOE regulations and tax dollars. At issue is the fundamental, Constitutionally-guaranteed right of state governments to manage their educational programs.
>
> It is happening because state and local educators, groaning under the burden of federal regulations and paperwork, have decided to fight back. In recent months, a growing number of school systems have rejected federal grants rather than complete the required paperwork. And many towns have considered the possibility of phasing out *all* federal funds in order to eliminate the red tape burden.
>
> The Florida state legislature is now considering a proposal to apply for and accept P.L. 94-142 (Education for All Handicapped Act) funds only under certain stringent conditions which reflect the educational needs and

legal restrictions of the state. If the application is rejected by the federal government, the Florida proposal calls for temporary state funding of the law while the case makes its way through the courts.

- Every state in the union will be watching that case in the coming months—because every state in the union is laboring under the oppressive weight of federal regulations. Each school administrator has experienced personally the trials and tribulations of the federal bureaucracy. But, the collective burden is staggering indeed. (p. 18)

Perhaps it is inevitable that local schools should find themselves burdened by the detailed and expensive procedures demanded by the state and federal bureaucracies. The situation is near threshold for a major backlash against this massive intrusion. Unless there is massive additional funding to local schools, the new procedures intended to guarantee service to children may simply diminish the services the children need. It is hoped that there will be moderation in the excesses of procedural demands, and the grand promises being made to children and their families will not be mutilated or consumed by distrust, excessive rule making, and the dehumanizing processes of sheer bureaucracy.

It is a time to consider carefully the conditions under which progress can be made under the press of massive governmental interventions. Clearly, it is not enough simply to write regulations and to create compliance mechanisms. It is necessary to create new awarenesses and deeply held human commitments, launch the necessary training programs, install the new systems for management of the new ventures, and undertake the careful evaluation of all activities. In other words, a strong, well supported developmental effort is required to parallel the strong regulatory effort. To a considerable degree, a strong developmental effort can serve to reduce the necessity for large regulatory efforts. On the other hand, strong regulatory approaches with only minimal developmental efforts risk backlash and vengeful attitudes. The field of special education is not safe from this sad fate at this time.

COLLECTIVE BARGAINING AND EXCEPTIONAL CHILDREN

Collective bargaining is "the process by which wages, hours, rules and working conditions are negotiated and agreed upon by a union with an employer for all the employees collectively whom it represents" (*Random House Dictionary of the English Language*). Teachers have access to formal collective bargaining in most states. Many have exercised that right through local groups affiliated with the National Education Association and the American Federation of Teachers. Others have formed collective bargaining units that are local and not affiliated with national organization. Still other teachers, especially in states where unionization is not accepted as a right of all public employees, form organizations to represent them, albeit informally, in discussions with employers about remuneration, tenure, and working conditions. In short, teachers more and more determine their roles and responsibilities among themselves and communicate their views to superintendents and boards of education who may have different views. Usually, discussions are held by the teacher representatives and administrators until a mutually acceptable meeting of minds occurs. Formal negotiations conclude in a collective agreement—the contract between an employer and a union in behalf of all the employees represented by the union—which contains in writing the agreed on schedule of wages, rules, and working conditions.

Sosnowsky and Coleman (1971) reported that although relatively little attention was given to special education issues in the collective bargaining of teachers before the 1970's, they could foresee potential issues. In the succeeding years, the special education issues have become much more prominent, not only at local levels but at state and national levels as well. Much of that attention has centered on what might be called the mainstreaming issues.

In general, the major teacher organizations (National Education Association and the American Federation of Teachers) have expressed favorable attitudes toward more inclusive or mainstreamed arrangements for exceptional students, but with qualifications. For example, in 1975 the Representative Assembly of the National Education Association (1976) adopted the following as part of their resolutions:

The NEA will support mainstreaming handicapped students only when—

- It provides a favorable learning experience both for handicapped and for regular students.
- Regular and special teachers and administrators share equally in its planning and implementation.
- Regular and special teachers are prepared for these roles.
- Appropriate instructional materials, supportive services, and pupil personnel services are provided for the teacher and the handicapped student.
- Modifications are made in class size, scheduling, and curriculum design to accommodate the shifting demands that mainstreaming creates.
- There is a systematic evaluation and reporting of program developments.
- Adequate additional funding and resources are provided for mainstreaming and are used exclusively for that purpose. (p. 19)

Similar resolutions have been adopted by NEA affiliate groups in many states.

In their 1976 meetings, the New York State United Teachers adopted a resolution calling for a moratorium on mainstreaming unless certain preconditions were met (*New York Times*, August 19, 1976). The

American Federation of Teachers Council (1977) commenting on regulations intended to implement Public Law 94-142, urged teachers to seek "improvements" in the "New Handicapped Law." In specific reference to the "least restrictive environment" concept, the Council reported that

> teachers have pointed out that already many local and state agencies use this as a budget-cutting device that proves to be anything but beneficial to either child or teacher.
>
> The AFT position is that the proper placement of children in regular classrooms can be accomplished only with an increase in expenditures needed to limit class sizes and assure adequate support personnel and services. (p. 9)

In April, 1977, the New York State United Teachers (NYSUT) recommended nonparticipation in federal programs under Public Law 94-142 because it sets up "obstacles and expenses which are inconsistent with the proper operation of educational programs" (New York State United Teachers, 1977).

Why I Cried, "Help!"
By Isabel Byron

Wednesday was not a good day at Julia Richman High School. The cold kept most of our 3,600 students (1,000 of them freshmen, 500 more total population than last year) and all of our 160 teachers (30 fewer than last year) in the school. It did not keep the hundred rovers in the classes, only in the halls. Teachers also took to the halls, voluntarily giving up one of their "free" preparation or lunch periods.

I patrolled third period with two very big men, all of us known for our excellent rapport with students. We were helpless, impotent, totally ineffectual as packs of 20 to 30 students stampeded down halls. The students were mainly freshmen; we could not identify them. They were safe in their anonymity.

Deans came by with walkie-talkies. I described a student who had broken into a storeroom on the third floor. We have all learned to look for distinguishing marks. This student had an earring in his left ear and a gold chain with his name, "Robbie," on it. The deans knew him: a sophomore, he had been in our school six weeks and had firmly established himself in the halls. He had already been suspended once. He was suspended again that day. Robbie is now safe. A child may be suspended twice each semester. Robbie must assault someone before we can remove him. At that point, he will be transferred to another high school in the city system, and we in turn will take one of their suspended students.

(continued)

> *(continued from page 689)*
>
> The bell rang and I went to a class I love. A successful pilot project, soon to be cut, this class has been told it is special, and it acts accordingly. Fostering a family feeling, working in small groups, calling homes, taking trips, keeping close tabs on them and they on each other, I have seen reading scores jump from 9.8 to 12.0 (the highest), from 5.0 to 6.7 (the lowest).
>
> I have watched them learn to write a logically constructed paragraph, write in full sentences, discuss the term "foil" in literature, write comparative essays, find and quote proofs in the text to support their hypotheses—these same students who one year ago grew angry or tearful when faced with a blank sheet of paper and a writing assignment. They speak knowledgeably of financial aid for college students; they take college applications home to parents, many of whom have never attended a high school graduation for their older children.
>
> Wednesday I could not smile at them. I felt abused; my body hurt. Franklin needed advice; I could not concentrate. I asked him to come in early on Thursday morning.
>
> Wednesday night I went to see "Marathon Man," a bad choice. The violence was overwhelming me when the fight began in the audience: "Please keep your voices down." "I paid my money, too." This escalated to "Call the security man." I answered silently "There is no one left to call."
>
> So Thursday, after I helped Franklin, taught my classes, broke up one fight, witnessed a second, saw Robbie trespassing, had him escorted out of the building, tutored three students in the use of "The Reader's Guide to Periodical Literature," attended a meeting on school security, graded one set of test papers and one of compositions—Thursday night, in public, I screamed, "Help!" (Byron, 1976)

Copyright © 1976 by the New York Times Company. Reprinted by permission.

A potentially difficult item of negotiation is class size in relation to to the placement of handicapped students in regular classes. In one major city, the following statement was prepared for negotiation by the Federation of Teachers:

> Teachers shall not be assigned students who qualify for special assistance (blind, deaf, physically handicapped, EMR, etc.) unless those students who are "mainstreamed" into a regular classroom setting, or into a cooperative alternative educational program, are counted as five (5) students for the established maximums. Further, before special student assignment decisions are made, a thorough briefing shall be provided (including the severity of the disability, previous educational experiences in special classes, family and medical data, etc.) in order for the teacher(s) involved to have full information to arrive at the final decision to accept or reject the students in question. (Minneapolis Federation of Teachers, 1975, Article IV, Subd. 3, p. 3)

The language was not adopted.

A different approach to the problem is seen in the deliberations of the American Federation of Teachers at its 1976 convention; there, emphasis was given to limiting the number of handicapped students assigned to any regular class to, preferably, two (*New York Times,* August 19, 1976).

One major difficulty in limiting class size is that it requires the designation-labeling of certain children as handicapped—creating a neater disjunction between "normals" and "handicapped" than can be justified. It divides children into two groups in a way that stigmatizes the handicapped students, especially those with behavioral (educable mentally retarded, emotionally disturbed, etc.) rather than physical problems. Certainly class size must be controlled if differences among pupils are to be respected, but better ways than adopting a simple "5 for 1" or "2 only" strategy must be found.

Perhaps the problem can be seen in other ways. Consider the following solution that worked in one school:

> Two third-grade teachers in a building had 30 pupils each. Three deaf children were to be assigned to them. The teachers' first reaction was to ask for a 6-for-1 reduction in class size; i.e., reduce over-all class size by six for every deaf child enrolled. But then they learned that a specialized teacher of the deaf and a teachers' aide would accompany the deaf pupils. Furthermore, the specialized teacher had a very strong background in languages and was very willing to help any child in the classes who had language-related problems. Instead of thinking in terms of two separate classes of 30 children each and three deaf pupils, the regular class teachers began to think of three teachers, one a specialist, and one aide working with a total of 63 children. In practice, the situation worked out well.

The Denver Classroom Teachers Association has negotiated and achieved a system for "class size relief" that is likely to receive a great deal of attention. It recognizes that class size problems are not measurable strictly in terms of numbers of children. A class size committee made up of five teachers and five administrators meets to parcel out classroom aides, teachers, and materials; the committee works in response to building committees (consisting of the school principal and several teachers—elected by colleagues) in each school building of the district (National Education Association, 1977).

A formula system is used as part of the Denver plan in which different "types" of students are assigned various weighting factors as follows:

Type of Student	Weight Factor
Normal functioning	1.0
Gifted students	1.5
Slow learners	1.5

Type of Student	Weight Factor
Emotionally disturbed	2.5
Identifiable perceptual and communicative disorders	2.5
Bilingual	1.5
Transient	1.5
Chronic absenteeism	1.5
Reading disability	2.0
Disciplinary problems	2.0
Significantly limited intellectual capacity	2.0
Non-English speaking	2.5
Hyperactive	2.5

(p. 10)

By applying the formula a teacher who has 30 children in a class might have a formula enrollment well above 30. We consider the classification (and potential labeling of children) parts of the Denver program objectionable; nevertheless it represents a forward step, particularly in the aspect of giving teachers a strong voice in making accommodations in each building.

Other topics that teachers frequently negotiate about now include the following:

1. Training for regular teachers and others as a precondition of mainstreaming.
2. Qualification of personnel for work with exceptional pupils.
3. Liability for accidents involving exceptional students.
4. Supplies, equipment, and instructional material necessary in mainstreaming situations.
5. Teacher participation in conferences, planning, and other professional matters.
6. Availability of supportive personnel—professional and paraprofessional.
7. Released time for parent conferences, planning, and professional growth.
8. Maintenance of alternative programs in addition to mainstreaming.

Special educators have every reason, we believe, to support the organized teaching profession in its negotiations on these topics; they are part of the attempt to construct more effective mainstream educational programs. It is not reasonable to assign children with special needs to regular classes except as training, instructional materials, consultation, and and helping hands of all necessary kinds are provided. Mainstreaming should not and need not, we think, become simply a device for reducing the costs of education. Passing handicapped children from one station to another for such a purpose would be cruel indeed. Mainstreaming is, instead, an endeavor in which all educators can join to create one unified and adequate school system to serve all students.

LOOKING TO THE FUTURE

The Schools of the Future

What will schools and educational systems be like in the future? We can hypothesize fairly safely that regular and special education will overlap to a considerable degree. The period of the late 1970's appears to be essentially one of renegotiation between special and regular education, of lowering the boundaries between the two, not only in the delivery of services in the public schools, but in all the administrative, training, and support systems that feed into the public schools as well. The renegotiations are going on in college teacher preparation programs, state departments of education, research centers, and elsewhere. Figure 14-1 is a conception of schools in the future in which the boundaries between regular and special education programs are open and special education can be described as mainstreamed, training based, and essentially noncategorical.

FIGURE 14-1
Education in the Future: A Projection

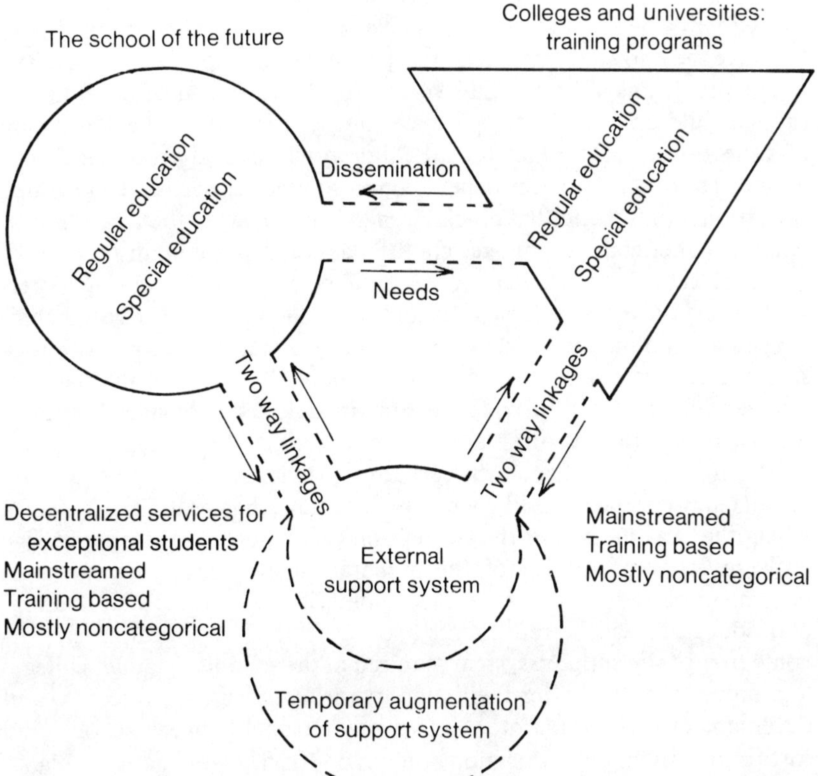

The school of the future

Colleges and universities: training programs

Regular education
Special education

Dissemination

Needs

Two way linkages

Decentralized services for exceptional students
Mainstreamed
Training based
Mostly noncategorical

External support system

Mainstreamed
Training based
Mostly noncategorical

Temporary augmentation of support system

The term *training based* (Lilly, 1971) connotes the strong emphasis that will be given to the training of all school personnel and the expansion of traditional regular education roles to include more functions relating to meeting the needs of exceptional children. It is assumed, for example, that special education teachers and psychologists will help to train teachers to perform some assessment functions rather than keeping assessment as an exclusive function of psychologists. It is also assumed that special educators and other specialists will be retrained for various consultation and support roles as they increasingly join forces with regular teachers to serve handicapped and gifted children in mainstream settings.

Given that Public Law 94-142 mandates individual educational plans for all handicapped children, we will probably see in the near future a strong move to individualize educational planning for all children. Indeed, Gilhool (1976) concluded an analysis of public policies on education as follows:

> Thus, special education may become general and general education, special. We are approaching the day when for each child, handicapped or not, the law will require that the schooling fit the child, his needs, his capacities, and his wishes; not that the child fit the school. That, I believe, is the purport of the so-called special education [judicial] cases. (p. 13)

We have the knowledge and technology, but we must put them to use.

The provisions in Public Law 94-142 for the early education of handicapped children leads us to speculate that, in the future, the continuum of education opportunities for all children will extend from age 3 or 4 to ages 18 to 21, the latter depending on individual needs. If integrated education holds benefits for children of school age, then certainly it must be beneficial for younger children as well. Many mainstream programs already have proven the value of peer age and cross age interactions and tutoring in elementary and secondary schools for both handicapped and nonhandicapped students and tutors and tutored. Although such tutoring is not possible at the preschool level, it is likely that peer interactions there can provide valuable models for behavior. We know that early experiences often are the most lasting; thus, if an integrated society is our national goal, the earlier we provide mainstream education for all children, the more likely we are to achieve that goal.

Another assumption of the conception (see Figure 14-1) is that college and university programs for the preparation of school personnel will become mainstreamed; that is, the boundaries between special and regular educators will be renegotiated so both kinds of educators can become part of the support system required in the schools. Mainly, colleges and universities will offer their support through training, research, and development activities. Note the two way channel between schools and institutions of higher education; the arrow from institutions of higher education to the schools is intended to represent the dissemination of research and development knowledge and theories of relevant disciplines, while the arrow from schools to institutes of higher education represents the transmission of needs from the real world of children and schools (Havelock, 1969).

Already colleges and universities are much engaged in the renegotiation process concerning regular and special education programs. Beginning early in the 1970's, the US Office of Education offered financial support in the form of so called "dean's grants" to assist colleges in revising preparation programs to broaden the roles of regular teachers in serving handicapped children. A similar set of grants to state departments of education has assisted in the in-service reeducation of regular teachers for the same purpose. Further, the federally supported Teacher Corps has made the installation of components relating to exceptional children a mandatory feature of each of the approximately 100 teacher preparation projects it supports across the nation each year. Under the Education Professions Development Act, beginning in 1968, strong support was offered to programs to revise special education teacher preparation programs to emphasize collaboration with regular teachers. Hardly any other innovation in teacher education has received as much support in recent years as this renegotiation of regular and special education roles. Despite these programs, the US Office of Education has been criticized by the Comptroller General of the United States (1976) for putting too little effort into revising regular teacher education.

Also depicted in Figure 14-1 are external support systems, that is, providers of technical assistance, research, development, demonstration, and evaluation expertise. Support systems are necessary to the development of quality in any field (e.g., agriculture and medicine) but they are critical to institutions and organizations during periods of transition. Given our present period of rapid change in and development of programs for exceptional children, the temporary augmentation of external support systems is essential to share national and regional resources that individual educational institutions and systems lack. The need for such support systems is reflected in the publications and training conferences conducted by such professional organizations as The Council for Exceptional Children in support of the rapidly changing field of special education. Several private corporations and universities also have developed nationwide technical assistance systems for educators and educational organizations. (For discussions of different kinds of support systems, see Reynolds, 1975).

For at least a decade, if not longer, such special support systems may be needed to aid both schools and institutions of higher learning to make the difficult transitions that are required. These systems may take a variety of forms, such as the Technical Assistance and Development

System at the University of North Carolina, which focuses on early childhood education and developmental disabilities; the Leadership Training Institute at the University of Minnesota, which concentrates on special regular education relations; the special technical assistance system to the field of learning disabilities conducted by National Learning Disabilities Assistance Project (conducted by the Network in Merrimac, Massachusetts) or the numerous technical assistance projects launched in or through state departments of education. Short term training efforts to implement some of the newly emerging concepts, such as "individualized educational programs," "nondiscriminatory assessment," and "due process" in placements, will have to be organized by different institutions or organizations that can provide the necessary expertise.

In-Service Education

Changes in special education are occurring so rapidly that training for new functions and roles will be an imperative for some time to come. More accurately, most of what is needed may be *retraining* for in-service teachers (both regular and special), school psychologists, and other school workers. The importance of in-service training emerges not only from the rapidity of the changes under way but from the facts of the manpower situation as well.

For many years in Minnesota, for example, the turnover rate for special education teachers was about 12% a year, that is, about 12 out of every 100 special teachers employed in any one year were not in the profession or the state the following year. Colleges and universities were required to prepare replacement personnel at the annual rate of about 12% of the total employed teacher work force. For program growth, still more new teachers were needed. At present, it appears that the turnover rate may be down to about one-third of the past rate or about 4%. The change in rate began to appear in the early 1970's coincident with the rapid decrease in elementary school enrollments. The story is similar in most parts of the nation. It seems evident that teachers who have jobs are keeping them.

The effect of this rapid reduction in turnover rate means that new roles in the schools no longer can be filled rapidly by new personnel. When new roles emerge, practicing professionals will need to be retrained to fill them, and if new functions are added to old roles, personnel now in the schools will require in-service training to carry them out.

Several particulars about the development of in-service education should be noted:

- Increasingly, in-service education is organized on a total school or district basis, thus linking the in-service education to specific programmatic changes occurring in the schools. Hence, in-service education is less often offered to more or less random collections of teachers who want to take a course but more often provided systematically for specific groups of personnel who are engaged in institutional change processes.

- More often, schools organize their own in-service education programs or negotiate with institutions of higher education for carefully tailored courses to meet local needs. Teacher centers and other organized projects, which represent permanent forms of collaboration between schools and institutions of higher education, are very useful for negotiating in parity the emerging in-service or continuing education* programs.
- Because of the growing strength and influence of teacher associations and unions, and the interest of teachers in influencing their own professional standards and practices, plans for in-service education are increasingly a subject of negotiation between administrators, institutions of higher education, or school boards and teachers' associations.

Thus, as we look to the future and at the developmental tasks to achieve desired goals, some new structures and roles must be considered in arranging the training components. Institutions of higher education, for example, have good reason to shift more attention to the in-service education of teachers and other school personnel; to do so, however, they must reach concordance with the institutional plans of schools and professional associations. Some educational leaders advocate that professional departments of colleges and universities be regarded as the training and development arms of the professions and seek much closer ties with professional associations; this view seems a likely trend in the future, especially in view of the growing political awareness and power of teacher associations and unions.

The subject matter for much of the in-service education that will be required to implement the mainstreaming philosophy is beginning to be clear. For regular teacher training, except for work toward supportive attitudes concerning exceptionality, instructional management is perhaps the central topic.

In a recent survey of objectives and competencies receiving the most attention in teacher education programs for mainstreaming, Goldhammer, Rader, and Reuschlein (1977) organized their findings around the

---

*Although the concepts of in-service and continuing education are sometimes distinguished quite usefully, the former referring to strictly local adaptation and training problems (e.g., preparing teachers for a reader series just adopted) and the latter referring to more general studies (e.g., a course on the latest theories or principles of language development), the distinction is not intended in these discussions.

following topics: nature of mainstreaming, nature of the handicapped, attitudes, resources, teaching techniques, learning environment, learning styles, classroom management, curriculum, communication, assessments of student research, evaluation of student progress, and administration.

A variety of systems and materials to assist in the training of regular teachers in these domains is becoming available. For example, the LOFT system (Learning Opportunities For Teachers), was developed by Barry and Susan Dollar and associates in the Houston School System; TTP (Teacher Training Program) was developed by Hafner, Parks, and others of the Texas Regional Service Agency XIII (Austin, Texas); and special compendiums of training materials have been developed at the Universtiy of Northern Colorado. The Leadership Training Institute (LTI) at the University of Minnesota has developed a substantial literature on mainstreaming topics that is available for use in the in-service education of school staff. (See Appendix B for a further catalog of these and other training systems and materials.)

CHANGE PROCESSES

People who are engaged in training processes of the kinds just described are among the first to admit the inadequacies of mere training as a means of accomplishing desired changes. Regular teachers who take courses on mainstreaming insist that their school systems revise their special education programs and provide the supports they require. Training must be imbedded in a larger set of change oriented activities if mainstreaming is to be accomplished.

When mainstreaming becomes the new strategy in a school system it may be necessary for at least the following changes to be made, somewhat in the order listed:

1. Top school leaders (school superintendents and other central staff members, leaders of professional associations, and members of boards of education) must be aware of new possibilities and make commitments to the specifics of a new orientation.
2. School principals and teachers must be given opportunities to study the possibilities of the new proposals and to participate in planning the change steps to be taken. Special training at an early date may be necessary and wise.
3. Needs assessments and plans should be developed in each school and in districts as wholes. Plans should be developed closely with parents, parent groups, and other organized interests in communities. Changes in services for exceptional children often draw high general community interest.

4. Training activities should be mounted in each school building, oriented at first to the specific problems and needs identified in the building. Teachers should be helped with their problems, recognizing that they already have many children needing special help in their regular classrooms. A bit later, there will be opportunities for exceptional children in special stations to be brought back into the mainstream; but teachers prefer to have their current problems recognized before more are urged on them.
5. Special education programs will need to be reorganized to begin to offer more support or indirect services and team cooperation to regular teachers. This reorganization may require the retraining of special education teachers, school psychologists, and others.

If the preceding steps are taken carefully, there is a good chance that the energies of regular and special education will be joined more effectively and that quality mainstream programing will emerge. Indeed, the scenario for change just described is derived from the dozens of schools in which serious efforts for mainstreaming have been undertaken in recent years with encouraging results.

A variety of models or systems for planning change procedures is available to educators who wish to develop mainstreaming models with all possible awareness and care. The Research and Development Center on Teacher Education, University of Texas, for example, has developed a Concerns-Based Adoption Model (CBAM) that can be adapted to local needs. The CBAM model focuses on the personal concerns of individuals when changes affect their life patterns. Hall, Wallace, and Doseth (1973) and others who have advanced the CBAM model have suggested that a highly reliable series of developmental stages of "concerns" is involved in all changes: awareness, exploration, early trial, limited impact, maximum benefit, and renewal.

By assessing the patterns of concerns to clients in the institution facing the change effort, presumably it is possible to tailor programs for maximum effects. The assumption is that until concerns at the early stages are satisfied, higher level tasks will be fruitless. Other approaches to change have been outlined by Havelock (1973), Miles (1964), Bennis, Benne, and Chin (1969) and others that give attention to fundamentals of organizational processes and developments as parts of the change process.

CONCLUSION

In preparing this book, our basic purpose was to communicate about change, about emerging new forms of education for students with special needs. In general, that change is in the direction of more inclusive arrangements in the schools, such that most exceptional children will be served in regular school programs rather than in special classes and other isolated stations. The changes represent, at root, moral issues. What do we think of human differences? How closely will we link our lives to persons who may be different? How much investment will we make in schools for literally *all* children?

Major conceptual shifts are involved as well, as in measurement, expectancy, classification, placement, and diagnosis. Broader units of concern are emerging so that we see the importance of broad ecological approaches to diagnosis and treatment.

Major role changes for all school personnel are inevitable. Regular teachers can expect to be confronted by increasing numbers of exceptional students in their classes and they will be expected to collaborate in their work with specialists who are now moving out of special centers in large numbers for more concerted efforts in the mainstream. Great demands for training educational personnel for new functions and roles already are evident.

Parent participation in the planning processes for the education of their exceptional children is increasing. Currently, neither they nor the teachers with whom they plan are particularly well prepared for their joint efforts. Schools may find it productive to train parents for participatory roles.

Massive new infusions of federal funds and regulations are in prospect; we must hope that there will be decent proportions of both. Working through all of the details of the expanding partnership with federal agencies will be difficult indeed; and in all of the negotiations the organized teaching profession promises to play a very large role.

At present, we are in a deeply challenging and promising period of service to exceptional children, but a difficult and dangerous period as well. The burdens of rapid change are great and much could occur that is negative and degrading. Still, there is reason to hope that the confluence of present trends will result in a strengthened capacity of schools to serve all children effectively. Special educators now have extraordinary opportunities to leave their special enclaves, taking with them their special children and resources, and to join with regular educators to create an educational structure based on providing every child with the services and opportunities necessary for his or her optimal development.

SUGGESTIONS FOR STUDENTS AND INSTRUCTOR

1. Review and discuss Hobbs' *The Futures of Children* (1975) on topics such as classification or funding systems.

2. Examine resolutions adopted in recent years by your state teachers' associations or unions as they pertain to mainstreaming. What implications do you see?
3. Check on the status of advisory councils in your state concerning the implementation of new federal laws relating to the handicapped (especially Public Law 94-142). What major issues and problems are being considered?
4. Consider the needs that exist in your community or state for an external "support system" in the field of mainstreaming. Are there such needs? Where are your schools getting the technical assistance they need? Are research and evaluation functions being performed adequately?
5. Check the special education funding system in your state, especially for its impact on mainstreaming. If you assumed that "programs follow dollars," what would you predict in your state for the future of mainstreaming?
6. Collect information on the number of different specialists (special education teachers, Title I tutors, speech clinicians, remedial teachers, psychologists, counselors, etc.) working in the typical school of your community. Examine the degree of coordination among services of such specialists. Get the opinions of school principals on this topic.
7. Examine the contracts now in force in your community governing the relationship of teachers and the local school board. What items relate to special education and what do they portend?
8. Write descriptions of what you think a school might be like when all of the principles and preferred practices discussed in this book are fully implemented.

TOPICAL BIBLIOGRAPHIES
Funding Systems

Bernstein, C. D., Kirst, M. W., Hartman, W. T., & Marshall, R. S. *Financing educational services for the handicapped.* Reston VA: The Council for Exceptional Children, 1976.

Gifford, B. R. *The cost of educating handicapped pupils in New York City.* (Special Report No. 2 on Assuring Equal Educational Opportunity for Handicapped Children in New York City.) New York: Board of Education of the City of New York.

McLure, W. P., Burnham, R. A., & Henderson, R. A. *Special education needs-costs-methods of financing.* Urbana-Champaign IL: Bureau of Educational Research, College of Education, University of Illinois, 1975.

Rossmiller, R. A., Hale, J. A., & Frohreich, L. E. *Educational programs for exceptional children: Resource configurations and costs.* (National Educational Finance Project Special Study No. 2). Madison: University of Wisconsin, 1970.

Thomas, M. A. Finance: Without which there is no special education. *Exceptional Children,* 1973, *39,* 475-480.

General Outlook for the Future

Elam, S. Special issue on special education. *Phi Delta Kappan,* April, 1974, *55,* 513-560.

Grosenick, J. K., & Reynolds, M. C. *Teacher education: Renegotiating roles for mainstreaming.* Reston VA: The Council for Exceptional Children, 1978.

Hobbs, N. *The futures of children.* San Francisco: Jossey-Bass, 1975.

Milofsky, R. D. Why special education isn't special. *Harvard Education Review,* 1974, *44*(4), 437-458.

Reynolds, M. C. *Futures of education for exceptional students: Emerging structures.* Reston VA: The Council for Exceptional Children, 1978.

Reynolds, M. C. More process than is due. *Theory Into Practice,* 1975, *14*(2), 61-68.

US Office of Education. *The condition of education.* Washington DC: US Government Printing Office (Stock No. 017-080-01678-8), 1977.

Warfield, G. J. (Ed.). *Mainstream currents: Reprints from* Exceptional Children *1968-1974.* Reston VA: The Council for Exceptional Children, 1974.

Wolfensberger, W. The future of residential services for the mentally retarded. *Journal of Clinical Child Psychology,* 1973, *2*(1), 19-20.

Categorizing—Labeling

Gallagher, J. J. The sacred and profane uses of labeling. *Mental Retardation,* December 1976, 3-7.

Hobbs, N. *The futures of children.* San Francisco: Jossey-Bass, 1975.

MacMillan, D. L., Jones, R. L., & Aloia, G. F. The mentally retarded label: A theoretical analysis and review of research. *American Journal of Mental Deficiency,* 1974, *79*(3), 241-261.

President's Committee on Mental Retardation. *The six-hour retarded child.* Washington DC: Bureau of Education for the Handicapped, US Office of Education, US Government Printing Office, 1969.

Collective Bargaining

The American Teacher, January 1977, p. 9.

Kirp, D. Schools as sorters. *University of Pennsylvania Law Review,* 1973, *12*(1), 705-797.

Sosnowsky, W. P., & Coleman, T. W. Special education in the collective bargaining process. *Phi Delta Kappan,* 1971, *52*(10), 610-613.

References

Abeson, A., Bolick, N., & Hass, J. *A primer on due process.* Reston VA: The Council for Exceptional Children, 1975.

Accreditation Council on Facilities for the Mentally Retarded. Chicago IL: The Joint Commission on Accreditation of Hospitals, 1973.

Aiello, B. (Ed.). *Places and spaces: Facilities planning for exceptional children.* Reston VA: The Council for Exceptional Children, 1976.

Aiello, B. A very special special teacher. *TEACHING Exceptional Children,* 1976, *9,* 4-5.

Ainsworth, S. The speech clinician in public schools: "Participant" or "separatist"? *American Speech and Hearing Association,* 1965, *7,* 495-503.

Albert, R. S. Toward a behavioral definition of genius. *The American Psychologist,* February 1975, pp. 140-151.

Alpiner, J. G. *The utilization of supportive personnel in speech correction in the public schools.* Denver: Colorado State Department of Education (Title VI, ESEA, BEH, US Office of Education), 1968.

Alvord, D. J. Innovation in speech therapy, A cost effective program. *Exceptional Children,* 1977, *43,* 520-525.

American Association of School Administrators. Court reinforces mainstream concept. *The School Administrator,* 1976, *33*(6), 12.

American Federation of Teachers Council. *American Teacher,* January 1977, 9.

Anderson, E. M. *The disabled school child: A study of integration in the primary schools.* London: Methuen, 1973.

Anderson, R.H. Ungraded primary classes: An administrative contribution to mental health. *Understanding the Child,* June 1955, 65-72.

Armor, D. J., Polich, J. M., & Stambul, H. B. *Alcoholism and treatment.* Santa Monica CA: Rand Corporation, 1976.

Axline, V. M. *Play therapy.* Boston: Houghton-Mifflin, 1947.

Baldwin, A. Y. Tests can underpredict: A case study. *Phi Delta Kappan,* 1977, *58*(8), 620-621.

Bandura, A. (Ed.). *Psychological modeling.* Chicago: Atherton, 1971.

Barbe, W. B. Evaluation of special classes for gifted children. *Exceptional Children,* 1955, *21,* 60-62.

Barsch, R. *Achieving perceptual-motor efficiency* (Vol. 1). Seattle: Special Child Publications, 1967.

Bartram, J. B. Prevention of mental retardation. *The Challenge.* Harrisburg PA: Department of Public Welfare, May-June, 1974, pp. 12-13.

Bateman, B. D. An educator's view of a diagnostic approach to learning disorders. In J. Hellmoth (Ed.). *Learning disorders* (Vol. 1). Seattle WA: Special Child Publications, 1965.

Bateman, B. Learning disabilities: An overview. *Journal of School Psychology,* 1965, *3*(3), 1-12.

Baumgartner, B. B. *Helping every trainable mentally retarded child.* New York: Teachers' College Press, Columbia University, 1960.

Baumgartner, B. B. *The trainable mentally retarded child.* New York: Teachers College Press, Columbia University, 1960.

Becker, W. C. Applications of behavior principles in typical classrooms. In C. E. Thorensen (Ed.), *Behavior modification in education.* Chicago: University of Chicago Press, 1972.

Bennis, W. G., Benne, K. D., & Chin, R. *The planning of change* (2nd ed.). New York: Holt, Rinehart, & Winston, 1969.

Bernstein, C. D., Hartman, W. T., Kirst, M. W. & Marshall, R. S. *Financing educational services for the handicapped.* Reston VA: The Council for Exceptional Children, 1976.

Bertness, H. J. 'Progressive inclusion: The mainstream movement in Tacoma. In M. C. Reynolds (Ed.), *Mainstreaming: Origins and implications.* Reston VA: The Council for Exceptional Children, 1976, 55-58.

Bettelheim, B. *The empty fortress: Infantile autism and the birth of the self.* New York: Free Press, 1967.

Betts, E. A. *Foundations of reading instruction.* New York: American Book, 1946.

Bijou, S. Theory and research in mental (developmental) retardation. *Psychological Record,* 1963, *13*, 99.

Bijou, S. A functional analysis of retarded development. In N. R. Ellis (Ed.), *International review of research in mental retardation* (Vol. 1). New York: Academic, 1966.

Birch, H. G. *Brain damage in children.* Baltimore: Williams & Wilkens, 1964.

Birch, J. W. *Retrieving the retarded reader* (revised). Indianapolis: Bobbs-Merrill, 1955.

Birch, J. W. et al. *School achievement and effect of type size on reading in visually handicapped children.* (Cooperative Research Project No. 1766, Contract No. OEC-4-10-028.). Pittsburgh: University of Pittsburgh, 1966.

Birch, J. W. *Mainstreaming: Educable mentally retarded children in regular classes.* Reston VA: The Council for Exceptional Children, 1974.

Birch, J. W. *Hearing impaired children in the mainstream.* Reston VA: The Council for Exceptional Children, 1975.

Birch, J. W., & Johnstone, B. K. *Designing schools and schooling for the handicapped.* Springfield IL: Charles C Thomas, 1975.

Birch, J. W., Matthews, J., & Burgi, E. *Improving children's speech.* Indianapolis IN: Bobbs-Merrill, 1958.

Bitter, G. B. (Ed.). *Systems O.N.E.* 1974. (Kits available from Educational Media Center, 207 Milton Bennion Hall, University of Utah, Salt Lake City UT 84112)

Blatt, B., & Kaplan, F. *Christmas in purgatory.* Boston: Allyn & Bacon, 1967.

Bloom, B. Learning for mastery. *Evaluation Comment,* May 1968, *1.* (Center for the Study of Evaluation, University of California at Los Angeles).
Blumberg, L. The case for integrated schooling. *Exceptional Parent,* 1973, *3*(4), 15-17.
Bond, G. L., & Tinker, M.A. *Reading difficulties, their diagnosis and correction* (3rd ed.). New York: Appleton-Century-Crofts, 1973.
Boote, K. S. *Principal and teacher perceptions of special education in-service programs for regular elementary teachers.* Unpublished doctoral dissertation, Temple University, 1975.
Borg, W. R. *Classroom management* (Protocol materials). Tampa: National Resource and Dissemination Center, University of South Florida (no date).
Bracht, G. H., & Glass, G. V. The external validity of experiments. *American Educational Research Journal,* 1968, *5,* 437-474.
Bradley, D. P. Expanded speech pathology services. *Prise Reporter,* June 1976, *7,* 1-3.
Bronfenbrenner, U. Developmental research, public policy, and the ecology of childhood. *Child Development,* 1974, *45,* 1-5.
Brotemarkle, R. A. (Ed.) *Clinical psychology: Studies in honor of Lightner Witmer to commemorate the thirty-fifth anniversary of the founding of the first psychological clinic.* Philadelphia: University of Pennsylvania Press, 1931.
Bruce, W. The parents' role from an educator's point of view. In W. H. Northcott (Ed.), *The hearing impaired child in the regular classroom.* Washington DC: A. G. Bell Association for the Deaf, 1973.
Budoff, M., & Gottlieb, J. Special class EMR children mainstreaming: A study of an aptitude (learning potential) X treatment interaction. *American Journal of Mental Deficiency,* July 1976, 1-11.
Buck v. Bell. 274 U.S. 200, 207(1927).
Burger, R., Ciani, N., Miller, H., Grigsby, C., Brown, R., Duffy, D., Yoh, B.L., Biacci, A., Wingate, V., and Duffy, J. *An introduction to individualized education program plans in Pennsylvania.* The National Learning Resource Center of Pennsylvania (443 South Gulph Rd., King of Prussia PA 19046), January, 1977.
Burrows, C., & Okey, J. *The effects of a mastery learning strategy on achievement.* Paper presented at the American Educational Research Association Annual Meeting, Washington DC, March 1975.
Byrne, M. C. *The child speaks.* New York: Harper and Row, 1965.
Byron, I. "Why I cried, "Help!" *New York Times,* August 19, 1976.
Caccamise, F. "Musts" for hearing people. *American Annals of the Deaf,* 1974, *119*(3), 296-297.
Cain, L. F., & Levine, S. *Effects of community and institutional school programs on trainable mentally retarded children.* (CEC Research Monograph, Series B, No. B-1). Reston VA: The Council for Exceptional Children, 1963.
Calovini, G. (Ed.). *Mainstreaming the visually impaired child.* Springfield IL: Instructional Materials Center, Office of the Superintendent of Public Instruction, undated.
Campbell, D. Blind children in the "normal" environment. *Understanding the Child,* June 1955, 73-76.

Cantrell, R. P., & Cantrell, M. L. Preventive mainstreaming: Impact of a supportive service program on children. *Exceptional Children,* 1976, *42,* 381-385.
Carter, J. L. Intelligence and reading achievement of EMR children in three educational settings. *Mental Retardation,* 1975, *13,* 26-27.
Cartwright, G. P. The relationship between sequences of instructional and mental abilities of retarded children. *American Educational Research Journal,* 1971, *1,* 143-150.
Center for Urban Secondary Students with Learning Disabilities. *Year end report, July 1, 1975—June 30, 1976.* Pittsburgh: University of Pittsburgh, Program in Special Education, 1976.
Coleman, P. G., Eggleston, K. K., Collins, J. P., Holloway, B. D., & Reider, S. K. A severely hearing impaired child in the mainstream. *TEACHING Exceptional Children,* 1975, *8,* 6-9.
Coloroso, B. Strategies for working with troubled students. In B.R. Gearhart & M. W. Weishahn, *The handicapped child in the regular classroom.* St. Louis: C. V. Mosby, 1976.
Comptroller General of the US. *Training educators for the handicapped: A need to redirect federal programs.* Washington DC: US Government Printing Office, September 28, 1976.
Conference on future structures of postsecondary education. Paris: Organization for Economic Cooperation and Development, 1974 (2 Rue Andre-Pascal, 75775 Paris CEDEX16, France).
Congressional Record Daily Edition. H7755. July 29, 1975.
Connor, L. E. Mainstreaming a special school. *TEACHING Exceptional Children,* 1976, *8,* 76-80.
Corson, S., & Makowski, R. *Skill-Log.* Unpublished manuscript, 1975. (Available from Western Illinois Association 0-3 Program, Regional Services, Macomb, Illinois.)
Cowen, E. L., Trost, M. A., Lorion, R. P., Dorr, D., Izzo, L. D., & Isaacson, R.V. *New ways in school mental health: Early detection and prevention of school maladaptation.* New York: Human Sciences, 1975.
Cox, C. C. The early mental traits of three hundred geniuses. In L. M. Terman (Ed.), *Genetic studies of genius* (Vol. II), Stanford CA: Stanford University Press, 1926.
Craig, S. B. Fifty years of training teachers of the deaf. *School and Society,* 1942, *56*(1449), 301-303.
Craig, W. N., & Salem, J. M. Partial integration of deaf with hearing students: Residential school perspectives. *American Annals of the Deaf,* 1975, *120* (1), 28-36.
Cromwell, R. Ethics, umbrage, and the ABCDs. In M. C. Reynolds (Ed.), *Mainstreaming: Origins and implications.* Reston VA: The Council for Exceptional Children, 1976.
Cronbach, L. J., & Gleser, G. C. *Psychological tests and personal decisions* (2nd ed.). Urbana: University of Illinois Press, 1965.
Cronbach, L. J. & Snow, R. E. *Aptitude and instructional methods.* New York: Irvington, 1977.
Cronbach, L. J., Gleser, G. C., Nanda, H., & Rajaratnam, N. *The dependa-*

bility of behavioral measurements: Theory of generalizability for scores and profiles. New York: Wiley & Sons, 1972.

Cruickshank, W. M., & Hallahan, D. P. (Eds.). *Perceptual and learning disabilities in children* (Vol. 1) *Psychoeducational practices*. Syracuse NY: Syracuse University Press, 1975.

Cuyahoga County Association for Retarded Children and Adults v. Essex. No. C74-587 (N.D. Ohio, April 5, 1976)

Cutts, N. E. (Ed.). *School psychologists at mid century*. Washington DC: American Psychological Association, 1955.

Dabney, M. G. Curriculum building and implementation in mainstream settings: Some concepts and propositions. In R. L. Jones (Ed.), *Mainstreaming and the minority child*. Reston VA: The Council for Exceptional Children, 1976.

Dacarie, T. G. A study of the mental and emotional development of the thalidomide child. In B. M. Foss (Ed.), *Determinants of infant behavior* (Vol. 4). London: Methuen, 1969, 167-187.

Davis, H., & Silverman, S.R. (Eds.). *Hearing and deafness* (3rd, ed.). New York: Holt, Rinehart and Winston, 1970.

Delacato, G. H. *The diagnosis and treatment of speech and reading disorders*. Springfield IL: Charles C Thomas, 1963.

Dell'Amore, J. Child abuse: Many unanswered questions. *Sharing*, Winter 1974, 3-9.

Delp, H.A., & Boote, K. Mainstreaming of the exceptional: In the future or now? *The School Administrator*, February 1975, pp. 18-19.

Deno, E. (Ed.). *Instructional alternatives for exceptional children*. Reston VA: The Council for Exceptional Children, 1972.

Deno, E. N. *Mainstreaming: Learning disabled, emotionally disturbed, and socially maladjusted children in regular classes*. Minneapolis: Leadership Training Institute, University of Minnesota, in preparation.

Dial, K.A. Program alternatives: Utilizing community and educational resources. *Invisible College on Learning and Behavior Problems of Handicapped Students in Secondary School Programs*. Reston VA: The Council for Exceptional Children, 1977.

Diana v. State Board of Education. Civil Action No. C-70 & 7RFP (N.D. Cal. Jan. 7, 1970 and June 18, 1973).

Dinger, J. C. Post-school adjustment of former educable mentally retarded pupils. *Exceptional Children,* 1961, 27, 353-360

Directory of Inpatient Facilities for the Mentally Retarded (HE 20.6202:In 7; sin 017/041/00090/8). Washington DC: US Government Printing Office, no date.

Distar Orientation. Chicago: Science Research Associates, 1971.

Doll, E. *Measurement of social competence*. Minneapolis: Educational Testing Bureau, 1953.

Doll, E. *Vineland Social Maturity Scale*. Circle Pines MN: American Guidance Service, Inc. 1953.

Dunlap, J. M. Gifted children in an enriched program. *Exceptional Children,* 1955, 22, 135-137.

Dreikurs, R., Grunwald, B. B., & Pepper, F. C. *Maintaining sanity in the classroom: Illustrated techniques*. New York: Harper & Row, 1971.

Drug crisis: Schools fight back with innovative programs. Arlington VA: National School Public Relations Association, 1971.

Dunn, L. M. Special education for the mildly retarded—Is much of it justifiable? *Exceptional Children,* 1968, *35,* 5-22.

Dunn, L. M. (Ed.). *Exceptional children in the schools: Special education in transition* (2nd ed.). New York: Holt, Rinehart & Winston, 1973.

East, L. A mainstreaming success story. *Today's Education,* Nov.-Dec. 1976, p. 71.

Education Policies Commission. *The purposes of education in American democracy.* Washington DC: National Education Association, 1938.

Enfield, M. L. *An alternate classroom approach to meeting special learning needs of children with reading problems.* Unpublished doctoral dissertation, University of Minnesota, 1976.

Engelmann, T., Osborn, J., & Engelmann, T. *Distar language: An instructional system.* Chicago: Science Research Associates, 1969.

Estroff, E. H. Polk County. *Talents and Gifts,* 1975, *17*(2), 10-11.

Eurich, A. C., Bronk, D. W., Millet, J. D., Perkins, J. A., & Wexler, J. Education. In *Public policy toward environment 1973: A review and appraisal. Annals of the New York Academy of Sciences,* 1973, *216,* 160-166.

Fant, L. J., Jr. *Say it with hands.* Washington DC: Gallaudet College Centennial Fund Commission, 1964.

Fant, L.J., Jr. *Ameslan, an introduction to American sign language.* Silver Spring MD: National Association of the Deaf, 1972.

Federal Register, 1976, *41*(96), 84.35.

Festinger, L. A theory of social comparison processes. *Human Relations,* 1954, *7,* 117-140.

Fitzgerald, E. *Straight language for the deaf: System of instruction for deaf children* (2nd ed.). Washington DC: The Volta Bureau, 1954.

Flanagan, J. C. Education: How and for what. *American Psychologist,* July 1973, 551-556.

Fogelman, G. J. (Ed.). *AAMD adaptive behavior scale* (1975 ed.) American Association on Mental Deficiency, 5201 Connecticut Ave. NW, Washington DC, 1975.

Fox, W. L., Egner, A. N., Paolucci, P. E., Perelman, P. F., & McKenzie, H. An introduction to a regular classroom approach to special education. In E. Deno (Ed.), *Instructional alternatives for exceptional children.* Reston VA: The Council for Exceptional Children, 1972.

Frankenburg, W. K., & Dodds, J. B. *Denver developmental screening test.* Denver: Project and Publishing Foundation, 1967.

French, J. L. *Educating the gifted, a book of readings.* New York: Holt, Rinehart, and Winston, 1959.

Friedman, R. J., & MacQueen, J. C. Psychoeducational considerations of physical handicapping conditions in children. *Exceptional Children,* 1971, *37,* 538-539.

Frostig, M. Visual perception in the brain injured child. *American Journal of Orthopsychiatry,* 1963, *32,* 271-280.

Gage, N. L. *Teacher effectiveness and teacher education: The search for a scientific basis.* Palo Alto CA: Pacific Books, 1972.

Gallagher, J. *Teaching the gifted child* (2nd ed.). Boston: Allyn & Bacon, 1975.
Gallup, G. *Gallup youth survey.* Princeton NJ: Gallup Polls, May 23, 1977.
Galton, F. *Hereditary genius.* New York: Macmillan, 1869.
Garber, H. L. Intervention in infancy: A developmental approach. In M. J. Begab & S. A. Richardson (Eds.), *The mentally retarded and society: A social science perspective.* Baltimore: University Park Press, 1975.
Garcia, F. Dade County Public Schools. *Talents and Gifts,* 1975, *17*(2), 7-8.
Gardner, W. I. *Learning and behavior characteristics of exceptional children and youth.* Boston: Allyn & Bacon, 1977.
Garmezy, E. The mother and infant care education project, Minneapolis Public Schools. *Sharing,* Winter 1975, 4-5.
Gearhart, B. R., & Weishahn, M. W. *The handicapped child in the regular classroom.* St. Louis: C. V. Mosby, 1976.
Gesell, A. *Gesell Developmental List.* New York: The Psychological Corporation, 1940.
Gilhool, T. K. Changing public policies: Roots and forces. In M. C. Reynolds (Ed.), *Mainstreaming: Origins and implications.* Reston VA: The Council for Exceptional Children, 1976.
Glaser, R. Educational psychology and education. *American Psychologist,* 1973, *28*(7), 557-566.
Glaser, W. *Reality therapy.* New York: Harper & Row, 1965.
Goertzel, V., & Goertzel, M. *Cradles of eminence.* Boston: Little, Brown, 1962.
Goldberg, I. I., & Cruickshank, W. M. The trainable but noneducable: Whose responsibility? *NEA Journal,* 1958, *47*(9), 622.
Goldhammer, K., Rader, B. T., & Reuschlein, P. *Mainstreaming: Teacher competencies.* East Lansing: College of Education, Michigan State University, April 1977.
Goldman, R., & Lynch, M. E. *The Goldman-Lynch sound and symbol development kit.* Circle Pines MN: American Guidance Service, 1971.
Goldstein, H. *The social learning curriculum.* Columbus OH: Charles E. Merrill, 1974.
Gordon, T. (with Burch, N.). *Teacher effectiveness training.* New York: Wyden, 1974.
Gorham, K. A. A lost generation of parents. *Exceptional Children,* 1975, *41*, 521-525.
Goss v. Lopez. 419, U.S. 565 (1975).
Gourley, T. J., Jr. Programs for gifted students: A national survey. *Talents and Gifts,* June 1976, pp. 31-32.
Gottlieb, J., Agard, J., Kauffman, N., & Semmel, M. Retarded children mainstreamed: Practices as they affect minority group children. In R. L. Jones (Ed.), *Mainstreaming and the minority child.* Reston VA: The Council for Exceptional Children, 1976.
Green, A., Gaines, R., & Sandgrund, A. Child abuse: Pathological syndrome of family interaction. *American Journal of Psychiatry,* 1974, *131*, 882-886.
Griffing, B. L. Planning educational programs and services for hard of hearing children. In F.S. Berg & S.G. Fletcher (Eds.), *The hard of hearing child: Clinical and educational management.* New York: Grune and Stratton, 1970.

Grogan, J. Local leaders in special education. *Reach Newsletter,* Oct.-Nov. 1975, p. 4. (Regional Resource Center, 5347 William Flynn Highway, Rt. 8, Gibsonia, PA 15044.)

Grossman, H. J. (Ed.). *Manual on terminology and classification in mental retardation.* Washington DC: American Association on Mental Deficiency, 1973.

Grotsky, J., Sabatino, D., & Ohrtman, W. (Eds.). *The concept of mainstreaming: A resource guide for regular classroom teachers.* King of Prussia PA: Eastern Pennsylvania Regional Resources Center for Special Education, 1976.

Gunzburg, H. C. *Progress Assessment Chart of Social Development.* Birmingham AL: SEFA Ltd., 1965.

Hall, G. E., Wallace, R. C., Jr., & Dosseth, W. F. *A structural model for developing a case study of PTE adoption: A developmental conceptualization of the adoptive process within educational institutions.* Austin: Research and Development Center for Teacher Education, The University of Texas, March 1973.

Halsey, A. H. (Ed.). *Ability and educational opportunity.* Report of the Conference Organized by the Office for Scientific and Technical Personnel of the Organization for Economic Cooperation and Development, June 1961. (Available in the US from OECD Mission, Publications Office Suite 1223, 1346 Connecticut Ave., N. W., Washington DC 20036.)

Haring, N. Application of behavior modification techniques to the learning situation. In W. M. Cruickshank & D. P. Hallahan (Eds.), *Psycho-educational practices* (Vol. 1). Syracuse NY: Syracuse University Press, 1975.

Haring, N. G., & Krug, D. A. Placement in regular programs: Procedures and results. *Exceptional Children,* 1974, *41*(6), 413-417.

Haring, N. G., & Phillips, E. L. *Analysis and modification of classroom behavior.* Englewood Cliffs NJ: Prentice-Hall, 1972.

Haring, N. G., & Schiefelbusch, R. L. *Teaching special children.* New York: McGraw-Hill, 1976.

Havelock, R. G. *Planning for innovation through dissemination and utilization of knowledge.* Ann Arbor: Center for Research on Utilization of Scientific Knowledge, University of Michigan, 1969.

Havelock, R. G. *The change agent's guide to innovation in education.* Englewood Cliffs NJ: Educational Technology Publications, 1973.

Hayes, G. M., & Griffing, B. L. *A guide to the education of the deaf in the public schools of California.* Sacramento: California State Department of Education, 1967.

Heiss, W. E., & Mischio, G. S. Designing curriculum for the educable mentally retarded. *Focus on Exceptional Children,* 1971, *3*, 1-10.

Heber, R. A manual on terminology and classification in mental retardation. *American Journal of Mental Deficiency,* 1961 (Monograph Supplement, 2nd ed.).

Hewett, F. M. *The emotionally disturbed child in the classroom.* Boston: Allyn & Bacon, 1968.

Hewett, F. M., & Forness, S. R. (Eds.). *Education of exceptional learners.* Boston: Allyn & Bacon, 1968.

Hildreth, G. H. *Educating gifted children at Hunter College Elementary School.* New York: Harper, 1952.

Hill, H. F. Vineland summer school for teachers of backward and mentally deficient children. *The Training School Bulletin,* May 1945, pp. 41-49.

Hillinger, C. Teletype communication puts the deaf in touch. *Los Angeles Times,* December 7, 1975.

Hirsch, S.P. Executive High School Internships: A boon for the gifted and talented. *TEACHING Exceptional Children,* 1976, *9,* 22-23.

Hively, W., & Reynolds, M. C. (Eds.). *Domain-referenced testing in special education.* Reston VA: The Council for Exceptional Children, 1975.

Hobbs, N. *The futures of children.* San Francisco: Jossey-Bass, 1975.

Homme, L. *How to use contingency contracting in the classroom.* Champaign IL: Research, 1970.

Howard, M. Improving services for young fathers. *Sharing,* Spring 1975, 10-22.

Hull, F. M., & Hull, M. E. Children with oral communication disabilities. In L.M. Dunn (Ed.), *Exceptional children in the schools.* New York: Holt, 1973.

Hunt, D. E. Person-environment interaction: A challenge found wanting before it was tried. *Review of Educational Research,* 1975, *45*(2), 209-230.

Hunt, J. McV. *Intelligence and experience.* New York: Ronald, 1961.

Hurlock, E. Developmental scale. In *Child Development.* New York: McGraw-Hill, 1966.

Hurt, M. *Child abuse and neglect: A report on the status of research* (Office of Human Development/Office of Child Development, Publication No. 74-20). Washington DC: US Government Printing Office, 1975.

International Herald Tribune, Paris, France, December 1, 1975, p. 14.

Jackson, D. M., & Boston, B. O. The future of the gifted and talented. *The School Psychologist,* Summer 1976, 4-15.

Janik, A., & Toulmin, S. *Wittgenstein's Vienna.* New York: Simon & Schuster, 1973.

Jenkins, J. R., & Mayhall, W. F. Development and evaluation of a resource teacher program. *Exceptional Children,* 1976, *43,* 21-24.

Johnson, D. W. & Johnson, R. T. *Learning together and alone.* Englewood Cliffs NJ: Prentice-Hall, 1975.

Johnson, G. O. Special education for the mentally handicapped. . .A paradox. *Exceptional Children.* 1962, *19,* 62-69.

Johnson, R. A., & Grismer, R. The Harrison School Center: A public school-university cooperative resource program. In E. Deno, (Ed.), *Instructional alternatives for exceptional children.* Reston VA: The Council for Exceptional Children, 1972.

Johnson, R.A., Gross, J.C., Nash, N., & Reynolds, M.C. Problem solving in Boston: A preliminary report. In M. C. Reynolds (Ed.), *National technical assistance systems in special education.* Minneapolis: Leadership Training Institute/Special Education, University of Minnesota, 1975.

Jones, R. L. (Ed.) *Mainstreaming and the minority child.* Reston VA: The Council for Exceptional Children, 1976.

Jones, R. L., & Wilderson, F. Mainstreaming and the minority child: An overview of the issues and a perspective. In R. L. Jones (Ed.), *Mainstreaming and the minority child.* Reston VA: The Council for Exceptional Children, 1976.

Joyce, B., & Weil, M. *Models of teaching.* Englewood Cliffs NJ: Prentice-Hall, 1972.

Kanner, L. *A history of the care and study of the mentally retarded.* Springfield IL: Charles C Thomas, 1964.

Kaplan, S. N. *Providing programs for the gifted and talented: A handbook.* Ventura CA: Ventura County Schools, 1974.

Keating, D. K. (Ed.). *Intellectual talent: Research and development.* Baltimore MD: Johns Hopkins University Press, 1976.

Kempe, C. H. A practical approach to the protection of the abused child and rehabilitation of the abusing parent. *Pediatrics,* 1973, *51*, 804-812.

Keogh, B. What research tells us about mainstreaming. In P. O'Donnell & R. Bradfield (Eds.), *Mainstreaming: Controversy and consensus.* San Rafael CA: Academic Therapy, 1976, 25-38.

Kephart, N.C. *The slow learner in the classroom.* Columbus OH: Charles E. Merrill, 1971.

King-Stoops, J. Critical factors in certain innovative British Schools. *Phi Delta Kappan,* November 1974, 215.

Kirk, S.A. *Educating exceptional children.* Boston: Houghton-Mifflin, 1962.

Kirk, S., & Johnson, G. O. *Educating the retarded child.* Boston: Houghton-Mifflin, 1951.

Klausmeier, H. J., Quilling, M. R., Sorenson, J. S., Way, R. S., & Glasrud, G. R. *Individually guided education in the multiunit school: Guidelines for implementation.* Madison: Wisconsin Research and Development Center for Cognitive Learning, 1971.

Klausmeier, H.J., Rossmiller, R.A., & Sailey, M. (Eds.). *Individually guided elementary education: Concepts and practices.* New York: Academic Press, 1977.

Klein, J. W. Headstart Services to handicapped: Mainstreaming the preschooler. *Head Start Newsletter,* 1977, *9*(6), 1-9.

Kohlberg, L. Stage and sequence: The cognitive-developmental approach to socialization. In D. Goslin (Ed.), *Handbook of socialization: Theory and research.* New York: Rand McNally, 1969.

Kolstoe, O. P. *Teaching educable mentally retarded children.* New York: Holt, Rinehart & Winston, 1970.

Koppitz, E. M. Special class pupils with learning disabilities: A five-year follow-up study. *School Psychology Digest,* Winter 1976, 45-50.

Kounin, J. S. *Discipline and group management in classrooms.* New York: Holt, Rinehart & Winston, 1970.

Kugel, R. B., & Wolfensberger, W. *Changing patterns in residential services for the mentally retarded.* Washington DC: President's Committee on Mental Retardation, 1969.

L'Abate, L., & Curtis, L. T. *Teaching the exceptional child.* Philadelphia: W. B. Saunders, 1975.

Lance, W. D. Who are all the children? *Exceptional Children,* 1976, *43*, 66-76.

Larry P. v. Riles. Civil Action N. C.-71-2270, 343 F Supp. 1306 (N.D. Cal., 1972).

Larsen, E.D. FOCUS: What makes it work? *Invisible College on Learning and Behavior Problems of Handicapped Students in Secondary School Programs.* Reston VA: The Council for Exceptional Children, 1977.

Levine, M. The academic achievement test. *American Psychologist,* March 1976.

Lilly, M. S. Forum: A training-based model for special education. *Exceptional Children,* 1971, *37,* 745-749.

Lindsley, O. Direct measurement and prosthesis of retarded behavior. *Journal of Education,* 1964, *147,* 62.

Lindsley, O. R. From Skinner to precision teaching: The child knows best. In J. B. Jordan & L. S. Robbins (Eds.), *Let's try doing something else kind of thing: Behavior principles and the exceptional child.* Reston VA: The Council for Exceptional Children, 1972, 2-11.

Lippman, L., & Goldberg, I. I. *Right to education.* New York: Teachers' College Press, 1973.

Litwak, E. & Meyer, H. J. The school and the family. In P. F. Lazarfeld et al. (Eds.), *The uses of sociology.* New York: Basic Books, 1967.

Loe, D. C., & Becker, L. D. Research interests of special education administrators. *Phi Delta Kappan,* February 1975, 430.

Lombroso, C. *The man of genius.* London: Walter Scott, 1893.

Lovatt, M. Autistic children in a day nursery. *Exceptional Children,* 1962, *29,* 103-108.

Love, H. D. *Educating exceptional children in regular classrooms.* Springfield IL: Charles C Thomas, 1972.

Lowenfeld, B. History of the education of visually handicapped children. In B. Lowenfeld (Ed.), *The visually handicapped child in school.* New York: John Day, 1973, 1-26.

Lundstrom, K. *Case studies in special education: Cuba, Japan, Kenya and Sweden.* Paris: The UNESCO Press, 1974.

Mackie, R. P. Spotlighting advances in special education. *Exceptional Children,* 1965, *32,* 77-81.

Mackie, R. P., & Dunn, L. N. *College and university programs for the preparation of teachers of exceptional children* (Office of Education Bulletin, 1954, No. 13). Washington DC: US Government Printing Office, 1954.

MacMillan D., Jones, R. L., & Meyers, C. E. Mainstreaming the mildly retarded: Some questions, cautions, and guidelines. *Mental Retardation,* 1976 *14*(1), 3-10.

Maeroff, G. I. Early entry in college hailed as blessing by U.S. prodigies. *New York Times,* November 9, 1975.

Mallis, J. A. Seminar for superior students. *The Clearing House,* November 1956, 175-178.

Marr, H. Education of the physically handicapped: An urban approach. *Newsletter,* Division on Physically Handicapped, Homebound and Hospitalized. Reston VA: The Council for Exceptional Children, September 1969. (Abstract)

Marshall, E. Teaching materials for children with learning disabilities. In W. M. Cruickshank & D.P. Hallahan, *Psychoeducational practices* (Vol. 1). Syracuse NY: Syracuse University Press, 1975.

Martin, D. L. The growing horror of child abuse and the undeniable role of the schools in putting an end to it. *American School Board Journal,* 1973, *160,* 51-55.

Martinson, R. *An analysis of problems and priorities: Advocate survey and statistical sources. Education of the gifted and talented.* Report to the Congress of the United States by the US Commissioner of Education and background papers submitted to the US Office of Education. Washington DC: Government Printing Office, 1972.

Martinson, R.A. Children with superior cognitive abilities. In L.M. Dunn (Ed.), *Exceptional children in the schools.* New York: Holt, Rinehart & Winston, 1973.

Martinson, R. A. *The identification of the gifted and talented.* Ventura CA: Office of the Ventura County Superintendent of Schools, 1974.

Marland, S.P., Jr. *Education of the gifted and talented.* Washington DC: Congress of the United States by the US Commissioner of Education, 1971.

Marland, S. P., Jr., *Education of the gifted and talented.* Washington DC: US Office of Education, 1972, p. 261.

Marland, S. P. Advanced placement. *Today's Education,* 1976, Jan.-Feb.

Mauser, A. J. As I see it: The gifted handicapped. *Talents and Gifts,* November 1975, p. 30.

McCarthy, J. J., & McCarthy, J. F. *Learning disabilities.* Boston: Allyn & Bacon, 1969.

McConnell, F. Children with hearing disabilities. In L. M. Dunn (Ed.), *Exceptional children in the schools.* New York: Holt, Rinehart & Winston, 1973.

McDonald, R.A.F. *Adjustment of school organization to various population groups.* New York: Teachers' College, Columbia University, 1915.

McLaughlin, T. F. Self-control in the classroom. *Review of Educational Research,* 1976, *46*(4), 631-663.

Mental Disability Law Reporter, July-August 1976, pp. 23-24.

Mercer, J. R. Cultural pluralism and the standardized testing movement. In G.R. Gredler (Ed.), *Ethical and legal factors in the practice of school psychology.* Harrisburg PA: State Department of Education, 1974.

Miel, A., & Kiester, E. K., Jr. *The shortchanged children of suburbia.* New York: Institute of Human Relations, American Jewish Committee, 1967.

Miles, M. B. *Innovation in education.* New York: Bureau of Publications, Teachers' College, Columbia University, 1964.

Minneapolis Association for Retarded Citizens. *Draft report of the special task force on implementing the least restrictive alternative.* Minneapolis: Author, 1976.

Minneapolis Federation of Teachers, Local 59. *Proposed Constitutional Amendment,* 1975.

Moore, M. W., & Peabody, R. L. *A functional description of the itinerant teacher of visually handicapped children in the Commonwealth of Pennsyl-*

vania. Pittsburgh PA: School of Education, University of Pittsburgh, 1976.

Morse, W. C. The helping teacher/crisis teacher concept. *Focus on Exceptional Children,* 1976, *8*(4), 1-11.

Morton, M. Your community—goldmine. *Talents and Gifts,* November 1975, pp. 25-26.

Mosher, R. L., & Sprinthall, N. A. Deliberate psychological education. *The Counseling Psychologist,* 1971, *2*(4), 3-82.

Moustakas, C. E. *Children in play therapy.* New York: McGraw-Hill, 1953.

Mullins, J. B. Integrated classrooms. *Journal of Rehabilitation,* 1971, *37*(2), 14-16.

Murphy, M. K. Harry Galanty. *Today's Education,* January-February 1976, pp. 29-30.

Myer, L. N. Personal communication, November 27, 1952.

Nagi, S. Child abuse and neglect programs: A national review. *Children Today,* 1975, *4*, 12-17.

National Advisory Committee on Handicapped Children of the U.S. Office of Education. *First Annual Report.* Washington DC: US Government Printing Office, 1968.

National Association for Retarded Citizens. Being retarded does not bother Danny Wheeler. *Mental Retardation News,* 1976, *25*(2), 8.

National Education Association. Class size formula may revolutionize teacher contracts. *NEA Reporter,* 1977, *16*(5).

National School Public Relations Association. *Preschool breakthrough: What works in early childhood education.* Washington DC: Author, 1966.

Newland, T. E. *The gifted in socio-educational perspective.* Englewood Cliffs NJ: Prentice-Hall, 1976.

Newman, R. The assessment of progress in the treatment of hyperaggressive children with learning disturbances within a school setting. *The American Journal of Orthopsychiatry,* 1959, *29*, 633-643.

Newman, R. *Psychological consultation in the schools.* New York: Basic Books, 1967.

New York State United Teachers. *New York Teacher,* May 8, 1977.

The New York Times, Sunday, May 18, 1975.

The New York Times, August 19, 1976.

Nober, L. W. *Hearing-impaired formal inservice program.* Columbus OH: National Media and Materials Center for the Handicapped, Ohio State University, 1973.

Noffsinger, T. *Observation of EMR students in special class and mainstream studies.* Mentor OH: Mentor Exempted Village School District, 1973.

Noffsinger, T., & Storms, W. *Special education cost study.* Mentor OH: Mentor Exempted Village School District, 1974.

Nolte, M. C. Why your school board should review and (probably) remake its policy toward pregnant school girls. *American School Board Journal,* March 1973, pp. 23-27.

North Carolina State Department of Public Instruction. *Rules governing programs and services for children with special needs.* Raleigh NC: Author, Division for Exceptional Children, 1976.

Northcott, W. H. (Ed.) *The hearing impaired child in a regular classroom: Preschool, elementary, and secondary years.* Washington DC: A. G. Bell Association, 1973.

Office of Demographic Studies. *Annual survey of hearing impaired children and youth, United States: 1970-1971.* Washington DC: Gallaudet College, March 1973.

Orton, S. *Reading, writing and speech problems in children.* New York: Norton, 1937.

Parke, R. D., & Collmer, C. W. Child abuse: An interdisciplinary analysis. In E. M. Hetherington (Ed.), *Review of child development research* (Vol. 5). Chicago: University of Chicago Press, 1975, 509-590.

Parker, C. A. (Ed.). *Psychological consultation: Helping teachers meet special needs.* Reston VA: The Council for Exceptional Children, 1975.

Paul, R. L. *An experience in deafness.* Pontiac MI: Oakland Public Schools, 1972.

Pegnato, C. W., & Birch, J. W. Locating gifted children in junior high school: A comparison of methods. *Exceptional Children,* 1959, *25*, 300-304.

Pennsylvania Association for Retarded Children v. Pennsylvania, 334 F. Supp. 1257 (E.D. Pa. 1971).

Pennsylvania Office of Children and Youth. *Won't you speak for them.* Department of Public Welfare, Commonwealth of Pennsylvania, February 1976.

Pennsylvania State Education Association. Tim Feiock—A tale of heart, courage. *Voice,* April 14, 1975, p. 7.

Pepper, F. Teaching the American Indian child in mainstream settings. In R. L. Jones (Ed.), *Mainstreaming and the minority child.* Reston VA: The Council for Exceptional Children, 1976.

Peterson, L. Pinellas County. *Talents and Gifts,* 1975, *17*(2), 10.

Pieper, E. *The Able Disabled Picture Kit.* Scotia NY: Author (R.D. 1, Ridge Road, 12302), 1975.

Pierson, D. E. The Brookline Early Education Project: Model for a new education priority. *Childhood Education,* 1974, *50*(3), 132-134.

Portland, Oregon, Public Schools. Public information brochure on the Holladay Center, no date.

Premack, D. Toward empirical behavior laws: I. Positive reinforcement. *Psychological Review,* 1959, *66*, 219-233.

President's Committee on Mental Retardation. *MR priority report: The retarded victims of poverty.* Washington DC: US Government Printing Office, 0-310-156, 1968.

President's Committee on Mental Retardation. Bureau of Education for the Handicapped, Office of Education, US Department of Health, Education, and Welfare. *The six-hour retarded child.* Washington DC: US Government Printing Office, 1969.

President's Committee on Mental Retardation. *Residential services for the mentally retarded: An action proposal.* Washington DC: US Government Printing Office, 1970.

President's Committee on Mental Retardation. *The decisive decade.* Washington DC: US Government Printing Office, 1971.
President's Committee on Mental Retardation. *Federal programs for the retarded—A review and evaluation.* Washington DC: US Government Printing Office, 1972.
President's Committee on Mental Retardation. *A friend in Washington.* DHEW Publication No. (OHD) 75-21010. Washington DC: US Government Printing Office, June 1975, p. 18.
Pressey, S. L. Concerning the nature and nurture of genius. *Scientific Monthly,* September 1955, pp. 123-129. (Reprinted in J. L. French, *Educating the gifted.* Columbus OH: Holt, 1959.)
A product of miracles. *Clark School Speaks,* 1976, *20*(8).
Prouty, R., & McGarry, F.M. The diagnostic/prescriptive teacher, In E. Deno (Ed.), *Instructional alternatives for exceptional children.* Reston VA: The Council for Exceptional Children, 1972.
Public Law 93-380, Section 404. *Federal Register,* May 6, 1976.
Putnam, J. F., & Chismore, W. D. *Standard terminology for curriculum and instruction in local and state school systems.* Washington DC: US Government Printing Office, (Catalog No. 5.223:23052, 1970).
Quie, A. H. *An address to the Executive Training Institute for Directors of Special Education,* June 8-12, 1970, University of Indiana, Bloomington.
Ramey, C. T., & Smith, B. J. Assessing the intellectual consequences of early intervention with high-risk infants. *American Journal of Mental Deficiency,* 1977, *81*(4), 318-324.
Rankin, A. Prodigy from Plumtree. *Reader's Digest,* August 1976, pp. 54-58.
Redden, M. R. *An investigation of mainstreaming competencies of regular elementary teachers.* Unpublished doctoral dissertation, University of Kentucky (Lexington), 1976.
Redden, M. R., Fortunato-Schwandt, W., Brown, J. W. *Barrier-free meetings: A guide for professional associations* (Publication No. 76-7). Washington DC: American Association for the Advancement of Science, 1976.
Redl, F. The concept of a therapeutic milieu. *American Journal of Orthopsychiatry,* 1959, *29,* 721-734.
Reger, R., & Koppman, M. The child oriented resource room program. *Exceptional Children,* 1971, *37,* 460-462.
Renzulli, J. S. *New directions in creativity.* New York: Harper & Row, 1975.
Report of the Ad Hoc Committee to define deaf and hard of hearing. *American Annals of the Deaf,* October 1975, pp. 509-512.
Representative Assembly of the National Education Association. Resolutions. *Today's Education,* March-April 1976, p. 19.
Reyna, J., & Bernal, E. M., Jr. Alternative identification strategies for Mexican American youngsters at the primary level. *Talents and Gifts,* March 1976, p. 9. (Abstract)
Reynolds, M. C. *Delphi survey.* Reston VA: The Council for Exceptional Children, 1973.
Reynolds, M. C. (Ed.). *Special education in school system decentralization.* Minneapolis: LTI/Department of Special Education, University of Minnesota, 1975.

Reynolds, M. C., & Balow, B. Categories and variables in special education. *Exceptional Children,* 1972, *38,* 357-366.

Reynolds, M., Birch, J., & Tuseth, A. Review of research on early admission. In M. C. Reynolds (Ed.), *Early school admission for mentally advanced children.* Reston VA: The Council for Exceptional Children, 1962.

Riesman, D. Notes on meritocracy. *Daedalus,* 1969, *96*(3), 905.

Rogers, C. R. *Client-centered therapy.* Boston: Houghton-Mifflin, 1951.

Rosensweet, A. "Give us compassion and help," handicapped urge. *Pittsburgh Post-Gazette,* Friday, September 17, 1976, p. 9.

Rosenzweig, L. E., & Long, J. *Understanding and teaching the dependent retarded child.* (2nd ed.). Darien CT: Educational Publishing, 1960.

Rubin, R., & Balow, B. Learning and behavior disorders: A longitudinal study. *Exceptional Children,* 1971, *38,* 293-299.

Russo, J. R. (Ed.). Mainstreaming handicapped students: Are your facilities suitable? *Education Digest,* 1975, *40,* 18-21.

Rucker, C. N. & Gable, R. K. *Rucker-Gable Educational Programming Scale.* Storrs CT: Rucker-Gable Associates, Rockridge, Box 201 C (Storrs CT 06268)

Salem, J. M. Partial integration at the high school level. *Volta Review,* 1971, *69,* 42-46.

Schaefer, E. S. Parents as educators. In W. W. Hartup (Ed.), *The young child: Reviews of research* (Vol 2). Washington DC: National Association for the Education of Young Children, 1972.

Schible, D. Right to education for all exceptional school-age persons, including gifted, made part of Pennsylvania school code. *Talents and Gifts,* November 1975, p. 22.

Schwartz, L., & Oseroff, A. *The clinical teacher for special education* (Vol. 1), *Establishing the model.* Tallahassee: Educational Research Institute, College of Education, Florida State University, 1975.

Sharing (News notes), Winter 1974, p. 28.

Shearer, D., Billingsley, J., Frohman, S., Hilliard, J., Johnson, F., & Shearer, M. *Developmental sequential checklist.* Unpublished manuscript, The Portage Project, Cooperative Educational Agency No. 12 (Portage, WI) 1970.

Shedd, M. R. The state-federal partnership: Making it work for schools. *The School Administrator,* 1977, *34*(5), 18-19.

Skinner, B. F. *Science and human behavior.* New York: Macmillan, 1953.

Skinner, B. F. *The technology of teaching.* New York: Appleton-Century-Crofts, 1968.

Sloan, W. Four score and seven. *American Journal of Mental Deficiency,* 1963, *68*(1), 6-14.

Sloan, W., & Birch, J. W. A rationale for degrees of retardation. *American Journal of Mental Deficiency,* 1955, *60,* p. 262.

Sloan, W., & Stevens, H. *AAMD—A century of concern.* Washington DC: American Association on Mental Deficiency (5201 Connecticut Ave., N.W., Washington, D.C. 20015), 1976.

Smith, J. David's story. *Programs for the handicapped,* April 12, 1976. DHEW Publ. No. (0-) 76-22000. (Room 3517, Switzer Building, 330 C Street, SW, Washington DC 20201.)

Smith, R. M. *Clinical teaching: Methods of instruction for the retarded.* New York: McGraw-Hill, 1968.

Sontag, E. Zero exclusion. No longer rhetoric. *Apropos,* Spring-Summer 1976, p. 3. (National Center on Educational Media and Materials for the Handicapped, The Ohio State University.)

Sosnowsky, W. P., & Coleman, T. W. Special education in the collective bargaining process. *Phi Delta Kappan,* 1971, *52,* 610-613.

Spache, G. D. *Diagnosing and correcting reading disabilities.* Boston: Allyn & Bacon, 1976.

Spears, H. Kappans ponder typical school procedures. *Phi Delta Kappan,* 1973, *54,* 615-618.

Sprinthall, N. A., & Erickson, V. L. Learning psychology by doing psychology: Guidance through the curriculum. *Personnel and Guidance Journal,* 1974, *52*(6), 396-405.

Stanwix House, Inc. *Functional basic reading program.* Pittsburgh PA: Author, 1970.

Stanwix House, Inc. *The best speech series.* Pittsburgh: Author, 1972.

State of Washington Department of Social and Health Services. Each one can learn. *Programs for the Handicapped.* Washington DC: US Department of Health, Education, and Welfare, Office for Handicapped Individuals, June 14, 1976.

Stevens, G. D. *Taxonomy in special education for children with body disorders.* Pittsburgh: Department of Special Education and Rehabilitation, University of Pittsburgh, 1962.

Stoddard, G. D. *The dual progress plan.* New York: Harper & Brothers, 1961.

Stoll, W. C. Guidelines for drug abuse education versus actual practice. *Phi Delta Kappan,* March 1974, pp. 489-490.

Stratton, J. The eye-music of deaf actors fills stage eloquently. *Smithsonian,* March 1976, pp. 66-72.

Strauss, A. A., & Lehtinen, L. E. *Psychopathology and education of the brain-injured child.* New York: Grune & Stratton, 1947.

Stutsman, R. *The Merrill-Palmer Scale.* New York: Harcourt, Brace, & World, 1948.

Sumption, M. R., & Luecking, E. M. *Education of the gifted.* New York: Ronald, 1960.

Suppes, P.A. A survey of cognition in handicapped children. *Review of Educational Research,* 1974, *44*(2), 145-146.

Swatzenbarg, P.A. "Mainstreaming" of handicapped children—Are we prepared? Unpublished manuscript, Department of Special Education, Utah State University (Logan UT 84322), Dec. 10, 1975.

Tacoma-Pierce County Cooperative Study. *Design for the education of exceptional children.* Tacoma WA: Tacoma Public Schools, July 1958.

Tacoma Public Schools. *Professional agreements between Board of Directors,* Tacoma School District No. 10 and the Tacoma Alliance of Education. July 1, 1972-June 30, 1974.

Talmage, H. (Ed.). *Systems for individualized education.* Berkeley CA: McCutchan, 1975.

Taylor, C. W. Be talent developers as well as knowledge dispensers. *Today's Education,* 1968, *57*, 67-69.

Terman, L. M. Mental and physical traits of a thousand gifted children (Vol. I) *Genetic studies of genius.* Stanford CA: Stanford University Press, 1925.

Terman, L. M. The discovery and encouragement of exceptional talent. *American Psychologist,* 1954, *8*(6), 221-230.

Terman, L., & Oden, M. *Genetic studies of genius. The gifted child grows up* (Vol. 4). Stanford CA: Stanford University Press, 1947.

Terman, L. M., & Oden, M. The Stanford studies of the gifted. In P. Witty (Ed.), *The gifted child.* Boston: Heath, 1951.

Terman, L., & Oden, M. Genetic studies of genius. *The gifted group at midlife* (Vol. 5). Stanford CA: Stanford University Press, 1959.

Thorndike, R. L. Mr. Binet's test 70 years later. *Educational Researcher,* 1975, *4*(5), 3-4.

Tobias, S. Achievement treatment interactions. *Review of Educational Research,* 1976, *46*(1), 61-74.

Tongue, C., & Sperling, C. *Gifted and talented: An identification model.* Division for Exceptional Children, State Department of Public Instruction, Raleigh NC, 1976.

Torrance, E.P. *They shall create: Gifted minority children* (cassette, side 1). Reston VA: The Council for Exceptional Children, 1973.

Torrance, E. P., & Myers, R. E. *Creative learning and teaching.* New York: Dodd, Mead, 1970.

Torres, S. (Ed.). *A primer on individualized education programs for handicapped children.* Reston VA: Foundation for Exceptional Children, 1977.

Trotter, V. Y., & Bell, T. H. Policy of the United States Office of Education on gifted and talented education. *Talents and Gifts,* 1976, *18*(2), 4.

Turton, L. J. Perceptual and learning disabilities in children. In W. M. Cruikshank & D. P. Hallahan (Eds.), *Psychoeducational practices* (Vol. I). Syracuse: Syracuse University Press, 1975.

Tyler, L. E. Design for a hopeful psychology. *American Psychologist,* 1973, *28*(12), 1021-1029.

UOP pharmacy student makes writing possible for cerebral palsy victim. *Programs for the handicapped,* Dept. of HEW, June 14, 1976. Washington, D.C.

Urbanowicz, L. Lack of pain no pleasure for Kelly. *The Turning Point,* Spring 1975. (Available from the Home for Crippled Children, 1426 Denniston Ave., Pittsburgh PA 15217)

US Department of Health, Education, and Welfare. *Education of the deaf.* A report to the Secretary of Health, Education, and Welfare by his Advisory Committee on Education of the Deaf. Washington DC: Author, February, 1965.

US Department of Health, Education, and Welfare. *Programs for the handicapped.* Washington DC: DHEW, Office for Handicapped Individuals, Washington, D.C. 20201, August 11, 1975, pp. 22-23.

US Secretary of Health, Education, and Welfare. *The problem of mental retardation.* Washington DC: US Government Printing Office, 1969.

Van Riper, C. *Speech correction: Principles and methods* (4th ed.). Englewood Cliffs NJ: Prentice-Hall, 1963.

Vogel, A. L. Integration of nine severe learning-disabled children in a junior-high school care program. *The School Psychology Digest,* Winter 1976, pp. 51-55.

Wallin, J. E. W. *The education of handicapped children.* Boston: Houghton-Mifflin, 1924.

Wallin, J. E. W. *Education of mentally handicapped children.* New York: Harper & Row, 1955.

Wardlaw, J. Mainstreaming that works. In P. H. Mann (Ed.), *Shared responsibility for handicapped students: Advocacy and programming.* Coral Gables FL: University of Miami Training and Technical Assistance Center, 1976.

Warfield, G. J. Mothers of retarded children review a parent education program. *Exceptional Children,* 1975, *41*, 559-562.

Warren, S. A. Letter to the AAMD Membership, March 19, 1976.

Wechsler, D. Intelligence defined and undefined; A relativistic appraisal. *American Psychologist,* February 1975, pp. 135-139.

Wendland, L. Personal communication, April 1972.

Wisland, M. V. *Psycho-educational diagnosis of exceptional children.* Springfield IL: Charles C Thomas, 1973.

Witty, P. The gifted child. *Exceptional Children* 1953, *19*, 255-259.

Wolfensberger, W. *The principle of normalization in human services.* Toronto: National Institute on Mental Retardation, 1972.

World Federation of the Deaf. *Gestuno.* London: British Deaf Association, 38 Victoria Place, Carlisle CA 11 HU.

Wyatt v. Aderholt, 334 F. Supp. 1341 (M.D. Alabama, 1971).

Wyatt v. Stickney. 344 F. Supp. 387 (M.D. Ala. 1972) Affirmed Sub. Nom. *Wyatt v. Aderholt,* 503 F. 2d. 1305 (5th Cir. 1974).

Yater, V. V. Personal communication, 1974.

Yoshida, R., MacMillan, D. L., & Meyers, C. E. The decertification of minority group EMR students in California: Student achievement and adjustment. In R. L. Jones (Ed.), *Mainstreaming and the minority child.* Reston VA: The Council for Exceptional Children, 1976.

Young, M. E. Mainstreaming and the minority child: The Philadelphia experience. In R. L. Jones (Ed.), *Mainstreaming and the minority child,* Reston VA: The Council for Exceptional Children, 1976.

Zajonc, R. B. Birth order and intelligence: Dumber by the dozen. *Psychology Today,* January 1975, *8*, 37-40.

Zawadski, R. F. A study of what regular classroom teachers consider deterrents to teaching educable mentally retarded children in regular classes. *Dissertation Abstracts International,* 1974, *35*(1), 292-A.

Zawadski, R. Unpublished research report. Victoria Center, University of Houston (Texas), 1973.

Ziegler, S., & Hambleton, D. Integration of young TMR children into a regular elementary school. *Exceptional Children,* 1976, *43*, 459-461.

Zigler, E. Controlling child abuse—An effort doomed to failure. In W. A. Collins (Ed.), *Newsletter of the Division on Developmental Psychology,* American Psychological Association, February 1976, 17-30.

Zigmond, N. *Child service demonstration center for urban secondary students with learning disabilities.* Pittsburgh: Department of Special Education, University of Pittsburgh, 1975 (mimeo.).

Zubin, J. Classification of the behavior disorders. In P.R. Farnsworth et al. (Eds), *Annual review of psychology.* Palo Alto CA: Annual Reviews, Inc., 1967, 373-406.

Appendix A
Organizations and Agencies Concerned with Exceptional Persons

Alexander Graham Bell Association for the Deaf, Inc.
3417 Volta Place
Washington DC 20007

American Association for Gifted Children
15 Gramercy Park
New York NY 10003

American Association on Mental Deficiency
5201 Connecticut Avenue, NW
Washington DC 20015

American Foundation for the Blind
15 West Sixteenth Street
New York NY 10011

American Printing House for the Blind
P.O. Box 6085
Louisville KY 40206

American Psychological Association
1200 Seventeenth Street, NW
Washington DC 20036

American Speech and Hearing Association
9030 Old Georgetown Road
Washington DC 20014

ARC Reprinter's Corporation*
21 Northampton Street
Buffalo NY 14209

Association for Children with Learning Disabilities
5225 Grace Street
Pittsburgh PA 15236

Association for the Aid of Crippled Children
345 East 46th Street
New York NY 10017

Association for the Education of the Visually Handicapped
919 Walnut, Fourth Floor
Philadelphia PA 19107

Association of Rehabilitation Facilities
5530 Wisconsin Avenue
Washington DC 20015

Bell & Howell Company*
Duopage Department, Micro Photo Division
Old Mansfield Road
Wooster OH 44691

Braille Circulating Library
2823 West Grace Street
Richmond VA 23221

---

*Suppliers of type enlargement materials

Clearinghouse on the Handicapped
Office of Handicapped Individuals
388-D S. Portal Building
Washington, DC 20201

Clearinghouse on Programs and
 Research in Child Abuse and Neglect
Herner and Company
2100 M Street, NW, Suite 316
Washington DC 20037

Closer Look
National Information Center for the
 Handicapped
1201 Sixteenth Street, NW
Washington DC 20037

The Council for Exceptional
 Children
1920 Association Drive
Reston VA 22091

Crane Duplicating Service*
P.O. Box 487
Barnstable MA 02630

Dakota Microfilm Services, Inc.*
North Central Office
501 North Dakota Street
St. Paul MN 55103

Division for the Blind and
 Physically Handicapped
Library of Congress
Washington DC 20542

Eye Gate House, Inc.
146-01 Archer Avenue
Jamaica NY 11435

ERIC Clearinghouse on Adult, Career,
 and Vocational Education
National Center for Research in
 Vocational Education
The Ohio State University
1960 Kenny Road
Columbus OH 43210

Gifted Child Society, Inc.
59 Glen Gray Road
Oakland NJ 07436

Large Type Books in Print
R.R. Bowker Company
1180 Avenue of the Americas
New York NY 10036

Library Reproduction Service*
1977 South Los Angeles Street
Los Angeles CA 90011

Muscular Dystrophy Association
810 Seventh Avenue
New York NY 10019

National Association for Creative
 Children and Adults
8080 Springvalley Drive
Cincinnati OH 45236

National Association of the Deaf
814 Thayer Avenue
Silver Spring MD 20910

National Association for Retarded
 Citizens
2709 Avenue E East
Arlington TX 76011

National Association for the
 Visually Handicapped
3201 Balboa Street
San Francisco CA 94121

National Center on Educational
 Media and Materials for the
 Handicapped
The Ohio State University
Columbus OH 43210

National Braille Press
88 St. Stephen Street
Boston MA 02115

---

*Suppliers of type enlargement materials

National Easter Seal Society for
  Crippled Children and Adults
2023 West Ogden Avenue
Chicago IL 60612

National Information Center for
  Special Education Materials
University of Southern California
University Park
Los Angeles CA 90007

National Diffusion Network
The Division of Educational
  Replication
US Office of Education
ROB 3, Room 3616
400 Maryland Avenue, SW
Washington DC 20202

National Foundation
March of Dimes
Division of Health Information
  and School Relations
1275 Mamaroneck Avenue
White Plains NY 10605

National Inservice Network
Indiana University
2853 East Tenth Street
Bloomington IN 47401

National Rehabilitation Association
1522 K Street, NW
Washington DC 20005

National Society for Autistic Children
169 Tampa Avenue
Albany NY 12208

National Society for Autistic
  Children
Information & Referral Service
306 - 31st Street
Huntington WV 25702

Orton Society, Inc.
8415 Bellona Lane
Baltimore MD 21204

Recording for the Blind, Inc.
215 East 58th Street
New York NY 10022

Singer Education and Training
  Products
Society for Visual Education, Inc.
1345 Diversey Parkway
Chicago IL 60614

United Cerebral Palsy Association
Program Department
66 East 34th Street
New York NY 10016

We Are People First
P.O. Box 5208
Salem OR 97304

Appendix B
Teacher Training Materials

The following is a beginning list of "mainstreaming" training systems, materials, and resources. They mainly represent materials developed in recent years to meet some of the urgent needs for training in the context of the renegotiation of special and regular education functions. It is unlikely that any trainer would wish to use these materials without modification, but there are extremely useful ideas, audiovisual materials, sets of readings, games, and other varieties of instructional aides that will be of value to virtually every instructor.

Following is a brief index of materials and resources that are described more fully in succeeding pages. A variety of materials are "noted briefly" in the last section of this appendix.

All Together Now: Presentations for The Council for Exceptional Children's Invisible College on Mainstreaming, Reston, Virginia

Classroom Management: protocol materials, University of South Florida, Tampa

Competencies for Teaching: individual instruction, classroom instruction, therapeutic instruction, and teacher education, Wadsworth Publishing Co., Belmont, California

Directory of Training Materials: From the Center for Innovation in Teaching the Handicapped, University of Indiana, Bloomington

Exceptional Teaching: By White and Haring, University of Washington, Seattle

Fundamentals, Operations, Resources, Environment (FORE): Los Angeles Public Schools and University of Oregon, Eugene

The Heart of Teaching: From the Agency for Exceptional Children, Bloomington, Indiana

Individualized Learning Materials (ILM) for Teachers, Supervisors, Principals, and Central Staff: University of Utah, Salt Lake City.

Information Center: The Council for Exceptional Children, Reston, Virginia

Leadership Training Institute/Special Education: University of Minnesota, Minneapolis

Learning Opportunities for Teachers: Accelerated Learning Systems, Austin, Texas

Let's Series Modules: Preparing Regular Educators for Mainstreaming (PREM) University of Texas, Austin

728 / Teaching Exceptional Children in All America's Schools

The Lexington Teacher Training Project: Agency for Instructional Television, Bloomington, Indiana
Mainstream: University of Connecticut, Wallingford
National Center for Educational Media and Materials for the Handicapped: Ohio State University, Columbus
National Instructional Materials Information System (NIMIS): Ohio State University, Columbus
The Preparation of Regular Classroom Teachers to Work with Students with Special Learning Problems: A Preservice Training Project; University of Northern Colorado, Greeley
The Principals' Training Program (PTP): Education Service Center, Region XIII, Austin, Texas
Public Law 94-142: multimedia package from The Council for Exceptional Children, Reston, Virginia
Special Education Administration Simulation in Monroe City (SEASIM): University Council for Educational Administration, Columbus, Ohio
Special Education Administrator's Simulation (SEASIM) for Rural/Sparsely Populated Areas: University of Minnesota, St. Paul
Special Education Administrators' Training Project (SEATP): University of Minnesota, St. Paul
Strategies for Training Regular Educators to Teach Children with Handicaps: Atlanta, Georgia
The Teacher Training Program (TTP): Education Service Center, Region XIII, Austin, Texas
Teaching Children with Special Needs: Maryland Instructional Television Series, Owings Mills, Maryland
Upset in Polymer: An Experience in Mainstreaming; Center for Innovation in Teaching the Handicapped, Bloomington, Indiana

Other materials briefly noted include:

Approaches to Mainstreaming: Teaching the Special Child in the Regular Classroom (Cejka & Needham)
Classroom Activities for Helping Children with Special Needs (Barbe)
Coming Back. . . or Never Leaving (Pasanella & Volkmar)
The Human Policy Press
IMPACT Workshop Kit
Learning Concepts
Mainstreaming, the Special Child, and the Reading Program
Parents' Magazine Films, Inc.
Special Education Placement: A Decision Systems Module
Special Education for Regular Teachers (SERT)
Training Materials (Non-categorical Centers)
Understanding Young Children (Mayer)
VIMCET Filmstrip-Tape Program for Teacher Education
What Is a Handicap

All Together Now:
Presentations from The CEC Invisible College on Mainstreaming

Purpose: These presentations provide a variety of professional viewpoints, research, and suggestions related to the process of mainstreaming handicapped children.

Brief Description of Materials or Service: An album of six audiotape cassettes and three books (1974). The recordings are conference presentations by special education specialists, state education personnel, local administrators, consulting and resource teachers, a teacher educator, and a management consultant.

Address and Phone: The Council for Exceptional Children, 1920 Association Drive, Reston, Virginia 22091, (703) 620-3660

Additional Description: The tapes included in the album are: Tape 1: *Mainstreaming: What Is It?;* Tape 2: *Planning at the State Level;* Tape 3: *Leadership of District Administrators;* Tape 4: *Teachers Help Teachers;* Tape 5: *Resource Rooms;* Tape 6: *Facilitating Change.*

The books included in the album include: *Special Education Delivery: The Need for Reform, Mainstreaming: Educable Mentally Retarded Children in Regular Classes* and *Mainstream Currents: Reprints from Exceptional Children 1968-1974.* They are also available separately.

Related Materials: Mainstreaming: Teacher Training Workshops on Individualized Instruction produced by The Council for Exceptional Children. This is a series of four in-service teacher training workshops providing 6 hours of training for use with regular class teachers and educators. Contents include a guidebook, 4 simulated learning activities, and one book.

Hawkins-Shepard, C. (Ed.). *Making It Work: Practical Ideas for Integrating Exceptional Children into Regular Classes,* CEC, Revised, 1978.

"Invisible College" program procedures by The Council for Exceptional Children on child abuse and neglect and learning and behavior problems at the secondary level. Each of these multimedia products includes an album of tape cassettes of presentations at special conferences and a full length book with each presentation as a chapter.

Classroom Management

Purpose: The classroom management materials were developed by Walter R. Borg of Utah State University as part of the national Protocol Materials Project, which are disseminated by the University of South Florida. *Classroom Management* is designed to teach teachers certain concepts and classroom management skills that relate to the rate at which disturbances and inattentiveness are likely to be present in the classroom. The material of this set may be used by individual teachers, small groups or large groups; they are useful both in preservice and inservice programs.

Brief description: Included are four multimedia protocol modules, each dealing with one important concept of classroom management. The research foundation for the modules comes from J. Kounin's *Discipline and Group Management in Classrooms.* (New York: Holt, Rinehart, Winston, 1976). The four modules are: Transitions, Group Alerting, Learner Accountability, Withitness.

Contact Person: Professor Walter R. Borg, Utah State University, Logan, Utah 84322

Address for Purchase: Protocol Material, National Resources and Dissemination Center, University of South Florida, Tampa, Florida 33620

Additional Description: Borg has reported the use and evaluation of these training materials in several settings. The results seem relevant in the present context because teachers who have been trained in *Classroom Management* by the Kounin/Borg approaches often achieve significant reductions in deviant behavior under both recitation and seatwork conditions. The number of students "off task" in classroom situations appears to go down following training.

Materials include films, reading materials, and a detailed instructor guide. Activities for classroom application are suggested as part of the training activities. Pairs or small groups of teachers in a building might easily collaborate in carrying out many of the suggested activities.

Related Materials: This training package is but one of many available through the National Resources and Dissemination Center at Tampa. For a catalog of other materials write to the Center at the address given above.

Competencies for Teaching:
Individual Instruction, Classroom Instruction,
Therapeutic Instruction, and Teacher Education

Purpose: Competencies for Teaching attempts to meet the need for a systematic competency based teacher education program based on a scientific study of effective teacher performance. The program attempts to integrate theory, methodology, simulation, and practice teaching into a competency based system with an equal effective system for accountability.

Brief Description of Materials or Service: The series consists of four self instructional volumes that can be used independently of each other, or, when adopted for course in the appropriate sequence, constitutes a complete system of competency based teacher education. The program is suitable for both preservice and in-service use. (1975)

Contact Person: Laurence J. Peter (author)

Address and Phone: Carol Butterfield, College Service Director, Wadsworth Publishing Company, Inc., 10 Davis Drive, Belmont, California 94002.

Additional Description: The fourth volume of *Competencies for Teaching, Teacher Education* serves two related purposes. First, it is a manual of instructions for installing and operating the competencies for the teaching system as a teacher education program; second, it is a textbook for students in teacher education. The first three volumes of *Competencies for Teaching—Individual*

Instruction, Classroom Instruction, and *Therapeutic Instruction*—can be used independently as texts for teacher education courses. *Individual Instruction* is a suitable text for courses in individualizing instruction and in competency based instruction with accountability. *Classroom Instruction* can be used in education courses in instructional objectives and classroom management. *Therapeutic Instruction* is appropriate for introductory courses in instructing exceptional children.

Through a developmental sequence, the program not only assures that students acquire knowledge of the "why" but performance skills as well. For example: Volume I: *Individual Instruction* concerns studies prior to the more complex process of group instruction. Once the student acquires the skills of interacting with one pupil, the next step would be Volume II: *Classroom Instruction.* From here, the student goes into Volume III: *Therapeutic Instruction* which deals with the acquisition of competencies required for effective parent teacher conferences, interdisciplinary communication, and counseling, as well as the skills needed in teaching handicapped children. A student who has completed these three phases may decide to move into Volume IV: *Teacher Education* and acquire the component skills required for teaching prospective teachers how to teach.

To help the students gain the maximum from this program, Volumes I, II, and III each provide: (a) a *textbook* that presents theory and methods of instruction, (b) a *workbook* that provides program instruction and simulation exercises; and (c) a *recordbook* for keeping an account of field experience.

Directory of Training Materials from The Center for Innovation in Teaching the Handicapped

Purpose: The Center for Innovation in Teaching the Handicapped at the University of Indiana is concerned with the design, development, and systematic evaluation of instructional materials for teacher trainers and preservice and in-service teachers of mildly handicapped children. The ultimate goal of CITH's activities is to improve the instructional accommodation and social assimilation of these children by improving teacher training.

Brief Description: CITH Training Materials include a variety of games, simulations, and multimedia packages designed by CITH for use with preservice and in-service teachers. Some of these materials are still at the prototype and evaluation stages; others are available for distribution. Ordering information should be requested from: Center for Innovation in Teaching the Handicapped, 2805 East 10th, Bloomington, Indiana 47401

Additional Description: Contents
Tips for Teachers: Preinstructional Competencies
Specifying Behavioral Objectives
Concept Analysis
Task Analysis
Lesson Planning Through Task Analysis
Lesson Planning Through Concept Analysis
Choose a Curriculum Package

Instructional Games for Handicapped Children
Teacher-Made Reading Materials for the Handicapped
Classroom Charts for Handicapped Children
Classroom Graphics for Handicapped Children
Designing Tutoring Materials

Tips for Teachers: Instructional Competencies
    Using Volunteers in the Classroom
    Parents as Partners in Teaching Handicapped Children
    Observing and Recording a Child's Behavior
    Informal Reading Inventory
    Teaching Reading to Handicapped Children
    A Decision-Making Model for Teaching the Handicapped
    Personalized Questions
    Troubleshooting in Teaching Concepts
    Improving Spelling Skills in Handicapped Learners
    Designing Art Experiences: Body Concepts

Instructional Development for Training Teachers of Exceptional Children
    How to Develop Teacher-Training Materials
    How to Analyze Your Trainee
    How to Analyze Teacher Training Tasks
    How to Analyze Teacher Training Concepts
    How to Develop Structured Roleplay Materials
    How to Develop Teacher Training Games
    How to Develop Audiovisual Training Modules

Games and Simulations
    Upset in Polymer: An Experience in Mainstreaming
    Naked Monsters
    GAMEgame
    Behavior Management Training Program
        Simulation Manual (1 per student)
        Instructor's Manual (1 per instructor)
        Roleplaying Materials Manual (1 for each group of 5)

Training Packages on Observation Systems
    Individual Cognitive Demand Schedule Training Package
    Indiana Behavior Management System-II Training Package
    Indiana Pupil Participation Schedule Training Package
    Affective Education Manual for Teachers

Exceptional Teaching (A Multimedia Training Program)

Purpose: This new program trains future and practicing special education teachers in diagnostic-prescriptive teaching. It supplies useful instructional strategies, practical behavioral principles, and daily classroom management techniques.

    It is designed to serve as a basic program for:
1. General (or generic) methods in special education (noncategorical survey of methods for special education majors).
2. Methods of teaching learning disabled children.

3. Behavior modification (Analysis and Modification of Behavior).
4. Diagnostic-prescriptive teaching (including continuous assessment).
5. Precision teaching.

It can also serve as core or supplemental material for:
1. Methods for teaching learning disabled.
2. Methods for teaching emotionally disturbed.
3. Methods for teaching mildly and moderately retarded.

Selected parts of the program can be used as supplements to:
1. Diagnosis, assessment, or evaluation of exceptional children (particularly Modules 2, 3, and 4).
2. Curriculum courses (particularly Modules 4, 5, and 7).
3. Survey courses (particularly Module 1 and parts of Module 5).
4. Field observation of practicum work.

Brief Description: Each module explains key concepts and procedures, and then the audiovisual materials demonstrate how real teachers work with a variety of handicapped learners. Students interact with text and media to assess their development of full mastery. The program is flexible enough for use in self paced, individual, or group paced classroom instruction, and works effectively in a combination of class meetings and individual work.

The program is both interactive and illustrative in the sense that the student uses text and media both for demonstration and for practice. The audiovisual materials are available in a number of formats in order to meet a variety of needs and hardware.

Contact Persons: Owen R. White and Norris G. Haring, Experimental Education Unit, University of Washington, Seattle.

Address and Phone: Charles E. Merrill Publishing Company, A Bell and Howell Company, 1300 Alum Creek Drive, Box 508, Columbus, Ohio 43216

Additional Description: The training program (a) prepares students in a comprehensive set of methods for teaching exceptional children; (b) focuses on observable academic and social classroom behaviors rather than on categories or labels; (c) presents material in small, easy to acquire steps; (d) reviews concepts and procedures at strategic points; (e) demonstrates and provides practice through multimedia with each procedure as it is used in real classroom by a variety of teachers; (f) provides for regular and frequent self assessment of skill mastery; (g) serves as valuable preparation for, or addition to, field observation and practicum work; and (h) serves as student paced or instructor paced material and functions as core or supplemental materials for a wide range of special education courses.

Contents:
Module 1: An Introduction to a Different Way of Learning
    Part 1. Teaching Is...
    MEDIAPAK A The Process of Teaching
    Part 2. How This Package Will Proceed

Module 2: Assessing Children: Movements and Measurements
    Part 1. This Child is an Individual Because...
    MEDIAPAK B This Child is an Individual Because...

Part 2. The Movement Cycle: A Precise Target for Precise Instruction
MEDIAPAK C Movement Cycles
MEDIAPAK D (1) David's Management Movements
　　　　　　　(2) Mike's Management Movements

Module 3: Assessment Results—Changes and Charts
Part 1. The Count: A Record of Movement
Part 2. Collecting the Counts
MEDIAPAK E Counting the Movements of Children
MEDIAPAK F I Can Do It Myself!
MEDIAPAK G Practices in Counting
Part 3. Movement Cycle Counts—Adjustment, Limits, and Change
Part 4. Charting the Course of Progress
MEDIAPAK H A Picture of Progress
MEDIAPAK I Using the Finder
MEDIAPAK J Charting Can Be Fun

Module 4: What to Do Before the Children Arrive...and Shortly Thereafter
Part 1. What's It All About?
Part 2. Probing a Child's Behavior: The Preparation of Inventories
Part 3. Probing a Child's Behavior: The Administration of Inventories
MEDIAPAK K Probing a Child's Behavior: Initial Assessment

Module 5: The Pain: A Prescription for Progress
Part 1. A Time and Place for Everything
Part 2. Getting the Movement Started
MEDIAPAK M Materials for Movement
MEDIAPAK N Instruction for Movement
Part 3. Consequences: A Reason for Movement
MEDIAPAK O Consequences: A Reason for Movement
Part 4. A Plan for Every Purpose

Module 6: Is It Working?
Part 1. Deciding Before It is Too Late
MEDIAPAK P (1) Alfred's Reading Program
　　　　　　　(2) Deciding Before It is Too Late
Part 2. Selecting a New Plan

Module 7: Building from Experience
Part 1. Basic Tools for Describing What Happened
MEDIAPAK Q (1) Finding a Line of Progress
　　　　　　　(2) Describing Lines of Progress
Part 2. Did It Work-Will It Work?
MEDIAPAK R (1) Describing Changes in Performance
　　　　　　　(2) Interpreting Performance Changes
Part 3. Evaluating Program and Curricula

Module 8: Quick Guides
1. The Process of Exceptional Teaching
2. Common Quantitative Formulas and Procedures
3. Guidelines for Precise Assessments
4. Charting Conventions

5. Minimum Celeration
6. Plans for Each Phase of Learning
7. The Split-middle Line of Progress
8. Program Evaluation

Components: (a) eighteen individual MEDIAPAK components, containing over 100 minutes of sound and film of teachers and classes that use *Exceptional Teaching* daily, (b) worktext, (c) instructor's guide, (d) module overviews and additional exercises, (e) transparent finders for student use with the text and extra behavior charts for instructor or student use.

Related Materials: Other training programs emphasizing behavioristic principles are:

Buckhalter, G., Presbie, R., and Brown, P. *Behavior Improvement Program.* Chicago, Illinois: Science Research Association, 1975.

The PASS Program. Eugene, Oregon: Oregon Center for Research in the Behavioral Education of the Handicapped, 1974.

Langstaff, A.L., and Volkmar, C.B. *Contingency Magazine.* Columbus, Ohio: Charles E. Merrill, 1975.

FORE (Fundamentals, Operations, Resources, Environment)

Purpose: System FORE is an individualized instructional system for teaching the three basic skills of language, reading, and math. It includes developmental sequences of skills, birth to prevocational skills in all three areas, assessment inventories, individual and group record keeping intruments, a materials retrieval system and procedures for establishing learning centers. As a general system for individualizing instruction, System FORE is a possible method of individualizing instruction to handicapped children in the mainstream.

Brief Description of Materials or Service: System FORE is comprised of four components—Fundamentals, Operations, Resources, and Environment.

Fundamentals are sequences of pupil objectives that provide the teacher with specific information about "what to teach." These include language sequences, reading sequences, and math sequences.

Operations help the teacher establish "where the pupil is" and "where he is going." These include assessing pupils, determining objectives, and grouping pupils.

Resources are lists of instructional materials that can be used by the teacher to teach specified objectives. Specific parts of commercial and other materials are identified that relate to specific objectives. Procedures for establishing a materials list catalog and a retrieval system in a region, district, or school are included.

Environment is the classroom arrangement that enables pupils to work on planned educational activities with appropriate materials. These are learning centers.

Together the components of System FORE offer a system of individualized instruction for individual teachers, schools, school districts, or regions. System

FORE is primarily an instructional resource and therefore would be most appropriate for teachers currently in service.

Contact Persons, Addresses, Phones:

Bob William, Los Angeles Unified School District, Special Education Division, 450 North Grand Avenue, Los Angeles, California 90014

Alan Reeder, Northwest Learning Resource System, Clinical Service Building, University of Oregon, Eugene, Oregon 97403, (503) 686-3591

California Learning Resource System, 600 South Commonwealth Avenue, Suite 1304, Los Angeles, California 90005, (213) 381-2104

Additional Description: The Los Angeles Unified School District received a Title III, ESEA grant to operate a project titled, "Assessment-Service Centers for the Handicapped." This project was designed to develop, field test, and implement over a 3 year period, a system for individualizing instruction in language, reading, and mathematics. System FORE was the product of that project.

Any system for individualizing instruction must consider a complexity of factors. From the pupils' point of view, every attempt should be made to assure that pupils (a) know where they are instructionally, (b) know where they are going, (c) do not fail, and (d) compare themselves with themselves rather than with their peer group. In addition, the system must provide the teacher with the following: sequentially arranged, measurable objectives,means for determining pupil's beginning instructional levels, means for measuring and recording pupil progress, means for providing and utilizing appropriate instructional materials, and means for delivering instruction at each pupils' developmental level. System FORE considers all of these factors and reduces their complexity within the four basic components of the system. The first of these components—fundamentals—although initially concerned with language, reading and mathematics, can, and in future revisions will, consider other academic skill areas as well as such fundamentals as motor skills, self help skills, occupational skills, etc. In addition, new sequences of objectives and instructional resources are continually being added to the system. The entire system is being used currently in various parts of the country.

The Heart of Teaching

Purpose: This series of films and videocassettes is designed to help teachers deal with the everyday professional problems that they themselves have identified as the most troublesome. The series was developed to meet a specific need identified by teachers: the need to understand themselves and their emotional responses to the daily experiences of their professional lives. When teachers know and accept their own feelings, they are better able to perceive and respond to the emotional needs of their students.

Brief Description: The series consists of 5-15 minute programs (4 dramatizations and a semidocumentary) that are available in film or color videocassette formats, viewers guides, and discussion leaders guide. While the programs can be viewed by teachers alone, discussion with other teachers is likely to yield greatest insights. Topics are: The Parent Crunch (communication), An Eye for

Change (professional growth), Last Hour Clash (frustration), Everyone is Something Else (individual differences), A Faulty Feeling (loneliness), and Teacher's Meeting (loneliness).

Address: Agency for Instructional Television, Box A, Bloomington, Indiana 47401

Additional Description: These materials were not designed to teach specific knowledge or skills, but rather to provide teachers with an emotionally charged experience, and an opportunity to reflect on it and to examine their feelings. A basic assumption is that by becoming more aware of how they themselves feel in similar situations, teachers will come to appreciate more fully their uniqueness as people and as professionals. The programs deal incidently with various professional topics such as grading, classroom techniques, and student discipline, however, in this series, these are not at issue. It is the feelings of the characters (anger, joy, compassion, anxiety)—how they express them and how they deal with them—that are significant.

Films may be previewed, rented, or purchased. The Agency for Instructional Television (AIT) is a nonprofit American-Canadian organization created to improve education through television and other techniques. A wide variety of materials besides *The Heart of Teaching* are available through AIT.

Individualized Learning Materials (ILM) for Teachers, Supervisors, Principals, and Central Staff

Purpose: ILM Learning Programs consist of series learning modules (LM's) that are designed for the development of competencies needed by teachers, supervisors, and administrators of educational programs. Each LM is based on an individualized and competency based format. Laboratory prepared, field tested modules are available in this series for the areas of: improvement of teaching, instructional supervision, education program planning and development, and the principalship.

Brief Description: Learning activities within each module are arranged in the following sequence: identification of competency(ies) and initiation of a log; taped flip-chart presentation; sources for further investigation; individual study; learning group activities where appropriate; performance product; and evaluation of learning materials and completion of log. Materials are provided to guide each phase of activity for each LM. However, this is *not* a programed sequence. These materials can be used for individual purposes and in different ways.

Individualization is designed into each LM by selection of *content, pacing,* and *depth* of study to be attained. Each person controls his or her own learning by deciding the content, pacing, and depth of study selected in terms of the desired competencies to be developed.

Contact person: Lloyd E. McCleary, Educational Administration, University of Utah (author)

Address: ILM Publishers, Inc., 1470 Wilton Way, Salt Lake City, Utah 84108

Additional Description: An ILM module includes:
1. A manual on the competency model, individualization concept, and learning format.
2. Supplementary materials on validated competency statements, competency profile forms, and content analysis of modules.
3. Cassette tape and flip charts for audiovisual presentation.
4. Study guide and log sheet including sources for investigation, individual study guide, learning group guide, performance product suggestions and evaluation form.

Each module contains materials for five individuals. Packets with any combination of study materials may be ordered by arrangement. Expendable, software materials may be reordered. See following list of topics:

The Teaching Act
The Teaching-Learning Process
Lesson Planning
Teaching Assessment: Content Analysis
Teaching Assessment: Interaction Analysis
Interaction Assessment: Climate Analysis
Models of Curriculum Development
Learning Theory: Four Basic Theories
Principles of Learning
Role of the Supervisor
Elements in Educational Program Planning
Forces in Educational Planning
Revolution as a Concept of Change
Program Purposes in Education
Instructional Objectives
Content and Process Instruction
T-Test: Confidence Intervals, Levels of Significance
MBO: Principles and Concepts
MBO: Applications to Schools
The Delphi Technique
Improving College Teaching: Exemplary Programs
Planning of Instruction: Organizational Concerns
Exemplary Programs in Early Childhood Education
Exemplary Programs in Elementary Education
Programs of the Middle School
The Secondary School Program
Programs in Higher Education
Role of the Principal
Toward a Helping Relationship
Communication and School Organization
Communication and Interpersonal Relations
School Organization as a Social System
Working with the Community
Conflict-Management and Resolution
Shared Decision Making
Time Management
Student Discipline: Issues and Conditions

Student Discipline: Applications in Schools

Evaluation—Purpose and Design

Evaluation—Data Collection

Evaluation—Data Description and Analysis

Evaluation Hypothesis Testing

Normal Curve, Probability, and Prediction

Organization: A 3 part Module

Organizational Analysis and Change

Organizational Analysis and Change: Process and Application

Program Development: Matrix for Decision-Making

Information Center— The Council for Exceptional Children

Purpose: The Council for Exceptional Children (CEC) Information Center is set up to provide a comprehensive data base of professional information, literature, and material on the education of handicapped and gifted children.

Brief Description of Materials or Service: The Council for Exceptional Children, as the major professional association in the education of exceptional children, provides a variety of products and services related to practice, training, and research for education professionals working with exceptional children. Bibliographies, including abstracts of each entry, may be purchased on the general topic of mainstreaming or on mainstreaming for special groups, such as the hearing impaired and on many other topics relevant to changing modes of service to exceptional children.

Address and Phone: Council for Exceptional Children, Information Center, 1920 Association Drive, Reston, Virginia 22091, (800) 336-3728, (In Virginia call (703) 620-3660 collect)

Additional Description: CEC maintains a comprehensive data base of professional material on the education of handicapped and gifted children. (In contrast, NICSEM/NIMIS I is designed to provide information about teaching and instructional materials themselves, rather than about the professional literature.)

The CEC Information Center also produces information products in both print and nonprint formats. Products and services such as the following are available for purchase: topical bibliographies giving an overview of the significant historical and current literature on a given topic; custom computer searches of the 20,000 citations in the CEC data base; Selective Dissemination of Information (SDI), a literature awareness service; *Exceptional Child Education Resources* (ECER), a quarterly, indexed publication containing bibliographic information and abstracts of all literature acquired by the CEC Information Center and stored in its computer data base; CEC periodicals, such as *Exceptional Children, TEACHING Exceptional Children, Insight, Education and Training of the Mentally Retarded,* and newsletters; almost 100 other publications and nonprint products; and the CEC microfilm library, which contains on microfilm the entire historical collection of CEC periodicals and other publications. The CEC Information Center was established in 1966.

Leadership Training Institute/Special Education

Purpose: The purpose of the LTI is to foster communication and the sharing of ideas in its area of concern. The LTI attempts to disseminate proved ideas and practices as widely as possible. LTI services would be equally useful to preservice and in-service training projects and they cover a broad range of ages and handicapping conditions.

Brief Description of Materials or Service: The LTI provides technical assistance and consultation on a project or contract basis to federally funded projects concerned with mainstreaming and teacher training. Currently these include the so-called "Deans' Projects." The LTI also provides, where possible, information and referral on matters related to special education and mainstreaming training by individual request, and has developed several publications on these topics.

Contact persons: Maynard C. Reynolds, Director; Karen Lundholm, Assistant to the Director.

Address and phone: Leadership Training Institute, 253 Burton Hall, University of Minnesota, Minneapolis, Minnesota 55455, (612) 373-4854

Additional description: Publications of the LTI include:

Reynolds, M.C., & Davis, M.D. (Eds.). *Exceptional children in regular classrooms.* Minneapolis: Department of Audio-Visual Extension, University of Minnesota, 1971.

Reynolds, M.D. (Ed.). *Psychology in the schools: Proceedings of the conference on psychology and the process of schooling in the next decade.* Minneapolis: Department of Audio-Visual Extension, University of Minnesota, 1971.

Reynolds, M.C. (Ed.). *National technical assistance systems in special education.* Report of the conference in Washington, D.C. (May, 1974). Minneapolis: Leadership Training Institute, University of Minnesota, 1975.

Reynolds, M.C. (Ed.). *National technical assistance system in special education.* Report of the conference in Washington, D.C. (May, 1974). Minneapolis: Leadership Training Institute, University of Minnesota, 1975.

Spicker, H.H., Anastasiow, N.J., & Hodges, W.L. (Eds.). *Children with special needs: Early development and education.* Minneapolis: Leadership Training Institute, University of Minnesota, 1976.

With The Council for Exceptional Children:

Birch, J.W. *Mainstreaming: Educable mentally retarded children in the regular classes.* Reston, VA: The Council for Exceptional Children, 1974.

Birch, J.W. *Hearing impaired children in the mainstream.* Reston VA: The Council for Exceptional Children, 1975.

Deno, E.N. (Ed.). *Instructional alternatives for exceptional children.* Reston VA: The Council for Exceptional Children, 1973.

Hively, W., & Reynolds, M.C. *Domain-referenced testing in special education.* Reston VA: The Council for Exceptional Children, 1975.

Jones, R.A. (Ed.). *Mainstreaming: The minority child in regular classes.* Reston VA: The Council for Exceptional Children, 1976.

Mainstreaming: Origins and implications, Minnesota education, 2(2), 1976 (reprinted by and may be purchased from The Council for Exceptional Children, Reston, Virginia)

Parker, C.A. (Ed.).*Psychological consultation: Helping teachers meet special needs.* Reston VA: The Council for Exceptional Children, 1975.

Thiagarajan, S., Semmel, D.S. & Semmel, M.I. *Instructional development for training teachers of exceptional children: A sourcebook.* Reston VA: The Council for Exceptional Children, 1974.

Weinberg, R.A., & Wood, F.H. (Eds.). *Observation of pupils and teachers in mainstream and special education settings: Alternative strategies.* Reston VA: The Council for Exceptional Children, 1975.

In preparation by LTI:

Deno, E.N., *Mainstreaming: Learning disabled, emotionally disturbed, and socially maladjusted children in regular classes.* (1977)

Freeman, G. *Mainstreaming: Speech handicapped children.* (1977)

Martin, G., & others. *Mainstreaming: Visually impaired children in regular classes.* (1977)

Reynolds, M.C. *Special education: a look to the future.* (1977)

Learning Opportunities for Teachers

Purpose: Learning Opportunities for Teachers (LOFT) is designed to train teachers in the manner in which they are encouraged to teach. The training *process* proceeds through five instructional management systems that sensitize the participant to the effects of possible current practices before proceeding to exploring and modeling the effects of more accommodative instruction. The training *content* is designed to provide the competencies for social interaction problem solving (discipline) and concept teaching and materials management.

Brief Description of Materials or Service: There are a total of 18 LOFT's and an assessment of instructional practices kit with followup materials. The training room is organized into learning centers with correlated games, show and tell materials, problem solving, self instruction, directed instruction, and reading articles. A filmstrip center is also available on request. A trainer manual, 18 games, 230 transparencies, 120 problem solving cards, 240 show and tell examples, and 90 reading articles comprise the training content (1976).

The LOFT is being used at both the university and school system levels for preservice and in-service teachers.

Contact Persons: Barry and Susan Dollar (co-authors)

Address and Phone: Accelerated Learning Systems, 7201 Woodhollow, Apartment 328, Austin, Texas 78731

Additional Description: The individual LOFT names are as follows:

1. Problem Solving Model
2. Consequences
3. Reinforcing Consequences
4. Punishing Consequences
5. Creating Reinforcers
6. Schedules of Reinforcers
7. Analyzing and Solving Problems
8. Contracts
9. Indirect Reinforcement Systems
10. Accommodating Differences
11. Specifying Concepts
12. Analyzing Tasks
13. Correcting Tasks
14. Sequencing Tasks and Concepts
15. Correlating Tasks
16. Testing Concepts
17. Accommodating Changing Differences
18. Learning Resources Management

Assessment of instructional practices is in terms of: (a) learning content, (b) learning style, (c) learning rate, and (d) learning environment.

Let's Series Module—
Preparing Regular Educators for Mainstreaming
(Project PREM)

Purpose: The Project PREM *Let's Series Modules* are designed to develop cognitive and attitudinal competencies for working with mildly handicapped students in the regular classroom.

Description: This series of 10 training modules in the form of individual learning packets could be used for both preservice and in-service training of regular educators, and is adaptable for use with supervisors, administrators, and principals. The modules are competency based and field tested (1976).

Contact Person: Donna Denney Haughton, Coordinator, Project PREM

Address and Phone: EDB 210, The University of Texas at Austin, Austin, Texas 78712, (512) 471-4161, Ext. 39

Additional Description: The *Let's Series Modules* is a series of 10 competency based filed tested training modules in the following areas:

1. Attitudes of teachers.
2. The concept and implementation of mainstreaming.
3. Characteristics and educational implications for handicapping conditions.
4. Individualizing instruction.

5. Communication skills development.
6. Social and academic integration of handicapped children into the regular classroom.
7. Testing and observation techniques.
8. Behavioral management techniques.
9. Sources and development of instructional materials.
10. Career education adaptations.

Each module contains a prospectus, goals and objectives, flow chart, pretest, specific objectives, learning alternatives, self assessment inventories, and a posttest.

The packets are available for cost of reproduction.

The Lexington Teacher Training Project
(Integration of Children with Special Needs in a Regular Classroom)

Purpose: The Lexington Teacher Training Project is designed to help teachers recognize and work with individual differences that affect children's learning development. It is also intended to help special education teachers apply their skills in the setting of the regular classroom. The overall purpose is to enable teachers to integrate students with special learning problems into the regular classroom—now an important part of the movement toward individualized instruction.

Brief Description: These materials consist of 10 color videotape programs of from 19 to 30 minutes, each with a printed guide.

Children with learning disabilities are looked on as being like all children: they have special strengths and special needs. To deal with the disabilities, which range from mild perceptual problems to severe mental retardation, teachers are shown a variety of teaching techniques as they are practiced in actual classrooms. Such methods include early assessment and diagnosis as well as activities devised to treat specific problems in handwriting, reading, and mathematics.

Throughout the programs the emphasis is on practical, effective techniques that any resourceful teacher can use on a step by step basis. Teachers are helped to identify problems accurately and then to solve them through carefully designed and monitored methods. For each of the 10 programs there is a detailed guide that contains suggestions for working with every child as an individual, specific objectives, discussion questions, pretests and posttests, bibliographies, extensive background information on particular learning disabilities, and suggested solutions to the problems examined in the programs. In addition, there is a comprehensive guide to all 10 programs for workshop discussion leaders.

The series was produced by the Lexington, Massachusetts, Public Schools with funds from the US Office of Education through Title III (ESEA) and Title VI (Education of the Handicapped Act) grants (1974).

Addresses and phones: Agency for Instructional Television, Box A, Bloomington, Indiana 47401, (812) 339-2203

AIT Southern Office, Suite 125, 333 Sandy Springs Circle, NE, Atlanta, Georgia 30328, (404) 252-6525

AIT Eastern Office, Suite 421, Reston International Center, 11800 Sunrise Valley Drive, Reston, Virginia 22091

AIT Midwestern Office, Suite 117, 5600 West Brown Deer Road, Brown Deer, Wisconsin 53223, (414) 354-8510

AIT Western Office, 1670 South Amphlett Boulevard, San Mateo, California 94492, (415) 574-3437

Additional Description: Following are descriptions of the 10 videotape programs.

1. *Diagnosis and Educational Planning.* A teacher, a physician, and a psychologist work together in a simulated evaluation of a student. Each specialist administers a set of tests to the boy, and then the three, acting as a team, summarize their findings in preparation for informing his family and reporting their specific recommendations in writing. The program demonstrates how such professional cooperation and interaction can be employed to produce for the student both a comprehensive diagnosis and an appropriate educational program.

2. *Early Assessment: Step to Planning.* A kindergarten teacher considers the children in her class and is concerned that several may have marked learning and behavioral problems in later years. The program follows her efforts to get a clearer sense of the children's needs and to adapt her own programs to meet those needs.

3. *After Assessment.* A kindergarten classroom is arranged in groups for auditory, motor, visual-motor, and visual perception skills. While the children work independently, the teacher works with one of the groups at a time. The varied levels of skills at which the children perform are closely observed.

4. *Every Child Can Learn.* The class is a combined third and fourth grade of over 50 children, team taught by math and reading teachers. The opening sequence is a math lesson in which one teacher guides students into groups and then works with those who need a more structured lesson.

5. *Together They Learn.* Retarded primary level children are shown working in different kinds of groups in an integrated class. A special educator, the regular teacher, and an aide offer all the children opportunities to work independently, in small groups, or in individual tutoring situations. The program focuses on math, reading, and science segments that demonstrate a range of teaching techniques. Playground activities that all the children share and enjoy provide further evidence of success of this school's integration process.

6. *Correcting Handwriting Problems.* While a class of primary students work in different subject groups, their teacher helps those who have problems in visual perception.

7. *Mastering Math Skills.* Third and fourth grade children are arranged in three groups after the results of a regularly given timed math test have been graphed to show their progress.

8. *Reading and Learning Styles.* Students in a first and second grade class

are grouped for a lesson according to their reading levels and learning styles.
9. *Developing Children's Languages.* The program focuses on first grade students of diverse racial, cultural, and national backgrounds.
10. *Every Student is Different: The High School.* The opening sequence dramatized ineffective teaching and the negative reactions of students. In this instance the teacher involved asks for help from a learning specialist, who offers concrete recommendations. Other scenes show a variety of teaching techniques in action and the successful responses they seem to elicit.

Videocassette copies of the 10 programs can be purchased for audiovisual use at a cost of $200 for each program cassette. Fifteen copies of the appropriate guide and one copy of the discussion leader's guide are included with each cassette ordered. A 10% discount is granted if all 10 program cassettes are purchased at one time. Previews of representative lessons are available on request at no charge to those interested in considering this series for in school use from the above addresses.

Mainstream

Purpose: Mainstream is a broad diagnostic-instructional system intended to help meet the needs of children who have behavioral and learning problems and who may have been labeled emotionally disturbed, retarded, or handicapped in some other category. The program includes assessment and evaluation, instructional tasks, and a procedure for integrating diagnostic information with instructional packages.

Contact Person: John F. Cawley, Professor of Special Education, University of Connecticut, Wallingford

Address: Educational Services, Inc., P.O. Box 771, Wallingford, Connecticut 06492

Additional Description: Mainstream involves use of 266 Desired Learner Outcomes (DLO's) stated in behavioral terms. The DLO's are related to over 9000 instructional tasks. Teachers can focus on one or a set of DLO's in three developmental skill areas—aural skills, visual skills, and social/emotional skills.

A *Behavioral Skills Inventory,* using criterion referenced evaluation of the developmental status of the learner, is used to design programs. The diagnostic system involves use of subtests from many of the widely known psychoeducational tests. *Instructional Components* contains instructional activity suggestions, all interrelated with DLO's and results of the *Behavior Skills Inventory.* A *Behavior Resource Guide* serves as a general organizing device for regular and special teachers who use the system.

Although this system is intended for children, it is perhaps best introduced through careful training of instructional staff. Educational Services, Inc., conducts special study institutes for this purpose.

National Diffusion Network (NDN)

Purpose: Disseminating exemplary programs developed with state or federal money is the business of the National Diffusion Network (NDN). In operation for approximately 4 years, the NDN is providing proven educational alternatives to local educators across the country. Programs are reviewed by the Joint Dissemination Review Panel, which is composed of 11 people from the US Office of Education and 11 people from the National Institute of Education. Highly effective programs are chosen to be Developer/Demonstrators, which means that selected programs will receive additional federal funds from NDN to enable the project's staff to work with educators elsewhere who would like to adopt or adapt the programs.

Assistance in matching district needs with available programs is provided by NDN State Facilitators. State Facilitators are involved in areas ranging from needs assessment through training and followup. Their role is to make educators aware of NDN and the programs it offers. State Facilitators also handle the logistics of adoptions as programs are moved across the state or the country.

Contact:
The Division of Educational Replication, US Office of Education, ROB 3, Room 3616, 400 Maryland Avenue, SW, Washington, DC 20202, (202) 245-2257 or 2243; or Educational Diffusion Materials/Support Center, Far West Laboratory for Educational Research and Development, 1855 Folsom Street, San Francisco CA 94103, (415) 565-3000.

National Inservice Network (NIN)

Purpose: The National Inservice Network (NIN) is a linkage agency designed to exchange information about inservice programs for regular educators. NIN is funded by the Division of Personnel Preparation, Bureau of Education for the Handicapped (BEH), United States Office of Education. The purpose of NIN is to assist educators in the implementation of the Education for All Handicapped Children Act (P.L. 94-142).

NIN has two components, a national and a states component, but the mission of each is the same: to help regular instructional personnel develop individual educational programs for handicapped children in the least restrictive educational setting. Eventually, it may be possible to demonstrate the usefulness of individualized planning for all children.

Contact: National Inservice Network, Indiana University, 2853 East Tenth Street, Bloomington IN 47401, (812) 337-2734.

Additional Description, National Component: The initial function of the national component is to link and support all regular education inservice projects currently funded by BEH. Later, new projects will be invited to join, and ultimately NIN will link a wide range of programs and resources designed to help regular school personnel meet the needs of special students.

The specific purposes of the national component of NIN are to:

- Prepare and share descriptions of funded training projects for the network members, potential adopters, and BEH.

- Survey project directors/staff concerning their needs for information and support.
- Convene interested project directors in miniconferences designed to meet expressed needs.
- Arrange site visitations and staff exchanges to link project directors/staff with potential adopters in Colorado, Indiana, and Maine interested in the project.
- Establish linkages to other diffusion networks to increase diffusion of REGI innovations.
- Establish a clearinghouse to collect and share resources with network colleagues and others.
- Prepare position papers on the development of a national network to diffuse innovations in regular education inservice.

The States Component: The specific purpose of the states' component of NIN are to:

- Assist SEA staff in the planning implementation, evaluation, and diffusion of LEA Model Regular Education Inservice (REGI) training programs (six per year).
- Prepare an ongoing in-state diffusion plan to spread components of LEA based innovations.
- Assist LEA's and SEA's in planning by linking them with model projects in the REGI national network.
- Disseminate state planning models with SEA staff to other SEA agency personnel in both regular and special education.

The State departments of education in Colorado, Indiana, and Maine are working with NIN in planning the inservice programs for the regular education staff.

National Information Center for Special Education Materials/ National Instructional Materials Information System 1/ (NICSEM/NIMIS 1)

Purpose: A computer based on-line interactive retrieval system specifically developed for the purpose of assisting teachers, parents, and other educators in locating information about instructional materials in the field of special education. Its ultimate objective is to provide users with as much information describing educationally appropriate special education instructional materials as is available and feasibly reportable.

Brief Description of Materials or Services: An on-line interactive retrieval system enables an individual to converse with a computer, asking questions and getting immediate answers. The answers are given in the form of information that includes bibliographic information and abstracts of descriptions of the material. Each NIMIS entry includes, if available, items of identification such as the following: author, title, publisher, price, abstract/description.

Contact: Information Specialist, NICSEM, University of Southern California University Park, Los Angeles, CA 90007 (800) 421-8711.

Additional Description: NIMIS provides descriptive information concerning instructional media and materials for a nationwide audience. The system now contains information on two types of materials:

1. Child use instructional materials/materials used by the teacher and/or child interacting in the process of education, diagnosis, instruction, and evaluation.
2. Teacher training materials—instructional materials used to train or assist teachers or teachers to be in the selection, utilization, design, or adaptation of media, materials, and educational technology (such as how to make and use transparencies).

Eventually, the system hopes to be able to store and retrieve instructional materials on the bases of the competencies to be achieved. This approach will facilitate matching appropriate instructional materials with the individual needs of exceptional children.

When NIMIS is in full operation, it is expected that about half the entries will be for nonprint materials such as instructional kits, teaching machines and programs, films, videocassettes, audiocassettes, filmstrips, games, toys, or transparencies.

Teachers or parents should first contact their local State Education Agencies. Appropriate instructional materials may be available to them. If not, persons at these local agencies can help the teacher formulate a request to NICSEM/NIMIS 1.

In order to make a thorough search, five items of very specific information are necessary:

1. Disability or handicapping condition.
2. Educational level of material needed.
3. Curricular area or general content area.
4. Specific concept or skills in that area.
5. Format of materials needed.

The Preparation of Regular Classroom Teachers to Work with Students with Special Learning Problems: A Preservice Training Project

Purpose: The purpose of the project is to provide college faculty with suggestions and materials that can be used to prepare the regular classroom teacher to work with children with special needs. Materials are aimed primarily at preservice preparation, elementary, and secondary.

Brief Description of Materials or Service: These materials consist of a set of 25 units each with goals, objectives, activities, evaluation, and resources identified. The materials are for the instructor's use as a guide and are designed for maximum flexibility. The instructor may select any number of units or parts of units, and sequence that seems logical.

Contact Persons: Barbara Fowler and Clifford D. Baker, Project Directors

Address and Phone: Department of Special Education and Rehabilitation, University of Northern Colorado, Greeley, Colorado 80639, (303) 356-9500

Additional Description: The individual units in 1974-1975 were as follows:

Section A—General
1. Overview of Handicapping Conditions
2. Mainstreaming: Who and Why
3. Delivery Systems
4. Understanding Students
5. Recognition of Teacher Attitudes
6. Pupil-Teacher Interaction
7. Learning Styles
8. Identification
9. Referral Process and Staffing
10. Behavior
11. Alternative Methods of Measuring Student Progress
12. Individualized Instruction
13. Facilitating the Integration Process
14. Media Materials

Section B—Elementary
15. Reading for Children with Special Needs
16. Math for Children with Special Needs
17. Spelling for Children with Special Needs
18. Handwriting for Children with Special Needs
19. Language for Children with Special Needs
20. Science for Children with Special Needs
21. Physical Education for Children with Special Needs
22. Music for Children with Special Needs
23. Art for Children with Special Needs
24. Social Studies for Children with Special Needs

750 / Teaching Exceptional Children in All America's Schools

Section C—Secondary
25. Adapting Curricula for Handicapped Students at the Secondary Level

The Principals' Training Program

Purpose: This training program is designed to achieve the following objectives: Objective 1: Each Participant will be able to demonstrate an understanding of the rationale for returning the handicapped child to the regular classroom. Objective 2: Each participant will be able to demonstrate an understanding of alternate administrative and instructional arrangements for programing for handicapped students in the regular classroom. Objective 3: Each participant will be able to demonstrate the skills necessary to administer building a special education program.

Brief description of materials or services: To achieve the objectives, a problem centered training program has been developed that is supported by a wide variety of media (audio, visual, and print). The instructional strategies include independent, small group, and large group settings with the major emphasis placed on the small group. Participants will be expected to gather and analyze data related to a variety of problems and share the data with group members (1975).

Contact Person: Donroy Hafner, Director

Address and Phone: Instructional Services, Education Service Center, Region XIII, 6504 Tracor Lane, Austin, Texas 78721, (512) 926-8080

Additional description: The kit contains the following resources:
1. A *Leader's Manual,* describing program sequence, activities, suggested workshop schedules, and optional activities with sample handouts that can be duplicated at the discretion of the leader. More specifically the *Leader's Manual* provides for the following:
    a. General workshop organization, small group organization, suggested timelines, and abstracts for each film, filmstrip, and reprint utilized in the training program
    b. A separate section devoted to each workshop objective which includes activity descriptions, leader scripts, participant material (printed on green paper in the same order as they appear in the *Participant's Manual*), and scripts for the filmstrips
    c. An appendix that includes materials for optional activities (these materials can be duplicated without prior permission), checklist of resources, and a glossary.
2. Instructional media that include eight filmstrips/audiocassettes, two 16mm color films, and seven transparencies. The use of all media is described in the *Leader's Manual.*
3. A *Participant's Manual* is included for the leader as reference material even though all the materials in the *Participant's Manual* are also included in the *Leader's Manual*. Enough copies of the *Participant's Manual* can be obtained for each workshop participant. It can be either for profit or free depending on how the leader wants to organize the workshop.

4. A *Book of Readings* is included that contains all the reprinted articles to be utilized by participants in their problem solving activities.

Note: A similar Teacher Training Program is also available from the same agency.

Public Law 94-142
(The Education for All Handicapped Children Act of 1975)

Purpose: This multimedia package was developed to help the field understand the many facets of Public Law 94-142, The Education for All Handicapped Children Act of 1975.

Brief Description: Included in the package are three captioned filmstrips and three audiocassettes, each designed to meet the needs of a different audience. A copy of the law, a question and answer document, and a printed copy of the script for each filmstrip is also included. Each script has a table of contents highlighting the issues presented on the accompanying filmstrip. Portions of the law upon which the narrative was based are reproduced in the printed copy of the script. Other laws and suggested resources have also been referenced in the scripts to help the presenter locate relevant material for expanded discussion. The law itself and the question and answer document may be duplicated for distribution to participants. The media package was designed to be used with an ordinary filmstrip projector and a cassette player. Audible bleeps on the cassette tape signal when to advance the filmstrip (1976).

Address and phone: The Council for Exceptional Children, 1920 Association Drive, Reston, Virginia 22091, (703) 620-3660

Additional Description: The three filmstrips in the package are as follows:

Introducing P.L. 94-142 (time: 20 minutes)
This material presents an overview of the law and is appropriate for anyone who wishes to gain familiarity with the main features of the Act's provisions. Although there is some overlap of concepts presented in all three filmstrips, the style of each presentation is different. The introductory filmstrip uses both photographs and drawings to illustrate the material. By reviewing the scripts in advance, a presenter can decide if the audience could benefit from viewing the introductory material before seeing either of the other two filmstrips.

Complying with P.L. 94-142 (time: 20 minutes)
This filmstrip was prepared for administrators who are responsible for developing and implementing state plans and local applications.

Three cartoon type characters are featured in this presentation: the yellow ball representing LEA's, the blue ball which stands for SEA's, and the orange ball, which depicts the US Commissioner of Education. The role of each agency is clearly illustrated throughout the filmstrip. Portions of the Joint Explanatory Statement of the Committee of Conference are included in the printed script to clarify certain aspects of the law.

P.L. 94-142 Works for Children (time: 14 minutes)

This presentation shows how P.L. 94-142 makes a difference in the lives of handicapped children and their families. It provides information to parents and advocates about the educational services and safeguards guaranteed by the act.

Photographs, depicting the effects of the law on the education of three children with different handicapping conditions, illustrate the provisions of the Act. The printed script includes portions of the regulations on confidentiality and suggests specific resources for further information on due process and the role of the parent surrogate.

Related Materials: A film entitled *Those Other Kids,* which was produced by The Council for Exceptional Children in collaboration with the Leadership Training Institute of the University of Minnesota, is frequently used in conjunction with materials that explain P.L. 94-142. The film, 26 minutes long, explains concepts of "right to education," "due process," and "least restrictive alternative." It may be purchased or rented from *Audio-Visual Education Services,* University of Minnesota, Minneapolis 55455.

Note: CEC conducts special training institutes, relevant to the implementation of P.L. 94-142, on topics such as the following: Placement of exceptional children, children's rights and professional responsibilities, least restrictive environment, due process, nondiscrimination in testing and evaluation, and child identification. Contact CEC offices for full information.

Special Education Administration Simulation in Monroe City (SEASIM)

Purpose: SEASIM curriculum experiences will provide individual participants with processes for assessing the quantity and content of information they presently have as resources for dealing with specific problems. The major goal of SEASIM is to increase behavioral repertoire (skills and strategies) utilized by the participants.

Through use of the SEASIM package, participants will have the opportunity to increase the numbers and kinds of responses, solutions, and strategies available for solving problems encountered in their job environments in light of the following:

1. Specific objectives they have developed.
2. Their rationale for selection of specific objectives.
3. Resources they have identified as being necessary and available for implementing their strategies.
4. A process for evaluating the strategy decision.

Brief Description of Materials or Service: SEASIM is a multimedia simulation package consisting of an instructor's manual, background booklet, case studies, office files, phone call interruption, films, filmstrips, audiotapes, transparencies, other expendable materials, and a series of other stimulus items. SEASIM is useful for preservice and in-service training of administrators and regular as well as special educators. SEASIM can be used as a complete package, or components can be selected to meet specific user needs.

Address and Phone: University Council for Educational Administration, 29 West Woodruff Avenue, Columbus, Ohio 43210, (614) 422-2564

Additional Description: The package consists of the following six major areas of focus:

1. *Continuum of services,* which includes process and content material on organizational theory; status of special education; relationship of special education and regular education; philosophies underlying continuum of services such as individualization of instruction, equal educational opportunities for all pupils, varied and diverse instructional arrangements and instructional systems.
2. *Identification processess,* which includes process and content material based on concepts found in item 1 above and expanding the materials/sections that focus on the issues more specifically involved in segregation.
3. *Placement procedures,* which are built on items 1 and 2, and include concepts of *teamwork* and other procedures, i.e., vehicles for making placement decisions about all pupils within the school.
4. *Curriculum,* which includes process and content material applicable to general curriculum development and implementation and also specific process and content material, which focuses on philosophies presented in items 1, 2, and 3 above and emphasizes factors and concerns that occur when a holistic approach to education is used; (holistic in this sense refers to the concept that curriculum for a school will include diverse instructional systems, some of which are presently labeled regular/special).
5. *Finance,* which includes process and content material applicable to implementation of programs. The finance issue is basic to all other sections in terms of making resources available for making programmatic decisions; this section also includes space allocation issues and transportation and attain, tie in with items 1-4.
6. The *Evaluation* section has the flexibility of being utilized separately as as unit, but is an integral part of each section; in each section, there is content and process materials which focus on evaluation as a process for making decisions, for administrative strategies, actions, and solutions.

Note: SEASIM is an urban simulation situation. A simulation similar in format has been adapted for rural and sparsely populated special education administration areas by Dr. Richard Weatherman, Department of Educational Administration, University of Minnesota, Minneapolis, Minnesota 55455 (612) 376-5052. (See: SEASIM—Rural/Sparsely Populated Areas, listed separately).

Special Education Administrators' Simulation (SEASIM) for Rural/Sparsely Populated Areas

Purpose: The Special Education Administrators' Simulation (SEASIM) for rural/sparsely populated areas multimedia simulation package was developed for training the special as well as the general educator. It is an adaptation of the Monroe City SEASIM developed by the University Council of Educator's Administration (UCEA), Columbus, Ohio. Rural SEASIM offers a generative process moving the participant from the development of information usage through its application on the job.

Brief Description: The Rural SEASIM package consists of the following seven major areas of focus in training: identification processes, placement procedures, curriculum review, delivery of service, resource allocation, evaluation, and communication. In addition, an early education simulation set is available.

Rural SEASIM materials are currently available in the form of instructor's and user's manuals, and are usually presented in a preservice or in-service workshop. Since some training in use of the materials is recommended, those wishing to instruct Rural SEASIM may wish to attend a Rural SEASIM workshop before using the materials.

While focused on administrators, Rural SEASIM would be useful in training virtually all school personnel (1976).

Contact Person: Richard Weatherman

Address and Telephone: Department of Educational Administration, University of Minnesota, 300 Health Service Building, St. Paul, Minnesota 55108, (612) 376-5052

Additional Description: Through use of the Rural SEASIM package, participants will have the opportunity to increase the numbers and kinds of responses, solutions, and strategies available for solving problems encountered in their job environments in light of (a) specific objectives they have developed, (b) their rationale for selection of specified objectives, (c) resources they have identified as being necessary and available for implementing their strategies, and (d) a process for evaluating the strategy decision.

There are a number of goals that can be identified for Rural SEASIM use in training general and/or special education administrators. Rural SEASIM is designed to assist participants to anticipate issues rather than react to a possible crisis. Rural SEASIM emphasizes both team and individual decision making processes as desirable elements of administrative skill. It focuses on the processes of special education administration rather than on the single role of a special education director. Rural SEASIM provides participants with insights into their own decision making and leadership styles. Through its approximation of the reality of school administration, it provides a variety of settings in which the participant must operate. Rural SEASIM employs many forms of media (audiovisual, written, data bank, critical incident) so that no single form is dominant. It is designed in such a way that males and females can assume all roles in the simulation and urban and rural school issues can be represented.

The Rural SEASIM materials are generally structured into a 3 day workshop experience for approximately 25 to 30 general and/or special educators. During the first day, participants are introduced to the simulation materials and assume the role of the director of special education. Throughout the remainder of the workshops, participants, through the vehicle of simulation, experience problems and issues relating to their roles in light of current educational practice.

Special Education Administrators' Training Project (SEATP)

Purpose: The Special Education Administrators' Training Project (SEATP) is designed to meet a current pressing need for administrator training in Minnesota and also to serve as a model to be replicated in training administrators in other states and areas of human services.

Brief Description: SEATP is a competency based training program developed from a system orientation model and used for the in-service and/or preservice education of administrators to promote educational effectiveness and efficiency. While SEATP is primarily focused on training special education administration competencies, the program would be extremely useful for training principals, superintendents, and school board members as well. The "program development" portion of the program would be useful training for regular educators concerned with mainstreaming: the materials are mostly self contained and are distributed as a large three ring notebook (1976).

Contact Persons: Richard Weatherman and Judith Wolf

Address and Telephone: Department of Educational Administration, University of Minnesota, 300 Health Service Building, St. Paul, Minnesota 55108, (612) 376-5052

Additional Description: SEATP's utilization of a competency based approach is an attempt to focus on education directly applicable to the administrator's actual job. As a result, SEATP can accommodate individual educational needs; procedures developed to identify and validate competencies, promote changes in existing curricular sequences to meet changing conditions, and allow replication of the model.

SEATP has seven basic features:
1. The objectives are stated as competencies of a director of special education (or other administrative position).
2. These competencies or performances are derived empirically from examination of the job existing special education directors perform.
3. There exists an identifiable core of minimum essential competencies for all directors of specialized positions, despite variations in individual job descriptions, scope of authority, line or staff designation, size of program, and single or multidistrict organization. These core competencies constitute the program curriculum.
4. Instruction received by a participating director of special education is based on individual needs as determined by prior and ongoing assessments.
5. Instruction is field centered, i.e., brought to the participant.
6. The types of instruction offered emphasize teaching of facts and concepts and the practice of skills relevant to performance in the position.
7. The bases for evaluation of the success of the training program are student practices, learning, and performance.

The SEATP format includes training in the following broad functions:
1. Devising ways of identifying children with special needs.
2. Assessing children with special needs in order to determine what kinds of special programs and services should be provided.
3. Planning the appropriate variety of interventions or program alternatives to mediate properly between the child's special education needs and tasks of rehabilitation and/or educational development.
4. Marshaling and organizing the resources needed in a comprehensive program of special education for exceptional children.
5. Directing, coordinating, and counseling appropriately in guiding the efforts of those engaged in the special education enterprise.
6. Evaluating and conducting research in order to improve special instruction and the quality of special services.
7. Interpreting and reporting information to gain public support and influence the power structure in helping to achieve program objectives.
8. Recruitment, selection, and training of competent staff.

Strategies for Training Regular Educators to Teach Children with Handicaps (STRETCH)

Purpose: Training modules were designed to help regular teachers increase their knowledge, understanding, and competencies in working with handicapped children.

Brief Description: Twenty modules, each including a half hour videotape cassette plus written materials.

Contact Person: Dr. Elouise Collins

Address: Project STRETCH, 2268 Adams Drive, NW, Atlanta, Georgia 30318

Additional Description: Subject matter includes introductory materials, identification procedures, and management techniques for all areas of exceptionality, with emphasis on serving exceptional children in regular classrooms. Suitable for television broadcasting.

Teacher Training Program (TTP)

Purpose: The TTP is aimed at building skills, concepts, and attitudes that are necessary for the regular educator to successfully mainstream handicapped students into the regular classroom. The program addresses areas of individualizing instruction, alternative behavior management strategies, and the interfacing of regular and special educator.

Brief Description of Materials or Service: The TTP is a multimedia program consisting of a facilitator manual, participant manuals, filmstrips, tapes, games, transparencies, and films. It is designed to be flexible, to provide resources to be used as a total program or in parts, to be developer free, and to practice what it preaches: individualized instructional strategies and processes. It is applicable for preservice or in-service training K-12 (1975).

Contact Person: Donroy Hafner, Director

Address and phone: Instructional Services, Education Service Center, Region XIII, 6504 Tracor Lane, Austin, Texas 78721, (512) 926-8080

Additional Description: The program sequence is as follows:

Phase I—Mainstreaming Group Activities is facilitator directed and involves the total group or small groups in activities related to the concept of mainstreaming and the special students involved. The duration of this phase of training is approximately twelve hours.

Phase II—Skill Building Individualized Activities focuses on skill building and problem solving related to individualizing and humanizing instruction. Participants work independently in small task groups at data banks. Each data bank addresses a particular concept or skill area related to individualization. Participants determine which data banks to work at according to their performance on a diagnostic pretest. The data bank topics are: assessment/evaluation, communication, curriculum, grading/reporting, influencing behavior, instructional management, learning environment, and learning style. Each data bank comprises approximately 4 to 5 hours of instruction.

Phase III—Implementation Take Home Reinforcement is the "take home reinforcement" phase of the training. It describes processes and provides resources for the gradual implementation of individualized instruction. Participants are called on to assess their own classroom setting, identify problem areas, and generate solutions for those problems, using skills they gained within the controlled practicum.

Note: A similar Principals' Training Program is also available.

Teaching Children with Special Needs
(Maryland Instructional Television Series)

Purpose: This is an introductory inservice training series for regular and special educators in the observation, identification, and management of children with special needs (K-3).

Brief Description of Materials or Service: The series consists of sixteen 30 minute lessons produced on color videotape, and a corresponding teacher's manual (1975).

Contact Persons: Videotapes—Frank Batavick; Manual—Eugenia Balsley

Address and Phone: Frank Batavick, Staff Specialist in Scheduling/Acquisition, Division of Instructional Television, Maryland Center for Public Broadcasting, 11767 Bonita Avenue, Owings Mills, Maryland 21117, (301) 356-5600 ext. 283.

Eugenia Balsley, Specialist, Curriculum/Development, Maryland State Department of Education, Division of Instructional Television, Garrison Forest Plaza, 10317 Reisterstown Road, Owings Mills, Maryland 21117

Additional Description: The lessons are available on several tape sizes for nonbroadcast use and are available individually or as a complete series.

Upset in Polymer: An Experience in Mainstreaming

Purpose: Although the participants in this set of role playing activities cannot be expected to come away with a predictable set of feelings or understandings, certain possible outcomes seem likely. First, these materials can help a staff cope with the anxieties about impending mainstreaming by exemplifying and personalizing some of these concerns. Second, the materials can stimulate discussion of the many problems in implementing mainstreaming within the participant's own school. Third, they can expose participants to the potential classroom use of group problem solving strategies such as role playing and discussion. And finally, by increasing group and individual awareness and by introducing problem solving techniques, these materials may facilitate planning activities in the school and participation in skill development activities which, in turn, may help solve future problems.

Brief Description: Upset in Polymer is a kit containing four audiotapes and six participant's manuals designed to allow participants to simulate/role play certain mainstreaming situations. The materials would be appropriate for both inservice and preservice training of teachers (1973).

Contact Person: Samuel Guskin, Project Director

Address and Phone: Center for Innovation in Teaching the Handicapped (CITH) Publications, School of Special Education, Indiana University, 2805 East Tenth Street, Bloomington, Indiana 47401, (812) 337-5847

Additional Description: Using an audiotape to provide settings and to pace the activities, and using player's booklets for further instructions, groups of five people simulate the events in a mythical school prior to, during, and just after a mildly handicapped child is integrated into a regular classroom. The participants role play and then discuss their role playing three times: once as teachers and a principal, once as teachers and parents, and once as a teacher and pupils. Then the participants simulate a planning session for the school district, thus summarizing and synthesizing their previous role playing activities.

Other Materials Briefly Noted

Approaches to mainstreaming: Teaching the special child in the regular classroom, Cejka, J.M. (Consultant), Needham, F. (Senior Editor). (Teaching Resources Corporation, 100 Boylston St., Boston, MA 20016, 1976). Filmstrips and audioscripts on *Individual Differences, Characteristics of Children with Special Needs, Organizing Your Classroom* and *Handling Behavioral Problems* are designed to help regular teachers meet the needs of exceptional children in their classes.

Classroom Activities for Helping Children with Special Needs, Barbe, W.B. (Ed.). Six separate, individually packaged activity units for six different groups of students with special learning needs (hyperactive, reluctant readers, misbehavior, slow learning, perceptually handicapped, underachieving).

Contact: The Center for Applied Research in Education, Inc., 521 Fifth Ave., New York NY 10017.

Coming Back...or Never Leaving, Pasanella, A., & Volkmar, C.B. Columbus, Ohio: Charles E. Merrill Co., 1977. A text for teachers on integration of mildly handicapped students in regular classes plus a set of five sound filmstrips on aspects of mainstreaming and a *Professional Supplement,* a sequence of exercises and training activities keyed to alter elements of the total program.

The Human Policy Press (P.O. Box 127, University Station, Syracuse NY 13210) publishes a variety of materials relating to deinstitutionalization, mainstreaming, and the general improvement of opportunities for handicapped persons. Of particular relevance in the present context are the following "slide shows":

- *Children Learn Together,* a set of 132 slides and script for narration on the integration of handicapped children into the schools, created by Ellen B. Barnes.
- *Where the Children Are,* a set of 129 slides and script for narration on institutions and alternatives, created by Douglas P. Biklen.
- *Handicapism: A Slide Show,* a set of 139 slides and script for narration on concept of handicapism, by Douglas Biklen and Robert Bogdan. Materials may be purchased from the Human Policy Press.

IMPACT. The IMPACT Workshop Kit, consists of six filmstrips with accompanying cassettes, the IMPACT box, manuals, and instructor's manual. These materials were developed by the staff of an experimental and demonstrative project in Michigan. Intended for in-service preparation of regular and special education teachers for mainstreaming. Contact: IMPACT, 711 St. Joseph Avenue, Berrien Springs MI 49103.

Learning Concepts (2501 North Lamar, Austin, TX 78705) has produced a series of paperback books on mainstreaming using a cartoon plus narrative format. Intended as a practical introduction for teachers. Topics are as follows: Mainstreaming Exceptional Children, Managing the Hyperactive Child in the Classroom, Mainstreaming the Gifted, Behavior Disorders: Helping Children with Behavioral Problems, Mainstreaming Children with Learning Disabilities, Mainstreaming the Mentally Retarded Child, and the Complete Series.

Mainstreaming, the Special Child, and the Reading Process. Includes teacher training packet with handbook by Harste and Atwell and videotapes by Guskin, Harste, Waremore, Shuster, and Burke. Intended for in-service education of teachers or for use by colleges in reading methods courses. Contact: Dr. Jerome S. Harste, Reading Program, Education 211, Indiana University, Bloomington IN 47401, (812) 337-0300 or 7167.

Parent's Magazine Films, Inc. (52 Vanderbilt Avenue, New York NY 10017) Four sound and color filmstrip sets on how parents can help their handicapped children are available, as well as four sound and color filmstrips on special education for children with special needs (behavioral and emotional disabilities, physical disabilities, intellectual disabilities, educational and language disabilities). These two sets of materials were produced in cooperation with staff of the Frank Porter Graham Child Development Center of the University of North Carolina.

Special Education Placement: A Decision Systems Module. Developed at the University of Connecticut by Professor Jack Cawley and associates, this training package is one of a number of "Decision Systems Modules" relating to changing practices in special education. This set consists of four 16 mm films and a student's guidebook. The module is now available through The Council for Exceptional Children, 1920 Association Drive, Reston, VA 22091.

Special Education for Regular Teachers (SERT). The staff of the Education Service Center (Region X) in Richardson, Texas, in cooperation with staff of the Special Education Department, East Texas State University, has produced a series of modules for the preparation of regular teachers to instruct exceptional children who have been mainstreamed. The total set is referred to as SERT—Special Education for Regular Teachers. Materials include readings, filmstrips, audiotapes and pretests and posttests. Topics covered are as follows: Comprehensive Special Education, Formal Appraisal, Team Planning for Student Program Management, Informal Assessment, Organizing Content for Individual Differences, Materials Selection, Classroom Management, and Evaluation of Instruction.

Training Materials: Staff of ten "non-categorical centers" in North Carolina have produced a variety of training materials on topics such as: formal and informal assessment, classroom organization for effective learning, basic teaching practices for individualization, self concept in the classroom, etc. Contact: Fred Baars, Division for Exceptional Children, State Department of Public Instruction, Raleigh NC 27611.

Understanding young children, Mayer, C.A. (Publication Office/IREC, College of Education, University of Illinois, 805 W. Pennsylvania Avenue, Urbana IL 61801, 1974). A series of five booklets for regular teachers to help them deal with exceptional children. Titles are:

The Handicapped Child in the Normal Preschool Class, 73 pp., (Cat. No. 114).

Emotional and Behavioral Development and Disabilities, 78 pp., (Cat. No. 115).

Learning Development and Learning Disabilities, 31 pp., (Cat. No. 116).

Language Development and Language Disabilities, 35 pp., (Cat. No. 117).

Intellectual Development and Intellectual Disabilities, 41 pp., (Cat. No. 118).

University of Wisconsin—Milwaukee has developed a series of modules for teacher preparation. Videotapes and printed materials are included and may be purchased at cost. Contact Susan Gruber at the Department of Exceptional Education, School of Education, The University of Wisconsin—Milwaukee, P.O. Box 413, Milwaukee, WI 53201, (414) 963-4029. Topics covered are as follows:

Understanding Individual Differences
Module 1: Legislation
  1. Historical
  2. 115—Wisconsin

3. Parent rights
4. Child rights
5. School based implementation—viewpoint: (a) parent, (b) teacher, (c) administrator, (d) taxpayer, and (e) businessman

Module 2: Philosophical considerations
1. Individualism
2. Issues facing teachers

Module 3: Human relations
1. Individual differences
2. Strategies for classroom use
3. Labeling issues

Module 4: Delivery of services
1. Description of program types
2. Supportive services within school
3. Parent support/involvement in program
4. Auxiliary services—community

Module 5: Characteristics which may suggest EEN
1. Unique learning patterns
2. Behavior patterns requiring intervention
3. Academic patterns which are unique

Assessing Individual Differences

Module 6: Observation
1. Presentation, analysis and application of four methods of observation
2. Techniques for recording and graphing

Module 7: Informal inventories
1. Academic
2. Social

Module 8: Diagnostic teaching

Module 9: Referral procedures and multidisciplinary team process
1. Determine when referral to MDT appropriate—through case studies
2. Describe referral process used by local systems
3. Awareness of formal assessment instruments used by MDT members
4. M-team staffing
5. Parent conferencing

Module 10: Teacher Variables

Programming for Individual Differences

Module 11: Environmental Control Strategies
1. Time-space arrangements in the classroom
2. Structuring classroom instruction to meet individual academic, social, and emotional needs

Module 12: Reading
1. Skills development

2. Selecting and adapting materials
3. Teaching strategies to meet varying needs

Module 13: Mathematics
1. Skills development
2. Selecting and adapting materials
3. Teaching strategies to meet varying needs

Module 14: Spoken and written language

Module 15: Application of strategies to other curricular areas

Module 16: Behavior managment strategies (individual focus)
1. Describe and explain behavior
2. Describe terminology and basic concepts of operant conditioning applied to behavior management
3. Describe terminology and basic concepts of counseling techniques applied to behavior management

VIMCET Filmstrip-Tape Program for Teacher Education. (Vimcet Associates, Inc., P.O. Box 24715, Los Angeles, CA 90024). A set of 30 filmstrip tape programs in areas of curriculum, instruction, and evaluation prepared by Eva L. Baker and W. James Popham, University of California, Los Angeles. Stress is on modern concepts of educational objectives, individualizing instruction, and criterion referenced assessment. Includes filmstrips, audiotape narratives, instructors manuals, statements of training objectives, and sample tests.

What is a Handicap. Four sound filmstrips, a teacher's guide, and 24 activity guides for use with regular students who increasingly meet handicapped students in their classrooms. They can be used individually or in small groups. Contact: BFA Educational Media, 221 Michigan Avenue, P.O. Box 1795, Santa Monica CA 90406.

Name Index

Aaronson, D. R., 511
Abel, G. L., 618
Abeson, A., 26, 46, 190, 290, 397, 438, 703
Abraham, W., 330
Agard, J. A., 90, 103, 329, 709
Agrault, E. W., 437
Aiello, B., 135, 152, 397, 438, 703, 729
Ainsworth, S., 502, 512, 703
Albert, R. S., 215, 259, 703
Allen, D., 378
Aloia, G. F., 701
Alpiner, J. G., 502, 703
Alvord, D. J., 502, 510, 703
Anastasiow, N. J., 511, 740
Anderson, E. M., 85
Anderson, R. H., 99, 379, 438, 703
Ankney, R., 391
Apolloni, T., 668
Aragon, J., 512
Arkell, R.N., 438, 602, 638
Armor, D. J., 660, 668, 703
Arnold, C. R., 480
Avery, C. B., 601
Axline, V. M., 360, 391, 703
Ayers, D., 328

Baars, F., 760
Baca, L., 153
Bagley, C., 391
Baird, O., 327
Baker, C. D., 749
Baker, E. L., 130, 762
Baldwin, A. Y., 122, 259, 703
Balla, D. A., 47
Ballard, J., 46, 47

Ballif, B., 511
Balow, B., 42, 119, 462, 480, 718
Baldwin, A. Y., 103, 258
Balsley, E., 757
Bandura, A., 503, 703
Barbe, W. B., 87, 152, 153, 259, 703, 728, 758
Bardon, J. I., 481
Barker, K., 511
Barnes, E. B., 759
Barnes, M., 196, 759
Barraga, N., 638
Barry, N. J., Jr., 103
Barsch, R., 360, 392, 703
Bartlett, J., 211
Bartram, J. B., 282, 284, 703
Batavick, F., 757
Bateman, B. D., 344, 360, 703
Bates, J., 231
Baumgartner, B. B., 297, 327, 704
Becker, W. C., 79, 371, 389, 480, 704, 711
Beers, C. A., 391
Beery, K., 45, 379
Begab, N. J., 47, 327, 328
Bell, A. G., 543
Bell, T. H., 720
Bellanca, J. A., 102
Benne, K. D., 698, 704
Bennett, V., 481
Bennis, W. G., 698, 704
Berg, F. S., 601
Berg, N. A., 437
Bergman, J. S., 327
Berlin, I., 481
Bernal, E., 218, 717

Bernstein, C.D., 677, 700, 704
Berry, P., 329
Bersoff, D.N., 391
Bertness, H. J., 79, 704
Beth, W. R., 259
Bettelheim, B., 360, 389, 392, 704
Betts, E. A., 350, 463, 704
Biacci, A., 131
Bijou, S., 53, 65, 273, 327, 704
Biklen, D. P., 759
Billings, H.K., 437
Billingsley, A., 103
Birch, H. G., 327, 359, 391, 704
Birch, J. W., 94, 95, 96, 118, 134, 152, 180, 219, 230, 244, 258, 260, 275, 277, 299, 302, 307, 329, 362, 392, 427-428, 438, 463, 495, 511, 545, 601, 704, 715, 718, 740
Bisek, J. H., 434
Bish, C. E., 215
Bitter, G. B., 559, 601, 704
Blackham, G.J., 389
Blacklow, J., 438
Blackwell, L., 152
Blakeslee, A., 637
Blatt, B., 314, 330, 704
Bliss, C., 412
Bloom, B., 460, 705
Blumberg, L., 406, 411, 428, 705
Bogatz, B., 152
Bogdan, R., 759
Bolick, N., 26, 190, 290, 397, 703
Bond, G. L., 392, 705
Bonet, J.P., 542
Boote, K. S., 93, 94, 96, 100, 705
Borg, W. R., 78, 102, 137, 373, 389, 705, 728
Bosco, J. J., 390
Boston, B. O., 198, 711
Bower, E. M., 389, 390
Bower, M. J., 153
Bowman, N. B., 289
Bracht, G. H., 61, 705
Braddock, D., 47
Braddy, N., 637
Bradley, D. P., 502, 510, 512, 705
Bradshaw, J. A., 102

Braginsky, B. H., 330
Braginsky, D., 330
Braidwood, T., 542
Braille, L., 14, 119, 616-617
Bransford, L. A., 153
Brawley, P., 527
Bridgeman, L., 14
Brolin, D. E., 329, 480
Bronfenbrenner, U., 259, 655, 705
Bronk, D. W., 52, 708
Brotemarkle, R. A., 357, 705
Brothers, R. J., 638
Brown, A., 327
Brown, J. W., 152, 717
Brown, P., 735
Brown, R., 131, 705
Bruce, W., 560, 705
Bruininks, R. H., 329
Buck, P. S., 330
Buchanan, R., 437
Buckhalter, G., 735
Buckholdt, D., 152
Budoff, M., 91, 705
Buell, C. E., 638
Bugental, D. B., 391
Bunch, G., 390
Burger, R., 131, 705
Burgi, E., 495, 511, 704
Burlingame, R., 602
Burnham, R. A., 700
Burrows, C., 460, 705
Burton, T. A., 327
Bush, W. J., 392
Butterfield, C., 730
Buys, C. J., 480
Bynum, M., 195
Byrne, M. C., 506, 705

Caccamise, F., 561, 705
Cain, L. F., 301, 327, 705
Callahan, C. M., 153, 481
Calovini, G., 438, 705
Campbell, D., 81, 705
Cantrell, M. L., 79, 80, 81, 706
Cantrell, R. P., 79, 80, 81, 706
Caplan, G., 481
Caplan, R. B., 47, 480

Cappa, J., 418, 428
Carter, J. L., 89, 706
Cartwright, G. P., 74, 706
Carvajal, A. L., 328
Castaneda, A., 103
Caudill, R., 511
Cawley, J. F., 191, 745, 760
Cegelka, W.J., 329
Cejka, J. M., 728, 758
Chevigny, H., 637
Chin, R., 698, 704
Ching, D. C., 391
Chismore, W. D., 717
Churchill, W., 211
Ciani, N., 131, 705
Clements, S. D., 348
Coleman, P.G., 82, 601, 706
Coleman, T. W., 688, 701, 719
Collins, E., 753, 756
Collins, J. P., 82, 706
Collmer, C. W., 655, 716
Coloroso, B., 372, 706
Connor, L. E., 82, 600, 706
Connors, C. K., 359, 390
Cook, V., 253
Cooke, T. P., 668
Corson, S., 649, 706
Cowen, E. L., 382, 386, 390, 706
Cox, C. C., 226, 259, 706
Craig, S. B., 17, 601, 706
Craig, W. N., 83, 586-587, 601, 706
Cromwell, R. L., 69, 103, 119, 706
Cronbach, L. J., 61, 65, 74, 144, 190, 706, 707
Cruickshank, W. M., 21, 54, 338, 342, 350, 360, 375, 391, 601, 637, 707, 709
Cunningham, S. A., 392
Curtis, L. T., 344
Cutts, N. E., 357, 707

Dabney, M. G., 140, 707
Dacarie, T. G., 265, 329, 707
Dahl, H. G., 438, 602, 638
Dailey, R. F., 668
Dale, D. M. C., 602
Dalenger, J., 510, 512

Davidson, M., 637
da Vinci, L., 212
Davis, H., 520, 601
Davis, M. D., 707, 740
Delacato, G. H., 359, 707
Del'Epee, C. M., 542
Dell'Amore, J., 655, 707
Dellas, M., 481
Delp, H. A., 100, 707
Dennison, A. L., 638
Deno, E., 46, 153, 190, 350, 444, 480, 707, 740, 741
Dial, K., 38, 707
Dibner, A., 437
Dibner, S., 437
Dickshoff, J., 637
Dinger, J. C., 270, 327, 707
Dodds, J. B., 301, 708
Doll, E., 274, 301, 326, 328, 707
Dollar, B., 697, 741
Dollar, S., 697, 741
Dopheide, W. R., 510, 512
Dorr, D., 382, 390, 706
Doseth, W. F., 698, 710
Douglas, W., 437
Dreikurs, R., 360, 708
Dryden, J., 200
Duffy, D., 131, 705
Duffy, J., 131, 705
Duker, S., 638
Dunlap, J. M., 86, 87, 259, 707
Dunn, L. M., 18, 21, 45, 275, 296, 298, 302, 314, 344, 601, 708, 713

East, L., 488-490, 507, 708
Edgar, E., 103
Egg, M., 191
Eggleston, K. K., 82, 706
Egner, A. N., 447, 708
Ehrhard, H., 248
Elam, S., 46, 701
Ellis, D. D., 152
Enders, M., 601
Enfield, M. L., 392, 449-450, 708
Engelmann, T., 472, 708
Erickson, V. L., 456, 719
Ernst, M., 601

Estroff, E. H., 248, 253, 708
Eurich, A. C., 52, 708
Evans, H. C., Jr., 527

Fairchild, T. N., 390
Fant, L. J., 527, 708
Fein, L. G., 481
Feiock, T., 415
Fellendorf, G. W., 601
Ferritor, D., 152
Festinger, L. A., 59, 708
Finger, J., 254
Fiscus, E., 391
Fitzgerald, E., 571
Flanagan, J. C., 94, 136, 708
Fletcher, S. G., 601
Fleigler, L., 215
Florio, J. P., 748
Flynn, T. M., 328
Fogelman, G. J., 275, 300, 326, 708
Forness, S. R., 296, 298, 348, 349, 710
Fortas, A., 335
Fortunato-Schwandt, W., 152, 717
Foulke, E., 638
Fowler, B., 749
Fox, W. L., 447, 708
Fram, J., 412
Frankenburg, W. K., 301, 708
Freeman, G., 511, 741
French, J. L., 87, 259, 708
Friedman, R. J., 401, 637, 708
Frohreich, L. E., 700
Frostig, M., 360, 708
Fudala, J. B., 511

Gadow, K. D., 390, 669
Gage, N. L., 462, 708
Gagne, R. M., 152
Gaier, E. L., 481
Gaines, R., 655, 709
Galanty, C., 195
Galanty, D., 195
Galanty, H., 195, 198
Gallagher, J. J., 103, 201, 210, 217, 234, 235, 241, 260, 668, 701, 709
Gallaudet, E. M., 543
Gallaudet, T. H., 14, 542

Gallico, P., 437
Gallup, G., 177, 709
Galton, F., 201, 259, 709
Garber, H. L., 281, 709
Garcia, D., 391
Garcia, F., 248, 250, 709
Gardner, W. I., 389, 709
Garmezy, E., 665, 709
Garrett, C., 602
Gault, G., 334
Gear, G. H., 103, 258
Gearhart, B. R., 343, 709
Gesell, A., 709
Getzels, J. W., 259
Gibbins, S., 47
Gibby, R.G., 328
Gifford, B. R., 700
Gilhool, T. K., 103, 693, 709
Giovanni, J. M., 103
Glaser, R., 57, 709
Glaser, W., 360
Glasrud, G. R., 148, 458, 712
Glass, G. V., 61, 705
Glavin, J. P., 389
Gleser, G. C., 61, 65, 190, 706, 707
Goertzel, M., 226, 259, 709
Goertzel, V., 226, 259, 709
Goffman, E., 328
Goldberg, I. I., 21, 25, 54, 709, 713
Goldhammer, K., 696, 709
Goldman, R., 506, 709
Goldstein, H., 103, 297, 709
Goodlad, J., 379
Goodman, H., 328
Gordon, T., 360, 709
Gorham, K. A., 174, 175, 176, 177, 179, 180, 181, 182, 709
Gottlieb, B. W., 328
Gottlieb, J., 90, 91, 328, 329, 705
Gourley, T. J., Jr., 218, 709
Gray, B. B., 511
Gredler, G. R., 102, 327
Green, A., 655, 709
Green, P., 438
Greenberg, M., 231
Griffing, B. L., 560, 562, 601, 710
Griffiths, A. N., 390

Grigsby, C., 131, 705
Grinspoon, L., 390
Grismer, R., 446, 711
Grogan, J., 315, 710
Grosenick, J. K., 46, 103, 702
Gross, J. C., 675, 711
Grossman, H. J., 272, 277, 327, 330, 710
Grotsky, J., 368, 374, 375, 710
Gruber, K., 618
Gruber, S., 760
Grunwald, B. B., 360, 708
Grzynkowicz, W., 390
Gunkel, P., 204
Gunzburg, H. C., 710
Guskin, S., 758

Hafner, D., 697, 750
Hale, J. A., 700
Hall, G. E., 698, 710
Hall, Jim, 201, 205
Hall, Joe, 201, 202, 203, 204, 205
Hall, Judy, 201, 205
Hall, T., 259
Hallahan, D. P., 338, 342, 350, 360, 375, 391, 707
Halsey, A. H., 65, 710
Hambleton, D., 88, 89, 327, 722
Hamblin, R. L., 152
Hammill, D. D., 46, 511
Hanes, M. L., 511
Hanks, K., 254
Hanninen, K. A., 637, 638
Haring, N. G., 53, 89, 329, 361, 371, 372, 385, 389, 466, 480, 710, 733
Harrison, R. H., 328
Harste, J. S., 759
Hart, J., 392
Hartman, R. K., 153, 704
Hartman, W. T., 677, 700
Hartup, W. W., 191
Hass, J., 26, 190, 290, 397, 703
Haughton, D. D., 742
Hauy, V., 616
Havelock, R. G., 694, 698, 710
Hawkins-Shepard, C., 438
Hayes, G. M., 562, 710

Hayes, N. E., 191
Healy, P., 254
Heber, R., 277, 710
Heinicke, S., 542
Heiss, W. E., 297, 710
Heller, H. B., 328
Hemmings, I., 602
Henderson, R. A., 700
Henry, N., 511
Henson, F. D., 260
Herron, W. G., 481
Hewett, F. M., 296, 298, 348, 349, 390, 464, 710
Higgins, S. T., 47
Hildreth, G. H., 86, 260, 711
Hill, E., 638
Hill, H. F., 17, 711
Hill, T., 231
Hillinger, C., 530, 711
Himmelstein, P., 328
Hirsch, S. P., 253, 711
Hively, W., 102, 131, 149, 152, 711, 741
Hobbs, N., 46, 67, 75, 102, 103, 328, 480, 683, 701, 711
Hoben, M., 638
Hodges, W. L., 740
Hodgins, A. S., 668
Hogan, H., 255
Hollingworth, L. S., 15, 259
Holloway, B. D., 82, 706
Holmes, O. W., 17
Holt, F. D., 481
Homme, L., 361, 389, 711
Horobin, G., 327
Howard, M., 666, 667, 668, 711
Howe, C. E., 329
Howe, S. G., 14
Hull, F. M., 487-488, 502, 511, 711
Hull, M. E., 487-488, 502, 511, 711
Humphrey, J. H., 392
Hunt, D. E., 71, 74, 120, 144, 151, 190
Hunt, J. M., 65, 645, 668, 711
Hunter, J., 253
Hunter, M., 378, 379
Hurley, R., 329
Hurlock, E., 711

Hurt, M., 655, 711
Hutt, M. L., 328

Iano, R. P., 328
Illsley, R., 327
Isaacson, R. V., 382, 390, 706
Itard, G., 14
Itard, J. W. S., 328, 330
Izzo, L. D., 382, 390, 706

Jackson, D. M., 198, 711
James, R. L., 103
Janik, A., 201, 711
Jefferson, T., 212
Jekel, J. F., 669
Jenkins, J. R., 46, 153, 370, 711
Jenkins, L. M., 153
Johnson, D. M., 329
Johnson, D. W., 78, 102, 139, 152, 711
Johnson, G. O., 103, 296, 328, 601, 637, 711, 712
Johnson, J. J., 103
Johnson, R. A., 446, 675, 711
Johnson, R. T., 78, 102, 139, 152, 711
Johnson, W., 511
Johnstone, B. K., 134, 152, 180, 244, 307, 427-428, 438, 704
Jones, B., 392
Jones, D., 270-272
Jones, R. L., 26, 28, 29, 100, 103, 140, 153, 328, 437, 511, 701, 711, 712, 713, 741
Jordan, J. B., 45, 46, 191, 328, 330, 389, 480, 481, 668
Jordon, L., 103
Josephson, N., 602
Joyce, B., 146, 153, 712

Kanner, L. A., 287, 328, 712
Kaplan, S. N., 242, 243, 260, 314, 704, 712
Kappan, D. L., 638
Karnes, M. B., 668
Kaswan, J. W., 391
Katz, L., 602
Kauffman, N., 90, 329, 709
Kaufman, M. J., 103

Kaufmann, F., 191, 258
Keating, D. K., 230, 260, 712
Keller, H., 14, 637
Kempe, C. H., 655, 712
Kennedy, J. F., 20
Kennedy, P., 600
Kenowitz, L. A., 103
Keogh, B., 90, 91, 100, 712
Kephart, N. C., 360, 712
Kicklighter, R., 481
Kiester, E. K., Jr., 97, 98, 714
King, A., 406, 411, 413
King-Stoops, J., 462, 712
Kirk, S. A., 296, 298, 314, 328, 343, 360, 601, 712
Kirp, D., 701
Kirst, M. W., 704
Klausmeier, H. J., 148, 458, 712
Klein, J. W., 712
Klerman, L. V., 669
Kobler, M., 391
Kohlberg, L., 146, 712
Kolstoe, O. P., 296, 712
Koppitz, E. M., 80, 81, 712
Koppmann, M., 84, 717
Korba, W. L., 191
Kounin, J., 78, 137, 373, 389, 712, 728
Kozloff, M., 152
Kraus, K., 201
Kroth, R. L., 191, 602
Krug, D. A., 89, 329, 710
Kugel, R. B., 314, 329, 712
Kunzweiler, C. E., 390
Kurtzman, D. H., 289
Kvaraceus, W. L., 191

L'Abate, L., 344, 712
Lance, W. D., 499-500, 712
Lane, K., 153
Langstaff, A. L., 735
Langton, P. G., 102
Lantzer, J. N., 103
Lanza, L. G., 46
Larsen, E. D., 8, 713
Larsen, L. A., 103
Larsen, S. C., 511

LaVor, M. L., 46
LeBoss, S., 250
Lee, R. C., 668
Lehtinen, L. E., 359, 391, 719
Leifer, A., 152
Leitenbert, H., 389
Lesser, G., 152
Levine, M., 713
Levine, S., 301, 327, 350, 705
Ley, D., 391
Lilly, M. S., 46, 692, 713
Lindsley, O. R., 53, 65, 326, 361, 713
Lippman, L., 25, 713
Litwak, E., 456, 713
Lloyd, L., 511
Loe, D. C., 79, 713
Lombardi, T. P., 327
Lombroso, C., 200, 201, 713
Long, J., 297, 717
Lord, F. E., 601
Lorion, R. P., 382, 390, 706
Lovatt, M., 82, 389, 713
Love, H. D., 215, 216, 217, 713
Love, L. R., 391
Lovitt, T. C., 389, 481
Lowenfeld, B., 615, 637, 713
Lucito, L., 103, 216, 258
Luecking, E. M., 226, 259, 719
Lukens, K., 438
Lukoff, I. F., 637
Lundholm, K., 740
Lundstrom, K., 23, 713
Lynch, M. E., 506, 709

Mackie, R., 18, 713
MacKinnon, D. W., 481
MacMillan, D. L., 100, 701, 713, 721
MacQueen, J. C., 401, 708
Madsen, C. H., 480
Maeroff, G. I., 231, 713
Maker, C. J., 260
Makowski, R., 649, 706
Mallis, J. A., 87, 260, 713
Maloney, M. P., 152
Marland, S. P., Jr., 198, 200, 232, 260, 714
Marquez, L., 512

Marr, H., 435, 713
Marsh, V., 637
Marshall, E., 704
Marshall, R. S., 677, 700, 714
Marsters, J. C., 527, 528
Martin, D. L., 654, 659, 714
Martin, G., 608, 638, 741
Martinson, R. A., 153, 221, 228, 229, 232, 236, 258, 714
Mathis, S. L., 602
Matthews, J., 495, 511, 704
Mauser, A. J., 205, 714
May, B., 381
Mayer, C. A., 760
Mayhall, W. F., 46, 153, 370, 711
McCaffrey, M., 669
McCarthy, J. F., 352, 360, 391
McCarthy, J.J., 352, 360, 391, 714
McCleary, L. E., 736
McClelland, D. C., 259
McConnell, F., 520, 523, 599, 601, 714
McDonald, R. A. F., 500, 714
McGarry, F. M., 445, 717
McGettigan, J. F., 328
McIntosh, D. K.
McKenzie, H., 447, 708
McLaughlin, T. F., 142, 714
McLure, W. P., 700
Mears, E. G., 601
Mefford, J. P., 327
Mercer, J. R., 299, 300, 327, 329, 714
Merkin, P., 153, 190
Merrill, E. C., Jr., 602
Metteer, R., 391
Meyen, E. L., 46, 329
Meyer, H. J., 456, 713
Meyerowitz, J. H., 329
Meyers, C. E., 100, 327, 713, 721
Miel, A., 97, 98, 714
Milazzo, T. C., 327
Miles, M. B., 698, 714
Miley, J., 248
Miller, H., 131, 705
Miller, K., 253
Millet, J. D., 52, 708
Milofsky, R. D., 701

Mischel, W., 102
Mischio, G. S., 297, 710
Mitchell, R., 438
Molloy, L., 438
Monroe, J. D., 329
Moore, J. J., 153, 714
Moore, M., 619, 627
Morehead, A. E., 511
Morehead, D. M., 511
Moreland, C., 419-420
Morse, W. C., 360, 363, 372, 376, 385, 389, 448, 715
Morton, M., 245, 715
Mosher, R. V., 456, 715
Moss, J., 103
Moustakas, C. E., 360, 715
Moyer, S. B., 392
Mullins, J. B., 403, 417, 437, 438
Murphy, M. K., 198, 715
Musgrave, G. R., 481
Myer, L. N., 461, 715
Myers, R. E., 242

Nagi, S., 655, 715
Nanda, H., 65, 707
Napier, G., 638
Nash, N., 675, 711
Nassar, C., 345
Nathanson, D. E., 190
Nazzaro, J. N., 46, 47, 153, 191
Needham, F., 728, 758
Newcomer, P. L., 392
Newland, T. E., 15, 215, 216, 260, 715
Newman, R., 83, 360, 391, 715
Nezol, A. J., 638
Nicol, E., 643
Nix, G. W., 602
Nober, L. W., 560, 715
Noffsinger, T., 98, 715
Nolte, M. C., 663, 664, 667, 669, 715
Northcott, W. H., 532-533, 559, 560, 562, 601, 602, 715
Novick, M. R., 152

Oden, M., 199, 201, 211, 213, 259, 720
O'Donnell, P., 378
Ogletree, E. J., 391

Ohrtman, W., 368, 374, 375, 710
Okey, J., 460, 705
Omenn, G. S., 390
Orton, S., 338, 359, 715
Osborn, J., 472, 708
Oseroff, A., 120, 718
Overman, P. B., 103
Owsley, P. J., 602

Paolucci, P. E., 447, 708
Panter, C., 438
Pappanikou, A. J., 191, 390
Parke, R. D., 655, 716
Parker, C. A., 56, 102, 481, 716, 741
Parks, A. L., 389, 697
Pasanella, A., 728, 759
Passow, A.H., 480
Paterson, L., 24
Patterson, R., 202, 205
Patterson, V. W., 102
Paul, J. L., 390, 716
Paul, R. L., 560
Peabody, R., 619, 627, 714
Pegnato, C. W., 118, 219, 258, 715
Pell, D. M., 437
Pepper, F. C., 140, 360, 708, 716
Pereire, J. R., 542
Perelman, P. F., 447, 708
Perkins, J. A., 52, 708
Peschka, C. M., 153
Peter, L. J., 730
Peterson, L., 248, 251, 716
Phillips, E. L., 361, 466, 480, 710
Phillips, M., 260
Piaget, J., 212
Picasso, P., 211
Picklesimer, R., 196
Pieper, E. J., 429, 437, 716
Pierson, D. E., 643, 644, 645, 716
Polich, J. M., 660, 668
Pollack, D., 601
Ponder, P., 638
Popham, W. J., 130, 762
Porter, D. O., 46
Porter, R. B., 327
Prather, D., 253
Premack, D., 467, 716

Presbie, R., 735
Pressey, S. L., 15, 227, 228, 230, 259, 260, 717
Prestwich, S., 153
Prouty, R., 445, 717
Purpura, D. P., 391
Putnam, J. F., 717

Quie, A. H., 21, 22, 681, 682, 717
Quilling, M. R., 148, 458, 712

Rader, B. T., 696, 709
Rajaratnam, N., 65, 707
Ramey, C. T., 322, 717
Ramsey, M. F., 395-397
Rankin, A., 717
Rapier, J., 437
Reagan, C. L., 392
Redden, M. R., 40, 94, 96, 152, 717
Redl, F., 360, 389
Reeder, A., 736
Rees, N. S.
Reger, R., 46, 84, 717
Reider, S. K., 82, 706
Renzulli, J. S., 153, 242, 258, 259, 260, 481, 717
Reuschlein, P., 696, 709
Reyna, J., 218, 717
Reynolds, M. C., 46, 102, 103, 119, 131, 149, 152, 230, 260, 452, 462, 480, 674, 675, 686, 694, 701, 711, 717, 718, 740, 741
Rhodes, W. C., 47
Richardson, S. A., 47, 327, 328, 437
Rieber, R. W., 511
Riesman, D., 28, 718
Risler, W. P., 327
Robbins, L. S., 480
Robbins, W., 103
Robin, S. S., 390
Robinson, 334, 335
Robinson, H. B., 327
Robinson, N. M., 327
Rogers, C. R., 360, 717
Rogers, G., 269
Rosenblum, G., 47, 480
Rosensweet, A., 418, 717

Rosenzweig, L. E., 297, 717
Rossmiller, R. A., 458, 700, 712
Rouse, J., 254
Rubin, E. J., 390
Rubin, R., 42, 718
Runion, H. T., 419
Russo, J. R., 433, 718
Rynders, J. E., 329

Sabatino, D., 368, 374, 375, 710
Sailey, M., 458, 712
Salem, J. M., 83, 586-587, 590, 601, 602, 706
Salvia, J., 102, 152, 153
Sangrund, A., 655, 709
Schaefer, E. S., 191, 281, 645, 718
Schary, D., 438
Schible, D., 200, 718
Schiefelbusch, R. L., 466, 511, 710
Schneider, S., 103
Scholl, G. T., 602, 637
Schrotberger, W. L., 638
Schultz, J. J., 390
Schwartz, L., 120, 718
Segars, K., 406
Seguin, E., 14
Semmel, D. S., 46, 741
Semmel, M. I., 46, 90, 103, 329, 709, 741
Sheare, J. B., 329
Shedd, M. R., 686, 718
Sheets, A. C., 314-315
Sheperd, G., 330
Silberman, A., 707
Silverman, S. R., 520, 601
Simoes, A., Jr., 391, 511
Simon, S. B., 102, 212
Simon, T.
Singer, S. B., 390
Sisk, D., 260
Skinner, B. F., 53, 65, 466, 718
Sloan, W., 17, 46, 267, 275, 277, 718
Smallwood, G., 512
Smith, B.J., 322, 717
Smith, J., 272, 718
Smith, L. A., 258
Smith, R. M., 296, 719

Snow, R. E., 74, 144, 190, 706
Snyder, L., 668
Sontag, E., 291, 292, 719
Sorenson, J. S., 148, 458, 712
Sosnowsky, W. P., 688, 701, 719
Spache, G. D., 392, 719
Sperber, R. L., 643
Sperling, C., 220, 259, 720
Spicker, H. H., 740
Spollen, J., 511
Sprinthall, N. A., 456, 715, 719
Stahl, R., 203, 204
Stambul, H. B., 660, 668
Stein, Z. A., 327
Stephens, T. M., 389
Stevens, G. D., 414, 719
Stevens, H., 267
Stilwater, R., 412
Stillman, R. D., 601
Stoddard, G., 55, 110, 719
Stoll, W. C., 719
Stoval, E. M.
Strattner, M. J., 602
Stratton, J., 719
Strauss, A. A., 359, 391, 719
Strodtbeck, F. L., 259
Stromer, R., 392
Stuckless, E. R., 601
Stuecher, U., 389
Sullivan, E. V., 190
Sullivan, H. J., 191
Sumption, M. C., 226, 259, 719
Suppes, P. A., 543, 719
Swatzenbarg, P. A., 93, 719

Talmage, H., 459, 719
Tarnopol, L., 392
Taylor, C. W., 238, 720
Taylor, O., 512
Terman, L. M., 15, 196, 199, 201, 211, 213, 228, 229, 259, 720
Teska, J. A., 668
Tewey, S., 669
Thiagarajan, S., 46, 741
Thomas, B. A., 480
Thomas, M. A., 327, 329, 330, 701

Thorensen, C. E., 481
Thorndike, R. L., 221, 720
Tinker, M. A., 392, 705
Tobias, S., 74, 144, 460, 720
Tongue, C., 220, 259, 720
Tonn, M., 330
Torrance, E. P., 153, 199, 242, 259, 481, 720
Torres, S., 157, 190, 191, 720
Toulmin, S., 201, 711
Trapp, E. P., 328
Trevena, T. M., 638
Trippi, J. A., 329
Trost, M. A., 382, 390, 706
Trotter, V. Y., 720
Tuttle, D. W., 638
Turton, L. J., 350, 720
Tuseth, A., 230, 260, 718
Tyler, L. E., 57, 329, 720

Upjohn, R., 419
Urbanowicz, L., 407, 720

Van Osdol, B. M., 329
Van Riper, C., 485, 511, 721
Vassar, W. G., 46
Velasquez, D., 212
Vergason, G. A., 46, 329
Verma, G., 391
Vogel, A. L., 84, 85, 720
Vogel, S. A., 390
Vogl, B., 407
Volkmar, C. B., 728, 735, 759
Von Braun, W., 204

Wagner, R. F., 390
Walker, V. S., 328, 330
Wallace, R. C., Jr., 698, 710
Wallin, J. E. W., 319, 328, 421, 542, 721
Ward, M. J., 438, 602, 638
Ward, M. P., 152
Wardlaw, J., 376, 381, 721
Warfield, G. J., 46, 188, 189, 701, 721
Warren, S. A., 267, 721
Waugh, K. W., 392

Way, R. S., 148, 712
Weatherman, R., 753, 754, 755
Wechsler, D., 209, 210, 721
Weil, M., 146, 153, 712
Weinberg, R. A., 102, 741
Weiner, B. B., 191, 481
Weintraub, F. J., 46, 47
Weishahn, M. W., 343, 438, 709
Weitbrecht, R., 529
Wendland, L., 404, 721
West, P., 602
Wexler, J., 52, 708
Wheeler, D., 268-270, 272
Whelan, R. J., 46, 329
White, B. C., 643
White, O. R., 733
Whitstock, E. L., 638
Wilderson, F., 26, 140, 712
Wilken, W. H., 46
William, B., 736
Williams, F., 220
Williams, N., 196
Wingate, V., 131, 705
Wise, J. H., 438, 602, 638

Wisland, M. V., 721
Witmer, L., 357, 358
Witty, P., 210, 216, 259, 721
Wolf, J., 755
Wolfensberger, W., 46, 47, 314, 316, 329, 701
Wolfson, I. N., 328
Wood, F. H., 102, 741
Wood, M. M., 390

Yahraes, H., 153
Yater, V. V., 560, 562, 602, 721
Yoh, B. L., 131, 705
Yoshida, R., 721
Young, L., 203
Young, M. E., 28, 675, 721
Ysseldyke, J., 102, 152, 153

Zawadzki, R., 92, 93, 94, 95, 96, 293, 721
Ziegler, S., 88, 89, 302, 327, 721
Zigler, E., 17, 47, 656, 721, 722
Zigmond, N., 362, 383, 384, 386, 722
Zubin, J., 68, 69, 722

Subject Index

Abacus, 632
Abused children, 283, 653-660
Acceleration, 203, 208
   age-grade, 230-235
   curriculum, 230-235
   See also Advanced placement
Acceptance, 187
Accidents, 283
   See also Traumatic injuries
Accountability, 54, 163-164, 175, 457, 551-552, 555
Adaptive behavior, 274, 275, 299-301
Advanced placement, 208, 232-235
   See also Acceleration
Affirmative action, 606
Aggression, 333
Alcoholics Anonymous, 659-660, 661
Alexander Graham Bell Association for the Deaf, 529
Allergies, 400
Altavista Elementary School, Altavista, Virginia, 488
American Association for the Advancement of Science, 40, 229, 399
American Association of School Administrators, 398
American Association on Mental Deficiency, 267, 318
American Council of the Blind, 609
American Federation of Teachers, 687-691
American Federation for the Blind, 609, 618
American Indians, 140-141, 646
   See also Minority groups

American Mental Health Association, 342
American Printing House for the Blind, 606, 629, 636
American Psychological Association, 57
American School for the Deaf, Hartford, Connecticut, 543
American Telephone and Telegraph Company, 529
Amniocentesis, 264-265
Aphasia, 521
Applied behavior analysis, 62, 65, 303, 361, 372, 466-467, 493
Appropriate education, 39, 58-59, 85, 111-112, 128, 290, 463
   See also Individualized education plan or program
Aptitude treatment interaction, 60-62, 69-70, 219, 240, 256
Architectural barriers, 133-134, 163, 205, 306, 427-428
Arkansas State Board of Education, 186
Arthritis, 400
Articulation defects, 494-496
Articulation test, 131, 494-496
Assessment procedures, 38-39, 107-151, 174-175, 223, 477
   See also Individualized education plan or program; School Psychologist
Association for Children with Learning Disabilities, 341, 342
Association for the Gifted, 229-230
Asthma, 400

Atlanta, Georgia, 195
Audiometer, 525
Auditory training, 496
Autistic, 81-82, 333

Battered children
　See Abused children
Behavior disorder, 83-85, 333-390
　See also Learning disability
Behavioral objectives, 612-613
　See also Individualized education program; Objectives
Blind, 81, 605
　See also Visually impaired
Blindisms, 614
Bliss Language System, 412
Bloomington Public Schools, Bloomington, Minnesota, 448-450
Braille, 606, 610, 616-618
Braille writer, 632
Braillist, 629
Brain damaged, 333, 486
Brain injured, 333
Bright, 208
Brilliant, 208
Brookline Early Education Project, 643-645
Bus service, 40, 43, 380, 399, 421, 597

California Association for the Gifted, 230
Cascade models, 31-40, 619
Categorical funding, 450
　See also Costs, Labels
Categories, 39, 67-75, 276-279, 445-452, 683-685
　See also Labels
Central Institute for the Deaf, St. Louis, Missouri, 575
Cerebral Palsy, 85, 400, 486
Chicago Public Schools, Chicago, Illinois, 584-586
Child Abuse Anonymous, 659-660
Child guidance clinics, 337
Clark County School District, Las Vegas, Nevada, 435

Clarke School for the Deaf, Northampton, Massachusetts, 528
Class management, 137, 427-428, 506
Classification, 67-75
　See also Categories, Labels
Cleft palate, 486
Cognitive development rate, 208, 195-258, 263-330, 441, 486, 537, 644
Collective bargaining, 311-313, 550, 555, 598, 687-691
Communication, 484-512
Communication aides
　See Interpreters
Community resources, 176-177, 555
Conference of Executives of American Schools for the Deaf, 533
Congenital anomalies, 400
Consultation, 55-56, 75, 80, 107, 137, 420, 457, 467, 556-558, 571-572
Consulting teacher, 55, 236, 447-448, 625-626
Convention of American Instructors of the Deaf, 533
Cooperative Special Rehabilitation Center, Minneapolis, Minnesota, 435
Costs, 19, 30, 84, 98-99, 382, 450, 646-648, 675-678
Council for Exceptional Children, 5, 25, 28, 174, 229, 318, 695
Council of Great Cities, 675
Counselor, 455-456, 557, 634
Courts, 24, 90, 236, 334
Creativity, 121, 208, 468-469
　See also Gifted and talented
Cretinism, 264
Crisis teacher, 364, 370, 374-375, 448
　See also Helping teacher
Criterion referenced measurement, 56-60, 127, 131
Cultural differences, 456
　See also Minority groups
Cultural electives, 109-111
Cultural imperatives, 55, 109-111
Culturally diverse gifted, 229
　See also Minority groups

Subject Index / 777

Curriculum, 143, 294-299, 424-426, 505

Dade County Public Schools, Florida, 248
Deaf, 525-526
　See also Hearing impairment
Decentralization, 39, 307-308
　See also Mainstreaming
Deficit, 69
　See also Discrepancy analysis
Deformities, 486
Delayed language, 333, 644
Demission, 51-55, 110
Developmental aphasia, 333, 486
Developmental retardation, 273
Diabetes, 283-284, 400
Diagnostic-prescriptive teaching, 445-446, 650
Diagnostic teaching, 127
　See also Assessment
Disability, 414-415
Disadvantaged, 66, 674, 682
　See also Minority groups
Discipline, 137, 379
　See also Class management; Crisis teacher
Discrepancy analysis, 64, 343-344
Disruptive, 333
Divergent thinking, 208, 468-469
Domain referenced measurement, 56-60
　See also Criterion referenced measurement
Down's syndrome, 116, 264
Dropouts, 380, 661
Drug handicapped children, 660-662
Due process, 24-27, 43, 54, 171-172, 223, 664, 685-687
Dyslexia, 333
Dysphasia, 521

Early childhood education, 66, 599, 633, 641-652
　Very early intervention, 448-449, 642-652

Educable mentally retarded, 89-92, 295-297
　See also Mental retardation
Educational diagnosis, 119-120, 124-125
　See also Assessment
Educational diagnostician, 107, 477
Educational handicap, 333
Educational measurement, 56-66
Educational plans
　See Individualized educational plan or program
Educational retardation, 544-545
Educational treatments, 69
Ego strengthening, 372
Emergencies, 631
Eminent, 208
Emotional blockage, 333, 336-339
Emotionally disturbed, 333, 614
Enrichment, 203
Epilepsy, 400
Evaluation, 129-133, 148-149, 162
Exceptional children
　defined, 9
　numbers, 41-42
　See also Categories, Labels
Exclusion, 43
　See also Demission
Excuse
　See Demission
Executive High School Internships of America, 253
Expectancy, 63-66, 441-442
Expel
　See Demission

Ferguson Florissant School District, Missouri, 646-647
Fitzgerald key, 571
Flexibility, 239
Foster home, 317

Gallaudet College, Washington, D.C., 543
Generic teacher certification, 441, 445-452, 693-697

Genius, 195, 202, 205, 208
Gifted and talented, 10, 86-88, 121, 195-258, 207
  Defined 195, 210-223
Gifted handicapped, 229, 397
Grading, 62-63
Grouping, 67-75
  See also Categories, Individualization, Labels
Group living, 265, 316-318

Halfway house, 317
Handicap, 291-292, 414
Hard of hearing, 526
  See also Hearing impairment
Health education, 283
Hearing aids, 524-526, 543
Hearing impairment, 82, 116-117, 123-124, 486, 514-602, 644
  defined, 516, 532-537
Helping teacher, 363-366, 447-448
Hemophilia, 85, 401
High achiever, 208
High-IQ, 208
Highly intelligent, 208
Hines Veterans' Hospital, Chicago, Illinois, 618
Holladay Center for Handicapped Children, Portland, Oregon, 432-433
Home for Crippled Children, Pittsburgh, Pennsylvania, 406-407
Homebound instruction, 664-665
Home-school telephone, 405
Hunger, 658
Hydrocephaly, 264
Hyperactivity, 333
Hyperkinetic, 333

Ida School District, Monroe County, Michigan, 573-575
  See Individualized education program
Immunization, 283
Impairment, 414-415
Incorrigible, 333, 334

Individualized education plan or program, 125, 150, 157-189, 545, 554, 659
Individualized instruction, 53, 100, 107-109, 112-116, 239-244, 266, 290, 294-301, 370-373, 424-428, 504-507, 560-573, 674
Individually guided education (IGE), 53, 458-459
Individually prescribed instruction (IPI), 53
Institutionalized racism, 28
  See also Minority groups
Instructional cascade 36-40, 620
  See also Cascades
Instructional materials, 136
Instructional methods, 144-146
Integration, 22-23, 100, 185-186
  See also Mainstreaming
Intelligence, 65, 209-210, 273
International Reading Association, 342
Interpreters, 595-596
Iron deficiency, 283
Itinerant teacher, 621-629

Job Corps program, 459-461
Juvenile courts, 334-336
  See also Courts
Juvenile delinquent, 38, 333, 334

Labels, 100, 118-119, 449
  See also Categories
Language arts curriculum, 209-210, 442-443, 505
  See also Curriculum
Language disabled, 333
Large print books, 606, 632
Las Vegas Association for Retarded Citizens, 269
Lawndale, Los Angeles County, California, 582-583
Leadership, 469-470, 633
Learning disability, 21-22, 64, 66, 83-85, 296, 333-390, 681-682
  defined 342-353

Least restrictive alternative, 22-23, 25-26, 39, 79, 363, 398
Lees-McRae College, Banner Elk, North Carolina, 526-528
Leukemia, 401
Lexington School for the Deaf, New York, New York, 38, 587-589
Liability, 111
  See also Accountability
Library of Congress, 606, 632, 636
Light perception, 614

Mainstreaming, 3-14, 22-23, 29, 38, 161-162, 289-307, 369-370, 379-381, 522-525
  academic, 5, 94-95, 185-188, 396-397
  cautions, 100, 234-235, 685-687
  defined, 5, 94, 99-100, 238-239, 420, 545-553
  physical, 5, 313
  policy, 25-26, 206-208, 236, 242-243, 293, 450, 487-488, 554-556
  research base, 76-101, 234-235
  social, 5, 39-41, 138-139
  See also Progressive inclusion
Major work, 208
Malnutrition, 283
Manual alphabet, 542-543
Marshall-University High School, Minneapolis, Minnesota, 434-435
Matching, 61, 70-75, 115, 256, 279-280, 294, 420, 545
Medication, 368-369
Mental Retardation, 263-330, 486, 493
  defined, 272-282
Mentally advanced, 208
Mentally ill, 333
Metabolic disorders, 282
Methods, 301-304, 371-373, 426, 461-477
Minimal brain dysfunction, 333
Minimal neurological dysfunction, 333
Minority groups, 27-29, 65, 120-122, 140-141, 218, 239, 643, 646, 673-674
  See also American Indian; Cultural differences; Disadvantaged
Minneapolis Association for Retarded Citizens, 188
Minneapolis Rehabilitation Center, Minneapolis, Minnesota, 435
Mobility, 20, 421, 617-618, 628-629
Modeling behavior, 174, 473-474, 490, 503, 614, 633
Mongolism
  See Down's Syndrome
Moral education, 303
Most able, 208
Most normal setting feasible
  See Least restrictive alternative
Multiply handicapped, 607
Muscular Dystrophy Association of America, 401

Narcotics
  See Drug handicapped children
National Association for Retarded Citizens, 19, 173, 265, 268, 270, 277, 307, 318, 323-324, 659
National Easter Seal Society for Crippled Children and Adults, 401
National Education Association, 687-691
National Epilepsy League, 401
National Foundation—March of Dimes, 401
National Society for the Prevention of Blindness, 605, 609
Neglected Children
  See Abused children
Near-genius, 208
  See also Genius
Neurologically impaired, 333
Nevada Advocates for the Mentally Retarded, 269
Newborn children
  See Early Childhood Education
New Jersey Agency for the Blind, 649
Normalization, 20, 316-317

Objectives
  behavioral, 612-613
  instructional, 128-130, 160
  See also Individualized education program
Observation, 127
Odessa, Texas, 38
Ontario Crippled Children's Centre, Canada, 412
Open Doors for the Handicapped, 402
Ophthalmologist, 629
Optacon, 610
Optometrist, 629
Oral method, 553-554
Orientation
  See Mobility

Parent norminations, 223
Parent organizations, 23-25, 185-189, 340
Parents, 26, 150, 162, 310, 339-340, 380, 502, 555, 564, 609, 633, 649-650, 659-660
Parent-teacher conference, 172-185, 384
Partial integration, 83, 320
  See also Mainstreaming
Partially sighted, 606, 632
Peer instruction, 470-471
Pennsylvania Association for Retarded Citizens, 24, 199
Pennsylvania Department of Education, 199-200
Perceptually handicapped, 333
Person-environment match
  See Matching
Phonetype, 528-530
Physical and health impairments, 394-438
  defined, 395-396, 413-416
Physically handicapped, 85-86
  See also Physical and health impairments
Physically impaired, 395-396
Pinellas County Public Schools, Florida, 250

Pittsburgh Association for the Blind, Pennsylvania, 649
Pittsburgh Public Schools, Pennsylvania, 288, 382-385
Placement processes, 25, 61
  See also Due process
Poliomyelitis, 401
Political power, 24, 28
Poisoning, 283
Polk County Public Schools, Florida, 251
Predelinquent, 333, 334
Pregnancy
  See School-age parents
Premack principle
  See Applied behavior analysis
President's Committee on Mental Retardation, 27
Preteach/teach/postteach strategy, 545-547
Prevailing and preferred practices, 10-14, 76, 151, 189, 223-226, 284-286, 353-356, 416-421, 497-499, 537-542, 635-636
Private education, 52-53, 678-679
Prodigy, 201, 231
  See also Gifted and talented
Progressive inclusion, 22-23, 30, 307-308
  See also Mainstreaming
Psychological block
  See Emotional blockage
Public education, 52-53
Public Law 94-142 (Education for All Handicapped Children Act), 27, 29, 43, 52, 162, 686-687
Pupil feedback, 471-472

Racial segregation, 27-28, 140, 141
Radiation, 283
Rancho Los Amigos Rehabilitation Center for Children, California, 404
Reader services, 632
Recording for the Blind, Inc., 632
Referral, 39

Rehabilitation, 19-20, 26, 29, 399, 402, 415, 500, 606, 662
Remedial case, 64, 66
Remedial education, 361-363, 369-370, 681-682
Residential schools, 15, 313-316, 551-552, 586-597, 618-619
Resource teacher, 446-447
Response contingent instruction, 384-385
  See also Applied behavior analysis
Retardation, 64, 66
  See also Educational retardation, Mental retardation
Rh factor, 283
Rheumatic fever, 401
Richardson, Texas, 507-509
Right to education, 23-27, 43-44, 112, 199-200, 289-290
Right to treatment, 24, 26
Roseville, Minnesota, 7-8
Rubella, 282, 607

School-age parents, 663-667
School psychologist, 384, 453-455, 502, 521-522, 557
  See also Assessment
Screening, 116-119, 609, 634
Services, 125, 160-161, 182
Sharing expertise, 444
Shopping, 339-340
  See also Parents
Sign language, 542-543
Simi Valley Union School District, Ventura County, California, 579-581
Sister Kenny Institute, Minneapolis, Minnesota, 435
Slate and stylus, 632
Social adaptation, 268
Social adjustment, 234
Social maturity, 234, 274, 644
Social worker, 456-457, 557
Socially disadvantaged, 234
  See also Minority groups
Socially maladjusted, 333, 334

Socioeconomic differences, 140-141
Special education, 3-14
  defined, 9-10, 115, 279-280, 694
  history, 14-23, 287-292, 356-363
Special School District of St. Louis County, Missouri, 575-576
Speech clinician, 500-504, 507-508
Speech correction, 490-491
Speech and language development, 490-491
Speech defect, defined, 492
Speech improvement, 490-491
Speech problems, 484-512
Spina bifida, 85, 401
Staff meeting, 340
Standardized tests, 127-128
Status offender, 335
Strauss syndrome, 333
Stuttering, 486, 493
Sub-average intellectual functioning, 273
Subtle neurological impairment, 333
Superior, 208
Suspension
  See Demission
Sweden, 22-23
Symbol systems, 209-210

Tacoma Public Schools, Tacoma, Washington, 188, 576-580
Talking books, 632
Teaching certification, 30-31, 310-311, 381
  See also Generic teacher certification
Teacher Corps, 695
Teacher organizations, 311, 380, 555, 662
Teamwork, 236-239, 292-294, 366-369, 380, 422-424, 553, 556-558, 620, 646
Teasing, 187, 408
Telebinocular, 609
Teletype Writers for the Deaf, Inc., 528-530
Thalidomide, 85, 265

Total communication, 543-544, 553-554
Trainable mentally retarded, 88-89, 289, 297-299
  See also Mental retardation
Transportation
  See Bus service
Traumatic injuries, 401
  See also Accidents
Tucson Public Schools, Tucson, Arizona, 645-647

Underachievement, 64, 66
United Cerebral Palsy Association, 173, 401
United Cerebral Palsy Center, Minneapolis, Minnesota, 435
Urbain Plavan School, Fountain Valley, California, 433
Utah State School for the Deaf, Ogden, Utah, 591-597

Village Nursery School, Amsterdam, New York, 429-432

Visual impairment, 116-117, 604-638, 644
  defined, 605-606
Voice problems, 496-497
Volunteer groups, 609-610, 636

Wasioja Area Special Education Cooperative, 164-171
Western Illinois Program, 649
Western Pennsylvania School for the Deaf, Pittsburgh, Pennsylvania, 590-591
Western State School and Hospital, Cannonsburg, Pennsylvania, 39, 314-315
Westside Community Schools, Omaha, Nebraska, 245

Yakima County, Washington, 411-415

Zero demission, 52
  See also Demission

DISCHARGED

DISCHARGED
DEC 1 0 1981

DISCHARGED DISCHARGED DISCHARGED

DISCHARGED
FEB 1 1 1981
DISCHARGED DISCHARGED DEC 8 1980

FEB 17 1981 DISCHARGED
DISCHARGED MAR 2 1984

DISCHARGED DISCHARGED

DISCHARGED DISCHARGED

NOV 15 1981
DISCHARGED DEC 26 1989
DISCHARGED

DISCHARGED
MAR 21 1990

DISCHARGED

DISCHARGED

APR 9 1983
DISCHARGED

DISCHARGED